Sha[illegible]

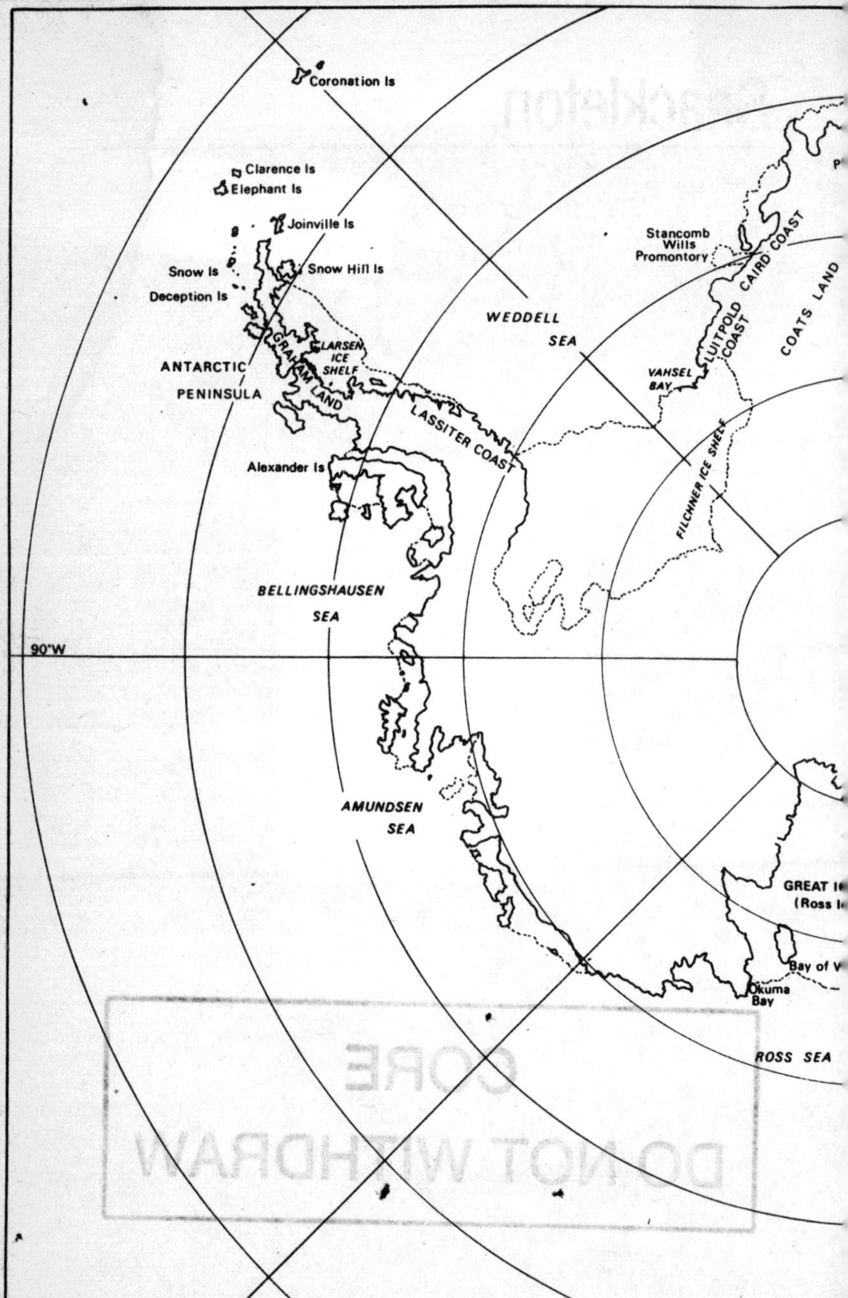

Coronation Is
Clarence Is
Elephant Is
Joinville Is
Snow Is
Snow Hill Is
Deception Is
ANTARCTIC PENINSULA
GRAHAM LAND
LARSEN ICE SHELF
WEDDELL SEA
Stancomb Wills Promontory
CAIRD COAST
COATS LAND
LUITPOLD COAST
VAHSEL BAY
LASSITER COAST
FILCHNER ICE SHELF
Alexander Is
BELLINGSHAUSEN SEA
90°W
AMUNDSEN SEA
Okuma Bay
ROSS SEA

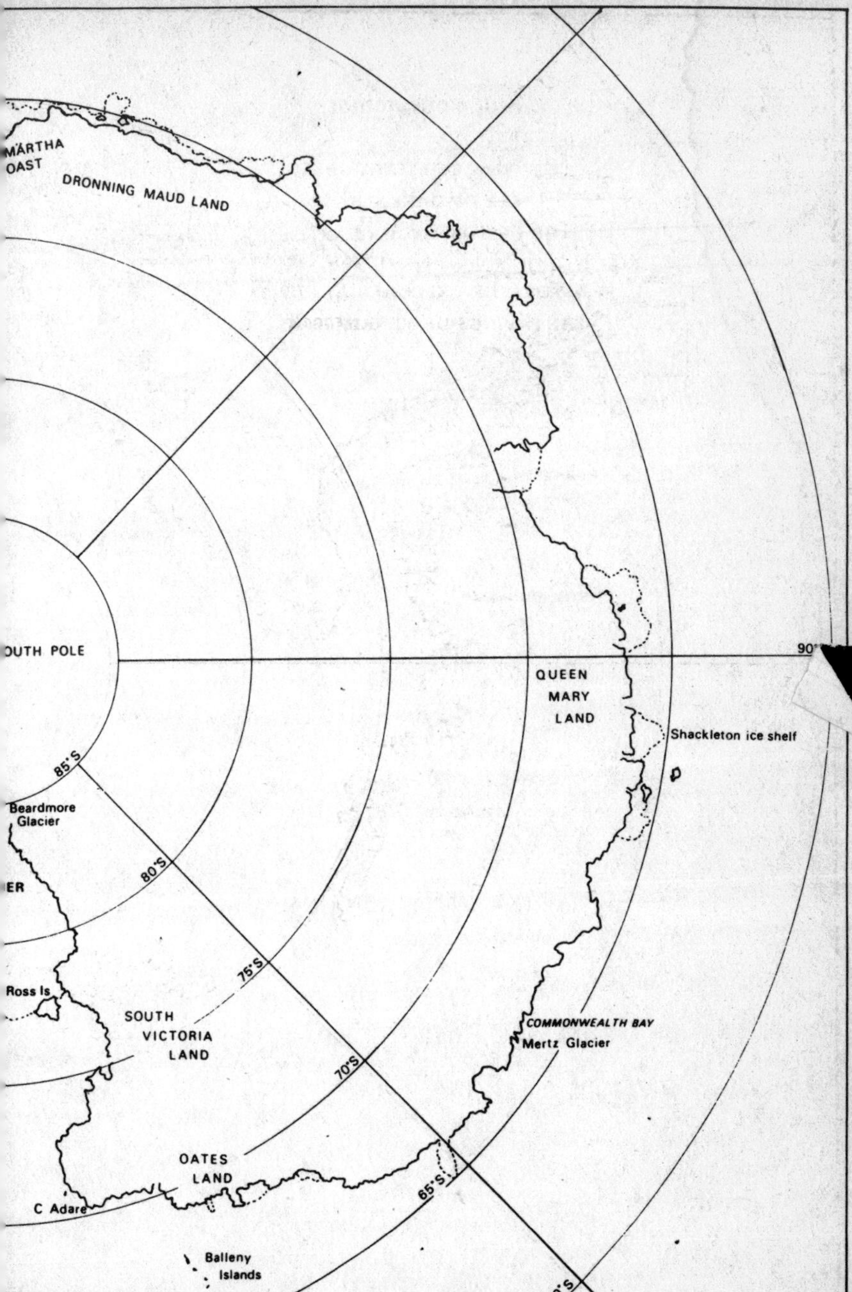

MARTHA
OAST
DRONNING MAUD LAND
OUTH POLE
90°
QUEEN
MARY
LAND
Shackleton ice shelf
85°S
Beardmore
Glacier
80°S
ER
75°S
Ross Is
SOUTH
VICTORIA
LAND
COMMONWEALTH BAY
Mertz Glacier
70°S
OATES
LAND
65°S
C Adare
Balleny
Islands
60°S

By the same author:

THE NEW TOTALITARIANS
SEA OF DARKNESS
THE LAST PLACE ON EARTH
Previously published as SCOTT AND AMUNDSEN
NANSEN: THE EXPLORER AS HERO
THE SAYINGS OF HENRIK IBSEN

Roland Huntford is the author of two polar biographies also published by Abacus; *Nansen* and *The Last Place on Earth: Scott and Amundsen's Race to the South Pole*, which was made into an acclaimed television series. For many years Roland Huntford was the *Observer*'s correspondent in Scandinavia, a job which he doubled with being their winter sports correspondent both in Scandinavia and the Alps. He lives in Cambridge and is a former Alistair Horne Fellow at St Antony's College, Oxford.

Praise for *Shackleton*:

'Mr Huntford is a model biographer . . . The account of Shackleton's last expedition is magnificent from the moment the *Endurance* is caught in the ice-pack right up to the crossing of South Georgia after the epic voyage in open boats across the savage seas, and the subsequent rescue of his marooned men. It is truly marvellous and marvellously moving, and it is impossible to suppose that any account of a triumph could so move one to tears of relief, joy and blind wonder.' Allan Massie, *Spectator*

'Magnificent . . . Huntford has done justice to this great and complex man. That, in itself, is a triumph.'
Sunday Times

Shackleton

Roland Huntford

"Sir Ernest Shackleton's name will for evermore be engraved with letters of fire in the history of Antarctic exploration."

Roald Amundsen

ABACUS

ABACUS

First published in Great Britain by Hodder & Stoughton Ltd 1985
This edition published by Abacus 1996
Reprinted 1997 (twice), 1999, 2000, 2001, 2002, 2004, 2007, 2009

A CIP catalogue record for this book is available from the British Library.

ISBN 978-0-349-10744-8

Printed in England by Clays Ltd, St Ives plc

Papers used by Abacus are natural, renewable and recyclable products sourced from well-managed forests and certified in accordance with the rules of the Forest Stewardship Council.

FSC
Mixed Sources
Product group from well-managed forests and other controlled sources
www.fsc.org Cert no. SGS-COC-004081
© 1996 Forest Stewardship Council

Abacus
An imprint of
Little, Brown Book Group
100 Victoria Embankment
London EC4Y 0DY

An Hachette UK Company
www.hachette.co.uk

www.littlebrown.co.uk

In Memory of
Torsten

Contents

Illustrations

[1]Mr Richard Greene
[2]GLC Photographic Department of Architecture and Civic Design
[3]Scott Polar Research Institute, Cambridge
[4]Canterbury Museum, Christchurch, New Zealand
[5]Alexander Turnbull Library, Wellington, New Zealand
[6]Department of Science and Technology, Antarctic Division Tasmania
[7]The Wodehouse Library, Dulwich College
[8]Private Collection
[9]The Hurley Collection/Scott Polar Research Institute, Cambridge
[10]Royal Geographical Society

Maps

Preface

This book grew out of my work on *Scott and Amundsen*, for at every other turn the shadow of Ernest Shackleton fell across my path.

Shackleton was more than a polar explorer; he was a hero, and a popular hero, of his own times. Under any circumstances, a biography seemed due. Only two have so far appeared, the last, by James and Margery Fisher, nearly thirty years ago. Since then, public records have been opened, new material has emerged.

That includes the diaries of Shackleton's followers. They are notably those of Sir Edgeworth David, Commander Lionel Greenstreet, Frank Hurley, Keith Jack, Ernest Joyce, Æneas Mackintosh, Sir Douglas Mawson, Lieutenant-Colonel Thomas Hans Orde-Lees, the Rev. Arnold Spencer-Smith. Other diaries of note have been those of Roald Amundsen, C. A. Larsen and Otto Nordenskjöld.

Before the age of air travel and universal radio, polar expeditions were essays in isolation. The participants were exclusively their own chroniclers. In piecing their story together, the proper foundation is obviously the private journal, even if written with an eye to publication. At the very least, it is free of hindsight. It breaches inhibition. Quotations do duty for historical dialogue. It produces an immediacy otherwise hard to achieve, but different viewpoints are desirable for a rounded picture of people and events. Historical authenticity is all.

For that reason, contemporary place-names have been used in this book. What is nowadays known as the Ross Ice Shelf appears as the Ross Ice Barrier or the Great Ice Barrier. Leningrad is called St Petersburg or, later, Petrograd. Oslo will be found as Christiania or Kristiania. Baia-Mare, now in Romania, reverts to Nagybanya in Hungary.

Similarly, in quoting from diaries and letters, the original spelling and punctuation have been left untouched. In units of measurement, too, the sources have been followed. Thus, altitudes appear in feet. The nautical (or geographical) mile has been used for polar land travel. Temperatures are given, not in Centigrade, but Fahrenheit. The pound sterling is the old, predecimalised kind. Conversions will be found later in the book, on page 701.

Acknowledgments

My thanks are firstly due to Mr Correlli Barnett, Keeper of the Records of Churchill College, Cambridge, Mr Clive Holland, and Professor F. H. Sandbach, of Trinity College, Cambridge. They gave me support when it was needed most.

Next, I wish to thank Mr R. F. Perachie and Mr Torkel Fagerli. Both selflessly helped me in my research. They never failed to answer any appeal, however troublesome or time-consuming. Without them, this book could hardly have been written.

To Frank Delaney, I am profoundly grateful for piloting me through the shoals of the Irish and the Anglo-Irish character.

Mrs Margery Fisher I thank for her generosity in placing at my disposal her transcripts of interviews with Shackleton's companions and contemporaries.

I am grateful to Mr A. G. E. Jones for generously sharing his unrivalled knowledge of polar history.

For frank and informative discussions on Freemasonry, I am particularly indebted to Mr J. Hamill, Librarian Curator of the United Grand Lodge of England.

Miss Irene Swinford Edwards, Mr Harry Joel, Mrs Peggy Sheridan Young and Mrs Alice Ireland, all good-humouredly allowed themselves to be interviewed.

For access to documents in their possession, I am extremely grateful to the following: Lieutenant-Colonel J. Kingsford Carson and Mrs Audrey Greenstreet, for the papers of Commander Lionel Greenstreet, RNR; Mr Christopher Dennistoun, for the papers of Mrs Caroline Oates; the Master and Fellows of Churchill College, Cambridge, for the Jutland Diary of Midshipman A. W. Clarke; Mr J. van Haeften, for the papers of Sir Philip Brocklehurst; Dr Derek Harbord, for the diaries of Commander A. E. Harbord, RN; Mrs J. Ruth Hatch, for the papers of Captain Rupert England; the Trustees of the Imperial War Museum, for the First World War letters of Captain A. D. Talbot, and the first-hand account of the Battle of Coronel written by an unidentified officer in HMS *Glasgow*; The Earl of Iveagh, for the papers of the first Earl of Iveagh; Professor Fred Jacka, Director of the Mawson Institute for Antarctic Research, Adelaide, for the papers of Sir Douglas Mawson; Mr Bjørn Tore Larsen, for the diaries of Captain C. A. Larsen; Miss Sue Limb for her notes of Violet Oates' copy of the Antarctic diary of Captain L. E. G. Oates; Mrs Jean Macklin for the papers of her late husband, Dr Alec Macklin; John Murray Ltd., for correspondence with C. D. Mackellar and Sir Ernest Shackleton; the Royal Archives, Windsor, for the diaries of King George V.

The late Mr R. W. Richards and "Bud" Waite provided much stimulating correspondence on Antarctic history, of which both were a part. Richards was the last survivor of Shackleton's Ross Sea Party. Waite was the discoverer of radio echo-sounding, the first reliable method of measuring the thickness of the polar ice cap.

I wish to thank too Dr Ian Calder, Dr John Dewhurst, Professor Rainer Goldsmith, of Chelsea College, London, Dr Derek Harbord, and Mr Denis Wilkins, FRCS, for the trouble they have taken to investigate and discuss Shackleton's health.

Once again, for their toleration of the bizarre conditions of authorship, I must thank my bankers, Coutts & Co.

For much patient help, I wish to thank: Churchill College, Cambridge, archives; Dulwich College, the Wodehouse Library (Mrs Margaret Slythe); Framnæs Mekaniske Værksted, Sandefjord (Mr Oscar Andersen and Mr Øyvind Freen); Hvalfangstmuseet (Whaling Museum) Sandefjord (Mr Einar Wexelson and Mrs Lorne Kirchoff); The Imperial War Museum; The Mawson Institute for Antarctic Research (especially Mrs Edna Sawyer for transcribing the diaries of Sir Douglas Mawson); The Mitchell Library, Sydney; John Murray Ltd., archives; National Archives and Records Service, Washington, DC (Miss Alison Wilson); The Public Record Office, London; The Royal Archives, Windsor; Universitetsbiblioteket (The University Library), Oslo (Mr Oddvar Vasstveit, curator of manuscripts); University of Glasgow, archives (Mr Michael Moss); University of Sydney, archives (Mr G. L. Fisher); Alexander Turnbull Library, Wellington, N.Z.

For help generously given, I thank Miss Hilary Bryans; Baron de Gerlache de Gomery; Mr Martin Gilbert; Mrs Nancy Mary Goodall; Mr Martin Gruselle of Baring Brothers and Co. Ltd.; Professor Sir Stuart Hampshire; Mr R. K. Headland; Mrs Kate Hedworth of Christie's; Mr Harald Horjen, of Aschehoug & Co., Oslo; Mrs Anne James; Mr H. J. James-Martin; Mr J. N. Littlewood of Rowe & Pitman; Dr Des. Lugg and Mr Robert Reeves of the Antarctic Division, Hobart, Tasmania; Mrs Anne Majgaard; General Sir James Marshall-Cornwall; Dr Laura Mill; Mr Bedford

Osborne; Miss Alison Paul of the Dunn Nutritional Laboratory, Cambridge; Rear Admiral M. J. Ross; Mr Edmund de Rothschild; Mr Malcolm Rumsey of Lloyds; Mrs Anne Sahlin; Mr Douglas Stevens; Dr Michael Stevens; Dr Charles Swithinbank; Group Captain J. D. Tomkinson; Mrs Joan Wooding.

Thanks are also due to The Associated Biscuit Manufacturers Ltd.; Australian Archives, Canberra and Brighton, Vic.; Bovril Ltd; The British Library, manuscript collection and Newspaper Library, Colindale; Cambridge University Library; Cayzer, Irvine & Co. (Union Castle Line); Central Library, Dundee; Companies House, The Devon County Librarian; The Durham County Record Office, Edinburgh Public Library; Eastbourne Central Library; the Guildhall Library, London; Gyldendal Norsk Forlag, Oslo; The Hertfordshire County Record Office; The Hocken Library, Dunedin, N.Z.; The Home Office; the Hudson's Bay Company; The Jockey Club; Det Kongelige Bibliotek (The Royal Library), Copenhagen; The London School of Hygiene and Tropical Medicine; Memorial University of Newfoundland; National Library of Australia, Canberra; National Library of Scotland, Edinburgh; National Maritime Museum, Greenwich; Naval Historical Library, Ministry of Defence; Norsk Sjøfartsmuseum (Norwegian Maritime Museum), Oslo; Otago Harbour Board, Dunedin, N.Z.; Registrar General of Shipping and Seamen; Public Archives of Canada; Riksarkivet (Swedish State archives), Stockholm; the Royal Aeronautical Society; the Royal Scottish Geographical Society; St Bartholomew's Hospital; the Somerset Record Office; the State Library of Victoria; Tekniska Museet (Technical Museum), Stockholm; The Tyne and Wear County Archives; University of Edinburgh Library; University Library, Dundee; University of Liverpool; Vetenskapsakadamiens Bibliotek (Library of the Royal Academy of Science), Stockholm; The Wellcome Institute for the History of Medicine; The Whipple Museum of the History of Science, Cambridge.

I made extensive use of the indispensable archives both at the Royal Geographical Society, and at the Scott Polar Research Institute, Cambridge. In the latter, I found most of the Shackleton material which was made available to me.

The author and publisher are grateful to the following for permission to use copyright material:

Mrs Alda Bittemor Amundsen for the diaries of Roald Amundsen; Mr M. L. Bernacchi, for the diaries of L. J. Bernacchi; Miss E. M. David for the papers of Professor Sir Edgeworth David; Faber and Faber Ltd. and Harcourt Brace Jovanovich Inc. for the quotation from *The Waste Land*; Mrs Minna Eyre for the diaries of Admiral Royds; Julian Ayer and Professor Sir Stuart Hampshire, for the diaries of Lieutenant-Colonel T. H. Orde-Lees; Dr Derek Harbord, for the diaries of Commander A. E. Harbord; Mrs J. Ruth Hatch, for the papers of Captain Rupert England; Mrs Margaret Hubert, for the diaries and manuscripts of Sir Raymond Priestley; Mr J. S. James, for the diaries of Professor R. W. James; Mr Bjørn Tore Larsen, for the diaries of Captain C. A. Larsen; Mrs Jean Macklin, for the papers of Dr A. J. Macklin; the Mawson Institute for Antarctic Research for the papers of Sir Douglas Mawson; Lieutenant-Colonel E. R. G. Oates, for the letters of Mrs Caroline Oates and Captain L. E. G. Oates; the Royal Archives, Windsor, for the diaries of King George V; Commander J. W. Skelton, for the diaries of Admiral R. W. Skelton; the Society of Authors for granting permission on behalf of the Bernard Shaw estate to quote from Bernard Shaw's letters.

I wish particularly to thank Mr Herman Mehren, for lending me his mountain hut in Norway; also my brother-in-law Mr Bertil Roos and sister-in-law Mrs Maja Pauli, for allowing me to stay at their summer homes in the Swedish countryside: all places of escape where this book was partly written.

If I have overlooked anybody, or failed to trace the correct copyright holders, I hope they will forgive me.

Acknowledgment of help does not imply endorsement of the views expressed in this book; I am answerable for them alone. Similarly, any errors are my responsibility.

Finally, I want to thank my wife and also my sons, Nicholas and Anthony, for their considerable patience while I was working on this book. They too have played their part.

Shackleton

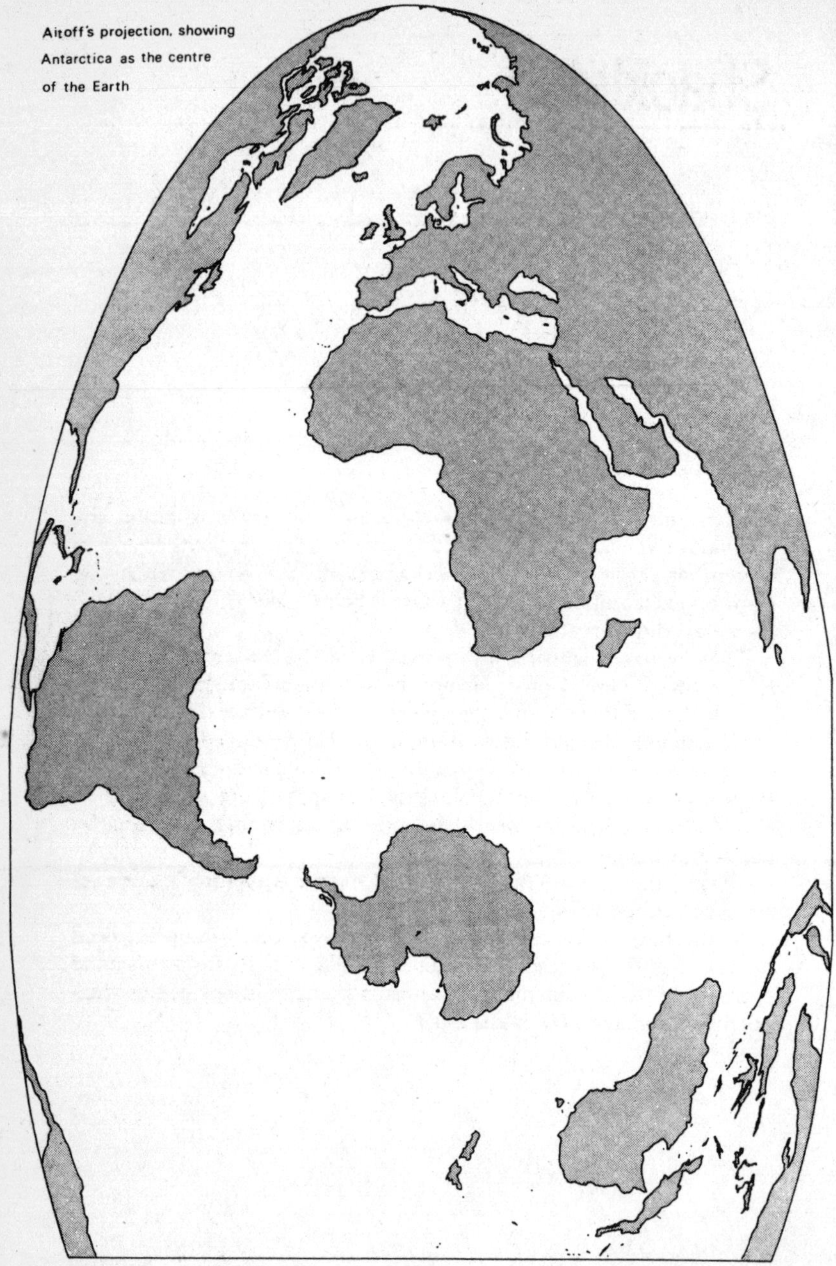

Aitoff's projection, showing Antarctica as the centre of the Earth

Prologue

"Great Shack!"

In the summer of 1909, some children were walking along the seafront at Sheringham, in Norfolk. One of them, as another was to remember down the years, "suddenly said: 'You know, when you want an exclamation, don't say "Great Scott", say "Great Shack!"' So we all did. Great Shack!"[1]

They were all cousins, by marriage, of the Antarctic explorer, Ernest Shackleton. Cousin or not, he was their idol. In his rivalry with Robert Falcon Scott, they were his devoted partisans.

Shackleton was an Edwardian hero. He belonged to the last epoch of terrestrial discovery before the exploration of space began. He hungered for the South Pole: "the last spot of the world," as he put it, "that counts as worth the striving for though ungilded by aught but adventure."[2]

During the Great War of 1914–18 even his country's enemies were concerned about his fate.

At the limit of his endurance in the snows, Shackleton believed he saw a ghostly presence by his side. To him it was a mystical experience – and it inspired a haunting passage in one of the great poems of our age, *The Waste Land*.

I

Anglo-Irish background

Ernest Henry Shackleton was an Anglo-Irishman. He thus belonged to an extraordinary breed.

From Sheridan and Goldsmith to Oscar Wilde and George Bernard Shaw, the Anglo-Irish have poured out playwrights in a flood. So too among soldiers; from Wellington to Alexander, the Anglo-Irish have begotten generals out of all proportion to their numbers. Jonathan Swift also was Anglo-Irish, Richard Steele as well. Playwrights, generals, satirists and wits; these were the characteristic Anglo-Irish products, interlarded with admirals and an explorer or two.

The Anglo-Irish formed, in the best sense of the term, an imperial governing class. They were the hereditary rulers of Ireland, when it was still England's oldest colony – a race apart, by definition Protestant, the so-called Protestant Ascendancy. Selection was rigidly by creed. They were privileged landowners. Urbane and civilised, yet also improvident and eccentric, they put their own stamp on Irish society. They were the descendants of English settlers implanted down the centuries in an attempt to solve the already too familiar Irish question, by Protestant colonisation over the heads of the indigenous Catholics. A more or less embattled minority, they had all the vigour of settlers surviving in a hostile land. Dublin society was their creation. They identified so passionately with the country they ruled that they considered themselves Irish, and English hardly at all.

The Shackletons came originally from Yorkshire. The founder of the family was Abraham Shackleton, a Quaker, who moved to Ireland early in the eighteenth century and started a school at Ballitore, near Dublin. One of Abraham's pupils happened to be

Edmund Burke, the political philosopher, among the greatest of the Anglo-Irish. One very Irish contemporary of Burke's wrote of how Philip of Macedon "thanked the Gods, at the birth of Alexander, not so much for their having blessed him with a son, as for that son's being born at a time when an Aristotle was living to superintend his education. Mr Burke's father must have felt similar emotions on finding a Shuckleton [*sic*] in his neighbourhood to train up the young orator."[1]

Henry Shackleton, Ernest's father, was Abraham's direct descendant in the fourth generation. He was brought up an Anglican, not a Quaker, of the first generation of apostates. He tried to enter the Army, but sickness stopped him, and he became a farmer instead.

It was in the green, fertile, rolling fields of County Kildare, among the most opulent of the Anglo-Irish that he settled, at a place called Kilkea. It was in the ancient English Pale of settlement which had existed since Strongbow and his Anglo-Normans originally conquered Ireland in the twelfth century.

Kilkea was a very Irish place. To the east, was a view of the mountains of Wicklow. Dublin was thirty miles away. On a rise lay an Anglo-Norman castle; started in 1180, incompletely rebuilt in the fifteenth century, and now the somewhat tumbledown property of the Duke of Leinster. Out among the fields lay the cottages of the Irish peasantry; and clustered around the crossroads in the protective shadow of the castle, were the homes of the Anglo-Irish gentry; large, rambling Georgian houses with a distinctive eighteenth-century air. It was in one of these, Kilkea House, that Henry Shackleton lived. There, in 1874, on 15 February, Ernest Shackleton was born, a Protestant from the Pale, a scion of the Ascendancy. In later years he liked to recall that he shared his birthday with Galileo.

Ernest Shackleton was the second child and elder son of a family that eventually numbered two brothers and eight sisters. Numbers, however, did not mean distress. There was enough to eat, and a comfortable home.

"In favourable circumstances," says an Anglo-Irish writer, "it must be admitted that in general the Irish are more amusing than the English or the Scots."[2] Bearded and upstanding, Shackleton's father looked the complete nineteenth-century patriarch, but he only played the part in moderation, and Shackleton escaped the grimmer versions of Victorian upbringing. His mother knew how to manage her husband and her children, giving them – perhaps on that account – a secure and happy home, wherever it might happen to be. Born Henrietta Letitia Sophia Gavan, she married Henry

Shackleton in 1872 and, on one side of her family, brought a touch of Irish blood into an otherwise pure Anglo-Irish lineage. Her virtues were total lack of pretension, and an unshakeable, almost exasperating optimism that recalls another Anglo-Irish remark about the Irish having "a certain fecklessness at worst, a trust in Providence at best".[3]

The tales clustering around Ernest Shackleton the child suggest an ordinarily troublesome boy, and very much the Irishman. They seem largely to illustrate persuasiveness, plausibility, and a capacity to hide shrewd calculation under onion skins of charm. In one, he induces a housemaid to help him dig in the garden for buried treasure, having first salted the claim with a ruby ring belonging to his mother. In another, he convinces one of his sisters that the Monument in London had been erected in his honour.

One tale at least has the air of authenticity. Because his nanny had made him afraid of thunder, he asked to be hidden in the nursery cupboard during a thunderstorm. In after years, he did not like this mentioned. Nonetheless, he grew up with the unique self-confidence that is the priceless gift of privilege, or a colonial upbringing, however poor the purse.

Shackleton's birth coincided with one of the disastrous periodic failures of the potato crop that are so much part of Irish history. That meant an agricultural depression and hard times for farmers, but Henry Shackleton had no sentimental devotion to the land. He was a typical Anglo-Irishman, and therefore a survivalist. In 1880, before it was too late, he left his acres for Trinity College, Dublin. He had been there before, becoming Classical Prizeman. Now, at the age of thirty-three, he began to read medicine and start a new career. He took his family with him. Ernest thus became, at a receptive age, an honorary Dubliner.

In 1884, immediately after qualifying Dr Shackleton crossed the water to settle in England for good. Two years before, not far from his Dublin home, had occurred the Phoenix Park assassination, when Lord Frederick Cavendish, the Chief Secretary for Ireland, was murdered by Catholic fanatics. The Irish Question was then in one of its periods of ferment; and since he believed in Home Rule for Ireland, Henry Shackleton sensed that Protestant power and English suzerainty could no longer be taken for granted. It was time to go. Just as Abraham Shackleton had arrived for the "great century" of the Anglo-Irish, Henry Shackleton left when they were in decline.

Money also had a hand in the move. Besides the agricultural decay that had driven Henry Shackleton off the land, better prospects lured him over the Irish sea. His first practice, at South

Croydon, was a failure, so after six months he moved to Sydenham. There he held his own, and there he stayed. It was in suburban London, therefore, that Ernest Shackleton passed the remainder of his boyhood.

His mother had by now become mysteriously an invalid, and was to remain one for the last forty years of her life. She spent her waking hours in her sick room, scarcely noticed by her family. It was Dr Shackleton who brought up his children, helped by his mother-in-law, and various female relatives who came over periodically from Ireland.

A male creature in an overwhelmingly female household, Ernest ran the risk of being crushed. He did not, at any rate, have an even submissive temperament but, in an Irish idiom, he was "down in the cellar or up in the garret". In spite, or because of this, his many sisters, to quote one of them, Eleanore, "all adored him". He had already learned how to charm his womenfolk into submission.

This all took place in a puritan menage where there was much Bible reading, in the sonorous language of the Authorised Version. The girls were not allowed out to parties, and there was a ban on all kinds of drink. It was Ernest, however, who put fervour into this cause. With his mobile and expressive face, he was the picture of intensity. He became a youthful advocate of abstinence, persuaded the servants to take the pledge, and his sisters to join him in the Band of Hope, a children's temperance organisation. Decked out in blue ribbons they would march past the pubs singing songs like,

> . . . once a mother's love
> Shielded me from all the cares of life,
> But a year ago, sorrow laid her low
> Mother died a wretched drunkard's wife.[4]

Until the age of eleven and a half, Shackleton was educated at home by a governess. He then went to Fir Lodge Preparatory School, down the road from his home, Aberdeen House in West Hill. Fir Lodge was run by a spinster of a certain age, "the redoubtable Miss Higgins (with her ear trumpet) and her Chief of Staff Miss Parry", to quote an old pupil. "Shackleton, whom I remember well," he said after sixty years,

> was a big strong well made youngster & being a little older had little to do with us smaller fry, but he was always friendly & good natured. I remember once meeting him in West Hill wearing a smart new suit which he explained he was getting used to before wearing it every day.

> His father . . . was . . . our family doctor . . . In spite of his alarming beard he was very kind & gentle . . . We often met the daughters walking two & two in the streets of Sydenham.[5]

It was in any case at Fir Lodge that Shackleton first learned the lesson of his background.

To be Anglo-Irish, in the words of John Beckett, an Irish historian, was to be "caught between two conflicting influences; Irish by birth and circumstances, they lived in a cultural atmosphere that was essentially English".[6] And, he went on to say, "the most pervasive Anglo-Irish quality is a kind of ambivalence or ambiguity of outlook, arising from the need to be at once Irish and English".

In Dublin, much effort had been spent on eradicating Ernest's brogue to make him speak like a little Englishman. But at Fir Lodge his speech stamped him as an Irishman. Indeed, on one St Patrick's day, he and a fellow-Irish pupil were compelled by their schoolmates to have a fight "in honour of the sacred memory of St Patrick". An Irishman in England Shackleton remained for the rest of his days.

In 1887 Shackleton left Fir Lodge to go to Dulwich College. "From what I remember he did very little work," an old schoolfellow remarked, "and if there was a scrap he was usually in it."[7]

Dulwich was not exactly one of the great public schools with aristocratic connections. In the words of one old boy, it was

> what you would call a middle class school. We were all the sons of reasonably solvent but not wealthy parents, and we all had to earn our living later on . . . Compared with Eton, Dulwich would be something like an American State university compared with Harvard or Princeton.[8]

This was not quite fair. Dulwich was founded in 1618, and it became a solid Victorian public school. It fulfilled its own aim of sending out imperial administrators. It produced a large number of businessmen. It was also a nursery for writers. Unlike most public schools, it was intended for boys living in the neighbourhood, and was therefore not predominantly boarding. It was within walking distance of the Shackleton home. In any case, it was what Dr Shackleton could afford, and Ernest entered as a day boy.

"It is very doubtful whether he was ever like other boys," *The Captain*, a schoolboy magazine, wrote of Shackleton's Dulwich days. It went on to say that he was "rather an odd boy who, in spite of an adventurous nature and the spirit of romance that was in him, loved a book better than a bat, solitude better than a crowd, his own companionship better than a mob of other lads, a boy who kept his own counsel, never except for brief moments let his thoughts show on his tongue – a grim, determined headstrong fellow of whom the discerning would prophesy great things, and the undiscerning miserable failure."

This was written twenty years on, by which time Shackleton had become one of the famous Edwardians. It was, as the writer frankly put it, an attempt to "reconstruct a man's boyhood out of the materials of his manhood".

The Captain was aimed at public schoolboys. It published, incidentally, some of the first stories of P. G. Wodehouse, one of the most celebrated Old Alleynians, as Dulwich Old Boys are called, after the Elizabethan actor Edward Alleyn, who founded the school. Shackleton was presented as one of their illustrious products, an exemplar of the working of the system, yet Shackleton himself complained that Dulwich had not

> taught me things . . . I never learned much geography at school, for instance. [It] consisted . . . in names of towns, lists of capes and bays and islands. Literature, too, consisted in the dissection, the parsing, the analysing of certain passages from our great poets and prose-writers . . . teachers should be very careful not to spoil their taste for poetry for all time by making it a task and an imposition.[9]

At school, as this indicates, Shackleton was unspeakably bored. As a result, he was usually near the bottom of his form. *The Captain* sympathised. The magazine was a bit of a maverick, discreetly campaigning for better teaching, and advocated engineering as a desirable profession for public schoolboys. From Shackleton's tale, this was the moral that it drew:

> The elemental forces of school life are a great unconscious training for a boy, and from these blind and semi-blind forces there emerge independence, grit, initiative and, once in a while, greatness.[10]

If you are unhappy at school, *The Captain* seems to be saying, do not despair; so were many famous men.

Not that Shackleton was a grand rebel or a spectacular misfit; he was simply unsuited to formalised academic schooling. "Education" then meant Latin and Greek, with Oxford or Cambridge the goal. Shackleton, however, was on the Modern side, which instead taught French, German and mathematics, intended for those going into business. This did not appeal to Shackleton. Nor did he excel at rugby or cricket. Indeed, he was ill at ease with team games. In most aspects of school life, therefore, he was out of place. He used to seek refuge, sometimes in reading, notably, like others of his kind, *The Boys' Own Paper*.

The *BOP* was a British institution. Every Saturday, for 1½d,* it dispensed an inimitable blend of escapism, practical advice ("How to tame a Snake"), moral uplift, true adventure, first class fiction, patriotism and blood and thunder serials like "Nearly garotted, a story of the Cuban Insurrection."[11] It was exactly calculated to inspire a late Victorian schoolboy like Ernest Shackleton. He had "dark hair & large grey-blue eyes", a school-friend's sister was to remember down the years. "He was always full of fun."[12] Of medium height, but broad-shouldered and pugnacious; nicknamed variously Mick, Mike, Mickey, and "The fighting Shackleton", an inveterate practical joker, the leader of a small gang of cronies and an occasional truant, he had the makings of a character from Kipling.

Shackleton's best friend at Dulwich was Nicetas Petrides, a boy of Greek extraction. They lived in the same road at Sydenham, West Hill, and used to walk to school together. On one seaside holiday at St Leonards, Petrides and his brother saved Shackleton from drowning. "For this," Petrides recalled, "we were duly rewarded by him by each being treated to an ice."[13] Not surprisingly, perhaps, Petrides' abiding memory of Shackleton was that even at the age of fifteen he could not swim.

Dr Shackleton wanted Ernest to follow him into the medical profession. Ernest, however, wanted to go to sea. In this, too, *The Boys' Own Paper* may have had a hand, with its nautical adventures, like *Great Shipwrecks of the World*, or perhaps even with its serialisation of *20,000 Leagues under the Sea*, which introduced Shackleton to Jules Verne's science fiction tale of the electric submarine *Nautilus*. Electricity was then the genie of the lamp, as the atom and the micro chip have since become, but Shackleton's response was wholly romantic. He saw himself as Captain Nemo, the mysterious captain of the *Nautilus*, a pirate, an Ishmael, a Robin Hood done up in sinister modern dress. It was an act of identification that persisted into adulthood, when Shackleton turned to Nemo as a *nom de guerre*.

The headmaster of Dulwich, A. H. Gilkes, was a legendary figure, tall, white-bearded, forbidding and patriarchal; "almost an incarnation", to quote someone recalling his schooldays, "of a boy's view of God". [14] Gilkes, however, was hardly the caricature of a Victorian martinet. Boys, he once said,

* A "penny ha'penny"; about 2/3p, but 11p in present terms.

> always should be treated with the utmost politeness and with everyone's best manners. Respectful kindness is more or less the secret of the whole matter, combined with a patience and a watchfulness and a trustfulness that never dies.[15]

Nonetheless, Dulwich was run with firm discipline; but Shackleton became known for the way he managed to avoid punishment under Gilkes' regime.

When, as frequently, he was late for school, Shackleton would start on a long and plainly fantastical explanation. Resisting all attempts by the master to cut him short, he would insist on telling his tale. Shackleton's excuses became a regular entertainment – so the story goes – in which the whole form was mesmerised by his very Irish capacity to grip an audience, and in the process he usually escaped the mandatory detention. Whether he actually believed what he was saying, was another matter altogether.

Evidently, Shackleton was not the usual kind of boy who keeps daydreams decently as daydreams. He inhabited the twilight world between imagination and reality and such people, as Dr Shackleton no doubt knew, will eventually go their own way, for better or for worse. Not that Dr Shackleton was exactly a model of conformity himself. He practised homeopathy, and thus was a medical dissenter, as his forebears had been religious dissenters. But he had learned not to resist the inevitable, and his son would be allowed to go to sea.

The Navy was one answer, but Dr Shackleton could hardly afford the fees for *Britannia*, the cadet training ship at Dartmouth. These were £70 a year whereas it had only cost £15 a year to keep Ernest at Dulwich. In any case, while the matter was being thrashed out, Shackleton passed the age limit for entry, which was 14½. There remained *Worcester* or *Conway*, the cadet training ships for the mercantile marine but, to quote Shackleton himself, "My father thought to cure me of my predilection for the sea by letting me go in the most primitive manner possible as a 'boy' on board a sailing ship at a shilling a month!"[16]

Dr Shackleton nonetheless had no wish to consign his son to a hell ship. Through a cousin, the Rev. G. W. Woosnam, who happened to be Superintendent of the Mersey Mission to Seamen, he secured a good berth with reasonable owners, the North Western Shipping Company of Liverpool. The ship was a full rigger called the *Hoghton Tower*. But before Shackleton could sail, he still had to endure one more term at school. Partly this was due to the necessary notice of removal; partly to the delay in preparing the ship for sea.

His chosen goal now within reach, Shackleton abruptly began to work more strenuously. For the first time at Dulwich, he worked hard. Looking back, he seemed to think that he was a kind of boy for whom school had ceased to be of any benefit, and that this at last had been acknowledged. Whatever the explanation, when he left Dulwich, at the end of the Lent term, 1890, he was near the top of the Lower Modern Fourth, the apex of his school career. He had just turned sixteen, and been at Dulwich a little less than three years. On 19 April he went to Liverpool to join the *Hoghton Tower*. The impression he left behind him, as one of his teachers put it, was that of "a rolling stone who would probably gather no moss".[17]

II

Round the Horn

In *Hoghton Tower* Shackleton was bound for Valparaiso round Cape Horn in a square rigged ship. It was the kind of first voyage that belongs to sailors' folklore.

Cape Horn has a special place in the mythology of the sea. The last outlier of the Americas towards the south, it juts out into tempestuous seas, a byword of danger and distress. There was, too, a mystique about the square rigger. Billowing with canvas under full sail, it possessed an incomparable beauty. It was also the fastest and the most dangerous sailing ship to handle. It produced its own breed of men. They and their ships were made to be driven hard.

A few days out, Shackleton discovered the literal meaning of the expression "learning the ropes". A ship is like a musical instrument, with her rigging and her sails the strings. In the rigging of the *Hoghton Tower*, there were over two hundred ropes, each with its own name. Shackleton had to learn them all. He was taught in the traditional way by the mate of his watch, who took him round the deck, pointing out the ropes, and examined him daily, helping memory by hitting him with a knotted rope end at each mistake. To confuse a clewline with a halyard, for example, or a lee brace with a weather backstay, could mean the end of the ship and everybody in her. The language of the sea is precise, and it must be learned quickly.

"I can tell you Nic," Shackleton wrote to his school friend Petrides from the *Hoghton Tower*, "that it is pretty hard work, and dirty work too. It is a queer life and a risky one"; he continued in his oddly punctuated, conversational style,

> you carry your life in your hand whenever you go aloft, in bad weather; how would you like to be 150 feet up in the air; hanging on with one

hand to a rope while with the other you try and get the sail in . . . and there is the ship rocking pitching and rolling about like a live creature. It takes you about an hour to get even a light sail in; so you can imagine how long it would take us to get a sail; with about 500 squ. feet of canvas in it in; even with 27 hands working. I can tell you its [*sic*] not all honey at sea.[1]

Numbed by the personal vindictiveness which, of all natural forces, only the wind suggests, Shackleton was learning the lesson of self-preservation, part of his initiation into an exclusive but dwindling brotherhood. *Hoghton Tower* symbolised the rearguard of the age of sail. Built of steel, of 1,700 tons displacement, Al at Lloyd's, she represented the sailing ship at the apex of its technical development, the last flowering before steam finally took over. The sailing ship only existed now by grace of the technical deficiencies of the steam engine and, as these were eliminated, sail was forced to retreat. By the time Shackleton went to sea, the sailing ship was doomed, but it survived as the scavenger of the oceans, picking up cargoes the steamers spurned. This usually meant unpleasant and dangerous cargoes: coal out from Britain to the East; nitrates (for fertilisers) home from the Pacific coast of South America.

Shackleton reached Cape Horn in the middle of the southern winter. Because it is against the prevailing winds, going round the Horn is usually harder east to west. It took the *Hoghton Tower* almost two months, fighting against the storms. To cap everything, there was the danger of icebergs on the prowl. Sometimes it must have seemed to a slightly frightened Shackleton that the ship was on the point of foundering, and possibly she was. It was, in short, a typical rough passage; the stuff of many a sailor's yarn.

Battered and seaworn, the *Hoghton Tower* ran for Valparaiso which she reached in the middle of August. From there she sailed for Iquique, a dreary tropical roadstead in Chile. There, for six monotonous weeks, she loaded nitrates and Shackleton learned how to work cargo in heavy boats through the surf – for Iquique did not offer the luxury of quays and cranes alongside. The *Hoghton Tower* returned to Liverpool at the end of April 1891, with food and water running out. It was all in the hard tradition of the age of sail.

So far Shackleton, or rather his calling, had been on probation. Now he had to decide whether to go home or be bound apprentice to qualify as an officer. It was the first great decision of his life.

"I think if I had hated the sea, I should have still stuck to it," Shackleton used to say in after years. "But I didn't hate it, although I found it a hard life."[2] Perhaps there was in this a grain of revolt against his father. Closer to the event, his captain, a strict but understanding man, said after that first voyage that Shackleton was "the most pig-headed, obstinate boy I have ever come across".[3] But beyond this did Shackleton perhaps sense that he was a kind of outcast, able only to approach contentment away from the mortal coil of life ashore?

In those days there was no wireless. Once out of sight of land, every ship was an island, each voyage an escape. On the *Hoghton Tower*, for all its hardship, Shackleton had the solace of being among others of his kind. They were epitomised in the captain who, afloat, was a kind of god but, as soon as he set foot ashore, seemed to shrink into the herd. They all seemed bound by some flaw that disqualified them from fulfilment on land.

So Shackleton chose the sea, and he signed his indentures. Before him lay at least four years hard sailing.

He returned to the *Hoghton Tower*; this time with an unsympathetic captain. Did he nurse a twinge of regret? "I suppose there must be a great change in our respective persons", he wrote to Petrides, who had now entered his father's firm of sponge merchants. "You will doubtless be a city man by this time." Perhaps Shackleton was wishing *his* father was a prosperous sponge importer, instead of a suburban doctor; for after the neat sheltered existence of a respectable London suburb, Shackleton was now having to learn to cope with men at sea:

> The characters you meet with [he continued his letter to Petrides,] are the most mixed kinds. for instance in the watch I am in viz.: – the starboard one; there is an American who had to flee his country for killing a coloured man; and another who was foreman in large timber works . . . another owner of a large cattle ranch in one of the central States of North America; they through various means have come down to a ships [*sic*] forecastle. Only the other day I saw a man stab another with a knife in the thigh right up to the handle . . .

"I suppose you have forgotten my existence altogether being away", Shackleton ended, "good bye old man always through life your true friend."[4]

On the *Hoghton Tower* Shackleton now shuttled between Liverpool, South America and the East: five times round Cape Horn; once round the Cape; each voyage an education on its own; half-way round the world without touching land; three or four months continuously at sea. In July 1894, he finally paid off in order to take his examination for Second Mate. He passed on 28 August. Six weeks later, he obtained his certificate for adjusting compasses. At the age of twenty Shackleton had become a qualified foreign-going Mate.

Shackleton left the *Hoghton Tower* with a reputation for being out of the ordinary. Men at sea, however, especially in sail, have always been varied to a fault and Shackleton was recognisably a type; or rather, as one of his shipmates later put it, he was "several types bound in one volume".[5]

He was still, for example, the proselytising abstainer of his schooldays. "I have 11 names down in my pledge book," he told Petrides, naively adding, "all of the fellows did not keep it, it is a great pity the way sailors spend their money; in making themselves lower than the very beasts." Nor, like other apprentices, was Shackleton sexually precocious.

> It is a hard job to keep straight here but I know where to go for help; so I am kept through the many temptations around me.[6]

"Communing with the stars" on watch kept him away from the women down by the dockside – Shackleton said, afterwards. He was, in the words of a shipmate, "a lad you could never get at, because when he wasn't on duty on the deck he was stowed away in his cabin with his books . . . He was full of it . . . he could quote poetry . . . And the other lads used to say 'Old Shack's busy with his books'."[7]

Browning, a standard favourite of the age, was the poet whom Shackleton could, and did, quote to anyone he could persuade to stand and listen. This was a legacy from home. Like many middle-class Victorian households, the Shackletons cultivated poetry, partly as entertainment, and partly as moral uplift. Shackleton himself, however, was not only reciting poetry; as his ship rose and swooped over the waves, he was secretly trying to write it as well, but he made the terrible discovery that the stanzas bore little resemblance to the tremendous emotions welling up within. It was the first, perhaps the greatest bafflement of his life.

Such was the mildly paradoxical figure with his fresh Second Mate's certificate in hand. Having left school with the stigma of being anything but scholarly, he had became "old Shacks" who was always "busy with his books". Now also muscular and agile after four years' shinning up the rigging, with his square jutting jaw, and eye a-gleam with stern purpose, he set out on the next stage of his career. He had to put in sea time to qualify for his First Mate's certificate. He nursed no romantic addiction to sail, and sought a change through a berth in steam.

Instead of doing the usual round of shipping offices, Shackleton went to an old school friend, Owen Burne, making intelligent use of the old-boy network. ("Favouritism," said Admiral Fisher, the great naval reformer, "is the secret of our efficiency!") Because Burne was a wine merchant, Shackleton assumed he must know some shipowners. Burne did and introduced him to Major Jenkins, senior partner of the Welsh Shire Line, who offered him a Fourth Mate's berth. As Burne himself told the tale:

> A few days later I met Jenkins and he said, "that's a rum fellow Shackleton," I said "what has he done," and his reply was he had been to see the ship and he did not like the 4th mates quarters but would go as third.
>
> I told him I was very sorry and asked him what he did about it and he said "I rather liked the chap and gave it him".[8]

The berth was on a tramp steamer called the *Monmouthshire*, and in the middle of November 1894 Shackleton shipped on her for China, Japan and the Straits Settlements, which began five years' sailing to the Far East and America.

On the *Hoghton Tower* Shackleton had made friends with a seaman of his own age, although apprentices, as future officers, were not supposed to mix with their social inferiors before the mast. An engineer on one of his later ships vividly recalled how, at the time, "a marked 'standoffishness' existed between officers and engineers, but Shackleton soon broke down the barrier".[9]

> "Do you know," I said to him, "I always thought that you belonged to the Ha! Ha! brigade, who considered engineers beneath their notice." "To tell you the real truth old man," Shackleton said, "I am of a retiring and nervous disposition, and prefer to remain in the background. I dislike being snubbed."[10]

Shackleton, at any rate, was proving to be at home with all kinds of men, but he was still "Old Shacks" always "busy with his books". Sometimes he was working for his First Mate's examination. More often, on his watch below, as he sat in his tiny cabin, which reverberated to the measured stamp of the ship's engines, he was reading for pleasure. It was very rarely fiction, more often history: "A certain type of history," as he once put it. "I read Motley's *History of the Dutch Republic* . . . and its fascinating story of the way that little nation became a great naval power and a great colonising race . . . Prescott I [also] read."[11]

As Shackleton tallied cargo under Eastern skies, the Union Jack often waved on the flagstaff at the port. Two out of every three ships he saw flew the Red Ensign. Everywhere, he could glimpse the White Ensign on a warship, a far-flung symbol of British naval might, policing the seaways of the world. He was tangibly experiencing the British Empire, the largest yet known, yet he chose to read about two other great empires: the Spanish and the Dutch. The trouble about British imperial literature was that, to a romantic like Shackleton, it seemed impossibly dismal (but not, of course, the deeds). It oozed high moral purpose. For vigorous reading, one had to look elsewhere.

Prescott, to whom Shackleton turned, is the historian of the Spanish American Empire; his heroes, the conquistadores of the sixteenth century, were explorers on a monumental scale, unburdened by moralistic delusions, conquering a continent with a handful of men; down-at-heel adventurers who made their fortunes by themselves. To Shackleton, this was notably inspiring. He found Prescott's romantic tale of Pizarro conquering Peru for his own unashamed gain conspicuously more attractive (and convincing?) than, for example, Livingstone gloomily trudging through Africa for the good of the natives' souls. So, Shackleton soaked himself in the heady stuff of personal fulfilment in the age of the individual, interlaced with the poetry of Browning, devoted to the inspection of his own soul.

In 1896 Shackleton, without much difficulty, passed for First Mate. In April 1898, he was certified as Master. At the age of twenty-four he had qualified to command a British ship anywhere on the seven seas.

Shackleton was then on another Welsh Line ship, the *Flintshire*. "Well Shacky," a shipmate recalled saying soon after,

> "what do you think of this old tub? You'll be skipper of her one day." "You see, old man," he said "as long as I remain with this company, I'll never be more than a skipper. But I think I can do something better. In fact, really, I would like to make a name for myself (he paused for a moment or two) and her." He was looking pensively over the sea at the moment, and I noticed his face light up at the mention of "her".[12]

Even allowing for the sentimentality of the age, it says something of Shackleton's personality that he could talk like this and get away with it. The "her" of this passage was Emily Dorman, a neighbour at Sydenham, and a friend of his sister Kathleen.

Shackleton had remained very much attached to his family. His sisters, one of them recalled with relish, he called his "harem":

> "Come all my wives," he would shout when he entered the house after a voyage. He would lie down and call out: "Come Fatima, tickle my toes. Come, oh favoured one and scratch my back." Of course we all loved it.[13]

It was probably inevitable that Shackleton would be attracted by one of his sisters' friends. He had met Emily Dorman at home in the summer of 1897 when she was visiting Kathleen. Shackleton was between voyages on the *Flintshire* just back from Japan. He was twenty-three, and she six years older, a tall, dark-haired young woman with a good figure; not exactly beautiful, but definitely attractive, and with a formidable hint of motherly firmness behind a soft manner. Had he heard of her before? Did his sisters arrange the meeting for reasons of their own? Shackleton, at any rate, was soon urgently in pursuit.

At the end of 1898 the *Flintshire* ran aground near Middlesbrough. Shackleton took the opportunity to beg 24-hours' leave and go home, ostensibly for his father's birthday on 1 January. At Sydenham, on the way, he visited The Firs, where Emily lived. She recalled how

> We spent the evening in the billiard room, – he told me how he loved me – I was deeply moved – I remember so well – because he put his cigarette on a ledge in the big oak chimney piece – & it burnt a deep dent – which we tried to rub out – and we often looked at it in after days – but no one else noticed it! . . . I let him out through the conservatory about 10.30 I think and he kissed my hand – he went home then to wish his father "many happy returns".[14]

It was the first time Shackleton had been seriously in love. Others before him had been interested in Emily, but Shackleton, in the words of a friend, gave an impression of "inexhaustible animal spirits, of exuberant vitality, of explosive energy".[15] This, perhaps, was what Emily hankered for, and perhaps, too, she dimly discerned that in the true Spanish sense, Shackleton was a kind of Don Juan; someone to whom the pursuit, not the conquest, was satisfaction.

In any case both were inhibited by the grotesqueries of Victorian morality. On the other hand, it lent piquancy to their affair. Browning became their bond, for Browning turned out to be Emily's favourite poet too, and they were soon presenting each other with his works. Browning also provided Shackleton with a vehicle for his thoughts, which he now proceeded to expound.

Loquacious and flamboyant as he was, Shackleton perhaps saw in Emily the first person to whom he could unburden himself.

"Listen," he wrote in one of the letters that now began to flow between them. "Listen, I do not want Paracelsus' happiness. I would attain, but the goal is that to which Aprile yearned."[16] To express himself, Shackleton had chosen one of Browning's more obscure works. Paracelsus is the hero of a long dramatic poem of that name, a kind of Faust figure, prepared to renounce love as the price for knowledge, fame and power. Aprile, one of the figures in the poem, takes the other view. Only love can make achievement worthwhile; "I would love infinitely," he is made to say, "and be loved."[17]

> What can I call success [Shackleton continued in his letter] a few years praise from those around and then down to the grave with the knowledge that the best thing has been missed: unless the worlds success brings that to pass and for me it seems a long way off.[18]

By the standards of the day, Emily Dorman was quite conventional. She appeared passive yet responsive. She knew how to flirt. Her aim, eventually, was marriage. Until then, she would live with her family. Afterwards, she would pass from her father's to her husband's care. She was with her family at Lugano, in the Alps, when Shackleton was at Port Said, on the way to China, suffering the miseries of separation and hope deferred. He wrote,

> It is because of my unhappy nature to stick to the truth to be true to others as to myself; that things seem so hard! I walk on Hells Paving stones burning my feet, yes twisting my hearts roots in the pain of it. Down in the dark with no ray of light . . . the other day you put life at its best about thirty years of age and the rest down hill . . .
>
> You ask me to tell you what I do every day. I think, curse it all, think again and hope; that is all, truly a happy life . . .[19]

Shackleton by now had had enough of tramping to the East. To improve his standing with Emily – and her father – he wanted something better. He left the Welsh Shire Line, and once more turned to his Old Alleynian friend, Owen Burne. This led, early in 1899, to a berth with the Union Castle Line.

The Union Castle Line belonged to the élite of the merchant service. It carried the mails between England and South Africa, one of the companies that maintained the communications of the Empire. From their red and black funnels to their red boot topping, its ships shone with immaculate paint – or as immaculate as coal-burning allowed. Brasswork glistened; officers gleamed in navy blue and gold braid. It was the next best thing to the Navy. It also meant the prospect of advancement to the top; and the chance of making useful friends among the passengers.

From this period, various tales became attached to Shackleton. In one, Lord Rothschild was a passenger on a ship in which he was serving and, after dinner one night, presented him with a magnificent cigar. Shackleton, so the story goes, carefully preserved that cigar, and on subsequent voyages would exhibit it to favoured lady passengers, recounting how he and Lord Rothschild had been "quite pally, you know".

In another story, a man fell overboard and a boat put out to rescue him. One of the ship's cooks and an officer were in the boat's crew; the cook dived in and saved the man, but in so doing tipped the boat, and the officer fell overboard. The officer received a life-saving medal, and the cook, nothing. Shackleton thereupon got his sister, Kathleen, to illustrate the scene, with the caption, "How ----- got his medal", and hung the drawing in the mess as a protest.

That at least was the tale that Kathleen told. She adored her brother Ernest. He it was who drove her to study art, saying that he himself was a frustrated artist, and that she must not end up one as well. She became a passable professional painter, convinced that but for Ernest she would never have had the courage to follow her bent. By her own account, another sister, Eleanore, was inspired by Shackleton to follow her vocation; and she became a nurse. Shackleton almost seemed driven to sustain his sisters against what he felt was the stultifying effect of his parents' household. He did not desert the house at Sydenham, but "home" to him meant the society of his sisters.

At all events, the Union Castle Line meant regularly coming home every two months instead of the long and indeterminate absences of the tramping trade.

It also meant passenger ships running to a timetable, and therefore also a routine of sorts. Down the Solent from Southampton, round the bulge of Africa, across the Bight of Benin, into the docks at Cape Town, under the blue flat-topped bulk of Table Mountain with its table-cloth of white clouds, and back; out and home again, voyage after voyage, six thousand miles each way. To most merchant officers it was an unattainable ideal.

When Shackleton joined the Union Castle Line, a shipmate recorded the now customary impression of someone "distinctive and a departure from our usual type of young officer". Shackleton, he went on,

> was contented with his own company – at the same time he never stood aloof in any way, but was eager to talk – to argue as sailors do . . . he had a quiet drawl in his ordinary speech but however slow his words his eyes were bright and his glances quick – When he was on a subject that . . . appealed to his imagination, his voice changed to a deep vibrant tone, his features worked, his eyes shone, and his whole body seemed to have received an increase of vitality . . . Shackleton on these occasions . . . was not then the same man who perhaps ten minutes earlier was spouting lines from Keats or Browning – this was another Shackleton with his broad shoulders hunched – his square jaw set – his eyes cold & piercing; at such a time he might have been likened to a bull at bay.
>
> But withal, he was very human, very sensitive. He quickly responded to his sympathetic nature and was slow to pass judgement on his fellows.[20]

But Shackleton was also noticeably restless. He was suffering the pangs of his love affair with Emily Dorman, and, as he explained in his outpourings to her, he was suffering the anguish of ambition stirring:

> A man should strive to the uttermost of his life's set prize. I feel the truth of it: but how can I do enough if my uttermost falls short in my opinion of what should take the prize?[21]

By December, promoted to Third Officer, Shackleton was transferred to the *Tintagel Castle*, trooping to the Cape. For in October 1899 the Boer War had broken out.

Shackleton's boyhood had been punctuated by imperial calamities. When he was seven, there was Isandhlwana, a defeat of the British Army (with firearms) by the Zulus (without); two years later, at Majuba Hill, the Boers had destroyed another British force and then, in 1885, occurred the all-British disaster: the romantic, useless death of General Gordon at Khartoum. Each defeat was eventually atoned for in what was to become an all too familiar pattern of final redemptory triumph after an overture of humiliation. The agents of revenge had been Generals Wolseley, Roberts, and Kitchener; the two former, the young Shackleton could note, Anglo-Irish like himself. All this prepared him for Spion Kop, Magersfontein, and the other preliminary disasters of the Boer War.

The soldiers on board the *Tintagel Castle* were going out, cock-a-hoop like a champion football team to an anticipated walkover. That disaster and disillusion lay in wait is beside the point.

Shackleton entered into the spirit of the troops. He was stirred by contact with men in the process of making history, one way or another.

During the summer of 1900, Shackleton was in London on leave, seeing Emily when he could. His intentions were what were then called "honourable", that is to say, marriage was probably in his mind. Emily's father, Charles Dorman, was a prosperous solicitor; a partner in a practice near the Law Courts in the Strand. As a person, he rather liked Ernest Shackleton, with his breezy kind of charm. As a prospective son-in-law, however, he was less sure. Even a Union Castle officer, Mr Dorman was now courteously hinting, especially one coming from an impecunious Irish family, was not quite what he expected. About the impecuniosity, Shackleton was only too ready to agree. But this particular Irish, or Anglo-Irish family, as he could argue, did have a coat of arms. In fact, he used it on his notepaper.

Then on 13 September, Shackleton wrote to volunteer for the National Antarctic Expedition which was in the process of being organised. Four days later, he visited the expedition offices in person to press home his claims.

III

A path to fame and fortune?

"And where," a journalist later asked, "did you first get the notion that you . . . would . . . become an explorer?" Shackleton replied,

> I think it came to me during my first voyage . . . I felt strangely drawn towards the mysterious south . . . we rounded Cape Horn in the depth of winter. it was one continuous blizzard all the way . . . Yet many a time, even in the midst of all this discomfort, my thoughts would go out to the southward . . .
>
> But strangely enough, the circumstance which actually determined me to become an explorer was a dream I had when I was twenty two. We were beating out to New York from Gibraltar, and I dreamt I was standing on the bridge in mid-Atlantic and looking northward. It was a simple dream. I seemed to vow to myself that some day I would go to the region of ice and snow and go on and on till I came to one of the poles of the earth, the end of the axis upon which this great round ball turns.[1]

Shackleton went even further:

> the unexplored parts of the world held a strong fascination for me from my earliest recollections . . . I read everything I could lay my hands upon which had for its subject Polar exploration. One of my favourite books was Dr Hall's *Life with the Esquimaux*.

None of this is actually implausible. Neither the North Pole nor the South Pole had yet been reached. *Life with the Esquimaux* had been serialised in *The Boys' Own Paper* when Shackleton, at school, was still amongst its readers. At that time, too, the *BOP* ran a lurid series on contemporary polar exploration entitled "The Thrones of the Ice King". The author, a Royal Naval officer called Commander Cheyne, was concerned to maintain British pre-eminence. After three hundred years in uninterrupted possession, the country had lost the record for the Furthest North. Cheyne was agitating for the resumption of British polar exploration, in the doldrums since 1876. "May England consider it time," Cheyne told *BOP* readers, "and not allow the final words 'Too late' to be inscribed on the tablets of her former daring achievements in the Polar regions."[2] He actually wanted to fly to the North Pole by balloon. The attempt was finally made, not by Cheyne, but by the Swede, Salomon Andrée, in 1897; and it ended in disaster.

What Shackleton told that journalist, however, was one thing; what he told his shipmates was another. Austin Hussey, a fellow officer, vividly recalled Shackleton explaining at the time that he had been attracted by the Antarctic expedition as an

> opportunity of breaking away from the monotony of method and routine – from an existence which might eventually strangle his individuality. He saw himself so slowly progressing to the command of a liner that his spirit rebelled at the thought of the best years of his life and virility passing away in weary waiting.[3]

Hussey also told a story of how "one rather pompous skipper", who had heard that Shackleton

> was "a bit of a poet" called to him when he was on the bridge keeping his watch "Is the glorious orb of day visible?" Like a flash Shackleton replied "The effulgence of King Sol is temporarily obscured by the nebulous condition of the intervening atmosphere." "Humph," said the skipper, who promptly retired. "Got him with his own tackle," quoth Shackleton.[4]

Shackleton might indeed rise to be a popular captain. He might just as easily end up as the everlasting First Mate; the "card"; that amusing Irishman remembered by so many captains on their way to the top. He might even turn out to be one of those pathetic drifters eking out a living in the China Seas.

Chance had played a part in Shackleton's approach to the Antarctic expedition; but haphazard, it was not. In March 1900, Shackleton had been on his second trooping voyage to South Africa in the *Tintagel Castle*. On board, he met a lieutenant in the East Surrey Regiment called Cedric Longstaff. Longstaff's father, Llewellyn Longstaff, happened to be the principal benefactor of the National Antarctic Expedition. Shackleton had already heard of the expedition and of Mr Longstaff, for a year before Mr Longstaff had donated £25,000, which had made the expedition possible.

In April 1899 the Prince of Wales (the future King Edward VII) became the expedition's patron; in June, the Government gave a grant. Meanwhile, at the end of March, there returned to Punta Arenas, in the Straits of Magellan, a Belgian Antarctic expedition under Adrien de Gerlache. In his ship *Belgica* de Gerlache had been caught in the ice, and drifted for almost a year over the Bellingshausen Sea as far as 71°36′ south latitude. It had been a nightmare, but it was the first expedition ever to spend a winter in the Antarctic. All this, of course, was reported in the press. After sixty years' quiescence, Antarctic exploration was being revived at last.

The British expedition was the brainchild of Sir Clements Markham, KCB, the President of the Royal Geographical Society. Shackleton applied to join the RGS. Proposed by a cousin, William Bell, he was elected a Fellow in November 1899.

The RGS was a typical Victorian institution, rooted in a desire for self-improvement and the propagation of knowledge. It welcomed anyone "interested in geography and discovery". It was synonymous with official British exploration, and associated with the opening up of Africa – too much so, perhaps. When Stanley found Livingstone, "The Council of the Society," to quote Hugh Robert Mill, its some time librarian, "thought it incongruous and almost an impertinence that a newspaper reporter should be successful where a British officer, backed by the authority of the Royal Geographical Society, had failed." The society institutionalised the geographical aspect of the British Empire, then at its high noon.

In January 1900, Shackleton offered the RGS an article on the winds and currents in the Atlantic, for its periodical, the *Geographical Journal*. It was gracefully refused on the grounds that everything had already "been worked out and published".[5] The journal used to keep Shackleton in touch with exploration, but it was the encounter with Cedric Longstaff that thrust opportunity in his path. He persuaded Longstaff to give him an introduction to his father.

At the end of May, meanwhile, when Shackleton had returned to London, *The Times* carried a report that attracted his very keenest interest. A certain naval lieutenant, soon to be gazetted Commander, Robert F. Scott, had been appointed to command the Antarctic expedition. Scott, said *The Times*, "possesses one absolutely essential qualification for polar work – youth", blandly going on to say that "As youth is essential, one without actual Polar experience has had to be selected . . ."[6]

Today, it seems inconceivable that anyone so blatantly unprepared would be chosen to lead a British national enterprise. Then, however, things were different. During the Boer War the *Westminster Gazette* could head a leading article "The Virtue of Unpreparedness", arguing that British aggression towards the Boers had been "finally refuted by the state of complete unpreparedness with which England entered the war."[7]

Shackleton could, at any rate, thoroughly applaud *The Times* when it declared that although Scott had no polar experience, "that is a small matter; any competent young officer will soon make himself familiar with what has been done and what remains to do."[8] Even more could he approve when *The Times* went on to say that "There can be little doubt that Lieutenant Scott will make the most of the splendid opportunity afforded him of . . . distinguishing himself as a leader."[9]

Exactly. If an obscure naval lieutenant, why not Ernest Shackleton? In seamanship, Shackleton had no reason to defer to Scott. Everybody knew that naval officers spent too much time in port. Although Scott had joined the Navy ten years before Shackleton first went to sea, in terms of actual sailing hours they were approximately level. And if youth was a criterion, Shackleton was twenty-six to Scott's thirty years. (Actually thirty-two. *The Times* had considerately, or in error, lopped off two years.)

There was other polar news to attract Shackleton's interest that summer of 1900. Carsten Borchgrevink arrived in London. Borchgrevink was the first man to winter on the Antarctic continent. He had done so at Cape Adare, the tip of South Victoria Land, during 1899. In an interview with the *Westminster Gazette*, Borchgrevink suggested that

> The Antarctic region may be another Klondyke . . . There are fish – fisheries might be established . . . There is quartz in which metals are to be seen.[10]

There spoke someone after Shackleton's heart. Borchgrevink was a restless, voluble and flamboyant Norwegian, with little more than ambition and personality on which to depend. In 1888, at the age of twenty-four, he went to Australia. At Melbourne, in 1894, after working variously as a labourer, surveyor and schoolmaster, Borchgrevink signed on a Norwegian sealer called *Antarctic* for a voyage to the Ross Sea.

Antarctic had been sent out to investigate Antarctic whaling and sealing. Along the way, Borchgrevink was in a boat's party that landed at Cape Adare, becoming one of the first men to set foot on the Antarctic continent. Then was kindled his ambition to become the first man to winter there.

Four years later, after much wandering, antagonism and setback, Borchgrevink finally managed to raise money in London for his own expedition. In a ship called *Southern Cross*, he then returned to spend his historic winter of 1899 at Cape Adare. He had done rather more. As the *Westminster Gazette* put it, Borchgrevink had been "Furthest South with sledge – record – 78 deg. 58 min."[11] This was the first time that anyone had claimed, in those words, to have set a southern record. Borchgrevink had opened the race for the South Pole.

For Shackleton, fretting in London on leave, it was a tumultuous summer. The war, of course, was the story of the day, and the tide seemed to have turned. On 19 May came the relief of Mafeking, and the outbreak of mass hysteria at the (delusive) prospect of imminent victory over the Boer. At the end of that month, however, Shackleton was touched personally by the war. His brother Frank was commissioned in the Royal Irish Fusiliers, bound for South Africa to take part in – so it seemed – mopping-up operations.

Borchgrevink, nonetheless, was front-page news. What with him and Scott on the one hand, and his brother and the war on the other, Shackleton was hounded by a haunting fear of being left behind, a man of action frustrated to the core. His twenty-sixth birthday had passed without a goal in sight. The National Antarctic Expedition seemed the gateway to salvation.

There was no obvious reason why the polar regions should appear to be the path to fame and fortune. Borchgrevink was a nine days' wonder, but the arrival of the polar explorer as hero was due to the illustrious Norwegian, Fridtjof Nansen. In 1895, Nansen set a new record – 86° 16′ – for the Furthest North. More important was the way he achieved it. For three years, he was lost in the Arctic. He had contrived a revolutionary method of freezing a specially built ship – the *Fram* ("Forwards") – into the sea ice and drifting with the pack. With one companion, Hjalmar Johansen, he had then made an epic dash north over the ice with dogs and sledges. That turned into a saga of survival. When Nansen came back to civilisation in 1896, he seemed to have returned from the dead. More to the point, the romantic image of a moody Viking, with an overwhelming force of personality, was the stuff out of which the press could make a popular hero. The world was so completely at his feet that, as Hugh Robert Mill described seeing Nansen off at Victoria after a visit to London, a page-boy from his hotel jumped on to the moving foot-board and seized Nansen's hand; and as he dropped off, shouted "I'm the last man to shake hands with him!"[12]

This was the folklore tugging at Shackleton's romantic imagination.

Armed with Cedric Longstaff's introduction to his father, Shackleton went down to visit him at his home in Wimbledon. Llewellyn Longstaff was a trained chemist, partly educated in Germany, which at the time was far ahead in chemistry. It was one of the secrets of her growing industrial power. Longstaff himself was a successful industrialist, a company director, and a retired Lieutenant-Colonel of Volunteers – whom the *Daily Chronicle* described as

a quiet, pleasant business-like man, barely sixty, his interest in Polar enterprise comes rather as a surprise to his friends, who have been wont to associate his liberality and good nature rather with promoting good relations between Yorkshire operatives and their employers.[13]

Like Shackleton, Mr Longstaff was a FRGS. Besides, he was pleased to receive anyone who had recently seen his son. He was overwhelmed by Shackleton's scintillating personality. When Shackleton asked his help in joining the expedition, Mr Longstaff could hardly refuse. It was only then, with Mr Longstaff's certain patronage, that Shackleton finally made his approach.

In October, however, when he went back to sea, it was under sentence of uncertainty. For months, his case hung fire. Shuttling between Southampton and the Cape, first on the *Gaika*, then on the *Carisbrook Castle*, Shackleton fretted under the suffocating sense of marking time. Meanwhile Llewellyn Longstaff had made it clear to Sir Clements Markham that he wanted Shackleton accepted. Sir Clements was anxious to oblige. He knew he would soon have to go begging for money again.

Sir Clements, in turn, told Scott; and Scott, saying that he "had no time to attend to it",[14] left the matter to Albert Armitage, his second-in-command. Armitage, as he put it, "made very full enquiries" about Shackleton,

and found every one speak well of him . . . The Marine Superintendent and his Captain in the [Union Castle] line both told me that he was more intelligent than the average officer. His brother officers considered him to be a very good fellow . . .[15]

Early in March 1901, Shackleton returned to Southampton on the *Carisbrook Castle* to find himself part of the National Antarctic Expedition at last. He had been appointed on 17 February,[16] while still at sea. He had leave from the Union Castle Line into the bargain, so that there was the belly-comfort of something to come back to. He paid off, and hurried to London to present himself at the expedition offices.

IV

National Antarctic Expedition

The offices of the National Antarctic Expedition bore, as one journalist put it, "a most business-like aspect. Skeleton sleighs are reared up in a corner, and on the floor are piles of sample skin suits to be worn amid the eternal ice and snow."[1]

This was the setting for Shackleton's first encounter, face to face, with Scott. Encased in the high white starched collars of the period, they tried to size each other up. They had much in common. Both were opportunists. Each doubted his own professional prospects. Neither was particularly interested in ice or snow or exploration as such, but both saw in the expedition a pathway to success. Each would cheerfully have done anything else that promised personal advancement. Both were burning with ambition. Shackleton, however, the Anglo-Irishman, half poet, half buccaneer, showed it openly. Scott, high-minded, and altogether more prosaic, hid it well.

Scott's "forte", in the words of a contemporary, was that he was "very prepossessing".[2] The same could safely have been said of Shackleton himself. Both he and Scott possessed charm, and each used it as he could, but one thing at least was clear to Shackleton, as he peered across the heavy, dulled oaken table, trying to make his leader out. Scott, newly promoted Commander and strangely awkward in his clothes, was the weaker personality and somehow uncertain of himself. He was distinctly on his guard. Shackleton knew why this was. He himself was an intruder; Sir Clements Markham had been crusading for a Royal Navy expedition.

Through precedent elevated to a principle, British polar exploration had become a naval preserve and, like most Englishmen of the day, Sir Clements considered the Royal Navy, then the largest on earth, the agent of national prestige. (Although as Captain Sir Seymour Fortescue rather acidly put it: "The ignorance of the British public of everything regarding the Navy can only be described as colossal."[3]) Besides, said Sir Clements,

> The Navy needs some action to wake it up from the canker of prolonged peace. Polar exploration is more wholesome for it, in a moral as well as a sanitary point of view, than any more petty wars with savages.[4]

Now seventy, venerable in appearance; high-minded, yet devious, cunning, complacent, self-seeking, and a master of intrigue, Markham might have stepped out of a novel by Trollope. He usually got his own way. The Admiralty, however, was not impressed with his plans for the expedition. Their lordships had lost interest in exploration a generation before, and declined to organise an expedition now; so Sir Clements had to settle for a private one manned by a naval crew. The Admiralty reluctantly agreed to lend some men, but not enough. The rest had, perforce, to come from the Mercantile Marine.

Shackleton, therefore, faced Scott as one of a not wholly welcome faction. Armitage, from the P. & O. Line, was the other officer on the expedition from the Mercantile Marine but they were two merchant officers amongst four naval ones. Each service regarded the other with a whiff of mutual disrespect, which went as far back as Elizabethan days. The merchant seaman felt that he did all the work; the naval, that he did the more honourable work of fighting. Such attitudes were hardened by the historical fact that the business of navigating warships used to be left to impressed merchant mates. The legacy of this was that the merchant service regarded the Navy with genial scorn, while the other way about, the feeling was of social superiority.

Shackleton knew only that his chance had come. Aptly for an Edwardian, it had come at the very start of Edward VII's reign. On 22 January 1901, as Sir Clements Markham recorded in his diary, Queen Victoria

> died at a good old age, after the longest and most prosperous reign on record. I first saw her when Princess, at a great dinner given by William IV, in August 1836 . . . Sixty years after I first saw her, when infirm and old, she gave me the acolade [*sic*] on both shoulders and called me "Sir Clements".[5]

After sixty-four years, the Victorian age had come to an end. "The sensation of universal change," wrote Lady Battersea in her diary, "haunted me more than any other sensation";[6] and as *The Times* put it in a leading article:

> We are finding ourselves somewhat less secure of our position than we could desire, and somewhat less abreast of the problems of the age than we ought to be, considering the initial advantages we secured . . . Others have learned our lessons, and bettered our instructions while we have been too easily content to rely upon the methods which were effective a generation or two ago.[7]

Yet only three weeks before, on New Year's day, *The Times* had written that

> We enter upon the new century with a heritage of achievement and glory older, more continuous and not less splendid than that of any nation in the world . . . with a people prosperous, contented, manly, intelligent and self-reliant, we may look forward with good hope to the storms and conflicts that may await us.[8]

A sense of foreboding was the hallmark of the Edwardians. The Boer War had sounded the tocsin. The British no longer felt unquestionably masters of the world. Germany, bursting with military and industrial power, was emerging as the national rival.

London, however, was still the capital of a world power and the hub of Empire. Shackleton was in the very centre of it all. Breezily settling down to work, he was at the least determined to enjoy every minute before sailing. He started by working at the expedition office. That lay in the very heart of the West End, a stone's throw from Piccadilly, in the old London University buildings in Burlington Gardens, at the corner of Bond Street. For the first time in his life, he had escaped from a provincial or suburban setting. No longer was he the abstemious young Puritan; now he smoked and drank regularly. He mingled in his off moments with the top-hatted and elaborately dressed saunterers, the women rustling with the frou-frou of silk. He imagined, no doubt, how nice it would be to have money of his own, lots of it, so that he could really belong.

To escape the murmuring of augurs, London was becoming a city of castles in the air. This absolutely suited Shackleton, for if ever there was a builder of such insubstantial properties, it was he. The National Antarctic Expedition soon became to him a certitude of fame and fortune, and this was the message he conveyed convincingly to Emily Dorman. Emily was now living in Wetherby Gardens, South Kensington, with her father, who had moved there the previous year from Sydenham. So Shackleton could prosecute his love affair without the surrogate of letters. By now he had decided that she was going to be his wife. She, on the other hand, was not so sure. He naturally favoured a whirlwind fulfilment. The whirlwind was there all right, but custom demanded a corybantic mating dance. Whenever he could, Shackleton was off to call on Emily, not by the newly electrified Underground but by hansom cab. London was still a city of horses, the sound of traffic still the clatter of hooves, its smell that of dung and urine. Nonetheless Emily Dorman was only – as she would still be today – about half an hour from the expedition office.

Equally important, in the office, Shackleton was at the centre of the enterprise. It was a place of potentially profitable contacts and not only among those connected with the expedition. He had, in any case, considerably impressed Sir Clements Markham, and frequently found himself asked to lunch at Sir Clements' home down in Pimlico, among the colonnaded porticoes of Eccleston Square.

Sir Clements saw in Shackleton something of himself; more so perhaps than he saw in Scott, his own particular protégé. Shackleton, as Sir Clements approvingly observed at the outset, though Irish, was "originally Yorkshire",[9] and Sir Clements, as he never forgot, was a Yorkshireman himself. Both were old public schoolboys – Sir Clements was at Westminster. Both had left school early to go to sea – Sir Clements in the Navy – and both made up for defective education by voracious reading. Shackleton, as Sir Clements put it, was "remarkably well informed considering the rough life he has led".[10] In his voluminous diaries, Sir Clements entered vivid pen portraits, biographies and genealogies of the young men whom he met. They were many, chiefly naval officers of whom he was very fond. The entries for the expedition members were detailed and discursive. Shackleton's lineage, for instance, was traced back three hundred years. The expedition, as Sir Clements summed it up,

> was fortunate in finding such an excellent and zealous officer as Ernest Shackleton . . . He is a steady, high-principled young man full of zeal, strong and hard working and exceedingly good tempered . . . A marvel of intelligent energy.[11]

Shackleton, meanwhile, did not spend all his time at Burlington Gardens. On 21 March, a bare fortnight after he returned to England, *Discovery*, the expedition ship, was launched at Dundee.

Discovery was probably the last big wooden sailing ship built in

Britain. She had steam auxiliary engines, coal fired. Polar navigation, however, still needed a wooden ship, for elasticity, to avoid being crushed in the ice. Sail was needed to eke out fuel. Because of its bulk, not enough coal could be carried and, away from bunkers, off the shipping routes, steaming range was limited.

Shackleton had made much of his experience in sail when he applied to the expedition. He was now sent up to help supervise *Discovery*'s acceptance trials off the Tay. Scott himself was usually absent being, in the words of the *Pall Mall Gazette*, "too busily engaged in organizational work in London".[12] As Shackleton had quickly learned, Scott was not yet secure in his post, and he had to stay in London to look after his interests. There was actually a plot to remove him from command, and it was during the climax of this cabal that Shackleton walked into the expedition.

About Scott's appointment, as Rear-Admiral Sir William Wharton put it, there had been "much indignation". The story started with Sir Clements Markham.

In April the year before, Sir Clements had asked the Admiralty for the loan of some naval officers. He then, in Sir William's words, calmly told the expedition's executive committee "that he did not name the officers, & that the Admiralty selected them themselves". That, Sir William agitatedly wrote to Admiral Lord Walter Kerr, the First Sea Lord, was "not correct".

Sir William was well placed to detect the brazen shiftiness of Sir Clements Markham, for Sir William happened to be on the executive committee himself. He was, moreover, the Hydrographer (chief surveyor of the Navy) and worked at the Admiralty. There, the "Antarctic documents", in his own words, "all come to me in connection with fitting out the expedition."[13] Sir William noticed that Sir Clements actually had written to Lord Walter asking for "Lieut. Robert F. Scott . . . to command the expedition."[14]

For twenty years, first as Honorary Secretary, and then as President, of the RGS, Sir Clements had campaigned for the resumption of British Antarctic exploration. This had virtually ceased since the great pioneering voyage of Sir James Clark Ross from 1840 to 1843. In a combative life, Sir Clements had fought for causes as diverse as the rehabilitation of Richard III and the abolition of flogging in the Royal Navy. It was, however, the campaign for Antarctic exploration that marked him most, because there he had the maddening experience of fighting against the compact indifference of British public life.

All the while, Sir Clements had been looking for the leader of the future expedition who, he decided, should naturally be a naval officer. Although his brief naval career ended in 1852 Sir Clements, through friends and relations, had maintained intimate contact with the service, and literally hundreds of officers passed under his review. Among them happened to be Scott.

Scott was a well built and, to quote one of his captains, an "amiable & promising young officer".[15] He was also rather dull and conventional, a contrast to the rebelliousness of both Shackleton and Sir Clements. He was born in Devon, the third of six children. He compliantly entered the Navy at the behest of his father, a not too successful Plymouth brewer. His mother was a dominating paragon of formidable respectability. He was an ordinary scion of an ordinary middle-class family. He was at home in an hierarchy. He was all that Shackleton was not.

Scott was good at passing examinations. Nonetheless, he somehow did not fulfil the promise he seemed to have shown. He himself feared for his promotion. To improve his professional prospects, he qualified as a torpedo lieutenant in 1893. The commander of the torpedo training school at Portsmouth was then complaining of the small number and poor calibre of applicants for the course. In any case, in 1899, as torpedo lieutenant on HMS *Majestic*, Scott chanced to meet Sir Clements Markham once more after several years.

Sir Clements by then had finally got the *Discovery* expedition under way. He was, however, still looking for a commander. For various reasons his first choices had all declined the bait; partly perhaps because Sir Clements had a talent for blighting the causes he espoused. So Scott, by now a very senior lieutenant, importuned Sir Clements; and Sir Clements, like many another manipulator, fell prey to manipulation himself. He adopted Scott as his candidate to command the expedition.

All along Sir Clements had hidden his own interest and insinuated that the Admiralty had appointed Scott. "The Admiralty," Sir William Wharton reminded Lord Walter Kerr, "took no such step . . . May I," he went on, "have your permission to quote this fact?"[16] Lord Walter replied,

> No objection, as no appointments have been made though officers asked for were promised to Sir C. Markham.[17]

All this, Sir William felt, was "most important". The executive committee

> had no authority to select the officers, especially the one for command, putting aside for the moment that Markham was acting without their knowledge, so it makes his action doubly reprehensible.

For the good of the expedition, Sir William concluded,

> it is absolutely necessary to nip at once the assumption of supreme authority on the part of one man or we shall be led we know not where & come to grief.[18]

The conflict went deeper than any naval doubts over a naval officer. Its roots lay in profoundly different views of polar exploration.

The expedition was jointly sponsored by the RGS and the Royal Society. The RGS put its money on geographical discovery, but the Royal Society, a scientific academy, was interested in science.

Sir Clements saw the explorer in his historical guise of a man who simply wanted to see what was over the next hill. Scientists, in his not unjustifiable opinion, were undesirable camp followers who impeded the business of discovery by pottering about in the field – "Mud larkers", Sir Clements liked to call them. "These mud larkers," he wrote to John Scott Keltie, the RGS Secretary, "coolly ask us to turn our expedition into a cruise for their purposes".[19]

Sir Clements wanted Scott to be not only captain of the ship, but undisputed commander of the whole expedition. The Royal Society, on the other hand, saw Scott merely as a skilled servant to transport their scientists. The scientific director, their nominee, would be overlord of the expedition. A feud was, naturally, the result and one which involved more than mere division of responsibility.

The scientific director was Dr J. W. Gregory. He was no academic dodderer and besides being a distinguished geologist, was an explorer in his own right. He had been to Africa, where he achieved lasting fame by exploring and naming the Great Rift Valley in Kenya. He was an accomplished mountaineer, and had been with Sir Martin Conway (a well-known climber) on the first crossing of Spitsbergen. He was one of the few men on the Antarctic expedition with any polar experience, and incontestably the most accomplished. He had, in the words of a friend, a "remarkable personality . . . free from assumption or arrogance [but] it was very unwise to assume that you knew more of any subject than Gregory did . . . as in the quietest possible manner he would produce some devastating facts, well attested but not widely known . . ."[20] Gregory voiced the fears of many when he wrote that

> Scott . . . has no experience of expedition equipment . . . On questions of furs, sledges, ski etc., his ignorance is appalling . . . he does not seem at all conscious of these facts or inclined to get [the] experience necessary.[21]

Shackleton might have laughed – or bridled – had he heard of this, for it applied equally, of course, to himself. Both he and Scott accepted the national myth that improvisation was best. Gregory, on the other hand, believed in proper preparation. He wanted the expedition members to "gain experience in ice work and on ski in Switzerland during the coming summer". He himself had gone out to Australia (he had recently been appointed to the chair of Geology at Melbourne University) where he proposed "taking out ski to practise on the Australian Alps this season and [I] think the others should arrange for similar training".[22]

To Sir Clements, this was unmanly and undesirable, although the expedition – usually called *Discovery*, after the ship – seemed conspicuously deficient in men with experience of snow and ice. In any case, Sir Clements seemed infatuated with Scott, and would tolerate no threat to his supremacy. Against him stood the Royal Society, but, in the words of one opponent,

> Markham is a man . . . the others are mere invertebrates . . . We all confess (as I do) to a sneaking admiration of Markham's energy & fighting power.[23]

In the middle of May, as Sir Clements had been scheming, Gregory was forced to resign. Scott was now not only captain of the ship, but the undisputed head of the whole expedition.

The consequences were fateful. They went far beyond personalities. Gregory was not the only competent leader available. There was his old chief in Spitsbergen, Sir Martin Conway. Better still perhaps, was David Hanbury, a young Englishman who had spent two years in the Canadian Arctic making himself into a master of polar travel, and who now happened to be in London. Neither was approached, however. Sir Clements seemed wilfully to have ignored the professional talent at his disposal and ensured that British polar exploration remained indisputably amateur.

"It seems doubtful," Gregory had written, when arguing for a captain from the merchant service, "whether a first-class naval officer would . . . be willing to bury himself in the Antarctic for three years, and whether the Admiralty would give the necessary leave of absence to any of its best men."[24] The Admiralty could hardly have put it better themselves. Previous naval expeditions had ended in disaster. They had no desire to risk public obloquy by taking responsibility for yet another questionable undertaking. It was only with almost comical reluctance that they had countenanced a naval commander for *Discovery*. In any case Scott, as Gregory put it, no doubt echoing Admiralty opinion, was "a mechanical engineer [referring to his torpedo specialisation], not a sailor".

> I think he is a poor organiser. His departments are in arrears and he is so casual in all his business. He appears to trust to luck what ought to be a matter of precise calculation.[25]

Amongst other things, this led to a last-minute rush, in dealing with which Shackleton bustled round to help. As Sir Clements noted at the end of April, Shackleton came

> to luncheon about the *Discovery*'s library. He is also getting plays and looking out for presents of wigs and dresses for the theatricals.[26]

Amateur theatricals were an absolutely essential part of Victorian polar expeditions, which Sir Clements was determined to preserve.

Early in June, *Discovery* sailed down from Dundee to the East India Docks in London for lading. Shackleton had signed on as Third Mate, and was given the job of stowing ship. This was the skill of the merchant, not the naval officer. Twice he was interrupted. He spent a few days at Aldershot with the Royal Engineers, learning to fly a captive balloon, which *Discovery* was taking for reconnaissance. (The Wright brothers' flight was still two years in the future.) Then Shackleton went down to the Thames estuary to test detonators for freeing *Discovery*, if need be, from the ice. The expedition's supplies meanwhile, were landing at the quayside haphazardly and late, so that Shackleton found himself working against time.

That could be said of his love affair as well. Emily was in love, or thought she was in love, with someone else.

> Well I know that I was the interloper [Shackleton wrote to her at a moment when the written, not the spoken word seemed best]: if a man who loves a woman much, so much that it seems his whole life hangs on her way with him, can be called an interloper. Child I suppose it is mans way to want a woman altogether to himself: I said it in the old days "Love me only a little, just a little" and now it seems as I grow older I am saying "Love me altogether and only me" And I know you told me all in the beginning: and I have nothing to offer you: I am poor: I am not clever, it is as wicked of me to want you to keep caring for me when my name is "Nemo" as it is to make or do other wrongs . . . when like today you spoke about him: something catches at my heart and I feel lost, out in the cold . . . why did I not know you first? Why did you not tremble to my touch first of all the men in this world. Of all tales

> of love and sorrow I feel ours stand out for there was no hope in the beginning and there is none now . . .[27]

But there was hope, of course; with Shackleton there usually was. *Discovery* sailed down the Thames on 31 July, as planned. Shackleton announced that *all* his family come to see him off in one place would be too much. He sent his three youngest sisters downriver to the Albert Docks to wave as *Discovery* sailed by. They were, as one of them recalled, "armed with semaphore flags (Ernest had taught us signalling), and as he passed we saw Ernest bring out a white handkerchief, then turn to someone, borrow another, then he signalled three times, 'Goodbye Helen, goodbye Kathleen, goodbye Gladys', in strict old nursery order of precedence."

By then, Shackleton had settled his affair with Emily Dorman – up to a point. He had more or less replaced the "other", and she had more or less agreed to marry him. He still had to secure Mr Dorman's approval, however, for Emily, although well past the age of majority, accepted the convention that a woman needed her father's permission to marry.

Shackleton delayed writing to Mr Dorman until London had been left astern. Before departing from the shores of England, *Discovery* had to swing compasses at Stokes Bay, near Portsmouth and there, between land and sea, Shackleton finally wrote to his prospective father-in-law. He was, as he put it, going on the expedition

> mainly for one reason . . . to get on so that when I come back or later when I have made money I might with your permission marry Emily if she still cares for me as I feel she does now: it is needless to say that I care for her more than anyone else in the world, but I fully see the difficulties in the way as regards my not having money, but time will overcome that and you not object [*sic*] if I have sufficient to keep her as you would wish . . . my future is all to make but I intend making it quickly: I would have spoken to you myself before only Emily had not given me a full answer. Now I feel it is all right so am asking you not now but when I have made money or position and money to marry her.[28]

Shackleton had, once more, eschewed the spoken word. He was probably correct. Face to face, Mr Dorman might well have said "no"; with pen in hand second thoughts could get to work.

At the eleventh hour, the expedition had been rescued from the glory-hole of esoteric enterprises. Sir Clements Markham may have been a wily and ruthless intriguer but no one, to quote Hugh

Robert Mill, who knew him well, could take him "for anything but the patriotic supporter of Church and State; the vehement supporter of England's glory in every path of enterprise".[29] In the words of Admiral Fitzgerald, an early supporter, the expedition encouraged

> that insatiable desire which our country has of planting the British flag upon every barren rock in the ocean and every desert sand in Africa, or every mount of snow or ice in the Arctic or Antarctic . . . I believe that desire would carry you to the moon if there were only a way.[30]

It was undoubtedly a patriotic, not to say an imperial venture; and Shackleton, at least now that he was on his way, was partly, like others, swayed by patriotism and the imperial sentiment. Indeed, as the expedition sailed, it became an antidote to the dismal news from South Africa, where the war dragged on and the British Army still seemed baffled by the Boer. As the *Morning Post* put it,

> Even in the last throes of an exhausting struggle, we can yet spare the energy and the men to add to the triumphs we have already won in the peaceful but heroic field of exploration . . .[31]

Or, to quote another kind of comment in *The Referee*,

> At the Pole, at the Pole,
> Britannia's pretty sure to reach her goal;
> Her ever-conquering legions,
> Will annex those distant regions,
> And make a new dominion of the Pole.[32]

The South Pole itself was the reason for the change of attitude. Just before departure it was officially announced that the expedition, in the words of a versifier, "means to reach the spot".[33] Press coverage was not exactly sensational because, as the *Daily Express* put it, "The South Pole has never caught the popular imagination as its Northern fellow has done":

> It is inconveniently distant from any European base. So its environment remains a kind of silence and mist and vague terrors.[34]

Nonetheless, it was well worth a paragraph or two. *Discovery*, said the *Daily Express*, would sail "with the hearty good wishes of all who hope that the race for the South Pole will be won by the first naval Power of the World".[35]

Before finally putting to sea, *Discovery* was commanded to Cowes to be inspected by the King. It was Cowes Week, the zenith of the yachting year, part regatta, part aristocratic social function, twin of Royal Ascot. After the years of his mother's dampening seclusion, Edward VII was making an occasion of everything he could.

Bearded, portly and a rake, Edward VII was, nonetheless, as Admiral Fisher put it, "every inch a King!" He loved dressing up and putting on a show, and was piped aboard *Discovery* wearing his admiral's uniform. The ship's company was mostly in naval uniform too. Even Shackleton sparkled with the scintilla of gold braid. With the help of Sir Clements Markham, he had obtained a commission in the Royal Naval Reserve, and he appeared in all the glory of a sub-lieutenant's single, twisted stripe.

In his guttural, almost German accent the King, with the legendary genial aloofness of the British royal family, spoke a few words to most on board, Shackleton included. Between them was a hidden bond. King Edward was a prominent Freemason. Less than a month earlier, on 9 July, Shackleton had become a Freemason himself. On 9 April, Scott had become one too.

On the face of it, the explanation was simple. Freemasonry was strong in the Navy. Admiral Lord Charles Beresford, Commander of the Channel Fleet, for example, was a well-known Freemason. So was Vice-Admiral Sir Harry Rawson, who had first recommended Scott for promotion. Sir Harry happened to be Grand Master of the Navy Lodge, into which Shackleton was initiated.

In the words of its Constitutions, Freemasonry

> is the centre of union between good men and true, and the happy means of conciliating friendship amongst those who must otherwise have remained at a perpetual distance.[36]

Or, as an eighteenth-century tract baldly put it,

> Masonry . . . provides . . . no small advantage to a man who would rise in the world.[37]

Nonetheless, Shackleton was not driven by self-interest alone. Freemasonry is many things. It is a fraternity, entry to which depends on the approval of the members. It is a secret society. It is an organisation for mutual help. It is also an ethical code. It promotes conviviality. According to a French writer, it mitigated the coarseness of eighteenth-century English drinking habits by a "sort of homeopathic treatment of a national vice, allowing Bacchus his share, but only his share".[38] Beyond all this, Freemasonry is a religion without church or dogma. It accepts those who believe in one God, by whatever name, and in whatever way.

It provides an outlet for religious feelings without the constraint of cult or clergy.

For Shackleton, this was important. The Masonic concept of God as the Great Architect of the Universe, the symbolic use of the craft of masonry, the regalia, the appearance of jewels and a blazing star in Masonic ritual, all appealed to his temperament. So too did the air of mystery, the promise of esoteric knowledge, the secret signs of recognition. The ceremony of initiation involved being led blindfolded into the Lodge with a halter round his neck and promising never to reveal the secrets of Freemasonry, to quote *The Complete Workings of Craft Freemasonry*,

> under the no less penalty on the violation . . . than that of having my throat cut across, my tongue torn out by the root, and buried in the sand of the sea at low water, or a cable's length from the shore, where the tide regularly ebbs and flows twice in twenty-four hours, or the more effectual punishment of being branded a wilfully perjured individual, void of all moral worth and totally unfit to be received into the worshipful Lodge . . . or society of men who prize honour and virtue above the external advantage of rank and fortune.[39]

All this seemed far removed from the company on *Discovery* – or was it? The King, after all, had once undergone the same ceremony as well.

With the King on board was Queen Alexandra, who particularly noticed Shackleton. The King's naval equerry, Vice-Admiral Sir Henry Stephenson, was present too. So was Llewellyn Longstaff, another Freemason as it happened. On the deck, other distinguished visitors strolled, and on the water round about lay the yachts of the rich and the great. It was different from the usual merchant ship's unremarked departure from dingy wharf or dilapidated jetty. Shackleton, in a few months had come far. He might almost pretend that he had arrived. At any rate, the obscure Third Officer of the *Carisbrook Castle* had become one of the accredited heroes pursuing Britain's imperial destiny. Emily had come down to see him off. How could Mr Dorman, a loyal subject, now be beastly to him in cold blood?

There could be no answer before *Discovery* finally left. Shackleton had seen to that. His letter to Mr Dorman was dated 3 August, a Saturday. The following Monday – the day of the royal inspection – was August Bank Holiday, and the next day – Tuesday 6 August – *Discovery* put to sea. Mr Dorman was only able to reply two days later. By then he had read in the press all about the royal scene on deck:

> My dear Ernest, I sincerely & heartily wish you a safe voyage & a happy return some 2 or 3 years hence having accomplished the arduous task before you & that you will be able to tell us what the Antarctic really is. I can only now say that if & whenever the time comes when you are in the pecuniary position you long for & that if you & Emmy are still of the same mind my consent to your union will not be wanting.[40]

Until this letter overtook him somewhere at a port of call, Shackleton would have to bear with the suspense.

V

Discovery

Shackleton was back on the familiar windjammer route, with its wide sweep down to the Cape, and then eastwards through the Roaring Forties to New Zealand. It was like the old days in the *Hoghton Tower*, although *Discovery* was no full rigger, but a barque.

Unexpectedly on board was Hugh Robert Mill, who had joined by what amounted to a pierhead jump. Almost a decade as RGS librarian had proved that he was a man with whom it was impossible to quarrel. At the eleventh hour, the scientific arrangements were suddenly found to be in total disarray. Although Mill had helped to organise the expedition, he had stood aside from the various controversies. Four days before *Discovery* left, Scott asked him to sail as far as Madeira and bring order out of muddle.

Geographer, meteorologist and oceanographer, Mill was a Scot from Caithness, near John o'Groats, and since childhood he had been in love with polar exploration. "No land," he explained, "lies between the shore of my place of birth . . . and the North Pole."[1] Poor sight and ill health – and Sir Clements Markham – however, had kept him away from the polar regions. Three years before, Mill had been asked to sail in a yacht on a summer cruise to the Arctic. Sir Clements refused to give him leave from the RGS. "The proper place of a librarian," as Sir Clements put it, "is in the library."[2] When the call to *Discovery* came, Mill had just left the RGS to become director of the British Rainfall Association, a forerunner of the Meteorological Office. Nonetheless, he dropped his work and went. It was a chance which, at the age of forty, he felt he could not miss.

Mill was expected to turn some of the ship's company into

scientific observers from scratch, following the expedition's philosophy, as it was expressed to the *Daily News*, that "there is nothing to learn that any smart naval officer cannot learn in a couple of days' time".[3] Replacing "naval" with "merchant", Ernest Shackleton wholeheartedly agreed. He cheerfully promised to take the density and salinity of the sea water during the voyage but, as Mill recalled,

> He found the minute accuracy required rather irksome and was long in grasping the importance of writing down one reading of an instrument before making the next.[4]

Nonetheless, said Mill, Shackleton's "inexhaustible good humour made correction easy".[5] Mill also had another point of view:

> I always associate Shackleton with the starlight of a summer night in the Bay of Biscay. I had known him for a year before, but it was on the bridge of the *Discovery* from midnight on, as the ship was rolling southward that I discovered his individuality and recognised how he differed in turn of phrase and trend of mind from the other splendid fellows [on board]. To tell the truth, I was at first surprised and a little alarmed at the ceaseless flow of quotation from the poets called forth by the summer night, the stars, the phosphorescence of the sea, and the thought of those he left behind him. Nor was it altogether pleasant to find that this young sailor was already familiar with every reference which rose to my mind from books I had read years before his thoughts had turned that way, and with many which I had never seen.[6]

Thin, quiet, bespectacled, Mill was every inch the academic. He ought to have been drawn more to Scott, who nursed scientific ambitions, than to Shackleton. Mill, however, did not share the reigning moralistic and exalted view of science:

> The tradition of inaccessibility is a challenge to humanity . . . the desire to wipe out *terra incognita* appeals more deeply to certain instincts of human nature than either science or trade, and the rough-and-ready test of highest latitude is in one sense a gauge of human progress.[7]

Frustrated in action, Mill sought vicarious experience through knowing polar explorers, and he had met most of them including Nansen. Like most Scots boys, Mill had been brought up on Carlyle and hero worship. The polar explorer he saw as the archetype of the heroic figure, and he evidently saw in Shackleton the closest approximation on board to his ideal. Mill did not, however, look through rose-hued spectacles and, as he put it afterwards, "To Shackleton the National Antarctic Expedition was an opportunity and nothing more. He would have tried to join just as eagerly a ship bound to seek buried treasure on the Spanish Main, or to scour the Atlantic in search of the Island of St Brendan".[8]

Perhaps there was a corner of Hugh Robert'Mill that would have done so too. At any rate, when he left *Discovery* at Madeira on 15 August to return to England, he and Shackleton had found in each other lifelong friends.

As the expedition sailed on from Madeira, Shackleton wrote in his diary:

> The ship steered badly, there being too much sail aft and not enough forward. I am afraid this . . . will be a serious matter when we get down South, but we hope to devise some way out of the difficulty. As we leave behind the stars under which dwell all whom I love, I feel that another link is snapping in the chain . . .[9]

This abrupt switch of thought was characteristic, but there was in any case good reason for Shackleton's sudden foreboding. *Discovery* was bound for some of the roughest waters in the world: after leaving Madeira sailing ships would pick up the north-east trade winds, and for a new vessel this was her first proper trial.

Most polar expeditions used converted whalers or sealers. Sir Clements Markham, when he first mooted the idea of building a ship specially for the purpose, considered doing so in Norway. "The cost would be much less than in England," he explained. "And, moreover . . . there are few, if any, wooden ships . . . built in England now-a-days."[10] Sir Clements wanted the work done by Colin Archer, the Norwegian of Scots descent who had built Nansen's *Fram*, the most famous polar ship of all. In the end, however, Sir Clements patriotically decided on an all-British ship instead. The upshot was that *Discovery* cost about twice what Archer would have charged (£45,000 against £20,000) and, as J. W. Gregory put it, was being "sent on a mission for which she is ill-fitted". Amongst other things, she was "under-rigged, [also] having insufficient coal capacity for wide-ranging geographical adventures".[11]

Discovery was built by the Dundee Shipbuilders, the last of the yards making the old Dundee whalers. Had Sir Clements not meddled with the yard, a Dundee whaler is what he would have got, and a proven, if expensive, polar ship. With his naval fixation, however, he insisted on a naval designer. He thus ensured an unlovely compromise.

Discovery was a barque; a three-masted vessel, square-rigged on fore and main, fore-and-aft on mizzen. Her masts were too short, and badly placed. Her lines were ugly and ineptly conceived. As she lurched over the South Atlantic swell, those on board were hardly comforted to know that W. E. Smith, the Admiralty constructor who designed her, also happened to have designed the Royal yacht *Victoria and Albert*, which threatened to turn turtle when launched, and needed 140 tons of ballast to float upright.

Outwardly, Shackleton was very much the breezy Irishman, the extrovert, the irrepressible optimist; but his shipmates would have been surprised to know his private feelings, as *Discovery* entered the tropics:

> The day is garish now, there are no shadows and often one longs even for the Shade of a city wall, but the sea is on every side; and all I want lies beyond it.[12]

And after crossing the equator, on 31 August:

> We have lost the Polar Star, and it will be a long, long time before the "old lost stars wheel back".[13]

Partly this was pining for Emily; but partly also because Scott lacked the gift of running a happy ship. "I have never thought him evil," Gregory's mother-in-law had written during the leadership controversy, "but he is an inexperienced young man without imagination, which will to some extent supply the place of experience".[14]

The physical state of the ship affected Shackleton as well. There is something peculiarly depressing about an instrument that does not function as it should, but it was not just a matter of *Discovery*'s stability and sailing qualities. "In the building of the ship," observed Charles Royds, one of the naval officers, "there have been one or two great mistakes made." He was scandalised to find that "with the exception of the bunker space there is not a single sounding well in the ship".[15] This meant that it was impossible to tell exactly where she was making water. All wooden ships leak; *Discovery*, because of what Royds called "downright carelessness & want of supervision", leaked more than most. The consequence was that suddenly the holds were found to be awash. This was Shackleton's department. He had to restow the cargo. Since he was a watch-keeping officer, that meant hard work in his watch below:

> I could work all day and all night too if Nature would allow it but now she is revolting and I find I must take more Sleep . . .[16]

He found, when they were restowing the cargo, that the dockers in London had broached a case of real turtle soup and, finding this particular luxury not to their taste, discarded it, half empty, in the hold, since when it had been quietly fermenting. But Shackleton, a merchant officer, was surprised by very little at sea, not even by the anomalous *Discovery*; a merchant ship manned both by naval and merchant seamen, and run as a man o'war. He had soon shaken down and was taking the measure of his shipmates.

It helped that Armitage was also a merchant officer. Armitage, heavily built and phlegmatic – "heavy cake"[17] he was called – had the melancholy talent to be second-in-command. Like Shackleton, he could deal with all the kinds of humanity afloat. So also, in another style, could Charles Royds, First Lieutenant, and senior naval officer on board.

Royds was the executive officer, the man who actually ran the ship – the buffer between the captain and the crew. He displayed infinite patience towards inferiors, and reserved ill-humour for his equals. Tall, well drilled, formal and immaculately turned out, Royds, to quote a naval rating, James Dell, was "absolutely navy from top to toe".[18]

Someone of a different stamp was the remaining deck officer, Lieutenant Michael Barne. Also from the Navy he was, however, less formal than either Royds or Scott. He had the face of a boy and the voice of Stentor. At home with small groups in close confinement, Barne was typically Navy, but a "small ship man".

Shackleton's chosen companion, however, was not a brother officer, but Dr Edward Wilson, the expedition's junior surgeon.

> He has quite taken me in his charge [Wilson wrote in his diary], and puts me up to endless tips and does no end of things for me.[19]

Wilson hinted at one reason for this when he blandly recorded how "Swinburne's *Leper** was read to me on the bridge last night by Shackleton".[20] The Third Mate of the *Discovery* needed a listener and, after Hugh Robert Mill had left at Madeira, Wilson was about the only man on board willing to play the part.

At the Cape, Shackleton hoped to meet his brother Frank, but when *Discovery* arrived there on 4 October, he found that Frank had been invalided home. *Discovery* in fact was late. She was no clipper.

* A somewhat foetid poem, which includes the lines:

Yea, he inside whose grasp all night
Her fervent body leapt or lay,
Stained with sharp kisses red and white,
Found her a plague to spurn away.

Her engines were too slow, and burned too much coal. Scott nonetheless had landed at the island of South Trinidad in the Atlantic and again, after the Cape, at Macquarie Island for a natural history excursion. "With the energy of enthusiasm," said Scott, Shackleton returned "with a unique collection of insects, plants & geological specimens";[21] or now, at Macquarie Island, with "the usual nondescript assortment unlike anything else got".[22]

To Shackleton, it all seemed unintelligent dawdling, but humouring your captain, as he well knew, was one of the rules of the sea. Scott was beginning to see the cruise of the *Discovery* as another voyage of the *Beagle*, with himself perhaps playing Darwin.

For the time being, however, Shackleton was most concerned with handling *Discovery*. She had turned out to be a worse sea boat than he had feared, She did not swoop over the long southern swell, she lumbered. Her steering gear jammed. She flew up into the wind against her helm. She lurched and kicked and broached to. As Shackleton was the only watchkeeping officer on board with much practice in sail, he felt acutely that the safety of the ship rested on himself.

On 28 November, the New Zealand coast finally appeared over the horizon. Just before midnight *Discovery* made Akaroa Heads, and dropped anchor outside Lyttelton. "Shackleton," said Wilson, "went off in a boat and pulled the old postmaster out of bed and made him give us his mails."[23] Shackleton wanted his letters from Emily, but he knew too that Wilson had left England a fortnight after getting married and also wanted letters from home.

VI

A protean world of ice

In New Zealand, Shackleton received the news that Mr Dorman had suddenly died. Emily was now in a position to decide on marriage for herself. She did not absolutely require her future husband to have reached 90° south latitude, so that in one sense Shackleton need not have come at all. On Christmas Eve, however, when *Discovery* left New Zealand and her dark, ungainly form headed at last south into the unknown, Shackleton was still on board; still, as he insisted, for Emily's sake.

"It is a difficult thing to write a diary", Shackleton remarked on New Year's day, "and keep the rubbish out."[1] Two days before, he had simply written, "There is nothing to say today so I will shut up."[2] That might have been because two stokers, in the words of Reginald Skelton, the chief engineer, were

> logged by Captain & paraded before Ship's Company for using discontented language on the mess deck about their food. Their grog & tobacco also stopped.[3]

It was Shackleton's first experience of naval discipline.

On 2 January, early in the afternoon, Royds sighted the first iceberg flat, gleaming dully and mysterious:

> Everyone came up to look see, & the Captain following too close on Skelton coming up the hatch got a nasty kick which cut his left eye & had to have it sewn.[4]

A few hours later *Discovery* crossed the Antarctic Circle, and the next day she reached the pack ice, having hardly had a blow all the way from New Zealand, 1100 miles or more. It was just as well. As her sluggish labouring revealed, she was dangerously overloaded. Shackleton, before leaving Lyttelton, had had to squeeze in a stupendous mound of extra stores waiting at the docks, and this before they crossed what Scott himself called "the stormiest ocean in the world".[5] Because of a drunken and unwilling crew, Shackleton had recourse to stevedores, the work, Scott recorded in naive surprise, being "exceedingly cheaply done considering the high level of wages in these colonies". Now strewn atop the deck cargo wherever there was space, were twenty-three sledge dogs, taken at the urgent advice of Fridtjof Nansen.

It was Nansen who gave the classic description of the pack ice, north or south. It was, as he put it, a world of its own, monotonous and simple,

> And yet it makes a rare impact on our senses. In its details it has forms changing interminably, and colours playing in all shades of blue and green; but overall, it is precisely by its simple contrasts that it has its effect . . . the drifting ice, a mighty white surface, curving into the distance as far as the eye can see . . . I will never forget the first time I entered this world . . . something white suddenly appeared . . . the first ice floe. More came; they appeared far ahead, with a squelching sound they glided past and disappeared once more astern. I noticed a strange glow in the [sky], strongest on the horizon, but it continued far towards the zenith . . . at the same time there was . . . a distant rumble as of surf beating on a shore. It was the pack ice ahead; the light was the reflection that its white surface always throws against the humid air.

This is the "ice blink" of the polar navigators; the distant warning of the pack:

> The sound [continued Nansen] came from the waves breaking against the floes, which cannoned against each other grinding and groaning; on still nights, it can be heard far out to sea.[6]

Such was the world into which *Discovery* now sailed. It was not the only expedition southward bound. On the other side of the continent, Otto Nordenskjöld, in his ship, *Antarctic*, was heading for Graham Land. Shackleton's fate was to cross that of Nordenskjöld.

Nordenskjöld was a Swede, although not exactly a typical one, and he was the antithesis of Scott. Where Scott was a servant appointed by others, Nordenskjöld had organised the expedition that he led, and financed it from private funds alone, fighting established opinion. Nordenskjöld, rather than Scott, therefore, typified the polar explorer of the age.

Quiet, withdrawn, physically unimposing, Nordenskjöld concealed behind a hopeful beard and a bland exterior quite considerable powers. He was an academic, a geologist from the University of Uppsala, and that, in Sweden, meant great authority and prestige.

At all events, Nordenskjöld was conspicuously better prepared than Scott. He had already been to Greenland, and led an expedition to Patagonia. Aware still of his own deficiencies, Nordenskjöld had taken a Norwegian whaling captain and crew for *Antarctic*. He wanted them for experience of ice. Now, at about the same time as *Discovery* in her quarter, *Antarctic* in the Weddell Sea was grappling with the pack as well.

"The captain himself," as Nordenskjöld described the classic scene, was "up in the crow's nest, from where he directed the maneouvring":

> The orders ring out incessantly, and the helmsman is hard put to follow the constant changes . . . From his lookout point, the captain chooses his point of attack approximately on the same principle as a billiard player, so that the chosen ice floe is not only pushed in the right direction . . . but the neighbouring floe, through cannoning, is set in motion, and makes way for the vessel. At full speed, we go ahead, then the engines are stopped, and immediately there is a violent shock, so that the vessel shudders in every joint, and the uninitiated might imagine that each moment was his last. So serious, however, it is not. Slowly, the colossal floe begins to move, slowly the vessel glides ahead, while both sides scrape against the ice with a long drawn out roar that deceptively reminds one of the rumbling of thunder.

Here, Nordenskjöld went on,

> there reigned a desolation and wildness which, perhaps, no other place on earth could show; I experienced a sense of helplessness as if standing alone and deserted amidst mighty natural forces.[7]

Scott was faced with the belt of pack ice guarding the Ross Sea. He passed through in four days, one of the fastest of the seven passages so far on record, and wrote,

> It was such a pack that no sailing ship & very few steamers could have won through . . . Ross' first voyage must have been attended with extraordinarily good fortune. Had he fallen in with such ice as we have met, he could not by any possibility have found his way through.[8]

Scott, naturally, had never seen the pack ice before. But, Sir James Clark Ross, to whom he referred, was, in 1841, the first to penetrate the unknown southern pack. Under any circumstances, with sailing vessels unaided by mechanical power, that had been a courageous feat. It was Ross who had discovered South Victoria Land and the open Ross Sea, into which *Discovery* was breaking. It was Ross who, to this day, discovered more of the Antarctic coast than any other man.

With land now in the offing, Scott was suddenly faced with the necessity of producing polar travellers. Also on the advice of Nansen, he had taken ski. One day when *Discovery* was brought up by the pack Shackleton, together with everyone else, was ordered out on to a convenient floe to start learning. Scott himself did not join. As audience, there was a liberal crowd of seal and penguin. North or south, the pack teems with life; and here its inhabitants had not yet learned to fear man. The seal barely moved out of the way, and the penguins gathered round squawking like spectators at an exhibition.

Improvisation was the order of the day. "We all found [the] ski (pronounced *shee*) . . . rather awkward" in the words of Clarence Hare, Scott's steward, "which is not surprising for the first time."[9] "I think my share of falls," Shackleton bleakly wrote, "was greater than the others."[10]

It was on 8 January that *Discovery* nosed out of the pack ice into the open water of the Ross Sea. She also found clear weather again after a long spell of dull and overcast skies. That day, Shackleton for the first time saw the midnight sun. That day too, for the first time, Shackleton saw Antarctica.

It was a distant prospect of mountains under the midnight sun. In Wilson's words:

> A more glorious sight can hardly be imagined, with immense snow peaks rolled up in a mass of golden clouds and flooded with golden sunlight.[11]

Shackleton, however, beyond invoking what he called his "lack of facility in explanation",[12] hardly recorded his impressions.

There was on board *Discovery* an Australian physicist called Louis Bernacchi, who had joined the expedition at Lyttelton. A common taste for poetry drew him to Shackleton but he was eventually led to remark that "although Shackleton was always alert for any new interest – always full of flashing new ideas . . . Antarctica to him did not exist".[13]

It was the inward, not the outer world that engrossed Shackleton. He did not share the semi-pagan nature worship in which Nansen and Nordenskjöld were steeped. Shackleton's impressions were probably akin to those of Scott, recording his first glimpse of the land ahead "which, so few having seen before, makes us almost feel explorers".[14] It was the Promised Land, with fame, fortune, heroic achievement, or so it seemed, waiting to be quarried from a cupola of ice.

The mountains rearing up ahead were the Admiralty Range of South Victoria Land. *Discovery* was closing Cape Adare, where Borchgrevink had become the first man to winter on the Antarctic continent.

Shackleton was in the landing party that, on 9 January, went away in one of *Discovery*'s whalers to leave a message for a relief ship, as instructed, at Borchgrevink's base. It lay on a spit of shingle with a colony of Adelie penguins.

> Such a sight! [Wilson remarked in his diary] The place was the colour of anchovy paste from the excreta of the young penguins. It simply stunk like hell, and the noise was deafening . . . And bang in the centre of this horrid place was the camp with its two wooden huts . . .[15]

But it was the first human habitation on the Antarctic continent. It was where Shackleton first landed. Bernacchi was in the party too. He had been there before, with Borchgrevink. Did he remember what he once had written in that deserted hut upon the shore?

> A year spent entirely within the Antarctic Circle . . . 365 days! A sequestration from all civilisation . . . The past year has been such an unhappy one & so full of hardships – that I would not voluntarily spend such another for fame & fortune combined.[16]

The date had been 1 January 1900, a mere two years before. Yet there he was, in the whaler grating on to the beach, already coming back.

Leaving Cape Adare, *Discovery* now headed down the coast of South Victoria Land. From this time Hartley Ferrar, the expedition geologist, had an abiding memory of Shackleton "standing at the bows, chewing chocolate, watching the icebergs".

He had other reasons to remember Shackleton. Ferrar was bullied by Scott who, as he told his mother, got to the point of "finally producing tears".[17] That was because Scott considered Ferrar "conceited". Ferrar happened to be a Cambridge man, hastily brought in as a substitute for Gregory, so hastily, in fact, that he only took his degree a month or two before sailing. Tall and athletic, Ferrar got a good second class in the natural sciences

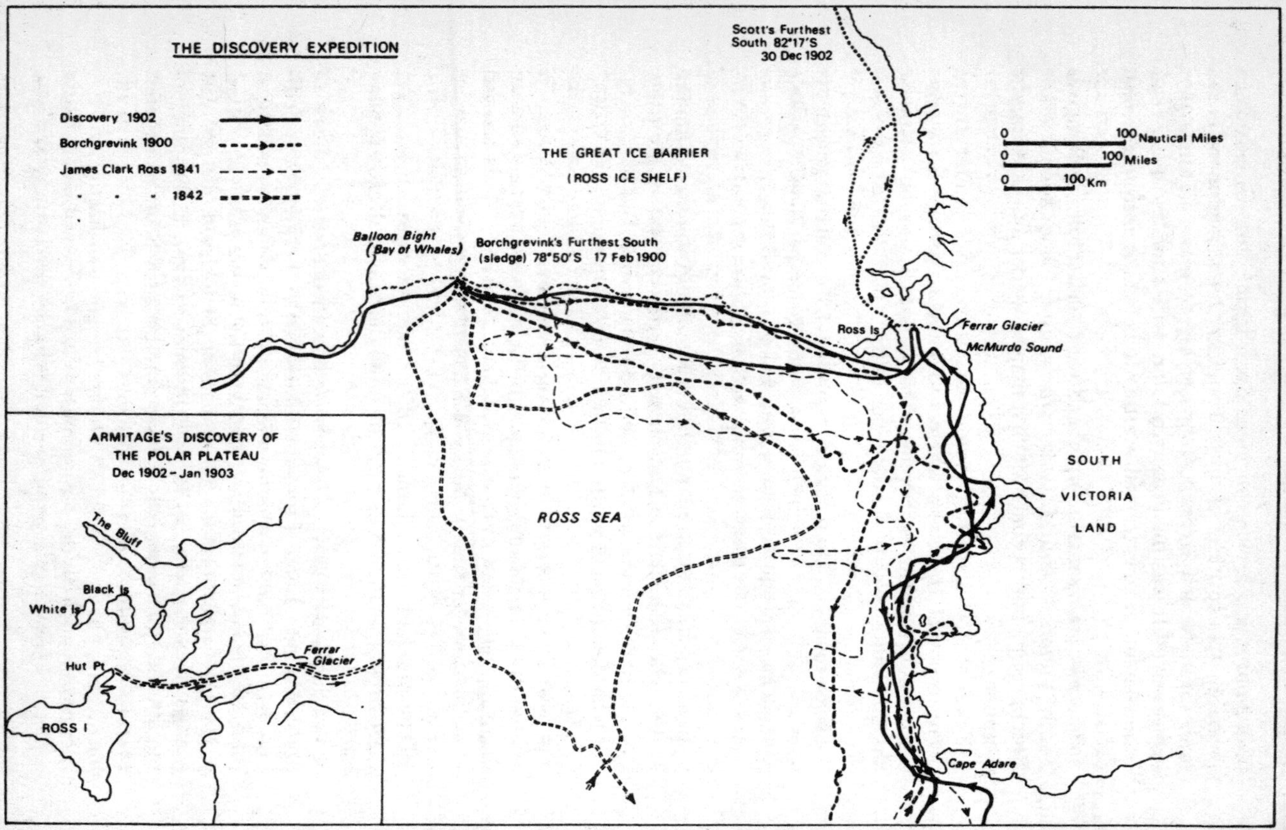
THE DISCOVERY EXPEDITION
Discovery 1902
Borchgrevink 1900
James Clark Ross 1841
1842
THE GREAT ICE BARRIER
(ROSS ICE SHELF)
Scott's Furthest South 82°17'S 30 Dec 1902
0 100 Nautical Miles
0 100 Miles
0 100 Km
Balloon Bight (Bay of Whales)
Borchgrevink's Furthest South (sledge) 78°50'S 17 Feb 1900
Ross Is
Ferrar Glacier
McMurdo Sound
SOUTH VICTORIA LAND
ROSS SEA
Cape Adare
ARMITAGE'S DISCOVERY OF THE POLAR PLATEAU
Dec 1902 – Jan 1903
The Bluff
Black Is
White Is
Hut Pt
Ferrar Glacier
ROSS I

tripos and rowed for his college (Sidney Sussex) too. He possessed the quiet, other-worldly Cambridge manner which, admittedly, can be a little disconcerting. Also, at the age of twenty-two, Ferrar was the youngest in the wardroom, and therefore a natural prey of bullying.

Shackleton took Ferrar under his wing, and Ferrar never forgot the way he stood by him in the face of Scott's baiting. Perhaps Shackleton felt a certain bond. Ferrar, a product of Oundle, was also a public schoolboy, and another Anglo-Irishman into the bargain. In after years, he always remembered Shackleton, the junior officer of *Discovery*, as "a wonderful leader", someone he would have "followed anywhere".

Discovery was now following in the tracks of Ross and his little squadron of *Erebus* and *Terror*. The constant spouting of whales induced Shackleton, on 11 January, to speculate whether Ross had been misled by the double blow of the Finn whale into believing it the Right whale.[18] By some peculiar coincidence, on that very same day, off Graham Land, C. A. Larsen, captain of Nordenskjöld's ship *Antarctic*, recorded similar speculations in *his* diary.

The Right whale was the commercially profitable species. It was, however, distressingly elusive. When Ross returned with reports of having seen it, he inspired a long, baffling hunt for Eldorado in the southern seas. A Right whale fishery would have meant a fortune without doubt.

Shackleton had other preoccupations. *Discovery* was coasting through treacherous polar waters, and he was still undergoing his baptism of ice. He was also hovering in uncertainty. Scott, as Wilson put it, had been "strangely reticent about letting a soul on the ship know what even his immediate plans are".[19] It seemed in keeping with the British official's apparently age-old mania for secrecy; or his belief that the repository of all wisdom lies in the official mind.

Discovery cruised on to the south. It was like going back in time to an Ice Age. To see any bare ground was a notable event. On 20 January, Shackleton led a party ashore to examine some rocks at a place on South Victoria Land since called Granite Harbour. With him was the senior surgeon and botanist, Reginald Koettlitz, a thin, melancholy man of German extraction, but rootless, with a passion for exploration. He had been with Armitage on the Jackson-Harmsworth Arctic expedition of 1894–7 to Franz Josef Land, and thus was one of the few on *Discovery* with polar experience. Shackleton wrote in his diary,

> Seeing some green stuff at the foot of a boulder I called [Koettlitz] to have a look at it. He went down on his knees and then jumped up,

> crying "Moss!! Moss!! I have found moss!!!" I said "Go on! I found it" He took it quite seriously, and said, "Never mind, it's moss; I am so glad." The poor fellow was so overjoyed that there were almost tears in his eyes. This was his Golconda* – this little green space in the icy South.[20]

At 76° 30′S, it was the most southerly plant yet found; this tiny bridgehead of life clinging to the edge of a sterile shore.

Through a protean world of ice, *Discovery* sailed on. In the water, sinister tabular icebergs, the debris of broken ones, polygonal floes, eroded bits, amorphous brash drifted by. On land, tongues, tumuli and towers tumbled outlandishly down to the sea, glinting dull green against grey waters.

Over the horizon to the south, there was rising steadily the smoking cone of Mount Erebus, the volcano discovered by Ross. On 22 January, *Discovery* sailed up under its ice-bound flanks, and then reached Cape Crozier, to the east, under Mount Terror, the extinct twin of Erebus. There now burst into sight the Great Ice Barrier, a vast ice cliff running eastwards from Cape Crozier as far as the eye could see.

The Barrier had been discovered by Ross. It forms the southern shore of the Ross Sea. It is in reality the edge of a mammoth shelf of ice, and is known today as the Ross Ice Shelf. To Ross, though, pre-eminently a seaman, it was a "barrier" to his ships.

Sir Clements Markham had told Scott to follow in the tracks of Ross and extend his discoveries to the east. Especially, Sir Clements wanted the other end of the Barrier fixed. *Discovery* therefore headed eastwards, and for a week cruised along the mysterious wall of ice, which rolled endlessly on, towering up, mast high. The swell, breaking against the ice front, roared and pounded, sending up cascades of spume. Wilson observed at one point that in the Barrier

> were the most wonderful bright blue caves, and the whole face was hung with thin icicles, which made the most fascinating grottos with the pure blue depths of the caves and cracks.[21]

Shackleton, on the other hand, was not as impressed by the Barrier as he had expected, not even after four hundred miles and the realisation that, with most of its bulk under water, it must have been a thousand feet thick. He was, as he said, occupied with "home thoughts from the ice".[22]

* In Shackleton's day, an expression for a "mint of money". Golconda was the old name of Hyderabad, in India, famed for its diamonds.

So far *Discovery* – to Scott's mild irritation – had been following in the tracks of Ross. On 29 January, she finally passed his Furthest East. From the captain down, everyone on board was now keyed up.

Next day, Thursday 30 January, as Royds recorded,

> it snowed hard all the time & was very thick & misty everywhere. We kept passing what was without any doubt snow covered land . . . at 6.45 p.m., in my last dog [watch] we, that is the Capt., Armitage, Koettlitz & self saw rocks sticking up through the snow, & at a good height up, so that at last we have really got the right stuff, and the "Discovery" has made a Discovery in real earnest . . .[23]

To Shackleton, it was

> a very definite discovery, and it does seem curious. It is a unique sort of feeling to look on lands that have never been seen by human eye before.[24]

The external scene had finally, as it were, broken in on Shackleton's thoughts. A semblance of personal achievement had appeared at last. This was indeed new land, part of the continental coastline jutting north to form the abutment of the Barrier. It was named King Edward VII Land (today, the King Edward VII Peninsula), in honour of the new monarch; the first geographical discovery of his reign.

Flushed with success, Scott now pushed on, for ahead lay another thousand miles of undiscovered coast, and apparently unlimited opportunity for fame. Heavy and difficult ice barred the way. "I am pretty confident," Scott had written to the RGS, that *Discovery* "won't *rise* to a squeeze." He meant that bad design, with straight sides, and a stern counter, ensured that, if trapped, *Discovery* would probably be crushed by the pressure of the ice. "So," he continued, "shall trust to luck to avoid that."[25] But in the evening of 31 January, when Shackleton took over the first watch (8 p.m. to midnight), he was faced with a notably unpleasant situation.

Discovery was embayed in compacted sea ice.

She was ringed by icebergs, like some polar Stonehenge of the Titans. Scott was below, although in such circumstances he ought to have stayed on the bridge. He had simply left orders to carry on east. Barne, the previous officer of the watch, had, in the naval manner of the day, blindly obeyed. In the process, he had lost his bearings. He knew he had sailed in through a narrow entrance. He could no longer say where it was. In the treacherous, shifting world of ice, drifting mysteriously in unknown currents, an entrance might no longer exist.

Shackleton grasped that the ship was in a trap. Orders or no, his only concern was to escape. He took *Discovery* right round the bay in search of the way out. When Scott appeared on deck at the end of the watch, Shackleton still had not succeeded.

Shackleton was now astounded to find Scott dissolve into something uncomfortably like panic. It was impossible to make him understand what was happening. Eventually, Shackleton went below, leaving Royds, who relieved him on watch, to deal with Scott.

Royds did not have much more success. By the time he too went below, at 4 a.m., he still had not convinced Scott that they were simply chasing their own tail. Scott seemed impervious to any argument; his orders were well-nigh irrational. According to the log, the ship went round in a complete circle three times. The pack ice was "very heavy, close and much hummocked".[26] At 7.30, as Royds put it in his diary,

> there was a panic . . . & at last managed to convince the capt; so we again turned back & at last got out of what at one time looked a very nasty position, as young ice was forming thickly & very quickly.[27]

It was not the first time that Scott had lost his head. Twice on the way down South Victoria Land he had allowed the ship to be trapped between an advancing belt of pack ice and the shore. It was Armitage who had taken over and saved the day, but a sense of ultimate purpose had been missing then, because Scott had so far divulged no plans. As if jolted by events, Scott now called officers and scientists into the wardroom and finally revealed what was in his mind.

For Shackleton, the essential point was that *Discovery* would winter in the ice. All along, he ardently wanted to stay in the south. Until then, no more than anyone else on board had he known whether *Discovery* would return to civilisation for the winter; much less who would land, and who sail back. Now all uncertainty was settled at a stroke.

Others were not so pleased. Some of the merchant seamen had signed on under the impression that it was for the round trip only, like any other voyage. Scott, however, did not tell the lower deck for another day or two.

Discovery, meanwhile, had put about, and was making her best speed back along her tracks to the west. Scott had had a fright, and wanted to get out of danger. Also, it was late in the season, and time to find a winter haven. On the afternoon of 3 February, at about 164° west longitude, *Discovery* entered an inlet in the Barrier. Here the ice front sloped down to the water like a natural quay. *Discovery* lay to. Shackleton, together with Scott and Reginald Skelton, the naval chief engineer, went ashore, put on ski, and tried to run towards the south.

Although Scott was curiously loath to admit it, they were following in Borchgrevink's wake. Bernacchi, once again, could say he had been there before. Two years earlier he had sailed with Borchgrevink in the *Southern Cross* up an inlet – not perhaps the same, it was difficult to say. In any case, they had berthed, and made the first landing on the Barrier, ever. This was the historic occasion when Borchgrevink reached his Furthest South and opened the race for the Pole. The real significance, however, was this. On ski, with dogs and sledges, Borchgrevink had travelled over the Barrier. He did not go far but, in the words of Bernacchi at the time, the surface appeared

> absolutely no obstacle to travelling being smooth & level . . . From their turning point furthest south nothing could be distinguished but the great level expanse of ice – extending out of sight to the South.[28]

Borchgrevink had proved that the Barrier was just another snowfield. He had shown the way ahead, and removed one mystery from the South. He was the precursor of continental Antarctic land travel, but he has never received the credit that is his due.

Unlike Borchgrevink, Shackleton and his companions did not find the Barrier surface "always very good travelling", as Skelton phrased it. "None of us are yet very expert on ski. So we do not get on very fast."[29] They soon returned.

Scott now decided to use his balloon. In the bitter breeze, this was not a simple performance. The balloon was made of cow gut, which needed careful handling. Filling it with hydrogen from the cylinders needed equal care.

Shackleton felt that here he would come into his own. He had had, after all, some training. Scott, however, although having none, insisted on going up first in order, as he frankly put it, to have "the honour of being the first aeronaut to make an ascent in the Antarctic regions".[30]

Shackleton was next. Into the rickety basket he clambered. Above him, the balloon, like a bloated tulip bulb, rose and billowed in the wind. Shackleton, to his own private satisfaction perhaps, climbed higher than Scott: to 650 feet. Precariously anchored to the snow by a frail-looking wire, he took the first Antarctic air photographs. They showed the white snow plain running free and unimpeded to the south. In the other direction, he could observe an equally interesting – and perhaps prophetic – sight. *Discovery* was snugly moored in an enticing natural harbour, protected by a narrow entrance. It was either a trap, or a base crying out to be used.

After Shackleton came down, it was Wilson's turn. He refused.

> As only one can go up at a time, I think it is perfect madness to allow novices to risk their lives in this silly way . . . Happily, after lunch, the balloon was found to have leaked to such an extent that an ascent was impossible, so [it] was emptied. and then it was found that had anyone used the valve in the morning, when the balloon was up, it would not have closed properly and nothing could have prevented the whole show from dropping to earth like a stone![31]

While all this was happening, *Discovery* was nearly crushed by a minor iceberg eddying in the tide. There was not enough steam in the boilers to move out of danger.

After a day at what came to be called Balloon Bight, *Discovery* sailed on. She now headed straight back for the waters under Erebus, where Scott had finally announced that he was going to winter. Ice had started forming on the sea, and it seemed time to go. On 8 February, *Discovery* arrived, and headed up McMurdo Sound.

McMurdo Sound is a wide waterway, thirty miles across and thirty miles long, sculpted out of ice. The western shore runs along the extremity of South Victoria Land, the eastern, along Ross Island, under Mount Erebus. Here *Discovery* seemed to be sailing through some outlandish dream world. At one point, a tongue of ice, mottled by volcanic grit, jutted out from the western shore. Scott saw the forms as "tombstones in a cemetery".[32] To Shackleton, on the other hand, "The whole place had a weird and uncanny look, and reminded me of the desert in 'Childe Roland to the dark tower came'."[33]* Scott had fallen back for an image on an underlying morbidity; Shackleton, as usual, to Browning.

At the head of McMurdo Sound, in a bay behind a promontory, *Discovery* found her haven. There, at 77° 50′ south latitude, she was

* "Then came a bit of stubbed ground once wood,
Next a marsh it would seem and now mere earth,
Desperate and done with . . .
Bog, clay and rubble, sand and stark black dearth . . ."[34]

runs one of the verses to which Shackleton refers.

warped into place to wait for the winter. Very close lay the edge of the Barrier, always accessible by a pass, soon called the Gap.

Among his plans, Scott had announced the attempt next summer to reach the South Pole. In preparation for this, he suddenly ordered skiing on the slopes above *Discovery*.

Ten years later Skelton, after a winter at Lenzerheide, in the Swiss Alps, ruefully remarked that it was "such a pity we had no one in the *Discovery* to teach us properly, because everything depends on first lessons".[35] Koettlitz was the instructor. He could ski, but a gifted teacher he was not. In any case, polar travel required cross-country skiing. These tyros on their farflung nursery slope were trying to learn the downhill discipline. Either way, Scott, who soon sprained a knee, was trusting to improvisation, even in the profoundly technical domain of skiing.

Shackleton incessantly tumbled about, finding – not entirely to his amusement – that, though uninjured, he was virtually the worst skier of them all. "Must practise the more,"[36] he noted laconically. He seemed not to have progressed much since his first steps in the pack ice. He never did really take to skiing. Nor was he made for dedicated practice; he wanted instant results.

Suddenly one day, soon after Shackleton's birthday, he found himself leading a party to spy out the start of the road to the south. At the time, he was immersed in nostalgia "thinking of home – have not had a birthday at home for nearly 12 years".[37] The order to go out was the finest birthday present he could possibly have had. In the course of his twenty-eight years, Shackleton had often taken the lead, but this was the first time that he had ever been put in command.

VII

Polar travel

Out into what he called the "weird white world".[1] Shackleton started just before midday on 19 February. It was, as perhaps he sensed, an historic occasion. Shackleton was leading the first major journey of the expedition, the first foray from McMurdo Sound. It was the start of the British route to the Pole. Chance played a part in the affair. By Scott's own account, he let Barne and Shackleton toss a coin for command of the party, and Shackleton won.

With Shackleton went Wilson and Ferrar; "Three polar knights",[2] as one contemporary put it. There was indeed a whiff of knight-errantry about their departure. Awkwardly accoutred in unfamiliar garments, they might well have been in armour. From a jackstaff on their sledge flew personal banners which, in the spirit of mediaeval chivalry, had been decreed for the officers by Sir Clements Markham. It was the first time they had been used. Each bore the owner's arms: "or on a fess gules", as the heraldic specification put it in the case of Shackleton, "three buckles on the field", with the motto *Fortitudine Vincimus*, "By endurance we conquer". Inspired by this, and Tennyson's *Idylls of the King*, Shackleton could see himself as a Knight of the Round Table setting off to do battle with the forces of nature.

Make-believe chivalry was still very much part of English life. In this case it was enhanced by the quixotry of the enterprise. Shackleton, Wilson, and Ferrar were all equally raw. Armitage, Koettlitz and Bernacchi, the men with polar experience, had been deliberately kept behind. Shackleton was to learn the hard way. He was quite content, however, for it was how he too had been cradled. Besides, in the country of the blind, as well he knew, the one-eyed man is – sometimes – king.

The day before Shackleton's departure there took place the first attempts at driving dogs. Armitage and Bernacchi were the protagonists, the former, as Royds put it, "driving them by means of a whip & hard treatment while the latter is using soft words and coaxing".[3] Neither was notably successful. Shackleton left the dogs behind, and harnessed himself and his companions to the sledge instead. They eschewed skis as well. Turning themselves into beasts of burden, they laboured across the snow on their own unaided feet.

It was a tableau that would have stupefied the eight other expeditions, of different nationalities, sharing the polar regions, north and south, with them. "Polar exploration without ski is extremely awkward," in the words of Otto Sverdrup, the Norwegian explorer now entering his fourth consecutive year in the Arctic, "without dogs it is impossible."[4] Only on *Discovery* were dogs and ski still considered doubtful innovations.

British polar explorers, at least of the official kind, had wilfully ignored the experience of others. They neglected ski. Likewise, they were obdurate in their prejudice against dogs for transport in the snow. Sir Clements Markham bore much of the blame. He had a talent for imposing the past on the present. Even so, the past had lessons for those willing to learn.

The Norwegians, after all, had shown the way. It was, however, not necessary to look to foreigners. Englishmen were pioneers in the spread of skiing from its Norwegian homeland. In Canada, Scots trappers and travellers of the Hudson's Bay Company had been object lessons in dog driving long ago. Thus William MacTavish from Norway House in 1834: "Transport in the winter is carried on by dogs yoked to a sledge . . . a man drives them, & it is scarcely credible the load these dogs will draw". Even then, there was an ingrained scorn for British official expeditions from polar professionals. "The mission was projected . . . without mature consideration and the necessary previous arrangements totally neglected", said Dr George Simpson, another Hudson's Bay traveller, of John Franklin, an earlier British polar hero, in 1821. Franklin, as he put it,

> must have three meals p. diem, Tea is indispensable . . . so that it does not follow if those Gentlemen are unsuccessfull the difficulties are insurmountable.[5]

The insularity that bedevilled polar explorers from Britain clearly extended to the British Empire as well. "You'll hear", to quote MacTavish again, on another contemporary expedition, "what a fine story they'll make out of this bungle, they will, you may be sure, take none of the blame themselves".[6]

Sir Clements Markham, however, ignored all this. His models were the very British naval expeditions that had excited the scorn of men like Simpson and MacTavish. They had signally failed with dogs, but performed prodigies of man-hauling instead. Sir Clements himself participated in one of those expeditions, fifty years before. It was a short interlude, and Sir Clements' only experience of polar exploration; but it was enough for him to assume immense personal authority. He extolled man-hauling, and deplored the use of ski and dogs.

Sir Clements was not dealing in rational argument, but seeing moral worth in doing things the hard way. That struck a deep chord among Englishmen. Sir Clements appealed also to the national sentimentality towards the dog, a fatal misunderstanding of the breed. It was coupled also with a romantic British preference for seeing men, rather than animals, at work.

Such was the historical background against which Shackleton set out. Over the sea ice he went, past killer whales cruising along the edge, and up on to the Barrier. He was heading south-east, for an unnamed *nunatak** later called White Island. Unused to the deceptiveness of clear air, the light of high latitude, and the foreshortening effect of snow and ice, he imagined the distance to be about ten miles; it proved instead to be eighteen.

Still, the terrain was flat and undisturbed. The snow was granular and firm. Under notably worse conditions, it was a distance that, away in the Arctic, Sverdrup was polishing off with dogs in six or seven hours. Shackleton and his men were nowhere near the end after that time, and they simply struggled on:

> The pulling [wrote Ferrar] was fairly hard . . . a wind carrying snow-dust caught us. We worked against this . . . hardly making 6 inches per step.[7]

This records the first Antarctic blizzard encountered by Scott's expedition on the march. "Snow-dust" was a graphic, homemade and wholly accurate term for what is known as drift. Antarctica is a desert, and fresh snowflakes falling are as rare as raindrops in the Sahara. Most blizzards simply sweep old, needle-like crystals of drift from one place to another. They are really dust storms in the cold.

Shackleton was also initiated into the strange conflict of polar travel, where cold and heat are bedfellows. The art is to balance the

* An Eskimo word meaning an isolated mass of rock piercing the ice.

two. It is easy enough to pile on garments while standing still; the difficulty is to protect the extremities without overheating the rest of the body while on the move. The key to this is proper ventilation.

Shackleton and his companions were dressed in Burberry cloth; a British product, at that time the most efficient windproof fabric known. The garments, however, were wholly unsuitable. They were too tight, without fixed hoods, and they generally ignored what other explorers had learned in the past fifty years. The upshot was that the three men were liberally frostbitten; Shackleton worst of all. Absolutely determined, however, to reach that elusive cone of rock, he nonetheless led on, far beyond the point where experience would have told him to stop.

They had a heavy sledge, crudely stowed with fourteen days' food, tent, furs, all surmounted by a pram, a Norwegian skiff adapted to launching and beaching, to act as a lifeboat in case the sea ice broke up.

Pulling all this and fighting the gale produced plenty of sweat which, in the end, drenched their underclothes and destroyed its insulation. They were dismal with clammy cold. By midnight they were thoroughly exhausted, battered by the incessant roaring of the wind and, though they did not understand it, dehydrated as well. It is a peculiarity of work in the cold that sweating is copious. Peary, Nansen, and others had already learned how vital it was to avoid sweating under polar conditions.

Except for one short rest, Shackleton and his companions had been trudging continuously for twelve hours. Since breakfast, they had eaten virtually nothing. Shackleton gave the order to camp. Not one of them had ever pitched a tent before. It reminded Shackleton of his first struggles aloft on the *Hoghton Tower* trying to set a topsail. Eventually the tent was, somehow, raised. Then a meal had to be cooked. That involved lighting the primus stove.

This was the first device for efficiently burning paraffin, and the first portable, high efficiency stove. By reducing fuel consumption, it vastly extended the range of unsupported travel. It was one of the technical advances that revolutionised polar exploration. Invented by a Swede called Frans Wilhelm Lindquist, the primus stove worked by vaporising paraffin under pressure applied by a small air pump. It could boil a pint of water in three minutes against ten minutes or more required by the old spirit lamps using wicks.

Lighting the primus stove, however, was not just a matter of striking a match and turning a tap. One had to know how to heat the nozzle with methylated spirits, how to pump, how to adjust the pressure. The primus had been on the market since 1892, but very few on *Discovery* had ever used one. Ferrar, at least, had taken the trouble to learn how to work it, but he had not yet applied his knowledge in the field, crouching in a tent. Eventually he managed it, but they were all three so exhausted that all they could stomach was a little cocoa.

Nor had any of them ever slept in a tent before; and never in a sleeping bag. In fact, they did not have sleeping bags, by now the customary gear among polar explorers. Instead, they had strange sleeping suits of reindeer pelts contrived by unnamed experts. Getting in was "like wrestling with a python",[8] as somebody put it, and that had to be accomplished in a crowded tent, the canvas rattling in the gale like the flicking of a damp towel. Their boots, in Wilson's words,

> were frozen to the socks, so that both came off in one and it took us all we knew next morning to tear the socks out. The sweat of one's feet had lined the boots with ice . . . I was constantly getting cramp in the thighs wherever I moved . . . the cold of the ice floor crept through and the points of contact got pretty chilly. We put Ferrar in the middle and though that was the warmest place, he was coldest during the night. I think he was most done up.[9]

After dozing fitfully for about an hour, they were woken by the silence of the wind suddenly dropping. They "rather tumbled everything into the pram",[10] as Ferrar put it, and hauled for four hours; "a rather different thing though now, with no wind and no drift and bright sunshine",[11] in Wilson's words. A mile or so from the island, they were stopped where the Barrier was cloven and crevassed.

Leaving the sledge behind, Shackleton led his men on, unroped. By all the rules, inexperience should have flung him to disaster in some chasm lightly bridged by snow. Except for dropping one foot into a hidden crevasse, however, he got them through to the island. Then, despite his ignorance of mountaineering, he led them safely to the top. By then, it was midnight on 20 February.

Having seen, Shackleton wanted to hurry back and tell his tale. He returned to the ship in a single day. Late in the evening of 22 February, after eleven hours' solid hauling, he arrived, "full of talk", said Royds, "as expected".[12]

In the bleak light of retrospection, Shackleton had merely blundered his untutored way over a few miles of snow and ice, and then up a not too impressive climb of a few hundred feet. But Balboa, first seeing the Pacific, could not have been more stupendously elated than Shackleton, as he stepped on to the summit of his nunatak. A silent white landscape dully glittered in the fading midnight sun. To the west, he saw a new range of unknown mountains. More, much more, southwards at his feet, the Barrier rolled on unhindered. Shackleton had found the road to the Pole. He was a discoverer; he had shown the way ahead. Beyond the mirage shimmering on the southern horizon, he could almost see El Dorado.

The day after his return was a Sunday. For church service Shackleton, as he noted in his diary, specially requested the hymn

> Fight the good fight with all thy might,
>   Christ is thy strength, and Christ thy right;
> Lay hold on life, and it shall be
>   Thy joy and crown eternally.[13]

The wardroom of *Discovery*, however, was designed to keep people in their place, not give the instant recognition that Shackleton craved; but at least he had the satisfaction of being the only one that season to attain his goal.

A dozen men tried to reach Cape Crozier, at the other end of Ross Island, with a message for the relief ship, a distance of barely forty miles. They failed. (Nansen had a dozen men with him for the whole three-year drift of the *Fram*.) Someone opened a tin of jam at a temperature of about −30°F. He "took out some on his knife & put it into his mouth," as Frank Wild, one of the naval seamen, told the tale. " The knife immediately froze fast to his lips & tongue & he had to keep it there until it warmed sufficiently for him to remove it without tearing a lot of skin away." On the way back another seaman, named Vince, fell over an ice cliff and was killed.

Before winter closed down, Scott himself went south to depot supplies out on the Barrier for the summer journey towards the Pole. He, too, failed.

Ignorance, inexperience and unpreparedness were the trouble. Shackleton was guilty of all three, he too. His short excursion, however, had stirred within him the feeling that, to quote one Irish writer, "Irishmen make better leaders than followers".[14] Within him burned the sacred flame of leadership. It was, perhaps, his redeeming virtue. For the moment, it simply intensified an acutely growing sense, before Scott, of playing second fiddle.

VIII

Polar night

"The whole arrangement," as Skelton put it, "can be improved by system."[1] He was writing of the technical deficiencies the Cape Crozier fiasco had so glaringly revealed, but he was practically alone in his concern. The wardroom seemed otherwise preoccupied. What, for example, was the expedition magazine to be called? On 21 March, a formal and argumentative meeting finally decided on *The South Polar Times*. As editor, the choice fell on Shackleton.

Until *Discovery* froze in, however, there was little peace of mind for editing. Like each other officer, Shackleton was perpetually worried about the safety of the ship. With every shift of the wind, wires and cables had to be adjusted. At last, by the end of March, the swell died down; the creak of working timbers ceased, *Discovery* was firmly embedded in the ice that now encased the bay. She ceased to be a living ship. Until she floated free once more, her officers were released from their over-riding care.

On shore, meanwhile, a wooden hut was built. Ordered from Australia, it had originally been intended for the landing party should *Discovery* not stay south for the winter. Since everyone now lived on the ship, it served as a store, and emergency quarters in case of fire on board. It was a gloomy place. It gave its name to Hut Point, a promontory of Ross Island on which it stood. The extreme tip was called Cape Armitage, after the second-in-command. Most of the local features, when *Discovery* sailed in, were as yet unnamed.

"I wonder how we will feel when the sun goes for a couple of months," Shackleton had written among the Cape rollers in August under clouded skies, "when we miss him so if he is away two days!"[2] On 3 March, with the midnight sun receding, he recorded that it was dark enough for the first time at McMurdo Sound to see the stars; "the heralds," as he put it, "of approaching winter".[3] Six weeks later, he marked the "creeping on of winter", with the Shakespearean tag, "Fear no more the heat of the sun, or the furious winter's rages though thy worldly . . ." leaving, as he often did, the ending in the air:

> . . . task hast done,
> Home art gone and ta'en thy wages;
> Golden lads and girls all must,
> As chimney sweepers, come to dust.[4]

Among the robust determination of the others *not* to be affected by the polar night, Shackleton's unease stood out.

The darkness was not the only explanation. It was in any case hardly absolute – at noon, even in midwinter, there was a faint red glimmer above the horizon to the north. There were the rippling curtains of the Aurora Australis, like Shelley's "orbed maiden", as Shackleton quoted in his diary, "with white fire laden".[5] Sometimes a cloud above Erebus glowed eerily with a dull red reflection from the crater. It was a foray, so it almost seemed, to another planet.

What Shackleton was troubled by was an aching fear of time and opportunity slipping by. He was, of course, only the junior officer on board. When the sun returned, he might so easily find himself the shipkeeper, condemned to wait behind while others collared all the glory in the south.

Once more he had to live in uncertainty and doubt; but he was not alone. Scott was secretive and morose. Not a word of his intentions did he discuss. Woe betide anyone who asked. Even the naval officers, accustomed to uncommunicative superiors, were ill at ease.

Gregory had anticipated something of the sort when he remarked that it was Scott's "first command and for a man who talks so much about discipline, I think it is a pity for his first command to be so unusual."[6] Under imaginative leaders, the polar winter was a crowded interval of preparation, but on *Discovery* it meant the torpid routine of a ship in port. In the spring, improvisation on the march could recommence but, until then, time, somehow, had to be made to pass.

Shackleton had sketched out a comprehensive plan of reading although it had nothing to do with the polar regions, for systematic preparation occurred no more to him than to his commander. "I can see no chance of doing the study I should like to during the winter,"[7] Shackleton, however, was soon writing. *The South Polar*

Times was absorbing his attention. He saw it, in fact, as something to fall back on, in case he did not go south. In any case, Scott would have the privilege, by contract, of writing the only authorised account of the expedition. Shackleton instead harboured a scheme to publish *The South Polar Times* on returning home. Shackleton indeed, as Armitage recalled, had "leanings towards Journalism".[8] *The South Polar Times* would be the entrée into Fleet Street, and hence the path to fame and fortune by another route. Of one thing, at any rate, Shackleton was now tolerably certain. Having once escaped, he was not going back to the mercantile marine.

With a nice sense of promotion, Shackleton launched *The South Polar Times* on 23 April, the day, as he put it, when "the sun disappeared from our view for 121 days and the long Antarctic winter has commenced".[9] It was of course (although he did not mention it) St George's day as well. The issue, he went on to say, "came out after dinner and was greatly praised!"

It was not, in fact, Shackleton's first experience of editing. Two years before while trooping in the Boer War, and together with the ship's surgeon, he had published a slim volume with the self-explanatory title *"O.H.M.S." an illustrated record of the voyage of s.s. "Tintagel Castle," containing twelve hundred soldiers from Southampton to Cape Town March 1900.* In his description of the departure:

> . . . We go! We are steaming into the blue, to the land where glory or death awaits us, and we're Britishers, we are men in a world of men. Our red flag waves on the steamer's stern with the Union which is ours the wide world over . . .[10]

Shackleton had already shown that he had the journalist's gift of being in touch with his public.

The South Polar Times was redolent of a school magazine. Besides the editing, Shackleton typed each issue out while Wilson, who was a fair painter, did the illustrations. Thus, frozen in at the edge of an uninhabited continent, at the other end of the globe, Shackleton learned the rudiments of magazine production. He rigged up an office in *Discovery*'s hold and, sequestered there week after week, he and Wilson worked.

Scott approved of *The South Polar Times*; he also wanted plenty of scientific observations. So, at the top of what was now called Crater Hill, Shackleton and Wilson obligingly established an extra meteorological observatory. "We want to take as much exercise . . . as possible," said Shackleton, "and this will be a useful way of doing it."[11] In his diary, "Went up Crater Hill with Billy",[12] as he called Wilson, became, throughout the winter, a constant refrain.

In a letter to his wife Wilson wrote,

> God knows it is just about as much as I can stand at times, and there is absolutely no escape. I have never had my temper so tried as it is every day now . . . You told me your Father had said I was a peacemaker [and] a little bit of peace-making is wanted . . . in this community of men . . .[13]

On the other side of the continent, meanwhile, Otto Nordenskjöld was writing that despite

> all the excellent qualities and goodwill . . . of my closest companions, nevertheless I had seen how difficult it is to unite round one interest personalities which in many respects are each others' diametric opposites.[14]

The only difference was that Nordenskjöld, philosophising over his leadership of the Swedish expedition, published what he wrote. Wilson very definitely did not, possibly because, as Hugh Robert Mill explained, it was "the fine tradition of British explorers [in] passing over . . . little squabbles and jealousies".

In any case, both were touching on a particular risk of polar exploration, that is, the strain of being cooped up for long in isolation. Friction is inevitable. The maddening proximity of a too familiar face may be a torture in itself. The clash of personality has always been a danger more sinister than climate or terrain. On *Discovery*, Scott responded by forcing everyone into the only pattern that he knew. He imposed a rigid, regimental kind of discipline that was actually a caricature of the Navy at the time. He paraded the men topsides thinly clad for captain's inspection, because that was the custom, although it was manifestly unsuited to the circumstances. He ordered the scientists – as he had told Sir Clements Markham – to keep a summary of their work in his cabin and write it up weekly.[15] "The thing that always used to tickle me," Shackleton afterwards recalled, "was the way . . . Royds used to put new snow on the . . . deck, getting the dirty stuff up before divisions."[16] At the time Shackleton was, perhaps, not so amused. It was noticed by the seamen; as most things on board usually are. Shackleton "hated any sort of formality", as one of the naval ratings vividly remembered. "He didn't fall in with all the views of all the naval officers."[17] Shackleton's walks up Crater Hill with Wilson were also to get away from the ambit of an unsympathetic regime.

Tall, thin, red-haired, with the ghost of a quizzical smile

hovering over slightly compressed lips, Wilson moved quietly among his fellows. Like Ferrar, he was a Cambridge man (Gonville and Caius College) and he displayed too the characteristic, withdrawn Cambridge manner. In Wilson's case, it was complicated by the fact that he was not too enthusiastically a doctor, but had a religious vocation in an evangelical way. Had he not been forced by custom to follow his father into medicine, he would undoubtedly have taken Orders. Except for a mysterious undertone of bitterness, he gave the impression, at twenty-nine, of all passion prematurely spent. He and Shackleton did not seem natural companions. Nonetheless, thrown together by chance, they found each other the most congenial company available.

Shackleton needed a listener still. It was not simply that he required an audience for his recitation; he could, and indeed did, dragoon others for that. (Skelton, for example, who actually despised poetry, or so he said.) Shackleton urgently wanted to talk about himself. Anyone else on board would have fled at the merest hint. It was Wilson's fate, as he once wryly put it, to have "confidential talks with various people who [have] confidences to bestow".[18] He was alone in being prepared to hear Shackleton out. From Shackleton, however, he got something in return.

Wilson had suffered from tuberculosis, and he may not yet have been completely cured. He was in any case someone of low vitality; and to that Shackleton, with his overflowing spirits, acted as an antidote. It was curiously similar to Shackleton's effect on Emily Dorman.

To Wilson, Shackleton harped on his ardent longing to go on the "southern journey" which now truly seemed the key to fame and fortune. The conquest of the Pole would put the world at his feet. Shackleton, however, was suffering from the protracted anguish of uncertainty. Wilson could sympathise, for the months passed, and Scott still revealed no plans. He remained withdrawn and secretive. Ennui had settled on the ship. While the dogs moped, neglected in their kennels, and blizzards swept down as a reminder of a world yet to be mastered, Shackleton succinctly wrote that he was "doing the same thing day after day".[19] Even *The South Polar Times* turned into a chore. To pass the time, Shackleton sometimes helped "Muggins" trawl for biological specimens through holes in the ice.

"Muggins" was what Shackleton called Thomas Vere Hodgson, the marine biologist. The wardroom mostly had nicknames. Almost all were Shackleton's invention. Hodgson was originally a Birmingham bank clerk, and virtually self-taught. Small, dark, shy and balding, he had a distinctive sense of humour, and a tendency to bungle meteorological observations. There was "a healthy catalogue of crime against me",[20] as he put it. "General conversation on the subject is not sympathetic." Shackleton found him quite companionable. "They would come back happy and filthy," said Hare, the steward,

> and unload their specimens on the wardroom table for . . . bottling, much to the disgust of some of the officers, and myself, when I might want to prepare the table for dinner.[21]

Which was all highly diverting; but scarcely the training they all so sorely needed.

In Scott, Shackleton, for the first time, was faced with a weak captain; or at any rate a captain with a conspicuously weaker personality than his own. Shackleton responded by dominating Scott. He assumed the psychological leadership. It was the sort of thing that happens on expeditions, the old battle for supremacy in the pack. While Scott seemed somehow to shrink into the background Shackleton obviously, too obviously, took the lead.

Barne, in after years, remembered him as "a grand shipmate and good company . . . a great raconteur, and he had a very pretty wit . . . he'd never rub anybody up the wrong way."[22] To Reginald Skelton, the naval chief engineer, on the other hand, Shackleton was simply " 'gassing' and 'eye serving' the whole time."[23] Wilson, again, thought that "Shackleton's conversation is sparkling and witty to a high degree. He has a wonderful memory, and has an amazing treasure of most interesting anecdote. That and his quick wit and keen humour are his strong points."[24] Bernacchi, for his part, considered Shackleton "a buccaneer in some of his ways, dominating, truculent and challenging. He could be very unpleasant if he were attacked."[25] Reginald Ford found a

> certain lack of consistency in [Shackleton's] character – you did not know where you were with him so certainly as with the others.

Ford was *Discovery*'s purser, and Shackleton's direct subordinate. Shackleton, Ford went on,

> told stories that were true only in the poetic sense. [But] I think that his good qualities and his charm and kindness when at his best, outweighed his faults in our eyes.[26]

Hare noticed that Shackleton had

> pronounced likes and dislikes. [He] was a man of many moods, soft spoken, quick brained, brilliant at times, but constrained when worried

> or under disturbing influences. His very handsome features plainly reflected these quick changing moods. His was no poker face . . .[27]

Such were the shifting views of Shackleton. It was part of his tantalising elusiveness; perhaps another facet of his Anglo-Irish ambivalence. In any case, said Hare, Shackleton was "the most popular of the officers among the crew, being a good mixer".[28]

However, since *Discovery* was run on naval lines, the gulf between officers and seamen was strictly maintained. This was only partly due to naval tradition; it accurately mirrored English social habits. In any case, it suited Scott's dependence for authority on hierarchy, rank, and drill. Even so Shackleton would often be found on the messdeck, talking to the men. He was not in fact the only officer to do so – Royds, for example, did so as well. Royds, however, was doing what he saw as his duty as an officer: affable and humane, he was ever conscious of the divide between the ratings and himself. Shackleton, on the other hand, ignored that divide. Social distinctions were meaningless to him. Being Anglo-Irish, he was in a sense classless. He took his friends where he found them, and this caused unease not only among the officers. As James Dell, a seaman, expressed it,

> To us on the lower deck, [Shackleton] was rather an enigma . . . He was both fore and aft, if you understand.[29]

Both sides of the social divide wanted to know where they stood.

Like a kind of hibernation, the dark winter rolled on, aimless and subdued. On 12 June however, Shackleton was writing in his diary that "we do not feel the long night as spoken about by the *Belgica*".[30] This was a comment on *Through The First Antarctic Night*, the book by an American, Dr Frederick A. Cook, about his experience on the *Belgica* expedition, under Adrien de Gerlache. Cook was trying to depict the true life of the expedition, instead of hiding behind the high-minded façade of an heroic convention. The ennui of *Belgica*, however, was not so very different from that on *Discovery*. The chief distinction was that whereas on *Belgica* there was insanity among the seamen, on *Discovery* there was fighting, partly due to drink. In any case, *Belgica* had been far worse off. She was drifting with the pack ice in the Bellingshausen Sea, none knew quite where. "In my view, the chance of being stuck," her Second Mate, a twenty-six-year-old Norwegian called Roald Amundsen, had written in his diary on 21 June 1898, "is as great as that of escape".[31] It was something that, under similar circumstances,

Shackleton might have to say himself. But for the moment Shackleton, no more than anyone else on *Discovery*, could hardly bear to face a mirror of his own condition. It was simpler to call the men of the *Belgica* "poor-hearted creatures",[32] as he put it in his diary that Thursday 12 June.

Next day Shackleton was unexpectedly summoned by Scott to his cabin, and told that he was going on the southern journey. The long torment of uncertainty was over.

The day before, it had been Wilson's turn. In his own words,

> The Skipper told me he had taken the long journey towards the South Pole for himself, and had decided that to get a long way south the party must be a small one . . . either two or three men . . . would I go with him? My surprise can be guessed. It was rather too good . . . to be true.

Wilson did not, apparently, have the same consuming desire as Shackleton or Scott for the Furthest South. It was in a spirit of fatalism that he had joined the Expedition. "I think I am intended to go," he had told his wife-to-be at the time.

> If I had tried to get it I should have had many doubts, but it seems to have been given to me to do.[33]

The southern journey, as he put it now, would be

> taking me right away from my proper sphere of work to monotonous hard work on an icy desert for three months, where we shall see neither beast nor bird nor life of any sort . . . and nothing whatever to sketch.

But, he went on,

> It is *the* long journey and I cannot help being glad I was chosen to go.[34]

Scott had originally intended taking Barne. Barne, however, had been badly frostbitten, and felt he would not be fit. Also, in Scott's eyes, he was responsible for the Cape Crozier disaster, and Vince's death.

Wilson was not obviously the next in line. Scott, however, was struggling with the lonely claims of leadership. Jealous and insecure, he mistrusted anyone in the naval hierarchy. He turned to Wilson for support. By the time Wilson was called into Scott's cabin to be told he was going south, he found himself in possession of a moral ascendancy over Scott. Shackleton, as Wilson himself put it,

> is still my best friend but . . . The Captain and I understand one another better than anyone else, I think. He has adopted every one of my suggestions.[35]

Wilson was a cardinal in spirit, the secret ruler in the shadows. It was hardly surprising, therefore, that in this case he was able to have his way as well. In his own words,

> I argued for three men rather than two [because] if one gets ill, all *could* get back if there were three. So eventually it was decided that the party should consist of three. "Who then was to be the third?" Scott said. So I told him it wasn't for me to suggest anyone. He then said, he need hardly have asked me because he knew who I would say and added that as a matter of fact he was the man he would have chosen himself.

Even if this was not strictly true, Scott was determined to take Wilson at almost any price.

> So then [continued Wilson] I told him it was Shackleton's one ambition to go on the southern journey. So it was settled and we three are to go.[36]

This was allowing sentiment to sway judgment; and medical judgment at that. As Wilson wrote to his wife,

> I feel more equal to it than I feel for Shackleton; for some reason I don't think he is fitted for the job. The Captain is strong and hard as a bull-dog, but Shackleton hasn't the legs the job wants; he is so keen to go, however, that he will carry it through.[37]

IX

Dogs and diet

This strange triumvirate was united only by their desire for the Furthest South and their ignorance of snow. Shackleton and Scott were both uncertain of themselves. Scott was uneasy in command. Shackleton was trying to get on, but still was not quite sure if he had chosen the right path. Scott was burdened by moral inhibitions and heroic ideals; Shackleton was free of both. Scott had formal rank and position; Shackleton remained openly the psychological leader. In between stood Wilson, a sort of *éminence grise*, with his enigmatic smile, exerting hidden power over both.

For his part Shackleton, like Scott, was infinitely glad of Wilson upon whom to lean. In any case, Shackleton felt a debt of gratitude to Wilson for it was to him, as well he knew, that he owed his chance of going south.

Shackleton could not yet follow his nature and talk openly about what had been decided. Scott insisted on concealing his plans for some time still. Amongst other things, he had to deal with Armitage, who had been promised the southern journey as part of the price for joining the expedition. Armitage, as he afterwards maintained, had been warned by two of Scott's "brother officers and one of the Committee of the Expedition that Scott could not be trusted to keep his word-of-honour promises".[1]

Under the surface ran obscure cross-currents. A week after the interview with Scott, Shackleton accompanied him to help Hodgson with his nets. "My hands stand the cold – pulling ropes out of the water," Shackleton pointedly remarked in his diary, but "the Captain gets chilblains."[2]

Time passed, the season ebbed. Scott still made no attempt to master a hostile environment or prepare for what he had set out to do. Things were allowed to drift. In the wardroom, chess and irrelevant debates passed the time. A midwinter theatrical performance diverted a messdeck sagging in monotony. *The South Polar Times* continued to absorb Shackleton's attention.

Royds was one of the few to grasp how behindhand was the work. He was in charge of preparing the sledging equipment. In the wardroom at the beginning of August he explained that to be ready in time, he would need extra help. Eight seamen had been detailed to dig holes in the ice through which Hodgson could trawl. Royds had taken one of them to speed the essential repair of vital sleeping bags.

> It was [wrote Royds] thoughtless of me to have said it at breakfast, as one is never quite certain how the land lies with the captain until that meal is over.[3]

Scott said furiously that on no account was anyone to be taken from *scientific* work, and so eight sailors continued to dig holes in the ice, while vital preparations languished. It all stemmed from an exalted view of science as moral uplift, peculiar to the British. *Dulce et decorum est*, ran an inscription on a monument in Sydney, commemorating an ornithologist speared to death by Australian aboriginals, *pro scientia mori.*[4]* That, too, was Scott's attitude.

In the application of scientific knowledge, however, Scott was hazier. Early in the season, against all warnings, he had put the lifeboats out on the sea ice. By midwinter, they were securely embedded in a solid frozen block. Ten sailors were now kept constantly at work chipping the boats free. Scott, as Royds put it,

> inquired about the picks & shovels which have been gradually getting lost & broken, & went for me about it. Like a fool, & not feeling fit I resented it, & said one or two things which I rather wish I hadn't.[5]

With inimitable and all too familiar logic, the seamen were no doubt deliberately breaking their tools so as not to work too hard.

On 7 July, with winter on the wane, Shackleton was suddenly put in charge of the dogs, and told to learn how to run them for the southern journey. Since the attempts to drive them in February, they had been ignored and left to languish in their kennels on the ice. Scott, however, had a sneaking suspicion that dogs might, after all, be the key to success.

Shackleton had, however, less than three months in which to

* "It is sweet and proper to die for science"; an adaptation of a famous Latin tag about dying for one's country.

learn how to handle dogs from scratch. Even so, he was undeterred. He cheerfully believed that was plenty of time to manage by hasty improvisation what had proved to require long and dedicated practice. Peary, for example, took two years to learn dog driving. Shackleton, so far, had not tried dog driving at all, but like everybody, or almost everybody, around him, he believed there was nothing the British sailor could not do.

Shackleton turned his overflowing energy on the dogs. Unfortunately, he was conspicuously disqualified for the task. He lacked the patience required for any kind of technical mastery; and certainly the kind of patience demanded by the dog. He lacked understanding, and furthermore did not really like dogs at all. The dogs of course sensed this and more.

All the attempts at driving them had so far been uniformly disastrous. Shackleton now fared no better. The incompetence of the expedition was all-embracing. A trained dog driver, David Wilton, a Scotsman living in Northern Russia, had actually volunteered for the expedition. He had been summarily rejected. Armitage, Koettlitz and Bernacchi, the old polar hands, had ignominiously proved to be amateurs with dogs. Shackleton alternately tried cursing and cajoling, wheedling and the whip; the dogs declined to respond.

For one thing, they were cruelly underfed. Despite there being seal for the taking, they had been deprived all winter of fresh meat. Instead, they were kept on a starvation diet of dog biscuits. No one seemed to grasp that these biscuits were intended to be mixed with meat. There *was* another kind, specially produced by Spratts as a full food for working dogs. It, however, was dumped, forgotten, in the snow, to be the salvation of another expedition fourteen years later. The outcome was that the poor maltreated beasts were unnecessarily fractious.

Even had they been properly in condition, Shackleton would scarcely have been better off. He did not know, for example, that the dog's natural gait, when pulling, is a trot. Also, it happens to match the pace of skiing. This was the momentous discovery brought back by Otto Sverdrup who, while Shackleton was beginning his experiments, returned to Norway after four years in the Arctic. Neither Shackleton nor anyone else on *Discovery*, of course, could really ski; they stumped along instead of sliding. So the dogs were compelled to walk, which did not suit them at all. Shackleton's catalogue of ignorance was long. The root of his trouble was that he was treating dogs like men or horses.

The upshot was that in the spring, when Shackleton followed Scott on three short experimental forays, the dogs performed exactly as they had done before. They slouched over the snow with their tails between their legs, and generally expressed mutinous resentment.

The first trip, north along the coast of Ross Island, started on 2 September. It was early for beginners' efforts. Only on 22 August, as Thomas Williamson, one of the *Discovery* seamen, feelingly recorded, was there "the 'return of old sol' [after] four long months . . . it looked something beautiful."[6]

Daylight was back, but not yet the warmth of the sun. Shackleton's second trip, south this time, in the middle of September, was still ominously cold. "Dogs not pulling,"[7] was his constant complaint on the march. A fortnight later, on the third preliminary excursion, he was still writing "dogs refused to pull".[8]*

Since returning from the first journey, Shackleton was unnaturally subdued. It was not only on account of the dogs.

> I hope that there will be nothing to throw me back from . . . the long South trip [he wrote] for I have been looking forward to it all the winter, but one always gets a bit anxious if one wants anything much . . .

The winter, he continued,

> has gone and half the things one desired to do have remained undone . . . I do hope that the time will go quickly on our journeys and so before we can realize it the relief ship will be down here with our letters and little presents from home.[9]

By now, Shackleton had started writing letters home. He even remembered to write to the manager of the railway bookstall at Sydenham station "so that people I know may not think that amid all this new life and excitement they are not forgotten at home".[10] Shackleton almost seemed to be saying his preliminary farewells. Early in October, after the third trial trip, he was writing in his diary that

* Royds, meanwhile, recorded "the first attempt at golf in these latitudes. Being such a beautiful day, I thought I would take a cleek & an iron, and potter about round the ship. I could hardly believe my fine drive; I swung easily, hit true & the little red ball simply flew . . . after I had had three really good drives with my dear old cleek, the head suddenly flew off. Fool that I was, I had never thought of the effect the temperature would have on the metal, although it was only −20° [F.] but sufficient to make that very hardened steel almost brittle; so came back to the ship, took my driver out but after two good drives the cold split the bone, so thinking Antarctic golf too expensive, I knocked off, having had a last good lofting drive over the ship."
[Charles Royds, *Discovery* diary, 30 September 1902.]

danger is rife and I say it without wishing to unduly exaggerate . . . one of our number [Vince] has lost his life and more than once the escapes have been a narrow margin . . . it is on one before a word can be uttered: and of course it is all part of the game. We did not expect a feather bed down here, and so de rien.[11]

Coming back through the disturbance in the Barrier, where it forced its way between nunataks into the sea, Shackleton and his companions had been careless. Men, dogs and sledges had repeatedly tumbled into hidden crevasses. They had all providentially been saved, but Shackleton was mildly shocked. Something else had shocked him more.

Within sight of the ship, Scott had suddenly pushed on alone in order to arrive first, leaving his companions to their own devices. By now, Scott's constitutional impatience had become a byword. But surely a captain's place was with his men – always? Worse still, among treacherous pressure ridges and unknown crevasses, Scott had cut a corner. He had taken an unnecessary risk. Shackleton, for all his flamboyance, disliked unnecessary risks.

His state of mind had other explanations, too. For some days after returning, he did not go out because, as he put it, he "felt pretty stiff".[12] Wilson, who had stayed behind, observed that Shackleton was "obviously a bit done up. He is very much thinner and has lost pounds in weight."[13] Perhaps Wilson uneasily saw the shadow over Shackleton's health that he had feared. Very privately Shackleton recorded that "coughing all night kept me awake".[14] Whatever else ailed him, Shackleton was now in the preliminary stages of scurvy. He had been half expecting it. It had broken out *en masse*, and Ferrar, amongst others, was already far gone, with the classic symptoms of bleeding gums and swollen legs.

The day before Scott had called him in to tell him he was going south Shackleton, as he put it in his diary, had been "rather bothered about the provisions".[15] Almost four months before, a seaman had already been showing signs of scurvy. The diet was evidently awry. That was Shackleton's responsibility. When the summons came, he first thought he was being called to account; but he was hardly surprised when he was not. Scott had long since borne out Gregory's warning that he was "so casual in all his business".

So too was Shackleton, up to a point. Where self-preservation was concerned, however, another side of him seemed to take over. That, in fact, had led to his first open clash with Scott. It was precisely diet and the fear of scurvy that was the cause.

Like the incapacity to deal with dogs, scurvy was the characteristic affliction of British polar expeditions. Shackleton did not exactly think of it in those terms, but his historical reading and lore had taught him that in food lay the danger that could kill. Scurvy, not cold or storm, was the greatest peril ahead.

We know now that scurvy is caused by an acute lack of vitamin C. It used to be a scourge, but not among the polar Eskimos. Those extraordinary survivors, clinging to life beyond the margins of the habitable world, knew in some way how to prevent vitamin deficiencies, long before vitamins were known to civilised man. They would, for example, travel far to eat the contents of a reindeer's stomach; the testicles of a musk ox, or the brains of the Greenland seal. All these are now known to be precise and potent sources of vitamin C.

When *Discovery* sailed, vitamins had not yet been discovered, so the exact cause of scurvy was still not understood. Two things, however, were certain. Down the ages, it had killed hordes of sailors and explorers. It was correctly associated with absence of fresh food, and fresh food was a certain cure. By the turn of the century, foreign polar expeditions and, indeed, British private ones, had learned to prevent scurvy by living off the land. Most British expeditions, however, like "Discovery", were under naval domination, and lamed by an official cast of mind.

In the British Empire, medical science seemed oddly inadequate. During the nineteenth century, for example, when the anaesthetic chloroform was first discovered, a British Army surgeon in India called it "a highly pernicious agent . . . That it renders the poor patient unconscious cannot be doubted. But what is pain? It is one of the most powerful, one of the most salutary *stimulants* known."[16] Overseas, indeed, the British often seemed to live as unhealthily as they could. British polar expeditions were in this tradition. They accepted conventional wisdom and brought with them their eating habits. That meant tinned food and salt meat, devoid of vitamin C.

Discovery people developed scurvy a few days after leaving the ship on the first spring journeys. The problem was not only what they had been eating in the snows. There was something wrong even with what they ate at home, indeed national diet had by now become a matter of official concern. The Boer War was the cause. When the Army suddenly needed large numbers of recruits, it found that healthy ones were comparatively rare. Something like sixty per cent were rejected as physically unfit. The alarming comparison was with Germany, the ever more probable enemy, where the equivalent figure was only a quarter. More alarming still, most of the British Army's rejects were due to malnutrition. The Army ordered an enquiry. The outcome was the eloquently named *Report of the Inter-Departmental Committee on Physical Deterioration* which found that the country was ill-nourished. The English working man, it concluded, although better paid than his continental counterpart, was worse fed. He ate the wrong foods. One of the witnesses, Sir John Gorst, MP, declared,

> Nothing is more deplorable than the general English labourer or labourer's wife in the presence of food. Where a Frenchwoman would make an excellent dinner an Englishwoman would almost starve . . . I have been in a great many poor people's homes both in England and France and I should say that, although an Englishwoman spends a great deal more on feeding her family than the Frenchwoman, the Frenchwoman gives them a great deal more food.[17]

So England was distinguished by being a country where to be poor also meant to be poorly fed. Nor did this affect only the poor.

By the time *Discovery* left New Zealand, Shackleton was appalled to discover that Scott's attitude to diet was that of a scientific dilettante. He accepted the fashionable view of scurvy as a kind of food poisoning, to be prevented by sterilisation, and more or less left it at that. Wilson, being also essentially conventional, agreed.

Koettlitz and Armitage, however, after two winters in the Arctic, could prove the connection with fresh food and the efficacy of living off the land. History of course has proved them right. Vitamin C is found only in fresh food. On the *Belgica* expedition, four years before, it was the commander's refusal to provide fresh seal (and penguin) meat that had caused a disastrous scurvy outbreak, killing one man.*

Shackleton ignored the theorisation that impressed Scott and took the other view. Since he was in charge of the food, he proposed enforcing his ideas. As soon as *Discovery* entered the pack ice, he decided to lay in stocks of meat from the seal littering the floes that drifted by. Scott refused permission – tinned food was good enough for him. But this was an issue over which Shackleton was not prepared to humour any captain. He grasped that Scott's objection was rooted in squeamishness, for Scott, as one of the seamen put it, "hated to see anything killed".[18]

Shackleton, however, was not concerned with finer feelings. After pertinacious cajoling, he finally compelled Scott on 15 January to

* See *Scott and Amundsen*, p. 63.

let him take some seal for the table. He was determined to keep scurvy at bay henceforth by serving fresh seal meat daily. The lower deck predictably objected to anything unfamiliar on their plates. Shackleton tried to overcome this by telling the cook to prepare the seal palatably; it has a strong fish-like taste, and needs some disguising. The cook, a New Zealand merchant seaman called Brett, strongly resented Shackleton's order; so strongly in fact, that he refused to obey.

Shackleton would have managed, somehow, in the way of the windjammer. Scott, however, took over. He put Brett in irons, and left him out on deck for a day. This was soon after arriving at McMurdo Sound, and it was very cold. It was naval discipline, but even the other naval officers disapproved. As a result, Brett was left with a consuming grudge; not against Scott, who had put him in irons, but against Shackleton, who had been the cause. His revenge was to serve seal so vilely as to offend even a boiler-plated palate. He over-cooked it, so that those who had the temerity to eat it obtained hardly any vitamin C.

In any case, Scott refused to allow enough seal to be killed. So, between his squeamishness and Brett's resentment, "A considerable amount of carelessness has been shown in the dietary regime during the winter", as Bernacchi put it when scurvy appeared, "seal flesh . . . has not been available . . . for the last month".[19] Thus, by an ironical twist, it was Shackleton who, having seen how to prevent scurvy, had been the unwitting cause of the trouble.

When scurvy broke out, Scott happened to be away, and Armitage was in command of the ship. Armitage, to quote Skelton, had "the knack of making himself popular".[20] At any rate, he overcame even Brett's sabotage, and succeeded where Shackleton and Scott had not. He achieved, according to Bernacchi,

> a great revolution in the dietary regime. Great variety & improvement in method of cooking has been acquired . . . Now we have seal meat every day & cooked in all manner of tempting ways, so that it is eaten with gusto and looked forward to.[21]

Because of the scurvy, the southern journey, which was supposed to have started in the middle of October, had been postponed.

Earlier, Scott reasoned, there had been no incentive to tackle the cook, or to question the diet since the health of all, as he put it, was "beyond criticism". Now that scurvy had appeared in epidemic proportions, he saw the point. Finally he was prepared to listen to Armitage and Koettlitz – and to Shackleton, who observed that

> People are not up to the mark. Seal is now the principal dish to be used: and as little tinned meat as possible . . . so that everyone will be well fit for sledging.

And, he added thoughtfully, "I [need] a great deal of sleep now."[22]

Nobody had yet mastered the art of dog driving; but nobody practised any more. As the start of the southern journey loomed up, Shackleton was concerned to "finish last number of S.P.T."[23] Others were preoccupied with matters equally irrelevant to what lay ahead. For, even after eight months, nothing was quite ready, and there was a last-minute rush. "Many of the things that are to be done now," in Ferrar's words, "were spoken about before the Winter began!"[24]

X

The southern journey

Finally, on 2 November, the southern journey started, but to the end, Scott remained unaccountably secretive.

Shackleton only discovered his intentions accidentally a week beforehand. Wilson had then asked permission to go hunting for Emperor penguins. Scott refused. In a few days, he said, they were going south. At the same time he told Shackleton to start practising the use of a theodolite. It would be needed for navigation on the march, but it was an instrument with which Shackleton was quite unfamiliar. He was accustomed to a sextant, the instrument used by sailors. The theodolite is used to fix position on land.

But for the intervention of a blizzard and another change of mind on the part of Scott, his companions would have had even less warning than they did.

Scott, in Wilson's words, had announced that there would be no sledging pennants

> on the southern journey. I said I should certainly not go without mine, if I had to sew it into my shirt. He said I could do that if I liked, but he wasn't going to take his, adding weight for mere sentiment. Shackleton agreed with me and we are both going to take ours.[1]

On the day of departure, however, the sledges bore the pennants of all three.

It was a Sunday morning; a cold, melancholy, windy day, with squalls of drift whirling out of the south. The landscape was shrouded by an overmastering veil of grey. Out on the sea ice, framed by the sombre dark hull masts and rigging of *Discovery*,

sledges, dogs and men were lined up ready for the start. The whole ship's company had turned out to cheer.

Shackleton, Scott and Wilson posed for a photograph in front of their sledges. Scott had a wide-brimmed hat tied around his chin. Their clothing was generally ill-designed, but their feet, at least, profited from previous experience. They were shod with finnesko, soft boots made of reindeer fur, specially tanned, with the hair turned outwards. The ancient ski-boots of the Lapps of Northern Scandinavia, finnesko* were a proven protection against cold, borrowed by explorers from native tribesmen adapted to polar conditions. The boots were filled with sennegrass, a Scandinavian plant that both provided insulation and absorbed moisture, so keeping feet warm and dry.

The cameras clicked; it was time to go. Not entirely to Scott's amusement, a bitch called Grannie marred the dignity of the moment by breaking loose and scampering off across the snow. It was, said Royds,

> really rather marvellous how these dogs know exactly what they are wanted for, as Grannie wouldn't allow anyone to come near her.

She was, he continued,

> eventually surrounded and headed back to the ship, where she was caught & triumphantly secured to her place in the traces.[2]

Then, like "three polar knights" once more, "they were away", as Bernacchi put it, "with banners flying in the wind, a small party but full of grit & determination".[3]

"They propose to be away for 91 days," Hare wrote in his diary, and

> in that time . . . they expect to get a very long way South. They have our best wishes. The Pole is too much to expect, with the number of dogs that they have. To get to the Pole and back, they would have to travel 1500 miles at the least . . . probably they will come to land, which will stop them from reaching a very high latitude.[4]

The captain's steward was being more realistic than the captain, for Scott believed that the Barrier ran right on to the Pole. It was all totally unknown, of course.

Shackleton set off in a spirit of effervescent optimism. He was

* A Norwegian word meaning Lapp shoes.

sure that the Pole lay within his grasp. He was inspired by what he called the "great send off". He was also agreeably surprised to find that "the dogs are pulling splendidly".[5]

It was an astonishing spectacle. This was the pioneer thrust into the hinterland, an event of considerable historic significance. The three men, however, were spectacularly inept and unprepared.

A practised dog driver, for example, would have been stupefied by the scene. Five sledges were coupled one behind the other in a train. In front, all nineteen dogs were harnessed in a single team. The arrangement was cumbersome and inefficient. The dogs ought to have been divided into several teams, each pulling one, or perhaps two sledges. Poor form and overloading could be detected in their gait. They were riding on pent-up energy alone.

The three men stumbled uncertainly over the variegated surface of the snow. They still did not believe in ski, because they still did not understand their use. Ski had been brought, but were riding on a sledge.

Soon after setting off, Shackleton started what Wilson called "a most persistent and annoying cough in the tent".[6] It was less than a month since Shackleton, after the third trial trip, had recorded how coughing had kept him awake all night, indeed a profound strain of apprehension ran through the letter he had left behind for Emily in case he did not return.

> Beloved, do not grieve for me for it has been a mans work and I have helped my little mite towards the increase of knowledge.

In this, there were echoes of Thomas Huxley's *Lay Sermons*, which he had then been reading. It was then, too, that Shackleton once more dipped into Browning, for the first time in months. That brought back memories of Emily with almost painful poignancy.

> You will always remember me my own true woman and little girl [he wrote]. I cannot say more my heart is so full of love and longing for you and words will not avail . . . Child we may meet again in another world, and I believe in God, that is all I can say, but it covers all things . . . if there is another world – and he wills it we shall find each other. I feel that there must be, this cannot be the end, but I do not know, I only believe from something in me . . .[7]

Not only did Shackleton seem ill at the start. Wilson also was feeling pain in his knees and hamstrings,[8] which a more experienced expedition doctor might have recognised as an early sign of scurvy.

Even with the fresh seal meat provided at the end of the winter, the expedition diet was showing a gross lack of vitamin C. It had provided about 6 milligrams per day, while the bare minimum to prevent obvious deficiency requires 10 milligrams per day. Once they started for the south, of course, Shackleton and his companions were cut off from any more.

Their sledging food was based on pemmican. This consists of ground dried meat mixed with fat. It was the only proven concentrated food and the staple then of all polar expeditions. The other main ingredient of their diet was a kind of hard biscuit fortified with gluten, a cereal protein. The pemmican was melted over the primus with a little water, to which was added broken biscuit, to make a kind of thick soup. This was called by English polar explorers their "hoosh". Besides pemmican and biscuit, the *Discovery* sledging diet consisted of a little cheese, chocolate, cocoa, sugar, oatmeal, pea flour, and a preparation based on bacon called "red ration". These were added as variations to the hoosh.

The science of nutrition was then in its infancy. With hindsight, however, and also by the light of contemporary knowledge, the diet of these men battling their way south had too little protein and fat and too much carbohydrate for hard work at low temperatures. Since it was devoid of vitamin C, the reappearance of scurvy was only a matter of time; they themselves only knew that they carried with them the shadow of a mysterious disease.

On 9 November, a week after starting, they were weatherbound. "It is most annoying," wrote Shackleton, "to lie here using up our provisions and not getting on at all."[9] A blizzard, as the diaries say, had stopped their march, but "blizzard" is an elastic and emotive word. It means, broadly, any wind driving snow with it. To be specific, as Shackleton keeping the meteorological log had to be, a wind of force three to four on the Beaufort Scale had blown up from the south-west. This is a moderate breeze, around twelve knots. The temperature was 4°F (or −16°C). There was low drift, but a clear sky. Shackleton was able to record the direction of Erebus' plume, fifty miles away. It would have been unpleasant to persevere since the cold would burn one's face. It was, however, far from unendurable. These were not the conditions that would normally stop polar travellers. A headwind of force six or seven, approaching a gale, was generally needed.

Scott and his men, nonetheless, were clearly overpowered by the weather. Partly, at least, this was due to the fact that they were unused to the conditions. Their clothes were badly designed, and let the wind through. Above all, it was because they were undernourished, and so they felt the cold more. All day, they stayed in their tent, without feeding themselves – or their dogs, closely tethered outside.

It was a Sunday and Wilson, propped up in his sleeping bag, held a kind of church service, reading the psalms, epistle and gospel for that day. One of the psalms happened to be number forty-six, *God is our Hope and Strength.* "Therefore will we not fear, though the earth be moved," it ran, appropriately, "and though the mountains shake at the tempest." Afterwards Scott insisted on a chapter of Darwin, which was his way of scoring off Wilson. Wilson was religious, Scott the reverse. Scott had brought the *Origin of Species*, in Shackleton's words, "to while away such days as these".[10] It was the bible of the agnostic. To please Scott, or in deference to his rank, it was read aloud by Shackleton and Wilson in turn.

This was Shackleton's introduction to Darwin, reading aloud in a tent on the edge of the unknown. "As natural selection works solely by and for the good of each being," Shackleton read out, "all corporeal and mental endowments will tend to progress towards perfection."[11] That was reassuring doctrine to hear while the snow hissed on the canvas of the tent, and nature with her little finger stopped the march.

"All of us," Wilson jotted in his diary, "very fit . . . except Shackle, whose cough seems very troublesome."[12] Next day the wind dropped and the cough, by coincidence or not, subsided.

Two support parties, meanwhile followed, man-hauling supplies. On 15 November, a fortnight out, the second, under Barne, turned back and finally, as Shackleton put it, "We are out on the long trail by ourselves."[13] It was the signal for a profound and sudden change.

Just before Barne's departure, Shackleton was writing:

> the dogs pulling very well . . . we did 10 miles today so are further South than anyone has been.[14]

and immediately after:

> We have not had very much luck today . . . we had very hard work with the dogs. we did not start till noon and only did 2½ miles for the whole day . . . We camped about 6 pm. as could not get dogs on.[15]

The conditions were not the cause. The day before, there had been a whiteout, "a blinding, shadowless whiteness, the most trying light there is in these regions," as Wilson put it, describing "large banks of snowdrift, which one discovered only by walking into and falling over".[16] Now, however, the endless white plain gleamed brightly under a cloudless sky and in the peculiar low, searing rays of the polar summer sun. The temperature was −11°F, and underfoot, a layer of soft, dry silky snow covered hard wind crust, bared here and there in long ridges and waves. It was the kind of perfect going to send a frisson of ecstatic pleasure through a proper skier or dog driver.

Shackleton, Scott and Wilson were already struggling, however. For one thing, the dogs were overloaded. When Barne turned back, they had to take on his loads in addition to their own. They were now pulling almost a ton and a half, which meant 150 lbs per dog, about twice what any experienced dog driver – let alone a humane one – would allow.

"Nobody seemed to know the habits of these dogs at all," as James Dell, the seaman (and a messdeck friend of Shackleton's) put it in after years, "noone . . . knew exactly what a dog would pull." Indeed, while Shackleton was straining inch by inch towards the south, back at base Dell, just as new to the game, was actually making himself into a respectable dog driver. He was using animals rejected for the southern journey as lazy or sick, together with some of the older pups.

> You can't make pets of dogs like that [Dell said]. If they'd got them to work [during the winter] instead of playing about with them, they'd have got something out of them . . . there was noone there who knew [that] a dog will never start a heavy load. Right from the start, I used to shake the sledge to get it alive, so they never had to make a standing pull. As long as they can get away, you can get along with them. I used to do twenty miles a day and laugh at it.[17]

As long as the support parties were with them the dogs, overloaded and ill fed as they were, nonetheless contrived to advance, because there was someone in front to follow. Now there was nothing ahead, they declined to pull. A forerunner was the key but Shackleton, Wilson and Scott all failed to see the connection. They were too cut off from nature to penetrate the animal world.

Relaying was now the only alternative. That is to say, the loads were divided; one half brought forward and afterwards the other, in a kind of leapfrog manoeuvre. It was, as Shackleton put it, "trying work, this going backward and forward: but it all helps out the scheme". For a whole month, they struggled on with what he called the "same old game".[18]

"The travelling," Shackleton tersely said at the end of November, "is awful."[19] At the end of each day, when camp was made, and the dogs were picketed in their traces, they seemed a little weaker, more fractious, than before.

This depressing struggle was peculiar to Scott's party. A month before, on his big journey over the Larsen Ice Shelf, in considerably worse conditions, Otto Nordenskjöld could write:

> That our march could be so quick, has its explanation in the fact that . . . we had such immense help from our dogs.[20]

At the other end of the world, meanwhile, Otto Sverdrup in the north summed up his experience by saying that

> one cannot think of anything more determined and tenacious than the Eskimo dog. [Its] capacity as draught animal and stamina are absolutely astonishing. when, in addition there is [its] great intelligence and devotion to its master, one can understand what importance [it has] for modern polar exploration.[21]

Shackleton, Nordenskjöld and Sverdrup never seem to be talking about the same kind of animals.

It was not only in the mismanagement of their dogs that Shackleton and his companions stood out. In every aspect of snow travel they were inexperienced and conspicuously inept. The sledges were so badly loaded that the runners were deformed, and dragged unnecessarily.

"We sink in about 8 in.,"[22] Shackleton noted on 21 November, an all too typical day, when they managed four miles after prodigious effort. The going was perceptibly better than that facing Otto Sverdrup in the Arctic a year before, when he was able to write that

> Everything went like a dream, both for animals and humans . . . be the going never so sticky . . . With our heavy load, we put 16 to 20 geographical miles behind us each day . . .
>
> Whatever the state of the snow, we skied by the side of the sledges, and under those circumstances, one can attain another kind of speed.[23]

Shackleton, Scott and Wilson, however, were still trying to learn how to ski as they went along. Constantly they were getting on and off their ski, wasting energy by sinking into the snow on foot; amateurs baffled by an unfamiliar technique. Sverdrup and the other masters of polar travel, on the other hand, were artists to whom the snow was their metier. A good day's skiing with an *obbligato* of soft snow rustling and the tingling rasp of ski racing over wind crust was an aesthetic experience. A dog team running sweetly was a triumph. The British party, in contrast, had only the goal ahead, with nothing but physical strength and dogged persistence and self-punishment to drive them on.

All this, repeated for the next decade or so, has been romanticised as the "heroic age" of British polar exploration. Like much heroism, unfortunately, it was wasteful and unnecessary, and often only a cloak for incompetence. Shackleton and his companions had, in short, made things difficult for themselves.

Technical ineptitude, however, was not the worst of the snares facing them as they fought on into the unknown. The human factor was lying in wait.

Shackleton had started off as cook, and he was concerned for the handling of the Nansen cooker. This was a fuel saving device, a complement of the primus, and an essential contemporary item of equipment. It was developed by Fridtjof Nansen for his journey to the Furthest North.*

Top heavy on the spindly primus, the Nansen cooker was easy to overturn. One evening, soon after starting from Hut Point, that is what Shackleton did. The hoosh was spilt, and the primus burned a hole in the groundsheet of the tent. Scott flew into a rage. Next day, he was still furious with Shackleton, and wanted to turn back.

In this crisis, it was Wilson who quietly took command. Scott, as he knew by now, had an unstable temper. It was difficult to decide the cause. For one thing, Scott lacked a sense of humour, which Shackleton so conspicuously possessed. On the other hand, as Wilson also knew, Scott suffered from some chronic undefined stomach trouble that could partly explain the irritability; or perhaps it was the other way about. Diet too may have had something to do with it for, amongst their assortment of deficiencies, was that of the vitamin B complex. This affects the nerves. Also, they were eating Plasmon, a product made of concentrated casein. This is the protein in milk and it can cause a food allergy.

Scott's outburst this time, however, went beyond losing his temper over trifles. Wilson grasped that the burning of the groundsheet was the trigger that exposed a profound dislike of Shackleton,

* To quote Nansen's own description, the cooker "consisted of a saucepan, and two containers to melt ice or snow . . . the saucepan, with the stove underneath, stood inside an annular container. From the burner, the hot combustion products rise in the space between the saucepan and the annular container. Over [the latter] was a tight fitting cover, with a hole in the centre, through which the hot air had to pass. Then it flowed under the bottom of a shallow . . . container, before being forced down the outside of the annular container by a cover enclosing the whole. There [the hot air] transferred the last of its heat to the outside of the annular container, and then escaped, more or less completely cooled".[24]

hitherto concealed. It was an uncomfortable revelation. Wilson was quietly appalled. The frontier of survival was no place for personal antagonism and he, unwittingly, had been the cause of the trouble. It was largely through him, after all, that Shackleton had been chosen for the journey. Wilson also still had nagging doubts about Shackleton's health. What did that cough mean? Perhaps, after all, it would be sensible to turn back before it was too late.

Wilson, however, told Scott they could not go back. There was public opinion to consider.[25] That argument was unanswerable. Scott therefore marched on, but Wilson had not made peace; he had only imposed a truce.

As long as the support parties were following, there was human company to mask the tension. When they left, what Shackleton called the "solitude and loneliness of it all"[26] closed in.

The tension between Shackleton and Scott was exacerbated by the sheer frustration of the struggle with their own inexperience. "It does seem annoying," as Shackleton put it on the last day of November, "that we have to haul so much to gain a distance of 4 or 5 miles daily."[27]

It was not only the relaying. The dogs now could not pull even the divided loads. They had lost all respect for their masters; and a dog will serve only those whom he respects. The men had to get into the traces and haul as well. That is to say Scott drove from behind, lashing the dogs on with his whip. Wilson and Shackleton did the hauling.

Shackleton in the traces seemed demoniac. He was, said Scott, "bent forward with the whole weight of the trace".[28] It was as if he were *willing* them all on to the Pole. There was urgency and passion in his every, jerking, step.

As Wilson told the tale, this was how the antagonism between Scott and Shackleton came to a head: Wilson and Shackleton were packing up after breakfast when Scott called out: "Come here you bloody fools."

They went over, and Wilson quietly asked Scott whether he was speaking to him.

"No, Billy," was the answer.

"Then," said Shackleton, "It must have been me."

There was silence.

"Right," Shackleton continued. "You are the worst bloody fool of the lot, and every time you dare to speak to me like that you will get it back."[29]

This was much more serious than the flare-up over the burnt groundsheet. Then Shackleton had at least controlled his temper. This was mutiny. Again, Scott wanted to turn; again Wilson stopped him with threats of what the world would say. Once more, Wilson imposed a truce. He now took over the moral leadership.

Shackleton and Scott were soon reading *The Origin of Species* to each other again. It was only a façade. Underneath, the tension ran on. Lying weatherbound in the tent on 6 December Scott, being the reader, chose the chapter on Instinct.

> No . . . animal [he read] performs any action for the exclusive good of another species . . . each tries to take advantage of the instincts of others.[30]

"Very interesting,"[31] was Shackleton's comment. Disappointment had much to do with the baring of the antagonism between Shackleton and Scott. It was, as Shackleton finally admitted on 19 December, "bad look out for good lat".[32] Scott had given up hope already, a month before.

When Shackleton recorded his own admission of defeat, they ought by contemporary standards to have covered 8° of latitude and put the 85th parallel behind them. In the event, they had barely crossed the 81st.

Sverdrup's performance in the north, directly transferred, would have put them past 86° S. There is also, again, a telling comparison with Nordenskjöld in Graham Land. At one point, on his traverse of the Larsen Ice Shelf, he covered fifty-one miles in three days. This is exactly what Scott managed the first twelve days after Barne turned back.

Wilson was neither surprised nor disappointed. " 'L'homme propose, mais le bon Dieu dispose,' is never out of my mind in all these preparations," he had written before starting. "I rather think that things will turn out rather differently to what is being arranged."[33] Neither Shackleton nor Scott could match this stoic detachment. Each had to face ambitions thwarted. Shackleton's castles in the air dissolved into a mirage. There would be no Pole; and therefore neither fame nor fortune. At least he masked his disappointment, while Scott morosely made his all too plain.

Shackleton was masking other things as well. After the beginning of December, he was tiring more than his companions. It was not only because he was now mostly ploughing through the snow on foot, instead of persevering with ski. Ominous remarks were appearing in his diary. "Fingers very sore," he recorded on 1 December; "legs tired or rather feet," the next day and, again, on 4 December, "feet tired". Was scurvy on the way; or something else?

"Chronic hunger," in Shackleton's words, had by now become the plague of himself and his companions. "Could do good feed," as he put it in a heartfelt jotting. "Anything would do."[34]

> We always dream of something to eat when asleep. My general dream is that fine three-cornered tarts are flying past me upstairs, but I never seem able to stop them. Billy dreams that he is cutting sandwiches for somebody else always. The Captain – lucky man – thinks he is eating stuff, but the joy only lasts in the dreams for he is just as hungry when he wakes up.[35]

"There is not really very much to tell about the journey," Shackleton wrote on another occasion,

> it is drag, drag and drive, drive from the time we get up until it is time to turn in.[36]

"Worst day," he recorded on 13 December, in a typical staccato note,

> heaviest snow. dist. less 2 miles. Dogs not pulling. No good. Must . . . struggle on. Even light loads too much . . . tired with hauling.[37]

Compared with all this self-inflicted misery, the normal hardships of high latitudes, like frozen boots, cold sleeping bags, a little frostbite, or a touch of snow-blindness, seemed to pale into insignificance.

Their misery, as Shackleton could hardly help noticing, was due to the captain's incompetence. They had started off insouciantly cooking and eating without limit. On 5 December, more than a month after starting, Scott had suddenly realised that without rationing, food and fuel would not last. Cooked meals were immediately cut from three daily to two. Food was drastically reduced. Their full daily ration gave about 4,200 calories. For the work they were doing, and the temperature, even that was too little. (They probably needed another five hundred to a thousand calories a day.) Now they were seriously underfed.

The dogs were even worse off. For the journey, their diet had been abruptly switched from biscuit to stockfish alone. Amongst other essentials, they were deprived of fat. Worse, the fish, now examined for the first time since its purchase in Norway eighteen months before, was found to be green with mould. That was too much even for the marvellous scavenging gut of a dog. The poor devils sickened, one by one. They got violent gastro-enteritis, passing blood in their stools. Probably they were poisoned by some kind of mycotoxin. This is the poison produced by a fungus, to which dogs are particularly susceptible.

That the cruelty with which Scott and his men treated their animals was due to ignorance and inexperience only aggravated their guilt. Not only were Scott's animals ill fed and lashed forward; they were forced to struggle on for hours at a time, when their nature craved frequent rests. Maltreated by uncomprehending masters, they nonetheless managed to survive for weeks. The first to die was a dog called Snatcher, on 9 December. By 20 December four more dogs had died and only fourteen were left.

It had taken seven weeks to reach the 81st parallel.

There was now obviously no chance of even approaching the 86° 14′ of Nansen's Furthest North, reached twelve years before. Shackleton would not be able to say he had been closest to either pole of the earth. That was the least consolation he had expected. He was baffled. The weather had been phenomenally kind. He was keeping the meteorological log, and since the start, had not had to record a single wind of gale force. "Calm" peppered the wind observations. Half the time there had been clear skies, as the sun dipped and circled around the horizon. Heat, not cold, had been chiefly noticeable. Circumstances could hardly be blamed.

Scott now decided to try and salve something from a depressing situation. On 15 December, he dumped much of his load at a depot, the second so far, labelled "B". That ended a month of relaying, in which he advanced a derisory 109 miles. He abandoned all his dog food. Travelling light, or relatively light, he proposed making a dash for the south, killing dogs along the way to feed each other.

The situation had been foreseen. No preparations, however, had been made for slaughter. Scott left it all to Wilson, who had to improvise a sickening butchery with scalpels from his medical kit. Once, when Wilson was snowblind, Shackleton had to butcher Brownie, the dog of the day. "Got his heart first time,"[38] he laconically noted. "Soft snow so bad for cutting up," he added, "body sinks in it as you cut away."[39] From all this Shackleton (and Scott too) acquired a mistrust of dogs and dog driving that was to have profound consequences.

At least they no longer had to relay. "It *was* a relief," said Wilson, "to at last . . . travel with the knowledge that we hadn't to cover the same ground three times over."[40] Still, in Shackleton's words, "Dogs great worry cannot make progress we desire," and "awful job dogs played out"[41] remained the constant theme.

"Hungrier than ever," Shackleton wrote on Christmas Eve,

> but tomorrow we shall be full I hope and then starve again I suppose . . . It is trying work but we are finding out new lands every day.[42]

Despite all their ineptitude, they had been discoverers since early in November. On and on rolled the Barrier without end, dazzling in the sunlight, undulating almost imperceptibly, ripples running in the snow like desert sands. Theirs were the first tracks in that snow.

"I feel open water SSE,"[43] Shackleton noted in his diary. On his right, to the west, he could actually see what he called "Interesting land. Mountains. Fine peaks."[44] This was an unknown mountain range sweeping on in a tremendous arc as far as the eye could see. Shackleton and his companions were uncovering another stretch of the Transantarctic Mountains. It was a continuation of the Admiralty Range and the mountains of South Victoria Land, discovered by Sir James Clark Ross.

The silence of the arid plain was eerie and oppressive. "How strange and weird it is to be out here," as Shackleton put it, "so many miles from all people!"[45] The only sounds were what the men themselves had brought into the wilderness; the creak of the sledges as they strained across the snow, the rustle of ski or, more often, the dreary sough of fur boots ploughing through the snow, the laboured panting of the dogs, the wan roar of the primus in the tent at day's end.

> What a little speck on the snowy wilderness is our camp, all round white save where the shadows fall on the snow mounds, and the sun shining down on it all. Ah well we will plod on and on until we find out all we can in the time allowed us: it is an unique experience.[46]

The hope was "to struggle on for another 3 weeks before turning back",[47] Shackleton wrote in the middle of December but "must look out possibility of no dogs for return".[48] Wilson, for his part, was soon writing darkly that "One *must* leave a margin for . . . bad travelling," as he phrased it, "and of course the possibility of one of us breaking down."[49] Scott alone recorded no such concern. He seemed obsessed with pushing on, incapable of thinking about getting back. Food had been reduced again to eke it out, without any idea of the consequences. There was very little margin to find the depot again. Shackleton, as he wrote up the meteorological log day after day, could only pray that the weather would hold.

On 30 November, Advent Sunday, Wilson (who noted Church festivals in his diary), had made an examination for signs of scurvy. It was the first he recorded since starting. In his words, "I found not a suspicion in any one of us".[50] Wilson was looking for the classic symptoms of discoloured gums and swollen legs that revealed the disease in an advanced state. On 21 December, the fourth Sunday in Advent, he found them.

At the next examination, on Christmas Eve, the symptoms had advanced. Wilson recorded telling Scott that "both he and Shackleton had suspicious looking gums".[51]

Wilson, paradoxically, felt a spark of relief. By now he had become distinctly anxious about getting back. Scurvy was a mysterious disease, but one thing was certain; untreated, it was a killer. Its appearance, he imagined, would be the one argument that would force Scott to turn before it was too late.

Scott, however, to Wilson's distress, could not be made to see reason. He absolutely insisted on going on yet further. They still had not reached 82°, and that magic line Scott was determined to cross, whatever the consequences.

On Christmas Day, there was an argument about going on. In the end, Wilson managed to wring from a frighteningly stubborn Scott a promise to turn on 28 December. Even so, this meant another week outward after knowing that scurvy had appeared. The risk was obvious, at least to Shackleton and Wilson. "We will not be going on further," said Shackleton, "as we are so far from our base. We hope to cross 82°S in two days anyhow."[52] A question mark against Scott's mental stability had now been entered; but scurvy does have mental side-effects.

They all three knew that they had not done particularly well. If this is what they felt alone in the snows, how would they appear to the world when they returned? By comparison with Nansen's crossing of Greenland fourteen years earlier, for example, they would appear notably unimpressive. To both Shackleton and Scott, the audience meant much. But Shackleton had no desire to be a dead hero. He wanted to get back alive.

On 28 December – Innocents' day, as Wilson recorded – the noon sight put them at 82° 10′south latitude. They had crossed the magic circle, at last. "I led," Shackleton remembered to write. That meant he was hauling, straining, shouting at the ever less willing dogs; but he was in front.

Scott now went back on his word. He still wanted to go on. Because their gums seemed better, he decided that the scurvy was on the mend. Wilson, of course, protested that this was an unjustified assumption. To see the point did not require medical training. Common sense was enough. Shackleton understood.

They were now at the mouth of a large inlet running westwards into the mountains on their right. Scott wanted to look at pressure ridges near the further shore. He was the perfect late Victorian scientific amateur.

Another reason for Scott's proceeding might have been that 10′ of latitude was a fragile margin. Instrumental error and recalculation might show that he had not actually crossed the 82nd parallel after all. A few more miles would help.

Next day, they woke to the first blow for three weeks. The wind, as on the last occasion, was only force three or four, but again it was enough to stop them. The implications were uncomfortable; for Shackleton and Wilson at least. They were 270 miles from base, nearly two months out, and with no margin for bad weather. They had scurvy, and still they were marching away from home. But again Scott refused to turn. Shackleton consoled himself with the thought that a promise had been wrung from Scott that this time, whatever happened, another two days would "see us on our way back".[53]

Instead of looking at ice ridges, Scott now decided he would swing west to the coast for geological specimens. Next day, 30 December, there was low fog and whiteout. The wind, however, had eased. Also, it had backed from south-west to north-east, so that it was no longer a headwind, but following. Going home, of course, it would be the other way about. Scott nonetheless insisted on pushing blindly on; first south-west and, when stopped by pressure ridges, he turned south. After four hours, they finally camped. The weather cleared enough for a meridian sight. It gave 82° 15′. That was to be their Furthest South.

What Shackleton did not record in his diary was that in the afternoon Wilson and Scott left him alone to guard the camp while they walked out to look up the inlet. "We saw nothing," wrote Wilson,

> and were compelled to return when we had gone a mile or two, as we were afraid of losing our camp, the weather was so thick.

That "mile or two", however, was to the south. Their Furthest South was 82° 17′. Shackleton's remained at 82° 15′.

Either way, it was, in Wilson's words, "not a . . . good record towards the South Pole." Nonetheless,

> we have had the unlooked for . . . interest of a long new coastline with very gigantic mountain ranges to survey which to my mind has made a far more interesting journey . . . than if we had travelled due south on a snow plain for so many hundred miles and back again.[54]

Running on into the haze, more mountains could be seen. "Our furthest south land chartered to 83°," Wilson summed up. "Just about 300 miles of new coastline we have got now."[55]

To Shackleton, this was no balm for baffled hopes although, in his own words, "it is a wonderful place and deserves the trouble . . . it takes to get here,"[56] and they had beaten "the record for the South by over 200 miles."[57] He had also left his name upon the map. His companions called the inlet at their Furthest South after him; but the Pole alone was what counted. 82° 15′ – or 17′ – was not much to bring home.

XI

Race for life

Still, it was with unmitigated relief and no regrets that Shackleton turned north. Nothing mattered now except getting back alive; to Shackleton nothing else had mattered for some time.

Wilson could only hope that he had persuaded Scott to turn before it was too late.

Turning is the moment when illusions are dissolved. Perhaps also because it was the last day of the Old Year, the dark feast of regret and self-reproach, Scott now displayed a somersault of feeling. With the event upon him he finally seemed to grasp what the others had long since feared, that the homeward march was going to be a race for life. From insouciance, he swung to the other extreme and, too evidently, plunged into dark despair. This particularly displeased Shackleton. He disliked what he called "pessimists".

It was over one hundred miles to the first depot. The dogs were rapidly failing. Food was so short that, in Wilson's words, "We *must* reach [the] Depot . . . before January 17th. This depot system," he thoughtfully continued, "has risks".[1] Their depot was fixed by landmarks in the mountains to the west, but the bearings were uncertain. It was marked by a single flag, and might be drifted up. They might easily miss it. The summer solstice had come and gone; the midnight sun was dipping perceptibly lower. The season had turned. There was a gathering chill in the air. Time was running out.

The first day's homeward march brought a clear sky and a following breeze. After four miles, Scott stopped, camped, and led off at a tangent to the west. He wanted geological samples from bare cliffs on the coast. His companions reluctantly acquiesced.

Crevasses stopped them. The only result of the excursion was the waste of half a day. Thereafter there were at least no more attempts to geologise. Scott finally grasped that now it really was time to head directly home.

The men were tired, starving, and weaker than they should have been. The dogs, said Shackleton, were "done for", and the surface of the snow was "so bad and heavy that it is a great job to do our mile an hour".[2]

Of the nineteen dogs that started, thirteen tortured wrecks remained. After a week, five were left and they, in Wilson's misleading words, were "only a hindrance".[3] With every sign of sanity, he and his companions yoked themselves, like oxen, to the sledges, while the surviving animals, as Shackleton put it, "walked either ahead or astern of their own sweet will".[4]

Their masters, meanwhile, still apparently in full possession of their senses, had finally abandoned their ski with the deliberate intention of trudging all the way back to the base on foot. Wilson spoke for them all with the illogical explanation that they could "make better way . . . though it is very heavy going".[5] They were convinced that it was impossible to haul on ski because it was impossible to prevent slipping back.

Back on *Discovery* lay a copy of Nansen's *First Crossing of Greenland*. Nansen had relied

> on the superiority of ski over every other means of transport over snow . . . Ski were an absolute necessity for us. Without them, we could in truth not have come far.[6]

It was not even necessary to learn from a foreigner. Also on a *Discovery* bookshelf rested *With Ski & Sledge over Arctic Glaciers* by Sir Martin Conway. He, like Shackleton, Wilson and Scott, had first seen ski in adult years. Sir Martin, however, had learned. After a few weeks on Spitsbergen, he was writing that, on ski, in any kind of snow, "we . . . could drag sledges with our full weight . . . Without ski, progress in any direction would have involved intolerable discomfort and labour".[7]

What distinguished Shackleton and his companions was that, weak as they were, they cheerfully proposed to endure the distress which Nansen and Sir Martin, in full health, had regarded with unmitigated horror.

They had not yet learned to ski, however; unable to glide, they plodded gawkily, like rheumatic crows, squandering energy with each step. Their equipment was against them. For one thing, their bindings were awkward and out of date. Their finnesko even were a handicap. Their turned up toes, to hook into the toe strap of the bindings, gave, for those with experience, the perfect freedom necessary for cross-country skiing. Unfortunately, however, being completely supple, finnesko give no built-in lateral stability, which meant that Shackleton and his companions found it hard to control their ski, their heels wobbling from side to side.

The heart of the matter, however, was that they did not understand waxing. Worse still, they still knew next to nothing of snow, which is a complex substance. The crux of waxing for cross-country skiing is to enable the ski to slide forward, but to stick backwards to give purchase for the thrust on the rear foot for the next step. The methods then available were either melting Stockholm tar on to the soles of the ski or (as Nansen did) attaching strips of sealskin along the mid section of the ski with the hairs pointing backwards. In fact, the cold, crystalline snow of the Antarctic would have worked very well on bare wood most of the time. In his ignorance Scott, however, had caused the ski to be soaked in linseed oil. This was a device actually used by downhill skiers and ski jumpers to obtain maximum glide, but in these circumstances ensured slipping backwards on a wide variety of otherwise enjoyable snow. Where life might depend on technique, these men were but beginners. Mile after mile, they floundered in the snow, where others would have floated everywhere on ski.

By 12 January, the dogs were down to two, Nigger and Jim. They were allowed to trot on, while the men dragged their food, in the vague hope of a pull from the depot. Also being dragged on the sledge were the ski.

The stage on which this heroic farce was being played is the greatest desert in the world. It is cold, but at least it is dry. In a sense, it is topsy-turvy land, where the natural state of water is solid. On 6 January, Shackleton recorded a warm blizzard, that is to say, the thermometer was above freezing point. The snow melted as soon as it fell. Everyone and everything was rapidly sodden and soaked. At that latitude, well south of the 81st parallel, it was a freakish misery. Soon, it was back to cold, comfortable temperatures again, where snow is dry and does not wet. But it was something to remember.

Yoked to the sledges, the three awkward figures, like failing beasts of burden, shambled on, sometimes breaking through wind crust and sinking, knee deep, into loose powder underneath. Scott was gloomy and gave no comfort. Thrown in upon themselves, all three were now troubled by inchoate doubts about survival. They hardly had the heart to talk. A skua sweeping out of the sky ten days after they started back was the first outside living thing in the arid sweep of snow. It was a reminder of the world. "How anxious I am for letters," now ran through Shackleton's diary, a constant theme.

On the morning of 10 January, when they set off, they were still thirty-three miles from the depot. That meant four days' travel at their present speed. Their food, they hoped, would last. There was no allowance for delay. But now, at the critical moment, a blizzard sprang up. The meteorological log told Shackleton that after more than two months, this was the first really stormy day, and first wind of gale force. Scott lamented over his bad luck. Shackleton considered himself outstandingly fortunate.

They could hardly see their hands in front of their faces through the drift. Shackleton and Wilson, at least, knew that it was march or die. The wind was with them. They groped their way a few miles on before the storm. "Tennyson's Ulysses," wrote Shackleton, "keeps running through my head."[8]

". . . I am become a name," one verse runs, "For always roaming with a hungry heart . . ."

Better known, perhaps are the lines

> . . . tho'
> We are not now that strength which in old days
> Moved earth and heaven; that which we are, we are;
> One equal temper of heroic hearts,
> Made weak by time and fate, but strong in will
> To strive, to seek, to find and not to yield.

What Shackleton did not record was that, in Wilson's words, he was "getting very short of breath".[9]

In Gregory's prophetic words: "One cannot expect men harnessed to heavy sledges to keep sufficiently alert."[10] Shackleton and his companions now needed all the alertness of which they were capable. Drift and fog shrouded the landscape. Everything melted into a pall of white. Their sledgemeter had broken down. That meant they could no longer reliably measure their distances. They did not have proper marching compasses. They could not navigate blind and could easily pass the depot in the mist.

On 13 January, they began to fear the worst. Cutting down an already attenuated breakfast in a last despairing attempt to keep food in hand, they set off. As usual now in a crisis, Shackleton was in front. "I steered," he said, "by the sastrugi."[11] (Sastrugi are wind blown waves or ridges in the snow. They follow the prevailing wind. In this case it was south-west.) At 11.30, he went on, "we were so played out that we put up tent for a rest". At noon, the weather lifted; and Scott, hurrying to take a meridian altitude, by chance saw the depot flag in the theodolite telescope, a single, insignificant speck miraged up over the horizon in a haze of white.

They cheered wanly; they had got through, if only just. There was food to eat. Relief just about lasted overnight. Next morning, before leaving the depot, Wilson found that they were all three still "scurvy tainted"; and as Shackleton put it, "I am especially so. De rien we shall soon be back."[12]

But would they?

> Since the last blizzard [Wilson wrote] Shackleton has been anything but up to the mark, and today he is decidedly short-winded, and coughing constantly . . . which [is] of no small consequence a hundred and sixty miles from the ship, and full loads to pull all the way.[13]

Wilson now might well feel his intuition confirmed. Shackleton did appear to have some constitutional flaw. He started coughing up blood. He ought of course to have been in bed. Instead, he was forced to race for home. Their loads had to be cut. "We threw away everything," said Wilson, "we possibly could dispense with."[14] That included ski. Wilson, however, admitting that their use meant "far less fatigue in this snow", insisted on saving one pair "for emergencies", as he put it, "to ease anyone who happened to go sick". But when, in the middle of the afternoon, they trudged out from the depot with Shackleton, in Wilson's words, "so seedy", those ski were riding on a sledge.

Nigger and Jim, meanwhile, followed behind, bedraggled but unharnessed, while their masters strained at the traces. There was still a vague hope of getting them to pull, some time; and with proper masters, they might have. The first day out from the depot, however, Wilson, remarking that they were now "utterly useless", put them down. In contrast, "How proudly and well he had strained to the last,"[15] had been Nansen's requiem for Caiaphas, his last surviving dog on the Arctic pack ice eight years before. "We were able," said Shackleton, the day the last dogs were put down, "to drag our loads fairly easily."[16] The "we" was misleading. The sledges were undoubtedly gliding better. They only marched for two miles, however, before hastily making camp. All night he coughed and gasped for breath.

Shackleton was now forbidden to pull. That left the whole load of more than 500 lbs for the other two. Fortunately scurvy in Scott and Wilson seemed once more on the wane. That is to say, the inflammation in their gums again happened to be subsiding. They were, however, weakening, and other symptoms, like swollen joints, were actually increasing. Nonetheless, they were at least steady on their feet. By comparison, Shackleton was becoming frighteningly ill. From his own diary, this is not absolutely clear: "Hope to be in full swing . . . tomorrow" on 17 January; "Still on sick list," the next day only hints at what was happening. "Have to go easy," runs one frank admission, "because of blood expect. [oration.]"[17]

It is Wilson who quietly tells the tale. "Shackleton," his diary records on 15 January, "had a very bad night [and] a bad day and was not allowed to pull." Next day, it was "Shackle looks very poorly indeed and walks along in his harness, forbidden to work either on the march or in camp"; and again, "The moment he attempts a job he gets breathless and coughs." Scott's comment was that Shackleton "has a terribly excitable temperament and it is impossible to keep him as quiet as we should wish".

With minor variations, that continued for the next week. All three by now looked like weatherbeaten scarecrows; but Shackleton undoubtedly seemed the weakest of them all. He finished each day panting, dizzy and exhausted. Only sheer will-power was keeping him going. On 18 January, however, even will-power failed. He collapsed with pains in the chest, and they had to stop after three hours on the march, with only four miles for the day. "We cannot," Wilson put the lurking thought, "carry him."[18] And Shackleton knew this only too well.

Reaching the next depot, exactly as before, was a race for life. There were a hundred miles to go. They had to do seven miles a day, or their food would run out. As usual, they had no reserves.

Paradoxically Shackleton's collapse probably improved their chances of survival. The necessity of getting him back as soon as possible was a frightening goad to his companions; they, but for great good luck, might themselves have been staggering through the snow. The sight drove them on faster than otherwise might have been the case. It quenched in Scott any lingering desire to dawdle. He pushed on while the going was good and made a beeline for the ship.

Because they were walking, not skiing, they often broke through the snow and fell into hidden crevasses. Their harnesses saved them, but for men with scurvy it was dangerous. One effect of the disease is to make blood vessels brittle, and even falling to the waist could cause a haemorrhage. As it was, on 16 January, Shackleton was badly shaken by one such fall. For hours afterwards, he felt ill and groggy.

On 21 January the surviving ski were removed from the sledge on which, for three weeks, they had been grotesquely dragged, and

Shackleton was finally put on to them. Even although he could not ski properly, plodding and not sliding, nonetheless he no longer sank into the snow. His unnecessary struggle had finally ceased. Perversely, this accentuated a growing sense of inadequacy. "My trouble," as Shackleton put it, "weighs on my mind for I would like to be doing more than just going along."[19] In this looking-glass world, it was *degrading* to resort to ski. Only an *invalid* saved energy. It was *manly* to struggle on one's own two feet.

The weather had forced Shackleton on to ski. For nine days it had been continuously calm. A force four wind now blew up. They were half-way to the next depot, and weakening still. The wind, providentially, was once more with them. A sail was improvised from a tent floorcloth on the forward sledge. The caravan floated over the snow before the wind too fast, however, for men on foot. Shackleton was put on the after-sledge to brake with a ski stick. That needed more strength than he could manage. He was then told to get off and follow at his own pace, while the others hauled back in front, to stop the sledges running out of control. It was then, in desperation, that he was put on ski.

Next day, 22 January, a "blizzard astern", as Shackleton put it, "gave us fine run of 10 miles".[20] Even with a "blizzard astern" it was a remarkable performance for someone made "breathless" in Wilson's words, by "the least exertion".[21]

Until then, together all day with the others, Shackleton at least had the sense of belonging; now, skiing alone behind the sledges with the others well ahead he was for the first time out of earshot, and uncomfortably suffered a sense of isolation.

It was in any case the opportunity for which Wilson had been waiting. In his own words, he "had it out with Scott".[22] Since turning home, Scott's latent dislike of Shackleton had turned into an obsession. There was no repetition of the earlier outbursts, but this was if anything even worse; constant nagging and malicious backbiting. "Lame duck" and "our invalid" were phrases he flung about.

The tension between Shackleton and Scott had in any case been rising. Even now, through their journals and letters, it can be felt: the clash of two contradictory and wholly irreconcilable characters, played out against the background of the hostile Antarctic world waiting to snuff them out.

By now Shackleton heartily reciprocated Scott's dislike. Even sympathy and help he took as insulting condescension. But Shackleton was ill, preoccupied with survival. He did not have the energy to hit back. That is partly the explanation of Scott's overbearing manner.

Scott had a strange, perhaps pathological contempt for invalids which he hardly took the trouble to conceal. Shackleton was clearly an invalid and manifestly now weaker than himself.

The mental side-effects of scurvy might partly have been responsible for Scott's behaviour. Whatever the explanation, the middle of a race for life was no time for quarrelling. It had to be stopped. In his calm, yet mysteriously bitter way, Wilson told Scott to exercise some self-control. Wilson was perhaps the only one able to address Scott in this fashion without causing an ungovernable fit of rage. After a volley of what Wilson called "home truths"[23] he persuaded Scott to stop harrying Shackleton.

Shackleton now seemed to be improving. On 25 January, he was allowed to pull once more. For ten days, he had been out of harness. Sick as he was, he took that as an affront to his manhood. It was consolation to be in the traces again and feel once more the jerk of the sledges against his gut. The same day, the familiar cone of Erebus with its plume reappeared over the horizon. They were nearing home.

It was high time. In Wilson's words, they were suffering from "a desperate hunger".[24] They were still eking out inadequate food. That was enough to explain why Shackleton recorded feeling the cold more than usual. In fact, the temperature was astonishingly mild for the season and the place.

Wilson and Scott were growing weaker. Swollen joints told a tale of scurvy once more advancing. The snow was "very deep and the walking very heavy", as Wilson put it, "so that we regret that we threw away our ski".[25] Even on ski, the strain of pulling exhausted Shackleton and left him in distress. After one day in harness, he was taken out again and the others, to his chagrin, continued to do all the work.

For three consecutive days the sun shone in a windless, cloudless sky. The going dramatically improved. Shackleton was able to ski with relative ease. He now went ahead to steer the course. The ice-clad landmarks on his left fixing the position of the depot shone far off like beacons in the sun.

> Cleared old [Mount] Terror [Shackleton wrote on 27 January] looks quite homely . . . Perhaps a little more than a week will see us at the ship again.[26]

These were the last words in his sledging diary.

Next morning opened fine and clear like the others. The depot lay only ten miles off. They dug into their scanty food for what Wilson called a "regal breakfast"[27] to celebrate, in the belief that they were home and dry. Less than an hour later they did penance for their presumption. The next depot, like the last, was ill-marked with a single flag. Now, just as every inch of visibility was vital, a gale roared down to turn the landscape into a boiling cauldron of drift. The sun was blotted out by scudding clouds. It was the first true blizzard of the whole journey. To Scott, the sudden turn of events was bewildering.

It was one stroke of luck that the gale was from the south; it was another that Shackleton, unburdened, could concentrate on his look-out's job ahead. During a short lull, he caught sight of the depot flag, a tiny dot at the end of a tunnel of white. A few hours later, they reached the depot. They were just in time. Soon after, the storm came down again.

Next morning, the storm was still raging, and Shackleton was ill once more, coughing and short of breath. It was more serious than before. Even at his worst, he had so far contrived not to be a passenger. Most of the time, he had managed to do the cooking, although the least exertion was a strain, and pumping the primus made him pant. Now, he lay prone in his sleeping bag, for the first time unable to move.

Wilson and Scott were still sick with scurvy. It was Shackleton's illness that gave them the illusion of health. When they stumbled on the depot, they were all on the verge of disaster. Now, however, they were as good as home. They were still sixty miles from the ship, but had all the food they needed. They were released from starvation and, worse still, the fear of starvation. They were no longer oppressed by a race for survival.

Shackleton, however, had reached a crisis. All day, while the blizzard roared and shuddered, he lay panting and restless in the tent. Wilson and Scott, meanwhile, read Darwin to each other. Towards evening, Shackleton took a turn for the worse. He fought for breath and could not sleep.

In after years Shackleton used to tell a story of hearing Wilson say to Scott he did not expect him to last the night. That made him determined, so he said, to pull through. Whatever it was, next morning – 30 January – Shackleton had pulled through, although he was livid, speechless and weak. He was in no condition to move. To save his life, however, he had to be hurried to the ship. In spite of everything, Wilson and Scott decided to travel that day.

Even kneeling to get out of the tent was agony for Shackleton. Outside, he staggered and tumbled about. He was lifted into his ski, and managed somehow to drive himself a few miles on.

The weather had eased. It was bright and barely cloudy. The sledges ran under sail before a following breeze. After an hour or two, Shackleton was in such distress, that he was placed on the rear sledge, and rode along for a spell. After lunch, he was put on his ski again, and somehow got through the day. At the end he was wheezing and gasping for air. Next morning, he was coughing up blood again. Nonetheless, he seemed somehow to gather strength. That day, it was the others, not himself, who were troubled. They were now at the point where the Barrier was broken by land as it flowed into McMurdo Sound. Plodding on foot, Wilson and Scott broke through snow bridges into crevasses beneath, saved luckily by their harnesses. Shackleton meanwhile floated safely over on ski.

The danger over, Scott swung from anxiety back to irritation. He now regarded the "sick man" as a burden stopping useful work like sketching and surveying.

On 3 February, they started off eleven miles from the ship. Half-way there, they were met by Skelton and Bernacchi, hurrying along on ski; the first human beings they had seen for almost three months. "Clean tidy looking people they were,"[28] as Wilson put it. Bernacchi's view of them, on the other hand, was of

> Long beards, hair, dirt, swollen lips & peeled complexions, & blood-shot eyes [which] made them almost unrecognizable. They appeared to be very worn & tired & Shackleton seemed very ill indeed.[29]

Bernacchi and Skelton insisted on hauling the sledge the last few miles to the ship. To their astonishment, the load which appeared such a strain for Wilson and Scott turned out to be no trouble at all. "In fact," said Skelton, "I could pull it myself."[30]

On *Discovery*, flags flew, a cheering party had been ordered up the rigging, naval style, and the welcome continued into the small hours with what Wilson called "drink and noise and songs".[31] Shackleton did not join in.

> I turned in at once when I got on board [he said], not being up to the mark, after having had a bath – that is the first for ninety-four days. It is very nice to be back again; but it was a good time.[32]

Despite the understatement, it was a very different Shackleton from the one who had come back a year ago from his first journey to the South with those "tremendous accounts" of which Skelton spoke, and when he "hardly stopped talking until everybody had turned in".[33]

XII

Invalided home

Neither Shackleton, Scott nor Wilson, were disposed to be absolutely frank about their experiences in the south. Skelton, however, did observe that they "could have done better",[1] while Hodgson, the biologist, remarked that they "seem to have had a far rougher time than they admitted at first". Hodgson also tellingly noticed what he called "some personal feeling"[2] between Shackleton and Scott.

The southern party returned to find a relief ship at McMurdo Sound. She was *Morning*, a converted Norwegian sealer, that had arrived ten days before. At first she meant simply fresh faces, a break in isolation, and much wanted contact with the outside world.

Discovery, however, was still firmly frozen in. Four miles of solid ice lay between her and *Morning*, anchored in the nearest open water to the north. About the middle of February, it became clear that *Discovery* would probably have to stay another year. Shackleton was then told by Scott that he was to go back on *Morning*, invalided home.

Shackleton, as Bernacchi put it, was "deeply disappointed & would give anything to remain. Although everyone is so anxious to return this year *with the Discovery* few are so poor spirited as to wish to return in the *Morning*."[3]

Shackleton refused to believe that sickness was the real reason for sending him away. Wilson, though still bedridden after the southern journey, was staying nonetheless. Hodgson, too, despite an acknowledged "weak chest" was going to remain. Shackleton turned to Armitage for help. As Armitage afterwards remembered, he was in "great distress".

> I consulted Koettlitz and he informed me that Scott was in a worse condition than Shackleton.[4]

It was not quite so simple. Koettlitz had been told by Scott to examine Shackleton. The instructions were formal, in writing, and left little doubt as to what was required. An executive officer, as Scott pointedly expressed it, "should in my opinion enjoy such health that [he] can at any moment be called on to undergo hardships & exposure".[5] Koettlitz was in an unenviable predicament. Like most doctors, he disliked giving professional opinions to order. Shackleton, he told Scott, had "practically recovered" from the effects of the southern journey

> but referring to your memorandum as to the duties of an executive officer I cannot say that he would be fit to undergo hardships and exposure in this climate.[6]

Scott privately decided that Shackleton had deceived both Koettlitz and Wilson, hiding shortness of breath and fits of coughing which were as bad as he had suffered on the journey south.[7]

Koettlitz was too astute to be hoodwinked by a patient. He was, however, uncomfortably aware that all was not as it should have been with Shackleton's health. So, for that matter, was Shackleton himself. When Koettlitz said that Shackleton had "practically recovered", he meant from scurvy to which, as he put it, his "breakdown was undoubtedly . . . due in great part".[8] Scurvy could explain Shackleton's symptoms on the southern journey. Panting, dizziness, coughing up blood, are all part of the pattern. But they are part of other patterns too. Shackleton himself had drawn a distinction between what he called his "scurvy signs"[9] and his other troubles. He may have had a form of pneumonia caused by microscopic ice crystals in cold air tearing the lining of the lung. It is found among elderly people during harsh winters in temperate climates. In those days, it was not recognised because the symptoms escaped detection by the stethoscope, and X-rays had hardly begun to be used medically. The doctors would have been genuinely puzzled. In a letter to Scott Keltie (but not in his report to Scott) Koettlitz wrote that Shackleton, besides scurvy, had been "attacked by a sort of asthma".[10] Recovery from scurvy was certain, that he knew. Asthma was another matter altogether.

Armitage, however, by now had taken Shackleton's side. As he put it, he

> went to Scott and asked him why he was sending [Shackleton] back. I told him that there was no necessity from a health point of view, so after much beating about the bush, he said "If he does not go back sick, he will go back in disgrace."[11]

Scott was referring, partly, to the now uncovered fact that Shackleton had, somehow, escaped the obligatory medical examination on joining *Discovery*. Scott was also hinting at the quarrels on the southern journey. Their fundamental incompatibility was now becoming uneasily apparent, even to the lower deck. "I think," said James Dell, "most of them sided with Shackleton."[12]

Few leaders find it easy to tolerate stronger men under their command. Shackleton had charisma and the power of self-presentation. Scott had neither. He was conventional and ordinary. Shackleton was a spiritual anarchist. He had shown up Scott's failings, and was a threat to his authority. That was his real offence. One way or another, Shackleton had to go.

Sickness came as a providential pretext. A sick Shackleton would be an admirable excuse for the shortcomings of the southern journey. A disabled companion would enhance the aura of heroic struggle and divert attention from the monumental bungling which Scott had to conceal.

As, on 1 March, Shackleton sadly plodded over the ice from *Discovery* to embark on *Morning*, it was with a tumult of emotion within him. Others were being sent home too. Most were also from the mercantile marine. Shackleton felt that he was a victim of a plot to get rid of the merchant seamen and turn the expedition into a naval one for the rest of the time. Armitage, having thwarted an attempt by Scott to send him home too, believed this as well.

In the certificate he gave Shackleton, Scott wrote:

> It is with great reluctance that I order his return, and trust that it will be made evident that I do so solely on account of his health and that his future prospects may not suffer.[13]

This, however, was not merely for public consumption. There was a little too much truth in it for comfort. Shackleton could not shrug off the doubts around his health. When Scott privately decided that until he left, he was in a "broken down condition",[14] there was in the taunt a grain of truth. Shackleton himself said of his departure:

> I went slowly, for I had only been twice out of the ship since I came back from the Southern journey.[15]

At Mauritius, while on the *Hoghton Tower*, Shackleton had contracted a mysterious illness. "Mauritius fever", it was called, at least by Shackleton himself. It may have been a virulent form of malaria, or even rheumatic fever, which can have lasting effects on the heart.

Shackleton was secretive about this, as he was secretive about everything connected with his health. He was lucky, or skilful, to have escaped the medical examination. Had he feared rejection? Now he was going home officially sick. It was a stigma almost too hard to bear.

A fellow Anglo-Irishman once said that Shackleton

> had this weird feeling he'd developed in Ireland. Some old nurse had told him that he would die at the age of 48 and he believed this, he absolutely believed it.[16]

Shackleton had just turned twenty-nine.

The wheezing in his lungs, a tightness in his chest, were not just an affront to his manhood. They were flaws threatening fulfilment, the tolling of the bell. As he left *Discovery* to start the long, unwished for journey back Shackleton "seemed very downhearted to leave us", in the words of a marine on board *Discovery*. "And I think all of our ships company are very sorry to lose him."[17] Shackleton felt the anguished sense, perhaps, of being a marked man:

> I left my home and all those who are chums as much as I ever will have any one for chums . . . it touched me more than I can say when the men came up on deck and gave me 3 parting cheers.[18]

Next day *Morning* set sail. Shackleton stayed on deck gazing at the edge of the ice as it receded, like some mysterious quayside in a distant port:

> Ah me it was a sad parting . . . snow was falling, and a dreariness seemed over all things . . . the sun came out in a blaze of glory and bathed the bergs in lights that were more than splendour: the small waves twinkled in the sunlight; waves not seen by me for more than year . . . one longed for a master hand to catch and hold for all time the wondrous beauty that was passing so quickly – Ah well. Mount Discovery away down South from us was a splendid sight standing out in the clear blue of the Southern sky. It was so familiar my home fading away. The beacon that guided us in our long journey to the North from the far South. I turned in and read for a bit but thoughts would go back to those I left on the floe.[19]

One of them was Scott, looking older, as everyone remarked, after the southern journey; the captain who in public had displayed so much solicitude while in secret planning to get rid of him. That was the figure that stuck in Shackleton's mind; the devious leader waving complacently at the edge of the ice, ready for another chance, while he was being sent back with nothing better than 82°15′ south latitude, a narrow escape, and the stigma of illness.

As the figure of Scott on the ice faded into the distance, Shackleton was overwhelmed by the conflict of emotion within him, and burst into tears.

For a few days, *Morning* picked her way through the pack ice, likened by Shackleton to "steering a bicycle through a graveyard".[20] He was steeped in melancholy and regret, but he was not a man to keep on looking astern:

> I am longing for the day to arrive when I can get ashore and then be off to England for now that I cannot go on with this work I must needs go back as soon as I can.[21]

In London, on 25 March, this cable was delivered to Emily Dorman:

> Broken down in chest returning southern sledge journey suffering scurvy and overstrain dont worry nearly well coming home . . .[22]

Thus did Shackleton mock himself with a parody of his hopes. He had sent the cable from Lyttelton, New Zealand, as soon as he landed there from *Morning*.

XIII

A new and better path?

On 12 June, after convalescing in New Zealand, Shackleton landed in England. He came unremarked by mailboat. It was not exactly the homecoming he had imagined for himself. At least he had recovered, and Emily was patiently waiting for him. He was, however, still ensnared by the Antarctic. A pressing invitation to visit Sir Clements Markham awaited him on arrival. The very next morning, he hurried round to Eccleston Square.

A tremendous scandal had broken out in the affairs of the expedition. It was the consequence of Scott's remaining for a second season in the south. On Shackleton, the irony was not lost. In the first place, allowing *Discovery* to be frozen in so that she could not escape was considered professional incompetence. It was the more so since Scott himself believed that *Discovery*'s defects meant that she risked being crushed by the ice. Moreover, the organisers had explicitly said that under no circumstances was he to stay for a second year. Sir Clements bore the brunt of the blame. Shackleton, being so far the only expedition officer to return, was the sole source of inside information. Sir Clements was making sure that he was the first of the expedition organisers to whom Shackleton talked.

Soon after, Shackleton received a telegram saying that

> The Admiralty will undertake rescue of Discovery. Committee appointed. Come to me. I wish to consult you.[1]

This was signed "Wharton" – Rear-Admiral Wharton, the Hydrographer who, as Shackleton well knew, was one of Scott's most powerful enemies at the Admiralty.

The expedition organisers had now run out of money. It was,

according to a headline in the *Daily Mail*, "POLAR EXTRAVAGANCE", caused by "LACK OF BUSINESS MANAGEMENT".[2] The government had had to be asked to pay for the next relief.

On *Discovery*, Shackleton had learned that naval intrigue was something to steer clear of. Since the Admiralty, as it turned out, now thoroughly mistrusted anything connected with Sir Clements, Shackleton felt he was being used against him. Shackleton looked upon Sir Clements as a friend, and ignored Wharton's imperious summons.

Morning was going out again, but the Admiralty, as it were, wished to keep an eye on her with a second relief ship of their own. They bought *Terra Nova*, a Dundee whaler of the very finest vintage. Despite his snub to Wharton, Shackleton was asked to help in fitting her out. To that, on Sir Clements' advice, he did agree, and much of August went on the work. He helped with *Morning* too. He was also helping in another, fateful quarter.

The previous November *Antarctic*, Otto Nordenskjöld's ship, had left Ushaïa, in the Beagle Channel, to fetch back the Swedish explorer. That was the last that had been heard of her. Three rescue expeditions were hastily being organised. One was from the Argentine where the government was sending out a gunboat called *Uruguay*. Commander Julian Irizar, the Argentine naval attaché in London, was given the command, and Shackleton helped Irizar as far as he could.

In the Weddell Sea, meanwhile, a hidden drama was unfolding. *Antarctic* had been crushed in the pack ice before reaching Nordenskjöld at all.

Antarctic's commander was an extraordinary Norwegian whaling skipper called Carl Anton Larsen, the pioneer of Norwegian Antarctic whaling. In some ways he resembled Shackleton. He was a great bearded figure with high cheekbones and hooded, but unfierce eyes, like a Viking chieftain in one of his civilised moments. He commanded by sheer force of personality; although it was a very different kind of personality to Shackleton's fluent Anglo-Irishness. Larsen had a sparing but equally eloquent use of words. "We'll have to change our hunting grounds," he had once told his men after a particularly bad season in the Arctic, "from the North to the South Pole, or thereabouts."[3]

That, more or less, was what Larsen had done. In 1893 he took *Jason* of Sandefjord to the Weddell Sea in search of new whaling grounds. During that voyage, Larsen had contrived to discover King Oscar II Land, and the Larsen ice shelf. Also, on an excursion over the pack ice, he became the first recorded man to use ski in the Antarctic.

Shipwreck was a new experience to Larsen. His reaction was wholly matter-of-fact. He was the captain. He had to save his men. He started by getting them all to the nearest land, which happened to be Paulet Island, at the mouth of the Weddell Sea.

When Shackleton met Irizar in London at the end of June, the castaways on Paulet Island were trying to survive the southern winter in a makeshift stone hut. Irizar, with his ship lying at Buenos Aires, was the nearest of the potential rescuers. Contact with him disturbed Shackleton's unquiet soul, for here was someone else soon off to the Antarctic.

Before leaving *Discovery* Shackleton, as Armitage vividly remembered, had sworn that "he meant to return and prove to Scott 'that he – Shackleton – was a better man than Scott'."[4] Yet now, when Shackleton was asked to sail out as chief officer on *Terra Nova*, he declined. It was tempting to turn the tables on Scott so soon by reappearing in the guise of rescuer; moreover officially pronounced, by an Admiralty doctor, "fit for Antarctic service."[5] Shackleton, however, was after something more.

For one thing, Emily had now decided to marry him. She had been left financially independent. Under her father's will, she inherited money in trust, with an income unconditionally for life. At that point it was about £700 a year. In those days, as Shackleton proved in an only mildly optimistic budget, that was enough to keep a couple in average middle-class state. It paid for two domestic servants. Other items included £24 a year for a trained cook, "coals and light per year £34. Kitchen and 3 fires all year £18. But it would be about £14 without 3 fires all year." "Clothes and personal for darling £150", was the largest single item after "food washing, extras . . . £260." Shackleton made the precise total £711; it should actually have been £721; but that was only an arithmetical error which did not affect the argument.

Shackleton was not the kind willingly to live off his wife. But he had not a sou of his own, and his expectations were approximately nil. To Emily, her money simply meant that her future husband would be spared the soul-deadening necessity of earning his living. "One must not," as she later remarked, "chain down an eagle in a barnyard."[6] Shackleton could devote himself to making a name, a fortune, a social position, and preferably all three.

All this, however, was not solace enough. Early in October, while deep in plans for marriage, Shackleton visited Sir Clements Markham "full of plans", in Sir Clements' words, "for another expedition".[7] Shackleton, in fact, had just written to Captain J. E. Bernier, a Canadian who proposed to reach the North Pole:

> My experience with the National Antarctic Expedition enables me perhaps to be of use . . . please understand that this is only for the regard that one explorer has to another, for there is no money question in it . . . the English nation wants men who will uphold their prestige.[8]

Soon after his return, Shackleton was commissioned by the *Illustrated London News* to write two articles on *Discovery*'s first season. The articles were uncharacteristic of their nominal author, and bore the imprint of Sir Clements' guiding hand. Shackleton lent himself to explaining away the expedition's various shortcomings. For his pains, when the news eventually travelled back to *Discovery*, he was accused by Bernacchi of having "managed to advertise himself extensively. From various accounts he does not seem to be quite playing the game".[9]

Shackleton advanced the virtuous plea that scientific work had been the real purpose of the expedition. "For the furtherance of . . . magnetic research," he wrote, "the Government had given £45,000 and . . . we have been successful in carrying out what was intended."[10] This, as both Shackleton and Sir Clements well knew, was specious reasoning. Later on, in an unprompted article for *Pearson's Magazine*, Shackleton showed what he really thought. The expedition, he wrote,

> was not fitted out with the idea of reaching the South Pole, but that, when all is said and done, is one of the main hopes of every explorer who goes into these inhospitable regions.[11]

This was the clue to getting his own back on Scott, and the germ of the idea with which Shackleton approached Sir Clements Markham. He was all for rushing back to the polar regions, north or south, with an expedition of his own, but the Pole itself *openly* his aim.

Sir Clements, in one way, could sympathise. The year before, on a visit to Norway he had, as he put it, found

> that young Roald Amundsen, the Norwegian who was in the *Belgica* is quietly preparing a daring . . . Arctic enterprise.

"Young" Amundsen (he was thirty-one, but Sir Clements was seventy) actually sailed from Norway for the Canadian Arctic five days after Shackleton landed back in England from the South. His plan, Sir Clements continued,

> is to reach the north magnetic pole . . . and to remain in its neighbourhood for two years, observing any change of position since

Ross's time. [Sir James Clark Ross, the first man to reach the North Magnetic Pole, in 1831.] There is at least no want of pluck and enterprise in the scheme. I wish Englishmen would do these things.[12]

In fact Amundsen really aimed at navigating the North-West Passage, the enterprise that for three centuries had been peculiarly British, but never yet achieved.

Sir Clements, somehow, preferred Englishmen to submit to institutionalised direction. He effectively discouraged Shackleton. But he always had the interests of his protégés at heart. To him, the Navy was the place for all right-thinking young men. He tried to obtain for Shackleton a regular commission. Naval officers then still had to enter the service as cadets. There was however a back door, for a small, select number, through the Supplementary List. Sir Clements, together with Sir William Huggins, the President of the Royal Society, wrote a heart-rending plea to the Admiralty. Sir Clements also got Lady Constance Barne, Michael Barne's mother, to approach an old friend of hers, Sir Evan MacGregor, the Secretary of the Admiralty. "I hope very much," she wrote, "Mr Shackleton may be successful, he strikes one as quite a first rate capable young man." Her son, she went on, had written to say "how very much he will be missed by the rest of the expedition".[13]

Lady Constance was the wife of a MP, daughter of the Marquis of Hertford, and grand-daughter of an admiral. Sir Evan, alas, had dealt with Sir Clements over the *Discovery* relief, and classified him as a "pachydermous gentleman".[14] Sir Clements' endorsement was hardly an asset and, as a result or not, the Admiralty declined to offer Shackleton a commission.

To Rear-Admiral Pelham Aldrich, this was "a thousand pities. His experience would be of possibly great value in the Service".[15] Aldrich was an old Arctic explorer himself, and it was through the *Terra Nova* relief, of which he was in charge, that he made Shackleton's acquaintance.

Shackleton himself may have been partly to blame for the Admiralty's rejection. Neither his refusal to sail on *Terra Nova* nor his snub to Wharton could have helped his case.

Shackleton did have something to fall back on, however. He was still formally on leave from the Union Castle Line, but the mercantile marine, as he had long since grasped, was no path to instant glory – any more than the Navy would have been. The South Pole also, for the moment, seemed a chimera. Shackleton looked for something else.

"Literature of sorts," a novelist of the period makes one of his characters say, "is the very thing nowadays; any fool can make a living at it."[16] Shackleton left the sea to try journalism instead.

It was the heyday of the printed word. After four hundred years, the printing press still reigned supreme. Fleet Street was "The Street of Adventure",[17] as one of its Edwardian inhabitants could seriously call it. It was still the capital of communication. It housed twenty-eight London daily newspapers. It was a place where one could not only become a writer, but where it was still possible to become a public figure as well. Some thought it was paved with gold; others knew it was lined with broken hearts. There, at any rate, Shackleton transferred the same exuberant hopes that he so recently had centred on the southern road.

Back in the Antarctic, Shackleton had already told Armitage that he "seriously thought" of trying journalism. OHMS and *The South Polar Times* had something to do with it. Perhaps, too, he had been spurred on by Emily. She was joint author of a book called *The Corona of Royalty*, about the coronation ceremony and regalia, published the previous year for King Edward VII's delayed coronation. Armitage, at any rate, observed that Shackleton "had certainly kissed the Blarney stone", seeing in him, with hindsight at least, the makings of "a great journalist".[18]

Shackleton proposed to capitalise on the Antarctic, but he could only do so while Scott was still in the south and out of the way. That was at best a matter of months. So he tramped – no, he tore – round the pavements of Fleet Street and its environs. One of the doors on which he knocked was that of F. W. Everett, editor of the *Royal Magazine*.

Everett, like everybody else, was not interested in Shackleton's propositions. He did, on the other hand, take him on his staff. As he later wrote,

> At first sight, it may appear strange that I should have offered a sub-editorship to a man like Shackleton. He had no experience of journalism beyond editing the *South Polar Times*, an interesting but highly unprofessional journal.

Thus, incidentally, died another hope of fame and fortune. *The South Polar Times* might be published as Shackleton had intended but it would be nobody's gold mine. Nonetheless, said Everett, "there was something about him that invited confidence".

At the age of thirty, Shackleton was old to be breaking into Fleet Street. But against this could be set qualities of boyishness, of extravagant enthusiasm, and what Everett called his "peculiar fascination and magnetism":

> His appearance, to begin with, was attractive. Extraordinarily powerful, he moved with the rolling sailor's gait and looked at you with his great, humorous dark-blue eyes which . . . had often in them the brooding eye of the dreamer . . .

"I never met a more exhilarating man," Everett went on, "a more genial, a better companion, a racier *raconteur*":

> He had the true sailor's love for spinning a yarn, and many are the work hours I wasted with the best will in the world listening to his stirring adventure in all quarters of the earth . . . his face, heavy and stern in repose, all alive and lit up with the excitement of retailing his hairbreadth escapes by field and flood. [His] deep, husky voice, rising and falling with the movement of his story [was] sometimes raised, by way of illustrating his point, to a rafter-shaking roar . . . Whether it was the . . . compelling gesture or the Irishman's natural gift for expression, he made us see the things he spoke of, and held us all spell-bound.[19]

Down in the Antarctic, meanwhile, when *Morning* and *Terra Nova* reached *Discovery*, Bernacchi remarked that Shackleton had "not carried out many of the promises he made . . . before leaving".[20] Fifty years on, this was something that another man on *Discovery*, Reginald Ford, could not forget. Shackleton, said Ford,

> made promises which he did not always keep . . . when he was leaving us he made notes of personal things which the members of the expedition needed and promised to send them to us by the Relief Ship . . . As far as I know not one of these commissions were executed.[21]

Yet Armitage could write that Shackleton "never spared himself at the expense of others, so that his men always knew that they could depend on him".[22] The fact was that Shackleton appeared differently to different people. Ford sensed what he called a "lack of unity in his character".[23]

Shackleton always lived intensely in the present. He might not remember all of the even recent past. Each promise that he made, he genuinely meant to keep; but sometimes he promised too quickly and too much. Time and circumstance might alter cases. Everett came close to the truth when he wrote that Shackleton was "in the best meaning of the word an egoist – a man who is furiously keen in his own concerns and the furthering of his career"; but still said, echoing Armitage, "he never forgets a favour or a friend."[24]

On the *Royal Magazine* Shackleton started at the very bottom of the ladder; he even had to write the jokes on the back page. ("Of the heroine in one of the latest sensational novels," ran a fair specimen, "it is said: 'Her eye chained him to the spot.' She must have been links-eyed.") But it was a start – exactly like *Discovery*.

> I am convinced [said Everett] that if he had gone to a stockbroker, a butcher, a carpenter or a theatrical manager and asked for a job, he would have got it . . . And none of these good folk would have repented taking him on.[25]

The *Royal Magazine* was a slightly superior monthly, aimed at middle-class suburbanites. It offered the now time-honoured formula of human interest, titillating fiction, useful information. "Considerable prominence has lately been given . . . to what is termed the 'physical degeneration of the race'," declared one issue at the time when Shackleton joined,

> and indeed a very little observation of the average man . . . will speedily assure one that these reports of our physical degeneracy have been in no way exaggerated.[26]

This introduced an article on the then vogue subject of "physical jerks". It neatly expressed a preoccupation of the world to which Shackleton had returned. While he was away, the Boer War had ended, and the Edwardian era had got into its stride.

It was a confused and heterogeneous age. The fear of physical degeneration had been released by what one official called the "avalanche of military incompetence"[27] of the war. There was a mood of melancholy abroad, a sense of failure of the will; "the weary Titan",[28] someone called the country. It was, on the other hand, in nearly every field, a creative age. It was opulent, light-hearted, an age of popularisers and showmen; and one of contrasts too, what one contemporary called "public penury, private ostentation".[29] War was admired as a character-building exercise to keep decadence at bay. It was an age of drifting disturbed by dreams of gore. It was also a bustling age, although the pace of change was, perhaps, too great. For all their doubts, the British still felt masters of the world. "It's . . . the richest town in the world, the biggest port, the greatest manufacturing town," H. G. Wells could still quite seriously make one of his characters say of London, "the centre of civilisation, the heart of the world."[30]

Into this highly charged and disturbing atmosphere strode Shackleton, restlessly aching to get on. Journalism, as he rapidly discovered, was a craft. There was no short cut to the top. When Scott returned, no doubt to be promoted captain, he, Ernest Henry Shackleton, would still be a nobody. After a very few months, Shackleton was looking for something else.

At this point, Hugh Robert Mill took a hand.

After ten years of marriage, Mill was resigned to being childless. He looked on Shackleton as a substitute son. Since their days together on *Discovery*, Mill had kept a kindly eye on him. They met regularly at the Royal Societies' Club (which Mill himself had helped to found) in St James's Street. "This never-to-be-forgotten-resort,"[31] as Mill called it, a gathering place of explorers (and other kinds of men), was Shackleton's first foothold in clubland. There, over regular lunches, Mill followed with growing concern Shackleton's quest for sudden fortune; he saw the restlessness and rootlessness behind the flow of talk.

Shackleton, as Mill discerned, wanted to be somebody at almost any cost. From his own family there was no help. Dr Shackleton had neither money nor connections. He was enmeshed by his unmarried daughters and invalid wife. Mill felt, and probably was, the only person who at this stage could give Shackleton the guidance of which he stood in need.

The secretaryship of the Royal Scottish Geographical Society in Edinburgh now happened to be vacant, and Mill persuaded Shackleton to apply for the post. For the moment, as Mill shrewdly guessed, Shackleton would be better off as a big frog in a small pool. Shackleton quickly grasped the point. The RSGS became to him a new and better path to the top. Thither he now swung the same sanguine zeal he had in turn devoted to *Discovery* and the *Royal Magazine*. It meant, he told Mill, "a great deal" to Emily and himself, "the loss or gain of this appointment".[32] Others wanted it too, "many", as Shackleton himself put it, "with splendid qualifications against me so I suppose that I am found somewhat lacking."[33]

Qualifications, happily, were not all. The high-minded façade of a learned society often hides nepotism and intrigue of Byzantine complexity. The appointment of a new RSGS secretary was no exception. Shackleton's friends, led by Mill, were wily, powerful and tough: committees were packed, adjournments gerrymandered, testimonials concocted.

> When I first met . . . Lieutenant E. H. Shackleton . . . on board the *Discovery* [Hugh Robert Mill cheerfully perjured himself], I saw that he was a painstaking scientific worker.*[34]

* See p. 46.

On 24 November, meanwhile, news arrived from Nordenskjöld. He had returned to civilisation, rescued by Commander Irizar. On 30 December, *The Times* published Nordenskjöld's own story of his two years on the shores of the Weddell Sea.

Within that tale were two sagas of their own. One was that of the castaways on Paulet Island. In the spring, with three companions, Larsen sailed in an open boat through violent, ice-infested waters to fetch help from Nordenskjöld on Snow Hill Island. On 8 November, Larsen reached his destination. The same day, such is the power of coincidence, Irizar arrived at Snow Hill in *Uruguay* to rescue them all.

About a month earlier, three more of Nordenskjöld's followers had arrived overland. The foundering of *Antarctic* had left them marooned all winter at a place they called the Bay of Hope at the tip of Graham Land. Theirs had been a Robinson Crusoe existence. When they met Nordenskjöld, J. Gunnar Andersson, their leader, described how Nordenskjöld's dogs "flung themselves aside at the sight of us savages".[35]

Irizar then picked up the men on Paulet Island and everyone got safely home. To this saga of survival, *The Times* devoted a whole page. (But it missed the news from Kitty Hawk, North Carolina, on 17 December, that two brothers Wright had become the first men to fly in a powered heavier-than-air machine.)

Nordenskjöld's was the first Antarctic expedition ship to be lost. The Weddell Sea was not to be trifled with. Both were lessons to be learned. But did Larsen's voyage sow the seed in Shackleton of an ambition to make a great open boat journey?

For the moment, however, Shackleton was more concerned with news from Edinburgh that never seemed to come. On 11 January 1904, after a long and nerve-racking wait, he at last found himself elected to the so much desired post of secretary to the Royal Scottish Geographical Society. "The world seems so bright and gay now," he wrote to Emily when he heard the news.

> I am so happy dearest thinking about all the times which are to be in the future . . . we do want to settle down and have our own house at last after all these years of waiting.[36]

XIV

"An east-windy, west-endy place"

A learned society was hardly Shackleton's milieu, especially in Edinburgh where, as Mill said, its "course was grave and ceremonial".[1] The Royal Scottish Geographical Society, however, was just another means to an end. It conferred on its office holders instant social status, providing, in other words, an entrée; and an entrée was what Shackleton urgently desired.

In Edwardian Scotland, parochial pride burned bright. On the Clyde, the shipyards were still busy night and day; in Dundee, men were still rich on jute. Edinburgh was a place of professional and social prospects. As Shackleton told Emily, "I feel that things will go on alright now, and straighten out for us."[2]

The first tangible result was that the remaining opposition among the Dormans to their marriage faded out. It was Herbert Dorman, Emily's elder brother, who mostly nursed the doubt. Head of the family since their father died, he was a lawyer, an executor of their father's estate, and considered himself his sister's guardian. It was not that Herbert disliked Shackleton personally; Shackleton was a frequent guest at his home in Sydenham. Shackleton had long since won the whole household over, both above and below stairs. "He was so nice to the maids when they waited at the table," one of Herbert's daughters recalled, "they almost dropped the things because he made them laugh so."[3]

Herbert's reservations were mainly financial. Shackleton's salary at the RSGS was £200 a year; "better than going to sea",[4] as he put it, but still exiguous, even for those days. It was intended as a part-time payment, Shackleton being the first incumbent to work full time. He would have to depend on Emily's income, at least to start with. Nonetheless, Shackleton the secretary of the RSGS was a better risk than Shackleton the merchant officer, Shackleton the journalist, or even Shackleton the explorer.

With his new position, Shackleton was worth a distinguished farewell dinner in London. Mill and Scott Keltie, the secretary of the RGS, were the hosts. One fellow guest was the private secretary to Lord Rosebery, the Scottish liberal peer; another promised "an introduction to Lord Kinnear, one of the first Law Lords of Scotland", as Shackleton told Emily, "so we can know them".[5] These were contacts of a standing which Shackleton had not before attained.

To the newcomer Edinburgh, as Hugh Robert Mill put it, was "an east-windy, west-endy place . . . meeting the world in a ring of cold shoulders draped with the sombre gowns of judges, church-leaders, professors and advocates".[6]

Shackleton left for this closed and clannish society at the end of January 1904. Everything seemed clear cut. He had his introductions, and hastened to break in. For a Third Mate in the Merchant Service, albeit a recognised explorer, it seemed a daunting task. Being Anglo-Irish somehow helped. It meant being classless and adaptable; not Scottish, but not quite an outsider either, and Protestant beyond a peradventure. Social bastions fell rapidly, one by one. The Dormans also provided introductions. Shackleton's fluent conversation and special personality did the rest. A lady who met him at a country house about this time called him

> a youthful and very modern mariner who . . . held us as spellbound as ever the Ancient Mariner held the Wedding Guest . . . during a motoring excursion in the midst of a furious snowstorm . . . the question "Do you love poetry" was shouted at me, and above the wind I heard the rhythmic chant of great lines . . .[7]

Shackleton, meanwhile, had his marriage to arrange. The wedding was provisionally set for April 1904, a bare three months after he had moved. Emily stayed behind in London while waiting to get married, and Shackleton it was who had to set up house. A week or two after arrival, with the aid of one of his contacts, he found his house, No 14, South Learmonth Gardens, then on the outskirts of Edinburgh, at a rent of £125 per year. (Not, as it happened, a particularly good bargain. A seven-roomed flat in the best suburbs of London could be rented for £50 a year.)

Things took their appointed course for a wedding of the day. At the end of March Shackleton wrote to Emily,

> I am glad my darling is getting nice jewellery. I only wish I could give you a lot beloved, but things will come on and soon we can do better.[8]

Emily Dorman was not what the Edwardians were beginning to call the "new woman". That is to say she was not in the van of the nascent female rebellion, no feminist fighting for women's rights, equality with men and the vote. She was conventional, submitting to the then accepted subservience to her menfolk – but perhaps not quite. In waiting for Ernest Shackleton and dismissing her earlier suitors, she was rejecting the mournful and smothering middle-class security that had a hand in shaping female emancipation. For she, of course, saw through Ernest Shackleton; and choosing him was in its way a mildly rebellious act.

A man, on the other hand, is known by his woman. Emily was passive; waiting to devote herself to her man. For Shackleton, with his overwhelming, dominating, perhaps domineering personality, there could be no other kind of woman. Emily took the revenge of her kind by mothering her man, and treating him in the dual role of master and child. This is touchingly illustrated by Shackleton's letters to Emily. "My Sweeteyes", they start, or "My darling Sweeteyes", going on sometimes to call her "child", or "little child",[9] but nearly always ending "Your boy", or "Your own boy".[10] "He will always be a boy you know,"[11] as Emily herself put it.

In London, on 9 April, the long wait of Ernest Shackleton and Emily Dorman at last came to an end, when they were married at Christchurch, Westminster. For his wedding breakfast, Shackleton went to Sir Clements Markham, at the familiar house in Eccleston Square. Sir Clements had been invited to the wedding, but was ill, and could not go, so Shackleton chose this way of including him. Sir Clements was now seventy-four, and in disgrace over the mismanagement of the *Discovery* and her relief. Shackleton did not want to desert an old friend. He had donated the fee for his article in *Pearson's Magazine* to the *Discovery* relief fund, not because the money was actually needed but because Sir Clements, as he told Emily, would be "awfully pleased". *Discovery* still clutched at him. It was to the expedition that he turned for his best man too. Cyril Longhurst, the secretary, filled the role.

A week before the wedding, *Discovery* actually returned to New Zealand, after her second season in the ice, with the record of the southern journey inviolate. When Shackleton walked up the aisle with Emily he was still one of the men who had reached the Furthest South. No finer wedding present could have been contrived. However Scott was someone, while Shackleton, as he had feared, was still a nobody. The prospect of this state of affairs persisting when Scott, after a few months, returned to England, was like a goad. Shackleton had to get on, quickly. He persuaded Emily to give up the honeymoon because, as he said, he had to get on with his new job.

"When I lie awake in bed," Shackleton wrote in one of the last letters to Emily before they were married,

> the firelight plays on your dear picture I long so for the real time when it will not be a picture but you yourself.[12]

This is the authentic echo of the dreamer to whom wooing and the fight are reality. Anticipation was all; attainment an anti-climax, and the whole concept of a honeymoon therefore repugnant. Emily did not discern this; or perhaps she did?

Shackleton was nonetheless honest when he said that he had to get on with his work. There was no time to lose if he were to have something to show by the time Scott landed back in England. That meant Edinburgh now, not mooning around the Lake District, as Emily wished. Not only a sense of frustration before Scott was driving Shackleton. His collapse on the southern journey seemed somehow to have marked him as a man apart and sown within him the seeds of a fear that time might be short.

> Never mind my beloved whether the days are dull or cold or dark [Shackleton had written to Emily before the wedding], we will be all brightness and light in our little house and we will have such happy times.[13]

At first, things promised to turn out as Shackleton sketched. Emily had charm. From her, he absorbed the social graces. Together, they were accepted into the most exclusive of Edinburgh social circles, although they could only entertain modestly in return. They rented a house for the summer at Dornoch, near the famous golf course, so that Shackleton even took up that socially desirable game. Emily played too, better than her husband, in fact. They made a conventional married couple on a delayed honeymoon.

But settling into their "little house" did not cure Shackleton's restlessness; it only altered its direction. And by now he was no longer happy in his work.

The RSGS was about twenty years old, ruled still by its founding fathers and, when Shackleton arrived, semi-somnolent. He had been put in to wake it up, but his sponsors got more than they bargained for. Shackleton was supposed to be a reformer, manipulating committees with his persuasiveness and charm. He was, however, alien to the forms of institutional life. Like a minor whirlwind, he swept through the society's modest and slightly dingy rooms in Queen Street. With a very personal blend of wheedling eloquence, genial hectoring, and quick action, he overcame the ossified mediocrities running the society. Within a week of his arrival, he had forced on them the daring innovations of a typewriter and, as he wrote to Mill,

> a telephone!! You should have seen the faces of some of the old chaps when it started to ring today . . . and . . . disturbed them in a discussion . . .
>
> There is [Shackleton went on] a certain lack of humour, notably in Finlay the late Interim [Secretary] . . . tact and humour were out for a holiday when Finlay's life called for his share.[14]

"I know you won't mind my open letter as you are one of the gifted discreet ones of this world," Shackleton continued in a telling declaration of friendship,

> I would so like to see you walk into my office some morning with that smile on your face and that epigram ready that I look at as inseparable to H. R. Mill. Often I think over our short trip [on *Discovery*] and thank the unfitness of preparation that gave [me] the opportunity of meeting you in such a practical fashion.[15]

In his office, when he was there, Shackleton was generally to be found smoking a cigarette and lounging about in a light tweed suit. That in itself had distressed the luminaries of the society from the start. Dark, formal garments were the order of the day. A story was also told of Shackleton surprising an assistant practising golf shots by driving a ball into heavy curtains at the end of one of the rooms. Instead of administering a rebuke, Shackleton is supposed to have borrowed the club, tried a few shots himself, and in the process driven a ball through a window pane into the street.

Shackleton soon arrogated to himself powers which the society never intended him to enjoy. He was by turns cheerful, charming, suave, autocratic and, when necessary, consummately rude. He was, perhaps, copying the legendary example of Sir Clements Markham. The rooms were dusted and tidied; meetings brightened, advertisements secured for the society's magazine. Audiences increased, membership rose, the academic ennui dispersed, and the society's public image was noticeably improved. This was all due to Shackleton and more or less accomplished by the time he went to London to get married. When he returned to Edinburgh after the wedding, therefore, his job was done. What remained was consolidation and routine. Neither was in his nature. The work now seemed a little hollow. Although he had had the satisfaction of establishing a personal mastery, his interest was now shifting elsewhere.

By the autumn of 1904, there were goads enough. In July, as RSGS secretary, Shackleton had organised the welcome for William Spiers Bruce. Together with Otto Nordenskjöld and a German, Erich von Drygalski, Bruce had been one of those who had led an expedition to the Antarctic at the same time as Scott. After two seasons in the Weddell Sea, Bruce was now returning to the Clyde.

Bruce was as determinedly a Scot as Shackleton an Irishman. In many ways they were a contrast. Where Shackleton – from time to time – saw the Antarctic as a path to fame and fortune, to Bruce, polar exploration was his ruling passion. A dark, squat, bearded, taut and highly strung man, he was a trained biologist, and had been one of the first to volunteer for *Discovery*, months before Shackleton himself. "For the past seven years," Bruce had written to Sir Clements Markham in April 1899, "I have been training myself with a view of making myself more efficient for Polar Service."[16] This included shipping on *Balaena*, a Dundee whaler, when she made a pioneer voyage in 1892 to the Weddell Sea. Sir Clements, however, was noticeably cool, for such obvious professionalism was considered less praiseworthy than to excel by unforced aptitude.

In the end, Bruce arranged an expedition of his own. He was the first British subject to organise a private Antarctic expedition. It was flaunted as a Scottish answer to *Discovery*; actually being called the Scottish National Antarctic Expedition. Sir Clements Markham took it as a personal insult.

The upshot was that, when Bruce returned to the welcome organised by Shackleton, he had discovered more of the unknown Antarctic coast than Scott. More to the point, perhaps, Bruce sailed up the Clyde on the deck of *Scotia*, his ship, while *Antarctic* lay at the bottom of the Weddell Sea. *Scotia*'s captain, a dour craggy Peterhead whaling skipper called Thomas Robertson, had brought his ship safely through the sinister Weddell pack ice that had defeated even Larsen. While *Discovery* seemed gloriously to enshrine the serene incompetence of British officialdom, Bruce was a glittering example of private enterprise. He had found the money, singlehanded, by asking a pair of wealthy philanthropists, the Coats brothers of Paisley, the sewing-thread magnates. They responded, and entirely, to the appeal of Bruce's personality. For Shackleton, *there* was an inspiring thought.

On 16 September, Shackleton saw Scott once more. It was at a lunch on board *Discovery* in the East India Docks to welcome the expedition back to London. It was their first encounter since eighteen months before when Shackleton had watched the figure of his leader recede and disappear, waving, at the edge of the ice at McMurdo Sound.

They had not exactly forgotten their quarrel; nor were they reconciled. They had tacitly agreed to bury the past. In fact, Shackleton had written to Scott, welcoming him back to England, and inviting him to the RSGS – "It will be a great thing for the Society if you can come up" – for its twentieth anniversary. When they finally met, it was with guarded neutrality, overlaid with public heartiness. But ringing in Shackleton's ears were still the mocking tones of unfulfilled desire. Where was his determination to go back to the Antarctic and prove himself a better man than Scott? Eighteen months on now, he was still stuck. Scott, meanwhile, had been promoted Captain; and a naval Captain then had a demi-godlike standing. Besides, as a result of *Discovery*, he was a national figure. By comparison, what was the Secretary of the RSGS? Even in Freemasonry, the disparity had grown. In New Zealand, on the way home, Scott had been raised to the Third Degree. Shackleton had not progressed beyond his initiation.

"I would like to see you come in", he had told Scott, writing about *Discovery*'s voyage up the Thames for her reception in London,

> but I . . . would only be in the way and I dont want to push myself forward as I have been so long apart from the show, though my heart [he tellingly added] has ever been turned South.

Shackleton also told Scott how, a few months after his marriage, he had tried once more to organise an Antarctic expedition of his own,

> but have given up the idea now – as there seems to be no money about and besides as I am settled down now and have to make money it would only break up my life, if I could stand it which Wilson thinks I could not.

However, Shackleton went on to tell Scott, perhaps with a tinge of bitter irony,

> I do hope to see you do the N.W. passage some time. I should think you could easily get an Expedition if you wanted to.[17]

The first real stab came early in November, when Scott gave his first lecture on the expedition in London, at the Albert Hall.

Shackleton had already lectured on his Furthest South. As a speaker, he displayed considerable flair. "A lot will be expected of you . . . in the way of lecturing," Mill had consequently told Scott, "so you had better be getting into practice."[18] Scott, in fact, found that Shackleton had stolen much of his thunder. Shackleton could hold an audience, which he could not. Scott responded with a twinge of jealousy. Of the southern journey he said, according to the *Daily Mail*, that he and Wilson

> on the way back . . . had to draw the sledge with their comrade who had become ill.[19]

That was Shackleton's agonising shame. He could not bear to be reminded that he had ever ridden on a sledge. It was a reflection on his manhood, blazoned out before an audience of 7,000 souls and reported in the press.

But Shackleton's new-found gift for *public* speaking was what partly had got him his job with the RSGS. His sponsors hoped he would breathe life into the public lectures and popularise the Society; justifiably, as it turned out. He had the common touch. This was not lost on the politicians among the motley cohort of acquaintances he had acquired, and he was asked to stand for Parliament.

Shackleton was hardly a political animal. That was, of course, no obstacle to a political career. Parliament was, on the other hand, another, heaven-sent opportunity in his fevered race for the top. "Lieutenant Shackleton," the *Dundee Courier* was able to announce on 16 November 1904, "is to uphold the Unionist cause in the next election." Shackleton, said the *Courier*, "was one of the party that had the honour of sledging to the most southerly point yet attained". So the Antarctic, after a fashion, had once more paid off. There was also something else. Shackleton, the *Courier* went on to say, had

> all the inherent characteristics of the Irishman – cheerful, optimistic, good-natured.[20]

"I am an Irishman," Shackleton himself publicly declared, "and I consider myself a true patriot . . . when I say that Ireland should not have Home Rule."[21] All along, Shackleton had shamelessly played on his Irishness. Sometimes, he almost seemed a professional Irishman, and Ireland, as usual, was bedevilling British politics.

Home Rule was one of the great issues of the day, and on that, no Irishman could remain absolutely cold. It was passionately espoused by the Liberals; and bitterly opposed by the Conservatives. To the Conservatives Home Rule meant, not local autonomy, but the first step to independence. That, they sensed, heralded the break-up of the British Empire. They stood for the continued union of Ireland with England; the "Unionist cause". Shackleton, however, was to stand for the Liberal Unionists. They were Liberals who had split off from the Liberal party in 1886 over Home Rule, and were now in all but name a branch of the Conservative party.

Shackleton was billed, to quote one headline, as "NOTED NAVAL OFFICER". That was stretching a point. When the Admiralty refused Shackleton a permanent commission, they offered instead special promotion to Lieutenant, RNR, because of "valuable services [to the] Antarctic Expedition".[22] As a pre-condition, however, Shackleton had to obtain a test certificate for drill, which he took as an insult. His failure to enter Dartmouth as a boy still rankled. "I did my best to get a commission in the navy when I had to go poor," as he put it publicly, "but I was refused."[23] Now, it had to be an instant permanent commission or nothing. In March 1904, when safely established at the RSGS, Shackleton resigned from the RNR. Nonetheless, when convenient he continued to use his rank.

The same issue of the *Dundee Courier* that reported Shackleton's political début also carried an account of Scott's lecture in Dundee. Scott was now on tour, lecturing on *Discovery*; and he was, after all, Captain, RN. For Shackleton to call himself Lieutenant, albeit very much by courtesy, and derived from Sub-Lieutenant (retired) of the Reserve, somehow made him seem less of a nobody. Shackleton and Scott appeared side by side on the same page of the *Dundee Courier*. Did some sub-editor sense the underlying rivalry?

Despite the report, Shackleton had not actually been chosen to contest the seat. He had only been recommended by the selection committee. A large faction opposed him as a carpet-bagger. After some tussle and intrigue, however, Shackleton was eventually adopted.

Shackleton had a capacity to make friends and enemies with almost equal ease. His entry into the RSGS, and his subsequent behaviour, generated a hostile clique. His enemies were only biding their time. The affair of his parliamentary adoption gave them the pretext that they sought. Indulging in politics, they said, was unbecoming to the dignity and impartiality of his office.

It was not only Shackleton's enemies who were perturbed. Hugh Robert Mill was upset as well. He felt that Shackleton had let him down; and wrote to tell him so. Shackleton was "much distressed about it", Dr J. G. Bartholomew, the cartographer, reported to Mill. Bartholomew was one of Shackleton's staunchest supporters at the RSGS:

> I do not take such a gloomy view . . . as you do . . . I love to see enthusiasm and if a man thinks he can run a Geogr. Society and be Prime Minister at the same time I would back that man – at all events I would not like to disillusion him! In the meantime my view is that if he undertakes that his candidature will not interfere with his secretarial duties no objections should be raised . . . It is not as if he were our Editor [of the Society's magazine] or *ever could be* – He cannot settle to sedentary work but is splendid at bustling around![24]

Mill was perhaps distressed by Shackleton's choice of party as much as by anything else. Mill was a Liberal (and "liberalism after all," to quote one historian, "implies rather more than a political creed . . . it is a profoundly conscience-stricken state of mind"), possibly even a sympathiser of the nascent Labour party. He was also a Home Ruler. His real concern, however, was that the anti-Shackleton movement within the RSGS now had wind in its sails. Shackleton was considered to be neglecting the society for his own affairs. Whispers reached as far as Scott in London. He took the trouble to warn Shackleton what was being said behind his back.

Shackleton replied, protesting a little too much perhaps,

> I cannot understand how the idea got around . . . My nominal hours of work are from 10 to 4.0 p.m., but during November and October I work from 9.0 to 11 p.m. The last secretary took four months holiday and held a lectureship at the University, so was not regularly in the rooms . . . I certainly do not sit in the office if there is nothing to do . . . I write this to you as you have been so intimately connected with my life that I feel I owe it both to you and myself that you should see how matters really stand.[25]

To Mill, Shackleton declared:

> I know you are a true and straight friend . . . I was more worried by your . . . letter than I have been by any uncomfortable circumstance that has happened to me for a long time, excepting the news that I had to come home on the "Morning" . . . for there are but few men amongst the many I know for whose opinion and friendship I care a damn about. This is plain speaking and I mean it to be plain.

"I want to get on in any line I take up," Shackleton frankly said,

> but I feel that in doing so I am perfectly honest . . . I want to do a little in the world to help it and no honest endeavour can be without its result. With life before me, and strength and hope, all these things which time will whittle down, I may achieve something before the period at which life grows stale and strength wanes and hope flies, or if it does not fly, assumes the dignified attitude of resignation.[26]

By now, Shackleton and the RSGS were both looking for a plausible excuse to part. What the society, like most of its kind, wanted, was a plodding mediocrity. That, Shackleton definitely was not. In any case the society could serve him no more. Politics gave him an honourable pretext to leave. In the middle of January 1905, therefore, he tendered his resignation which, after six months' grave debate, the society was pleased to accept.

XV

Prospects, but no work

When Shackleton first arrived in Edinburgh, he had stayed with a member of the RSGS council called William Beardmore at Tulliecrewan Castle, his country home. This was a social conquest of no little weight. Beardmore was a rich, Clydeside shipbuilder and industrialist. Elspeth, his wife, was completely charmed by Shackleton. Through her, at any rate, Beardmore promised Shackleton a job if he did not get into Parliament. The future seemed more or less assured.

The Dissolution, however, hung fire. Shackleton was not the first politician to bank mistakenly on an imminent election. Patiently to nurse a constituency was not in his nature. A burst of oratory during the campaign, when it came, he believed, would pull him through.

Meanwhile, on 2 February 1905, Emily had given birth to their first child. "Good fists for fighting!" Shackleton is supposed to have said when he saw the infant. It was a boy, christened Raymond Swinford. (Emily's mother was born Swinford. She was descended from Catherine Swynford, the wife of John of Gaunt.) A reasonably large family had always been part of Shackleton's scheme of things.

The only trouble now was that he had prospects, but no work. For the moment, therefore, Shackleton turned to other, apparently more profitable things; exactly as he had done at the RSGS when it began to pall. The gossip was right. Shackleton *had* been spending society time on his own affairs. He had started dabbling in business. He saw commercial agents making money effortlessly, so it seemed, from commissions. He tried to do the same, quietly, so that his name did not appear, through a firm called the Scottish Agency. A quick fortune, however, was decidedly elusive. Now, released from the constraint of regular work, Shackleton intensified the chase.

He was inspired by the example of his brother. Frank Shackleton was just then moving into the glittering world of company promotion. More to the point, perhaps, Frank was making his entry into the social upper reaches of Edwardian London. "Extremely good looking", in the words of a friend, "and extremely depraved",[1] Frank Shackleton was an admired newcomer to an influential homosexual set. His friends included Lord Ronald Sutherland-Gower, an unworldly but wealthy Bohemian (a trustee of Shakespeare's birthplace at Stratford-upon-Avon), and his nephew, the Duke of Argyll, brother-in-law of the King. Soon, no one quite knew how, Frank had a luxurious flat at 44, Park Lane. He was unashamedly on the make.

Frank was two years younger than his brother, and followed him to Dulwich. On leaving school, in 1893, at the age of seventeen, Frank worked at gardening, which he proposed to make his profession. Meanwhile, he evinced an interest in heraldry, as a result of which, in 1897, he met Sir Arthur Vicars, a fastidious and ill-fated Anglo-Irishman who was Ulster King-at-Arms. Frank was then trying to find work at the College of Arms in London. He failed but, in 1899, Sir Arthur made him assistant secretary (unpaid) at the Office of Arms in Dublin. Soon after, Frank joined the Army to fight in the Boer War. In 1903, on his discharge, he was made Gold Staff by Sir Arthur at his little heraldic court in Dublin Castle. Now in 1905, Sir Arthur promoted Frank to Dublin Herald. These grandiloquent appointments were sinecures with social advantages. They required only a token presence in Dublin, and Frank spent most of his time in London. Besides the flat in Park Lane, he was now sharing a house in Dublin with Sir Arthur.

In the meanwhile, Frank somehow acquired land near Paignton, in South Devon. There he commenced rose-growing and, incidentally, established a third residence. In 1905, as Ernest was leaving the RSGS, Frank formed the West of England Rose Farm Limited to take over the business. All the shareholders were members of the Shackleton family, Ernest among them.

Frank, in the words of a niece was "a thinner edition of Uncle Ernest, and he wore beautiful clothes".[2] Both brothers were persuasive, gregarious, and possessed of an insatiable zest for living. Each nursed an invincible belief in Eldorado round the next corner. Underneath all his foppishness, however, it was Frank who had the true financial passion. He was a dedicated man, prepared to work and wait. Ernest did not see the hard work and shrewd judgment that went into making seemingly effortless fortunes. He thought, as usual, that a little bustling around would bring the desired results.

Waiting for the general election, meanwhile, Shackleton returned to an earlier enthusiasm. While on the *Royal Magazine*, his waning faith in journalism had been revived by Niels Grøn, an enterprising and eccentric Dane, of whom the Danish Dictionary of National Biography said that "nobody seems to have fathomed the economic foundations of his existence or the other riddles of his career."[3] Grøn had spent some time in America. There, amongst other things, he was a confidential agent of the Danish government in the prelude to selling the Danish West Indies to the United States. When Shackleton met Grøn, he had arrived in London pushing *Potentia*.

Potentia was to be a press agency with a difference. Its aim was to promote international understanding by distributing a special kind of news guaranteed to be the unvarnished and pellucid truth – none genuine without the name *Potentia* – together with authoritative and uplifting articles written by the finest intellects in every civilised country throughout the world. It would "show Truth Dominant and unite those who in its cause have stood everywhere as strangers",[4] in Grøn's own words. "I feel," Shackleton had told Emily, "that that is going to be the great thing of the future."[5] That had in fact been the danger signal that originally made Mill send Shackleton to the RSGS.

Grøn, undeterred, followed Shackleton to Edinburgh. *Potentia* was incorporated as a company, and Shackleton helped Grøn with contacts. William Beardmore bought shares, so did Frank Shackleton. In fact, the shareholders covered a motley sample of British and continental life. *Potentia*, however, produced no fortune overnight, and Shackleton's enthusiasm soon faded. Now, with time on his hands, his hopes revived, and in September 1905, still waiting for the general election, he visited Belgium to promote *Potentia*, together with Charles Sarolea.

Sarolea was Lecturer in French at Edinburgh University. A Belgian of terrifying omniscience, he was one of Shackleton's eclectic coterie of friends. Within a year of meeting, they became brothers-in-law, Sarolea marrying Emily's elder sister Julia, *à deuxième noces*. Sarolea himself, a man of almost aggressive vivacity and violent enthusiasms, was attracted by Shackleton's "combative Irish temperament", as he put it, and his "wonderful vitality".[6] When Shackleton introduced him to *Potentia*, he embraced *Potentia* heart and soul.

On the strength of Grøn having "got in with the Royalties of many countries," Shackleton wrote to Emily from Brussels,

"Potentia seems to be doing very well." In Brussels, he also told her, "one can keep a carriage and live in luxury on £600 a year." Sarolea, he went on, would get Grøn an interview with Prince Albert of the Belgians. "I will also meet him so things are looking up." Prince Albert was politely unimpressed. Once more, Shackleton's enthusiasm waned and *Potentia* was soon driven from his mind.

Shackleton had been persuaded to put into *Potentia* five hundred pounds that he could ill afford. It was the last he saw of his investment, for *Potentia* never existed except as a paper company. Grøn was not an ordinary fraud. Seven years older than Shackleton, and of distinguished appearance, he was a kind of idealist, and monumentally persuasive. He spent much of his time staying with wealthy acquaintances, "resting and recuperating", as he put it, "from overwork of the Brain".[7]

What drove *Potentia* from Shackleton's mind was the publication, in October, of *The Voyage of the "Discovery"*. This was Scott's "official" account of the expedition. It made his name. To Shackleton, it was a fraud and a public humiliation. It reopened all his old wounds.

In 1903, after the first season on the *Discovery* expedition, Scott had sent home a report which was published in the *Geographical Journal*. When he came to the southern journey, Scott had written of the "sudden break-down of . . . Mr Shackleton", who was "feeling the strain of our recent work more than Dr Wilson or I were."[8] Scott managed to omit all mention of scurvy. Shackleton appeared as the sole cause of failure. It was all thoroughly misleading. Scott, on the other hand, had been writing under strain. Shackleton was then willing to give him the benefit of the doubt. Now, in *The Voyage of the "Discovery"*, Shackleton found everything repeated, together with a suspicion of doctored facts.

In the account of the southern journey, Shackleton found once more Scott's declaration at the Albert Hall that he had been carried on the sledge. Now when he told his own tale, Shackleton was quite prepared to admit, as he did in *Pearson's Magazine*, that he "broke down"; that his companions did all the pulling; anything at all, in fact, except that he ever had a ride. Scott said in the book that Shackleton was carried on the sledge on 21 and 30 January 1903. Shackleton himself recorded on 21 January that he "sat for an hour" on the sledge, although it was to "put brake on"[9] to stop overrunning while under sail. Scott had omitted any reference to manoeuvring the sledge. Shackleton was so sensitive on the point that the whole episode was reserved for his very private diary. Not even Emily was allowed to see it. For her, he typed out a copy, from which he suppressed all reference to riding on the sledge.

The second incident was even more degrading to Shackleton. "Our invalid," wrote Scott, "was so exhausted that we thought it wiser he should sit on the sledge, where for the remainder of the forenoon . . . we carried him."[10] By then, Shackleton was so ill that he had ceased keeping a diary. At the time, Wilson recorded that "Shackleton . . . has been very weak and breathless all day, but has stuck to it well and kept up with us on ski."[11] Whatever the truth, it was Scott's version that prevailed. Moreover, Shackleton had to sustain patronising references to "poor Shackleton", "our invalid", "our poor patient".[12] Nor did it help when Scott wrote that he was "pretending to be stronger than he is"[13] for this contained a grain of truth.

There was, however, yet worse to come. On the southern journey, scurvy was mentioned now. In describing its first appearance, however, Scott, purporting to quote his diary, wrote that "We have decided not to tell Shackleton for the present . . . but I am not sure he does not smell a rat."[14] Shackleton was being presented as a child unfit to be trusted with the truth. Moreover, he could see himself the victim of a fraud. Scott's drift was that Shackleton alone suffered from scurvy at the start. Shackleton, however, could read in his own diary that "medical exam^{tn} shews Capt. & I to be inclined to scurvy"[15] and, did he but know it, Wilson's diary said the same. Shackleton would not by now, perhaps, have been surprised if he had learned that Scott's supposed quotations from his diary had been composed in retrospect.

Scott's skilfully contrived narrative used Shackleton as the excuse for the poor southern record. That Shackleton found dishonest and insulting. The ironic truth was that his breakdown probably saved them all by forcing them to hurry on the return from the Furthest South.

But the most humiliating thrust of all was Scott's version of the aftermath of the journey:

> Shackleton at once took to his bed, and although he soon made an effort to be out and about again, he found that the least exertion caused a return of his breathless-ness . . . he would creep into his cabin and there rest until the strain had worn off . . . I was the least affected of the party.[16]

For some time, Shackleton had managed to regard Scott with indifference. *The Voyage of the "Discovery"* turned that to smouldering scorn and dislike. Scott, though he did not know it, was playing with fire.

Shackleton belonged to a breed that never forgave and never forgot. He felt himself the victim of a humiliating fraud. Besides, Scott was still a Freemason, and he had sworn an oath "on no account to wrong" other Freemasons, "or see them wronged".[17] Shackleton happened to take that seriously. Worse still, Scott, by exposing the physical flaw that was Shackleton's shame, had uncovered a corner of the truth.

Since his collapse on *Discovery*, and Koettlitz' diagnosis, Shackleton probably accepted that he was an asthmatic. Asthma then covered a host of nebulous chest complaints. True asthma, as now understood, is a bronchial attack triggered by an allergy or some outside physical cause. With its sense of gasping for breath, its unpredictability, it can be quite frightening. If that really was Shackleton's trouble, he could nonetheless have been perfectly well between attacks, and that would explain why he was passed "fit for Antarctic service" by the Admiralty doctor in 1903.

Exactly what ailed Shackleton, however, remained an enigma. Koettlitz' was only one opinion, but Shackleton shied away from doctors. Perhaps he was afraid of what he might find. If for no other reason, in the Edwardian cult of manliness, sickness was a stigma. In any case, his health remained part of the secret core of himself he shared with nobody at all. For all his breezy talkativeness, he was essentially a private person.

One thing was all too clear. Shackleton was now smoking heavily, which would have exacerbated his condition, whether it concerned heart or lungs. Whatever the exact reason, he gave the impression of feeling more and more a marked man.

The Voyage of the "Discovery" unleashed within him the demons of wounded pride, fear of time running out, and hunger for revenge. Not even Emily could console him for that. Satisfaction would only come from a return to the Antarctic and an attempt to outdo Scott.

Shackleton immediately made his first serious attempt to raise money for another expedition. He got as far as printing a prospectus. His ship, he said, would be "specially built – small but strong – fitted with a forty h.p. Petrol Motor, with which she would be capable of doing five knots . . . Ammundsen [*sic*] is attempting the North-West Passage with a vessel only half this size."[18]

Shackleton had clearly been inspired by the first despatches from Roald Amundsen, prominently published by *The Times* exactly at this time. Amundsen was on King William Land, in the Canadian Arctic, whence his despatches had been carried by Eskimo messenger and the North West Mounted Police. Amundsen's ship, *Gjøa*, reported *The Times*, was "fitted with a small petroleum motor, by means of which she can make about four knots".[19] The prospectus proved of little help. The men of means whom Shackleton approached all declined to help. For one thing, the palpable mismanagement of the *Discovery* expedition had generated a suspicion of polar exploration. For another, the shadow on Shackleton's health, so newly dramatised in *The Voyage of the "Discovery"*, made him a risk that potential investors were reluctant to accept.

Just before Christmas, the new election was at long last announced, and the Antarctic faded once more into the background. Shackleton's imagination soared beyond the technicalities of getting into Parliament, and the back benches, to the magic circle of political office, fame and fortune. The Palace of Westminster, gleaming dully over rainy pavements, now supplanted the South Pole in the role of Eldorado. Revenge on Scott was not only to be found, perhaps, in the snows.

The bustle of an election suited Shackleton's spirit. He was exactly the man for charging from one meeting to another, cramming three into the time for two. This was a practical necessity then, for the personal appearance was the candidates' only method of exposure. At that time, election days were spread over a fortnight, and Dundee was to poll on 16 January. That gave Shackleton about three weeks in which to campaign.

It was no ordinary election into which Shackleton had strayed. Liberals and Tories were then playing the great game of In and Out. The Tories had been in power for seventeen out of the past twenty years and the country was tiring of them, as it had tired before of the Liberals. It was, perhaps, the Liberals' turn again, but this time it was not quite the old familiar roundelay. The Labour party was fighting its first parliamentary election in force.

Dundee, a Liberal, indeed a radical, stronghold, was one of the constituencies in which a Labour candidate was standing. To contest the seat for the Unionists, an invincible optimist was required. Shackleton admirably filled the bill. "Since coming to Dundee," wrote the *Dundee Courier*, a Unionist organ, "the Lieutenant's breezy personality and his attractive manner have gained him much popularity."[20] Shackleton, said "A Working Man" in a letter to the editor, "has won friends in Dundee whose opinions are as far apart from him as are the Poles."[21] Shackleton found it hard, however, to distinguish personal popularity from political trends, even though he had at least one lesson in the essential irrelevancy of the individual candidate. "Come over to our side," one Labour heckler called, "and we'll put ye in!" It was party, not the person that counted. One candidate in that election at least understood it very well. Winston Churchill, already a Conservative MP, had crossed over to the Liberals.

Dundee was one of the old two-member constituencies, elected in a single poll. The voters were tough, forthright, combative, and given to what the *Dundee Courier* called "Breezy Heckling". It was an atmosphere in which Shackleton thrived. He was never at a loss for words. He could handle a large, organised meeting as well as an impromptu gathering on the quayside or at the factory gates. His one weakness was a lack of power hunger, the necessary attribute of a politician.

Emily wanted to follow her husband round the hustings. It would, however, as he put it, "not be of any use darling . . . though I long to see your sweet face."[22] So she followed Ernest's campaign through his own scrappy letters instead: "I addressed 5 meetings today over 2000 people."

> We had a rowdy meeting . . . heckling right up to 10 p.m. I had most as usual because I was in an Irish district. I am making a good many friends . . . I am eating plenty and taking Champagne.[23]

From one dingy hall to the next, Shackleton trudged the constituency trail. Stronger ties between Britain and the Empire; female suffrage, peasant proprietors, the importation of Chinese coolies into the South African gold mines, belong to the list of long dead issues on which Shackleton was expected to offer an opinion. On the whole, he was content to hammer away at the party line. The real Shackleton, however, kept on breaking through. Asked "as an Irish landlord" whether it was fair to subsidise Irish landlords (another burning issue of the day), Shackleton answered, "I wish to goodness I was an Irish landlord. All the land I own is just enough for me to hang my washing on Monday morning".[24]

Many of Shackleton's speeches have a familiar ring. There was, as he put it, "something wrong with the trade of the country".[25] Unemployment was high. Exports had shrunk. "Continental competitors" were the cause, especially the Germans. Shackleton did not suggest that this might have been due to the German ability to work harder and produce better products at a lower price. Instead he repeated the party line, which he probably believed, that the Germans were succeeding, not because of industrial superiority, but because of their subsidies. "Such transactions [are] dishonest. They amount to a direct blow at our commercial interests."[26] "But for the Greater Britains beyond the seas," Shackleton told a working-class audience, "we would feel the pinch of foreign competition even more." He was arguing for protectionism, which the Unionists (more or less) upheld against Free Trade, in which the Liberals (more or less) believed. Germany was both the model and the fear and, like his fellow-campaigners, Shackleton played on this. Where party priming failed, he could always improvise, and raise a laugh. "An unskilled workman," ran a characteristic flash, "is one who looks around and when he sees a job runs away from it."[27]

It was all to no avail. "I got all the applause," as Shackleton put it, "and the other fellows got all the votes."[28] In the early hours of 17 January, when the poll was declared, one Liberal and the Labour man had been elected. Shackleton had been beaten into fourth place. He was in good company. Balfour, the Conservative leader, and out-going Prime Minister, had lost his seat. Both had been engulfed by a gigantic and unprecedented Liberal and Labour landslide. Shackleton had taken part in perhaps the most significant event of the Edwardian age.

Balfour was one of the few in England to sense the rumblings of the political earthquake that was to change the face of Europe. "This election," he wrote the day after his defeat to Francis Knollys, the King's secretary, "inaugurates a new era." The sudden emergence of the Labour party as a parliamentary force was its salient fact. What had happened was something more than "ordinary party change". It could only be understood in terms of "the same movement which has produced massacres in St Petersburg, riots in Vienna and Socialist processions in Berlin."[29]

To Shackleton, on the other hand, the outcome simply meant that, as a short-cut to success, politics had failed. Without regret, he turned his back on the shattered allure of Parliament, and moved on.

The election took place in the aftermath of the Russo-Japanese war, and this provided Shackleton with his next money-hunting opportunity. The war had been a humiliating Russian defeat, leaving her troops in a state of disaffection. The Russian government urgently wanted to bring them home from the Far East before mutiny broke out. Overland, it was impossible. Ships were the only answer, but the Russians owned too few and so they had to charter foreign tonnage, quickly. This was exactly the chance for which Shackleton and what he called his "little steamboat company"[30] had been waiting.

The company was promoted by George Petrides, the brother of Nicetas Petrides, Shackleton's school friend, and himself another Old Alleynian. Some months before, George had given Shackleton an interest in the company. When the Russians came into the market, early in the election campaign, George and the company chairman were soon negotiating with their representatives in London.

The chairman was an accountant called Thomas Jehu Garlick, who was heavily involved in Frank Shackleton's company promotions. By now, Frank, to quote an erstwhile guest at his and Sir Arthur Vicars' Dublin ménage, was widely considered "a shady customer in every respect".[31] This company, however, was reasonably genuine. Little more than a fortnight after the poll, Shackleton was in London, helping the proceedings.

Emily was distressed. She wanted her husband at home. "But I must do something," Ernest wrote. He was "in the City late and early", as he told her. "It is awfully exciting."[32]

Shackleton loved the special aura of confidence and consummate money-making that clung to the sober top-hatted crowds thronging the pavements of Bishopsgate and Cheapside. He bustled from one office to the other, extravagantly keeping hansoms waiting at the door. He was, as usual, larger than life. His big face eloquently reflecting the thoughts within, he was almost the caricature of the City hanger-on, thirsting for a quick fortune. Quick, it had to be, because Shackleton was now in financial straits; and Emily's income, as it turned out, could not really keep them both in style.

The company was highly speculative. It owned no ships, and had been promoted to charter as required. It was perfectly suitable for George Petrides, with his finger in many pies, including, as it happened, some of Frank Shackleton's enterprises. It was less appropriate for Ernest Shackleton, who saw it as a sole and certain scheme. If everything succeeded, "you can come down to London with me," Shackleton wrote to Emily, "for we will have plenty of money and I must be on the spot."[33]

Garlick and Petrides, however, were doing the actual work. Shackleton, so he understood, was to be traffic manager when the deal was actually done. What he did not grasp was that, in the friendliest possible way, he was simply being used. It was his name as an explorer that his friends wanted. *That* had a cachet; indeed, a respectability which, in the right hands, on the right prospectus, could be turned into a profitable asset. But the role of sleeping partner was not for him. He was consumed by a thirst for action. Having touched the world of finance, he immediately saw himself as a great financier. For the moment, he was fobbed off with talking to Sir Sydney Boulton, a Lloyd's underwriter, about insuring the putative ships.

Sir Sydney's wife, Shackleton wrote to Emily, in a rare personal comment, was "very dowdily dressed but was quite nice".[34] Sir Sydney happened to be an old friend of Emily's.

Early in February, the Russians offered a contract to take 40,000 troops from Vladivostok to the Black Sea, at £40 a head for officers, and £12 for other ranks. "My 1000 shares will be worth £4,000 in a few days,"[35] Shackleton wrote exultantly to Emily. He foresaw a glorious total profit of £30,000 and, as he put it, "things will be all right with us for ever".[36] Yet while Shackleton was dreaming in tens of thousands, another part of him was worrying whether his brother Frank would send him a promised £40. He had to tell Emily that he could not come up to Edinburgh on a flying visit although "I want to see you so much Sweeteyes," because "Time and money are both short just now."[37]

Frank Shackleton was in financial difficulties himself. "They could easily have been relieved had I chosen to go to my family," he later blandly said, "but for various reasons I did not care to do so, and I borrowed money from a money-lender."[38] He did so on the security of Sir Arthur Vicars, who took some of the proceeds. It was out of this dubious transaction that Frank found the money to help Ernest.

To Ernest, the £40 was only a temporary help until the Russian deal was clinched. But when Garlick wanted to take him to St Petersburg to talk to the Russians, Shackleton refused. Underneath all his sanguine flamboyance there remained a hard core of self-preservation. The Russians, as usual, were Asiatic in their dealings. They used shady intermediaries. The negotiations with Petrides' company had been a blind. The purpose was to press down the prices of the Hamburg-American Line, which had already secured the bulk of the contract, the remainder being parcelled out among other German firms. By the middle of February, Garlick's and Petrides' deal had collapsed. Once more, Shackleton's dream of instant fortune faded.

It did not quell his optimism. Sir John Boraston, the chief Liberal Unionist agent, had half-promised some kind of job as a consolation for not getting into Parliament. In a few days that faded too. Shackleton therefore grasped the lifeline held out to him by William Beardmore. Within a fortnight he found himself in Glasgow, at the Parkhead Engineering Works.

From the glamour of the City to the industrial clatter of the Clyde was hardly a congenial transition, but Shackleton characteristically transferred Eldorado to the new milieu. After the first few days he was already writing to Emily:

> I may become a director before very long, If I had say ten thousand pounds in the business it would pay from 10% to 14% and then the directorship is at least worth one thousand a year so we ought to do very well.[39]

Very possibly that is what Elspeth Beardmore had led Shackleton to believe.

Beardmore himself was a great deal less forthcoming. "The greatest captain of industry",[40] as a rebellious employee and trade union adversary admiringly called him, Beardmore was distinguished from most industrialists by a higher technical training. He had invented nickel-chrome armour plate, which was now much in demand since the Royal Navy, at last, had started modernising itself to meet the growing German threat.

"I have made Parkhead famous," Beardmore used to say. He had devoted his life to building up the works, and it rolled the heaviest armour plate in the country. When Shackleton appeared, Beardmore had just diversified into shipbuilding, and was finding he could not yet compete with the established yards. Poor management was leading him into financial difficulties. In any case, a directorship for Shackleton would scarcely have been a serious possibility. To oblige his wife, however, Beardmore was prepared to help him over an awkward patch with a sinecure at thirty pounds a month.

After his momentary daydream of mythical dividends and illusory boardroom seats, Shackleton soon realised that Beardmore was not going to mean a fortune overnight, any more than Russian soldiers, Parliament, *Potentia*, or the *Royal Magazine*. For his part, Beardmore shrewdly guessed that to Shackleton Parkhead was just one more staging post on the road to somewhere else.

At Parkhead, Shackleton was an early kind of public relations officer. He was employed to charm potential customers; to talk and entertain, and generally lend lustre by his presence. Also, he was made secretary of a committee to evaluate a new German gas engine. Keeping minutes, as Shackleton had long since discovered at the RSGS, was hardly his metier. He, however, persuaded Mr McDuff, Beardmore's personal secretary, to do most of the work – as perhaps Beardmore suspected that he would. "He'd come in and talk and keep me from my work," said McDuff, echoing Everett on the *Royal Magazine*, "but

> I liked it . . . even if I was in the thick of things I'd give them up to do what he wanted – I'd such a liking for the fellow . . . I couldn't refuse Shackleton anything within reason.[41]

Newly built but drab; all sober mahogany, ornate wrought iron and solid, polished granite; redolent of solemn endeavour, the Beardmore offices were hardly Shackleton's milieu. As the year wore on, he grew more obviously restless.

In the middle of October, *The Times* published a leader called "Arctic Exploration", a review of the year in the North. One American, Wellman, twenty years before his time, was trying to reach the North Pole by airship; another, Robert Edwin Peary, was preparing an attempt on the same goal – again – using dogs and sledges. But, said *The Times*,

> The completion of the North-West Passage by the Norwegian expedition on board the Gjøa – a unique achievement – . . . will probably rank as the outstanding feature of the year in the annals of polar exploration . . . Captain Amundsen has carried out his programme almost to the letter . . .[42]

On 31 August, Amundsen had arrived at Nome, Alaska – the first man to bring a ship through the Arctic channels connecting the Atlantic with the Pacific. To Shackleton, it meant a catalogue of frustration. Here was Amundsen, following his destiny, while he himself was languishing in an office, still baffled, at the age of thirty-two, and hungering for attainment. The Antarctic began to stir again at the shifting core of Shackleton's desire. "What would I now give to be out there again," he wrote to Hugh Robert Mill, "and this time really on the way to the Pole."[43]

Mill was still director of the British Rainfall Association in London. He had long since forgiven Shackleton for leaving the RSGS and, with some anxiety, followed the waywardness of his protégé. Shackleton, on the other hand, clung to him as perhaps his only true friend, a father figure, and a confidant.

When, inevitably, he realised that Beardmore's would only be another temporary expedient, Shackleton gave up plans of moving house. He kept on his household in Edinburgh, and commuted by train instead. For Beardmore, he also went regularly to London, "only down on business", as he took care to write to Mill, "so I never have time to move about in the social way".[44] This was not strictly true. He managed to meet friends, and visit theatres, as indeed he told Emily. But he was also seeing an American girl friend, a Miss Havemeyer, who lived at Walton Street, South Kensington.

Shackleton was not exactly being unfaithful. Emily was pregnant again. She had been thirty-seven when Raymond was born. That was old to be having a first baby and, even under favourable circumstances, childbirth then among middle-class women was unpleasant. "Dont worry little girl if there is to be No 2", Shackleton had tellingly written from London when the new pregnancy was still uncertain.

You will not be a worry to anyone and least of all to your husband so Cheer Oh Sweeteyes. After all it is better to have the two and then you will have done, if we have not two you would always be wanting the other one.[45]

The intensity of Shackleton's eyes hinted at warm wellsprings of passion. The complexities of a wife living with a distaste for everything connected with childbirth, were too much for him. He needed a woman, all the time. He was virtually driven to find satisfaction outside his home.

At this point, he was also seeing a great deal of Elspeth Beardmore. "I have had a beastly time of it the last few days," he once wrote to her from Parkhead in the autumn of 1906 when they could not meet,

and only wish I could have seen you . . . for you are always so cheerful and make me feel so much better after I have seen you.

The least thing, he explained, upset

Emmie . . . very much just now . . . Raymond has become very poorly . . . you can well imagine that with all these worries . . . it has been a bit of an effort to keep things going brightly; and outside my own house I hear that my father who has worked as doctor on the heart . . . is getting very deaf . . . He writes me a doleful letter and ends up with a request for some money as he has so many expenses and is unable to take heart cases as he cannot hear people's hearts beating and tells me he has to spend £80 on mourning for my sister as an aunt has died, it is perfectly ridiculous to you . . . mourning for a relative they have never seen . . . in Ireland. I sent him some money and my opinion on such proceedings. I have had a fine lot of worry this past week and the one bright spot was seeing you. Don't think me a grumbling person, Elspeth but you have always been such a real friend and confidant to me that it is to you alone I can talk. I am doing my best [at the office] and I think I am helping things along . . . but even that is difficult for you can understand there are differences of opinion . . . Don't mind this dreary letter Elspeth and let me see you soon. My little troubles are not much in reality but they are real all the same . . . You looked so beautiful the other night.[46]

Emily did not understand what was going on; or perhaps she did? Years later she said to Hugh Robert Mill,

I must have failed him somehow – perhaps I was too sure . . . I am conscious of my own limitations. He sat so lightly to the things of this world – and was big, where I am often small. I looked after the small things and they rather stifle the soul. I am always sorry for "Martha". I expect she would much rather have been "Mary" . . .[47]

Childless, and destined to remain so, Elspeth Beardmore understood Shackleton's aspirations. She could see that he had now turned once more to the Antarctic as his outlet for ambition. To Emily, he could hardly speak about it. She wanted him to stay at home. It was Elspeth who encouraged him to go out and fulfil his destiny, and it was to her that he turned to talk about his plans. For now, Shackleton saw the tantalising prospect of his expedition edging within reach. Miss Elizabeth Dawson-Lambton had lent him £1,000.

Elizabeth Dawson-Lambton, "Old Liz" to her servants, was a wealthy maiden lady, connected with the Earls of Durham. Nearly seventy years old, she migrated between boarding houses and her two maiden sisters' homes in Devon. Thin and frail, all caps and curls surrounding a small face, she was not unfeminine in the style of another age. She was philanthropic and touched by eccentricity – one of her causes was supporting the last survivors of the Charge of the Light Brigade.

"Old Liz" had also been among *Discovery*'s benefactors. Shackleton had first met her in 1901, when he showed her over the ship before sailing. Since then, her heart had beaten warmly for him. She had a special lace collar she wore only for him. Like Elspeth Beardmore, she applauded his Antarctic yearnings and her £1,000 was the expression of what she felt.

It was the start for which Shackleton had been longing. Nothing else, however, was even remotely yet in sight. With Elizabeth Dawson-Lambton's permission, Shackleton gave his brother the £1,000 to invest until it was required. With the inspiration of that first instalment, Ernest Shackleton tried once more to raise the money for an expedition of his own.

To Frank Shackleton, Miss Dawson-Lambton's money was a timely windfall too. He appropriated every penny to help finance one of his company promotions. Of this, Ernest was quite unaware. To him Frank, as a mutual acquaintance put it, was still the "genie who had given him the golden lamp".[48] "Old Foozle" was how Lord Ronald Sutherland-Gower, whose financial adviser Frank Shackleton was now scheming to become, genially preferred to call him.

Ernest Shackleton, meanwhile, when he could take time off, was urgently trying his luck again in the City. He had decided to finance his putative expedition like a company promotion. The road back to the Antarctic started in Throgmorton Street. He began by trying his brother's City friends. Among the more respectable was a certain Douglas Spens Steuart. Early in 1907, Shackleton actually persuaded Steuart to invest in his expedition.

In the words of a Scottish friend, Shackleton was "unique in his love of talking big and his ability to do big things. The two qualities seldom go together."[49] Perhaps this glinted through his buccaneering figure to distinguish Shackleton from the other camp followers milling round the pavements of the City. And Shackleton, like Borchgrevink in his day, had suggested that the Antarctic might be another Klondyke; a source of minerals and precious stones. He did so not only to impress Steuart, but because he happened to believe in it himself. The Edwardian City was an enterprising mart. A vague anxiety hung over the land; an unresolvable depression and expectation of war. Quick returns before the deluge were what the City wanted. In his quest for big money, quickly, Shackleton was in tune with the spirit of the place.

Steuart was a mining engineer, partner in a City firm of consultants, and therefore accustomed to speculative schemes. Antarctic minerals were a gamble as safe as some being aired on the Stock Exchange. Still, it was an investment in which the prudent financier would prefer to risk other people's money rather than his own.

On 27 December 1906 – four days after Emily Shackleton gave birth to her second child, Cecily – Steuart incorporated a company called the Celtic Investment Trust to develop mining interests he owned in Cornwall, Mexico and Siberia. Frank Shackleton was also involved in the promotion. Very likely Elizabeth Dawson-Lambton's £1,000 did double duty, as it were, by giving Frank, like Ernest Shackleton, the wherewithal to impress Steuart. Steuart, at all events, earmarked 10,000 shares for the Antarctic enterprise.

At this point, Hugh Robert Mill met Shackleton by chance in the corridor of a sleeping car at Euston going to Glasgow. To Mill, Shackleton was now the businessman settling down to a career:

> I remarked in saying goodnight that now he would be content to leave the south Pole alone. Like the Ancient mariner, he held me with his glittering eye until he unfolded the scheme of his new expedition, told of . . . the funds secured, and all plans made for sailing . . .[50]

Underneath the flood of visionary optimism, however, Shackleton was not naive. Celtic was still a paper company and its shares had no value, yet. Nonetheless, Shackleton could truthfully say that he had "City backing" now. Like many another hopeful, he was rushing to strike while the iron was hot. When he ran into Mill, he was on his way to solicit Beardmore's support.

William Beardmore, as the archetypal captain of industry, was diligent, determined, and autocratic, displaying a wonderful moustache, and always smoking a cigar; stern and formidable to face. Underneath it all, however, he concealed a charitable streak. That Shackleton had already discerned, and on that he now proposed to play. With Steuart's promise in his hand, he possessed the necessary confidence. Besides, Elspeth Beardmore had prepared the ground.

Beardmore probably saw through the tale of "City backing" with which Shackleton confronted him. He chose, however, to take the magic password at face value, and he did not remind Shackleton that when he came to Parkhead less than a year ago, it was under protestations of having renounced polar ambitions. Beardmore had partly succumbed to Shackleton's Irish blend of calculating charm and visionary conviction. Besides, of Shackleton it could be said, as Ibsen made one of his characters say of Peer Gynt in the play of that name, that "he was too strong. There were women behind him".[51]

It was accepted in Beardmore's office, and later became a tradition there, that Shackleton and Elspeth Beardmore were having an affair. Beardmore himself was certainly growing a little suspicious of his wife's protégé. Sending him to the other end of the world was a chance tactfully to get rid of an unwelcome guest. He agreed to help the expedition.

Like Steuart, however, William Beardmore was reluctant to risk money of his own. Instead, he guaranteed a loan of £7,000 at his bankers, the Clydesdale Bank. The condition, as Shackleton put it in his letter of agreement, was that "the first profits of the expedition will be given up to you to an amount which will release the guarantee".[52]

On the face of it, this was qualified and grudging. It was not to be compared, for example, with the £20,000 for Jackson by Alfred Harmsworth, or the £25,000 by Llewellyn Longstaff for Sir Clements Markham and *Discovery*; both outright gifts, not loans. These, however, were support for men who, whatever their faults, were dedicated to their aims. Shackleton, on the other hand, by now appeared to be a not too successful opportunist. Given this, Beardmore was being conspicuously generous. Seven thousand pounds was not much, but it was enough for Shackleton to launch his enterprise.

Among polar explorers, Shackleton was the only one who openly promoted his expedition as a commercial venture. His aim was to be first at the South Pole. Money would flow from telling the story in books, lectures, newspapers and the exciting innovation of the cinematograph. For Steuart, Shackleton held out as well the enticement of mineral rights.

Meanwhile, the Marquis of Graham allowed his name to go forward as a patron of the expedition. The marquis was a Beardmore director, besides being, with William Beardmore and Shackleton, a fellow *Potentia* shareholder. It says something for Shackleton's mesmeric persuasiveness that he had managed to overcome the misgivings of three reasonably astute Scottish businessmen. Perhaps it spoke for the lucky star under which he believed he had been born. With Beardmore's guarantee, "City backing", and the prestige of a titled associate, Shackleton was on his way, at last. The shadow of three and a half years of bafflement started to dissolve.

The worst part of the whole affair was breaking the news to Emily. Until the enterprise seemed certain, Shackleton had kept her in the dark.

To be told that her husband was planning to leave her for one of the poles of the earth, was hardly joy to a woman in the throes of post-parturitive depression. But, as Emily wrote in after years to Mill,

> I never wittingly hampered his ardent spirit, or tried to chain it to the domestic life which meant so much to me. He used to say he went on the Discovery "to get out of the ruck" for me! – it was *dear* of him to say it because I cannot flatter myself that it was only for me – it was his own spirit "a soul whipped on by the wanderfire".[53]

After almost three years of marriage, Emily accepted that it was her fate to give Ernest Shackleton the security of a home and of a patient, waiting wife that he needed to come back to. It was his fate to be restless when he was actually there.

He now persuaded her – although perhaps not quite – that the South Pole was what would make them rich and happy ever after. In any case, Emily swallowed her distress. There was, as well she knew, no choice. Released from the humiliating frustration of insolvent hope, Shackleton now swept into action like a gale.

XVI

British Antarctic Expedition, 1907

Beardmore committed himself on 8 February 1907, a Friday. On Monday, 11 February, Shackleton was in London, at the RGS, talking to Scott Keltie. In the same room stood Roald Amundsen and Fridtjof Nansen. It was an extraordinary scene. Towering over Shackleton by half a head the two Norwegians, like philosophic Vikings, personified polar exploration in its most professional and intellectualised form. Amundsen had come to lecture that evening to the RGS on his attainment of the North-West Passage. Nansen, now the first Minister in London of a newly independent Norway,* was there as his mentor.

Amundsen was also in London with plans to discuss, for he now wanted to be the first man at the North Pole. He had just asked Nansen to lend him *Fram* for the attempt, but Nansen was still tormented by the desire of his youth for the South Pole, and half believed he might soon need *Fram* himself.

Of this, Shackleton was completely unaware. To him, Nansen and Amundsen, celebrities though they might be, were merely competing for attention. Talking characteristically in bursts, with long silences in between, Shackleton nonetheless managed to buttonhole Keltie for half an hour. "After many mysterious questions and hints," as Keltie recorded the conversation, "Shackleton suddenly told me he had got enough money for an expedition, somewhere about £30,000."[1]

Shackleton had come to ask, bluntly, for the support of the RGS and the patronage of the King. He spoke also to Sir George Taubman Goldie, the RGS President. Shackleton, said Keltie,

* Norway had become independent in 1905, after almost a century of Swedish rule and, before that, four centuries under Denmark.

> wanted me to take the matter up in the press, but I said I could do nothing at all in the present stage, but he had better do it himself.[2]

Goldie, too, was strangely cool and non-committal.

Keltie, besides his work at the RGS, also wrote for *The Times* on exploration. Shackleton took him at his word. He immediately left and, through a raw and rainy afternoon, went to Fleet Street to give the Press Association his news. He then hurried back to Edinburgh to plunge into his preparations.

The following day, his announcement was printed in *The Times*, and in the next column was the report of Amundsen's lecture to the RGS:

> Dr Nansen . . . said that . . . the . . . secret of [Amundsen's] success . . . was that . . . he acquired knowledge . . . and then bought his ship, instead of doing what most . . . explorers had done, bought the ship first and then acquired the requisite information . . .[3]

Since sailing away from McMurdo Sound four years before, however, Shackleton had acquired no new snow technique, but he was determined not to repeat Scott's mistakes. He was also determined to get away this year. Few polar explorers have worked in quite that rush.

Shackleton's impatience had many strands. It was part of his character. He was driven by the fear of being forestalled, since Nansen was not alone in yearning for one of the last great geographic goals. Interest in the Antarctic was beginning to ignite. Within a year two congresses had been held, and plans were being aired. In France, for example, Dr J. B. Charcot, and a flying pioneer, the Count de la Vaulx, had proposed to reach the South Pole by balloon and motor sledge. More seriously, Henryk Arçtowski, one of Amundsen's old companions from *Belgica*, had Belgian backing for an expedition. Arçtowski, too, had visited Scott Keltie to talk about his plans. More than all this perhaps, Shackleton was afraid to give his backers time for second thoughts.

First, Shackleton needed a second-in-command. Back in Edinburgh, the day after meeting Keltie, he wrote to Edward Wilson, his companion at the Furthest South. "You know me well enough to know that we can work together," Shackleton wrote, "Come, Billy, Don't say No till we have had a talk," he pleaded. "Don't say No at all."[4] Wilson, however, had started research into a disease that was killing wild grouse on the Scottish moors. He could not leave. Shackleton responded with a flood of entreaty, mostly by telegram. "It is," he wired, "the country before the grouse."[5]

With superb panache, Shackleton called his very private venture the "British Antarctic Expedition, 1907". His idiom was a hybrid of patriotism and company promotion. Besides, he frankly admitted, in persuading his backers he had used Wilson's name. Beardmore, Shackleton told Wilson, had now written to say he "hoped you would come".[6] Also, said Shackleton, "My friend the Marquis of Graham . . . knows all about . . . the importance of your coming".[7]

Wilson, however, was adamant. "Don't waste any more money on long telegrams,"[8] he wrote. "This," Shackleton telegraphed in reply, "is almost as bitter a disappointment as when I left Discovery."[9]

> I don't want to make it harder, Billy, my friend, but I am sad at heart.[10]

It was not only as a friend, moral guarantor and support that Shackleton wanted Wilson, but also as a doctor he could trust. If asthma was troubling him, the heart palpitations that sometimes follow in its wake would have haunted him even more. He dreaded the sentence of infirmity an unsympathetic medical practitioner could impose. "If I am not fit enough to do the southern Journey," he had pleaded with Wilson, "there could be no one better than you."[11] He was afraid that unless he did things quickly, he would not do them at all.

"You will probably get better advice than I can give," Wilson consoled him by replying, "but when we meet I shall consider it my duty to give you a tip or two!"[12]

Wilson's refusal was one more bitter bafflement. Was the work on grouse disease the real reason or merely a pretext? But there was no time to brood. Shackleton turned to the next person on his list. He wrote to George Mulock, the naval lieutenant who had replaced him on *Discovery*. Mulock, too, declined, remarking casually that he had "volunteered to go with Scott".[13]

Shackleton, in his own words, "took the letter to the Geographical and saw Keltie".

> I said "What is the meaning of this?" Keltie said "Oh! Mulock has let the cat out of the bag." I said "Is Scott going to go?" He said "Yes. He is thinking of going, but it is a secret."[14]

Now, Shackleton began to understand the atmosphere at the RGS when he went there to announce his expedition: the coolness of Goldie; the hint of shiftiness behind Keltie's impenetrable eyes framed by a slightly unfashionable beard.

The revelations of subterfuge and competition did little more, at first, than spur Shackleton on. A few days later, however, two letters arrived from Scott himself, the first contact Shackleton had had with him for two years. In a copious and emotional flow of words, Shackleton was startled to find himself accused of thwarting Scott's life's work.

Scott had learned of Shackleton's intentions from *The Times*. The "NEW BRITISH EXPEDITION TO THE SOUTH POLE", as the headline put it, would

> go down to the winter quarters of the Discovery . . . After landing a shore party . . . the ship will proceed back to . . . New Zealand, thus avoiding the risk of being frozen in like the Discovery.

And, *The Times* continued, developing the theme,

> the main object . . . is to follow out the discoveries made on the southern sledge journey from the Discovery . . . It is held that the southern . . . party of the Discovery would have reached a much higher latitude if they had been more adequately equipped for sledge work.[15]

The drift was clear. Shackleton's enterprise was born out of an obsession with *Discovery* and its captain. Anything Scott had done, Shackleton would do better.

The nub of what Scott now wrote to Shackleton was that he himself had also decided to return and outdo the *Discovery* expedition. He, however, had a natural right to the *Discovery* quarters, and therefore ordered Shackleton to change his plans, leaving the entire Ross Sea region to him. Before Shackleton had time to reply – if indeed he intended replying – to this demand, a telegram arrived from Wilson saying that Scott had written to him as well, and asking whether Shackleton had informed Scott before making the announcement.[16] Once more he was playing conciliator in the same uneasy triad of the southern journey.

By now, Shackleton regarded Scott as a faintly ridiculous figure. Wilson at least was someone to be taken seriously, but Shackleton decided after all to reply to Scott.

Scott's reaction could be ascribed to an overwrought mind. HMS *Albemarle,* the battleship he was commanding, had rammed HMS *Commonwealth* on manoeuvres off the coast of Portugal. That was on 11 February – the same day, as it happened, that Shackleton was revealing his plans in London to Keltie, and at the very hour, 8 p.m., when Amundsen was starting to lecture to the RGS on his conquest of the North-West Passage. Later, when his ship limped into Gibraltar for repairs, Scott saw *The Times*, with its report of both; including Nansen's declaration that he "hoped, in fact he knew, that they might some day see Captain Amundsen start on another expedition".[17]

Scott's naval career was now possibly at stake. In the circumstances, Shackleton answered him more considerately than he otherwise might have done. What he sent was nonetheless a challenge.

Scott had, in effect, claimed that his desires conferred prescriptive right. "My desires were as great", Shackleton pointedly replied,

> if not greater, than anyone else's to return, seeing that I was cut off by a premature return . . . from . . . the [*Discovery*] expedition.[18]

Shackleton had "monies definitely promised", as he put it, and he would be "ready to start in October". Keltie, on the other hand, Shackleton added, had himself said "We do not know whether [Scott] will be going . . . we do not know whether he has got any money yet."[19] Shackleton then sent the letter to Wilson for approval. That, as far as Shackleton was concerned, was the end of the matter.

Wilson, however, swiftly replied advising him

> to offer to retire from McMurdo Sound as a base . . . I do wholly agree with the right lying with Scott to use the base before anyone else.

To Shackleton that came as a shock; and another blow followed, as Wilson continued

> One's motives are always mixed, but I think that the tarnished honour of getting the Pole even, as things have turned out will be worth infinitely less than the honour of dealing generously with Scott. One never loses by being quixotic – if this really appears to you quixotic.[20]

Wilson, to Shackleton, had so far been something of an ideal. This was a kind of treachery. Something feline and sinister had crept out from behind the mask. Shackleton, as Charles Sarolea put it, "belonged to a bygone age – to the age of Froissart and Queen Elizabeth rather than to our own".[21] He was certainly confounded by Wilson's high moral tone.

Scott's assumption of prescriptive right was certainly preposterous, arguably pathological. The barren lands were surely anybody's game. Although Peary in 1886, for example, had tried to make the first crossing of the Greenland Ice Cap, that did not prevent Nansen stepping in two years later to snatch the prize. Wilson had, however, invoked the chivalric delusion of the Edwardian gentlemanly ideal. If Shackleton was closer to the Elizabethan viewpoint of seeing men as they were, rather than as they ought to be, he was, even so, not entirely proof against his schooling; nor against Wilson's quiet, ruthless, mental bullying. Shackleton, in Keltie's words,

> told me that he has not slept for three nights. He has evidently been thinking of alternatives. He talked of the Weddell Sea . . . and even hinted that he might turn his expedition towards the North Pole . . .[22]

Behind the moralistic turmoil Shackleton, in a characteristically Irish way, was looking out, clear-eyed, in shrewd judgment. Not plagued by jealousy himself, he nonetheless discerned its workings in Scott; perhaps also the traces of *folie de grandeur*. In any case, he could see that behind the lofty talk Scott was bent on stopping him at almost any price.

Scott was a naval captain, and a protégé of the establishment that had the power to obstruct. Shackleton, as he would have been the first to admit, was an outsider. He had no money yet, only promises. If Scott publicly opposed him or, more ruinous still, intrigued behind the scenes, his backers might change their minds. A mere whisper, however egregious, of not "playing the game", might be enough.

Two years before Scott had revealed his tactical weaknesses; in the aftermath of the *Discovery* expedition, he had declined an invitation to receive a decoration in Stockholm. "I am dependent on our Admiralty as my employers," he explained,

> and after a recent interview I quite came to the conclusion that it would not do for me to prolong my absence from the Naval Service.[23]

Since then, little had changed. For fear of what the Navy would say, Scott had to keep his plans secret until he was ready. That did not stop him using a young officer on board *Albemarle* to type out his letters to Shackleton. "I got no thanks for my slow and imperfect typewriting,"[24] the officer later recalled. He had to bear the brunt of Scott's anger and frustration.

For the moment, in any case, the Navy required most of Scott's attention, and the Navy would keep him out of the country for some time yet. Shackleton therefore had the advantage, both of Scott's fear of exposure, and in being the man on the spot. He had to exploit the situation while he could. On 4 March, before Scott had a chance of coming back, Shackleton visited Wilson at his home near Cheltenham in the hope of coming to an accommodation. Wilson, however, was implacable. He insisted on the renunciation of McMurdo Sound.

Shackleton hastily agreed, too hastily perhaps. It was, however, the price of propitiating Wilson's moral scruples; hence of preserving his mediation, and buying Scott off. Immediately, from Cheltenham, Shackleton cabled his decision to Scott; only to be told by Wilson that he must not "on any account make up . . . new plans until you know definitely from Scott what limits he puts to his rights".[25]

> His rights [Shackleton replied] end at the base he asked for . . . I fully appreciate your desire that everything should be peaceful . . . but there are limits to what one may give in . . .

If, Shackleton went on, Scott demanded more than the *Discovery* base,

> I cannot see that he will be upheld by anybody . . . but whether he is upheld or not . . . I shall fight . . . my limit has been reached.[26]

Scott did limit himself for the present to McMurdo Sound. In any case, some of his anger had been diverted on to Keltie. To begin with, Scott assumed that Keltie had told Shackleton about his own plans, to warn him off, and therefore that Shackleton had acted deliberately to forestall him. When Scott found that Keltie had kept silent, he assumed that Keltie was trying to stir up trouble. This, however, was unreasonable. Scott had repeatedly told Keltie to keep his plans secret; and Keltie was only being all things to all men; as the Secretary of the RGS needed to be:

> Supposing . . . I had told Shackleton of your plans when he rushed in here upon us that day [he replied smoothly to a tirade of reproach from Scott] I am quite sure it would never have restrained him from doing as he did, and then probably you might have blamed us for telling him.[27]

With that, Scott fervently agreed, expounding as he did so on what he considered Shackleton's "disloyalty", and claiming that Shackleton owed everything to him. "You will no doubt be first in the field," Keltie meanwhile wrote to Shackleton, "and so have the start of any other expedition."[28]

Almost in the same breath, Keltie was consoling Scott with the thought that Shackleton might "have to return . . . without doing much. Then of course it would be your opportunity."[29] The RGS, he assured Scott, would "do nothing whatever that will involve any responsibility for Shackleton's expedition", although, as he put it, "You will admit that we could hardly ignore it . . . altogether . . . At the same time you need not have any doubt that if the two expeditions are to set out on which side the heartiest wishes for success will be."[30]

With smooth ambivalence, Keltie informed Scott that Shackleton "told me he had been planning something of the kind ever since he came back, probably to prove that though he had been sent home, [from the *Discovery*] he is quite as good as those who remained." He went on reassuringly,

> As to Shackleton's capacity as a leader and his staying powers, I think you and I take the same view. He looks strong enough, but it is clear I think that he is not absolutely sound, and Heaven knows what may happen if he starts on his journey Pole-wards.[31]

Shackleton's appeal had centred on working along the one known route to the Pole. Deprived of this by Scott, he fell back on King Edward VII Land instead. That was the mysterious coast which Shackleton had been the first to sight from the deck of *Discovery* five years before. "I have given up a certainty almost," he told Wilson, "for a very uncertain base."[32]

Shackleton's first task was to reconcile his supporters with this setback. That was why he had swallowed his combativeness and compromised so rapidly with Scott. Speed was all. It was worth anything; even a hostage to fortune in the shape of a rashly given promise.

During one of his earlier attempts to organise an expedition Shackleton had asked Albert Armitage, second-in-command of *Discovery*, to join him in the same capacity. Armitage, as he put it, was still gripped by "the restless craving to be on the 'Long lone trail once more' ".[33] He had fleetingly considered an expedition of his own. But settled down now as a P&O captain, he recognised wistfully that his exploring days were over. He did, however, give Shackleton his plans. So highly did Shackleton think of them that now, as he frankly put it, "I have adopted them entirely as my own".[34]

Long before Scott's assumption of prescriptive right, Armitage actually proposed abandoning McMurdo Sound for a base further to the east. His reason was that the south-easterly trend of the mountains promised an easier route to the Pole. Shackleton was therefore able to present the retreat forced upon him as a blessing in disguise, and his supporters accepted the change of base. On 25 March, Beardmore signed the guarantee. That seemed to remove the last obstruction. At last Shackleton could devote himself to the actual business of organising his expedition.

XVII

Seven months to prepare

Shackleton had allowed himself a bare seven months to prepare everything from scratch. He therefore had to be in the centre of things and temporarily abandoned Edinburgh for London. There, he opened an office at 9, Regent Street, overlooking Waterloo Place.

To cope with workaday detail, Shackleton installed a business manager. This was a shadowy member of his circle called Alfred Reid who, with varying success, had done the same work for other expeditions. Shackleton was nonetheless "working from 6 a.m. to very late at night", as he told Elspeth Beardmore:

> I have been hoping for a line from you . . . there are 1000 and 1 things to do and the time seems all too short to do them in.[1]

From Emily, Shackleton had been unable to hide all his fears about his health. She had joined him with the children in London and, for the time being, they were all living in a furnished house in Palace Court, Bayswater. She now finally persuaded him to see a heart specialist.

> I think he examined the specialist instead of the specialist examining him! [in the words of a doctor who knew Shackleton well]. I know the fellow never got a chance of listening to his heart . . . He may have been afraid that he wouldn't be fit to go . . .[2]

Shackleton's first concern was to find his men. He began by harking back to *Discovery*. Besides Wilson, Armitage and Mulock, he asked Barne, Skelton, Hodgson and Ferrar, almost all the old *Discovery* officers and scientists, in fact. For a variety of reasons, they all declined to go. It was, perhaps, just as well. Shackleton was trying to revive the *Discovery* expedition, with himself replacing Scott in the lead. That would have been a doomed attempt. He was now forced to look elsewhere.

To Arthur Schuster, professor of physics at Manchester University, Shackleton wrote asking for help in finding a physicist for the expedition. Shackleton was not the least interested in science, of course; he was a Pole-seeker pure and simple. But he understood the importance of a scientific halo in acquiring respectability and support. The letter to Schuster, however, sets out Shackleton's physical specifications for his followers. "A man between the ages of 27 and 35 would be most suitable," Shackleton explained. He himself was now thirty-three. And, he added, with thought also of himself: "he must be free from any heart troubles – in other respects physique will not be of such vital importance."[3] That aside, Shackleton worked on no very obvious principle, except that he was not looking for polar experience, or even familiarity with ice and snow. He was feeling his way towards leadership, and instinctively avoided anyone whose authority might be a challenge to his own. Besides, in England, polar exploration did not yet exert a universal fascination. To find his followers, he had to depend on his personality. He turned to amateurs and gentleman adventurers, like himself.

By May, he had found most of them. "One is a Baronet!!" he told Elspeth Beardmore, "but he is a really good chap."[4] This was Sir Philip Lee Brocklehurst, of Swythamley Hall in Staffordshire. Sir Philip was a characteristic example of how Shackleton found his men. They met, as Sir Philip told the tale, in the flat of "Shackleton's American girl friend", Miss Havemeyer, whose acquaintance they shared. Even there, Shackleton talked of the expedition that was, some time, to be. That was on one of his visits to London in 1906. Sir Philip was fired by the idea, and immediately offered to join. Sir Philip Brocklehurst was everyone's idea of a sporting baronet. An Old Etonian, he was tall, upstanding, splendid in hunting pink and, when the time came, in an Army officer's uniform. When he met Shackleton, he was at Trinity Hall, Cambridge, which he left without taking his degree, but where he boxed, as a lightweight, and got his Half Blue. That impressed Shackleton: he loved boxing; although he conspicuously avoided putting on the gloves himself. Perhaps he felt he was not fit enough.

Sir Philip also impressed Shackleton by being rich and well connected. Sir Philip, for his part, admired Shackleton because he was "Bohemian", "fond of the ladies", and "extravagant with taxis".[5] He offered to contribute to the expedition funds, or rather, since he was only nineteen, and still a minor, his mother would do so. Shackleton met her, overwhelmed her with his charm, and promised to keep her son in mind. He was as good as his word. Now, in May 1907, he telegraphed Sir Philip confirming his appointment – Shackleton generally preferred telegrams to letters. Sir Philip thereby became the first subscribing volunteer on an Antarctic expedition. "Take up a course of practical surveying," Shackleton then wrote with instructions to turn him into a useful expedition member. "Learn to take your latitudes and longitudes with the theodolite. Learn to take bearings with the compass."[6]

One of Sir Philip's acquaintances was a loquacious but perceptive Scots traveller and author from the Western Highlands called Campbell Mackellar. Unmarried, grey-haired, and the personification of Scottish nationalism, Mackellar was at one time a landowner in Scotland; his present interests were in the Balkans. "Polar explorers," he somewhat surprisingly said, "are my heroes."

> [They] have to possess the very highest qualities in man – physical and moral courage, endurance under terrible privations in terrible climates . . .[7]

Mackellar saw this as redemption for what he called "our decadent Empire". He had actually travelled in the East, and seen the evidence of decline. "An impudent native," he wrote of an incident on Java, "came up to me and said 'All German man now; Englishman no good now.' " How, asked Mackellar, "has this idea so quickly spread?" Partly, he decided, "because *it is true*". Mackellar, having met Shackleton through Brocklehurst, succumbed to his personality, and decided he might be an agent of regeneration. " 'This is the man, and this is the expedition,' I said to myself." Indeed, Shackleton saw himself in the same kind of light. Mackellar became one of his staunchest supporters, if a gushing one.

Like most contemporary polar explorers, Shackleton took care to consult Nansen, for Nansen had attained the status of an oracle, and was still conveniently on his doorstep, in the Norwegian Legation at 36, Victoria Street. Shackleton now perceived that Nansen, as he put it, was "not very keen on his job as Minister, so perhaps he may want to be off to the ice again".[8]

> 'This life has become a wilderness [Nansen even then was writing to Eva, his wife]. I . . . let the years glide by . . . conducting meaningless negotiations on all kinds of meaningless subjects . . . I long only to break these chains.[9]

An austere, self-possessed and enigmatic Titan, the hero of the greatest polar saga of the age, Nansen was inwardly mourning for the embers of desire. "After my return from the Arctic, I will go to the South Pole," he had said fourteen years before, "and then my life's work will be finished."[10] Those were the words that mocked him, as Shackleton, bursting with vitality, eloquence and optimism, appeared before him asking for advice. Shackleton lay directly athwart Nansen's path. It was not so very different from Shackleton's clash with Scott. Nansen, however, was a big man, and a stranger to envy. It was regret that tortured him. But Shackleton did not appear the threat to Nansen that he was to Scott. In Nansen's words, Shackleton was spending "too little time over his preparations"; he was "bound to experience disappointments with things he had never tried properly".[11] Shackleton was expecting to do in weeks what had taken Nansen years. Even Amundsen was contemplating two years at least before *he* felt prepared to sail.

Patient experiment, however, was not in Shackleton's nature. He was, in the words of an acquaintance, "one of the broad gauge individuals". He brushed aside awkward detail to be considered later, in the field. To Nansen, this was incomprehensible and, because it was defying Fate, profoundly shocking. The other side of that coin, which Nansen found hard to fathom, was that someone like Shackleton was only true to himself when improvising, fighting against the odds. He would wither in the face of systematic preparation, and only in a crisis did he come into his own. Shackleton was the inspired amateur in all respects.

When they discussed transport, Nansen was nonplussed. Ski and dogs were by now the proven means of polar travel. Almost twenty years' experience, from Nansen's own first crossing of Greenland, to Amundsen on the North-West Passage, had made the point. Yet here was Shackleton now showing an irrational prejudice against ski. It was no use reminding him that they had saved his life on the southern journey of the *Discovery*, when he was sick and ailing. Moreover, since then skiing had gone through rapid technical development. Bindings had improved. Two sticks, instead of one, had become usual. Better wax was on the market. But ski were associated in Shackleton's mind with weakness, and therefore as something to be spurned. In any case, he had never managed to ski well, and did not wish to expose that frailty to the world. The dedication needed to master skiing, like any other craft, was foreign to his nature. Shackleton proposed *walking* to the Pole and back. In a Norwegian, that would ordinarily be taken as clear evidence of insanity. In Shackleton, however, the aberration could be put down to the proverbial eccentricity of the English.

There was something even more bizarre yet to come. Instead of dogs, Shackleton had decided to take horses.

To Nansen, it was like going back in time. Eleven years before, he had walked along a frozen foreshore on Franz Josef Land with Major Frederick Jackson and, as Jackson put it, "discussed plans for reaching the South Pole. I strongly advised the use of . . . horses".[12] Jackson was the leader of the Jackson-Harmsworth expedition. The talk about horses occurred four days after their legendary meeting at Cape Flora, on 17 June, 1896, when Nansen appeared out of the mists at the end of his saga in the pack ice.

Frederick Jackson was the archetypal hunting, shooting, and fishing man. He was a big game hunter. He was unregenerately horsey. By his own account, his three years on Franz Josef Land had been largely devoted to proving that horses could be used at high latitudes.

Shackleton at first seemed to have drawn from his own experience the logical conclusion in favour of dogs. "We only had twenty-three dogs when we started," he had written about a year after his return from *Discovery*. "I wish we had had about sixty or seventy, for then I think we could have reached the Pole."[13] As Nansen discerned, it was Jackson who had made Shackleton change his mind. In Jackson's words, "Shackleton consulted me in reference to taking ponies on [his] South Polar expedition . . . we had many conversations [about] his preparations."[14] Tall, moustachio'd, garrulous, with gleaming eye, Jackson was just the type to impress "his brother explorer",[15] as Shackleton himself wrote to him, more so than the withdrawn and intellectual Nansen.

Shackleton had been led to Jackson through Armitage. In Franz Josef Land, Armitage had absorbed Jackson's views on horses, and during the *Discovery* expedition, frequently brought them forth. In his own Antarctic plans, Armitage proposed using horses in preference to dogs.

"Some misunderstanding must lie behind the English view of the use of the Eskimo dog in the polar regions," Amundsen once was moved to write. "Could it be that the dog has not understood his master? Or is it the master who has not understood his dog?"[16]

Jackson himself made the point in his own diaries which offered copious and prophetic proof of the horse's drawbacks in the snow. On a glacier, for example, one horse "dropped all four legs into a crevasse . . . We had not proceeded a hundred yards further before she dropped her hind legs into another yawning chasm."[17] Meanwhile, some dogs pulling another sledge had trotted safely over the same snow bridges that collapsed under the horse's hooves. In that climate horses, as Jackson put it, suffered

> from irritation of the bowels. [They] require such a quantity of physic . . . They are always wet, or else their coats are hard-frozen; lumps of ice dangle from them.[18]

The horses died off one by one. The dogs, on the other hand, as even Jackson had plainly proven, were superbly adapted to the conditions. "In spite of the trouble . . . I am thoroughly satisfied with my experiment," he nonetheless wrote. "Horses . . . proved to be an unqualified success."[19]

The horrible incompetence of the dog-handling under Scott gave extra point to Jackson's argument, and Shackleton veered round to the classic escape of blaming the servants for the faults of the masters. He himself was indifferent to animals. Dogs were, of course, more intelligent than horses, and therefore harder to control. Anybody could, somehow, drive a horse. Horses therefore it would be; and the fact that every ounce of fodder would have to be shipped to the Antarctic, let alone the other proven drawbacks of the breed, did not enter his sanguine calculations. Nothing that Nansen could say would make Shackleton change his mind.

Shackleton went down to the City, and ordered twelve Manchurian ponies through the Hong Kong and Shanghai Bank. Nansen might, indeed, have wondered why Shackleton had bothered to consult him at all.

In the third week of April, Shackleton visited Christiania to buy polar equipment. He was just one more in a succession of explorers who had sailed up the fjord on the self-same errand. Norway, after the achievement of the North-West Passage by Amundsen, was all the more the heartland of polar travel. Shackleton, as he told the press, "wanted very much to consult Amundsen". But Amundsen was "travelling about the Country here being fêted", Shackleton wrote to Keltie, "and I expect within a month will suffer from overfeeding".[20]

Despite the predominance of their illustrious compatriot, Norwegian journalists were considerably interested in Shackleton and his preparations. "For the first time in the history of Polar exploration", a Christiania newspaper reported in covering Shackleton's arrival on the mail boat from Hull, he would "take a motor car".[21]

Those were the days of motor pioneering, and the idea was in the air. That Shackleton became the first to put it into practice, was due to William Beardmore. Beardmore had recently taken over the Arrol-Johnston works at Paisley to save it from bankruptcy. Arrol-Johnston was the only Scottish motor manufacturer, and Beardmore wanted Scotland to have a motor industry of its own. From Arrol-Johnston, he now ordered a specially built motor car for Shackleton, and gave it free, partly for advertisement.

> Under favourable circumstances [to quote an interview in *The Car*] Lieutenant Shackleton computes that the machine can travel 150 miles in twenty four hours and . . . he thinks there would be a fair chance of sprinting to the Pole.[22]

Shackleton, as the *Morning Post* reported,

> does not anticipate that . . . his task will be comparable in severity with Prince Borghese's drive from Peking to Paris, because the Antarctic surface will be so incomparably better.[23]

There was something in this. Prince Borghese had rattled and bumped over the rutted mule tracks of China and the sleepers of the Trans-Siberian railway. His drive, the longest motor journey yet made, was an epic proof of what the car could do.

The motor car, however, was still notoriously unreliable. The machine broken down by the roadside, its flustered driver in shirtsleeves and waistcoat bent over the engine, was a stock Edwardian lampoon. Little was known about the behaviour of the petrol engine in extreme cold; nor had anybody yet developed a workable traction system for snow. Arrol-Johnston were hopefully using tracked rear wheels with runners bolted on to the front ones for steering. Shackleton optimistically proposed taking it south without testing it first under working conditions.

One thing at least was clear to anyone familiar with snow. It was unsuited to the wheel. "We predict," in the words of a Norwegian journal, that Shackleton's

> automobile will only prove usable on the fixed ice along the coast and that he will not drive many miles with it into the hinterland before it lies in a crevasse or is stuck in a snowdrift.[24]

This was not the utterance of a romantic diehard. In the snows, there was no room for breakdown or doubt. In the muddy deadwater between one technology and another, it was safer to rely on the perfection of the known until the new was reliable. That, in a sense, was what Shackleton was trying to do when he ordered horses.

Now, in Christiania, there was another attempt to make him change his mind and depend on dogs. Nansen had given him an introduction to Gunnar Isachsen, who had been with Otto

Sverdrup in the Arctic on the second *Fram* expedition. That was the enterprise which perfected the use of dogs and ski in polar travel. Isachsen tried to convey to Shackleton what he had learned. Gruff and severely Nordic, Isachsen was hardly the type to appeal to Shackleton, especially when he suggested that if the dogs were unsatisfactory, "we can safely assume that it is the masters who need training".[25] In any case, Isachsen, like Nansen, was a foreigner.

One of the aspects of the British Empire in decline was a depressing insularity. For half a century Britain had enjoyed what one Foreign Secretary called "Splendid Isolation".[26] That not only meant she was without friends; she was in a self-imposed intellectual quarantine. Most Britons complacently ignored what came from abroad, and Shackleton was no exception. So, although he had been led to Norway in search of equipment, he was impervious to the ideas of his hosts. In any case, he had been faced with an irritating setback. He had originally appointed as his agent D. M. Crichton Somerville, an expatriate Englishman in Christiania, who posed as a polar expert, and had been involved in fitting out *Discovery*. Shackleton arrived to find that Somerville had wasted two precious months, and done nothing. Shackleton had to start everything from scratch himself, and Isachsen stepped in to help.

It was going to be a race to have everything ready in time, for most items had to be specially made. Very little could be bought over the counter. L. H. Hagen, one of the first mass producers of ski, agreed to build the sledges. Shackleton, however, had to telegraph Keltie urgently to send over a surviving specimen of the *Discovery* sledges – also Norwegian made – as a pattern.

At that time, fur was still the only effective armour against cold. Shackleton had hurriedly to order sleeping bags of reindeer fur – perhaps the most efficient natural insulator, weight for weight – and gloves of dog or wolfskin. One firm of furriers specialised in the field: Møllers of Drammen, about two hours on the train from Christiania. There, Shackleton had to rush as soon as he arrived. Møllers usually wanted a year's notice to make sure of proper pelts but they patently warmed to Shackleton's personality and sympathised with his predicament. They promised to have everything finished in a month or two, and delivered in London ready for shipping by the end of July. They even, as Shackleton told Keltie, were "getting special Finsko [*sic*] from the Lapps, of better quality than we have had on the *Discovery*".[27] By this, he meant finnesko made with fur from the leg, the hardest wearing reindeer fur.

Shackleton had also come to view a ship, for Norway remained the prime source of vessels for the ice. He was working through Adrien de Gerlache, commander of the *Belgica* expedition.

Helpful, goatee'd and precise, de Gerlache was a disappointed man. He had been the first man to winter in the Antarctic and had virtually opened modern Antarctic exploration, but he had never received the recognition that was his due. Still commanding *Belgica*, he now hired out himself and his ship for polar expeditions. When Shackleton approached him, he was at Sandefjord, the whaling and sealing port at the mouth of the Christiania fjord, preparing for an Arctic cruise under the Duke of Orleans. From the ships laid up around the fjord, de Gerlache chose for Shackleton one called *Bjørn* ("Bear"). So, from Christiania, Shackleton hurried down to Sandefjord.

Bjørn was a wooden sealer of 500 tons, only three years old, with plenty of cargo space and berths for fifty men. She had powerful engines, and in two Arctic seasons had forced pack ice as dense as that in the Ross Sea.

Having secured his equipment, and found something close to the ideal expedition ship, Shackleton left Christiania at the end of April brimming over with confidence and pleasure.

Back in London, he found that Douglas Steuart was not, after all, going to pay his promised contribution. Instead of the £30,000 on which he had perhaps too blithely counted, Shackleton could now only be sure of Beardmore's £7,000 and, perhaps, Elizabeth Dawson-Lambton's £1,000. *Bjørn* alone cost £11,000. The whole existence of the expedition was suddenly once more in doubt.

It was enough to induce despair. Shackleton, however, now drew on his determination to survive. He gave up *Bjørn* and sought what he could afford. This proved to be a sealer from Newfoundland for £5,000. She was called *Nimrod* "but," Shackleton wrote to Elspeth Beardmore, "I am going to change her name to *Endurance*".[28] This was a reference to his family motto, *Fortitudine Vincimus*; "By endurance we conquer".

Built in Dundee, *Nimrod* was forty-one years old, and a mere 300 tons. Like most sealers, she had both sails and auxiliary steam power, but her top speed was exactly six knots. When she arrived in the Thames in the middle of June, she turned out to be even punier by comparison with *Bjørn* than the figures hinted. Her engines were weak and decrepit. She was a battered tramp, a grim and soiled little hunter of the seas. In the end the name *Nimrod*, perhaps for the allusion, was allowed to stand. Nimrod, in the Book of Genesis, is "the mighty hunter before the Lord"; Shackleton was probably thinking, however, of Milton's interpretation as a "mighty hunter and his prey was man".[29]

Originally, to command his ship, whichever she might be,

Shackleton had asked William Colbeck. Colbeck had captained the *Discovery* relief ship *Morning* on which Shackleton had sailed home from the south. Colbeck, who had also been with Borchgrevink on the *Southern Cross*, was the most experienced Antarctic navigator in England. "I could not wish for anyone better than you," Shackleton had written soon after announcing his expedition,

> You should have a salary of not less than £500 a year and . . . a bonus of £2,000 out of the proceeds of lectures, etc., if the Expedition is successful.

Colbeck, however, had a comfortable berth with the Wilson Line on the Norwegian run across the North Sea. He did not really like Shackleton, and was unmoved by his economic blandishments or his talk of "a number of strong friends"[30] who knew his owners. To command his ship, therefore, Shackleton also had to make do with second choice. On Colbeck's recommendation he took Rupert England, who had been First Mate on *Morning*, and also came from the Wilson Line. Recently, England had been sailing on the west coast of Africa. Coming home, incidentally, he had met Dr William Michell, a Canadian, who became ship's surgeon on *Nimrod*.

Nimrod's Chief Officer, John King Davis, applied for the job, in his own words, "on the spur of the moment" when led by chance to the expedition offices. A serious red-headed Anglo-Irishman, he vividly remembered his first interview with Shackleton who was

> dressed in a blue suit . . . He had thick black hair carefully brushed down and parted in the middle, heavy eyebrows, a piercing glance and a clean-shaven jaw of the variety known as "bulldog". There was about him the unmistakable look of a deep-water sailor.[31]

Behind that look was a very worried man, however. Shackleton had hastened to pay for *Nimrod* while the going was good. He then had just enough money for her vital refit. That included changing her original schooner rig to a barquentine.* The ship at least was safe, but very little more.

Shackleton's brother, having first, by his introduction to high finance, enabled the expedition to be born, was now the threat to its existence. It had been Frank Shackleton's irregular dealings in the Celtic flotation that lay behind Steuart's defection. Yet worse was the snowballing effect of Frank's increasingly shady reputation. To add to his other peccadilloes, he was now on the brink of bankruptcy.

* A three masted vessel, square-rigged on the foremast; fore-and-aft, on main and mizzen.

Ernest Shackleton walked alone. He had no committee to confer respectability on him by association. To keep his creditors at bay, he could count only on himself, on his self-control, and on his overwhelming Anglo-Irish confidence. It was a complicated gamble. He had a reasonable chance of getting *Nimrod* safely away but no more. A brother's bankruptcy would be a calamitous liability. It would threaten Ernest Shackleton's credit, and without credit he, and the expedition, were lost.

Besides all this, "Scott", Shackleton wrote to Elspeth Beardmore, had been "a bother as well".[32] Shackleton imagined that the question of a base had been settled: McMurdo Sound for Scott, King Edward VII Land for himself. But when Scott came back to England in *Albemarle* early in May, he returned to the attack. In several uncomfortable talks Shackleton discovered, with a mixture of annoyance and amusement, that Scott really did seem to believe that the whole Ross Sea belonged to him. Scott still considered him a poacher, and wanted him to go elsewhere.

Scott now displayed an impressive capacity for defensive whining, which in the end, wore down even Shackleton. He managed to make Scott understand that his plans could not be altered any more; but he succumbed to Scott's demand for a formal agreement of demarcation. To that, Wilson now lent his moral backing. Once more Shackleton visited Wilson, and at his dictation, put his signature to a declaration, of which these were the operative clauses:

> I am leaving the McMurdo sound base to you, and will land either at the place known as Barrier Inlet or at King Edward VII Land whichever is the most suitable, if I land at either of these places I will not work to the westward of the 170 meridian W. . .
>
> If I find it impracticable to land at King Edward VII Land or at Barrier Inlet . . . I may possibly . . . try and land to the west of King Wilhelm II Land . . .
>
> I think this outlines my plan, which I shall rigidly adhere to.[33]

It was a promise which Scott had no right, and which no reasonable person would have dared, to demand. In those remote and dangerous regions, it was playing with fate. But to Shackleton, getting rid of Scott was worth paying almost any price. He signed this extraordinary document, as he might have done anything else, to avert yet another threat to his plans.

Meanwhile, less than a month before *Nimrod* was due to sail, the Irish crown jewels were stolen.

XVIII

When *Nimrod* sailed

The theft of the Irish crown jewels was an Edwardian melodrama, in which the chief actors drifted to disaster and death. It even inspired a Sherlock Holmes story: *The Bruce-Partington Plans.*

The jewels were the insignia of the Order of St Patrick, the knighthood of the Anglo-Irish, and a symbol of the Protestant Ascendancy. They were worked in diamonds, rubies and emeralds, and worn on formal occasions by the Lord Lieutenant of Ireland as Grand Master of the Order. Today they would be worth at least £1,000,000. They were kept in a safe at the office of the College of Arms in the tower of Dublin Castle, where Sir Arthur Vicars held court, and Frank Shackleton occasionally appeared. Between 11 June 1907, when they were last seen, and 6 July, when the theft was discovered, the jewels must have disappeared. So much is clear. To this day, the crime has not been solved or the jewels, officially, recovered. The evidence pointed to an inside job; and Frank Shackleton was a prime suspect.

To Ernest Shackleton, a bankrupt brother would have been menace enough; but what would be the effect on his creditors of one indicted for a crime? Ernest Shackleton was, at this point, in a state of financial desperation. *Nimrod* needed a refit from maintruck to keel. Luckily Green's, at Blackwall, down the Thames, was still in business. This was one of the last of the old wooden ship repair yards, used to the swift rehabilitation of floating wrecks that was a feature of the age of sail. The refit, however, cost far more than Shackleton had bargained for. Credit was not to be considered, and Beardmore's £7,000 would not stretch.

Shackleton had to raise another £8,000, quickly. On 15 July, he asked the Earl of Iveagh to guarantee a loan at Lloyds Bank. They were not acquainted; but the earl, Edward Guinness of the great Dublin brewing family, was a known philanthropist. He was then, fortunately, at his London house in Grosvenor Place.

"Your fitness," wrote Sir Clements Markham, in one of the testimonials that Shackleton hastily drummed up, "may be assumed from your previous service in the Antarctic . . . when you yourself proved to be sound, thorough and reliable. You were enthusiastic but with judgment," he continued, "additional aid . . . would be well bestowed."[1]

After two days, the Earl of Iveagh agreed to help. The fact that he was a Knight of St Patrick, and thus peripherally involved in the crown jewels affair, may have had something to do with the case. Perhaps, as a fellow Anglo-Irishman, he also appreciated Shackleton's engaging cheek. The fact that he too was a Freemason, like Shackleton, and therefore obliged to help a brother-Mason, may have tipped the scales. In any case, what the Earl actually did was to promise to guarantee £2,000 provided Shackleton found others to bring the amount up to £8,000. Within ten days, Shackleton had, somehow, contrived to do so. The other guarantors were the Duke of Westminster, Sir Rupert Clarke, Bart (a rich Australian), and Lady Brocklehurst; and in this, Lady Brocklehurst was undoubtedly the key.

Under his astonishingly confident surface, the strain was nevertheless telling on Shackleton. He poured out his feelings to Elspeth Beardmore. "I almost imagined you had forgotten all about me", he wrote on receiving a long-awaited letter,

> but I now know you have not . . . I know you can sympathise with my longing to be out at my own work and now it all lies before me and it is my one great chance you will understand all it means to me and I will always be thinking of you and wondering how you are getting on and will remember all the times we talked over the future which even now is in the knees of the Gods . . .[2]

Marriage, alas, had shown Shackleton how sadly little he and Emily had in common. Emily gave patience, tolerance, loyalty, devotion; everything, in fact, but sympathetic understanding of his aspirations. For that, Shackleton had to go elsewhere. At home, he was safe, but lonely; outside, where he found companionship, he was damned by insecurity. It was his fate, perhaps, to be divided against himself.

Against all this, the practical preparations for the south seemed somehow to pale. Hagen sent the sledges; Møllers, the furs, in reasonably good time. Away from the technicalities of snow travel,

Shackleton was sensible and innovative. The Discovery hut, built up board by board, had been appallingly cumbrous to erect. Shackleton, following Nordenskjöld in Graham Land, had his hut built instead in prefabricated sections for simplified assembly. In diet, too, Shackleton tried to avoid repeating mistakes. Pemmican remained the staple. Biscuits, however, he had specially made with wholemeal flour and Plasmon.

At all costs Shackleton was determined to get *Nimrod* away by the first week of August, as he originally had planned. This was not only because she was a slow sailer and had to get to the ice in time, but also because the funds that he had raised were nowhere near enough to settle all his bills. That meant his credit had to stretch until territorial waters were left astern. Creditors were, unfortunately, growing restless. As sailing day approached, the rustle of writs was in the air.

Desperate straits require desperate measures. For months, Shackleton had been vainly hoping for royal patronage. Finally, on 25 July, he wrote to Lord Knollys, the King's Secretary, with a direct and blunt request. "I have asked the Marquis of Graham, who knows me well, and who knows all about the Expedition, to write to you as well," Shackleton explained, "also Colonel Brocklehurst,* the Queen's Equerry, who is cousin of Sir Philip Brocklehurst, Bart., one of our staff . . . I would not have left this until so late a date," Shackleton concluded, "only my finances of the Expedition were not entirely assured until quite lately."[3] That was an understatement, to say the least. It was not until that very day that Shackleton had finally got all his guarantors together, and pledged himself "to make no profit, by lectures or Book, on the return of the . . . Expedition until the Guarantee . . . which Lord Iveagh has signed, is released."[4]

On the morning of 29 July, a Tuesday, General Sir Dighton Probyn, Keeper of the Privy Purse, privately saw Alfred Reid, the expedition secretary, at Buckingham Palace. By special messenger, Sir Dighton then sent Shackleton a letter to say that the King could not grant the expedition his patronage.

> Should, however, your Ship "Nimrod" be at Cowes when The King and Queen are there next week [Sir Dighton explained], I am authorised to inform you that Their Majesties hope to be able to inspect the Vessel.[5]

Next day, *Nimrod* left her berth in the East India Docks to begin her voyage. In the Thames Estuary – having no wireless – she was

*Colonel John Fielding Brocklehurst, later Major-General Lord Ranksborough. He had been with Gordon in the Sudan.

overtaken by a naval torpedo boat with a message now *commanding* her to Cowes to be inspected by the King on Sunday.

The King's hesitation had been due to Shackleton's financial uncertainty, but the theft of the Irish crown jewels had radically altered the case. If Ernest Shackleton's insolvency was aired, Frank's affairs would almost certainly be dragged into the open as well. That was distinctly undesirable, for Frank was now involved in circles uncomfortably close to the throne. Royal recognition of Ernest would keep his creditors at bay, blanket both brothers, and avert potentially discomfiting disclosures. In any case, King Edward almost certainly knew more about the expedition than he cared openly to admit. He recognised in Shackleton someone who might just conceivably turn out to be an ornament of his reign. In the background, too, lurked the Masonic connection. All things considered, giving *Nimrod* a royal send-off seemed a sensible proceeding.

On the way to Cowes, Shackleton insisted on putting in at Eastbourne to let Elizabeth Dawson-Lambton come on board. A Victorian figure in bonnet and the lace she put on only to meet Shackleton, she inspected *Nimrod* before the King did. It was a gesture of gratitude to the mother, in a sense, of the expedition; and one which Edward VII would undoubtedly have approved.

On Sunday afternoon, the King boarded *Nimrod* in Cowes roads. Like *Discovery*'s farewell, six years before, it was Cowes Week; this time, however, it was not subdued by Queen Victoria's death, but flaunted its full Edwardian splendour as the culmination of the London season. It was a spectacle to sum up the age. Like huge butterflies on the water sailed the long vanished fleet of big yachts: opulent craft with gaff rigs, vast spreads of canvas, and crews of thirty men or more. By day, it was a regatta; by night, ashore and afloat, to the haunting melodies of Strauss, there were extravagant dinner parties and balls. Over it all, presided the genial, rakish figure of the King; determined to enjoy himself while he could, and expecting everyone else to do so too.

Nimrod was taking part in a naval occasion, which *Discovery* had been denied. In sinister grey, barbed with guns, two hundred warships lined the pale waters of the Solent. It was the first review of the new Home Fleet, the most powerful naval force in the world. Like a dwarf beside Leviathan, *Nimrod* was given the berth of honour next to HMS *Dreadnought*, the flagship of this colossal assembly, the most powerful man o'war in existence, the first modern battleship. For Ernest Shackleton, the King could hardly do more.

"War in the old days made *men*," Shackleton began his introduction to *Nimrod*'s shipboard magazine, *The Antarctic Petrel.*

> We have not these same stirring times to live in and must look for other outlets for our energy and for the restless spirit that fame alone can satisfy.

That was, in Shackleton's words, his answer "to a question which has been put to me on several occasions viz. Why seek the Pole?"[6]

With the King, as he was piped aboard *Nimrod* on 4 August under a cloudless summer sky, was a swarthy, taciturn figure with no apparent interest in the polar regions. This was the legendary Admiral Sir John ("Jackie") Fisher, First Sea Lord, architect of the naval might on display. On *Discovery*, as Shackleton could hardly fail to recall, Scott had had to make do with a naval equerry. Besides the King and Queen Alexandra, and Admiral Fisher, there were the Prince of Wales (later George V), Prince Edward (later the Duke of Windsor), the Duke of Connaught, and Princess Victoria. In most ways, Shackleton had gone one better than Scott. "The Queen," as Shackleton told Elspeth Beardmore, "gave me a flag. This is the 1st time that it has been done."[7]

Just before going over the side, the King extracted a medal from his back pocket, and pinned it on to Shackleton's jacket, saying

> When Captain Scott left in the Discovery I conferred the Royal Victorian Order on him. I now do the same to you . . .[8]

"And that", as Shackleton put it, was "the final touch to the social side of the show".[9]

There was one disappointment. In their original agreement Shackleton had made *Nimrod* over to William Beardmore so that in his words, "you . . . will place her . . . in the Royal Yacht Squadron as a yacht of yours as since 1842 no Antarctic exploring vessel has flown the White Ensign."[10] That was another way of going one better than Scott for, outside the Navy, flying the White Ensign was the exclusive privilege of the Royal Yacht Squadron.

Shackleton was not merely demanding a favour. The Royal Yacht Squadron was a citadel of social exclusiveness. Mere industrialists were unwelcome. Shackleton offered to help Beardmore get in. This was not as fanciful as it first appeared. Shackleton had developed his talent for making acquaintances in high places; also he was showing a gift for advancing other people's affairs. Amidst all his difficulties, he was "keeping well in touch" with the secretary of the Royal Yacht Squadron, he told Elspeth Beardmore in May. Also he was lobbying Lord Leith and Sir Allan Young (an old Arctic explorer) to support her husband's entry. Despite all Shackleton's efforts, however, William Beardmore was only elected a membe. or. 5 August, the day after *Nimrod*'s inspection by the King. That morning, as she sailed out into the Channel she had to make do, like *Discovery*, with the Blue Ensign.

Nimrod touched first at Torquay, where Emily and the children were waiting, for they had not been at Cowes. Frank Shackleton was also at Torquay, where he now had a house, The Knoll, and where he was now trying to rest from the furore of the Irish crown jewels. Together they all visited *Nimrod* anchored in the bay. At the Torbay Hotel, that evening, Shackleton gave a dinner for the captain and the crew. "Everyone," John King Davis recalled in after years, "felt proud, excited, and full of hope."[11] Next day, 7 August, *Nimrod* weighed anchor and at last sailed away from England for the south. The Mayor of Torquay came down to say goodbye. "Fine send off," to quote *The Antarctic Petrel*, "Good bye to our Commander whose last words were 'Play the game.'"[12]

Nimrod at least had got away; but despite royal recognition, the whole enterprise could founder yet. Money remained a desperate, dismal, intractable problem. To try and resolve his predicament, Shackleton stayed behind, and arranged to follow on by mailboat. "Things have been very bad for me," he wrote to Elspeth Beardmore:

> and many have been my troubles apart from the work of the Expedition which has kept me going night and day to say nothing of my having been laid up and bowled over by overstrain with all the anxiety of the Expedition which I have run so far by myself.[13]

At the last moment William Bell, the cousin of Shackleton's who had proposed him for the RGS, providentially gave him £4,000. That brought the total fund up to £20,000. It was still not enough. Douglas Steuart could save the situation, and Shackleton tried him once again. But Celtic shares remained illusory, and therefore Steuart's promised contribution. So, as *Nimrod* crawled down the Atlantic to New Zealand round the Cape, Shackleton had to trudge round again with the begging bowl. Campbell Mackellar now provided financial, besides verbal aid.

Shackleton decided he should get out while the going was good. "In the wildest last," he wrote to Elspeth Beardmore on 3 September, "I send you a line."

> I will not see you to say goodbye, but you will have a long letter en route.[14]

Shackleton was then down at The Knoll, snatching in peace and quiet the last few days together with Emily and the children, as he thought. "Ernest has got to go," as she put it, "and so the only thing to do is to make it as easy for him as possible."[15]

Then a message of distress arrived from Frank. He had been called to Scotland Yard and told, as he put it, that he "might be arrested on suspicion" of having stolen the Irish crown jewels. "I expected to be arrested next day."[16] Ernest had to put off his departure. He could not leave his brother in the lurch. In the event, Frank was *not* arrested. At this calamitous juncture for his brother, however, Frank was faced by dishonoured bills. The details were unsavoury, but Ernest, from family feeling and self-interest, was obliged to help. He borrowed another £1,000 from William Beardmore, and redeemed the bills. Frank, as Ernest hopefully wrote to Elspeth Beardmore, was now

> out of his troubles and will pay me back all the money he owes me which is well over 4 figures; he . . . is really trying to live quietly and is not doing anything on the Stock Exchange. I wonder [he added in an inconsequential aside] where Niels Grøn is I hear nothing of Potentia at all now.[17]

But what Shackleton did not know was that to put back Elizabeth Dawson-Lambton's £1,000 into the expedition funds, Frank had carried out a fraudulent transaction with Celtic shares.

Shackleton had promised to pay Beardmore back his £1,000 within three weeks. "Often I have sat down to write," he said after a month in a letter to Elspeth Beardmore,

> yet felt somehow I couldnt as it has always stuck in my mind that you cannot think much of me whilst I had not paid back to Will all the money he so generously lent me.[18]

Shackleton finally left, on the last day of October, without repaying the loan. His departure, despite royal recognition was, like that of *Nimrod*, relatively obscure. Very few went down to see him off at Charing Cross. He travelled by the overland route; across the Channel, by special train from Calais to Marseilles, there to catch the waiting P & O liner – in his case RMS *India* – through Suez. It gave him a few extra days at home.

"I shall not be really happy," Shackleton wrote in farewell to Elspeth Beardmore, "until I see the last of the ship and we are out on our own on the ice."

I . . . will not be back for 2 years and then I hope to have got the Pole safe for this country . . . I wish I could see you and have a long talk . . . it is so hard to write it all and explain all things.[19]

From Marseilles, just before embarking, Shackleton telegraphed "Good bye" to Elspeth, but the image haunting him was that of Emily, who had come as far as Dover to say farewell:

I can see you just as you stand on the wharf and are smiling at me [Shackleton wrote along the way]. My heart was too full to speak . . . If I failed to get to the Pole and was within 10 miles and had to turn back it would or will not mean so much sadness as was compressed into those few minutes.[20]

Although he might not perhaps have put it exactly that way, Shackleton was suffering last-minute twinges of conscience. He had left Emily to fend for herself. She did, however, have her £700 a year, and her brother, Herbert, to look after her while her husband was away. Shackleton, perhaps, had been counting on that. The eye, in one Irishman's expressive phrase, was watching what the heart was doing. By now, in any case, Herbert was Shackleton's, and also the expedition's, solicitor.

"I wish I was back in windy Edinburgh with you," Shackleton wrote to Emily. That was the constant theme in the letters he poured out during the long voyage.

It gives me a lump in my throat when I think of my family and I see the mothers on board ship with their children, and I am going so far away from all I love.

At home, as Shackleton well knew, he fretted under domesticity, impatient with his children and his wife. It was only in parting, somehow, that his feelings seemed to flower. Yearning for what was out of reach seemed to the Irishman in him a necessary state of mind.

"The work is a great one and we are going to win through," he told Emily. "When I come back," he added, in words already familiar to her from *Discovery*, "I promise you darling Heart that never will I go away on this sort of thing again."[21]

The expedition, as Shackleton put it, with characteristic baldness,

owes nothing to the world at large and yet it may help the honour of the country: if successful there will be ample money . . . for us to live our lives as we wish.[22]

But he also promised Emily,

> I shall not run any risk, for the sake of trying to get the "Pole" in the face of hard odds.

This was a world away from the witless valour that was the Edwardian gentlemanly ideal, as it was from any unconscious seeking for martyrdom. Shackleton had learned his lesson from *Discovery*. It was not an Englishman speaking, but an Anglo-Irish survivalist:

> I have not only myself but you and the children to consider . . . if inclined to do anything rash I will think of my promise to you and not do it . . . I promise you darling that I will come back to you safe and well if God wishes it and also that I will not be sharp and hasty with the men.[23]

"We intend to do our best but not to do anything foolhardy at all," Shackleton repeated along the way, "for life is short enough and I do not think it is worth it."[24] The Anglo-Irish paradox within him was vividly illustrated by the fact that, while one part of him was professing this superbly rational credo, another was clutching at a scheme in which sanity was sorely stretched.

For Shackleton was proposing not only to reach the South Pole, but to cross the Antarctic continent as well. He had actually ordered a light portable boat – named *Raymond*, after the son he had left behind – which he intended dragging 2,000 miles to the other side. There, he would cross the Weddell Sea to a rendezvous with *Nimrod*. That in between lay uncharted waters and the unknown centre of a continent were unconsidered trifles. The Pole had dissolved into a milestone along the way. At the misty centre of Shackleton's dream lay an epic voyage in an open boat.

XIX

A broken promise

"We cannot cross the sea on the other side," Shackleton was writing to Emily on the first day of 1908, "as the boat *Raymond* never was sent out through some rotten mistake":

> Still darling you can be relieved on that point for it was a very uncertain proposition at the best. The more I think of it, the more I see that we ought to come back from the Pole, the conquest of the Pole ought to be enough for us to do and there will in this be money enough.[1]

This was Shackleton's farewell, written from New Zealand as he left for the south, jerked back to reality perhaps by the act of leaving civilisation behind, but pursued by dreams of fortune, like Nemesis, to the last.

Shackleton had landed in Australia a month before to find that an extra £4,500 promised by his cousin William Bell would not, after all, be forthcoming. American bank failures (said Bell) were the cause. Shackleton had counted on that money to pay the wages of *Nimrod*'s crew, and to refit her for his relief. There was no question of any more money from home. It was the old familiar predicament – but not quite. In Australia, Shackleton had come into his own.

"Indifference and the struggle to try and do something of which every one did not approve," he said at one of the receptions to which he was hauled, "has been our experience in England."

> You [he went on] have the enthusiasm for the glory of the Empire which keeps you from the condition of the people in the old lands, who are smoothing down into a state from which I hope the expedition will shake them.[2]

All this, as Shackleton well knew, was precisely what Australians wanted to hear. He did not, however, have to depend wholly on his rhetoric and personality.

At Sydney University there was a Welsh-born professor of geology called Edgeworth David. Shackleton's expedition struck David as an opportunity to spend a different kind of long vacation by visiting the Antarctic. Ostensibly, his aim was professional improvement by observation of an Ice Age in being. He wrote asking to make the round trip in *Nimrod*. Shackleton agreed. David heard the news just as he was starting on a field trip to Mount Kociusko in September. He seized the opportunity to begin learning how to ski and how to build igloos.

David was then almost fifty years old. Short, frail, with high cheekbones, a crinkled face, and the suspicion of a squint from peering into a microscope, he was infinitely professorial. When he and Shackleton met, in December, Shackleton, in his own words, found that he could "charm a bird off a bough".[3] Shackleton seemed to have met his match. Each prepared shamelessly to use the other.

David inspired an old pupil, Douglas Mawson, to follow in his footsteps. Mawson was now a lecturer at Adelaide University. When Shackleton touched at Adelaide on his way out from England, Mawson managed to talk to him, and to ask if he too could join the expedition. What then happened was vintage Shackleton. A few days later, Mawson received a telegram from Shackleton in Sydney, appointing him physicist "for the duration of the expedition".[4] Mawson had only asked for the round trip on *Nimrod*. He was a geologist, not a physicist. "After a few days consideration",[5] as he put it, he nonetheless decided to accept.

Leo Cotton, yet another geologist, was to sail out and home in *Nimrod*. Bertram Armytage, from Melbourne, who had been at Jesus College, Cambridge, and fought in the Boer War, was accepted for the shore party. Their presence on the expedition – as Shackleton no doubt had calculated – meant an Australian interest.

Emergent colony as she was, Australia was both emotionally tied to the mother country, and nervously in search of a national identity. Antarctic exploration was one means to that end. Twenty years before, the Geographical Society of Melbourne had actually asked Baron A. E. Nordenskiöld, the illustrious Swedish explorer (and uncle of Otto Nordenskjöld) who had first conquered the North East Passage to lead an Australian expedition to the south. Nothing came of it, but Shackleton offered another opportunity along that road.

That, at any rate, was what David was able to exploit when

he decided to help Shackleton out of his financial straits, and save the expedition. David – the Professor, or the Prof., as he was universally called – was no cloistered academic. He was a public figure of immense prestige, to whom many a legend clung. He was famous for an elaborate and sometimes cunning courtesy. Also, a factor Shackleton certainly had not ignored in taking him, he had powerful political friends. David swiftly persuaded the Australian Prime Minister, Alfred Deakin, to make up for William Bell's abortive contribution with a government grant of £5,000. "There is," David told a member of the Cabinet, "a very fair chance of the South Pole being actually reached . . . and Lieut. Shackleton seems to me to be just an ideal leader for . . . this work."[6]

In the middle of December, Shackleton hurried on to rejoin *Nimrod* in New Zealand. "It will only be a short while before I am out again to see you,"[7] he had written to Joseph Kinsey when last he was there, on his way home from *Discovery*. Five years had passed since then.

Kinsey, bearded, philanthropic, cultivated, English born and rich, was a Christchurch shipper. He had helped the *Discovery* expedition, and Shackleton had then made friends with him. Now, upon a cable, he had agreed to be Shackleton's agent in New Zealand. He went beyond that, and took Shackleton under his wing. So did New Zealanders at large. Like the Australians, they warmed to his disarming lack of humbug. The government greeted him with a grant of £1,000, which Shackleton proceeded to spend.

The grant offended Alfred Deakin. He believed that the Australian grant of £5,000 was to "meet all your necessities",[8] as he cabled Shackleton. With the New Zealand money, Shackleton cabled back, he had

> altered ship accommodation increased clothing food . . . to enlarge work of expedition shifted navigation bridge for better navigation in ice renewed parts of main engine cost of this work is additional to that of satisfying urgent needs for which five thousand asked.[9]

"Trust that total contribution from Australia will not be less than five thousand,"[10] David cabled in his turn to Deakin; and it was not.

At Lyttelton, meanwhile, *Nimrod* was berthed, and the various strands of the expedition were brought together. Out on Quail Island, the quarantine station, the Manchurian ponies were being broken in. After a three week passage from Tientsin, by way of Hong Kong, they reached Sydney one morning, and the ship taking them to New Zealand sailed the same afternoon. The local agent felt he could "hardly expect such good luck . . . as . . . Shackleton's again".[11]

Until the last moment Shackleton, to use one of his favourite phrases, was rushing "day and night". He had the gift, however, of not communicating a sense of panic. Without apparent fuss the Blue Peter flew, as planned, on New Year's Day. By then, *Nimrod* was impressively overloaded. Her Plimsoll line was nearly two feet under water; her freeboard, a bare 3ft 6ins. Her decks were crammed with cargo, including the ponies, and the motor car in a crate. Stow as he could, however, not even Shackleton could quite cram a quart into this pint pot. *Nimrod* was just too small. Five ponies and a variety of stores had to be left behind. Well might Shackleton rue the lack of a few thousand pounds that deprived him of *Bjørn*; now, as it happened, laid up for the winter in Norway.

"Oh Child I do want so much to have you with me now," Shackleton wrote to Emily in his last letter home. "My heart is just all going out to you and wanting you so much," but, he continued with his strain of contradiction, "In a few hours we will be off . . . and there will be some rest and peace."[12] Nothing could destroy the sensation, as *Nimrod* drew away, of leaving behind the mortal coil of life ashore. Shackleton was still the true sailor; at ease only when the gangplank was up, and the quayside had started to recede.

The farewell was a colonial version of that at Cowes; with the white sails of a regatta, warships anchored in the roads, a tug coming out with a cable from the King. There was this difference. *Nimrod* was the centre of the stage. A crowd had gathered to say goodbye; exactly as they had done for *Discovery* and Scott. But now they were cheering for Ernest Shackleton. Thirty thousand people had gathered round the wharf, more than on that previous occasion and, as Shackleton could hardly fail to observe, rather more enthusiastic. To the strains of brass bands playing *Auld Lang Syne*, and the thunder of salutes echoing along the mountains framing the shore, *Nimrod* sailed up to the Heads and started for the south. The same "passion for adventure" that was driving Shackleton, a local newspaper was inspired by the scene to write,

> was at the bottom of the rise of the British Empire . . it was won . . . by men who could not endure the little life of a small island

remembering, nonetheless, to add a virtuous caveat. "The voyagers of the *Nimrod* take their mission seriously," the leader writer said, "their undertaking is not to be justified by a mere enjoyment of strange sensations in a strange land."[13]

It was the culmination of an astonishing year. Ten months

before, the expedition was little more than a hope; now Shackleton was heading for his goal – pursued, to the last, by dreams of opulence. "I have a splendid friend here Mr. G. Buckley," he had written to Emily, "he has given me £500 and if I get the Pole will give me £1,000 more."[14]

George McLean Buckley was a wealthy farmer, whose vision extended beyond his fields. Nearly six feet three inches tall, he was handsome, easy-going, in the process of running through a fortune, and a devoted yachtsman. He was in fact aboard *Nimrod* as she departed. He had come down to see her off and, on the spur of the moment, decided to sail as far as the ice. Now he was southward bound in the clothes he stood up in – a natty summer suit.

Shackleton had firmly imposed the sailor's superstition that taking money to an unknown country meant bad luck. He insisted on everyone turning out their pockets and handing over all coins to Alfred Reid to take ashore. The only money officially on board was a silver threepenny piece nailed by a lady to the mast. Other talismans were a horseshoe and a sprig of heather, both given to the ship by Campbell Mackellar.

With the other part of him, Shackleton was quite down to earth. He had told Emily, for example, not to let Reid know that expedition funds were to be used for her upkeep. Herbert Dorman, moreover, was "not to suggest that I may make money out of this for I cannot tell what we will do till the job is really done".[15] But underneath it all, he was still the frustrated poet and lovelorn boy:

> I could make a wondrous story
> Of thy beauty and witching grace,

as he put it in verse to Emily on the way out from England,

> My hand in writing falters
> My eyes grow dim with tears
> For long long days are before us
> To be filled with hopes and fears . . .[16]

"Sweetheart" he wrote (in prose) in farewell from New Zealand,

> though I may be disappointed I will come back to the loving arms and soft embraces of you my wife and in the joy of seeing you . . . and our children all will be forgotten.[17]

"Oh that such beaming smiles should so soon fade away,"[18] wrote *Nimrod*'s Second Officer, Arthur Harbord, in his diary, as she cleared Lyttelton Heads. All ships have their own style of riding to a seaway: some swoop; others heave. This one, as Harbord had ample opportunity to ascertain, shuddered and lurched. The great consolation was that an uncomfortable ship, on the whole, is a safe ship. Things were complicated by the fact that *Nimrod* was under tow.

To make her passage, *Nimrod* needed her engines and, ten days before sailing, it had dawned on Shackleton that he could not take enough coal without endangering his ship. Partly this was due to sheer lack of bunker space. Also, coal was needed as ballast for the return, because there was no ballast to be found in the Antarctic. It was an oversight caused by Shackleton's inexperience of command, and the only solution was to have *Nimrod* towed to the ice. Shackleton appealed to the New Zealand government, and they offered to pay half the cost. The Union Steamship Company of New Zealand supplied the ship, and waived the remainder of the expenses. Such was the sympathy that Shackleton had managed to excite.

The towing vessel was a tramp steamer of 1,200 tons, the *Koonya*. One of the company's senior captains, Frederick Pryce Evans, was put in command, with instructions that the tow "was to be performed as completely as possible and nothing short of demonstration of its impracticability was to excuse failure".[19]

From the moment that *Nimrod* nosed into the open sea, a gale seized her in its grip. For ten days, veering and backing all over the westerly quarter, the wind roared and shrieked and tore at the overloaded hull. As Harbord wrote,

> I have never seen such large seas in the whole of my seagoing career, one moment we can see the keel of "Koonya" and the next we cannot see the truck . . .

"Everything upside down," he continued on the third day out, "occasionally men."

> Some of us are over the seasick stage and we no longer want to die . . . The "Koonya" kindly enquired how our passengers were feeling and drew our attention to the simple life of a sailor.[20]

These were the circumstances under which the whole landing party was gathered for the first time. They were living in part of the after hold converted at Lyttelton into sleeping quarters of a kind. Fourteen human beings were crammed into an unventilated space which, as one of them said, was "not fit for 10 dogs".[21] Yawing, lurching, flung about and drenched, they made each other's unvarnished acquaintance. *Nimrod* was one of the smallest ships to go south for over sixty years.

The core of the landing party was a group that had sailed out from England all, for economy, in a single cabin on a one-class emigrant ship called the *Runic*. Their nominal leader was Jameson Boyd Adams, of whom a cabin mate said that "we didn't like him very much but he clearly had his points – some of them, indeed, were very sharp".[22] Tall, rough-spoken, and very much the sea-dog, Adams began life like Shackleton. Originally intended for the Navy, Adams failed to gain entry. In 1893 at the age of thirteen, he joined the merchant service instead and ever since had been at sea. By 1902, he had his Master's ticket; but he was still the frustrated naval officer. As second best, he had joined the Royal Naval Reserve and, in 1906, a newly fledged RNR lieutenant, he was in HMS *Berwick* when she anchored in the Firth of Forth exactly opposite the cottage at Queensferry the Shackletons had taken for the summer. A message had promptly arrived on board from Shackleton, inviting the wardroom officers to tea. Adams was among those drafted to accept. In his own words,

> we . . . called on Shackleton and . . . stayed . . . until ten o'clock at night, talking about his expeditions and his ambitions . . . and as we were going over the side, I said to Shackleton "If you go again will you take me with you?"[23]

It was the first time they had met.

A year later Adams was at Portsmouth, still a RNR lieutenant on HMS *Berwick*, when suddenly his captain announced that he was to be given a regular commission. To get that, without going through Dartmouth, was like passing through the eye of the proverbial needle. Adams' career was made; his ambition achieved. In his own words, he

> went down to the wardroom to celebrate . . . I hadn't been [there] for two minutes when a signal came down . . . from Shackleton. "Will you come as my second in command".

It was the first sign of life from Shackleton since their meeting the year before.

> I went up to the bridge, and said to my Captain "Sir, I've changed my mind already: this is my offer and I'm going to take it. The Navy can go by." Quite dramatic.[24]

That, at least, was how Adams liked to tell the tale.

A total contrast to Adams was Raymond Priestley, a shy young cricket-playing innocent from Tewkesbury in Gloucestershire. A few months before boarding *Runic*, he was finishing his second year at University College, Bristol. "That fateful morning," as he liked to tell *his* tale, he was in the library, while a distinctly reluctant candidate was being interviewed on behalf of Shackleton for the post of geologist. Priestley's brother Bert, a botany lecturer, happened to walk into the room, whereupon the interviewer said,

> "What about your younger brother . . . He's a geologist isn't he?" Bert said he would ask me and as he passed through the library . . . he saw me there. "How would you like to go to the Antarctic?" he said . . . "I'd go anywhere to get out of this place," I said. It was as casual as that.[25]

Soon after, Priestley was summoned by Shackleton to his office in London for inspection. As he recalled in later years,

> I remember very little about the interview, except that . . . Shackleton asked me "Would you know gold if you saw it?" I made no bones about that.[26]

A few weeks later Priestley received a telegram from Shackleton asking why he was not in London collecting his equipment. That was how he learned of his acceptance.

Yet another type was Eric Marshall, the chief surgeon. In Priestley's words, he had "the build and arrogance of the class rugger forward".[27] That is precisely what he was. Newly qualified from Emmanuel College, Cambridge, and St Bartholomew's Hospital, Marshall had rowed for the one and played in the scrum for the other. Born in Hampstead, the son of a solicitor, and the product of a minor public school, he originally intended to take Orders. He met Shackleton, by chance, at a house party in 1906. Shackleton poured out his usual cascade of talk from the half-world of his hopes and plans. Marshall impulsively offered to join him when the time came.

Ernest Joyce, a strange mixture of fraud, flamboyance, and ability, had little in common with Marshall, Adams or Priestley except that chance also had brought him to the expedition. He was on the top of a bus passing the expedition offices in Regent Street one day when Shackleton happened to be looking out of the window. The top decks of London buses were then open to the skies and Shackleton – so the story goes – recognised Joyce, a naval petty officer on *Discovery*. He sent someone out to fetch him, and engaged him on the spot. Chance, in varying degrees, also gathered in George Marston, the expedition's artist, who had "the frame and face of a prizefighter", as Priestley put it, "and the disposition of a fallen angel";[28] Bernard Day, the motor mechanic, "cynic and philosopher", and Roberts, the cook.

Such, more or less, was the *Runic* party. On the long voyage out from England, they discovered the deepest cleavages among themselves, and laid down lifelong rivalries and friendships. Also, in Priestley's words, they ended up in "Oyster Alley", as they mysteriously dubbed their allotted place in *Nimrod*, "with esprit-de-corps laid on with a trowel".[29] Sir Philip Brocklehurst escaped this formative experience. Paying his own way he had very sensibly come out on his own, first class, reserving the foetid discomfort of *Nimrod* for the last lap from New Zealand. Adding clique to clique, at Lyttelton, David, Mawson and Armytage, the Australians were decanted into "Oyster Alley". There, they joined James Murray, the expedition biologist, and Alistair Forbes Mackay, the second surgeon. Murray and Mackay were both Scots. Murray, dark, bearded, squat and irrepressible, came from Glasgow. Mackay, on the other hand, broad, muscular and strangely lopsided in appearance, was a Highlander with an erratic streak. The son of an Army officer he had served in the Boer War, and briefly been a naval surgeon. Reputedly, he had once been kicked in the head by a horse. Both he and Murray were inveterate wanderers.

Finally, in "Oyster Alley" was another wanderer, Frank Wild. He was the one man whom Shackleton deliberately sought out. Wild was a Yorkshireman, quiet, modest, wiry, and intermittently pugnacious. They had met on *Discovery* when Wild, although lower deck, was the friend, after Wilson, that Shackleton had chosen to make. Wild belonged to a new breed of naval rating. Higher pay and long service engagements had started to bring into the Navy at the turn of the century a better class of man, more educated and ambitious than before. Many, like Wild, were merchant seamen, tired of looking for a new ship after every voyage, and attracted by the security of naval service. Yet that did not exactly describe Wild, for he very soon grew discontented with naval routine, and he volunteered for *Discovery* within two years of joining the Navy.

In the background there lurked some flaw that haunted Wild. Perhaps Shackleton saw there a mirror of himself. The son of a schoolmaster, Wild had a better education than most naval ratings. Before entering the Navy, he had tried to get his mate's certificate, but something stopped him; probably drink. Through the winter on *Discovery*, Shackleton helped him in an ambition to make up for lost time by teaching him navigation; and as soon as he knew he was going south again, he asked Wild to come. Wild jumped at the chance.

In Lyttelton, at the last moment, Shackleton had added one more to the landing party. This was Æneas Mackintosh, who had started out as *Nimrod*'s Second Mate. Mackintosh had been lent by the P & O Line; he was competent but uninspiring. It was hard to understand what Shackleton saw in him, unless it was similarity of background. Mackintosh was apparently related to the then head of the clan, and therefore belonged, in a way, to the gentry. He too had been to a minor public school – in this case Bedford School – and, self-willed, had gone to sea.

Such were the men with whom Shackleton proposed to be marooned on the frontiers of survival. They were a peculiar mélange. Since experience of snow and ice was not required, they were a crowd of polar amateurs and, to that extent, it was a repetition of *Discovery*. Shackleton, however, was not another Scott, playing coolly with his men like pawns for his own ambition. Shackleton had contact with his companions. He seemed to rouse the rootlessness and restlessness that were the common ingredients of their make-up. Perhaps, underneath his apparently arbitrary choice, Shackleton was following some arcane method of his own. As he later rationalised it,

> The qualities . . . necessary to the explorer are . . . in . . . order of importance: first, optimism; second, patience; third, physical endurance; fourth, idealism; fifth and last, courage . . . Few men are wanting in courage but optimism nullifies disappointment and makes one more ready than ever to go on . . . Impatience means disaster . . . Physical endurance . . . will not compensate for the first two moral or temperamental qualities.[30]

As the days wore on, *Nimrod*'s voyage turned into a nightmare, and Shackleton had every chance to put these axioms to the test. "The dear old tub," as Harbord put it, was "riding the mountainous seas like a parson on a cab . . . Water is coming on board by the ton."[31] Constantly it filtered down into every nook and cranny of the hull. "We can't help wondering what it feels like to be dry," he wrote again on the eighth day out.

> See this little wardroom of ours. The same as when in Lyttelton, and yet as totally different. The curtains dirty and grubby are swinging jerkily to the movement of the ship. The walls, once white are splashed all over with ink where the unbreakable inkpot has strayed in its hurry to elude a thirsty pen; the mast has on one side of it, distinct traces of

oily fingers that have rested there, while the rolling has delayed their owner on his way to his room. There's an old dripping and soaked oilskin lying on top of an empty, and cold looking stove.[32]

Harbord was another not quite ordinary seaman. A Yorkshireman from Hull, he came of a long line of Norfolk squires and belonged, as it were, to the penniless gentry. As he was acutely conscious, he could trace his forebears back to the Elizabethan Navy, indeed, he saw himself sometimes as a displaced Elizabethan. Now twenty-four, he had been sent to sea at the age of twelve by his father, a merchant captain, to knock him into shape, and had been sailing ever since. He joined *Nimrod* in Lyttelton from *Ionic*, a White Star liner, to replace Mackintosh, who was expecting to stay in the south. Restless and ambitious, Harbord instantly took to Shackleton as the man who had plucked him out of routine.

Harbord had a lively interest in human personality. Behind Irish blarney, he believed, there was often little of substance, merely charm. But if one added drive, and performance, one had a lethal cocktail; and that, broadly, was his view of Shackleton.

The character of everyone on *Nimrod* was being shown up by the storm. The ship's officers felt on trial. They were not exactly afraid, for all had been trained in sail. But none had yet navigated so small a ship in such high latitudes, and the shriek of the wind in the rigging seemed of an unfamiliar pitch. Shackleton was conspicuously restless, but Harbord felt that he had the knack of making one feel guilty if one did not come up to scratch.

On the ninth day out, the storm reached its climax. "Everything moveable washed away from decks," the ship's log chronicled with sober eloquence. "Squalls of hurricane force . . . Blinding spray overall . . . shipped heavy sea . . . smashing bulwarks,"[33] it noted, as *Nimrod* shuddered to the sea, jerking 50° sometimes each way, as if she would roll her masts out.

"Not more than one skipper in 100," wrote Marshall that day, "would have hung on to us as Evans has done."[34] Even from a landlubber that was fair praise. The tow rope was 400 yards long, and a single mistake would have snapped it off – or worse. Shackleton, as Marshall meanwhile put it, was "in disagreeable surly mood", and Frank Wild thought they were going to founder.[35]

Shackleton was in an unenviable predicament. He commanded the expedition, but Evans and England were the captains of the ships. By the custom of the sea their word was law. It was divided command; something with which Scott had not been burdened; for on *Discovery* he was captain too. Shackleton, although formally qualified, had never actually commanded a ship; worse, there was an unspoken doubt whether he could do so, and here he was not even on the crew list. Technically, he was a passenger. He could only watch helplessly and wait.

It was now, at the height of the storm, that Shackleton had graphically demonstrated for him the grotesque drawbacks of ponies in the polar regions. Hundreds of bales of fodder encumbered the ship, endangering her stability, while there was unlimited seal meat for carnivores on the shores ahead. At least three men, at the cost of much danger and discomfort, had to tend the creatures in their stalls night and day. The ponies could not cope with the heaving decks. In every lurch there was peril. One vicious sea sweeping inboard knocked a pony on his back. He had to be put down; and only nine were left. Nine sledge dogs, meanwhile, descendants of Borchgrevink's dogs, left behind in 1900, and acquired in New Zealand as an afterthought (perhaps the lingering effects of Nansen's pleading), were perched out of the way. Even though they were whining and growling, and swaying on their feet like their masters, they could look after themselves.

> On going aft [Marshall wrote as the gale shrieked to its climax, on the evening of 9 January], a huge sea came on deck & left me hanging on to life line with a seething mass of water up to my waist. Its goodbye to anyone who lets go . . . Two men at wheel, one has just been thrown over it. Never seen such seas running and hope may never again but withal a magnificent sight.

The knowledge that they were far off the shipping lanes, and utterly alone, heightened the nervousness and tension. Some of the sailors blamed the storm on an albatross that Wild had killed at the start of the voyage. Marshall considered that there were "at least two Jonahs we can do without". One was David; the other Mawson, who was "useless & objectionable, lacking in guts and manners".[36] Mawson, he added,

> lay in a sleeping bag at one end of the bridge vomiting when he rolled to starboard, whilst the cook handed up food from the galley beneath him. He did no watches.

Marshall himself was "sick as hell", as he put it, but even without the depressing effect of seasickness, he was unlikely to get on with a typical Australian. Mawson, in any case, was austere and forthright – rather like Marshall, in fact.

On 10 January, the weather started to ease. Shackleton, nonetheless, had a twinge of conscience. He had been blown over the

170th meridian west – the invisible frontier he had been forced to promise Scott he would under no circumstances breach. Now he had to claw his way back out of "forbidden territory". But he had survived.

Four days later, the first icebergs appeared, gleaming dully like shields floating on the sea. For Shackleton it was a kind of reunion, and a milestone on the way. "We will be all right for money if the Pole is reached," he now repeated to Emily in a letter to be sent back with *Koonya*, "and of that I feel very hopeful."[37]

Next day, 15 January, almost exactly on the Antarctic Circle, a white strip appeared on the horizon. Although ice blink was absent, it was assumed to be the pack ice guarding the Ross Sea. *Koonya*, being of steel, could go no further. It was time for her to turn. A heavy swell was still running, and dropping the tow was not easy. First a boat was rowed painfully from *Nimrod* to *Koonya* carrying Buckley, who was going home, Captain England to talk to Captain Evans, and the mails.

One of the letters was from Edgeworth David to Sydney University, requesting leave of absence for a year. It appeared to be a spontaneous decision. In fact, before sailing, the Prof. had wanted, not merely the round trip, but the whole expedition from beginning to end, although he preferred not to say so openly. His wife or the university might object. He therefore concealed his true intentions until he was safely out of reach, and then presented a *fait accompli*, knowing he would be incommunicado for a year at least.

The Prof. – although that too was concealed for some time – was to be head of the scientific staff. Marshall had early heard the rumour. "A great pity," was his comment, "as . . . Prof. David . . . has S. under his thumb." David, as Marshall tellingly remarked, would "take all the credit for the scientific results".[38] To put it another way, however, David would secure for the expedition a patina of intellectual virtue and for that reason Shackleton had been the Prof.'s willing accomplice.

Twenty live sheep (despite all the seal waiting in Antarctica) had been brought on *Koonya* all the way from New Zealand, and by now they had been slaughtered and skinned. Because of a rising sea, they could not be rowed across, but had to be drifted across on a line. Only ten got through; and so, luckily, did the boat with Captain England.

Captain Evans, meanwhile, felt it was high time to move. He cut the tow and, in Harbord's words, "with the dip of flags, the late tow boat steamed away and left us watching her through the fog that was quickly gathering".[39] *Nimrod* took eight hours to get in her cables, and then got under way. By the small hours, the fog had cleared, and she reached the white band on the southern horizon.

It was not the expected pack ice. Instead, *Nimrod* was faced with icebergs covering the sea from horizon to horizon. They spanned five degrees of latitude; concentrated in two belts each a hundred miles across. There was always open water; a labyrinth rather than an obstacle. Previous expeditions had seen nothing like it. *Nimrod* had to dodge in and out among the bergs. At one point all hands were called on deck to wear ship; that is, to swing her round by using rudder and sails.

> Hear S. [Shackleton] was very unwell after pulling on a rope [Marshall noted in his diary]. Will not hold myself responsible until he allows me to examine him. Something wrong?[40]

In the evening of 20 January, at 72° south latitude after exactly four and a half days among the bergs, *Nimrod* ran out into the open Ross Sea, dark smoke belching from her stovepipe funnel to spread a lonely streak on the empty horizon. Her longitude was 179° W., still in forbidden waters. She headed south-east towards the fateful 170th meridian, Scott's frontier.

New Zealand was two thousand miles astern. Journey's end was looming up. Shackleton now announced a change of plan. Instead of going to King Edward VII Land, "I have decided," as he had already written to Emily by *Koonya*, "to winter at the Barrier Inlet."[41] This was exactly what Armitage, in his original plan, had proposed. It was a radical proposal, for nobody had yet dared to stay on an ice shelf, for there was the nightmare risk of the ice calving and sending the whole base on an iceberg out to sea.

"Barrier Inlet" was Scott's "Balloon Bight"; where Shackleton had landed from *Discovery*. Tellingly, Shackleton was using another name.

By landing at Barrier Inlet Shackleton, as he told Emily, repeating Armitage's opinion, would "only be 660 miles from the Pole".[42] In other words, he would be almost a degree closer than at "Scott's" base at McMurdo Sound, and save 120 miles on the journey. Besides, as he put it, he would have "a straight road to the south and *no* crevasses . . ."[43]

Vividly, Shackleton remembered the view from the balloon six years before; the unbroken white plain rolling uninterruptedly south as far as the eye could see. Just as vividly, he recalled the disturbances in the Barrier at McMurdo Sound where it flowed between mountains to the sea. Perhaps King Edward VII Land would turn out to be even more treacherous.

Early on 23 January for the first time on the voyage, a proper ice blink appeared. The whole southern horizon glowed with a white incandescence. Towards nine o'clock, in the words of John King Davis,

> a hard white line, as if drawn by an enormous ruler, began to materialize out of the blink, becoming sharper . . . as we drew near, until at last it stood fully revealed as the Great Ice barrier itself.[44]

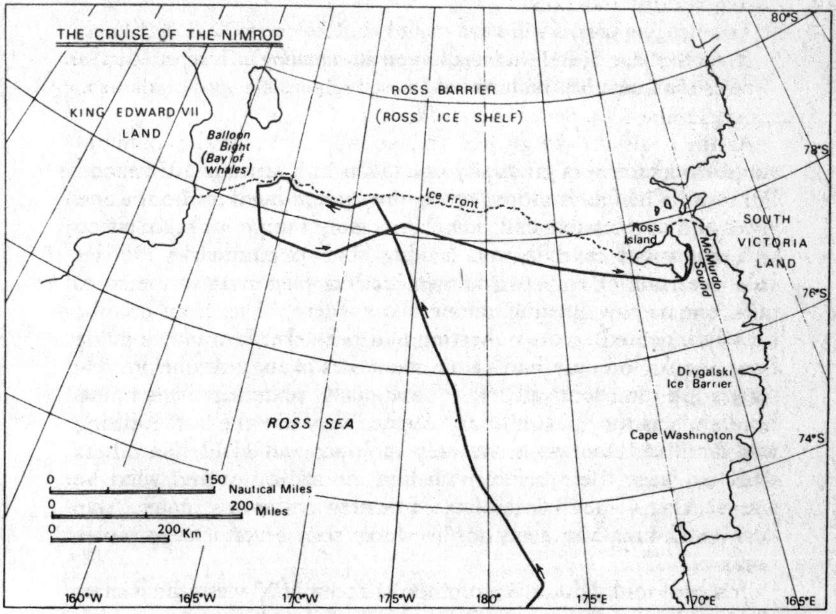

Nimrod now turned east to cruise along the Barrier a mile or two offshore, looking for "Barrier Inlet". All day long, the starboard bulwarks were crowded with men gazing at the endless ice cliff of the Barrier face; "an eighth wonder of the world", as Edgeworth David put it.[45] Nature had arranged things for the occasion. The wind dropped. The first skuas and petrels swooped out of a cloudless sky. "The sea," wrote Priestley, "is beautifully calm, scarcely a ripple on the surface & though the thermometer is down to 19°F it does not seem as cold as on some winter days in England."[46] Whales spouted in grey, open water, broken only by an occasional iceberg far off to port, or a small floe drifting lazily by, sometimes with penguins, or barking seals on top, like decorations on a cake.

Swiftly the degrees of longitude dropped astern for, at that latitude, due to the convergence of the meridians, the degree of longitude is only twelve miles, instead of sixty at the equator. In the middle of the afternoon, *Nimrod* passed the 170th meridian west. Shackleton had crossed the invisible frontier at last, and a mood somewhere between relief and hope surged through the ship. Barrier Inlet could be, after all, the secret of success. Plans were confidently aired.

> Two sledging parties will start about Feb. 15th one to K. E. VII Land, & another due South [Marshall wrote in his diary]. If we can do 200 miles shall beat Southern record.[47]

As the southern sky glowed yellow and red under the midnight sun, Shackleton was gradually overtaken by a sense of bafflement. For most of its four hundred miles, the sombre-hued ice front was a sheer and inaccessible cliff, sometimes more than mast high, pitted with enormous caverns, and lacking obvious landmarks. Barrier Inlet was one of only two known landing places. It was easy to miss: one narrow opening among many where the ice front became heavily indented. Scott's charting had been sketchy, and to guide him, Shackleton only had vague memories of six years before. He stayed up on deck all night, anxiously scanning bights and headlands as they passed. Each seemed very like the last. Nothing was familiar. Even with the help of Joyce and Wild, the others who had been there before with him, he could not find what he was seeking. The Barrier face, Priestley ominously noted, was "evidently breaking away for we have seen several large pieces break off".[48]

Just past midnight, at a longitude of about 165° west, the Barrier face suddenly fell away to the south-east in a broad bay, which Shackleton did not recognise, but which he identified with what he called Borchgrevink's Bight. That was where Borchgrevink presumably had landed in 1900. It would have been Barrier Inlet's neighbour to the west. It was not what he was seeking; but it was the first even faintly possible landing place.

Shackleton and Captain England had agreed that they had until 1 March to find a base. After that, *Nimrod* risked being frozen in. It was now only 24 January. England, however, was manifestly anxious to regain civilisation as quickly as he could. He wanted to land. Shackleton, however, with a touch of impatience, declined to accept the first likely looking place. In any case, this bay was frozen over with an unbroken sheet of ice, and the Barrier edge was some way off. England took *Nimrod* on further east to continue the search.

There was a hint of nervous tension in the way he gave his orders to the helmsman.

At 7.30 a.m., a little bight appeared where the Barrier came down to the sea. It was at about the position of what is now called Kainan Bay, around 165° W. Shackleton did not recognise it at all. *He was now east of where Barrier Inlet ought to have been.*

Nimrod put in and moored to the edge of the bay ice. Observations were taken to fix her position; four times over. Her latitude was 78° 20′ S, which put her *south* of *Discovery* in 1902.

Barrier Inlet existed no more. The ice had calved, taking it out to sea.

Here, on the other hand, was a possible landing place. These, however, were sketchily charted waters. England was now distinctly nervous, and Shackleton manifestly uncertain. They withdrew to the cabin that they shared, to breakfast there alone, instead of in the wardroom, and talk things over in private. This break in routine sent an indefinable frisson through the crew.

Between Shackleton and England there was by now a hint of underlying strain. England was a Yorkshireman, the son of an Anglican curate. Conscientious, hard-working, respected by his superiors, he was a model of caution. He had been a good first mate, but this was the first time he had been captain of a ship. In any case, he now considered Shackleton a little too rash for comfort, and was distinctly reluctant to try conclusions with the ice.

The upshot was that no attempt was made to get ashore. *Nimrod* put about and continued east to make for King Edward VII Land. This part of the Ross Sea, as Shackleton knew only too well from *Discovery*, was too treacherous for comfort.

Nimrod was soon threatened by pack ice bearing down from the north. She only just managed to escape in time from being crushed up against the Barrier. A promise, especially given to someone now taking on the colour of a vindictive enemy, could hardly be pursued against nature. *Nimrod* put out to sea. There was talk of making for McMurdo Sound. Marshall was disturbed. A promise to him was a promise. In his own words, Shackleton had "given his word to Scott, that under no circs. will he go there".[49] Together with Adams, Marshall "had a talk with S.", as he phrased it in an agitated entry in his diary. "Returning to look at Borchgrevink Bay [Bight] & see if possible to land & winter there."

After six hours' steaming back upon her tracks, *Nimrod* reached Borchgrevink's Bight; but Borchgrevink's Bight it was not. The truth now gradually dawned. When the Barrier calved, it had sent not only Barrier Inlet out to sea, but Borchgrevink's Bight had broken away as well. A single large bay remained in their stead, where "whales", to quote the ship's log, were "spouting all around".[50] The place was spontaneously named the Bay of Whales.

Shackleton was now faced with the crisis of his life. A belt of solid, gleaming sea ice still kept *Nimrod* several miles off the Barrier front. The logical procedure was to sheer off, wait for the ice to move out, and then put back. Shackleton, however, had just gone through the unnerving experience of finding that what once seemed solid had turned out to be thoroughly impermanent. It was like going through an earthquake.

The Bay of Whales was in fact vastly preferable to the now vanished inlets. Their entrances had been narrow, masked, and easily blocked by the caprice of the ice, which turned them into potential traps. The new bay had a wide, clear, easily recognisable approach. It had other advantages too. Seal and penguin abounded, so there would be no lack of food. Most important of all, Raymond Priestley noted that behind the Bay of Whales the Barrier was undulating, with

> convex slopes separated by . . . fairly long flat stretches. This looks as if it were probably due . . . to the fact that the ice had passed over land of a low-lying character.[51]

Priestley was right. What he had seen was Roosevelt Island, a domed feature in the ice sheet, discovered twenty years later from the air. Shackleton himself had seen the same feature in 1902; so, for that matter, had Borchgrevink two years earlier, and James Clark Ross sixty years before that.

Shackleton, however, declined to land. "I am thankful," he wrote, that the ice "went out before we arrived . . . otherwise I would have landed and the whole thing might have gone this year."[52] He now associated the freakish belt of icebergs at the entrance to the Ross Sea with the break-up of the Barrier front. It was quite plausible, for Antarctic icebergs are formed by the calving of the continental ice. In his own words:

> The thought of what might have been made me decide then and there that under no circumstances would I winter on the Barrier, and that wherever we did land we would secure a solid rock foundation for our winter home.[53]

David backed that decision; indeed, he might have been the cause. It was a case of the halt leading the blind. Professor as he was, David knew little more about ice than Shackleton. In truth, the calving of the Barrier meant stability for what was left, besides ten miles off the journey to the Pole.

Marshall was not happy as *Nimrod* turned about. Alone of those on board, he was prepared to land, for to him, the Bay of Whales was unquestionably the key to the Pole. His distress was compounded when he heard, once more, that they were on their way to McMurdo Sound. "If this is so," he wrote in his diary, "he [Shackleton] hasn't got the guts of a louse, in spite of what he may say to the world on his return." Marshall was preoccupied with the promise to Scott. Shackleton, he went on,

> has made no attempt to reach K. E. Land. In short he & England funk it . . . Got very angry when I told him I was sorry he had not made an attempt on K. E. Land. Tried to make me believe that he had done as much as any human being could. I think Prof. had a talk with him for 1½ hr. later he turned round heading east to make another attempt. Went to bed with mind more at ease.[54]

Shackleton, normally the most decisive of men, was now torn by indecision, and beset by conflicting advice. He bore the same moral burden as Marshall; but what Marshall did not know was that England had been secretly urging an immediate turnabout for McMurdo Sound. England understood the force of Shackleton's promise to Scott, but to him a seaman who could even think of denying a haven to another was a monster. England only knew that time wasted on looking for a landing place meant danger to his ship. Beneath his feet he had a strained and overburdened hull. *Nimrod* could not move properly under sail alone. Safely to return to New Zealand, he was going to need every ounce of coal, and here it was being frittered away for a whim. Reluctantly, he agreed to try, just once more, to reach King Edward VII Land. He gave Shackleton forty-eight hours' grace. After that, they would head for McMurdo Sound.

Hardly twenty-four hours later, *Nimrod* was jammed once more against impenetrable pack. Once more Shackleton and England retired to their cabin for a private discussion. "I felt keenly the probable ending of the whole expedition," said England,

> & . . . laid the whole thing before [Shackleton], the shortage of coal – the futility of trying to reach K. E. Land for I knew then that we should have to return and – though it cut him terribly he saw I was right & was reluctantly compelled by his duty to the Expn. to return & break his word to Scott. I felt . . . for him & for his feelings but I had to speak as I thought & I knew the probable disaster if [he] did not.

"A/C [altered course]," in the words of the ship's log, "returning to Westward side of Ross Sea."[55] Thus in the terse language of the mariner was the moment of high drama put on record. *Nimrod*, finally, was heading for McMurdo Sound. "Sick at heart", was how Harbord conveyed the mood on board. "Words cannot describe Shackleton's disappointment."[56] The time was 6.30 in the afternoon of 25 January. As England put it,

> The *Antarctic* foundered & the *Belgica* wintered unprepared . . . thro' not recognising the force & power of such a pack. Another hour would probably have seen us embayed & I will not look further than that.[57]

All – or nearly all – moral scruples had been resolved. Even Marshall was more or less content. "At any rate," he said, "we have had a try for it."[58]

In one sense, England had taken the responsibility of having broken his word off Shackleton's shoulders. England it was who had taken the decision to turn. It was the captain of the ship alone who had the power to decide.

That consolation could not last long. The day after turning, *Nimrod* sailed over the 170th meridian west. Crossing this "forbidden" line brought home to Shackleton the enormity of what he had been compelled to do. It goaded him into a long, agonised letter to Emily.

"Child o'mine," he wrote, "I have been through a sort of Hell":

> You . . . can . . . realise what it has been to me to stand up on the bridge in those snow squalls and decide whether to go on or turn back my whole heart crying out for me to go on and the feeling against of the lives of the 40 odd men on board: I swept away from my thoughts the question of the Pole of the success of the Expedition at that moment though in doing so I know now that in my calmer moments that I was wrong even to do that: that my money was given for me to reach the Pole not to just play with according to my ideas of right and wrong, that I had a great public trust which I could not betray . . . my duty to the country and King since I was given the flag for the Pole . . . just imagine this and think that . . . I had the success from the world's point of view and the eyes of the world on us, then it will come home to you what those hours meant to me . . .

"My heart was heavy within me," he wrote of his failure to land where he wanted,

> my private word of honour my promise given under pressure was the one thing that weighed in the balance against my going back at once.

However, he went on,

> My conscience is clear but my heart is sore . . . but I have one comfort that I did my best . . . and if the whole world were to cry out at me which I am sure they would not even then I would not worry myself for I know in my own heart that I am right.[59]

Shackleton also felt betrayed by a brother Mason. It was Scott, after all, who had put him in this predicament. Scott, once more, had transgressed the charge "on no account to wrong" other Freemasons, "and to view their interest as inseparable from your own".[60] The fact that Scott had now resigned from Freemasonry made little difference to Shackleton.

His shipmates sympathised with his evident distress. Marshall was moved to write an apologia on the spot, intended for the RGS. The alternative to renouncing McMurdo Sound, he said,

> was going back to New Zealand – not one of [us] would have gone back to New Zealand so . . . Shackleton . . . was plainly justified in going to . . . McMurdo Sound . . . as he had his supporters to consider and was bound to carry his expedition through.[61]

Nonetheless, as Shackleton himself put it,

> I had promised and I felt that each mile I went to the West was a horror to me.

Nothing could hide that from Shackleton, not all his reasoning, the sympathy of his companions, nor the fact that Scott had taken an advantage that no human being could take with impunity.

But it was Shackleton who had broken a promise. The Irishman within him perhaps sensed it as a curse. As the glinting shore of the Bay of Whales dissolved into the haze, he could only cling to his double-edged belief that he was following his star.

XX

McMurdo Sound

"It seemed as though it were only yesterday that I had looked on the scene,"[1] wrote Shackleton of his return to McMurdo Sound. Through an intermittent veil of snow, the smoking cone of Erebus, the distant glitter of the Western Mountains over purple-grey waters, Castle Rock, Observation Hill, and all the familiar landmarks from *Discovery* loomed up again like a nostalgic vision from the past.

Shackleton needed the *Discovery* base at Hut Point. It was always in contact with the Barrier. The start of the road to the south did not risk floating out to sea with the break-up of the ice, and of no other place could that be said. Besides, Hut Point was the only safe anchorage in McMurdo Sound. But between *Nimrod* and Hut Point, at the end of the Sound, sixteen miles of solid ice were interposed. "It really seemed as though the fates were against us,"[2] Harbord was driven to record.

It was now 29 January. *Nimrod* had arrived ten days earlier than had *Discovery* in 1902. There was still a month before the ship faced the danger of being frozen in. At the *Discovery* quarters, she could be discharged within forty-eight hours. On the face of it, therefore, Shackleton could afford to wait for the ice to break up but England was growing visibly anxious to be off. Besides, the ponies were in miserable straits. For a month they had been cooped up on board. On them, the Pole depended. They had to be got ashore without delay. Even so one more, injured during the voyage, had had to be put down, and only eight remained.

Shackleton refused to abandon hope of reaching the *Discovery* quarters. For two days he steamed up and down hoping that the ice would go out; haunted by the spectre of 1903, when it did not. He

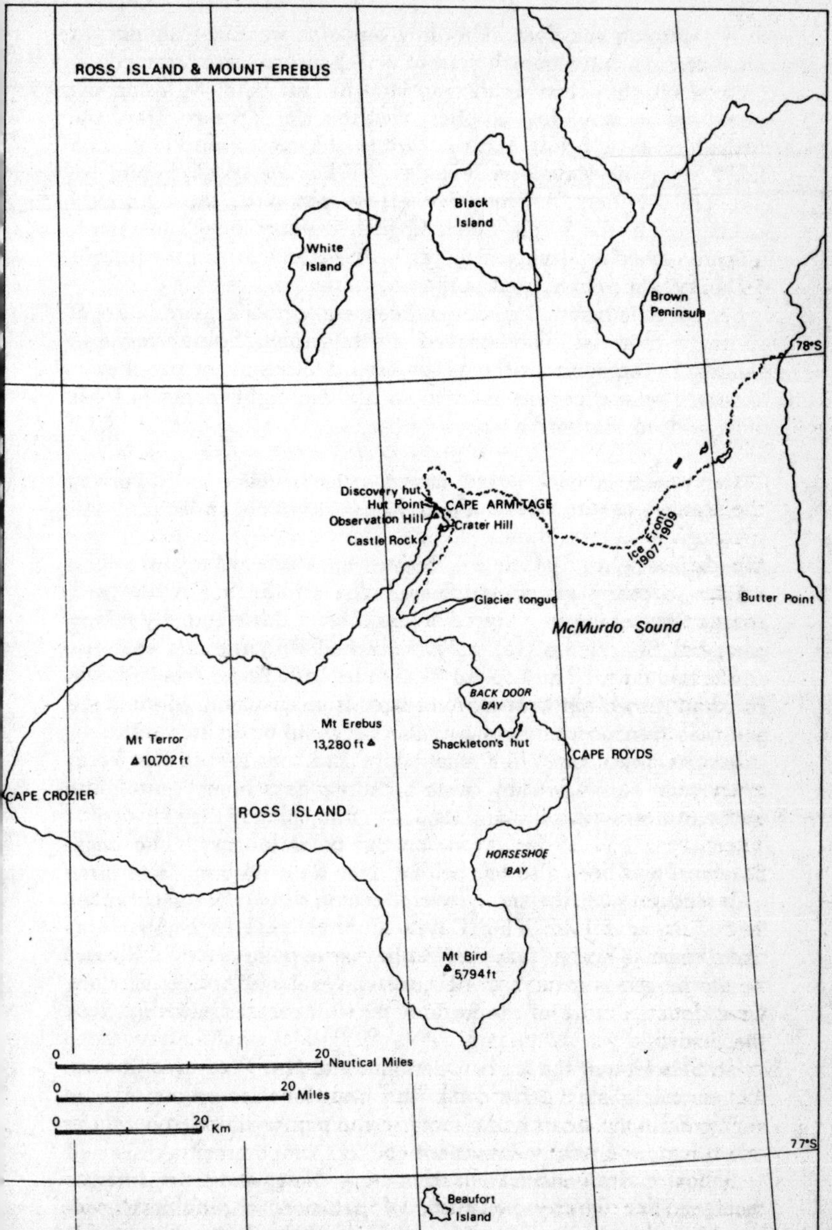

ROSS ISLAND & MOUNT EREBUS
Black Island
White Island
Brown Peninsula
78°S
Discovery hut
Hut Point
CAPE ARMITAGE
Observation Hill
Crater Hill
Castle Rock
Ice Front 1907-1909
Glacier tongue
Butter Point
McMurdo Sound
BACK DOOR BAY
Mt Erebus
13,280 ft
Mt Terror
10,702 ft
Shackleton's hut
CAPE ROYDS
CAPE CROZIER
ROSS ISLAND
HORSESHOE BAY
Mt Bird
5,794 ft
0
20
Nautical Miles
0
20
Miles
0
20
Km
77°S
Beaufort Island
169°E
168°E
167°E
166°E
165°E

tried ramming the floes. The only outcome was an insignificant advance, and extra punishment to a ship already overstrained.

So Shackleton then decided to land at Hut Point by using the motor car to haul his supplies over the ice. Bernard Day, the mechanic, as a result became "quite the most important man here", to quote Raymond Priestley. "When we speak to him we take off our hats."[3] Protective grease removed, incongruously looking ready for a spin down English country lanes, the Arrol-Johnston stood on deck, waiting to be tried. At noon on Saturday 1 February, she was hoisted outboard.

Bent double before the bonnet, like a contemporary caricature of an early motorist, Day heaved at the crank. Spluttering and banging in the polar air the motor, after a false start or two, began to run. The sea ice was covered with about eight inches of loose snow and, in Harbord's words,

> The wheels in duty bound turned violently round . . . burying themselves to such an extent that the car moved not an inch.[4]

After a few hours, the car was hoisted back inboard again.

Like so many historic moments, the significance of the first attempt at driving in Antarctica was lost on those actually taking part; but Shackleton was only concerned with the fact that the device had failed. The hopeful "150 miles in 24 hours" towards the Pole had turned out to be a product of his imagination. More to the point, as transport in the snow, the car could be written off.

Adams, Joyce and Wild, meanwhile, had been sent to Hut Point to try man-hauling. They came back two days later "quite done up", as Priestley put it, "and turned in immediately they arrived".[5] The horses had to be saved for the polar journey. The dogs, however, had been also left behind. Nor were ski used. The three men trudged over the snow-covered ice on their own unsupported feet. This, said John King Davis, austerely making comparisons from *Nimrod*'s bridge, was the "Stone Age of polar travel".[6] Surely, he was moved to remark, of all those who explored Antarctica, "few have done so more uncomfortably or with greater hardship than the British".[7]

To Shackleton, the ice between him and Hut Point was now an insuperable obstacle. He could only wait for it to go out. Under such conditions, Scott had dissolved into panic. Shackleton, on the other hand, normally impatient, bossy, temperamental, seemed somehow to draw inspiration from crisis. Now, under pressure, he displayed an impressive mask of patience, cheerfulness, self-confidence, and calm. Underneath, he was horribly worried and uncertain. Many people can control their emotions. Shackleton had the rarer gift of not communicating his fears. England, on the other hand, was baring an uncomfortable degree of nervousness and tension. From the start, he had been manifestly highly strung; but now the doctors began to wonder if he was ill. He was painfully anxious to be off.

The weather was unpleasant and unstable. On 3 February, in the middle of the afternoon, it began unexpectedly to clear. Shackleton suddenly felt that he had to seize the opportunity. He announced an immediate landing on Ross Island as close as possible to the Barrier edge. This happened to be Cape Royds, the rocky promontory named after Charles Royds, the First Lieutenant of *Discovery*. By evening, *Nimrod* was alongside.

Under the opalesque slopes of Erebus, Cape Royds lay in an impressive setting. The ice falls of the volcano, however, cut it off overland. The sea was the only way across. The anchorage was virtually unprotected. There were twinges of regret at having retreated from the Bay of Whales. Cape Royds, however, would have to do.

As the waters were uncharted, Shackleton took a boat to sound the approaches. At one point, he actually handled the lead himself, saying the leadsman needed a rest. Fetching an unknown shore is a delicate manoeuvre. These waters were notoriously foul. Everyone knew how *Discovery* had struck a hidden reef just as she was leaving, four years before. Shackleton wished to be sure of the vital soundings. He also wanted to calm England by demonstrably taking responsibility in a crisis.

As soon as he had finished sounding, Shackleton went ashore in search of a site for his hut. He found it about two hundred yards inland, on the level, ice-free floor of a small, protected valley. Not far off, in his own telling words, he

> came across the camp where Captain Scott and Dr. Wilson spent some days in . . . 1904 whilst . . . waiting for the relief ship.[8]

Unloading began under the midnight sun, glowing ember-red against the emerald of ice and snow. Wandering about, with an eye-patch, was the tall, melancholy figure of Mackintosh. He had been struck in the right eye by a hook while hoisting a barrel of beer out of the hold. Marshall had had to remove the eye – the first major operation in the Antarctic. Mackintosh was doubly miserable, because now he could not stay with the shore party, and would have to go home in the ship.

After a few hours, a south-easterly blizzard blew up; or, in the precise terms of the ship's log, a SSE wind, force 5 (20 knots), with snow and fog. Erebus and everything else was blotted out. More to the point, it turned Cape Royds into a lee shore. *Nimrod* lay in a crescent of bay ice that ran south-east from the cape, and heavy grating sounds suggested an imminent break-up. *Nimrod*, as Harbord put it, had to "cut and run".[9]

All that day, 4 February, *Nimrod* stood off in the Sound, moored to the ice. Next evening, the weather had eased enough for England to bring her in again but only, in Marshall's words, "after terrible waste of time & bad seamanship". This was partly pique at losing thirty-six hours when every minute told, but also much unnecessary hauling could have been avoided by mooring *Nimrod* opposite a snow ramp leading to the shore. England, as Priestley put it, was "afraid to take the ship in so close".[10]

In the afternoon of 6 February the wind freshened once more and *Nimrod*, for the second time, sheered off. She had been alongside for only eighteen hours, but at least the dogs, horses, motor car, hut elements, and a lifeboat for the base had now been landed. A party under Adams stayed behind to build the hut and to look after the animals. Shackleton deliberately remained on board.

When *Nimrod* returned, on the afternoon of 8 February, Shackleton found the men at Cape Royds in a mutinous mood. It had been calm and mostly fine inshore. Two more whole days appeared to have been unnecessarily lost. The general opinion, as Frank Wild put it, was that England had "entirely lost his nerve & is, in fact off his rocker".[11] This put Shackleton in a predicament, for Wild echoed a corner of his own thoughts. To make England come in this time, he had to use all his powers of persuasion, although conditions, even out in the Sound, were hardly threatening. The wind was moderate and offshore. The ice was not moving. Nor were currents a hazard. England, on the other hand, was captain, and Shackleton had to uphold his authority. Shackleton had already reprimanded Marshall after hearing him publicly condemn England, but this was considered "giving in" to England. The men crowding round Shackleton on the beach to have their say were all of the shore party – Adams, Wild, Mackay, Joyce, Brocklehurst and Marston. For good or ill, Shackleton would have to share isolation with them for a year.

In the midst of this upsetting scene, *Nimrod* unexpectedly stood out again. Shackleton ran down to the edge of the ice foot, and signalled urgently for a boat to come and take him off. He found England on the bridge, by the engine-room telegraph. England had again sheered off for no apparent reason – the sea was calm, the wind had dropped, and the weather showed no signs of breaking up. With some difficulty, he persuaded England to go in again. *Nimrod* headed for the shore, dead slow.

Exasperated, Shackleton seized the engine-room telegraph and rang up "full speed ahead". England told him not to interfere with the navigation of the ship and, pulling at the handle, ordered "full speed astern".

Between the expedition leader and his captain, conflict was inherent. The one was devoted to the attainment of his goal; the other, to the safety of his ship. Shackleton was England's employer; but he could not give orders, only directives. On the bridge, the captain was absolute master. Shackleton had broken the law of the sea, and he knew it. England stopped the engines and, once again, he and Shackleton went into their cabin for a private talk.

Up on deck Harbord, watching penguins on a floe, was asking himself: "Can it be the absence of civilisation that makes us see so many human traits in the bird-fish."[12] Isolation, as everyone more or less discerned, was intensifying strain.

Nothing in Shackleton's experience had prepared him for the confrontation with which he now was faced. He was used to riding rough-shod over opposition; or ingratiating himself with recalcitrant objectors. Here, neither would suffice. Shackleton, confronting England in the cabin, had to face an unpalatable fact. "England," he had written to Emily by *Koonya*, "is a splendid man good sailor."[13] To England himself, Shackleton had said in written orders: "You will know by this time my feelings towards you, both as regards my opinion of you as a seaman, and also as regards those more intimate qualities that go to make a man . . . I feel assured that in placing the honour and responsibility of the Expedition in your hands I am not erring in judgment."[14] That was hardly three weeks before. Shackleton now believed he had made a mistake. England's failings, he feared, were risking the expedition.

Shackleton now asked England to hand over command on the grounds that he was ill. This was not a specious pretext. Two days before Marshall had "long talk with S. re Eng", as he recorded in his diary, "much worried but suggested course to take".[15] Although not exactly ill, England was in a state of mind where his judgment was impaired.

Shackleton and England were both under intolerable strain. For both it was their first experience of command; both were men of powerful emotion. The difference was that Shackleton could hide his feelings behind a mask of self-confidence. On the other hand, "it gave me a fit of the blues to look at England", as Dunlop, the red-headed Chief Engineer from Ulster put it, "he seemed half dead, with a long-drawn, god-forsaken expression on his face".[16]

While the ship was stopped, and moving gently with the tide, the drama below decks took its course. There was no shouting and very little talk. With an effort, Shackleton controlled his temper. Underneath the calm the tension was almost unbearable. England was oppressed by worries for which he was not prepared. Methodical and precise, he found Shackleton's personality distressingly antipathetic. Antagonism was exacerbated by their having been forced to share a tiny cabin for weeks on end. "All my discipline & order have had to be altered for the good of the cause," England had written to his fiancée in New Zealand, "I am growing more & more alone in myself . . . 'tis a strange work that we have undertaken . . . I broke down and shook like ague," he wrote after the strain of trying to land on King Edward VII Land and at the Bay of Whales, "and I fell into a restless troubled sleep for 10 hours."[17]

Now England found there would be no time to ballast *Nimrod* for the homeward run. She would be unstable, and risked turning turtle in a gale. All that England could do was to reduce top hamper by removing topmasts. Shackleton previously had announced, via *Koonya*, that he was going to make his base at the Bay of Whales. Until *Nimrod* got through, therefore, nobody would know where to look for him. To England, it was a terrifying burden on his conscience.

In other polar partnerships, such as Nansen and Sverdrup, Nordenskjöld and Larsen, the captains had been men with a lifetime's experience of ice. Their leaders never questioned their authority. Shackleton and England, however, were equally *in*experienced. Also, England felt his future was at stake. So, too, was Shackleton's. Their interests, unfortunately, diverged.

England, in any case, refused to hand over command. He could not legally be removed until *Nimrod* returned to port. Shackleton had to accept the situation. England, as Shackleton eventually told him, was "quite capable of undertaking any ordinary navigation job", but ought to avoid "Arctic or Antarctic work".[18] That came close to the truth. England was at heart an ordinary ship's officer, perhaps not too happy in seas where someone extraordinary was needed.

The two men were not long in the cabin; but their confrontation was unnerving. When they returned on deck, the tension between them was rapidly sensed and spread from man to man.

The engines were restarted. With the gentle ripple of her prow, *Nimrod* came alongside once more. Much ice had disappeared and now she was close up against the east side of Cape Royds in what was dubbed Front Door Bay. Once more there was the drudgery of hauling cargo over the ice from ship to shore. A derrick was rigged to hoist loads up an inconvenient cliff.

The quarrel with England paradoxically revived faith in Shackleton. He was still learning the art of leadership; and between passivity and self-control, the division is hair-fine. His companions grasped however that, whatever had happened in the cabin, England had been steadied. They had to finish unloading while the captain's nerve, and the weather, held. As Davis wrote,

> With twenty four hours of daylight men worked until they were completely exhausted . . . this period of our lives became . . . a veritable day without end.[19]

In the afternoon of 11 February the ice finally broke up, and *Nimrod* sheered off again. She had been alongside seventy hours, her longest continuous stretch. By then, most of her cargo had been discharged. It was an illustration of how Shackleton, though an amateur in polar travel, was a professional and innovative seaman. He had never forgotten his experiences on *Hoghton Tower*, humping cargo at Iquique through the surf. For *Nimrod*, he had everything repacked in identical cases, thirty by fifteen inches square. An early use of the module in packaging, it saved space and simplified stowing. Moreover, the cases, 2,500 in all, were made of three-ply wood, saving four tons all told. The dimensions and capacity of each case were such that it could be handled by one man. That single piece of forethought probably turned the scales, and allowed *Nimrod* to be unloaded in time.

Meanwhile, it seemed Shackleton's fate to be pursued by the might-have-been. "Large quantities of ice," as Harbord put it, were "drifting down from the southward which means that the ice in McMurdo Sound is breaking up in good style."[20] When *Nimrod* stood off, she found open water within eight miles of Hut Point. Over half the ice was gone.

Shackleton, having stayed behind at Cape Royds, was faced with another crisis. To save time, some material had been dumped at a cove called Backdoor Bay on the optimistic assumption that the ice would not go out so close to shore. The dump now stood on a remnant jutting out like a shelf. A widening crack hinted that it, too, was about to disappear. It carried thirty tons of vital stores, including fodder for the horses. To help move the dump to safety Shackleton signalled for extra men from the ship. "Every man jack worked like a bally nigger," in Harbord's words, "but he got more than a nigger's praise from Shackleton who was delighted to see everybody come right up to scratch in such an emergency." By midnight, the work was done.

> Everyone feels relieved [Harbord continued], especially so when after . . . about half an hour . . . there was a loud crash, and the very piece of ice that the stores had been standing upon, fell into the sea with a mighty crash.[21]

Harbord was now back on the ship. The stores for the winter had admittedly been saved, but on *Nimrod*, hove to in a gathering gale out in the Sound, there remained supplies for the polar journey, and most of the winter's coal for heating the hut. The more or less unspoken fear was that England might yet run for home and leave the landing party in the lurch.

When the ice was in, it formed a natural jetty. Now that it had disappeared, *Nimrod* could hardly come alongside any more. The rest of the unloading would have to be done by boat. Shackleton believed that if England had shown stronger nerve earlier on, all the trouble now would have been saved.

For the first time, there was a heavy running swell, and an intermittent, treacherous wind. England kept in the offing, coming in when the weather eased to ferry boatloads ashore. For the oarsmen it was a fight with freezing surf. To save time, Shackleton finally ordered England to land his main sledging supplies on Glacier Tongue, an extraordinary ice formation like a natural harbour mole down the Sound.

On 14 February, *Nimrod* returned to Cape Royds, having been away for three days. Shackleton was furious at what he considered an inexplicable delay on England's part in carrying out his orders. Edgeworth David had to intervene in order to prevent a quarrel.

The next day, Shackleton went on board, and ordered England to sail down the Sound to investigate the ice. There was now open water right up to Castle Rock, four miles from the *Discovery* base. Perhaps, if Shackleton had been more certain of his men, he might then and there have ordered the transfer of a depot party by ship to go out on to the Barrier. Perhaps, too, he felt a twinge of regret at not having imposed his will on England and waited to establish his base. It was at any rate a renewed sense of bafflement.

The crew liked England, more or less, for not risking the ship. The shore party disliked him because, in their eyes, his exaggerated caution had jeopardised their safety. At the last moment, England refused to land all the coal that Shackleton wanted, because he wanted more for the voyage back. As Priestley wrote,

> If Capt. England refuses to . . . give us any more I don't know what we shall do.

rnest Shackleton's birthplace, Kilkea House in County Kildare *(top)*.

he house in Sydenham, South London
'here Shackleton spent his boyhood.

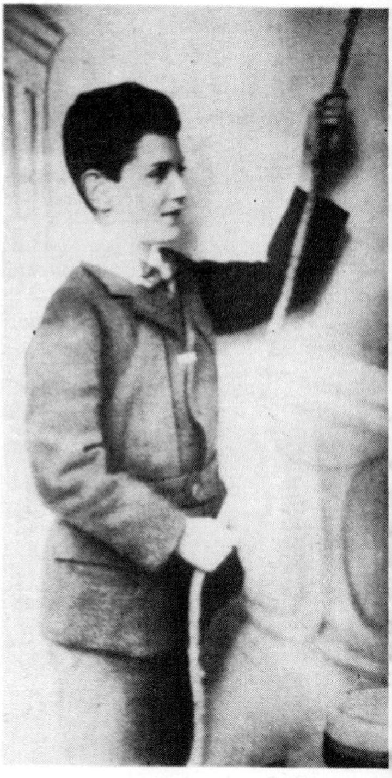

Shackleton at Dulwich College.

On board *Discovery* in Lyttelton harbour, 1901 *(top).* Left to right: Dr Edward Wilson, Lt Ernest Shackleton, Lt Albert Armitage, Lt Michael Barne, Dr Reginald Koettlitz, Lt Reginald Skelton, Cdr Robert Falcon Scott, Lt Charles Royds, Louis Bernacchi, Hartley Ferrar and Thomas Hodgson.

Shackleton, Koettlitz and Scott on ski.

Shackleton in 1902 on return from his first snow journey, which marked the opening of the British route to the South Pole.

Discovery with the shadow of the balloon on the ice, 1902. This was the first aerial Antarctic ascent, and the place was named Balloon Bight.

Shackleton, Scott and Wilson starting off on their southern journey, November 1902.

Shackleton on board *Morning* in New Zealand after being invalided home. On the right is Dr George A. Davidson.

Shackleton on the bridge of *Nimrod* at her moorings off Temple Pier in the Thames.

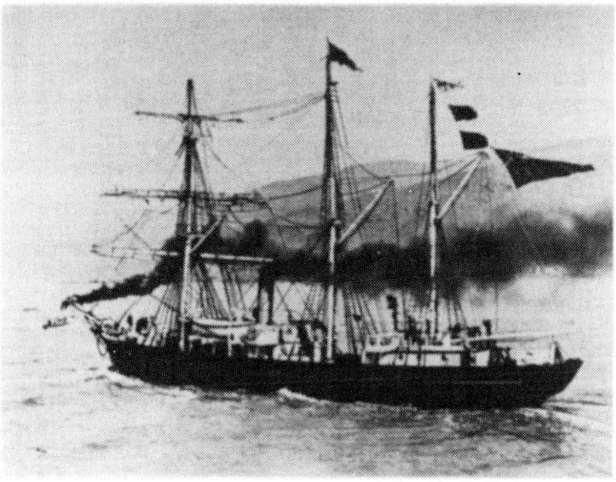
Nimrod leaving Lyttelton harbour, 1 January 1908.

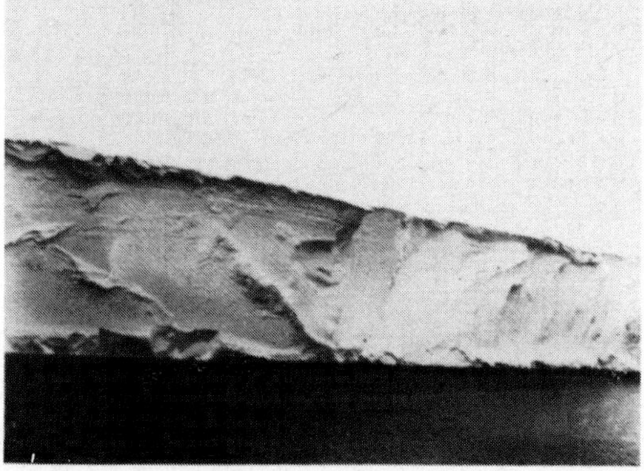
The 100-foot-high ice front which forms the edge of the Ross Ice Shelf, photographed during the *Discovery* expedition.

Sic transit gloria mundi. Shackleton's Furthest South, 9 January 1909. From left to right: Adams, Wild and Shackleton (Marshall was the photographer).

Less than three years later Amundsen passes the same latitude, but he paid generous tribute to Shackleton's achievement (see title page).

Shackleton feted as a national hero in 1909. *Above,* a luncheon on 13 December 1909 at the Berkeley Hotel to celebrate his knighthood. Left to right: Campbell Mackellar, Æneas Mackintosh, Dr Alistair Forbes Mackay, Bernard Day, Alfred Reid (standing, under the palms, a waiter), E. M. Joyce, George Maclean Buckley, Sir Ernest Shackleton, Frank Wild, Sir Philip Brocklehurst, (sitting back) Bertram Armytage, George Marston, John King Davis, S. Roberts.

Left, back at his old school, Dulwich.

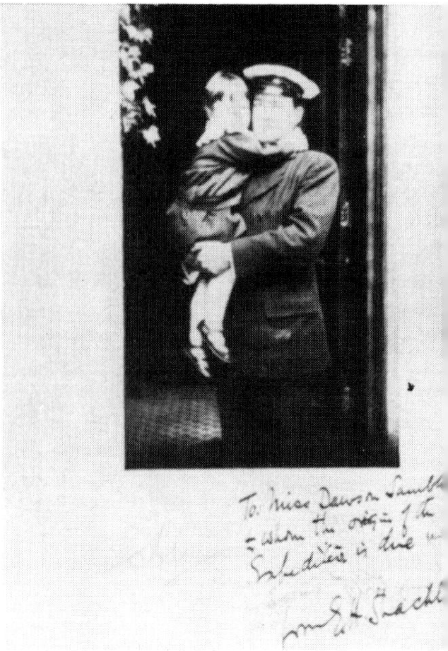

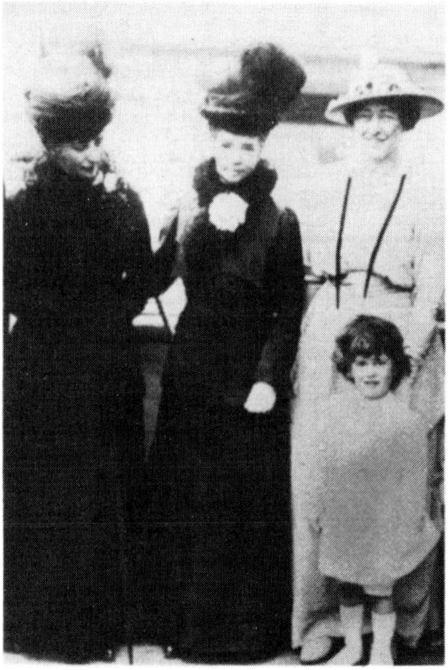

Top left, Shackleton with Emily in Copenhagen in 1909. *Top right,* Shackleton with daughter Cecily in a photograph dedicated to Elizabeth Dawson-Lambton. *Bottom,* Emily Shackleton with Queen Alexandra on the left and her sister the Dowager Empress of Russia in the centre. The photograph dates from 1914 and the child in the foreground is Edward Alexander, later Lord Shackleton.

The hut was in fact virtually complete, but it revealed a distressing deficiency:

> The temperature . . . within three feet of the stove . . . was . . . 13°F. of frost . . . what it will be like in the winter if the coal supply gives out I don't like to think.[22]

On 18 February, while Shackleton was on board arguing with England, the wind shifted to ESE, a blizzard roared down from Erebus, sweeping sheets of snow off the land. *Nimrod* once more stood off. This, however, was much the most serious affair. England had been taken by surprise. The ship was blown out to sea. Shackleton and some of the shore party were caught on board. In the lulls, the sea was freezing over. *Nimrod* drove fifty miles northwards out of McMurdo Sound before she was brought under control. It was early in the morning of 22 February before *Nimrod* closed Cape Royds again. By then, those ashore had made up their minds she would not return; so too perhaps had some on board.

In a surf boat, through the rip and surge of the swell, Davis then ferried a few more loads of coal ashore. It made the total stock eighteen tons; enough for a year but no more. After dumping the last sacks Davis reported to Shackleton. As Davis wrote in after years,

> My memory retains a picture of him . . . fists on hips and brow knitted in thought. It was a characteristic pose . . . "Well done!" he said, "Now get away as soon as possible and tell the Captain to sail at once. Goodbye." I remember exhorting my tired and grimy rowers to put their backs into it.[23]

With a puff of smoke from her funnel, *Nimrod* swung slowly round and, tossing jerkily in the swell, she gathered way.

"I have been through much that I cannot write," Shackleton said in his last letter to Emily. *Nimrod* left him with another shaft of bafflement. As she came in for the last time to put him ashore, he had seen that the ice had broken up as far as Hut Point. "Prospice," Shackleton ended his letter, "Prospice." This was their private greeting; a reference to Browning's poem of that name. It was Shackleton's battle cry. "I was ever a fighter, so – one fight more/The best and the last!" ran his favourite lines, "For sudden the worst turns to the best to the brave."[24]

On *Nimrod*, Davis found England looking

> tired and ill . . . he said . . . "I want you to take over for the time being . . . I must get some rest." It was more than twenty four hours

> before we saw the Captain again and he then looked a different man. It had been [his] first proper rest . . . since leaving New Zealand, nearly eight weeks before.

For the following year, England was carrying precisely worded orders. If, Shackleton had written, he was not back from the polar journey by 15 February 1909, England was to

> return as early as possible to McMurdo Sound in 1910 . . . You are not to delegate this work to any other Expedition that may possibly be going to the above place.[25]

"I write this as a definite instruction," Shackleton declared, "though I know well it is the last thing you would allow should occur." Shackleton was haunted by the fear of being rescued by Scott. That would be an unbearable disgrace. "It is to you alone," Shackleton told England, "that I look for my ultimate relief."[26]

XXI

The conquest of Mount Erebus

"Glad to see the last of her & England," Marshall remarked, as the black hull of *Nimrod* melted into the grey-green waters, and disappeared from sight. "Rotten orders," he went on, "Unnecessary rush."[1]

Shackleton had undoubtedly sent *Nimrod* off in a hurry. He unceremoniously bundled the crew members on shore back to the ship. There were no goodbyes and, amongst other things, he left four sledges still on board. It was as if he wished to break the link with the outside as quickly as he could. "There were times," admitted Marshall, "when more than one of us thought of returning with *Nimrod*."[2] Shackleton sensed that. In the unsettling aftermath of the quarrel with England, he wanted no opportunity for second thoughts.

Mackintosh, in Marshall's words, was "to bring ship down next time. England got his congé".[3] The whole landing party knew it. Shackleton had decided that England was a threat to his authority. Either way, to uphold morale ashore he had to be quit of England, and be seen to have done so.

For the sake of morale on board *Nimrod*, on the other hand, England had to be kept in ignorance until journey's end. So, as he paced the bridge with the comfortable heave underfoot of *Nimrod* running free, and the satisfaction, as he felt, of a job well done, he carried, all unknowing, the death warrant of his hopes. "I cannot have England down again," ran a letter from Shackleton to Emily in the mailbag carefully guarded by England himself in his cabin, "he is ill and has lost his nerve and . . . has given me an awful time of it."[4] Also on board were sealed orders from Shackleton dismissing England from his post. They superseded the open ones in which Shackleton had entrusted England with defending him from possible rescue by Scott.

At Cape Royds, *Nimrod* had left an eerie desolation. There was no jetty, no friendly buoy to mark the harbour channel; only a dark surf hissing on an arid shore lined with frozen spray. The men who stayed behind were now marooned. There was no radio, with its ambivalent power of instant contact to break the isolation. For a year at least, they were as effectively cut off from the world as if they had been on another planet suspended out in space. They were vaguely haunted by the thought that on the whole mysterious continent to the edge of which they clung, they were the only men.

Their tensions were accentuated by the descent of isolation. Because of his personality, Marshall recorded some notably outspoken signs. "Shacks & I are polite but distant," as he put it in his diary,

> never will be any confidence between us. Having not an iota of respect for him, it is only course & I am content.[5]

Marshall had various grievances. So far, not a single Sunday service had been held and, from the day the ship left Cape Royds, Shackleton announced that Adams was second-in-command. "Not straight",[6] Marshall wrote, especially as, in his view, "Adams was the most insubordinate of the shore party".[7] He felt that he had been promised the position; but Adams was just as sure that Shackleton had promised *him*.

Marshall did not exactly show his feelings. He was, however, a man of rigid moral probity and, as so often is the case, a bit of a misanthrope. The real point was simply, as he had discovered too late, that he and Shackleton did not get on.

When *Nimrod* sailed, the hut first had to be completed, and order brought to the snow-covered jumble of stores standing where they had been dumped ashore. It was rough, cold, windy, harsh and uninspiring work. "Sh. devilish surly in morning," Marshall observed on one occasion, "improved slightly as day went on."[8] Shackleton, as one of his companions, an Ulsterman, put it, had

> absorbed most of the Irish temperament . . . He'd got a temper which flared up very quickly too . . . We could always tell when things were bad by watching him come into breakfast . . . if Shackleton didn't say good morning to us, we kept very quiet at breakfast time![9]

Shackleton, meanwhile, had to face the fact that he was not only marooned, but hemmed in. The ice along the shore had long since floated out to sea, cutting the road to the south. Until McMurdo Sound froze over again, there was no escape. There was no way of laying depots for the southern journey before winter came. No more visibly useful work was in sight. The Pole suddenly seemed swathed in doubt. To avert frustration, and check disturbing undercurrents, Shackleton had to find some outlet for pent-up energy. He proposed the ascent of Mount Erebus, still as yet unclimbed.

The idea may have been Edgeworth David's; but Shackleton willingly took it as his own. They discussed it with Marshall on 2 March; on 3 March, Shackleton declared the work of settling in to be completed. Next day, he announced the climb, and the day after, it had started.

For some time, Marshall had been trying to give Shackleton a medical examination. Shackleton had consistently refused. This partly explained Marshall's rising antagonism. He was brooding over the incident of Shackleton having been taken ill on the voyage down.* He suspected Shackleton of being unfit and trying to conceal the fact. He was privately predicting that the expedition would succeed only if Shackleton "does not start on Southern journey as he hints".[10] Marshall now declined to pass Shackleton fit for the ascent of Erebus unless allowed to examine him once and for all. Shackleton evaded the issue, and elected to stay behind.

David, Mawson and Mackay went instead, together with Marshall, Brocklehurst and Adams. What lay ahead was scarcely a climb. It was a scramble up a high but unprecipitous volcanic cone, but the ludicrously accoutred sextet that ambled off that Wednesday morning scarcely seemed to belong to the nation that pioneered modern mountaineering.

Mount Erebus, sweeping almost to the height of the Matterhorn, straight up from the sea, is one of the great vistas of the world, although its technical difficulties are approximately nil. It is nonetheless a snow and ice peak. Its wide fields of névé and open flanks in any case were the kind reasonably to be expected on the polar journey.

Shackleton, however, had with him no trained mountaineer. Nor had climbing equipment been brought. The only footwear was smooth-soled, finnesko and Northern Swedish ski boots. The latter were really finnesko made of cowhide instead of reindeer fur. They were brought because of a misconception that only soft footwear could prevent frostbite. A frenzied bout of improvisation preceded the start. For a better grip, Edgeworth David attached a few strips of leather to his ski boots. Crampons were improvised out of nails

* See p. 200.

stuck through pieces of leather, the last being finished only at midnight, a few hours before departure.

The approach slopes were wide, mildly rising, with mixed going over wind-packed crust and a little blue ice sprinkled with snow. To carry all their equipment, the six mountaineers hauled behind them a sledge weighing 600 lbs. "We were struggling for some time, mostly on our hands and knees," David recorded. There was "no breath for talking".[11]

> Occasionally we came to blows, but these were dealt accidentally by a long armed finnesko-shod cramponless sledger, who whirled his arms like a windmill in his desperate efforts to keep his balance after slipping.[12]

After two days of this sort of thing, the slope increased, the sledge could be taken no further and the climb itself began. The altitude was 6,000 feet, almost half way up the mountain.

Shackleton had made David, Mawson and Mackay the summit party, with Adams, Marshall and Brocklehurst in support. The former were now supposed to go forward and the latter to return. Leadership, however, was confused. Shackleton had put David in charge of the summit party, but Adams was in overall command. Adams also wanted to be among the first to climb an Antarctic mountain. He chose now to go forward with all six. Unfortunately, there was not enough equipment to go round. On the side of the mountain, more improvisation was required. The sledge had to be depoted, but no rucksacks had been taken. Carrying devices had to be contrived with odd straps and stumps of Alpine rope. "We each," David recorded, "had to carry a weight of about forty pounds."

> We filed off in a procession more bizarre than beautiful. Some of us with our sleeping bags hanging straight down our backs with the foot of the bag curled upwards and outwards, resembled the scorpion men of the Assyrian sculptures: others marched with their household gods done up in the form of huge sausages; yet another presented Sindbad, with the place of the "Old Man of the Sea" taken by a huge brown bag, stuffed with all our cooking utensils; this bag had a knack of suddenly slipping off his shoulders, and bow-stringing him around his neck.[13]

For three days they struggled up the mountainside, sliding and slipping on wind-packed snow. They had no proper tents, for the poles were too cumbersome to carry. They sat in the open to eat – "we munched in silence",[14] in David's words – and bivouacked by spreading tent cloths over their sleeping bags. They survived a blizzard, which pinned them down at 10,000 feet for thirty-six hours without food.

On the way, Brocklehurst celebrated his twenty-first birthday, suffered from altitude sickness, and wanted to turn back. David, however, was determined to go on. "Your personal safety," as Mawson had ruefully told him, "you always place in such light regard."[15] Nor was Adams the man to consider a sick companion. Brocklehurst was forced to go on. He got frostbitten feet, but refused to change from ski boots to finnesko. Mackay, too, began acting irrationally. They were all roped up part of the way; not because the slopes were particularly steep, but because there were not enough crampons to go round. At one point Mackay suddenly unroped, struck out on his own across a hanging glacier, cutting steps with his ice axe, and fainted in the process.

On Tuesday, 10 March, after five days of self-imposed struggle, they reached the summit and saw "the great shadow of Erebus", as David recorded in his diary, "on [a] sea of cumulus".[16] Brocklehurst, too weak for the last few thousand feet, had been left behind in his sleeping bag. He thus missed being one of the first men to look down into the crater of Erebus. What the others saw were clouds of steam rising from large holes far below. Periodical booms were heard from the bowels of the mountain. Marshall fixed the altitude by hypsometer. This was simply a small cylinder in which distilled water was boiled, and the temperature measured. It is based on the fact that the temperature at which water boils drops with height above sea level. It was then the most accurate known method of measuring altitude. The summit of Erebus turned out to be 13,500 feet above sea level.

Since at high latitudes the air is thinner and the effective altitude higher, the men on top of Erebus felt the consequences. After three hours, they scurried off down the mountain as quickly as they could, picking up Brocklehurst on their way. Again they were overtaken by a blizzard, but reached the sledge in time to pick up their tent poles and make a proper camp before the full fury burst on them. Next morning, it had blown itself out, and at 5 a.m., they continued on their way. Slithering down, they had to manipulate the sledge. "Many upsets," Marshall recorded laconically. "Commenced to blow."

> Depoted sledge, started to tramp it. Fell 100ds of times, bruised all over dead tired lost bearings. Arrived hut 11 a.m. nearly dead . . . very thankful to be back.[17]

Staggering out of the drift, they were cheered by the men who stayed behind. They had made ludicrously heavy weather of a simple climb; but they had succeeded in the first ascent of an Antarctic peak. It was only a month after landing, but already the expedition had its first achievement to show.

The taste of victory eased the path of leadership. The underlying fear with which Shackleton had to deal, which muted even the conquest of Erebus, was what would happen if *Nimrod* did not get through. Because the world would not know where they were, they might not be found again. Everything turned on England, the captain under sentence of dismissal, and whose judgment they had been led to doubt.

In case no ship returned next year, Shackleton had been airing the idea of sailing the lifeboat left by *Nimrod* to fetch help from New Zealand. That was another version of his dream of making a great open boat journey. Larsen, rowing from Paulet Island to Snow Hill on Nordenskjöld's expedition, had shown what could be done. Shackleton had to keep alive the belief in escape, and quash a lurking terror of being trapped.

On 6 March, while Shackleton's men were still climbing up the slopes of Erebus, *Nimrod* raised Port Chalmers, New Zealand. For some time Harry Dunlop, the chief engineer, had been uneasy. He was carrying sealed orders from Shackleton dismissing England, and he knew the contents. Perhaps Shackleton had chosen to confide in Dunlop, as a fellow Irishman; perhaps also because, as an engineer, and not a deck officer, he would be distanced from his captain. Nonetheless, as the voyage went on, Dunlop found it hard to face England across the wardroom table. When *Nimrod* reached Port Chalmers, Mackintosh, by previous arrangement, went ashore to go on ahead to Christchurch. Dunlop gave him the letter of dismissal. It was addressed to Joseph Kinsey, who would hand it to England.

Two days later, *Nimrod* was sailing up past Akaroa Heads, to Lyttelton, where her voyage would officially end. Dunlop could stand the deception no longer. On his own initiative, he prepared England for what was in store. England was numbed by what he heard, and when he received Shackleton's letter he was considerably distressed; especially when he read "that you are resigning on account of your health being impaired".[18] "'tis a lie," England wrote to William Colbeck. "I was dismissed."[19] It was true, of course.

> You will please sign off the register as master [Shackleton had baldly written]. I do not wish you to be a loser by this unfortunate state of

your health, and I have instructed . . . Kinsey . . . to pay your salary regularly until my return . . . I advise you to take a prolonged rest at home.[20]

England thought that Shackleton was using illness as a pretext to avoid public embarrassment. By his own letter, on the other hand – "knowing the state of mind and health you are in at present", as it began – Shackleton clearly believed that England had been ill. Shackleton connected this with the fact that, early in 1907, England had been invalided home from West Africa with sunstroke. Of this, Shackleton had been unaware when he appointed England.

In any case, illness offered a convenient cover to conceal the quarrel at McMurdo Sound and to save the expedition from scandal. It had the opposite effect, of course. "Illness" smacked only too obviously of a smokescreen, especially with the unspoken stigma of "mental" hanging in the air. It left England in considerable distress, for his whole seagoing career now seemed in jeopardy: "I cannot fight or attack," he wrote in a letter home, "until [Shackleton] returns, if he ever does".[21]

"EXPLORERS FIGHT" was the resultant headline in the *Daily Mail* and, with variations, elsewhere too. This derived from *Nimrod* sailors, in their cups or not, talking about the moment in McMurdo Sound when England seized the engine-room telegraph out of Shackleton's hands. Journalists at Lyttelton very properly wanted to get to the bottom of the story. Someone said that Shackleton – or was it England? – had been knocked down, and behind the gossip and the headlines lay, as usual, a psychological truth.

To Scott, at least, it made titillating compensation for an earlier *Daily Mail* headline "MESSAGE FROM THE ANTARCTIC", over a story which announced: "Lieutenant Shackleton is camped near the foot of Mount Erebus, the most southerly of volcanoes".[22] Rage, jealousy and high moral indignation, in that order, were Scott's reactions to Shackleton's breaking his promise to keep away from McMurdo Sound.

Scott could only too vividly imagine the barrier rolling on uninterruptedly to the Pole. Shackleton could hardly fail. Scott's fiancée, Kathleen Bruce, offered the consoling thought that Shackleton would "soon break down",[23] but Scott saw himself forestalled, beaten, his ambition in the dust. He turned to his faithful friends, as he thought, in the RGS.

Shackleton, Scott wrote to Scott Keltie, was a "liar",[24] adding that he had suspected all along he would break his word. Never would he have anything more to do with Shackleton. Scott, however, found his friends uncomfortably cool. The whole affair, Scott Keltie, in his own words (but not to Scott) found "painful". To Sir Clements Markham, he wrote,

> Personally, I am all with Scott . . . but don't you think it places the [Royal Geographical] Society in an awkward position, supposing Shackleton should return successful, that is to say . . . having reached the Pole or somewhere near it . . .[25]

That, of course, was the rub. Keltie, at heart a shrewd Edinburgh Scot, grasped that the society would make a spectacular fool of itself if it disowned a possible hero on a debatable moralistic point.

Sir Clements Markham was thinking along the same lines when he wrote to Emily Shackleton:

> I strongly advised Dr. Keltie not to put anything in the RGS journal about the reasons for giving up King Edward VII Land, and he has taken my advice. The reason is that an excuse would be implied; when the public are not aware that any excuse is needed.[26]

"The England affair," as Sir Clements told Keltie, "had better be hushed up," sagaciously adding "I suppose there are two sides to the story."[27] To Emily, Sir Clements went on to say that

> It is a pity that Ernest worded his promise [to Scott] so strongly, and now the best thing is that nothing more should be heard about it.[28]

Victory, as Sir Clements knew, would be an incontrovertible argument. Before that, even his personal devotion to Scott would have to bend.

It was not only the England affair and his broken promise to Scott with which Shackleton was burdened. When obtaining the Australian and New Zealand government grants, he had promised in return to let *Nimrod* carry out oceanographic and magnetic surveys while waiting to sail on his relief. On the voyage south, he had decided that this would be an unjustifiable risk. *Nimrod* was in no condition to sustain the extra cruise. With *Koonya* he had sent back a categorical order that *Nimrod* was not to leave Lyttelton before sailing south again. He knew therefore he would be reproached with having obtained government money under false pretences. Dealing with this embarrassment was one more task with which Joseph Kinsey found himself unexpectedly faced. More seriously, he found that there was no money to send *Nimrod* down again.

Emily was left to her own devices. She it was who had to bring her husband home. Her brother Herbert who had volunteered to act as the expedition's solicitor, was actually saddled with the work. It was, as he put it, "more than I ever bargained for".[29] Shackleton had left an impressive welter of confusion behind him. £7,000 was desperately needed before *Nimrod* could sail. Herbert Dorman, as he told Emily, felt "inclined to pass the whole thing on" to Frank Shackleton; but on Frank, he added, "I can't rely." Shackleton's backers had mostly turned away. William Beardmore, as Herbert Dorman told Emily, was "vexed" because of the unrepaid loan of £1,000 to Shackleton before he sailed; more, perhaps, because "E. never wrote from N.Z. Of course", Herbert added, "I know nothing about it."[30] Unfortunately, at this point, with the affairs of the expedition in conspicuous disarray, the truth about the £1,000 emerged.

To enquire into the yet unsolved theft of the Irish crown jewels, a quaintly named "Viceregal Commission" had been appointed. It sat in Dublin Castle. On 16 January, 1908, the same day, incidentally, that his brother, on *Nimrod*, was passing through the first belt of icebergs guarding the Ross Sea, Frank Shackleton was giving evidence. What Frank called his "monetary difficulties" were touched on and Frank candidly admitted that he "borrowed money from a money-lender".[31] These loans, another witness told the commission, were "paid off, as a matter of fact . . . by Mr. Shackleton's brother".[32] The witness was another shady character, Francis Bennett-Goldney, Mayor of Canterbury, who happened to have backed the bills.

In this piquant way, Beardmore discovered why Ernest Shackleton had borrowed the £1,000. It was not, as he had imagined, for the expedition, but to save his brother from insolvency. The two were, of course, closely interwoven. Had Frank Shackleton gone bankrupt it would have destroyed what remained of Ernest Shackleton's credit. To save himself, therefore, Ernest had had, at whatever cost, to save his brother. With none of this did William Beardmore sympathise. He refused categorically to help with Shackleton's relief.

That was not the end of the story. The commission could not decide who had stolen the crown jewels. It did, on the other hand, exonerate Frank Shackleton. The commission, however, was widely regarded as a sham. For one thing, although presided over by a judge, and conducted with all legal trappings, it was clearly usurping the functions of a court of law. It was designed, like so many commissions, to obfuscate the truth. By the King's command, Frank had resigned from the College of Arms. So, too, had

Sir Arthur Vicars; for having introduced Frank Shackleton to Dublin Castle, so it was said.

Frank, meanwhile, was questioned by the police. Their investigation into the disappearance of the crown jewels happened to overlap another into (the then criminal offence of) homosexuality in high places, and Frank Shackleton was one of the names that appeared in both. "An abandoned ruffian",[33] was what Augustine Birrell, Chief Secretary for Ireland, called him. Frank was not arrested, so the story went, nor brought to trial, because if he was indicted, he would reveal a scandal of colossal proportions which touched the Court, and which would give the nationalists a golden opportunity to bring British rule in Ireland into disrepute.

In England, none of this, on the whole, was taken too seriously. It seemed to be another misty Irish farce, hovering no doubt on the brink of tragedy. For the moment, it was an amusing embarrassment for the Liberal government, and an equally amusing piece of salacious gossip.

Frank's shady reputation, however, now enveloped Ernest Shackleton as well. The trouble was that in other directions Ernest himself was a little suspect now. His financial insouciance had caused offence, and his backers all declined to give any further help. The quarrel with England also played its part. During the summer England returned home to Hull, bringing home his bride. He had married his New Zealand fiancée and decided to leave the sea. Did the incident on *Nimrod* show that he was unsuited to command a ship? Had it broken his nerve? In public he was impeccably loyal to Shackleton; but still the question mark remained.

The upshot was that the months passed and money for Shackleton's relief seemed as far off as ever. At least Emily Shackleton now discovered who were her husband's friends. "This 'little show' as your husband calls it is going to be a big one I expect,"[34] wrote Campbell Mackellar. "On this midwinter day of the Southern Hemisphere," Hugh Robert Mill wrote to her on 22 June,

> I cannot help thinking of you and of the object of your thought. The worst of the darkness is over now with every day bringing the sun nearer . . . whether my friend Shackleton brings back the South Pole or not I am quite sure he will bring back a splendid record – and much do I look forward to hearing him recount it![35]

XXII

Midwinter

In the hut at Cape Royds, midwinter was, according to Antarctic custom, being celebrated as Christmas; as indeed it might have been if history had been made in the southern, instead of the northern hemisphere.*

Let us join Shackleton and his men after dinner on 23 June. Most of them we have already met on *Nimrod* or the slopes of Erebus. Mackay is missing. He has retired to bed after consuming two thirds of a bottle of whisky. All the rest are there, however, in their paper hats, masks and false noses. To the general relief George Marston, the artist – "Putty" – has not made an embarrassing exhibition of himself again by dressing up as a woman, down to lipstick, powder and rouge. Conversation is heated, vinous but, on the whole, clean. Shackleton will tolerate no smut, and his disapproval has long since been respected as a command. The only way of dealing with sexual deprivation, he has decided, is by pretending that women do not exist.

Streamers, crackers and champagne cannot quite disguise the fact that they are living in a small, dark, and cramped hut. Something is wrong with the insulation. A few feet away from the stove, the temperature on the floor is below freezing. There is no proper furniture. To save money and also space on *Nimrod*,

* The southern hemisphere, according to Dante in the *Divine Comedy*, was where Satan landed when he fell from Heaven. All the land which, until then had been concentrated there, migrated in horror to the northern hemisphere, leaving only Mount Purgatory behind, a place, as Dante put it,

> by no means fit
> For a king's palace, but a natural prison,
> With a vile floor, and very badly lit.[1]

Not a bad preview, in fact, of the modern theory of continental drift.

Shackleton deliberately left everything to be improvised out of packing cases, including all the bunks and partitions for the sleeping cubicles. The long table around which they are sitting has been made by Murray; a bit roughly, perhaps, but it serves. It is designed to be hoisted out of the way on pulleys to the ceiling when more space is needed or the floor has to be cleaned. During a storm, the floor buckles, and the whole place sways and creaks. Sometimes it seems that another demented gust would carry it away. It is like the overcrowded fo'c'sle of some cranky ship. In Shackleton's words, however, it is the "whole inhabited world to us".[2]

The young fellow with the hopeful moustache, near the foot of the table, is Raymond Priestley. He has been put in his place by Adams, the loud, hectoring, sharp-faced figure sitting opposite. Earlier in the winter, Adams had told Priestley to exercise the horses. Priestley objected. He did not like horses. Science, he said, was his job. Adams, as Priestley later told the tale, thereupon rounded on him and said:

> "You needn't think, Priestley, that you were taken on this show because you were a great scientist." I didn't. He went on "I was present when Shacks interviewed you . . . He was worried at the time because he had got hold of a lot of real hard nuts." He had – Adams was one of them. "When you left the room," Adams continued, "he turned to me and said 'Well! Anyhow I can manage that fellow!' "[3]

Priestley got the point. Everyone was expected to do his share of all the chores. Soon afterwards he was writing,

> I have heard it said that a well-managed expedition was nothing but a glorified picnic with a spice of danger, & our stay here has certainly upheld the truth of the remark.[4]

This is Raymond Priestley's great adventure. It has got him away from the hedgerowed confines of Tewkesbury, and here, at 77° 31′ south latitude, he has had his first drive in a motor car. He is also one of the most percipient members of the expedition.

> I can quite understand what Wild said about men getting panic struck [on *Discovery*] & rushing back to the . . . ship when left alone on the ice . . . in the winter night. either there are weird noises going on on all sides . . . & you fancy you can hear footsteps behind you, or you hear nothing but are oppressed by the still more weird silence.[5]

It is Priestley, too, who has articulated the fear haunting the outwardly festive scene. A mysterious disease had started ravaging the ponies. It turned out to be volcanic grit around their stalls that they were perversely eating. By the middle of March, three ponies had died. That left five, and Shackleton's absolute minimum was six. "If we lose many more," wrote Priestley at the time, "our chances of getting to the Pole will become chimerical."[6] Since then, one more had died, and only four remained. Also, Priestley reflected,

> It has become a very grave question whether or not we shall be able to get to Hut Pt. over the sea-ice . . . every blizzard has broken the ice . . .[7]

Shackleton, sitting at the head of the table, pulling yet another cracker, and puffing at a cigarette, gives no sign of these or other worries. He has contrived to keep his men reasonably happy; happier at least than he had been on *Discovery*. It is hard to say exactly how Shackleton has done it. Privately, with Brocklehurst – whom, incidentally, he has persuaded to invest in some shares he was promoting – he will laugh at Scott.[8] So partly, perhaps, it is a conscious effort to avoid the same mistakes.

On practically every point, as Wild and Joyce, the old *Discovery* men can observe, Shackleton is a notable contrast to Scott. Shackleton is informal and unfussy. He delegates well, but takes an obvious interest in each man. He has the knack of making everyone feel that he is important to the expedition. Above all, he can hide his feelings, although not always suppress his emotions. He is moody, but not morose. A suspicion of a frown behind the infectious humour and the ready laugh betrays the eye that is always watching and the temper that can so easily flare up.

This is shrugged off as part of the Irish temperament, for it is as an Irishman amongst Englishmen that Shackleton is seen. His temper comes and goes quickly. "He'd probably laugh about it afterwards," as one of his companions puts it. "Very much of a boy at heart."[9] He is at any rate not jealous, class-conscious, or dependent on hierarchy. Behind everything lies the mysterious force of leadership. That everyone, with more or less enthusiasm, accepts. "The power was in himself," as Harbord said on *Nimrod*, "it was not outside".[10]

Around the more or less scruffy gathering, there is a touch of the academic common room. Six of the thirteen men in the hut have been to university. This is something new in polar exploration. The company is predominantly middle-class; on the other hand a broad social range is represented; from Sir Philip Brocklehurst, Eton and Cambridge, to Roberts, a rough diamond, the cook. Sir Philip likes being a bit of a rough diamond too. In any case, they all live together without distinction. That is Shackleton's style. There is none of the separation of wardroom and messdeck so conspicuous on *Discovery*. Shackleton has also managed to avoid fragmentation into cliques, although some people have naturally gravitated together. Priestley, for example, is great friends with Murray, possibly because Murray is imperturbable and humorous. Indeed, they share a sleeping cubicle, coarsely called the "tap room", because Murray is suffering from chronic diarrhoea.

Pulling a cracker with Shackleton is the picturesquely dishevelled, yet somehow dignified figure of Edgeworth David. His Welsh origins run strong. He maintains a compulsive flow of talk. A bit of an actor, he regularly entertains his companions with spirited readings from Dickens. Today, naturally, it has been *A Christmas Carol*.

In Marshall's words, David has Shackleton "under his thumb".[11] Although Adams is formally second-in-command, David is psychologically so. Perhaps that is why Shackleton wanted him. To anyone versed in the intellectual thuggery of the academic world, the tortuous byways of expedition psychology are child's play. Unobtrusively, he smooths over tensions. David is a peacemaker; a pillar of this little enclosed society, a "tower of strength" as Shackleton himself says, with "such a good influence over all the men".[12]

David also leads the Australians, Mawson and Armytage. They are the one true clique in the hut. Nationalism is their bond, and ambivalence towards the mother country. Mawson, tall, bleak-eyed, is abrupt, austere, and not universally popular. Armytage's haunted eyes hint at some private hell. He has an irritating, or amusing, habit of saying "what what". He is intermittently depressed, for which Shackleton who, next to loyalty, demands optimism from his men, has little sympathy. He has lectured Armytage severely about his inability to get on with anybody else. What Shackleton does not understand is that Armytage is brooding on his sense of uselessness which the expedition has only partly relieved.

The outsider at the party, somehow, is Eric Marshall. He is sitting at the foot of the table aloof, barely entering into the spirit of the feast. His companions shrug it off as bad temper or arrogance. It is not as simple as that. Marshall has proposed a winter journey to Cape Crozier, at the other end of Ross Island, to collect the eggs of the Emperor penguin. Shackleton has that very day scuppered the idea. "It is certain to be a tough job," Marshall has admitted, "as there will be very little light & probably low temperatures."[13]

To Shackleton, that is an unacceptable risk for a bird's egg. It will jeopardise the polar journey.

Marshall, in one of the outbursts that pepper his diary, has already written:

> When [Shackleton] took me on he thought he had got a fool. No doubt he was right. He had got a man who was fool enough . . . to take him at his word . . . to disregard & refute certain reports we had heard re him . . . To spend £90 in prep . . . for Expedition . . . To have sacrificed an appointment & prospects in order to join hands with a coward, a cad, who was incapable of keeping his word.[14]

This hardly helps to put Marshall in the party spirit. He is probably relieved when, around midnight, Shackleton retires to his cubicle – the only private one in the hut – and goes to bed.

Soon afterwards, in Marshall's words, Wild

> showed sign of being drunk, & was anxious to make a row, but after a little while persuaded him to turn in. Was seriously thinking of getting him outside to give me a hand with the ponies & then giving him a damn good hammering, as he was becoming very talkative and objectionable & Shacks was evidently afraid to come out and stop him, although awake and hearing all he said.[15]

Shackleton, of course, has deliberately gone off to let his companions relax. However genial, he is still a leader, and therefore a constraint. Also it is an opportunity to eavesdrop and learn a little more about his men. In any case, Wild has been looking for a leader to whom to attach himself; but he is not yet sure that in Shackleton he has found what he seeks. If nothing else, the party has shown that Wild's burden is drink. Shackleton can sympathise. He knows that unless he controls himself, it could be his problem too. Between them, Shackleton and David have prevented most discontent, but in a small, isolated group, it cannot be entirely avoided.

At the beginning of August, Mackay suddenly went for Roberts, the cook, with whom he shared a cubicle. The casus belli was that Roberts put his feet on Mackay's sea-chest to lace up his boots. Mackay, much the bigger and stronger, tried to wring Roberts' neck. He might have succeeded if Mawson, who was bigger and stronger still, had not intervened. It was "the first disagreeable fracas", in Priestley's words, and it was "lucky evidently that the Winter [was] almost over instead of just beginning".[16]

In Marshall's version, Shackleton was

> in a regular panic about it & threatens he will shoot [Mackay]. This is the 2nd time he has said [so]. He is so easily frightened that he is not to be trusted with a pistol . . . Mac quite all right but *slightly* eccentric & quick tempered.[17]

Partly this expressed the vein of bitterness within Marshall, partly genuine disgust with human flaws. He was appalled when Shackleton "lost his temper . . . with pups & made violent efforts to kick them".[18] Marshall was discovering that leadership is distinct from worthiness or likeability. He was also suffering the shafts of frustrated ambition. Morally, he felt superior to Shackleton, but Shackleton was the leader he would like to have been.

Marshall's real concern now was with the polar journey "on which", as he frankly said, "all my ambitions are centred".[19] He had digested the deficiencies in Shackleton's preparations – nobody with farrier's experience, for example, had been brought. Nobody, therefore, could pare the ponies' hooves, and the only way to keep them trimmed was by constant exercise around a snow-free patch of volcanic grit. Moreover, although dogs had been brought there were no experienced dog drivers. Joyce, who was in charge of the dogs, had only been, as Marshall drily put it, "on the Discovery Expedition, where all the dogs died".[20]

It was the health of the humans, however, that preoccupied Marshall. The wrong man on the road to the Pole could kill them all. The choice, he had determined, would be his, as doctor. In England, Shackleton had promised Wild, Adams, Joyce, Brocklehurst and Marshall places on the polar party. Shackleton, said Marshall, "should never have made these rash promises".[21]

Marshall had decided to "plough" Joyce, as he put it. For one thing, Joyce's liver was affected by drink. Also Marshall, in his own words, was convinced that Joyce "had a myocarditis [a form of heart disease] in a very early stage".[22] Above all, Marshall believed that Joyce was mentally incapacitated for the southern journey. He considered him of limited intelligence, resentful, incompatible with the others. It was a dangerous combination, threatening breakdown and disaster. Mentally, Marshall was not sure of Adams either, although physically he passed him. "I saw much on Erebus," Marshall darkly recorded, "to make me doubt his nerve and judgment."[23]

It was Shackleton himself, however, who was causing Marshall the greatest perplexity. In after years, Marshall categorically asserted that "Shacks was never physically fit to carry out any of his programmes",[24] but at the time, he was grappling simply with a sense of something awry. For example, Shackleton started an anti-swearing club which Marshall joined "on condition he did same in our anti-smoking [club]".[25]

Early in the winter, Marshall recorded going for a walk with Shackleton who, as he put it, was "thinking of his 'past' & anxious as to how much I know".[26] Marshall believed that Shackleton was harbouring a secret. It was at any rate now painfully clear that Shackleton was anxious to keep doctors at a distance.

On 3 June, after months of argument, Marshall finally compelled Shackleton to let him examine him. What Marshall found was a "pulm[onary] systolic [heart] murmur".[27] It was still present five weeks later. Marshall did not know exactly what it meant. He was not a heart specialist. At that time, in any case, diagnosis of heart disease was still rudimentary. The murmur could well have been "functional", that is, not a symptom of disease. People then condemned to an invalid's life would today run marathons.

Since his collapse on *Discovery*, and possibly before, Shackleton had been pursued by the spectre of weak heart and lungs, but particularly a weak heart. Perhaps he was what today is called a "cardiac neurotic". His avoidance of doctors nourished imagination. The fear was real enough to him. Marshall's stethoscope probably first gave form to an inchoate dread. In any case, doctor and patient were now equally confused. Shackleton somehow persuaded Marshall to pass him for the southern journey. For that, Marshall never quite forgave himself. He had allowed his medical judgment to be overriden by sheer force of superior personality. Perhaps that helps to explain the thread of discontent running through his diary.

Early in the winter, as a result of frostbite on the ascent of Erebus, Marshall had had to amputate one of Brocklehurst's big toes. More to the point, after the operation Brocklehurst was "very down"; he "seems to have no guts", as Marshall brutally put it.[28] The matter had been clinched at the end of July, when Brocklehurst showed an irregular heartbeat: "on history and condition told Sh. could not pass him for South".[29] Shackleton, said Marshall, was "afraid to tell Brocklehurst he cant go [and] will try and buy him off. Whole expedition being risked by fear of speaking out."[30] Shackleton, in fact, did remove both Brocklehurst and Joyce from the southern party. Except where he himself was concerned, he unreservedly followed Marshall's professional advice.

So, in the end, Shackleton, Adams, Marshall and Wild were going south. Marshall could only hope that it was the right choice. There was in any case "never any question of Wild not going", in Marshall's words, "as I regarded him as the fittest in the party".[31]

Scurvy was Marshall's great concern. "I was well aware," he

said, surveying the history of polar exploration, "that we had not a hope of achieving anything worthwhile unless we could beat this scourge."

> Before going South, I had hoped to add something to our knowledge of Scurvy and interviewed several men who were reputed to have knowledge of the subject, but it seemed largely "guess work".[32]

Nobody in fact yet knew what caused scurvy, but shortly before Marshall left England, there appeared in the *Journal of Hygiene* a paper by two Norwegian doctors, Axel Holst and Theodor Frølich. They had induced scurvy in guinea pigs by withholding fresh foods. It was the first systematic experimentation in the disease since the great pioneering clinical trials of James Lind, a Scottish naval surgeon, in the eighteenth century.

Holst and Frølich, like Lind, showed that scurvy was a deficiency disease. They also showed, however, that scurvy was prevented by some substance, as yet unknown, but which was destroyed by prolonged cooking. This was an accurate description of vitamin C, which was not to be isolated and identified as the anti-scurvy vitamin for another quarter of a century. (The very word "vitamin" did not yet exist.) Conventional wisdom explained scurvy by food poisoning, to be prevented by sterilisation at high temperature, but Marshall was unimpressed by conventional wisdom. He had the insight to follow Holst and Frølich, against the established authorities.

That is to say, Marshall proposed to prevent scurvy with fresh food from the start. In New Zealand, he had acquired (the word "scrounge" did not yet exist, either) a load of the season's tinned and bottled fruit. He especially took tinned tomatoes, which had just come on the market; and which now are known as a good source of vitamin C. Above all, throughout the winter, Marshall insisted on plenty of fresh, underdone, seal meat.

The first danger sign was an epidemic of minor cuts that refused to heal. "Such microbes as have survived the cold," said Priestley, "seem possessed of extraordinary vigour."[33] That was the prevailing view. Marshall disagreed. From careful reading, he recognised it as an early sign of scurvy, whereas Wilson, on *Discovery*, had only known the advanced symptoms. Marshall got Shackleton to have more seal meat served. Again, he was quite remarkably ahead of his times. By accepted modern standards, Marshall was providing his companions with about twice the amount of vitamin C required to maintain health. His idea was to "prime" everyone with fresh food for the long sledge journeys ahead.

Sledging began on 12 August. The days were light again, but the sun had not yet returned. It was, as Shackleton well knew, far too early and too cold. He was left, however, with no choice. He had to carry out all the preparation stopped the previous autumn by the disappearance of the sea ice. At least now McMurdo Sound had frozen over again. Shackleton had to blood his tyros, and move supplies along his line of march. He had two and a half months in which to do so.

David, Mawson and Mackay were going northwards on a journey of their own towards the South Magnetic Pole; insurance, as it were, against not reaching the geographical Pole. No experienced Antarctic travellers, however, could go with them. Shackleton and Wild were going south. Joyce was not passed fit for a long journey, and this one would be just as demanding as the southern journey.

Shackleton began by leading David – who was to command the Magnetic Pole party – and Bertram Armytage on a reconnaissance to the *Discovery* quarters at Hut Point. From there, he went a little way on to the Barrier to sample the surface. The last time he had seen those surroundings, had been that day, five and a half years before, when he had staggered back out of the south, wasted and ill.

Shackleton returned to Cape Royds on 22 August, the day the sun returned. At least he had found the sea ice safe, and the southern road whole again. David and Armytage had also, in Shackleton's words, "received a good baptism of frost".[34] Thenceforth, every week, Shackleton sent a party to Hut Point with supplies to build up an advance base. In rotation, all the novices were initiated into snow travel.

By contemporary standards, it was a grotesque performance. Nobody was on ski; it was man-hauling all the way. The four remaining ponies had to be saved for the polar journey; the dogs stayed behind at the hut, where they had languished since landing in January. "From past experience", Shackleton declared he knew that "dogs would not travel when low drift was blowing in their faces".[35] This was nonsense. The winter, after all, had passed almost as uselessly as on *Discovery*, even down to the production of a magazine; this time called *Aurora Australis*. A small printing press had been brought along, while on *Discovery*, *The South Polar Times* had to make do with a typewriter. *Aurora Australis* was the first work to be printed in Antarctica. Shackleton, however, had neglected to learn more about dogs, ski, or the technique of snow travel.

The work culminated in a spring depot journey out on the Barrier. Shackleton took the polar party of Adams, Marshall and Wild, together with Joyce and Marston. They left on 22 September, by motor car. They only travelled eight miles, which was as far as hard wind-packed snow covered the sea ice. The engine was running well in the cold but the wheels, as usual, failed at the first hint of drift snow. Thereafter, they had to climb out and yoke themselves to the sledge, as usual. It was nonetheless an historic little event, the first use of mechanical transport on a journey in the polar regions.

On 13 October, having got his depot out a hundred miles over the wind-blasted snowfields to 79° 36½′ south latitude, Shackleton returned to Cape Royds. A week earlier, Edgeworth David, Douglas Mawson, and Alistair Mackay had started across McMurdo Sound for the Magnetic Pole, they too "with motor car",[36] in David's words. After a few miles drift snow, as usual, forced the car to turn and they were decanted on to their own two feet. David, as Mawson put it, was

> so covered in clothes that he can hardly walk . . . He wears at least 1 singlet and 1 shirt, Jaeger wool waistcoat – waistlet sweater, blue coat and burberry drawers – blue pants, double seated burberry pants, fleece lined balaclava and fleece lined helmet . . .[37]

The dogs still stayed at home. David, Mawson and Mackay were going to man-haul every mile, and they had a long way to go.

With Edgeworth David away, Shackleton for the last few weeks before leaving was seen to be in absolute command.

XXIII

"A glorious day for our start"

> Last night as we sat at dinner the evening sun entered through the ventilator and the circle of light shone full on the portrait of [King Edward VII], Slowly it moved across and found the portrait of Her Majesty [Queen Alexandra]: it seemed an omen of good luck for only on this day and at that particular time could this have happened and today we started to strive & plant Her flag on the last spot of the world that counts as worth the striving for though ungilded by aught but adventure.

Such was the way Shackleton recorded his departure for the south. The date was Thursday, 29 October 1908. It was 10 a.m. when he led off through the snow and scree down from Cape Royds to the sea ice. As he put it,

> At last we are out on the long trail after 4 years thought and work. I pray we may be successful for my Heart has been so much in this.

It was, Shackleton wrote in his usual, tumbling, unpunctuated style, "a glorious day for our start. Brilliant sunshine and a cloudless sky. A fair wind from the north in fact everything that could conduce to an auspicious beginning".[1]

Like a reminder of menace in the glittering white landscape, Erebus reared its ice-clad crater ominously up above. Against this backdrop Grisi, Socks, Quan and Chinaman, the four surviving ponies, each harnessed to a sledge, each with a member of the polar party at his head, started ambling southwards over the ice.

Half an hour earlier the motor car had broken the eerie silence with its stutter, and started off, hauling a sledge; Day sitting to attention at the wheel. His passengers were Joyce, Brocklehurst,

Priestley, Armytage and Marston, following Shackleton in support. It was a strange contrast to the wayward technical retrogression for which the ponies stood. After a few miles, however, the hard wind crust ended, the drift snow began and the car, as usual, had to stop. The support party got out, hitched themselves to the sledge and, with a jerk and a heave, to a sardonic farewell from Day, they began hauling, like beasts of burden, to the south.

At Cape Royds, the dogs remained behind in frustration, their growls and whines following their masters until they faded away in the distance. The only spectators were Murray and Roberts, who were staying behind, alone, to look after the hut. They "had done for me all that man could do in their own particular work", Shackleton wrote in the first page of his sledging diary,

> and as we turned . . . and saw them standing on the ice by the familiar cliffs I felt that we must do well even for their sakes.[2]

Shackleton meant what he said. His thoughts for Murray and Roberts were different in kind from Scott's naval expectation of duty from his minions.

Shackleton was also haunted by the orders left behind by Scott, which he considered had been criminally vague and, in case of disaster, would have burdened subordinates for the rest of their lives with a sense of guilt. So, before departure, Shackleton carefully drafted letters to his companions.

"In view of the fact that I am shortly to proceed on a sledge journey," as he put it, typically, to Marshall, "and in case I do not return from the same I here place in writing all matters . . . affecting yourself in connection with the . . . Expedition":

> In the event of any action being brought against you in connection with your medical opinion the action will be defended by my executors: I have accepted all your medical opinions and acted accordingly . . . On hearing your opinion that neither Brocklehurst nor Joyce were fit for the Southern Journey I rejected them: Your responsibility ceased when you gave me your report.[3]

Especially, Shackleton left behind unequivocal instructions for relief. Scott had left none at all. Shackleton, however, did not regard rescue as disgrace. Indeed, as far as he was able, he would make absolutely certain of rescue should the need arise. If he was overdue, a search party was immediately to set out.

Precise orders on the subject were addressed to James Murray.

whom Shackleton had put in command while he was away. More: if Shackleton and Adams both failed to return, Murray was to take command of the whole expedition, by-passing both Marshall and David. It was, on the face of it, a surprising choice. Murray was a mere scientist. In his own words, when he joined the expedition, he had

> only recently recovered from an extensive general breakdown in health . . . I had rheumatism, inflamed eyes, and God knows what not . . . I was just a little bit uneasy in my mind at foisting upon Shackleton such a wreck of humanity.[4]

He was a polar tyro too. Shackleton, however, discerned in him something more. A grocer's son, Murray had begun by studying medicine, then turned to art, worked as a sculptor, and finally found his metier in marine biology. He was self-taught. He followed his bent with a combination of enthusiasm and pertinacity. Behind a joking and bumbling exterior was the one man, so Shackleton felt, in whose hands he could safely leave his life.

Where the present was concerned Shackleton, in his own very candid words, by contrast, was "working to the bare ounce".[5] The contradiction disturbed neither him nor his companions.

At Hut Point, a mere twenty miles along the road to the south, the peculiarities of his transport forced Shackleton to halt. One pony had gone lame. From the depot left by *Nimrod* at Glacier Tongue, a quarter of a ton of maize had to be hauled and ground up for pony fodder. Shackleton, meanwhile, made a quick trip back to Cape Royds to fetch equipment left behind, including wire rope for tethering the ponies, since they were chewing their leather halters.

"It is a mercy", wrote Shackleton when Adams was kicked by a pony, but rapidly recovered. "I cannot imagine what he would have done if he had been knocked out for the Southern Journey."[6] Leaving Adams behind did not bear thinking about. He would have taken over command at base. Shackleton therefore would have gone south knowing that his life might depend on someone whose judgment, he now agreed with Marshall, was erratic.

It was on 3 November that, in Marshall's words, they finally were "off for the great event".[7] Shackleton, as Wild recorded, was "rather irritable and excited".[8] That was in a cipher used by Wild in his diary for such remarks. Marshall, by contrast, put everything *en clair*. Shackleton, on the other hand, mentioned his companions only when forced to by events and then only in a neutral or sympathetic way. Censure he reserved for his thoughts. He was

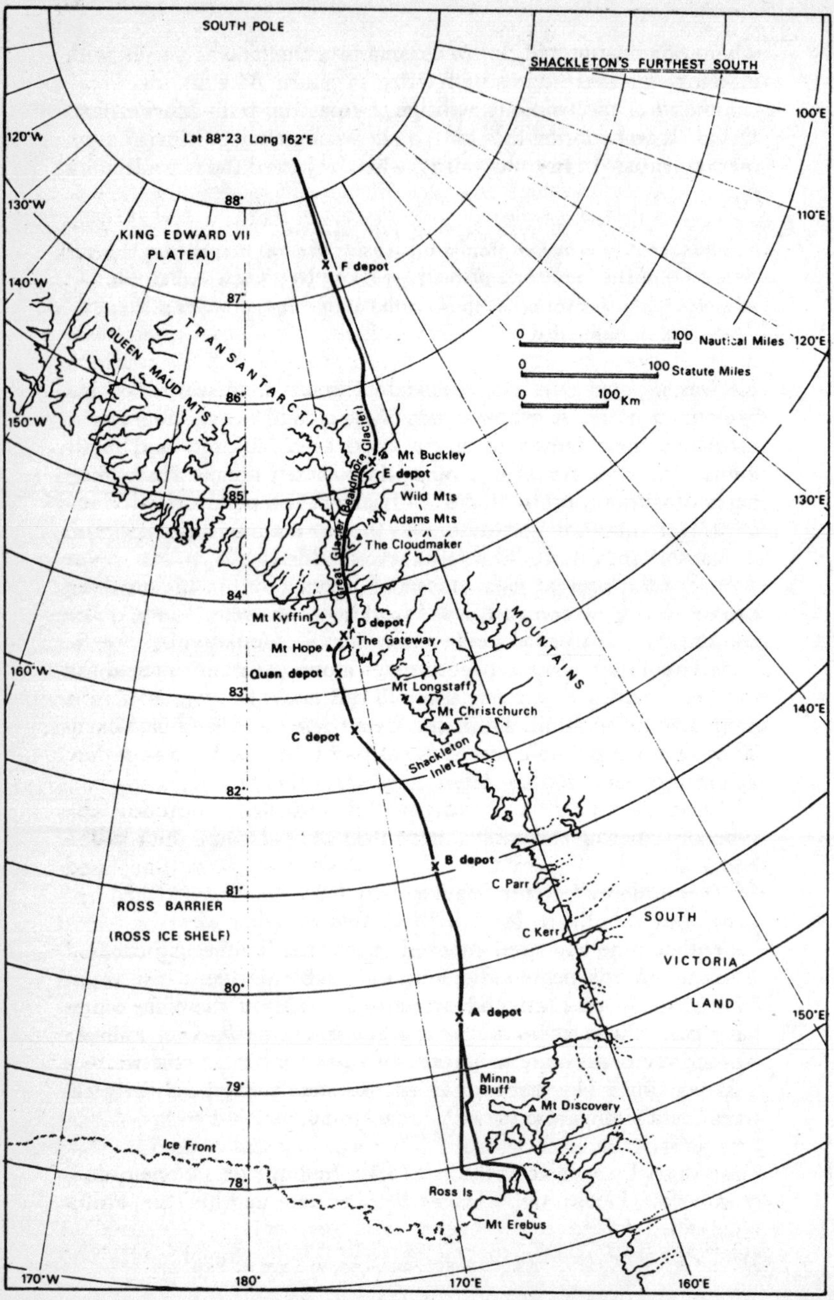
SHACKLETON'S FURTHEST SOUTH
SOUTH POLE
Lat 88°23 Long 162°E
KING EDWARD VII PLATEAU
F depot
TRANSANTARCTIC
QUEEN MAUD MTS
0 100 Nautical Miles
0 100 Statute Miles
0 100 Km
Great Glacier (Beardmore Glacier)
Mt Buckley
E depot
Wild Mts
Adams Mts
The Cloudmaker
Mt Kyffin
D depot
Mt Hope
The Gateway
MOUNTAINS
Quan depot
Mt Longstaff
Mt Christchurch
C depot
Shackleton Inlet
B depot
C Parr
ROSS BARRIER
(ROSS ICE SHELF)
SOUTH
C Kerr
VICTORIA
LAND
A depot
Minna Bluff
Mt Discovery
Ice Front
Ross Is
Mt Erebus
120°W
130°W
140°W
150°W
160°W
170°W
180°
170°E
160°E
150°E
140°E
130°E
120°E
110°E
100°E
88°
87°
86°
85°
84°
83°
82°
81°
80°
79°
78°

not exactly introverted, but his diary was concerned mainly with himself.

Five years, eight months and three days before, Shackleton had left the same Hut Point to sail away unwillingly in the relief ship; "a beautiful day", as he had then written, "but a sad one indeed for me".[9] Now, on another "beautiful fine day",[10] as he put it, he was at last leading his own men south. Unseen by all save Shackleton, the shadow of Scott pursued him as he started across the sea ice from Hut Point. The night before, Shackleton had slept in the old *Discovery* hut; "never", he pointedly remarked, "a very cheerful place",[11] and now full of ghosts. Right up to the start, there were echoes of *Discovery*. At the edge of the Barrier, where the southern road began, men and ponies posed with chivalric pennants and Queen Alexandra's Union Jack for Brocklehurst to photograph.

Then the strange procession got under way. Like mythical beasts in a dream landscape, the ponies trooped out into the long white plain. Since landing, they had stayed on the rocky tip of Cape Royds. Now, for the first time, they moved across deep snow, and so for the first time displayed their drawbacks in the polar environment. Starting off across the Barrier, they ran into long sweeps of drift snow "sinking in up to their bellies", to quote Shackleton, "and always over their hocks",[12] where dogs, as he knew, would have kept on top, as would men on ski.* Instead the men, too, sank in at every step. The support party, as if in a nightmare was floundering before their sledge, and the polar party had to take turns helping them to haul. For three terrible days they struggled on like this.

The support party had come to help Shackleton negotiate the crevasses where the Barrier flowed past the mountain spur called the Bluff. On the third day out, Wild was snowblind, and Brocklehurst kindly wrote up his diary for him:

> They will keep edging towards the Bluff instead of keeping out God knows why . . . Ghastly wind getting up . . . after lunch . . . Grisi . . . put his forefeet down a hell of a crevasse and . . . after changing the course due east Wild stuck his thumping great feet down another . . . Shacks decided to pitch camp as it was impossible to see . . . the weather getting thicker every minute. Four tents were pitched and the gents split up a bit owing to the fact that the supporting ---[13]

Alas, we shall never know more. "I have had to tear out one page", Wild wrote, when sight returned. The language of Sir Philip

* The pressure of a horse's hoof is 15 lbs per sq. inch; of a dog's paw, 3½ lbs per sq. inch; of a man on foot, 2¼ lbs per sq. inch., and of a man on ski, ½ lb per sq. inch.

Brocklehurst, Bart, of Swythamley Hall was "rather lurid" he explained, in code.

On 6 November, the first blizzard of the journey kept them in their tents. All day, as the drift hissed and the canvas flapped, and the wind shrieked outside like some monster at the door, they stayed in their sleeping bags where, as Shackleton put it, "each person has a little home where he can read and write and look at the Penates & Lares brought with him".[14]

Six years before, at the identical stage of the journey, he had also been weatherbound and reading. Then, it had been *The Origin of Species* out aloud to Scott; now it was *Much Ado About Nothing* to himself. He had allowed each man one volume for the journey. His own was Shakespeare's comedies. Marshall took George Borrow's *The Bible in Spain*; Adams, *Travels in France* by Arthur Young, and Wild, Dickens' *Sketches by Boz*. At this point too Shackleton, on the return journey lying gasping for breath, had overheard Wilson say he did not expect him to last the night, and had sworn he would survive. "We only had a couple of biscuits each for lunch," Shackleton now wrote in his diary, no doubt remembering Scott's improvidence,

> for I can see that we must retrench at every setback if we are going to have enough food to carry us through.[15]

After nine days, Shackleton had covered fifty-four miles. On 10 November 1902, nine days out on *Discovery*, the figure had been thirty-seven miles. The difference was not enough. Even without haunting comparisons from the past, the arithmetic was simple. The Pole was 747 miles from Cape Royds. Shackleton had started with ninety-one days' food. That meant covering sixteen miles a day out and home.

Beyond the Furthest South in 1902, it was terra incognita. The Pole might well be on the Barrier; perhaps even on sea ice, and plain sailing all the way. Even so, sixteen miles a day was asking much, even of the technically most accomplished travellers of the day. Shackleton's daily average was less than six miles, and already he was a hundred miles behind. By his own, wholly optimistic assumptions, the Pole was already out of reach. "With careful management," he now wrote in his diary, "we can make [our food] spin out to 110 days."[16] Given that, he need only do twelve and a half miles a day to get to the Pole and back. Admittedly he had twice exceeded that figure, but he had no margin of safety. Now he had 110 days in hand. "Then," in his own words, "if we have not done the job in that time it is God's will."[17]

The support party, meanwhile, had been relieved of most of their loads, and turned out to be a drag. On 7 November, the wind having dropped, they were sent home. With three cheers wanly tinkling in the silence, they parted and, as Shackleton put it, "we are out at last quite on our own."[18] He could only hope that the support party would get back safely. Joyce, their leader, was to bring out supplies to a depot off the Bluff. Shackleton absolutely depended on those supplies to get him home.

For the moment, it was the road ahead that counted. Soon after starting, Shackleton had run into the crevasses round the Bluff. In turn everyone put his foot into the depths; if on ski they would mostly have floated over. It was calm all right, but with clinging fog and overcast sky; and a white-out had come down. Under the snow bridges, the crevasses were impossible to detect. To go on was suicidal. Shackleton stopped and camped again after scarcely half a mile. He was pinned down all that day and the next as well. He dared not move until the light improved. "It is a sore trial to one's hopes," Shackleton wrote, "to lie and watch the drift on the tent side and to know that our valuable pony food is going."[19]

Shackleton did not reveal his worries. To his men, he seemed a pillar of patience. They, for their part, consciously or not, were watching to see how he behaved. As a leader, Shackleton was on trial. So too was his transport.

Standing still, "the ponies", Shackleton had to observe, "felt chilly".[20] Thus did he discover the obvious. The species is built to dissipate heat, not conserve it. Every square inch of hide can sweat. All day, Shackleton and his companions were in and out of their tents cosseting their ponies with blankets and shelter from the wind. The animals were off their feed and, to save fuel, the men had to give up their own hot lunch to boil up a hot mash. Dogs, as Shackleton even now would find it hard to admit, would have looked after themselves. With their thick fur, sweating almost only through their tongues and paws, they were superbly adapted to the environment. They would simply have buried themselves in the snow and kept warm until they were ready to run again.

Six years before, also on the eleventh day out, Shackleton had done ten miles, so now, he reckoned ruefully, he was ten miles behind. Next day, 9 November, it was calm and clear at last. What the sunshine showed was that they were trapped in a labyrinth of crevasses revealed only by the collapse of the undulating snow-mantle concealing them. In Shackleton's words, "There was nothing for it but to trust in Providence we had to cross . . . the crevasses . . . somewhere."[21]

Adams had "the place of honour in the front", Wild pointedly observed. Wild blamed Adams for getting them into this mess by persuading Shackleton to steer too close to the Bluff. It was, Wild felt, a kind of poetic justice that they "had not gone half a mile before . . . Adams . . . pony Chinaman went down a crack".[22] With the combined struggles of three men Chinaman managed to scramble to safety; another graphic demonstration of a pony's drawbacks in the snows. One man can jerk a dog, even two dogs at a time, out of danger.

But now their luck turned. In Marshall's words, "were v. surprised to get out of . . . crevasses in about 2 miles".[23] Shackleton was not surprised. He had already quoted his favourite Browning tag, "When things seem the worst, they turn to the best."

In the afternoon "the land had its usual attractions,"[24] Wild caustically noted, and they were heading for danger again "until," as he put it in cipher, "I spoke about it when Shacks altered [course], he always listens to me now." The sledgemeter (a bicycle wheel rigged behind one of the sledges with a counter to register the distance) announced 12½ miles for the day. For the first time they had done the distance needed to reach the Pole in time. "Weather looking promising," Marshall noted, "Everything more hopeful."

"Got up in blizzard," Mawson meanwhile was writing that same day, two hundred miles to the north, "did 5m . . . We have travelled these 2 days in heavy brash ice . . . It is now very bad."[25]

For five whole weeks, Mawson, David and Mackay had been man-hauling along the coast of South Victoria Land, and covered barely 120 miles. Still they had not found the way inland they sought through the twisted coastal ramparts of glacier, ice shelf and mountain wall. Shackleton at least had something solid underfoot. Mawson and his companions were in the strange half-world between land and sea; crawling along the fragile frontier strip of ice that formed a precarious coastal path. At any moment it might break away and sweep them in a current out to sea.

Shackleton also had the advantage of dry snow. Here it was a clinging mass made sticky by salt and damp from the sea. Boots were sodden, and the sledge refused to slide. Mawson, David and Mackay had to relay every mile.

From Shackleton, Mawson had orders that, after returning to base, he was to proceed to any

> spot you think you may find minerals of economic value or precious stones . . . Your orders are final and are not to be departed from unless in the case of illness, accident, shortage of provisions or lack of time.[26]

Mawson was anxious to comply. Within the austere man of science there lurked a treasure hunter. Condemned to man-hauling, he saw the opportunity fading away. Edgeworth David bore the brunt of his irritation. David's legendary politeness now became to Mawson

> the way . . . the Prof . . . will take all day putting roundabout questions . . . in order to get a simple yes or no answer. This worries one almost to distraction.[27]

This echoed Wild's almost simultaneous complaint (in cipher) on the southern road:

> I pray daily that Adams may be struck dumb, his incessant idiotic chatter would make a saint curse. His pony is getting like him and don't pull.[28]

Even after another month, Mawson was still complaining:

> The Prof is certainly a fine example of a man for his age . . . but he is a great drag . . . He . . . does not pull as much as a younger man . . . seeing that he travels with thumbs tucked in his braces and [from his] general attitude one concludes he lays his weight on harness rather than pulling. Several times when we have been struggling heavily with hauling he has continued to recite poetry or tell yarns.[29]

David, for his part, told Mawson – politely – that he was not as he used to be, which provoked an argument, while Mackay sardonically looked on.

Mawson's acid judgments may partly have had a physical cause. He was suffering intermittently, as he fought his way through the coarse grained slush and ice, from violent diarrhoea. In any case, succinctly damning David as "full of great words and deadly slow action,"[30] Mawson, by his own account, had early seized the psychological leadership.

Mawson understood priorities. He realised that without concentrating on the Pole, it was out of reach. That, the others did not understand. They frittered away time on geology.

> No allowance [Mawson wrote in his diary] has been made for the impossibility of speedy return – due to certain open water coast – and the Prof's idea of ½ ration scheme for 2½ months with same amount of work is ridiculous . . . I came to the conclusion that . . . we must . . . preserve a full ration of sledge food for 480 m. journey [and] in order to make this possible we must live on seal flesh and local food cooked by local means as much as possible.[31]

These ideas, Mawson with laconic arrogance recorded, were "carried unanimously".

This happened on 29 October, the day that Shackleton started from Cape Royds. Since then, Mawson and his companions had been living on seals killed along the way. During the winter, Mackay had experimented with blubber stoves. "At the time," in David's words, "his experiments were not taken very seriously";[32] but now Mackay came into his own. To save paraffin for the primus once they struck inland, they had to cook with blubber, and Mackay it was who, out of a biscuit tin, improvised a stove.

So as not to make inroads on the sledging ration, all the biscuits were being saved. The sudden deprivation of fibre and carbohydrates took its toll. That partly explained Mawson's diarrhoea. With abundance of fresh meat, however, scurvy was certain to be kept at bay. Slowly, they inched their way along the coast.

XXIV

Furthest South

"I am beginning to think we shall get to the Pole alright," Frank Wild was writing in his diary on 25 November, "but," he added, "am doubtful about getting back again."[1] That was the day before Shackleton wrote that "We have passed the Furthest South yet reached by man . . . we are in Latitude 82° 18½'S".[2]

Marshall unequivocally echoed Shackleton's delight. "Just beaten Scott's record," in his own words, "Celebrated it at dinner by drinking healths in orange curaçao given by E.M.L. [a mysterious lady friend]."[3]

It was not only the record but, in Shackleton's words, that

> this we have been able to do in much less time than we did on the last long march when with Captain Scott we made 82°16½' Furthest South.

They had covered in twenty-nine days a distance that had taken Scott fifty-nine days. They were doing thirteen miles a day now, which meant they were drawing ahead of Scott at the rate of nearly ten miles a day. More to the point, they were covering the daily twelve and a half miles needed to keep up with their own timetable. Around New Year's day, they could expect to be at the Pole.

There were, however, reasons for the bleak undertone of Wild's bafflement. Earlier on, Shackleton had been worried by the difficulty of finding the depot he had laid in the spring. It was "just the same", his own words, "as picking up a buoy in the North Sea with only distant mountains for bearings".[4] The depot was a moderately large snow cairn, difficult to see against the snow around. It was marked by a single flag. Luckily the weather was right, and it was found.

The depot, on the other hand, held only four days' pony food and a gallon of paraffin. Would it not have been wise to have concentrated all efforts on the southern journey, and moved more supplies out on the trail?

Huge sastrugi rippled the Barrier, with soft snow in between. "We have never seen the surface alike for 2 consecutive days," as Shackleton put it. "The Barrier is as wayward and changeful as the sea."[5] Wild, meanwhile, talked about "the rotten monotonous trudge through 4 to 6 inches of soft snow".[6] But to a skier, that was recognisably good going. As Amundsen had succinctly recorded on the North-West Passage, in soft snow, "the pedestrians sank in deeply [while] I had ski and . . . glided on top."[7]

The ponies cost much effort in their care. As Shackleton wrote,

> The poor . . . beasts . . . break through the crust . . . and flounder up to their hocks . . . It seems to savour of repetition to write down each day the heavy going and the soft surface.[8]

At each camp, the ponies had to be rubbed down and covered with blankets and a snow wall had to be thrown up to shield them from the wind. Every morning snow had to be scraped off their hooves, where it had balled up during the night. Much energy was squandered on grinding up their compressed Maujee ration, for which the deadweight of a pestle and mortar had to be carried. All this was in addition to the normal work of camping.

In other aspects, too, Shackleton's preparations were faulty. Foreign explorers by now had adopted the Eskimo anorak or parka which, with its attached hood and sophisticated design, had turned out to be the best cold-weather garment. Shackleton persisted with the ill-designed jacket used on *Discovery*. Lacking a fixed hood, it had to be combined with a complicated outfit of caps and helmets to protect the head. That let in cold air through the gap around the neck. Also, Shackleton had decided that, in his own words, "except for the hands and feet, in the way of personal clothing, and the sleeping bags for camping, furs are entirely unnecessary".[9] Without fur around the face, he suffered needlessly from cold. Tents, too, had not been improved since *Discovery*. Shackleton used the same awkward model, slung over a framework of five bamboo poles, like a tepee, without a sewn-in floor cloth, and difficult to erect in a gale.

Away from the technicalities of snow travel, Shackleton was sensible, innovative, and open to informed advice. He had two tents, with two men in each. Every Monday, to prevent irritation, ennui and division, there was a rotation of tents and duties.

Particularly in food, Shackleton took care to avoid old mistakes. He had, for example, ordered special biscuits fortified with Plasmon, the concentrated milk protein already tried on *Discovery*. The effect was to make the proportion of protein in the diet fifty per cent higher. By modern ideas this is correct. Marshall, however, was bothered by the quantity of food. The original daily ration gave 4,300 calories, about the same as on *Discovery*, but was it enough? Marshall had gone through his textbooks again and again, without being sure. Nutrition as a science was still in its infancy, and Marshall could only hope that he and Shackleton were right. Besides 7½ oz of pemmican and 16 oz of Plasmon biscuits per man each day, there was some cheese, cocoa, pure Plasmon tea, oats and sugar, making 34 oz in all. There was too much carbohydrate, too little fat, and none of the as yet undiscovered vitamin C. Marshall, at any rate, felt that the ration, somehow, was too low; and now that they were saving food, it was lower still.

Meanwhile, cold and exposure remorselessly weakened the ponies. On 21 November, at 81°S, the first one, Chinaman, had had to be put down. Marshall had with him a revolver to kill humanely, and avoid the frightful butchery under Scott.

Chinaman at least meant more food for his masters. Most was depoted for the return; but some meat was now added to the rations. It would keep them out longer. Marshall was more concerned that it was "a great change having fresh meat. Should lose danger of scurvy with this addition."[10] He was now in Shackleton's tent, and cook for the week. As he broke the block of pemmican and stirred it in the pannikin for dinner that evening, while he pumped the primus to give its comforting roar, Marshall could only hope that he had got the diet right.

The main medical trouble, so far, had been an aching tooth of Adams', which Marshall had drawn without anaesthetic at the second attempt. The first had failed because, not having brought dental forceps, Marshall only succeeded in breaking the tooth.

It was Shackleton, however, who continued to make Marshall professionally wary. So far, Shackleton had only suffered from snow-blindness, "a particularly unpleasant thing", as he put it. "One first begins by seeing double then the eyes feel full of grit and it makes them water. Eventually one cannot see at all."[11] It was his fault, through not wearing goggles, and hardly qualified as illness. Still, Marshall felt there was something not quite right. At any rate, they all crossed Scott's Furthest South with a clean bill of health.

The complex emotions of revenge, and of putting their feet, in Adams' words, "where nobody has ever put their feet before",[12] masked the clawing of uncertainty. Only three ponies remained, all manifestly weakening, with the Pole still almost five hundred miles off.

Beyond the last known landmarks of Shackleton Inlet and Mount Longstaff, ice-flanked, glinting mountains opened up, never seen by human eyes before. In Shackleton's own words,

> The whole place seems so strange and unlike anything else in the world . . . when the hazy clouds spring silently from either hand and drift quickly across our zenith not followed by any wind it seems almost uncanny. Then comes a puff of wind . . . seeming to obey no law acting on erratic impulses. It seems as though we were truly at the worlds end and were bursting in on the birthplace of the clouds and the nesting home of the four winds and that we mortals were being watched with a jealous eye by these children of Nature.[13]

On 29 November, a mysterious disturbance began to affect the Barrier. For weeks long, regular undulations had been sweeping south, like the rollers of a frozen sea. Huge waves now started to run diagonally across. The hollows were filled with soft snow, in which the ponies sank once again up to their bellies. Only two were left now, for Grisi, Marshall's pony, had been failing, and was put down the day before. Now the men were hauling with the ponies, two to a sledge.

For some time, in Wild's words, "we have noticed quite a brilliant gleam of light in the sky above the southern horizon which we cannot account for."[14] With more experience, they would have understood. To begin with, the new land they were raising stayed out of their way, to the west. By 1 December, Shackleton was writing that

> Ahead of us, we can see the land stretching away to the East with a long white line in front of it that looks . . . as though there were great pressure ridges in front of us . . . It seems as though . . . there is going to be a change in some gigantic way . . . We fervently trust it will not delay us in our march South.[15]

It was at this point that they began to slip behind their timetable, which had assumed no obstacle on the way to the Pole, besides the survival of the animals. The same day Quan, Shackleton's pony was shot, like the others, and his carcass depoted for food. Socks, belonging to Wild, was the last one left; and the Pole was still more than four hundred miles off. The men, trudging through lakes of loose, abrasive drift snow, like desert sand, were now all hauling a quarter of a ton more. "Our appetites," as Shackleton put it, "are increasing at an alarming rate . . . after the heavy pulling."[16] It was an elementary physiological fact which, in planning, had not been taken into account. That the weather was now astonishingly good, seemed somehow to lose its importance.

> We are [wrote Shackleton] ever adding to the chain of wonderful mountains we have found At one moment our thoughts are in the grandeur of the scene the next of what we would like to eat . . . for we are very hungry and we know that we are likely to be for another three months.[17]

At the lunch rest next day, 2 December, in Shackleton's words,

> we had got close enough to the disturbance ahead of us to see that it consisted of enormous pressure ridges running a long way East and not the slightest chance of our being able to get Southing any longer on the Barrier.[18]

They were moving SSE along the coast. Behind the disturbance, mountains ran across their course. Shackleton now had to decide whether to turn south immediately, or carry on in search of a gap. But he was the precursor. There was nothing to guide him. His intuition was all he had on which to rely.

It was a crisis, perhaps the crisis of the journey, and it was mirrored by a crisis in command.

They were now about 83°20′S. In a week they had beaten Scott by a whole degree.

> I was here asked to tell Boss he "had done damned well & had done enough" [Marshall obscurely wrote in his diary]. I replied "there is nothing to stop anyone turning back".[19]

They had started off without exaggerated respect for Shackleton. "Boss" was a nickname coined by Wild since the journey began. It was not wholly complimentary, for his personality was irritating his companions, and hunger sharpened their sensibilities. Marshall blamed Shackleton's "ignorance & incompetence", as he put it, for the death of Quan. "Any other horse," he had written in his diary while Quan was still alive, "would have gone under with the treatment he has had from Sh."[20]

"Shall be glad to get out," Wild, now sharing Shackleton's tent, wrote in cipher,

> Would not take it on again for five pounds a day [he added, darkly, still in cipher, repeating his old concern]. If we get the Pole 'twill be sheer luck, and we shall be luckier still to get back.[21]

Wild was still searching for a leader to whom he could become attached. So too was Adams. Neither was at all sure that Shackleton was his man. Adams, so far, directed all his hero worship towards his old Captain, on *Berwick*, the future Rear Admiral Hood, a doomed figure, fated to go down with his ship. Why in any case was Adams here, heaving at a sledge in the snow, past the 83rd parallel? He did not exactly seem attuned to the polar regions. He liked to justify himself by saying that he wanted "to see that England got where she should get". If it was "a question of trying to get to the South Pole, I want . . . to be the one chap, that's all".[22] Perhaps Shackleton, seeing El Dorado over the mountains looming up ahead, so uninhibitedly consumed by personal ambition, was too formidable for comfort; especially at close quarters. The force of leadership he undoubtedly possessed; but accepted leader he was not.

By the early afternoon of 2 December, the pressure ridges ahead were "looking v. nasty", as Marshall put it; like the ocean swell breaking on an unknown shore. As they ran far to the east so, in his words, "It was unanimously agreed to change course going S. to what appears to be the Golden Gateway to the S."[23]

"The Golden Gateway," in Wild's more earthbound language, was a glacier which "s. of us opens up leading through the mountains . . . almost due South".[24] Flanked by two low peaks, it looked like the classic image of a pass.

There is a mystical symbolism about a mountain pass, the promise of undefined hope, but to Shackleton the "Golden Gateway" meant disillusion. It destroyed his hope that the snow plain would roll on the way to the end. "But after all," as he put it in his diary, "we must not expect to find things cut and dried . . . and suited to us in such a place."[25]

So they headed for the "Golden Gateway". Labouring across glittering ridges of ice, the four men and their one patient pony faced oblivion at every step. They were crossing a sea of veiled chasms. Their lives hung upon the caprice of snow bridges draped over the abyss underfoot. By late afternoon, they had hauled as far as they could manage, and there they camped, among the crevasses. "If we can land tomorrow," said Shackleton in his diary, "it will be the pioneer landing in the far South."[26]

Next day, it was agreed, they would climb the rock dome on the east of the Golden Gateway and spy out the way ahead. Leaving Socks tethered, but unguarded, all four men left camp at 5.30 a.m. The weather, astonishingly, continued fine. The Golden Gateway glittered like a crystal in the morning sun. Shackleton and his companions were travelling light, with nothing but a few biscuits and a little chocolate for their lunch. They had been seduced by the distortion of perspective in the snows. The distance to the foot of the mountain turned out to be closer to seven miles instead of the four they had imagined. Soon after the start, they had to circumvent a chasm in the ice sheet. It was only after seven and a half hours' hard plodding through a maze of crevasses that they reached the foot of the mountain and could start the climb.

In Alpine terms, the climb was hardly worth the name. It was more a scramble up about 2,000 feet of weathered granite line with ice and snow. With an Alpine rope, ice axes, and ski boots lightly nailed, they were not badly equipped. Unfamiliarity with the mountain world, however, made everything seem worse than it was. They worked their way up, praying that the weather would hold. At 3 p.m., after two hours' climbing, they reached the summit slope, and moved up the last few hundred yards. Wild was ahead, and suddenly gave a shout. Shackleton, who was last, hurried at the sound and, in his own words,

> there burst upon our vision an open road to the south for there stretched a great glacier running almost South and North between the great mountain ranges.

They were not quite at the summit yet. They scrambled up the remaining ridge and

> From the top we could see the glacier stretching away inland till at last it seemed to merge into inland ice.[27]

The Golden Gateway, after all, had been an illusion. It was not the pass over the mountains; only a side entrance to the glacier:

> Where the glacier fell into the Barrier the pressure waves were enormous and for miles the surface of the barrier was broken up. This was what we had seen ahead the last few days and now understood the reason of the commotion in the Barrier surface.[28]

It also explained the "gleam in the sky" recorded by Wild. It was the blink of the glacier.

The Golden Gateway avoided the upheaval. It was, in fact, the only possible entry to the glacier. It had been the illusion that brings discovery in its wake, the key to the key. But as, simply, the Gateway it has come down to us.

Seven years before, on *Discovery*, Shackleton had stood upon another pinnacle, White Island, and discovered the start of the road to the Pole;* now perhaps he had found the end. What he could not know was this. For three thousand miles what are now called the Transantarctic Mountains wind across the continent, barring the way to the inland ice. Shackleton had found one of the negotiable gaps, and one of the very few, with its long, gentle rise, open to the technique at his command.

Mount Hope was what the four men spontaneously named the summit on which they stood. "Shall never forget the 1st sight of this promised land," Marshall characteristically wrote in his diary, "The Almighty has indeed been good to us."[29] In equally characteristic style, Wild said:

> The view was well worth double the labour. The glacier . . . must be the largest in the world . . .

"Glacier" hardly conveyed the feeling. This was a monstrous estuary of ice, "at least 30 miles in width", as Wild put it, "and we could see over 100 miles of its length";[30] remarkably accurate estimates, as it turned out.

The headwaters of this monster were hard to conceive. There was a sense of irresistible, pent-up power behind its forms, like a tide caught in a moment of full surge. The impression was so overwhelming, Shackleton and his men found it hard to name their discovery. For the moment, they called it the Great Glacier, or simply The Glacier. It ran like a highway to the South. Shackleton decided to travel up it and strike inland. His companions plainly agreed.

They ate their frugal lunch, hurried off the mountain, and after three hours returned to their camp. By then, Shackleton was snow-blind again. He received scant sympathy because, in Marshall's words, "he will not wear goggles".[31] Shackleton had taken them off when the sun was obscured by cloud, in order to see some crevasses clearly and guide his companions through.

Within him, a disturbing tumult of images revolved. Like a glittering serpent the glacier wound its way to the heights. It was overshadowed by the dark vision of summits in the sun sawing the horizon to the south-east. They continued for "about 150 miles," thought Wild.

> that would be about 86 S. Lat . . . if we keep to the Barrier, we shall . . . find our way barred by impassable mountains.[32]

* See p. 69.

That explained the decision to strike up the glacier. Heading for those mountains, Shackleton had imagined, on the other hand, he could have travelled at least another hundred miles closer to the Pole before the climb began. It was where he would have been had he started from the Bay of Whales.

Next day, 4 December, the crossing of the Gateway began. From Mount Hope, there had appeared to be a safe road free of crevasses. "Looking at it from above," to quote Wild, "and keeping to it from below, we found to be different matters altogether."[33] What they had to negotiate was a gentle snow saddle rising and falling gently about two hundred feet, with crevasses concentrated at the junction of the Barrier.

Marshall, Adams and Shackleton led the way, man-hauling a sledge weighing 650 lbs. With ice axes, they deliberately holed the snow bridges ahead of Wild, following with Socks and the second sledge

> so that Socks [as Wild put it] could see . . . the . . . crevasses . . . and then I took him over with a rush, and the good little fellow cleared them all splendidly.[34]

By late afternoon they were through the Golden Gateway, down on the other side, and camped by the side of the glacier, ready to ascend. "The weather," said Wild, was "still all we could wish for",

> today we have been marching stripped to our shirts. We are all getting very sunburnt . . . I really believe we shall reach the Pole but we shall as surely miss the ship.[35]

The first day on the glacier they began to feel like true discoverers. Nothing had prepared them for the sensations by which they now were overwhelmed. They seemed engulfed by the outlandish stream of ice. Far away, mountains lined the other shore like the comb along the back of a dinosaur. In Shackleton's words,

> We 4 are seeing these great designs and the play of Nature for the first time, and possibly this may never be seen by man again.[36]

The following day, Wild "had a long yarn with S.", as he recorded, in cipher, "find he is not such a ----- as I thought".[37]

It was not only that Shackleton had led – not driven – them there. The first day on the glacier was the real start of danger. It seemed to inspire him, and he started to display a blend of daring and self control. With every appearance of unconcern, Shackleton camped that evening on a bridged crevasse, under a stupendous granite pillar threatening stonefalls at any time. It was, however, the only patch of snow within sight. Glaciers have many aspects. This one then, at that place, was swept clean to the blue ice. On that, in Shackleton's opinion, it was "impossible to spread a tent", and "Providence," as he said, "will look over us".[38] Was this his Anglo-Irish fecklessness, or faith? Whatever it was, it impressed Wild, at least.

The granite pillar was an unmistakable landmark. There, Shackleton lightened his loads with a depot, the fourth along the way.

Next day, 6 December, Shackleton was again in agony from snow-blindness. His goggles continually fogged, so that he could hardly see where he was going "but," as Wild admiringly put it, "he would not give in". The sun shone from a cloudless sky; but over the mountains, banks of cirro-cumulus driving, like puff-balls from the south, warned of the threat behind even the finest day.

They were crossing the turbulence at the edge of the glacier, "an awful place", said Wild,

> exactly like a rough sea in appearance, but in every hollow there was a crevasse . . . the strain on one's nerves was greater than on the muscles, although goodness knows that was bad enough.[39]

The surface alternated between blue ice and patches of heavy, slushy snow. It was a place to try even trained mountaineers. Without crampons, and unroped, they slithered ominously on the edge of the abyss, their sledges pitching and yawing behind. Without technique all they had to offer were prodigies of endurance.

Socks was the most grotesque anomaly. This would have been hard enough for a dog's claws; it was no place for the hooves of a horse. Since his masters had seen fit to bring no farriers, Socks was unshod, so that he had not a vestige of a grip. Over the mauvais pas, he was a passenger. Both sledges had to be manhandled, and steps cut for him to get across.

The third day on the glacier brought a cataract of masked crevasses. It began in deep, coarse-grained snow, made mushy by the sun. The tell-tale hollows, like tarpaulins loosely draped, hinted at the abyss underfoot. The men, being without ski, were naturally sinking knee deep. Socks went down as far as his girth. Nobody knew when there was a chasm underfoot or not. Twice, Socks put his hind legs into space. The greater risk, Shackleton decided, was to stop and search for a road. Some snow bridges slowly sagged;

but held up long enough to be crossed in a rush. The safest course was to push on blindly, Shackleton trusting, as always, in his lucky star.

So far, he had kept to the side of the glacier. The chaos was due to tributary glaciers debouching from the nearby mountains into the main ice stream. So, to escape the pressure, and the deep soft snow gathered there, Shackleton turned towards the middle of the glacier. The snow now became firmer, the going better. Marshall, Adams and Shackleton were man-hauling ahead. Afterwards came Wild leading Socks and the second sledge exactly in their wake. About an hour after lunch, in Marshall's words,

> Wild shouted for help & turning round saw [him] partly down a huge hole sledge jammed at edge & Socks gone altogether. Rushed to his assistance with a rope, but on arrival he had climbed out & was deadly pale. Swingletree* had carried away & noble little Socks had found a resting place at last . . . Not a sign of him down this terrible abyss & not a sound to be heard.[40]

Socks had paid the penalty of his breed. His hooves had broken through a snow bridge that held men on foot. Marshall now recalled that

> after shooting my pony I had suggested the replacement of Socks swingletree with mine which was copperbound and reinforced. Had this been done it would not have broken and we should have lost Wild, pony & sledge!

Shackleton allowed no time for the working of shock. Coupling the sledges together, he got his men immediately marching again, hauling the pony's load as well. They were now pulling half a ton. Just before camping, Shackleton and Marshall broke through a snow bridge, and were saved only by their harness from being swallowed by the abyss below. "This," said Marshall, "has upset Sh. & he is not in good form."[41]

Marshall was still more concerned over the loss of Socks. He had counted on him as meat on the hoof to make the seven weeks' food they were carrying last for another fortnight. Now it was a matter of reducing rations yet again. Their food was down to 3,000 calories a day or less, when, working as they were, in that climate, they

* A cross bar, attached to the traces at the ends, and to the vehicle by a pivot at the centre, so as to give the horse freedom of movement. Depending on the point of view, it is the weak link in a harness, or a safety device. What had happened here was that the impact had snapped it across the middle.

needed 5,000 calories. They needed no numbers to measure their discomfort. "Marching 5 hours on 4 bisc. & 2 oz. choc. & tea," as Marshall put it on 9 December, "is pretty stiff."[42] They had forgotten what it was like to feel properly fed. They would have to live with hunger for no one knew quite how much longer yet.

Not hunger but scurvy was still Marshall's true concern, however; for Socks was to give fresh meat to continue keeping it at bay. Scurvy now must be only a matter of time.

With this in the background, the passage of the 84th parallel and, on 10 December, the shattering of Scott's record by two whole degrees of latitude, passed without remark. They were now 3,000 feet up, and just 360 miles from the Pole. They camped that day under a conical peak which from afar had seemed like a volcano with a permanent vapour crown. It turned out to be an ordinary mountain, its summit merely wreathed in cloud. It was named the Cloudmaker, to join the now distant Erebus and the Bluff as great landmarks along the way.

Like primitive tribesmen, Marshall, Adams and Wild sat round one afternoon grinding the remainder of their pony fodder between stones picked from the surface of the glacier. It was a waste of precious energy, but the proper pestle and mortar had been jettisoned far behind, and no one knew whether there would be any more stones ahead. Pony fodder was now needed for the men.

The weather continued fair, with occasional breezes but sinister banks of cumulus were rolling down from the south. The glacier was like a slumbering monster, waiting to swallow the intruders. It was not particularly steep, but Shackleton and his companions were unprepared for what they had to face.

They had reached a point where the glacier was picked clean of snow. It was evidently that kind of season. The bare ice, fissured and broken, glinting dully blue and green, rolled treacherously on. They changed from finnesko, intended only for snow, to ski boots. Even so, fields of sharp ridges made walking a torture. Sledge runners were ripped and scored. The only sounds were laboured panting, the creak of the harness, and the rasp of the sledge heaving over the ice. Over all lay the pall of fear.

Without crampons, each step was an essay in uncertainty where "many times a slip meant death", in Shackleton's words. It was "a constant strain on us all both to save the sledges from . . . going down a crevasse and to save ourselves as well".[43] Worse still was the mystery of what lay ahead. This easily outweighed the sensation of advancing into the unknown with every step. One thing at least was clear. The sheer size of the glacier hinted at the mass on which it fed. Shackleton was heading for a vast ice cap on which the Pole would probably be found.

They had now been climbing for a week, and still the glacier uncoiled in endless waves and subtle contours that veiled what lay ahead. Each day began with the tantalising hope that it was the last of the climb, and ended, after what were becoming ritual narrow escapes from crevasses, yet higher still. "We are getting South," was the way Shackleton chose to put it, "and perhaps tomorrow may see the end of these difficulties. Difficulties are just things to overcome after all."[44]

On 16 December, they all squatted round the roaring primus in Marshall's and Adams' tent – Marshall was cook again that week – and waited for their sadly inadequate meal in a more hopeful frame of mind. They could even forget that to eke out their food marginally digestible pony fodder was boiling in the pot. Outside, to the south, under a finger-striped sky of stratus clouds, was a hazy cupola that must have been the inland ice. There were ice falls ahead. The head of the glacier was in sight.

Next day, under the rocks of a nunatak he called Mount Buckley, Shackleton made another depot. To get there had meant an undignified struggle over eleven miles of bare ice slippery as glass. Mount Buckley, however, was the last landmark by which a depot could safely be fixed. It was the western sentinel of the pass to the heights. They had indeed reached the head of the glacier, or at least the top of the valley down which it flowed, like a massive torrent in profound slow motion.

Shackleton had decided, on the assumption that he was virtually on the plateau, to make a final dash for the Pole. Everything superfluous was dumped under Mount Buckley. Even warm clothing was left behind. In Shackleton's own words, "we have burned our boats".[45] Nobody objected. "Only about 300 miles more," as Marshall put it, more or less approvingly, "Should do this in 3 weeks travelling light."[46] Three days earlier, both Marshall and Wild were afraid of missing *Nimrod*, and being stuck for another year. Now, in Wild's words, "We are . . . very hopeful of doing the job and of getting back in time to catch the ship."[47] Such was the surge of optimism that followed on accomplishment.

Since crossing the Gateway they had travelled nearly a hundred miles and risen six thousand feet. In twelve days they had found the way to the heights. They had just crossed the 85th Parallel. At the same stage, six years before, as Shackleton with vengeful pleasure now recalled, Scott had only just reached 81° S, and his prospects were fast fading. His feelings, in varying degrees, were shared by his companions.

Other thoughts were not so comforting. Along the glacier, on slippery patches, or where the long waves rose up, Shackleton and his companions had often had to relay. It was, as Marshall said, "heart breaking work", doing the same distance twice over broken ice for hours on end. Their best day's run had been twelve miles; their average barely eight miles. Since the end of November, they had been steadily losing ground. They were now nearly a hundred miles and ten days behind their own timetable. Their already meagre supplies were being dangerously over-run.

"Tomorrow," said Frank Wild, after climbing an ice ridge ahead of Mount Buckley to spy out the land, "we . . . ought to be on the plateau . . . and then Ho for the Pole."[48] But tomorrow came, and tomorrow after that, and still the climb went on.

Ice is almost like a fourth state of matter; it is a solid that flows. That was the force of nature with which Shackleton and his men were grappling. This was the ice stream from the hinterland. Here the ice cap, two miles thick, crept over the lip of the plateau, to be rammed up against the coastal mountains and channelled to feed the great glacier as it started its journey to the sea. Like the frozen headwaters of some mighty river, the ice surged down in a savage, shattered and crevassed cascade of enormous standing waves.

Against this, Shackleton and his men now fought. The slopes were sometimes so steep that they had to unyoke and haul the sledges up on the Alpine rope like a tug o'war. The blue ice of the days before had given way to snow in one of its most treacherous forms; a thin, brittle wind crust that looked solid to the eye. It masked the crevasses, so that day after day everyone repeatedly broke through, saved only by their harnesses from falling into the fathomless pits below. "We are," Shackleton said, "always glad to meet crevasses with their coats off i.e. not hidden by . . . snow."[49] By now, each slope was no longer assumed to be the last. "We have finally decided," as Shackleton put it, still climbing four days after the summit supposedly had been reached, "to trust nothing by eyesight".[50]

The climb that never ends is like a penance out of purgatory. Frustration, fury, self pity, follow in its wake. This intensified the conflict and stress Shackleton and his companions were now undergoing. Man-hauling was the crux. There was a complex interplay between the four human beings imprisoned on the trace.

Adams was "working into my hands", Wild had written, in cipher during the first week of the climb, "He had a row with S. today [because he] does not pull". As for Marshall, said Wild, he

> does not pull the weight of his food, the big hulking lazy hog. S. pulls like the devil . . . I would tell M. and A. what I thought of them only for the sake of poor old S.[51]

"While the rest of us were tearing our hearts out up the steep slopes," Wild was still complaining on 19 December, Marshall "was walking along with a slack trace."[52]

With animals for company, dog drivers do not brood so unrelievedly on each other's failings. Shackleton and his men had no such relief, and it is an obsession of man-hauling to believe that others are not pulling their weight. Of that, however, nobody accused Wild. To Marshall, he was always a "great little man. He just did not fit into our modern way of life, and I don't blame him."[53] Perhaps Wild took pleasure in the thought that he, the smallest of them all, was working hardest. In Shackleton, at any rate, he had now, at last, found the leader for whom he was searching.

To Marshall, on the other hand, Shackleton was the scapegoat. "Following Sh. to the pole," he had written, "is like following an old woman. Always panicking."[54] His irritation was connected with the fact that he had the burden of the navigation. He it was who had learned to use the theodolite, and scorned Shackleton because he found it hard. It was not only a matter of the meridian altitude, when the sky was clear. Marshall also was surveying the new land. That meant fifty or sixty angles squinting through the instrument after the day's run, while his companions were relaxing.

"As cook," Marshall also complained to his diary, "Shackleton is hopeless."[55] This, however, concealed the fact it was not so much as leader that Marshall was thinking of Shackleton, but as patient. Shackleton, Marshall recorded on 19 December, was "rather done"[56] and, two days later, that he was "feeling our high altitude";[57] that is, more than the rest. They were then at 7,000 feet, still climbing, and still hoping, with a touch more desperation each day, that the summit was finally in sight.

"All round us are pressure ridges mounds and cracks," Wild was still writing on 23 December; "the view is exactly like one would see from a small boat in a very rough sea."[58] Two days later he wrote,

> May none but my worst enemies spend their Xmas in such a dreary God forsaken spot as this. Here we are . . . farther away from civilisation than any human being has ever been since civilisation was.

That was a record of a kind. It intensified the forlorn sense of desolation. To make matters worse there was, in Wild's words, "half a gale blowing and drift snow flying and . . . 52° of frost".[59]

For a whole week on end, that wind had blown incessantly from the south. Gone was the calm and sunny weather of the lower glacier. Their faces were cracked and blistered from the gale that clawed and froze. They were entering another climate and another world. At least the disturbance in the ice was beginning to fade.

At the night camp, for Christmas dinner, they allowed themselves a little extra food so that "for the first time for many days," as Wild put it, "I feel replete and therefore I will not make any nasty remarks about anyone, although I should very much like to".

It was a time for stocktaking. Huddled together for warmth in one tent, with the comfort of crême de menthe and cigars dragged all the 550 miles from Cape Royds for Christmas day, Shackleton and his men discussed the way ahead.

They were now 9,500 feet up and, by the midday sight (a torture of freezing fingers to Marshall with the theodolite), at latitude 85° 5′S. They were 250 miles from the Pole. They had less than one month's food left. On their best form so far – thirteen miles a day during November down on the Barrier – it was more than a month's travel to the Pole and back to where they were. They had actually done nine miles that day, and their daily average was down to nine-and-a-half miles. Their line of retreat was growing slimmer by the hour.

Shackleton nonetheless believed the Pole still to be within his grasp. He made his companions think so too. Whatever the private demons that had goaded each of them so far, Shackleton was able to drive them on with a simple fear they all could understand. Unless they actually reached the Pole, they would only have shown the way for someone else to follow and reap what they had sown.

Marshall had serious misgivings. Their body temperatures, which he was carefully monitoring, were now two degrees under normal. How long they could survive, he could only guess. Nonetheless he, too, as doctor, agreed to go on. Once more, equipment was jettisoned. Food was reduced once again to spin it out to six weeks. That would still leave them up on the heights at the end of January, and the season was already on the turn.

Like four scarecrows they set off on Boxing day. They had thrown away all spare clothing, and carried only what they stood up in. They had abandoned their spare sledge runners, and trusted to the old, worn and deformed ones left on their single remaining sledge. There was something feckless in this tableau. They had no furs to protect them. Altitude, cold and starvation were taking their toll. In Shackleton's words, "We are so tired after each hour's pulling we throw ourselves on our backs for 3 minutes spell . . . but," he went on, "it is hard to know what man's limit is for pulling."[60]

On 28 December, the last of the coastal mountains disappeared, curving in a distant crescent towards the south-east. It was as if they had lost contact with the earth. They were like insects alone in a waste of ice and snow. They were still rising, but perceptibly less than before. At least they had left all crevasses and disturbance behind. The surface was smooth, and each step no longer meant fear. They had reached the domed summit of the ice cap.

But they were starving. They were not only growing thinner and weaker, they were not eating enough to maintain the body's heat. Adams' temperature was nearly four degrees below normal. Under ordinary circumstances he would have been nearly dead. "Head wind . . . & low temp.," as Marshall succinctly wrote, "take it out of us."[61]

"Thank God," Shackleton said, "our thoughts can fly across the wastes . . . to those . . . who are thinking of us now."[62]

In London, at his offices near the Law Courts, Herbert Dorman was still grappling with the financial disarray his brother-in-law had left behind. *Nimrod*, nonetheless, had already started on her voyage of relief. "I suppose Ernest must now be thinking of turning back," Herbert wrote to Emily on 29 December. "I often wonder how far he has got. The time will soon slip by."[63]

> The Pole is hard to get [Shackleton was actually writing that same day at about 86° 40′ south latitude], but we will, Please God get there.

Shackleton was not even prepared to contemplate the prospect of turning before 31 December. That was the day on which he, Wilson and Scott had started north in 1902. Willpower, endurance, ambition, pride, were driving Shackleton on. The instinct of self-preservation alone remained to call him back.

They were all in a woeful state. A constant bitter headwind with 40° of frost pierced their ill-designed and inadequate clothing to flay them on the march. They were starving. Their peril was compounded by man-hauling, and by shuffling sometimes knee deep in fine, dry snow, squandering their precious strength. Also they were weakening from dehydration. With a bare minimum of fuel for the primus, they could not melt enough snow to give them the water that they needed.

They were crammed all four into one tent, the cloth of which was worn so thin that it let the wind blow through. Their sleeping bags had become a hard mass of rime, with little warmth. They could hardly sleep for cold. Every march was like a scene from the lowest circle of inferno. Through the incessant whine and roar of the wind they struggled on the trace, stumbling over the sastrugi against the arid needles of the drift that scoured and shaped the wilderness. The sledge, now deformed and half wrecked, was hard to move, and dragged to the right. For a few days after Christmas, they just managed to keep up with their target of twelve and a half miles; but only after hours of debilitating struggle.

Still the Pole hovered tantalisingly within reach. "Tomorrow," Shackleton had written on 28 December, "I . . . hope . . . to make 15 miles at least"; but they did not. So, he said, "we must risk a depot at 70 miles off the Pole and dash for it then."[64] After four miles next day, 30 December, a blizzard stopped them in their tracks. It was the first time they had been weatherbound since early in November. That did not make it easier to bear. "I cannot express my feelings," Shackleton wrote in his diary.

> All day we have been lying in our sleeping bags trying to keep warm and listening to the threshing drift on the tent side . . . Our precious food is going and our time also . . . We lie here and think of how to make things better but we cannot reduce food now and the only thing will be to rush all possible at the end . . . It lies with Providence to help us more.[65]

"Last day of the old year," Shackleton had written in another diary, exactly six years before, "and today we turned back after a blowy night."[66] "Still we are getting South," he now could say when, once more in a sledging diary, he wrote, "The last day of the old year." The blizzard had blown itself out, and the sledge was deeply drifted up, but get away they did. It was, in Shackleton's words,

> the hardest day we have had almost pulling through soft snow uphill with a strong wind and drift all day.[67]

Somehow they dragged themselves another ten miles.

Next day, the first day of the New Year, the wind dropped, the sky was clear, and Marshall got his first sun sight since Christmas day. The latitude was 86° 59′ at noon. That evening; or perhaps some time next morning, they passed 87° 6′, which was Peary's furthest north in 1906. "Thus," wrote Shackleton, "have beaten N. & S. record."[68] The Pole was less than 180 miles off. He had come three-quarters of the way. He had overcome Scott by almost three hundred miles. It was poor comfort. Unless Shackleton reached the Pole, it could only be a temporary triumph.

His hopes now turned on the surface of the snow. A tough, thick wind crust bearing men on foot was what he needed. It was asking a great deal. In any case, the cold, the rarefied air, the wind sweeping drift from one part of the arid uplands to the other, were all against it, if Shackleton could have read the signs. In camp on New Year's day he still believed in a better tomorrow, but tomorrow when it came brought snow into which, as usual, they sank up to their ankles. It took all day to struggle ten miles "though the weights are fairly light", he said.

> We are weakening . . . from want of food . . . We are not travelling fast enough to make our food spin out and get back to our depot in time.

It was the first note of pessimism since leaving Cape Royds sixty-six long days before. He went on,

> I cannot think of failure yet I must look at the matter sensibly and the lives of those who are with me. I feel that if we go on too far it will be impossible to get back over this surface and then all the results will be lost to the world.[69]

In the quiet and desultory talk in the tent this was not voiced. Shackleton still presented an optimistic front. Marshall and Wild at least now had their private fears.

Neither Adams nor Marshall, Wild had written on New Year's eve, harping on his usual theme,

> have been pulling a damn and consequently . . . I am beginning to be doubtful of success . . . If we only had Joyce and Marston here instead of those two grubscoffing useless beggars we would have done it easily.[70]

It was a comforting illusion.

Marshall faced a dilemma he had half foreseen. Since 27 December Shackleton, as Marshall put it, had been "suffering from extreme headaches and giddiness".[71] On New Year's day Marshall "called for camp at 5.30 as Sh. was done & he was suffering terribly from his head".[72] Now again, on 2 January, Marshall had to insist on "camp about ½hr. before time as . . . Sh. bad."[73]

> Shacks [he wrote laconically in his diary] won't stand a higher Alt.[74]

They were now at 11,000 feet, and climbing still. All were suffering from the altitude, for the human body needs time to acclimatise to the thin air, low pressure and oxygen deficiency of great heights. There is a kind of threshold, usually at about 10,000 feet. Above it, the symptoms of altitude sickness become plain. The pulse races, and every breath is a gasp, as heart and lungs struggle to feed the body with enough oxygen. Every movement is an effort. In the polar regions, because of thinner air, the effective altitude is higher than it appears. Besides, short of fuel, they were drinking too little and therefore a prey to dehydration.

Even so, to Marshall, something indefinable still set Shackleton apart. His pulse was disturbingly weaker than the others. Ought he ever to have been passed fit for the journey? Wild and Adams were by now, especially in this extremity, both Shackleton's more or less unquestioning followers. Marshall stood outside this. He knew only that unless Shackleton turned back, soon, he would collapse. But even as a doctor, how much authority did Marshall have? In his diary, Shackleton refused to admit any physical weakness; however, Wild also divined something awry.

The 3 January began with the rare comfort of a hard surface but soon, as Marshall put it, "again on came soft stuff".[75] Once more they were reminded of how they were at the mercy of the snow. The conditions were beginning to tell. Each morning, their now threadbare outer garments were frozen stiff as armourplate. So too were their finnesko. What was more, the lamp wick used as boot laces had chafed through. There was no reserve. The laces had to be knotted, catching the snow under the finnesko and making it ball up. That had to be periodically cleared, which meant extra stops and more delay. After ten hours' floundering and drag in the face of the incessant bitter wind from the south, they barely forced themselves on another ten miles. At least the sky was clear. At lunch, Marshall put up the theodolite, and got another sunsight.

That evening, after the sadly inadequate little pannikin of pemmican; in the mournful silence after the roar of the primus ceased, they discussed what was to be done. The figures were eloquent and simple. Marshall's sight put them at 87° 22′. They were 158 miles from their goal.

At best, this meant arriving at 90° S on 17 or 18 January. Even assuming quicker marches on the way back, that would leave them out on the Barrier in the middle of March still trying to get home. Not even the fear of having to admit defeat would make them take that risk.

So, as Wild put it, "We have come to the conclusion that we cannot get to the Pole". Shackleton, he remarked in cipher, "is very disappointed".[76]

Now they had to turn before it was too late. To Marshall, that meant at once. According to Adams, Shackleton, however, said to him: "You'll stick by me if I go on".[77] Wild was willing to follow too. Marshall believed that Shackleton was on the verge of collapse, while a slight swelling on Adams' legs, and discoloration of one foot *might* have meant scurvy on the way. Grasping that argument would now be an even greater peril than disease, he had reluctantly to bow to the majority.

> We can now definitely locate the South Pole on the highest plateau in the world and our geological work and meteorology will be of great use to science [Shackleton wrote in the interior dialogue of his diary]. But all this is not the Pole.[78]

Shackleton had not quite resigned himself to defeat. At least he would get within a hundred miles of the Pole. He still clung to the shadow of hope that a miraculous change in wind, weather and snow would let him snatch victory at the eleventh hour. He persuaded his companions to make a final dash. With the insight that they all were weakening, he decided once again to lighten the sledge. The remaining food and fuel was divided. Enough was now depoted – they all hoped – to carry them, on half rations, back to their last proper depot at the head of the great glacier, 150 long miles away. They took with them exactly ten days' supply.

In the wide, featureless sweep of snow on the roof of the world, there were no landmarks to fix the depot. It was, once more, marked by a single flag. They had not the strength to build cairns along the way. Shackleton banked on fine weather. To find his way back to this forlorn outpost at 87° 22′S, he depended on his footsteps in the snow – alone – "a risk", as he acknowledged, "that only this case justified".[79]

In any case, when they started off at 7.45 a.m. on 4 January, their footsteps were clear enough. Sinking through soft snow, as usual, well above their ankles, they were paying yet again for their prejudice against ski. All day they fought against a headwind, force five. Technically, this is a "fresh breeze", about 20 knots. At sea, it means, for example, yachts heeling to the wind, and spray against a summer sky. In the mountains, on the other hand, to quote one textbook definition, the snow drift blown along by this kind of wind, "gives a sensation of the face being whipped".[80] This hardly begins to express what Shackleton and his companions went through that day.

There were 50°F of frost (−28° C), and all they had between that and their skin was one worn set of underwear, a thin Burberry windsuit and, in Shackleton's words, "no [under]trousers and

2 guernseys".[81] Everything else had long since been jettisoned to save weight. When Marshall "took or rather tried to take our temperatures", said Wild,

> his clinical thermo was not marked low enough to take any except mine. The other three were therefore below 94.2° which spells death at home.[82]

"All nearly paralysed with cold",[83] Marshall jotted in his diary. That day had clearly shown that although they were now only dragging 70lbs each, "we . . . found we could do no better," in Wild's words, "than we did a fortnight ago with 200".[84] "The end is in sight," Shackleton was forced to agree. "We are weakening rapidly."[85] The fact that their sledgemeter told them they had covered twelve-and-a-half miles, their old timetable minimum for victory, suddenly seemed academic.

Logically, it was now really time to turn. Shackleton, however, still burned with the desire to go on. The Pole, he finally admitted, was out of reach, but he was still determined to advance to within 100 miles of it. He was equally determined to survive. By some unspoken device, he conveyed that to his companions and, against their own judgment, they agreed to follow him a little further into the wasteland.

They were now on the borders of survival. Marshall insisted, and Shackleton agreed, that they shorten their march and increase their food. They would go on for only three days more. That, to quote Wild, doubtless echoing Shackleton, as he harangued in low tones to the drumming of the tent wall in the wind, while they shivered in their sleeping bags and fought the sour gnawing of hunger,

> should put us within 100 miles of the Pole. It seems hard that we cannot do the remainder, but as it is absolutely certain we should all die if we did, it would not do us or the world much good.[86]

So, like failing beasts of burden, they hauled their ill-sliding sledge, dragging foot after weary foot through deepening drifts, against the pitiless wind from the south. On 6 January the thermometer showed 57°F of frost. They were all frostbitten. "Things were so bad," said Wild, "that we had to camp at 4.30 or I really believe we should have collapsed."[87] It was the worst day of the whole journey so far. At least it was the last agreed day out.

"Tomorrow," Shackleton said nonetheless, "we march South with the flag. 88° 5′ South tonight."[88]

Tomorrow, however, brought a "blinding, roaring blizzard", as

Shackleton put it, "wind 80–100 [miles] an hour",[89] which kept them tent-bound, and the day after it was the same. They could do nothing but lie in their sleeping bags, battered by the enervating howl of the storm and beat of the canvas; pressed more and more uncomfortably up against each other by the weight of the drift, ominously piling up outside.

They were, in Shackleton's words, "suffering considerably physically from cold . . . and . . . hunger but more mentally". This was not because, as he put it in one of his laborious jottings made with freezing fingers clutching at a stump of pencil, of their "chief anxiety that our tracks may drift up" – that was certainly "A serious risk . . . . but we had to play the game to the utmost and Providence will look after us." What fundamentally was troubling Shackleton was that

> we cannot get on South and we simply lie here shivering. We must do something more to the South even though the food is going and we weaken lying in the cold for . . . even the drift is finding its way into our bags which . . . are wet and damp enough as it is . . . we must get within 100 miles of the Pole.[90]

Unless Shackleton actually believed that they were within one hundred miles of the Pole, Marshall feared disaster. Since 3 January, at 87° 22′, he had got no sun sight. He depended on dead reckoning and the sledgemeter. Yet though weakening and in worsening conditions, they suddenly appeared to increase their daily run from ten to thirteen miles.

Shackleton could not allow his companions to brood in isolation in their sleeping bags. He read aloud, with Wild, *The Merchant of Venice*. There, on the Antarctic ice cap in a blizzard, was surely the most outlandish stage for Shakespeare yet.

> So may the outward shows be least themselves:
> The world is still deceived with ornament . . .
> How many cowards, whose hearts are all as false
> As stairs of sand wear yet upon their chins
> The beards of Hercules and frowning Mars
>
> Who, inwards searched, have livers white as milk;
> And these assume but valour's excrement to render them redoubted![91]

Outside the wind swept and roared and shook the tent in squalls.

At 2 a.m. on 9 January, after raging for sixty hours, the blizzard dropped. Two hours later, with nothing but some biscuits and a little chocolate in their pockets for lunch, the four men left the camp for their last southwards dash.

The blizzard had hardened the surface. Without the burden of a sledge, they found the going appreciably better. From 4 a.m. to 9 a.m., they marched as hard as they could.

"We have shot our bolt," Shackleton said simply at the end, "and the tale is 88 23S. 162 E."[92] That is undoubtedly what he believed. It was overcast, with a high veil of alto cirrus clouds. Even had the sun been shining clear, there would have been no observation. The theodolite had been left behind because of weight. Nor was there any question of waiting until noon for a meridian altitude. They had come as far as raw courage could bring them.

Every minute now counted. Without instruments the run from the camp could only be guessed. Upon Marshall, as navigator, the responsibility lay. 88° 23′ put them ninety-seven miles from the Pole. They had reached their goal of consolation. Now they were going to need all their reserves of moral strength to get back.

With him, Shackleton had carried Queen Alexandra's Union Jack mounted on a bamboo pole. This he now planted in the snow to mark the Furthest South; and also a small brass cylinder containing some of his Antarctic stamps. "With a few well chosen words," as Wild put it, he "took possession of the country."[93] Shackleton named it the King Edward VII Plateau.

They then photographed each other with the flag streaming in the bitter wind. There was no inducement to linger. Each in his own way was troubled by the unsaid thought: they had now to retrace their steps over 730 miles. Would they get back alive? After a very few minutes, they were on their way again, homeward bound at last.

Perversely, the weather now cleared. The sun, in its unfamiliar low orbit, came weakly out. Among them was a whiff, perhaps, of regret for the might-have-been. It was not wholly shared by Marshall. Shackleton, as he put it, had

> qualities which produced a ready response . . . His great passion was an inordinate personal ambition which knew no limits and sometimes . . . soared . . . beyond the physical efforts of which he was capable.[94]

Now, as they hurried through the snow with the wind behind them at last, cracked and blistered faces no longer tortured by the drift, it all suddenly seemed a "nightmare story", as Marshall turned round and told Shackleton, a journey that should not have been attempted *from that base* [Cape Royds] for the sole purpose of getting to the Pole, and the mentality of any man who tries to defend this basic decision is warped.[95]

Was this a reproach for not having started from the Bay of Whales? Had they done so, they might have been at the Pole by now.

Shackleton pretended that even from where they were, a little more food would have got them through. But, in Marshall's very private words, he "showed physical weaknesses which unfitted him for strenuous conditions at high altitudes".

Did he realize that given the necessary . . . supplies . . . he was physically incapable of achieving the Pole . . . and returning to Base?[96]

Perhaps Shackleton did. Perhaps that had helped him to turn.

Even so, it had taken courage of a special kind to turn, after coming so far, and with the Pole almost within reach. It was arguably one of the bravest acts in the history of exploration. Any fool can go on blindly forwards. It required insight and moral courage to turn back; especially when it meant publicly admitting defeat and to a despised rival.

In any case, Shackleton had set a marvellous record. He had beaten Scott's Furthest South by 360 miles. He had made the greatest single leap forward to either Pole of the earth that anyone had ever achieved. Of that, he could never be deprived. He had shown the way to the heart of the last continent. Whoever finally reached the Pole would have to follow in his wake. Still, all that, as Shackleton said, was not the Pole. He had come all this way, it seemed, merely to suffer once more the dull ache of bafflement, only a little more uncomfortably than before. All that was left was to rush home as quickly as he could and snatch a temporary triumph.

The weather held and, at about 2 p.m., helped by a following breeze, they returned to their camp. They had been on the march for ten hours almost without pause. Exhausted as they were, some instinct made Shackleton drive them on yet further. Swallowing some tea, they struck camp, and within half an hour were yoked once more to the sledge. They managed between four and five miles to the north before the day was out. They believed they had done forty geographical miles when they collapsed into their sleeping bags, faint and exhausted but, in Shackleton's words, "Homeward Bound":

Whatever regrets may be we have done our best. Beaten the Southern Record by 366 miles the North by 77 miles. Amen.[97]

"It has indeed been a risk leaving our food on this great white plain," he soon was saying, "with only our sledge tracks to guide us back."[98]

Snow, however, is like engraver's plate. Its markings are hard to erase. The wind had scoured the terrain ahead, but where the sledge had run before, the tracks were raised in relief, like the imprint of a mould. By 11 January, they had led straight back to the depot dumped despairingly eight days before at the last observed latitude of 87° 22′. "Had we missed it," as Marshall noted in his diary, "our chances would have been nil."[99]

Their chances were still not exactly high. Shackleton expected there to be "little in the locker"[100] by the time he reached the next depot. That was at the head of the glacier, 180 miles off. The distance had taken seventeen days on the outward journey. There remained barely ten days' food, at half rations, for the return. At least, they now had the help of the persistent wind from the south. They improvised a sail on the sledge from a tent floor cloth, and were more or less blown along.

Even so, they were handicapped. Without ski, they had to run to keep up with the sledge, as it pitched and tossed over the sastrugi. They had to waste even more precious energy braking the sledge, instead of coasting along, as a skier would have done. At night, hunger, cold and altitude kept them awake. Shackleton's feet were now frostbitten and cracked, and causing him great pain. Nonetheless they forced themselves along eighteen and nineteen and twenty miles a day.

They lost their sledgemeter; so their navigation was now reduced to guesswork. Enveloped in clouds of drift sweeping from the south, they had only their ever fainter outward spoors to lead them back. On 16 January, as Wild put it, "our eyes were gladdened by the sight of land".[101]

It was the first time for almost three weeks. The coastal mountains, the first milestone on the way home, had reappeared. The strange disorienting wilderness of unrelieved snow had been left behind. Against all odds they had, so far, survived.

XXV

March or die

"I hereby take possession of this area now containing the Magnetic Pole for the British Empire," Edgeworth David was saying that same day in another part of the inland ice: 72° 25′ south latitude, longitude 155° 16′ east, to be exact. He hoisted the Union Jack on a tent pole. "Three cheers for the King," he scribbled in his diary. "Mawson photographed us."[1] They at least had reached their goal. Even as David spoke the Magnetic Pole pulsated and moved on. Now he and his companions also had to turn and hasten home. Their tale was more or less that of Shackleton. "Most miserable travelling," as Mawson put it tersely, "Always cold wind – surface soft and bad."[2]

Nearly eight hundred miles to the south, a day or two later, Shackleton and his companions, in Marshall's faintly disbelieving words, were "still on the trail".[3]

On 18 January, Mount Buckley hove into view. That was the depot mark. Their lives still hung upon a thread. They had reached the crevassed outflow of the ice cap; the labyrinth through which they had to find safety again. The depot was still far away; and a storm would snuff them out. Fear and hunger goaded them on long past the supposed limits of endurance. "Never will I refuse a hungry man a feed, & [I will] feed the hungry whenever possible!" Marshall was moved to write – "if," he added as an afterthought, "willing to work!"[4] In his distress, Marshall had preserved his professional detachment. They were weakening from malnutrition, that he could see, but at least, after eighty-eight days, he could find no sign of scurvy.

For two days, they continued their headlong race for life. The snow had turned into a hard wind crust since they had last been there. Down the waves of the ice cataract, they rushed pell mell through the frozen headwaters of the glacier, sledge under full sail, bumping recklessly down, before a constant following gale. On 19 January, they covered twenty-nine miles, having "crossed hundreds of crevasses wide and narrow," as Wild phrased it, "all at the run."[5] Starvation, not the danger of falling down a crevasse, was their all-consuming fear. Wild wrote that same day,

> I don't know how [Shackleton] stands it; both his heels are split in four or five places, his legs are bruised and chafed, and today he has had a violent headache through falls, and yet he gets along as well as anyone.[6]

The next day, 20 January, the descent went on, helter-skelter, down the slopes around Mount Buckley at the head of the glacier. The distance was only thirteen miles instead of twenty-five miles the day before, but it was much harder. Soon after starting, they ran on to bare ice, and began slipping and falling. "I took charge," Wild wrote, in cipher, "or we should have lost sledge."[7] It was lowered with the Alpine rope, using an ice axe driven into the snow as a bollard. About midday, they reached the depot. It was just in time. They had exactly one day's food in reserve.

The depot meant not only food. Now they had extra clothing again; also the second tent, dumped on the outward journey to save weight. Loading up, they hauled on urgently another few miles along a gentler slope where the glacier proper began. Storm squalls knocked them over, and Shackleton fell noticeably more than the others. Towards evening they ran out on to a terrace of hard snow and there, tired, and bruised from all the falls, they camped. The wind by now had dropped. They were down to 6,000 feet and at last could breathe again without effort. "Bad as the day has been," in Shackleton's words, "we have said farewell to that awful Plateau."[8]

After supper, he collapsed.

His companions were not surprised. "For a good six weeks," said Wild, Shackleton had been "doing far more than his share of work."[9] In Marshall's words, "we shall have to push on at all costs, & carry him on sledge if necessary."[10]

For all of them, survival seemed to hang upon a thread. From the depot they had just picked up, to the next one at the foot of the glacier, was a hundred miles. Climbing, it had taken a fortnight between the two. They now had barely five days' food.

All next day, 21 January, Shackleton was "very ill", as he himself admitted. He rode on the sledge now and then. Most of the time, however, he managed to walk, while his companions did all the work, although Wild, by now absolutely Shackleton's man, was still brooding over Marshall's trace being "as slack as ever, though only three of us were in harness".[11]

Somehow, Shackleton got through the day, his pulse racing, irregular and, Marshall noted, "thin and thready". When they camped, his pulse was still irregular, his temperature was nearly 100°, he could not eat, and now he had diarrhoea.[12] Exactly what was the matter, Marshall could not say. Asthma and altitude might have been involved. Everything was so confused. They were all starving, and, on Shackleton's medical history, perhaps he simply had a constitutional flaw which malnutrition found out. Vitamin C deficiency, after all, was looming up. In any case, the pattern was uncannily like that of the southern journey on *Discovery*: collapse after prolonged exertion, six years before, almost to the day. Whatever the cause, Shackleton was weak and fighting for breath. He had nonetheless forced himself to march fifteen miles. To Marshall, however, Shackleton was a patient who had brought at least some of his troubles on himself. He was also a leader who had trusted a little too much to luck for comfort.

Shackleton was "better & able to assist sledge a little," Marshall noted the following day, 22 January. "V. fortunate," he drily added. They were now on the sharp, blue rippled ice of the middle glacier, with another twenty miles of this torture to go. The sledge by now was almost wrecked. Almost half of one runner had been ripped away, and there was no material for repairs. Shackleton, at least, continued to improve, and started eating again. He was tired, however, and still not strong enough to pull.

Marshall, Wild wrote on 24 January,

> is certainly bucking up, he has been pulling almost his share today, so I think he must be getting scared about the food.[13]

And well he might. The depot was still over forty miles away. Not quite two days' eked out food remained; and they were doing only fifteen miles a day now, struggling through fragile wind crust, and loose drift snow like quicksand.

The weather, incredibly, had held, with beautiful, clear skies, sunshine, and a moderate following wind. "If we should happen to have a thick day tomorrow," as Wild wrote on 25 January, "I don't suppose anyone would have the chance of reading this."[14]

After breakfast the next morning, they came to the end of their food. The depot was still twenty miles off, they thought. Soon after starting, they lost their way. Snow had blanketed the glacier since they climbed up, and made the contours unrecognisable. Without a map, they were trapped in an unfamiliar labyrinth of pressure ridges and hidden crevasses. Heavy going and doubtful snow bridges slowed them up. Shackleton tried to lead, but he was still too ill, and Marshall soon took over.

In the afternoon, they seemed no nearer their goal. They were failing from hunger and exhaustion, and were hardly making half a mile an hour. All food had gone.

Marshall had prepared for a crisis such as this. From 5.30 p.m., he dosed everyone hourly with "Forced March" tablets, a cocaine preparation, which "sustains strength", as the makers put it, "without subsequent depression."[15]

Somehow they kept going. Their discomfort was intensified by thirst. Time seemed to lose its meaning. "I cannot describe adequately the mental and physical strain,"[16] Shackleton wrote. What etched itself into Marshall's consciousness was

> a brilliant sun with never a cloud, with our shadows crawling round every point of the compass as day passed into night, again to day and then to night, with the snow plain still stretching far ahead and the mountains always seeming within easy reach yet never attainable . . . Except for the swish of the deep snow as we shuffled through it [he continued], complete silence reigned, broken at times by the tinkle of falling ice into the crevasses over which we were passing.[17]

The four men resembled grotesque caricatures by some mad engraver: hollow-eyed, faces burned, blistered and deformed by sunburn and frostbite; scarecrow figures stumbling through the snow. Shackleton, however, was not only starving like the rest; he was still ill. All his willpower was needed simply to survive.

By the early hours of 27 January, Marshall, effectively taking over command, had found a way out of the crevasses, and led his companions on to the right track again. The depot was then only two or three miles off. The rock pillar under which it lay was clearly in sight. By then, even the "Forced March" tablets were exhausted.

In reaction, Wild collapsed, and they had to camp until late morning. An hour after starting Adams sank in his tracks, mumbling a demand for half an hour's rest, and fell asleep in the snow. He was immediately kicked, and told the half-hour was up. Nothing could rouse him. Shackleton and Wild were not much better off. Only Marshall had a reserve of strength. He now made up for slacking on the trace if, indeed, he ever had been slacking.

Leaving the others behind, Marshall set off alone the last few miles in a desperate attempt to fetch food. "Reached depot in about 25 min. after falling into 3 crevasses covered by recent heavy fall of snow,"[18] he tersely recorded. Each time he saved himself by flinging himself forward as the snow collapsed, in the hope that he was crossing the crevasses at right angles.

Taking a little food from the depot, with its single pennant fluttering in the breeze, Marshall returned without mishap to his companions. In Shackleton's words, "Only an all merciful Providence has guided our lives to . . . safety."

They had been forty hours without solid food: "The hardest and most trying days we have ever spent in our lives," said Shackleton, "and which will ever stand in our memories."[19] Even after eating, they were so exhausted, mentally and physically, that they had to sleep before facing the last mile or two ahead. The going was treacherous; fresh snow on slippery ice, without cohesion. Early in the morning of 28 January, they finally all reached the depot. Stopping only to load the sledge, they crossed the Gateway and, by 3 p.m., were camped on the Barrier again.

> It is with a feeling of relief too intense for expression that we left the glacier [said Shackleton], for the strain has been great and we know that except for blizzards and thick weather, which two things can alone prevent us from finding our depots in good time, we will be all right.[20]

Next morning, after two hours on the march, the air was thick with falling snow, soon driven before a heavy gale, force nine, nearly fifty knots. It was a freakish, warm blizzard. Visibility was practically nil. Landmarks were blotted out. Since they were manhauling, rather than on a ski, the snow was sticky and impassable. So even although it was, as usual, a following wind from the south, they had to stop and camp. "Had this occurred a few hours earlier," Marshall remarked, still shaken by events, "we should not have reached the depot."[21]

When Shackleton collapsed, Marshall had naturally taken charge. Despite Wild's obsessive belief that he was not pulling his weight, this reflected the hierarchy of the group. Adams had been exposed: he was only titular second-in-command.

Marshall's attitude to Shackleton now was partly admiration for a plucky patient. Shackleton, in his words, "has stood it wonderfully", while "Wild and Adams", he noted in awe, were "rather played out".[22] Shackleton might have suffered an attack of asthma, as Koettlitz suggested on *Discovery*, but there was also the heart murmur Marshall had found. The symptoms were still anything but clear cut. Marshall was simply glad to have got Shackleton down from the heights alive.

Back on the Barrier, Shackleton recovered sufficiently to reassert his command.

In the small hours of 30 January, the blizzard stopped. "After spending 3/4 hour digging out our sledge & tents from the drift," in Shackleton's words, "started 8.15 a.m. . . . It was clear . . . as we started but soon began to snow and became very thick". This was precisely as they had to cross the crevasses where the Barrier joined the land, but now Shackleton simply drove on, trusting, as usual, to his lucky star:

> Steering on a [compass] course, we came through the crevasses without even touching one though every time before in broad daylight and good light we have had to turn & twist to avoid them.[23]

This was the last full entry Shackleton made in his diary. It was not, anyway, the kind of diary written with one eye on the public. He was truly the man of action, and did not care what others who came after him might think. Crisis released in him some fierce internal reserve of power and made him concentrate on survival. For his diary, he could spare the energy only for disconnected jottings.

The depot had only been a tenuous respite. The next one was sixty miles off, at 82° 39′, where Grisi's meat was stored. On the way out it had taken them five days to travel between the two; and now, when they set off, they had exactly five days' food, at half allowance. It was six weeks since they had eaten a full meal, yet suddenly they were oppressed by a frightful hunger, far worse than anything before, and they began rapidly to weaken. To make matters worse, when they started on the Barrier, Wild suddenly developed a violent dysentery, which weakened him yet more. Somehow he had to drag himself along; for now it was, literally, march or die.

Marshall blamed the trouble on bad pony meat from the last depot, at the bottom of the glacier. It could also have been advance warning of scurvy; or even simply lack of carbohydrates. They were living off pemmican and pony meat, with only four thin biscuits each a day now. Underlining every word, Wild wrote on the last day of January that Shackleton

> privately forced upon me his one breakfast biscuit, and would have given me another tonight had I allowed him. I do not suppose that anyone else in the world can thoroughly realise how much generosity and sympathy was shown by this; I DO by GOD I shall never forget it. Thousands of pounds would not have bought that one biscuit.[24]

For twelve miles and more each day, Wild had to drag himself through soft snow, sinking knee deep at every step. There were no ski for an invalid, as on *Discovery* for Shackleton.

On 2 February, just as food gave out, they reached the next depot; three hundred miles from home. "Only 5 miles awful surface," Shackleton tersely jotted next day, "all touched dysentery."[25]

"The Prof.," Douglas Mawson said that same day, several hundred miles to the north, "was now certainly partially demented."[26] David, Mawson and Mackay were camped on the coast on the Drygalski Ice Barrier, waiting for the ship. The return from the Magnetic Pole, in Mawson's words, had meant "despair, disappointment, hard travelling, agonising walking".[27] It was the mirror of what Shackleton was going through. The strain had been so great that David, somewhere up on the Inland Ice, had said that had he "known the magnitude" of the journey, he "would not have undertaken it".[28] Mackay, as Mawson had recorded at the end of January, had

> told the Prof . . . that he would have to give me written authority as commander, or he would as medical man pronounce him insane.

Part of the strain was the uncertainty of relief. The captain of the *Nimrod*, whoever he now might be, had no rendezvous, because plans had been so vague. On this score, Shackleton was not now uncritically admired. There was no certainty even that any ship would come; and now, with open water all along the coast, a ship was vital for escape.

On 4 February, during the afternoon, they were in the tent having a gloomy meal of penguin liver fried in blubber when, in Mawson's words,

> a shot rang out – in a second I had overturned the cooker and was through the door where the bow of the Nimrod was just appearing round a corner in the inlet . . . Just as I was descending to the lower shore the snow gave way and down I went some 18 ft. on to the middle of my back . . . After some trouble I was hauled up safely by the crew.[29]

Nimrod's new captain was Frederick Pryce Evans, who had commanded *Koonya* the year before. His side of the story was also one of drama and uncertainty.

Evans did not quite approve of Shackleton. Firstly, there were the circumstances in which England had been dismissed. Then, he arrived at McMurdo Sound on 5 January to find orders of the vaguest kind. Shackleton had simply told the Captain of the *Nimrod* to look for David and his party along the coast of South Victoria Land. It meant searching every inch of broken, ice-infested shore through foul waters, imperfectly charted, for two hundred miles. Armytage, Brocklehurst and Priestley, meanwhile, were in the Western Mountains, also waiting to be picked up, and, somewhere in the south, Shackleton was hidden.

At Cape Royds, Evans found Murray, Marston, Day, Joyce and Roberts: "a mixed lot", as he put it, "ill-naturedly sceptical of what those still absent on sledging adventures might achieve".[30] Evans carried orders from Joseph Kinsey putting him in command if Shackleton should be delayed. It was no time for divided authority. When he discovered that Murray had been left in charge by Shackleton, Evans quite simply seized command by superior force of personality. A Welsh-born New Zealander, six feet tall, with piercing eyes, Evans, like Shackleton, possessed the quality of leadership, but in a more naked, despotic form.

Evans first had to rescue the men strung out along South Victoria Land. On 24 January, he sailed to Butter Point, on the other side of McMurdo Sound, and without difficulty picked up Armytage, Brocklehurst and Priestley. "Their normal social relations," Evans was half amused to observe, "had been suspended," and replaced by a "primitive . . . unmannerliness [which] demonstrated . . . how queer these people had become under the influence of prolonged and trying association with each other."[31]

To find David, Mawson and Mackay, however, was more difficult. All that Evans could do was to search the broken, icebound coast of South Victoria Land and hope he missed nothing on the way. On 4 February, after a nerve-racking passage through shoals and floes and icebergs, he made Cape Washington, the northernmost point of the sweep ordered by Shackleton. Still David had not been found. Shortage of coal dictated a return direct to Cape Royds, leaving the three men to their fate.

John King Davis, still first officer, had been worried by the thought of some grounded icebergs he had sighted in a snow squall at 4 a.m. Under Evans' cross-examination, he felt they might have masked an inlet in the Drygalski Ice Barrier. As Davis told the story, Evans left the bridge to finish his breakfast, giving him until then to make up his mind.

> I passed an exceedingly troubled twenty minutes [Davis said]. Fortunately, when the Captain returned to the bridge he had rephrased his question. Fixing me with his cool and disconcerting gaze, he said: "Are

you sufficiently uncertain of what you saw to make it worth my while to return to those bergs?" And I found myself answering without the slightest hesitation, "Yes!"[32]

So *Nimrod* turned on her tracks. The weather had now cleared, and behind the bergs there now distinctly appeared the inlet in the ice cliff where David and his companions were found. They had only arrived a few hours *after* the ship had passed on her way north. "Therefore, in some strange and providential way," as Davis put it, "my mistake in not taking the ship closer inshore to examine the tabular bergs . . . had made their rescue certain and assured!"[33]

They were "a curious looking little group", as Evans put it. "Abnormally lean . . . they were the colour of mahogany with hands that resembled the talons of a bird of prey." David was hobbling about; Mawson's nose was horny with frostbite. They had trudged and hauled twelve hundred miles, a triumph of sheer endurance.

Evans now had an inkling that Shackleton's survival might be hanging in the balance. On 11 February *Nimrod* returned to McMurdo Sound, but of the southern party there was no sign. They had been expected back at the beginning of the month.

Meanwhile, on 15 January, Joyce had set off to put a depot at the Bluff, as Shackleton had ordered. Alone among Shackleton's men, Joyce believed in dogs. Since the spring, he had been training the animals, and now he took them along. It was the first journey of the expedition in which dogs were used.

Joyce was hampered by certain limitations. The dogs had to be held back because, as he put it, "a man cannot keep pace with dogs".[34] That was because, like everyone else under Shackleton, Joyce was without ski. Also, the dogs were harnessed in tandem, not fan fashion. That meant that when one fell into a crevasse, he would drag the others with him, making rescue harder. But the dogs proved their worth. Blizzard and the caprice of snow were reduced to their proper proportions.

With him, Joyce had Day, Marston and, from the ship, Æneas Mackintosh who, despite the loss of his eye, had refused to stay at home. They all took turns riding on the sledge. The dogs, pulling a hundred pounds each, scampered unconcernedly along, snow spurting from their paws. Technically, it was the most impressive performance of the whole expedition.

On 31 January, having made the depot without noticeable hardship, Joyce returned to Hut Point, and by 8 February, after a storm or two, he was back at the depot with a second load.

Joyce expected to find Shackleton waiting there; but he was not.

"As our orders were to return on the 10th if the Southern party did not turn up," Joyce said, "we began to feel rather uneasy." They were weatherbound, perhaps by choice, until 11 February. "During every lull," in Joyce's words, "we . . . looked round the horizon with the glasses, expecting every minute to see the Southern party loom out of the whiteness."[35] He also laid out a line of flags towards the Bluff across Shackleton's course to make sure he did not miss the depot.

Whatever his faults, Joyce was someone who knew when to disobey orders. After the blizzard dropped, he raced south for two days, still failed to find Shackleton and, regretfully, turned north. On 20 February, he and his companions reached Hut Point again, to find *Nimrod* waiting offshore. "They have performed some wonderful marches," wrote Mackay, now recovered – physically at least – from his man-hauling ordeal, "and are loud in their praises of the dogs".[36]

That same day, at 79° 36′ south latitude, Shackleton and his companions stumbled into the depot laid during the spring. For the first week of February their dysentery had continued. Each camp, as Marshall put it, was "like a battlefield".[37] Adams was passing blood but, on the sledge, he was forced to drag unnecessary weight.

Travelling south, Shackleton had collected rock samples; on 10 December from the Cloudmaker, and on 17 December from a mountain at the head of the Beardmore glacier. He was hoping for economic minerals, if not precious stones, even on the road to the Pole. Also, geological samples would be proof of his journey, besides earning kudos for devotion to science. For men weakened by malnutrition, however, it was an indefensible burden.

By the middle of the month they had recovered, at least from dysentery; but still they were walking shadows of themselves. Wild recorded,

> We get now less than 1½ cups of [pony] meat a day, six biscuits . . . three spoonsful of pemmican; a spoonful of sugar in our tea & cocoa. How is that for more than 50° of frost and a heavy sledge at 14 miles a day and underclad.[38]

"We have a great deal to be thankful for," he wrote nonetheless. They were able to pick up the cairns they had built on the outward journey. Wind and weather remained astonishingly fair and,

> had the surface been the same as it was when we came down, we should all now be dead without a doubt.[39]

A single blizzard would have finished them off. Even one day's deep snow would have been too much, because they were now too weak to lift their feet clear. They could survive only if the snow continued as a wind-packed crust which both supported a moving human foot and allowed a sledge to slide.

Over the endless rolling, featureless white plain of snow, they drove themselves along, scarecrows hauling at the sledge. The shaft of polar autumn was in the air. The sun, when it came through a high veil of cloud, spiralled lower. The only sounds were the scrape of the runners, the pad of finnesko on the snow, the sough of wind in surges, pushing them on, like the tide towards a distant shore.

On 13 February they reached their depot "B" at 81° 4′ S, where Chinaman had been put down three months before. They arrived, once more, with food running out. There were no reserves for the next stage either. They had been out for 108 days and survived 1100 miles so far; there were still 230 miles to go.

Shackleton had defied nature; nemesis was at his heels. Cold, starving, weakening, he and his companions should by now have been dropping in their tracks. There remained the moral factor. Different though they were, Shackleton, Wild, Marshall and Adams had this in common. They were uninfected by heroic longings. They wished only to survive, even though it meant coming back with only failure to report.

It needed, nonetheless, a touch of leadership to drive them on and draw out their reserves. Shackleton now seemed to come into his own. It was, again, as if supreme danger was necessary for self-fulfilment. He possessed some magic that overcame seemingly hopeless outer circumstances. Wild had surrendered most obviously to this power. By now he alone was still keeping a full diary, "for the sake of others",[40] as he put it.

One day, while Shackleton and Wild were sharing a tent, Shackleton suddenly asked Wild if he would return with him to make another attempt on the Pole. The situation was grotesque. They were at the extremity of starvation. It was so cold that, in his diary, Shackleton had been unable to write more than a sentence or two. They were in the middle of the Barrier, and survival was still no more than a chance. "This trip," as Wild had put it, when he was somewhere about 82° S, in the throes of dysentery, "has completely cured me of any desire for more polar exploration."[41] Nonetheless, in his own words, when Shackleton, shivering in his sleeping bag, asked him to come back,

> without any hesitation I replied "yes"! We then went on to discuss details. Shackleton was sure that he could raise sufficient funds in Australia to return [this] year.[42]

Wild actually believed it (so, perhaps, did Shackleton), and he drifted into his fitful, cold-ridden sleep, considerably uplifted.

When they left the depot at 79° 36′, they had exactly four days' food; with luck, it was four days to the Bluff.

Now another worry was oppressing them. Shackleton had left orders that, if they were not back by 1 March, they were to be considered dead, and the ship could sail without them. It was now 21 February. They had exactly a week in hand; but on the way out, it had taken a week from Hut Point to the Bluff, still forty-five miles off.

Shackleton now began to discuss an open boat journey in case they missed the ship. Round the primus over their thin meals in the tent; resting on the sledge, during halts, while the drift whirled about their feet, and the cold cut them to the bone, he sketched out the details. They would sail to New Zealand in the lifeboat at Cape Royds. It would only take a month or two. They could still enjoy the fruits of their achievement. He made it all sound credible. A great open boat journey was still one of his ambitions. In any case, his talk lifted his companions over their worries and fears.

But now they were at the end of their tether. Shackleton was again suffering from headaches. Yet at least the weather held miraculously still; there was a moderate following wind and hard snow crust. On 22 February, as Wild put it, they had "nearly everything to be thankful for".[43] During the morning they saw tracks in the snow; not theirs, and outward bound. It was the first trace of other people for three and a half long months. From the detritus in the snow, Shackleton deduced there were four men and dogs, "all well, smoking & plenty of food".[44]

Like a finger thrust across their course, the Bluff was now in sight. The tracks unmistakably ran from it. They must surely belong to the depot party. Joyce had done his job. Until then, the existence of a depot had to them been a matter of faith alone. The empty tins littering a camp site were a different make from those landed the year before, and thus Shackleton learned that a relief ship had arrived. That removed another gnawing doubt. Light of heart they plodded on, the jerk of the harness on their bellies no longer quite the discomfort it had been. That night they camped only twelve miles, as they reckoned, from the Bluff. With safety in sight, they cheerfully ate almost all their remaining food. But in those last twelve miles, a storm could still snuff them out.

Next day, however, the weather still providentially held and, more important, the snow as well. Like a vision in the desert, a huge snow cairn appeared late in the morning, miraged up. At

4.30 p.m. they reached it. "Good old Joyce," as Wild's expressively laconic diary entry put it: "Bluff dept. Hoosh. Defeat."[45]

They were now flooded with food. Not only essentials had been dumped. Starchy delicacies had also been charitably left. After months of starvation, they wolfed everything indiscriminately. A note from Joyce explained that it was *Nimrod* that had arrived, and also about the change of command.

It was now 23 February. *Nimrod* was only bound to remain for six days more. Shackleton led his men on with all possible speed. On 25 February, a blizzard blew. It would have been possible to travel but Marshall, hitherto the fittest of them all, collapsed with fierce cramp and diarrhoea. He ascribed it to sudden over-eating after starvation. All day they were tent-bound, Shackleton, in Marshall's words, "v. restless to get away".[46] It was still about fifty miles to Hut Point; but far longer, in fact, because of a detour towards the east to avoid the crevasses around White Island.

For two days, Marshall suffered greatly, but kept on marching. He never complained, but on the afternoon of 27 February, he collapsed again, and could no longer carry on. In less than forty-eight hours, *Nimrod* was due to sail. Hut Point was still thirty-three miles off. Shackleton pitched camp, dumped everything but the bare essentials and, leaving Marshall, with Adams to nurse him, drove on with Wild to fetch help and catch the ship.

In Wild's words,

> After we had covered a mile Shackleton stopped and grasping my hand said "Frank old man, it's the old dog for the hard road every time." He and I were then 35 . . . and the two we had left behind were under thirty.[47]

The snow, now hard and gritty, like a dusty road, still held; so did the weather, still with a following wind, although veering a little westerly. Through the driving curtains of cloud and drift, there loomed up ahead the gloomy peak of Erebus, like the ancient Greek entrance of the underworld after which it was named. It reminded them, if they needed reminding, that, unless their luck held until the end, they could still be lost.

After twelve hours on the march, "our progress", as Wild put it, became "a ghastly struggle".[48] Adams had been trusted to pack the food bag. When they took it off the now lightly laden sledge, they discovered that he had put in enough for one meal only. By the end of the morning of 28 February, it was all finished. Still there remained something like fifteen miles to go. Within a few hours, *Nimrod* would have leave to sail.

The mental strain, for Wild at least, was well nigh insupportable. What Shackleton was feeling, he did not reveal. From 25 February, he had ordered a constant look-out from Observation Hill, near Hut Point. They were now well within sight. To be conspicuous, Shackleton kept sail up on the sledge. In the sun, now shining fitfully through hazy clouds on the rippled snow, he stopped to flash a mirror. There was no answering signal from the heights.

Early in the afternoon, open water showed up ahead. An hour and a half later, the weather finally broke. Like the fall of the final curtain after some epic drama, a blizzard shut off all landmarks with a hissing veil of drift. Shackleton, however, had seen enough to get his bearings. The Barrier edge was close. The *Discovery* hut was within reach.

During a lull, Shackleton saw what he thought were men in the offing. "Our sledge seemed to grow lighter",[49] in his words, but the men, "turned out to be a group of penguins at the ice-edge".[50]

It was now 4.30 p.m. Shackleton and Wild had been marching for thirty-six hours with three hours' rest. They were weak, starving again, still inadequately clothed, and their finnesko were practically worn through. Wild's feet were starting to freeze. The *Discovery* hut was less than four miles off; but the sea ice had all gone out, and they were cut off by open water lapping at the edge of the Barrier. "It seemed the last straw,"[51] was all that Wild could say.

There was a short way round. Even in distress and under strain, however, Shackleton preserved the judgment to see that in the blizzard it was too dangerous. He decided to make a long, but safer detour around Castle Rock. Abandoning the sledge and all equipment, he and Wild started walking as fast as they could contrive. Unbelievably, the hard snow held, as it had done all the way from the foot of the great glacier.

> Weary, footsore and famished [said Wild] those hills seemed to be miles high instead of the actual 1,000 feet and when finally we came into sight of the hut and saw no signs of life we were past speech.[52]

"I presented my protest to the skipper", Mackay meanwhile was recording on board *Nimrod*. "The result was a long confabulation in whispers."[53]

Shackleton had been given up for dead. It was a matter of arithmetic. He had started out with food for 91 days. He had now been out for 120 days. Evans was preparing to land a wintering party to "find the bodies", as he put it. Mawson was to be in charge. Mackay was protesting at his own exclusion. Evans "explained to Mackay in Mawson's presence", as he blandly put it, his "reasons for not appointing him".[54] It was, in Mackay's words,

> *Unjust in the gravest sense of the word*! Because (other things being equal) men should be chosen who are most closely bound to the missing members of the expedition by the ties of old friendship and natural affection. This point will become most important if letters, perhaps addressed to individuals, or relics of the missing people are found.[55]

Out of loyalty, some of Shackleton's companions nonetheless had wanted to set off south quickly on a search. To Evans, however, since it seemed merely a matter of "finding the bodies", as he ghoulishly insisted on saying, it could therefore wait. Like many of his kind, he was tough, but limited. He knew all about the sea; but on land his judgment failed, and about polar travel he knew nothing whatsoever. For that matter he was not, any more than England, really compatible with Shackleton, nor could he be expected to grasp his peculiar combination of dashing insouciance and shrewd caution.

Evans, insisting now that he was permanently in command, over-rode all the orders that Shackleton had left behind. That included the vital instruction:

> In the event of the non arrival of the Southern party by the 25th February, 3 men [are] to proceed at once to the south on the 168th Meridian in search of the Southern party.[56]

Moreover, besides a watch being kept from Observation Hill, the *Discovery* hut was supposed to be constantly supplied and manned. Only if he had not returned by 1 March, Shackleton stipulated, was he to be given up for lost.

Like Rupert England before him, however, Evans' chief concern was for the safety of his ship. On the one hand, he was threatened by being frozen in; on the other, he was afraid of being wrecked by wind and current on some uncharted reef. Since 25 February, he had kept *Nimrod* sheltering off Glacier Tongue "in inactivity", as Mackay bitterly put it, "absolute inactivity".[57]

Through the chill eddies of the dying storm the two ragged figures half ran, half stumbled down the last few hundred yards to the hut. It was cold, deserted, and boarded up.

Nailed to a window was a letter from Edgeworth David, courteous as ever, to say that everyone else was safe and sound. This was good news; for until then, Shackleton had assumed that some disaster had interfered with his orders about relief and keeping watch. Now, something more sinister loomed up. A sense of betrayal hung uneasily in the air. David announced that the ship would be sheltering under Glacier Tongue until 26 February. After that, so he seemed to say, she would sail. It was now 8 p.m. on 28 February.

"To give way to despair," said Wild, "was not possible for Shackleton."[58] Lying in the snow was the wreck of an old outbuilding. Shackleton tried to burn it as a beacon, just in case *Nimrod* still was in the offing. The wood, however, refused to ignite. Shackleton then tried to tie a Union Jack to the cross on the heights commemorating Vince, who was killed on the *Discovery* expedition. By now, however, both Shackleton and Wild were so cold that their fingers literally could not manage the knots. They returned to the hut, scraped up some food and, without sleeping bags, tried to pass the night, as Wild said, "almost paralysed with cold". It was, as Shackleton put it,

> indeed a different home-coming from what we had expected . . . we had never imagined fighting our way to the back-door, so to speak, in such a cheerless fashion.[59]

From the past, came the distant, mocking memory of cheers and bunting that had welcomed him – or rather Scott, Wilson and him – back to the same place on *Discovery* from that other journey south.

"We are all in a state of the most painful anxiety," Mackay was writing on board *Nimrod*. "And . . . we are all made uncomfortable by the rather hole-and-corner business that is going on."[60] Mackay meant, still, the choice of the wintering party that was to establish Shackleton's fate. "Colonials being in power," in Priestley's words, "it was [to be] an entirely Colonial party,"[61] that is to say Australians and New Zealanders alone.

That, said Mackay, was "to the discredit and dishonour of the British members of the land party".[62] The squabbling was still in progress on 1 March, as *Nimrod* finally approached Hut Point to land the wintering party. "As a sop to Shackleton",[63] Priestley noted, Joyce had been added to their number.

"We had almost overlooked the fact that we were in the Land of Surprises," wrote Harbord, still *Nimrod*'s second officer, "but we were reminded of it very forcibly when we saw two men on Hut Point waving a flag."[64]

"No happier sight ever met the eyes of man,"[65] was how Wild put it, when *Nimrod*'s crow's nest appeared out of the frost smoke hanging over the water. Yet he and Shackleton could not respond to the jubilation which greeted them as they came on board. The simple question "Did you get to the Pole?" sung out by one of the sailors sobered them.

Failure is the inability to achieve one's aim. By that test, Shackleton had failed. He did not try to deceive himself. That was the burden he had borne, from the moment that he turned, for almost seven hundred miles. "No" had to be the answer to the question. His rider that "we got within ninety seven miles . . . !"[66] delighted his companions, but his own words, "all this is not the Pole," welled up to mock him.

When Shackleton came over the side, it was like the leader returning from the dead. Evans shrank to being the captain of the ship again. Shackleton resumed command. He could not rest, however, while Marshall and Adams were still out on the Barrier.

Shackleton had had no proper sleep for fifty-four hours. There were several men on board, rested and well fed, who could have led the relief party. Shackleton insisted, however, that it was his duty as leader to go back himself.

He had told Marshall he would return with the dog team;[67] but the dogs were being humanely rested at Cape Royds. So it had to be man-hauling to the bitter end.

Wild was too weak to follow, and had to stay on board. Shackleton took with him Mawson, Mackay and a reputedly athletic stoker called McGillan. It was Shackleton who cooked and tended the party on the march. Reaching Marshall and Adams the following afternoon, Mawson, McGillan and Mackay turned in for a rest. Shackleton cooked a meal and helped to break camp. Two hours later he gave the order to start, and in the evening of 3 March returned to Hut Point, two days after leaving the ship. Marshall had recovered sufficiently to get through under his own steam.

Even now, Shackleton had to face a kind of bafflement. He had told Evans to wait with *Nimrod* at the edge of the Barrier, and save him the long tramp round the bay. "For some occult reason," as Harbord pointedly remarked,

> we . . . anchored to . . . Glacier Tongue . . . leaving the party who had made a forced march from the South to get to the Hut as well as they might. This meant a very heavy and long trek over the glaciated hill sides where . . . Vince lost his life.[68]

Shackleton had to jettison one of his two sledges and most of his equipment. So, in Mackay's words, we arrived at the hut without a cooker. Here Shackleton's resourcefulness came out; for he soon had an excellent hoosh cooked . . . in an old butter-tin. We burned a flare, by simply opening a tin of carbide, pump-shipping [urinating] on it, and setting a light to it.

Calcium carbide had been used to provide acetylene for lighting. Applying water generates the gas. As Mackay wrote,

It went off with a slight explosion. It was seen by Mackintosh, on . . . the ship . . . and in a few hours we were on board.[69]

For five days, Shackleton had been almost continually on the march; in the past forty-eight hours he had covered sixty miles. To Marshall, after Shackleton's collapse, this was thoroughly confusing. Or was it sheer will-power overcoming physical weakness? In any case, Marshall himself was in no condition to insist on examining Shackleton; so the mystery remained.

Nimrod had by now picked up the dogs and the men waiting at Cape Royds. Baggage, however, still remained ashore. Shackleton nonetheless gave the order to sail as soon as he returned on board. He only had a temporary triumph in his hand. In bringing it to market, every hour would count. It was now 4 March. The season was on the wane. McMurdo Sound was already white and choked with the freezing of the sea. There was every chance of being trapped for another year at least.

So the end of the business [as Mackay put it], is that [we are] homeward bound, bumping our way through this season's ice, which is in the form of pantiles, some three or four inches thick. I have left a great many things behind that I am very sorry to lose.[70]

As *Nimrod* passed Cape Royds, "we all turned out to give three cheers", in Shackleton's words,

and to take a last look at the place where we had spent so many happy days. The hut was not exactly a palatial residence . . . but, on the other hand it had been our home for a year that would always live in our memories . . . We watched the little hut fade away in the distance with feelings almost of sadness, and there were few men aboard who did not cherish a hope that some day they would once more live strenuous days under the shadow of mighty Erebus.[71]

Pursued by a following gale, *Nimrod* drove through the grinding garland of ice and headed north into the gathering dusk.

XXVI

National Hero

"You have been fêted both in the south and in the north since your return from your famous expedition, but . . . nowhere have hearts beat [*sic*] more warmly for you."

These words were addressed to Shackleton on the balcony of a hotel in Christiania. Below, in autumn darkness, flames flickered red on upturned faces. The university students had come to greet him in a torchlight procession. By his side, Roald Amundsen, the conqueror of the North-West Passage, was making the speech customary on such occasions:

> Nowhere has the admiration for your great achievement been greater than here, and perhaps no assembly has been better qualified to judge of your undertaking than the assembly you see before you this evening.[1]

Amundsen spoke in a strange, reedy English, with a heavy, sing-song Norwegian accent and the charged, halting cadence of someone striving to express deep emotions in a foreign tongue. Cheers punctuated every sentence.

"Never before in all my life, have I received such a marvellous, enthusiastic reception", said Shackleton, stepping forward to reply:

> Never before have I seen such a sight as I see now before me, of all the torches lit in my honour . . . Never has an honour made such an overwhelming impression on me . . . I thank you from the bottom of my heart. More, I cannot say now. But I say again: this evening I have been overwhelmed, yes really overwhelmed.[2]

It was 15 October, 1909. On 23 March, at Stewart Island, off New Zealand, Shackleton had returned to civilisation. Since then, he had swept along on a tide of popularity. He could hardly have done better if he had actually reached the Pole.

At home, Shackleton had become a national hero overnight. Edwardian England knew how to honour success, and its ultimate reward was the exclusive, scintillating and exacting summer social round called the London Season. Of that, Shackleton was "the undisputed Lion", as one gossip columnist authoritatively put it. "If he only charged a small fee like Pooh Bah, in *The Mikado*, for dining at suburban dinner-parties, he could make an absolute fortune."[3]

For the Season, Shackleton's homecoming could hardly have been better timed. On 16 June, two days after his arrival, he was entertained to dinner by Mrs Eckstein at No 18, Park Lane. She was the wife of Frederick Eckstein, a de Beers diamond magnate, and one of the Rand millionaires who were lavish then in London. There were five hundred guests, ranging from the Duke and Duchess of Teck to Frank Shackleton and some of his shady City friends. The table decorations exactly mirrored the taste of the age, as the *Morning Post* reported:

> A green and blue gauze were put together to look like the sea, and between the folds fishes were placed. On the top of this a large sheet of plate glass was laid, edged around with seaweed. In the centre was a model of the *Nimrod* made entirely of flowers, the ropes done with white heather and a Union Jack flying from the topmast.[4]

That was followed by a dinner at 55, Harley Street, the home of a cousin by marriage, Mr Frederick Swinford Edwards, a successful surgeon. There, only eighteen guests took their places round the mahogany table, because the dining-room could take no more. Polar decorations were confined to miniature sledges at each place.

All summer long, Shackleton was fêted in various style between these two extremes. His days were crammed with teas, luncheons, dinners and receptions. His list of engagements read like the roll-call of society. He basked in the limelight "without the pride", as he put it, "that apes humility".[5] It was, after all, the reward which, honestly, he had sought. In his own words, "The world was pleased with our work, and it seemed as though nothing but happiness could ever enter life again".[6] With infectious gusto, he was hurrying, like a true Edwardian, to squeeze every drop of pleasure out of his success before it was too late.

It was not only public enjoyment. When Shackleton visited Hugh Robert Mill, at his home in North London, Mill's eleven-year-old niece remembered asking for Shackleton's autograph, and "he kindly obliged in dashing style [with] the text . . . 'We glory in tribulations also'."

> There was constant talking and a good deal of laughter, as everyone seemed very happy . . . Mrs Shackleton was most attractive [and her] dress I thought lovely. I . . . remember it was long, pale apple green adorned by slightly paler tassels. She seemed bright and happy – and no wonder.[7]

Shackleton's square figure, with heavy shoulders, surmounted by bulldog jaw and black hair parted in the middle, became familiar from peering out of press pictures. To begin with, at any rate, Emily was by his side. Well groomed and well dressed in the elaborate style of late Edwardian fashion, she appears, a background figure, yet not exactly shy. "I have never sought publicity", she once said, "never desired that the world should know of the share I had in his life."[8] Nonetheless, the fact was she enjoyed sharing in her husband's acclaim.

Underneath the surface, things were not so simple. Recognition of Shackleton's true achievement, as Amundsen suggested, first came in Christiania from the torchlight crowd. They nearly all ski'd and went out into the snows. They could put themselves in Shackleton's shoes; they could understand what he had achieved despite the inadequate preparation, poor technique, defective equipment, and his incomprehensible prejudice against ski. "It is so much the more marvellous," Nansen had succinctly written to Emily Shackleton, "that he could do all he has done."[9]

"I must write and congratulate you and through you the Royal Geographical Society upon this wonderful achievement", Amundsen had spontaneously written to Scott Keltie when Shackleton's news first came through. Amundsen was only one of many explorers to heap congratulations on the RGS. Otto Nordenskjöld, for example, wrote to say that Shackleton's expedition was "remarkable . . . not only for its Southern record but also for being the first that has opened . . . the central Antarctic regions".[10] All this bore out Keltie's precautionary remarks to Scott and Sir Clements Markham that the RGS "could not ignore" Shackleton.[11] Amundsen continued in his letter to Keltie:

> When I first heard of it, I thought it was some news brought up for sentiaation [*sic*] – especially [he perhaps unfairly added] coming from the "Daily Mail" but now . . . there is no more place for doubt. The English nation has by this deed of Shackleton's won a victory in the Antarctic exploration which never can be surpassed.[12]

When Shackleton visited Christiania, it was to lecture to the university students and the Norwegian Geographical Society. The first flush of welcome was past. This was part of a calculated garnering of recognition as the prelude to a commercial tour.

On the face of it, Shackleton's appearance was hardly worthwhile. At the lecture to the Geographical Society, there were only a few hundred selected guests in dress and decorations at banqueting rooms down by the fjord. Christiania, after all, was a small city.

Nonetheless, Norway was still the heartland of polar travel. Christiania audiences had seen the greatest explorers of their generation pass through. Nansen went to hear Shackleton. He sat through the lecture, his evening dress worn like a suit of armour, and not by a tremor over his granite features did he reveal the tumult of emotion within. Of course he respected Shackleton for what he had done. He was relieved, nonetheless, that Shackleton had not quite taken the game. The South Pole, in his own poignant words, "the crown of my work as an explorer",[13] might yet be his to win.

Amundsen was in the audience too. Hawk-nosed and enigmatic, encircled by a pool of loneliness, he was transfixed by the saga that Shackleton had come to tell. After the lecture and the cheering came a banquet where Shackleton had to reply to after-dinner speeches. "I shall never forget the look on Amundsen's face while Ernest was speaking," Emily said in after years. "His keen eyes were fixed on him, and when Ernest quoted [Robert] Service's lines,

> The trails of the world be countless, and most of the trails be tried,
> You tread on the heels of the many, till you come where the ways divide,
> And one lies safe in the sunlight, and the other is dreary and wan,
> Yet you look aslant on the Lone Trail, yet the Lone Trail lures you on . . .

"a mystic look softened them, the look of a man who saw a vision."[14]

Amundsen, as he listened, was perhaps thinking of another verse by another poet; something by one of his own countrymen, much quoted:

> He who goes first into the fray,
> Triumphs not; he only fights and falls.[15]

A month before, Robert Peary and Frederick Cook had both returned to civilisation, each claiming to have reached the North

Pole. For all of Nansen's longing for the South Pole, Amundsen had by then finally obtained *Fram* from him. His own expedition was a reality, his declared aim the North Pole too.

"The race for the Pole," as Shackleton put it, was "after all, a stupendous sporting event."

> There isn't glory enough for more than one Pole "discoverer", . . . and unless I can be the first to get there I have no particular desire to get there at all.[16]

That also expressed Amundsen's feelings only too well. From one end of the earth to the other, he swung the goal of his desire. "More than anyone else," in Amundsen's words, Shackleton "had managed to lift the veil that rested over Antarctica.

"But a little patch remained."[17]

By the time Shackleton arrived in Christiania, therefore, Amundsen had decided to go south instead. Of this, Shackleton, like everyone else, had no inkling, for Amundsen concealed his true intention. His secrecy had many strands; fear of what his backers would say, fear of being forestalled, fear of Nansen, an instinct, perhaps, not to show his hand too soon, an almost superstitious dislike of saying anything before the event.

Shackleton, on the other hand, believed in blazoning his intentions to the world. Time, in any case, was running out for him. He had been Furthest South – but for how much longer yet? When Amundsen said to him that "nowhere have hearts beat more warmly for you", it was with hidden ambivalence. Shackleton was the man who had shown the way.

When Shackleton and Emily left Christiania at 7 a.m. on 17 October, a Sunday, Amundsen was down at the railway station, alone, to see them off. For Emily, Amundsen had a farewell bouquet of flowers. She was, he understood, the poignant figure of the woman who waits.

Shackleton returned from Christiania with Amundsen's unfeigned generosity ringing in his ears. He felt he had been accepted by a critical and knowledgeable public, for in this, as in many other things, the Norwegians were people of extremes. Nationalistic to a degree, they yet accepted Shackleton as an explorer, untinged by national partisanship.

In England, things were more complicated. When Shackleton reappeared from out of the ice, on the black and weatherbeaten *Nimrod*, he was like a corsair coming home. Breezily untainted by virtuous intentions, innocent of cant, he was uninhibitedly patriotic, not to say imperialist; and always with an eye to the main chance. He was out of time and out of place, and just the character to cheer Edward VII, resting in the sunshine at Biarritz.

"His Majesty," in the words of the *Daily Mail*, when the news of Shackleton's achievement came over the wire, "declared it the greatest geographical event of his reign."[18] The King had, as usual, got it right.

In a typical comment, the *Sketch*, said:

> It is one of the symptoms of this age of nerves and hysteria that we magnify everything, that our boasts are frantic and our scares pitiable, that we call a man who plays well in a football match a hero, and that all successes are triumphs . . . but Lieutenant Shackleton is in that rank of heroes whose names go down to posterity . . . Just now, when we are all feeling a little downhearted at seeing our supremacy in sport and in more serious matters slipping away from us, it is a moral tonic to find that in exploration we are still the kings of the world.[19]

This was still the constant theme three months later when, on 14 June, Shackleton made a triumphant entry into London. "Of . . . Antarctic exploration," as the *Daily Graphic* tellingly put it, "the crowds which . . . made the Strand echo with their enthusiastic cheers know little." That, however, did not matter.

> What they honour is the indomitable spirit of the man who strove with amazing pluck and resourcefulness to do what no other man had done before . . .
>
> It is pleasant to think that in spite of the moanings we hear from time to time on the decay of British manliness, our people are still as swift as ever to . . . idolise the Man of Action.[20]

In more exalted spheres, the same thought was hammered home. "When one remembers what he had gone through," said Lord Halsbury (a famous lawyer, and a former Lord Chancellor), in proposing Shackleton's toast at a lunch given in Shackleton's honour by the Royal Societies' Club,

> one does not believe in the supposed degeneration of the British race. (Hear hear.) One does not believe that we have lost all sense of admiration for courage [and] endurance . . . (cheers.)[21]

The unspoken but underlying fear was of Germany, the rising power that was threatening Britain in almost every field. This was illustrated, too, at the Royal Societies Club lunch. "We live in days of naval stress," said Sir Arthur Conan Doyle, the creator of Sherlock Holmes; also the self-styled spokesman of the "man in the street",

> and when the trouble comes our cry will be for men, not ships. We can pass the eight Dreadnoughts, if we are sure of the eight Shackletons.

It was during one of the recurrent naval scares. Both in quality and numbers, the German fleet threatened British naval supremacy, and a campaign had been mounted to build eight new Dreadnoughts, as battleships then were called. "We want eight," was the cry, "and we won't wait."

Shackleton, said Conan Doyle, in his speech, turning to another subject,

> is an Irishman. As a fellow-Irishman I take pride in the thought. These are times when a religious and racial problem of most complex character may cause antagonism between the islands, may even cause you to have hard thoughts of the gallant race who are your neighbours. When such a time comes, think of what you have on the other side. Think of what Ireland has done for the Empire. Think of the great men the Wellingtons the Wolseleys, the Robertses . . . Finally, think of that flag flapping down yonder on the snow field, planted there by an Irishman.[22]

It was not only by Conan Doyle that Shackleton was now claimed as Irish. "SOUTH POLE ALMOST REACHED BY AN IRISHMAN," ran the headline in the Dublin *Evening Telegraph*, which went on to trumpet that Shackleton was "a scion of a well known anglo-Irish family".[23] "Let there be no mistake," said the *Weekly Freeman*, a nationalist journal, "the Shackletons are Irish."[24]

The *Dublin Express* hoped that Shackleton,

> would not dispute an explanation of his . . . success which should attribute it in some measure . . . to the qualities which were his heritage as an Irishman, the dash and buoyant enthusiasm, the cheerful and unshakeable courage . . .

Nor did Shackleton dispute it. In December, when he visited Dublin, he talked about returning to his native land. It was a quarter of a century, he said, since he had left, an obscure and unknown boy, but Irish he remained.

Almost alone in the British press, the *Dublin Express* made one telling point. Shackleton, it reminded its readers, was rightly proud of [having] penetrated . . . furthest South . . . he was even more proud of the fact that his was the first Antarctic expedition to return with a record, not only for winning more regions for the flag, but for doing this without the loss of a single life. It must have been a hard and bitter thing to have to give up when within striking distance of the South Pole.

Nonetheless, the *Dublin Express* went on,

Shackleton did the right thing in refusing to sacrifice the lives of others so willingly . . . placed at his disposal . . . it is a brave thing to turn back . . . [25]

The same point had been made by Amundsen when he told Keltie: "What Nansen is in the North, Shackleton is in the South."[26] Nansen was admired by his countrymen not so much because in his time he had come closest to a pole of the earth, but because on 8 April 1895, at 86°14′ north latitude, before it was too late, he deliberately turned. It was perhaps the hardest thing he ever had to do. That, partly, was what was in Nansen's mind when he wrote to Emily Shackleton that

If you have done a thing you are satisfied with . . . then you have indeed every reason to be happy . . . And I think indeed, that your husband and yourself, who allowed him to go, and have waited for him, have done a deed you have every reason to be satisfied with and proud of, a deed which could not have been done better.[27]

Before he left *Fram* to fight his way over the Arctic pack ice, Nansen had told his companions that the Pole was not worth a human life. Polar exploration was also Amundsen's obsession, but it was not a pretext for useless heroism.

No doubt, if Shackleton had been prepared to kill himself and his companions, he could have reached the Pole and, with luck, achieved posthumous glory. The real, largely unsung courage of Shackleton was that he *had turned back*. He was prepared to live with the might-have-been. "Only 97 miles off," as he expressed it to Elspeth Beardmore, "*You* can realise my feelings."[28]

To Emily, in her own words,

The only comment he made to me about not reaching the Pole, was "a live donkey is better than a dead lion, isn't it?" and I said "Yes darling, as far as I am concerned," and we left it at that.[29]

Amundsen who, so far, had achieved precisely what he had set out to do in the snows, could understand Shackleton's feelings only too well. In England, on the other hand, Shackleton's great act of courage in deciding to turn was consistently ignored. It lay outside the national ethos. Shackleton, in a typical newspaper comment, was "the stuff of which the Gordons and the Livingstones are made".[30] A martyred hero, it seemed, was what the country was looking for. Shackleton, so the thinly veiled thought suggested, ought to have gone on, even if, in the process, he killed himself. There was an undercurrent of feeling that his decision to turn was not so much courage as a want of tact.

"The English public," as Campbell Mackellar, now one of Shackleton's most strident supporters, put it, was

> greatly given to ignoring, and even denying honour or aid to the living: and then exalting them into heroes . . . when they are dead and going to extremes over it. It is false sentiment, and a rather cheap form of national applause.[31]

Even so, few explorers had received the welcome that Shackleton now enjoyed. The polar regions somehow caught the public imagination. They were mysterious, remote, the ultimate desert, the last great blanks on the surface of the earth, the threshold of outer space, half-way to the moon, away from human beings. It was part of the shrinking stage for the individualist.

Shackleton had the right kind of adventures: terrible (if really unnecessary) suffering; hairbreadth escapes, a near miss, a happy ending by the skin of his teeth. He was the personification of sheer physical courage, which was what the nation most admired. He was a vehicle of insular self-congratulation, ignoring the ominous fact that his inability to attain his goal was a measure of technical insufficiency which no amount of courage could overcome. He was portrayed by the press as that core of the English myth, the "splendid failure".[32] He gave the crowds an opportunity for hero worship and vicarious adventure. It was not only that he had nearly reached the South Pole. Until Cook and Peary returned, Shackleton was the man who had come closest to either pole of the earth.

All this, however, was merely the raw material of success. To transmute it into triumph, the correct personality was needed, and that, Shackleton undoubtedly possessed. He had all the instincts of a showman. When he returned from the expedition, by the P & O liner *India*, via Suez, he transferred at Port Said, like others in a hurry, to the mail packet *Isis*. This took him to Brindisi, on the heel of Italy, and the boat train across the Continent that was supposed to save a day or two. Armitage, his old companion from *Discovery*, was captain of *Isis*. For that reason, Shackleton was on the bridge as they berthed at Brindisi, instead of with the other passengers at the rails. Armitage remembered how Shackleton

> wanted, so he said, a "catchword". He walked up and down . . . muttering several phrases to himself.
>
> "I've got it at last", he cried, "Death lay ahead and food behind, so I had to return".[33]

Shackleton arrived at Brindisi on 11 June, a Friday. He could have reached home quietly thirty-six hours later. In freely given interviews to the press, however, he announced that he would actually arrive in London on the Monday, at Charing Cross Station, at 5 p.m.

"In his photographs," as the *Daily Telegraph* vividly reported from Brindisi, "Mr. Shackleton is nothing more than an intelligent but ordinary naval officer. In reality, he radiates the fascination of an indefinable force":

> But all this energy which breathes in the masculine and rigid lines of his face is illuminated by a gentle glance. If he has the face of a fighter, he has the look of a poet; one must be both fighter and poet to accomplish what he has done.[34]

Shackleton appealed to journalists. As a polar hero, he was the creation of the press. When he emerged from Charing Cross station, the crowd was there to meet him. It was the opening of an uninterrupted season of acclaim. On one occasion men were said to have removed the horses of his carriage and drawn it along instead. Exactly where this happened is hard to tell. Family tradition puts it in his home suburb of Sydenham, but it has the quality of myth. Shackleton had the world at his feet.

"It was *lovely* having him back again", Shackleton's sister, Kathleen, wrote to a correspondent,

> He *is* & always has been my hero – its rather nice isn't it that the man you like best in the whole world is your own Brother! Nothing can ever alter our Relationship, whereas one loses other friends so easily.[35]

Underneath the hero-worship and the glory, however, there was an elusive note of bafflement. On *Isis*, Armitage had

> noticed a great change in . . . Shackleton . . . He was no longer so dreamy; he was full of a restless, nervous energy.[36]

Eric Marshall, for his part, felt that Shackleton was "knocked off his balance by a 'near success'."[37]

Kathleen had not received back the same brother who had sailed away, nor Emily the same husband. He had become a public figure; but it is much too simple to say that fame had gone to his head. It was impossible to go through what he had undergone without being marked by the experience.

XXVII

Sir Ernest's debts

"A professed liar," Scott had called Shackleton when he learned of the landing at McMurdo Sound, "a plausible rogue."[1] He refused to associate with him ever again, but in the event, like Keltie, the RGS, and almost everyone else who had sat on the fence, he found Shackleton's reflected glory irresistible. When Shackleton returned in triumph to London, Scott was among the notabilities gathered on the platform at Charing Cross station to meet him.

To Scott, however, Shackleton remained the unlicensed intruder. Scott still considered the *Discovery* base, if not the whole Ross Sea, exclusively his domain, but he knew that success was its own justification. He had to be content with watching in the shadows while Shackleton enjoyed the limelight and charmed the public in a way of which he knew himself to be incapable.

Sir Clements Markham also found a share in a popular triumph hard to pass by. "As an old friend of eight years standing", he wrote in a letter waiting for Shackleton on his return,

> you will receive my very cordial welcome as coming from one who has watched your career with the interest of a sincere friend.[2]

But privately the "sincere friend" had had other things to say. "The arrangements about depôts, food &c." Sir Clements wrote to Keltie,

> seem to have been very harum-scarum, and it is a wonder they ever got back.[3]

Shackleton's failure to reach the Pole, Sir Clements said,

was due to faulty management . . . pushing on with half rations &c. &c., and he reached a very high latitude by risks which ought not to be run . . .[4]

This was trenchant criticism, and it echoed Nansen's point of view. At the age of seventy-nine, Sir Clements had not lost his touch. "Shackles," he wrote to Scott, "is suffering from swollen head."[5] That was because Shackleton had cabled from New Zealand that he wanted "Albert Hall and King's presence"[6] for the big meeting on his return. "It was not at all necessary," Keltie austerely replied, "for you to remind me about the Albert Hall and the king."

You do not need to do anything more than you have done already in the Antarctic, to obtain the appreciation and the reception which you deserve . . . To use an old Scotch expression "Keep a calm souch and a dark look-out."*[7]

Behind all his flamboyance, that was exactly what Shackleton was doing.

"The King," Sir Clements crowed to Scott, "is not coming."[8] The Prince of Wales, however, soon to become George V, did go to the Albert Hall where Shackleton, as he noted, "gave us an excellent lecture . . . He also showed us many beautiful photographs and cinematographs . . . The whole thing was a great success."[9] In the end, Shackleton confounded Sir Clements, and lectured before the King too; privately, by royal command, at Balmoral, in September. "The King," Shackleton reported to Emily, "enjoys a joke very much: He asked me a lot about Cook and Peary and Scott: he seems to know everything that is going on."[10]

In June, a few days after returning to London, Shackleton was entertained to dinner at the Savage Club. Scott was in the chair. "If I had a hand in rocking his Antarctic cradle," he said of Shackleton in proposing his health, "I am very proud of it."[11] Immediately after dinner, Shackleton made some excuse, departed, and did not return. Scott was surprised. He ought not to have been. Even in the determinedly convivial surroundings of the Savage Club, Shackleton did not wish to be talked of as a baby, especially by the man against whom he had fought so hard to erase the stigma of weakness.

Besides, Scott, in the same breath had publicly revealed his intention to go south again and try for the Pole. On 12 September,

* "Be quiet, and keep a good lookout."

he officially announced his new expedition. "Probably Mr. Shackleton could have done the work a great deal better," Scott said a month later at a meeting in the Mansion House to raise funds, "but he could not arrange the matter." His own expedition might fail, Scott darkly added, "but their supporters would never have cause to doubt the story they would have to tell".[12]

The background to this particular bitterness is curious. Some time before, Scott had received a mysterious envelope from the *Nimrod* expedition. Inside was a blank sheet of paper. Scott, and his wife Kathleen, were puzzled and annoyed. The incident made its way into a novel called *The Turnstile* by the contemporary best-selling author, A. E. W. Mason, like Shackleton, an Old Alleynian.

Mason knew Kathleen Scott. The hero of *The Turnstile* was Scott, thinly disguised as an Antarctic explorer called Harry Rames; characterised as "complacent and cunning". Shackleton appears as another explorer called Walter Hemming. The plot was partly based on their rivalry. This is how the blank sheet of paper appears:

> "Mr. Hemming sent it?" . . . cried Cynthia. [Kathleen Scott.]
>
> "Without a doubt!" . . . Rames . . . thrust the letter . . . into Cynthia's hand.
>
> "You open it. You can tell me what it says."
>
> . . . She tore open the envelope . . . she did not speak a word. Rames' heart sank.
>
> "Then he has reached the Pole?" he asked with studied carelessness.
>
> "I don't know," Cynthia replied, in perplexity . . . She was holding a single blank sheet of note-paper in her hand . . . "do you understand it?"
>
> "Yes. He has failed."[13]

"If Shackleton ever did anything of the sort," Raymond Priestley said in after years, "he would have done it in the spirit in which Mason has put it . . . I should like to think he did!"[14]

It now seemed that all Shackleton's struggle had merely been to break the trail for his enemy. "Another 50lb of food," as he soon was saying, to anyone who cared to listen, "would have taken us to the Pole and back."[15] Was this his great delusion? Was this the regret with which he was prepared to live? Even before he landed back in England, he was full of plans to go south again. Had he forgotten his distress at high altitude? Had he forgotten his bout of asthma, or whatever it was, going down the glacier? With hindsight, Marshall was beginning to think in terms of a heart attack. All Shackleton knew was that he wanted to go back and, perhaps, still beat Scott to the Pole.

Emily was disconsolate. "Never again," Shackleton had written to her from Australia, "will there be such a separation as there has been. Never again will you and I have this long parting that takes so much out of our lives."[16] But, as she put it,

> when a man's heart is set in that direction, & especially when he is so suited for the work one has to put one's own feelings aside – though you know how terribly hard it is sometimes.[17]

Despite his sudden fame, however, Shackleton found another expedition still a distant prospect. His bafflement was compounded by something else. Soon after returning from the Antarctic, he met Edward Wilson at Wilson's wish, to clear the way for Scott. Wilson was going south with Scott again, and wanted a declaration from Shackleton that he was not returning to McMurdo Sound or, indeed, the whole Ross Sea. For the second time, Shackleton found himself forced by Wilson to write a letter of renunciation to Scott.

> Your expedition, [he wrote therefore] will not interfere with any plans of mine. If I do any further exploration it will not be until I have heard news of your expedition, presuming that you start next year.[18]

Shackleton would rather have written that to anyone else on earth. Just as bitter was the change in Wilson's attitude to him. "I was glad to find that we could meet & speak together in a friendly manner", said Wilson, but he was no longer quite Shackleton's friend. "I allow that you were in a very difficult position," as Wilson put it in a long, unforgiving comment on Shackleton's landing at McMurdo Sound,

> That you know – But I wish to God you had done any mortal thing in the whole world rather than break the promise you had made.[19]

Wilson, despite the bitter undertone, was right; as Shackleton perhaps obscurely felt. Of course, the original promise was unreasonable. It was something Scott had no right to demand. "Shackleton," as Marshall then had said, "was plainly justified in going to McMurdo Sound." Shackleton, nonetheless, had broken a promise. He had committed the awful finality of a moment's surrender. The stain was indelible, as, perhaps, with anguish he had discerned at the time. Would he be believed or trusted again?

"When Lieutenant Shackleton returned," the *Saturday Review* wrote in September,

> there were half-a-dozen keen minds at work . . . calculating mileages . . . setting one statement against another, so that if any discrepancy existed it would be brought to light. Some of these perhaps were critics who had predicted . . . failure, anxious to vindicate their own prescience at the expense of the explorer's reputation.[20]

In this, as in other things, the *Saturday Review* was well informed. When the news from *Nimrod* first arrived, Sir Clements Markham, then visiting Portugal, wrote to Keltie casting doubt on Shackleton's latitudes. "I do not," said Sir Clements, "see how it is possible."[21] Sir Clements declined to believe that Shackleton moved as fast as he did, or faster than Scott.

After hearing from Sir Clements, Keltie wrote with polite urgency to Shackleton in Australia that

> I suppose you made pretty sure what latitude you reached. I do not know you said anything about the instruments you had with you, and of course the difficulty of taking any observations under the conditions must have been fearfully trying, but still, I have no doubt you established your latitude to your complete satisfaction.[22]

"As if," Shackleton wrote bitterly to Hugh Robert Mill, "I had not taken all possible means in my power to ascertain the exact position . . . You can rest assured," he went on, in a pointed reference to a scandal on *Discovery*, "that there is no confusion between true and magnetic [bearings] as regards the winds."[23]

Despite his disbelief in Shackleton's mileages, Sir Clements could not help admiring what Shackleton had done. "Shackleton," he wrote to Keltie at the RGS, when first he heard the news, "certainly ought to have the Patron's Medal for this year. It will be a serious mistake if this is not done."[24] "Something," Sir Clements later generously went on to say, "should be allowed for his very impulsive character."[25]

Early in April, when Sir Clements returned to England, he still seemed to be suspending judgment. On 13 April, Scott came to dinner and, as Sir Clements recorded, "does not believe in the latitudes".[26] Scott had already announced to Keltie that he would not credit anything Shackleton might say, unless it was supported by the "ample testimony" of others. Sir Clements now became relentlessly mistrustful too. "From the moment that Shackleton broke his word," as Marshall put it, forty years later, "he was 'suspect'."[27] To Shackleton's face, Sir Clements and Scott were civil. Sir Clements even asked Shackleton for "the pleasure of your company at dinner"[28] soon after he returned. By stealth, however, Sir Clements and Scott proceeded to spread rumours that Shackleton had faked his latitudes.

The rumours remained rumours. A popular hero with royal recognition, Shackleton was now more or less secure. But the rumours persisted, and caused him a great deal of bitterness and distress. It more or less sealed his contempt of Scott. On the rare occasions they met in public, he too was civil. They never met again in private.

If Amundsen was content that a "little patch remained", why was Scott discontented yet? Amundsen, though he passionately wanted to win, wished failure on no one. Scott, on the other hand, seemed to be consumed by a secret and morose jealousy. His wife had comforted him with the prediction that Shackleton would collapse one way or another. They had got their way, after a fashion. The Pole, after all, had been left, as Scott thought, to him; and Shackleton had shown the way. Towards Shackleton, however, Scott, unlike Amundsen, was incapable of gratitude. Scott seemed to resent those to whom he owed a debt. On *Discovery*, he had belittled the achievement of Sir James Clark Ross by suggesting that luck alone enabled Ross to get through the pack ice and discover the Ross Sea while he, Scott, had to fight ill fortune.[29] It was not a long step to accuse a living rival of deliberate falsification.

The truth, in any case, was not simple. Soon after returning from the Antarctic, Shackleton presented his southern journey records to the RGS for investigation. The RGS was not pleased. Although the society was quite willing to bask in Shackleton's reflected glory, it evinced the strongest desire to evade any kind of responsibility. Nonetheless, it was the national repository of geographical wisdom, and its imprimatur guaranteed the authenticity of any exploration. They could not refuse to check Shackleton's observations. A. E. Reeves, the Society's map curator and navigational authority, did the work. The theodolite taken by Shackleton "compares well", as Reeves put it, "with the instruments carried by other Polar explorers who have often had a small sextant, used with either the natural or artificial horizon".

> I have [he said] examined the original notebook containing the . . . observations which were taken by Dr. Marshall and checked by Mr. Shackleton and Mr. Adams.[30]

All three were trained in navigation. Shackleton and Adams, however, being seamen, were used to sextants. Marshall had learned to use the theodolite. Reeves went on to explain:

> I have . . . recomputed the latitudes, using more correct refraction tables. In no case does my result differ from that previously obtained by Mr. Shackleton by more than about one minute, and in the furthest south observation the agreement was within a few seconds [of] arc.[31]

That was the last observed latitude, on 3 January, of 87°22′. When Scott returned to the Antarctic, he would "no doubt", as Marshall ironically put it, be "investigating the genuineness of our claims",[32] chiefly by the charting of the landmarks.

Compared with modern surveys, their readings stand up well. Mount Hope, for example, Shackleton, or rather Marshall, put at 83°35′S; today it is given as 83°31′S. Mount Buckley, at the head of the plateau, lies at 85°4′S on Marshall's map; the modern position is 85°5′S.

Of 87°22′ there could be no reasonable doubt. The question was, what came after? Everything then turned on dead reckoning. That meant distance and course made good. The one depended on the sledgemeter; the other on accuracy of steering. Marshall assumed a course absolutely due south so that every step meant that much more latitude.

It is not exactly clear why Marshall took no sights after 3 January. According to the meteorological log, he could have done so, not perhaps at noon, but at other times for so-called ex meridian altitudes of the sun. All four men were, of course, by then very cold and miserable. "This wind is killing", as Marshall himself recorded on 4 January. "Last night was so cold & hungry for last 5 hours was unable to sleep."[33] There was no energy left over for setting up the theodolite and taking complicated sights. Nor was there perhaps the will. Marshall knew that Shackleton desperately wanted to get within a hundred miles of the Pole. So perhaps did Marshall himself. To break the magic frontier of double figures possessed a significance they had since had every opportunity to appreciate. Marshall, however, understood that survival depended on turning soon enough. It was safer to depend on the slight haziness of dead reckoning than the implacable certainty of an instrument, and risk the temptation to go the one extra fatal mile.

In the last resort, the Furthest South depended on the dash from the final camp. That assumed sixteen nautical miles in five hours, and another sixteen back to camp in the same time. Even for trained skiers in good conditions that, at 10,000 feet above sea level, would have been a respectable performance. Those men, however, were not skiers. They were on foot, sinking into the snow at every step. They were near the end of their tether. It is very likely that the distance south felt like sixteen miles. It is unlikely that they actually covered sixteen miles.

Nonetheless 88°23′ was not only what Shackleton claimed. It was what all the diaries said. It was what everyone wanted to believe. In the end, everything rested with Marshall. Significantly, perhaps, that day, alone, on the whole journey his diary records no run, but merely that "we hoisted Queens Flag in DR [Dead Reckoning] Lat. 88°23′S".[34]

They were unlikely to have covered more than ten miles out and ten miles back. At best that put them at 88°16′S; 104 miles from the Pole, just short of the magic line. Allowing for deviations from the ideal line of march since the last astronomical fix at 87°22′, it may have been a few miles further off. Almost certainly they had crossed the 88th parallel. 88°10′ was the likeliest Furthest South. But 88°23′ was what the records said. It all depended on Marshall's estimate. Did he suspect that, consciously or not, he had connived at a necessary deception?

The responsibility, in the end, as navigator, was Marshall's alone, and he could never be sure if he had told the truth or not. In figures, it was all so insignificant. It did not alter the nature of the deed. Marshall had not crossed the line separating self-deception from deliberate lying. But he was incorruptible and an enemy of cant. For the rest of his days, the uncertainty preyed on his mind. "The story of the British attempt to [*sic*] the South Pole," Marshall said in after years, "is not a pleasant one!"[35]

The British public, at any rate, were satisfied. 88°23′; ninety-seven miles from the Pole, was good enough for them. But did Shackleton himself nurse a tiny doubt? "I have so much to say and tell as I used to say in the old days", he wrote to Elspeth Beardmore as soon as he returned to England. His reunion with Emily had not been quite what he had expected: he had grown away from her, somehow. Elspeth Beardmore, he now felt even more strongly, was the one woman who understood him. Her position was not easy, however. "It is due more to Will than to anyone else that the Expedition was enabled to go at all", as Shackleton told her. "I want to name one of our big new mountains after you and mountains & glacier after Will."[36] In the end only the great glacier up to the polar plateau was named, simply, Beardmore.

Shackleton did however mark his overflowing capacity for affection unequivocally on the map of Antarctica. On the voyage out to join *Nimrod* in 1907, he fell passionately in love with a girl called Isobel Donaldson. It was more than just a shipboard romance, but when he returned home, he prudently broke it off and refused to see her any more. He did, however, name a mountain after her. To this day, Mount Donaldson, overlooking the Beardmore Glacier, remains a memento of the affair.

William Beardmore, at any rate, was not to be repaid by seeing his name – or was it his wife's? – on the map. His guarantee had to be released. "Will you tell him," Shackleton wrote to Elspeth, "that now the money will be all right."[37] In June 1909, this was touchingly optimistic. The return to civilisation meant debts which no one quite knew how he was going to clear. He himself had cheerfully inflated hopes of what he was about to earn. He was writing a book about the expedition. That, together with lecture tours, he expected to produce £50,000. From the *Daily Mail* for the story of the Furthest South he had actually received £2,000.

Shackleton also hoped to make a quick £20,000 or so from sales to collectors of special New Zealand stamps for the expedition, overprinted "King Edward VII Land".[38] Shackleton had persuaded the New Zealand authorities to constitute him postmaster so that he could open the first Antarctic post office, complete with special cancellation stamp. Dealers, however, were less than enthusiastic: the issue was arguably not genuine, since it too obviously had a philatelic aim, nor was it immediately clear that Shackleton was entitled to sell the unused sheets for his own benefit. The stamps joined *Potentia* and the Russian soldiers in the limbo of faded money-making schemes.

Such was the state of affairs when, early in August, and for the third time in his career, Shackleton went to Cowes. Now he was there as a celebrity, by invitation. He was the guest of Sir Donald Currie, Chairman of the Union Castle Line, his old employer. He joined a large, distinguished party on board the *Armadale Castle*, Sir Donald's latest ship, anchored in the Solent.

Emily was there as well. To her, there was something incongruous in the scene. Cowes Week, the culmination of the London season, was the epitome of opulence, and the late Edwardian sumptuousness was accentuated by the visit of the Tsar, albeit not so much for the regatta, as for the Fleet review. Shackleton, as usual responding to his surroundings, played up to the glitter of the rich and the great. Emily could see only the façade of success and, behind that, little more than debt.

On board the *Armadale Castle*, Shackleton met Sir Henry Lucy. Sir Henry was a journalist. Tubby, shock-headed, greying and voluble, he was a self-made man from Lancashire. Like many another, he instantly was mesmerised by Shackleton's personality.

Meanwhile, out of earshot, in another part of the deck, Emily quietly told Lucy's wife the baleful truth behind Shackleton's spirited appearance of success. To this, Emily herself bore ironic testimony. She happened to be wearing a brooch made of five diamonds in the shape of the Southern Cross, a gift from her husband to remind her, as he whimsically said, of the time that he was under the constellation of the Southern Cross, while she remained under the Great Bear. It would have cost about £150. Was her talk a calculated indiscretion? Lucy was no ordinary hack. He was "Toby M.P." of *Punch*: caricatured as the White Knight from *Alice through the Looking-Glass*, the first of the modern political journalists, the first to be on intimate terms with politicians, almost part of the apparatus of power itself. Perhaps that explained his recent knighthood, the first given to a working journalist.

Lady Lucy told her husband what Emily had said. Until then, Sir Henry, like almost everyone else, assumed that Shackleton had found fame and fortune too. Now it was borne on him not only that this was an illusion, but that "Shackleton," as he put it, "was not the man to go about whining at the cruel irony of fate."[39] Emily understood the power of the indirect approach, through womenfolk.

"It appeared to me," as Sir Henry put it, "that if the truth were made known to the public the reproach of leaving the gallant explorer in the lurch would not lie against the country."[40] He quickly planted in the *Daily Express* a piece making it known that behind the celebrity was a man still in a financial predicament. Shackleton, more worried than he cared to admit, seized the opportunity to reveal his deplorable finances. The bank loan, he explained, was his burden. To repay it, and release the guarantees of £20,000, he only had until the following July.

"Though England takes credit for his work, and annexes himself as an Englishman," the *Cork Examiner* waspishly commented,

> she has not contributed anything towards the expense of the expedition . . . It will be of interest, to see how the Government (which always pleads that the Treasury is financially embarrassed when anything is wanted for Ireland) rises to the occasion.[41]

The *Examiner* was not alone. A positive outcry erupted in the press. The *Kentish Mercury*, for example, recalled when Shackleton set out, that "The Government declined to help . . . and the Royal Geographical Society . . . was even less disposed to assist, if that were possible."[42] Unfavourable comparisons were freely drawn with government aid to Scott and *Discovery*. This was, perhaps, connected with sympathy for the underdog. Shackleton was, after all, very much a private adventurer, while Scott, as we would say, belonged to the establishment. "It is not nice to think," as the *Dundee Advertiser* put it, in a typical Edwardian comment, "that after efforts which have brought the country some credit," Shackleton might face

> a heavy loss. If [he] is left single-handed to liquidate the bill of the expedition it will be far from creditable to a country flushed with wealth the lavish expenditure of which on self-indulgent extravagance is in evidence on every hand.[43]

This sort of reaction left politicians in little doubt over Shackleton's place in the public's heart. On 11 August, within forty-eight hours of his revealing his predicament, a palpably arranged parliamentary question on help for Shackleton was tabled from the government benches for the Prime Minister, Herbert Asquith. A week later, in answer to another "inspired" question, by Robert Harcourt, member for Montrose, Asquith told the House that the government would make Shackleton a grant of £20,000. In between, Shackleton had seen Asquith at the latter's urgent request.

"Just think," Shackleton wrote exultantly to Emily, "your Boy getting £20,000 from the Country: What oh!!"[44] Characteristically, he named certain Antarctic mountains he had discovered after Asquith, Lucy and Harcourt, all three. "I appreciate the generosity of the government, representing the British nation," Shackleton more soberly told journalists, "and believe it will be popular."[45]

That was a shrewd hit. Politicians, too, had discovered the attractions of Shackleton's reflected glory. That Shackleton had stood against the government in the last general election caused no *arrière pensée* on Asquith's part. "The Government," said Asquith in a letter to Shackleton,

> are impressed . . . by . . . the efficient and economical manner in which your whole enterprise was conducted, as is shown by the fortunate return of the entire party, and of the comparatively small total outlay incurred.[46]

"A very nice letter, don't you think?" Shackleton said, showing it to a journalist for publication. It was a not so veiled allusion to the extravagance of the *Discovery*, and thus another dig at Scott. For Asquith, with another general election in the offing, it was good publicity, too.

The whole expedition, Shackleton said, cost about £45,000; half what was spent on *Discovery*. Shackleton never actually produced detailed accounts. He vaguely announced that the balance of

£25,000 was covered. Some debts were possibly written off. "I expect with the government grant and my lectures," he told Lord Iveagh in one of the more explicit statements of his affairs, "I will make up all the liabilities."[47] The main thing was that with the government grant Shackleton could clear off his guarantees. His guarantors were well-known. Beardmore was an Admiralty contractor. Lord Iveagh was a friend of the King. The Duke of Westminster, too, was close to the Court. Bailing Shackleton out made political sense in more ways than one. For in the background lurked Frank Shackleton.

The theft of the Irish crown jewels had not yet been solved. Frank Shackleton, however, was by now widely assumed to be the thief, and it was an open secret that the affair had been hushed up. "No one knows how [Frank] Shackleton gets his money," wrote Sir Arthur Vicars, after a long visit to London in that summer of 1909, "his own family don't know. He bought since the robbery an £850 Motor Car." Frank had moved from Park Lane and now, as Sir Arthur reported, "lives in a huge house, beautifully furnished, at 29 Palace Court".[48]

That was in quite fashionable Bayswater. It would not have escaped notice that Ernest and Emily Shackleton were staying with Frank at the same address: they had decided to leave Edinburgh, and were looking for a house in London. It would not do for Ernest Shackleton to be thrown on his brother's charity; he had to be kept out of Frank's clutches.

Early in November, seven and a half months after he had returned to civilisation, Ernest Shackleton found himself Sir Ernest, knighted in the Birthday Honours. In the previous July he had been made a CVO. The short interval between the decorations, taken together with the wait for the knighthood, hinted at strange events behind the scenes.

The Royal Victorian Order was in the sovereign's personal gift, and the CVO was clearly intended to treat Shackleton equally with Scott. The delay in the knighthood was due partly to the necessity of waiting for Shackleton, as it were, to be made respectable. That, the parliamentary grant accomplished. "It is safe to say," in the words of the *Daily Mirror*, amid a flood of unanimous approval, "that none of the honours will be more popular with the general public."[49]

With his knack of making friends in high places, and by sheer force of personality, Shackleton had overcome official indifference, and the institutional bastions of mediocrity. He could now drop "Lieutenant"; he used to say he only called himself Lieutenant to avoid confusion with David Shackleton, a Trade Union leader with whom he had little sympathy. His standing, socially, had been secured. His success, however, remained mysteriously flawed.

At the time of Shackleton's parliamentary grant, one newspaper had hinted: "It has been suggested more than once in certain quarters . . . that the money he has been making . . . was going into his own pocket. Now that the real facts of the case have been made known that insinuation is finally disposed of, and the general public regard . . . Shackleton with even greater admiration and respect than before."[50] The smear, Shackleton knew, could not entirely be wiped out. He imputed it to Scott. As it was, Scott was manifestly trying to interfere. He had even written to Sir Philip Brocklehurst asking for details of the quarrel between Shackleton and England. Sir Philip replied, politely, that it was none of Scott's business.

As far as William Beardmore was concerned Shackleton assumed that once the £1,000 debt was settled, all would be well again. Beardmore, however, Scottish, forthright, and a model of financial probity, would neither forgive nor forget. It hurt Shackleton to find that, even when he had made amends, the stain could not be removed.

Late in the summer of 1909, *Nimrod* returned to England. Shackleton fitted her out as a floating exhibition of expedition relics. From entrance fees, he made the substantial sum of £2,000. Every penny, as *The Times* approvingly reported, he gave away to charity. He had done the same with lectures in New Zealand and Australia. John King Davis, who had succeeded Evans as *Nimrod*'s captain, was not amused. "Shackleton," as he put it, "had not yet paid in full the salaries owing to members of the expedition."[51] Shackleton, however, was not selfish. He wanted to share the spoils. He never forgot his men. Always he used "we" and "us"; never "I". He lost no opportunity to say in public what he owed his companions. He invariably tried to have some of them with him at meetings, dinners and receptions.

To follow him around required stamina and perseverance. After a week or two the pleasures, for most, began to pall. Armytage, Adams and Brocklehurst soon withdrew. Marshall, faintly disgusted with all the ostentation, left for Dutch New Guinea on another expedition. Raymond Priestley belonged to the hard core of statutory companions maintained by Shackleton, as it were for the Season. Wild, Joyce and Day were the others. They were all, for different reasons, at a loose end. For several months, they lived, to quote Priestley,

> in one room with two beds in the Blackfriars Road. At night we dressed for dinner and plunged abruptly into an entirely different world . . .

> Shackleton . . . was cashing in on an astounding record of success . . . and there never was a more generous man . . . We could have had almost anything for which we dared to ask.[52]

The contradictions in Shackleton's nature were such that, while showing towards his men true generosity of feeling, he could actually fail to pay what he had promised. Adams and Sir Philip had to remind Shackleton of his obligations; and, as a result, Shackleton and Adams fell out for a time. It was not exactly that Shackleton was irresponsible. The grand gesture it was that appealed to him. Giving publicly to charity was a gesture of the grandest kind. It played up to the gentlemanly pretence that money really did not count.

In Shackleton's case, that happened to be the truth. Money meant, literally, nothing to him. Nor did a person quite exist for him unless actually in sight. From Mackellar, for example, Shackleton had borrowed £150, and forgotten to repay it. "I wrote to him to write off this debt as a contribution," in Mackellar's words, "& added £100 to make it £250, but he barely acknowledged it." Nonetheless, he went on, in a typical reaction, "It is a pity that my circumstances were not different for I would willingly have paid *everything* myself."[53] Shackleton had the gift – or curse – of driving people to extremes. With equal ease he could provoke implacable antagonism or compel blind loyalty in all circumstances, among all conditions of men, even against their better judgment.

At the end of March, when Shackleton had reached New Zealand from the Antarctic, he knew only too well that the book of the expedition would have to be written in a rush. Like everything else, it would be a race to profit while he could. In London, William Heinemann, an astute and successful publisher, was impatiently waiting for his manuscript. Nine simultaneous translations into foreign languages had been arranged. Since Nansen returned from the North, there had not been such interest in a book of polar exploration.

Shackleton could not sit down and produce a sustained narrative. He somehow lacked the calm. He could not bear to shut himself away and work. He wanted to be among people and enjoy his fame from the start. The pen was not his metier. As he once succinctly told Emily, "I can talk much better than I can write."[54] He gave a kind of proof on landing in New Zealand by making a record, the first polar explorer to do so. Down the years, his voice still distantly crackles, summarising his attainment in the South, "for the first time returning without the loss of a single human life".[55]

To meet his deadline, indeed to write his book at all, Shackleton needed an amanuensis. Edward Saunders, a reporter on the *Lyttelton Times*, at Christchurch, was recommended; by Sir Joseph Ward, the Prime Minister of New Zealand, no less. Shackleton asked Saunders to travel with him to England and work for £10 a week, all expenses, and return passage paid. Saunders jumped at the offer. So at intervals squeezed in between lectures, interviews, receptions, or simply bouts of uncontrollable restlessness, Shackleton told his tale to Saunders. On trains and mailships; in hotels and country houses; all the long way home, and for three frenetic months thereafter, Shackleton paced to and fro, dictating in staccato bursts. He found it hard to work for longer than an hour at a time, but that gave Saunders a chance to transcribe his notes.

Saunders was not quite an ordinary ghost writer, however. He was young. He had found his niche as a reporter in New Zealand, where the way to an editorial chair was clear. So it was not for the money alone that he had taken on this task; he was a Boswell looking for a Johnson. He had already interviewed Shackleton for the *Lyttelton Times*, and fallen under the spell of his personality. He now joined the band of Shackleton's devoted followers, so that what might have been soul destroying hack work turned into the great adventure of his life.

> If I said that any chapter was simply my transcription of notes taken down from Shackleton's dictation, I should be telling an untruth [Saunders explained in after years]. If I said that any chapter was entirely mine, I should be telling an untruth. My work was complementary to his. I could say that Shackleton had a remarkable gift of literary suggestion . . . and that when his interest was stirred at critical portions of his narrative, he had a command of vivid, forceful English . . . Shackleton and I understood each other thoroughly.[56]

As a result, *The Heart of the Antarctic*, as it was called, bore none of the tell-tale stiltedness of most ghosted work. The book appeared early in November, an unprecedentedly quick five months after putting pen to paper. *The Times* set the tone. *The Heart of the Antarctic* was "The book of the season". It was, said the *Manchester Guardian*, "The best book of Polar travel which has ever been written."[57] "The success of the book", as Shackleton put it, was "largely due" to Saunders. "I cannot speak too highly of him in every way."[58] Shackleton wanted Saunders' name on the title page, but Saunders refused. The book, as he afterwards said, "should stand without any attempt being made to explain just how [it was] produced".[59]

"These two splendid volumes," as *The Times Literary Supplement* said in its judicious way, "form the permanent record of an expedition which will always be remembered with pride wherever the British flag flies."[60] Shackleton did not actually produce the whole of both volumes. He allowed his companions to tell their own tales.

The *Observer* did remark that "None of the [Southern] party would seem to have been . . . experienced . . . ice men . . . with . . . a . . . feeling for treacherous snow and ice".[61] Shackleton seemed to bear that out when he wrote: "I do not think that I could suggest any improvement in equipment for any future expedition."[62] On the other hand, in Christiania he had admitted that "if we had had ski on the southern journey, and understood how to use them like Norwegians, we would presumably have reached the Pole."[63] Either way, the *Observer* had made a rare statement of an obvious conclusion.

In the chorus of praise, one note sadly jarred. "We may surely be left to cherish a hope," wrote Scott Keltie in the *Sphere*, "that the Union Jack will be carried across the hundred miles or so which have been left untrodden by Shackleton and planted at . . . the South Pole . . . This, we may be assured," Keltie continued smoothly, "will be accomplished by Captain Scott within the next year or two . . . It is right," he added, trimming his sails skilfully once more to the wind, "that Captain Scott should complete what he has so well begun."[64]

Away in Christiania Amundsen, secretly planning his journey south, was also pondering Shackleton's experience, and he had now decided to land at the Bay of Whales. Of this, Shackleton, naturally, was unaware. But Keltie's pointed comment reminded him, with a stab, that he seemed fated to struggle hard merely for someone else to reap the fruit. Shackleton had brought the South Pole into the popular consciousness. He had given Antarctic exploration prestige. It was his example that was now sending five thousand volunteers to Scott's expedition.

Publication of *The Heart of the Antarctic* was for Shackleton in any case a kind of anti-climax. It marked the end of the great wave of welcome. His companions, most of them, were trying to return to the daily lives from which they had been plucked. One at least, sadly, did not succeed. Back in Australia, Bertram Armytage failed to find a meaning in existence. Having put on full dress and decorations, he shot himself in a Melbourne club.

Shackleton was now left to soldier on alone. On 1 November, he started on his main lecture tour. With the large, black and white fragile glass lantern slides of the age, carefully packed in solid wooden boxes, he followed the well trodden trail from one auditorium to another. First of polar explorers, he also had a film to show. The cinema, like wireless and the gramophone, had been invented. All this, however, was still in its infancy. Lecturing in person remained the only means of profiting from the spoken word. While Amundsen and Scott had the exhilaration of preparing their next expeditions, Shackleton faced the grind of paying off the debts of the last one.

In six months he was to lecture at least 123 times and to travel twenty thousand miles in two continents every inch by boat or train. "Never before," as his agent, Gerald Christy, proudly put it, "has such a long list of lectures been set down . . . for one single tour."[65] It was enough to break a lesser man. Yet Shackleton somehow managed to make his well-worn text sound fresh each time. It was genuinely infused with zest. His lectures were not money-making drudgery alone. They were also to prolong the moment of fame. Scott, as Shackleton believed, or hoped, would probably fail. Then, it would be his chance again.

Meanwhile, he sought to squeeze every ounce of applause and recognition out of his Furthest South while there was yet time.

XXVIII

Hungarian mines

Early in 1910 Shackleton crossed the Channel on the continental leg of his lecture tour. Being pitchforked into the charged atmosphere of the Central European capitals, was almost like living through his first welcome all over again.

"We have had *6* nights in bed and 5 on the train since we started," wrote Emily's sister, Daisy Dorman, from Vienna on 9 January, "the anniversary," in her words, "of Ernest's 'Furthest South.'!"[1] Daisy had joined Shackleton and Emily for their tour.

Shackleton by now was every inch the famous explorer, a blend of bluff sailor, genial buccaneer, fetching raconteur, and modest but scintillating man of action. Partly it was another form of his bewilderingly shifting self, partly a pose for a purpose. Ever the eye was watching for effect.

Shackleton had the Irishman's "terrible gift of intimacy". He could buttonhole an audience as if it were one man in a corner. Whether he was faced with watch-chained Lancashire worthies in dingy meeting halls, or charming Viennese cynics under gleaming chandeliers, the effect was approximately the same. Shackleton was at home with all men, without distinction of morality, language, class or country. Journals as far removed as *Aftenposten* of Christiania, and *Pester Lloyd* of Budapest responded to his personality:

> Shackleton . . . captivated by his modesty, as he stood there forthright and unaffected, and spoke with undisturbed calm about dangerous, daring deeds. He constantly amused his audience with a little joke, a dry remark, which he let drop, without a single, self-satisfied smile to disturb the calm on his sharp drawn features.[2]

Shackleton . . . speaks with a clear, calm, voice . . . he ornaments the description of his journey with a humorous depiction of the life of the expedition members.[3]

Shackleton, however, was not quite an ordinary explorer simply telling his tale. When King Edward VII knighted him, it was not only, perhaps, with the South Pole in mind. An explorer could be an ambassador as well as anybody else.

Shackleton was making a foray into a lost world. It was a place where the Habsburgs were coming to the end of their tolerant, muddled rule over the now vanished empire of Austria-Hungary. It was also the disturbing world of Germany under the Hohenzollerns. "I do think the Germans are funny", Daisy wrote to her sister-in-law, "they seem to eat all day . . . speeches between every course & nothing but drinking healths etc!" They were, she went on, echoing many a contemporary English traveller,

all most kind and hospital [*sic*] & they all pretend that the idea of war with England has never occurred to them!! . . . I must say they all talk awfully nicely of the English as if they like them immensely, perhaps they are all arrant humbugs!! I can't tell at all what they are aiming at.[4]

In fact, the Germans were openly announcing that they proposed to fight England for her "place in the sun". This was the last age when sovereigns had a hand in policy. Edward VII was desperately trying to avert war.

All the world, as the King well knew, loves a title. Plain Mr Ernest Shackleton might be dismissed as an itinerant adventurer; Sir Ernest to the Germans ought to be *hoffähig*: fit for the Court. So he was. The Kaiser himself wanted to meet Sir Ernest; possibly because his name, too, was on the Antarctic map; Kaiser Wilhelm II Land, discovered by the German expedition under Drygalski in 1901. Prompted perhaps by King Edward, the Kaiser commanded a private lecture. It was held, not at the imperial palace in Potsdam but in the more intimate surroundings of the house of Herr Dernburg, the Colonial Minister, on the outskirts of Berlin. There, into what one foreign correspondent called "a brilliant assembly, including the British Ambassador and all the members of the Embassy",[5] marched the Kaiser, fiercely moustachio'd, eye a-gleam, withered arm hidden in an Admiral's uniform, every inch his caricature.

In the Kaiser, the imperial family and others, Shackleton "created great enthusiasm", to quote Campbell Mackellar, with his titled German relations and Court connections. German antagonism to England was rooted in the belief that the Englishman was now decadent, and therefore no longer deserved his power. When Shackleton appeared, notably before Prince Henry of Prussia and German naval officers,

> they saw in his breezy personality [as Mackellar put it] more of their ideal of what they had imagined the conquering Briton to be more than in anyone else, and no longer believed the species was extinct.[6]

Did Shackleton have a tiny effect on policy? It was at any rate an age where the effect of personality on human affairs was openly admitted. With an introduction from Prince Henry of Prussia, Shackleton, when he visited St Petersburg, was given an audience with the Tsar Nicholas II. Perhaps, like the Kaiser, that unhappy monarch saw in Shackleton a sign that the British, after all, were not quite universally effete. Shackleton, was certainly at ease with the autocrat of all the Russias as he was with everyone else. He was told that his audience would last fifteen minutes, and no more. Instead, so the story goes, he stayed two hours, walking up and down the audience chamber at the Winter palace, side by side with the Tsar, talking all the time.

But it was in Hungary that Shackleton found himself feeling most at home. Perhaps there is an affinity between the Irish and the Hungarians. Both are flamboyant, irrepressible, with an unmistakable flair; both, more than most, are the prisoners of geography. Living in the shadow of stronger and, in the case of the Hungarians, culturally alien neighbours, they have had a frightful, bloody and vengeful history. Both have a fierce sense of national identity. Both, in their day, provided illustrious figures for their imperial partners; and both have some fatal flaw that has hindered full national achievement. Whatever their troubles, the Hungarians and Irish have been free of a chip on the shoulder. In both, charm is part of their apparatus of survival; and both are thoroughly ambiguous.

On 11 January, at any rate, when Shackleton's lecturing took him to Budapest, he was suddenly among people as charming and plausible as himself. Budapest, in the last days of the Habsburg monarchy, the air tinkling with café conversation, gilded domes glittering by the Danube, downstream from Vienna, was still a place to conjure up illusions overnight.

In his lecture, Shackleton had talked of Antarctic mineral wealth. Among the reception committee was the President of the Hungarian Geographical Society, Professor Ludwig Löczy, who talked of gold nearer home. At a place called Nagybanya, in north-eastern Hungary (now Romania), there was a reef where, Shackleton was confidentially informed, lay mines waiting to make a fortune for percipient investors. Depressed by German financial domination, Hungarians were ever on the lookout for investment from elsewhere. Of course, they also wished this illustrious and entertaining stranger well.

Shackleton, by now, was on the way to clearing off his debts. From his lectures, his book; with the help of friends and the income of his wife; he could look forward to a future reasonably secure. The prospect of gold, however, fired the treasure hunter in him. In the reef of Nagybanya he now saw his El Dorado. Aflame once more with the idea of a fortune just over the hill, he returned at the end of January to London.

There, he found Douglas Mawson, now also gripped by the polar mania. Mawson had come all the way from Australia with ideas for another Antarctic expedition. Shackleton had kept on his expedition offices at 9, Regent Street, and gave Mawson the run of the place. "Shackleton," in Mawson's words, "came in early to the office one morning and said to me 'I have decided to go to the coast west of Cape Adare'."[7] Mawson was "rather taken aback", especially when Shackleton told him "you are to be chief scientist". Exploring west of Cape Adare was what Mawson proposed. It was his plan that Shackleton had calmly annexed.

Mawson had also been talking to Scott about joining his expedition. Shackleton, however, as Mawson tersely put it, "was anxious that I should not go with Scott".[8] "I can get the money," said Shackleton, "and that," he persuasively argued, "will be your trouble were you taking it yourself." Mawson, in his own words, "decided to fall in with him". With Scott, in any case, Mawson felt increasingly ill-at-ease while, as he baldly said after being introduced, "I did not like Dr Wilson".[9] He did not elaborate.

Once more, Shackleton felt an almost manic hunger for achievement before it was too late. Ashore, in over-civilised surroundings, there was no time. "I . . . will cast round for something more . . . in the way of exploration",[10] he now wrote. It was Mawson who providentially arrived with a plan to give form to his nebulous intention.

Shackleton plunged instantly into preparations. *Nimrod* was being sold, and money he had none, but he immediately started looking for another ship. He turned once more to Adrien de Gerlache. By the middle of February, de Gerlache had found three Norwegian vessels, including the well-remembered *Bjørn*. Whereupon Shackleton telegraphed him "Fix nothing this year";[11]

writing then to Scott: "I am preparing [an] expedition to . . . Antarctica commencing in 1911".[12] Mawson, Shackleton gleefully announced, would be coming with *him*.

> I do not intend to make any efforts towards reaching the South Geographical Pole . . . The *Expedition* is purely *Scientific*.

That was true, to a certain extent. Should Scott happen to fail, however, Shackleton would be conveniently placed for another attempt on the Pole. Meanwhile, there remained the question of finance.

When Shackleton said he could get the money for a new expedition he meant, among other things, from his Hungarian gold mines. He proposed, somehow, to buy them, and he now wanted Mawson to come in with him.

In Antarctica, Mawson had been prevented by circumstances from prospecting, but that had not quenched his own treasure-hunting streak. Digging for gold, after all, was part of Australian folklore. Now, when Shackleton asked him to report on the mines at Nagybanya, he instantly agreed. It would make an entertaining interlude before returning to Australia. As assistants, Shackleton sent Mackintosh and John King Davis, both still at a loose end, and both, like Mawson, provisionally booked for the putative expedition. So, "feeling capable of anything",[13] as Davis put it, off they went from Ostend on the Orient Express to Nagybanya, which they found to be a small, more or less industrial town set among the low, fir-clad foothills of the Carpathians, and there they set to work.

Shackleton, meanwhile, on 19 March, sailed on the *Lusitania* for a lecture tour of the United States and Canada. "Do not see Scott about the new Expedition",[14] he hurriedly wrote to Mawson just before departure.

Emily was with her husband. "Has Lady Shackleton accompanied her pet lion", a gossip writer wickedly asked, "to keep off the kisses which ladies of the land of Equality are so free?"[15] To an American journalist, at any rate, Emily appeared "unlike many of the wives of great men", but had "a distinctly original personality, separate and apart from her distinguished husband".[16] Emily was "statuesque . . . She impresses one as a woman of unusual force and intelligence".[17] Nonetheless, as she told *Woman at Home* before sailing, she desired "nothing so much as to be considered merely the wife of Shackleton".[18] But in America, freed from constraint, Emily allowed herself rare moments of public self-revelation. "I am so different from my husband, who sees the broad lines of everything", she told the *New York Times*:

I am afraid I only see the small things – you will agree when I tell you that what [has] impressed me most in America is . . . the abundance of . . . iced water.

Emily was actually impressed with America because "here if a girl of the middle classes wishes to study or to . . . work . . . she does not lose caste . . . But in England we still have the old notion that a girl should not work . . . and consequently you find houses full of girls who are dependent on their families for support . . . and who make life miserable for themselves and the persons around them because they have no suitable occupation". That came from the heart. Perhaps she, too, yearned for a career of her own. "I think fairy tales are to be blamed for half the misery in the world", Emily tellingly continued,

I never let my children read them . . . I think the moral is reprehensible, "And they were married and lived happily ever afterward".

Is it a wonder that when a girl has such things dinned into her . . . from the time she can . . . understand anything that she grows to think marriage the only thing in the world for her? And how wrong that is![19]

In the ambience of the New World, Shackleton, too, was more expansive even than usual. His lectures, understood at home to be devoted to clearing off his debts were, he now explained, to raise funds for his new expedition.[20]

"I hope not", was Emily's melancholy comment. However, she added,

We live through everything when we have to . . . That's all I can say about it. And now my small son is beginning to say he is going to be an explorer. Oh, dear. Well, he is just 5 . . . so I dare say it is early to worry about it.[21]

In the gold reef at Nagybanya, Mawson, meanwhile, had finished his survey. It was time to return to Australia. Shackleton, however, had as usual failed to keep in touch. Mawson changed his plans and travelled via America to meet Shackleton on the way.

Shackleton had started off on his American tour with every hope of repeating his now customary triumph of the Furthest South. He met President Taft at the White House; he was lionised by the Anglophile "upper crust" of New York and the Eastern States. To Arçtowski, of the *Belgica* expedition, now living in America, Shackleton had "changed for the better . . . I didn't like him very much before, but it pleased me . . . to see that his great success had not turned his head . . . the simplicity of his manner was charming".[22] Shackleton, indeed, showed sides of himself that went down well in the new surroundings. "AMERICAN AFTER DINNER STORY TELLERS," as one headline put it, "HAVE NOTHING ON SHACKLETON."[23] He was "that most rare of men, an English wit";[24] he "made good" with an "air of genuine democracy".[25] Having passed the 150th repetition of his lecture, he could still more or less truthfully say "I enjoy it, for I don't mind talking about something I know about".[26] In New York, at one of the endless lunches in his honour, he declared that "The Anglo-Saxon world will eventually own the two ends of the earth". That was a graceful reference to Peary, who was present. "We are", as he put it, "the twin nations and should own them."[27] The idea of Britain and America ensuring Anglo-Saxon world power was just coming into vogue.

The lecture audiences rapidly tailed off, however. Partly this was due to bad management; more, perhaps, to circumstances. Polar exploration did not hold a very high place in America. Doubts over Peary's claim to have reached the North Pole, and his quarrel with Cook, now denounced as a fraud, made matters even worse. The trouble was that Shackleton seemed larger than life at home, but here he was cut down to size. Shackleton was not the first European celebrity to be dwarfed by the sheer scale of the United States.

On 13 May, Mawson caught up with Shackleton at Omaha, Nebraska. It was about their expedition that Mawson had mainly come to talk. Shackleton, however, was more interested in Mawson's news that the gold mines at Nagybanya were genuine, promising a reasonable yield. Since the lecture tour had manifestly flopped, Shackleton, in Mawson's words, now had other "get-rich-quick schemes in view". To those, Nagybanya came as an opportune addition. Late that night, in an Omaha hotel room, filled with the smoke of Shackleton's interminable cigarettes, Mawson drew up an agreement between them. It took the form of an undertaking by Shackleton to float a company to work the Hungarian gold mines and also, incidentally, to pay Mawson the salary still owing to him from the *Nimrod* expedition. The final clause ran,

> I intend to proceed with . . . an Antarctic expedition to commence in the latter half of 1911, and shall appoint D. Mawson as director of the scientific [side] . . . In the event of my not accompanying the expedition as commander D. Mawson will be in charge and I shall still use my influence with my supporters in regard to raising the necessary funds.[28]

Next day, Mawson left Shackleton at Omaha to continue his journey to Australia. "I felt," Mawson said, "that the chances of his going to Antarctica had lessened."[29]

In London just at this time, the name of Sir Ernest Shackleton, CVO, the celebrated explorer, was appearing among the directors of the North Mexico Land and Timber Company. This was Frank Shackleton's latest promotion. His brother's reflected glory lent lustre to the prospectus. For three years now, Frank had been tenaciously pursuing his quest for fortune in the City. He was a generous soul. He not merely wanted to use his brother's name; he wished him to share in the proceeds as well.

The company was registered on 5 May 1910. The next day, King Edward VII died. Ernest Shackleton was in Chicago when he heard the news. Thinking of what the King had done for him, it was, he told the *New York Times*, "a great blow to Antarctic exploration".[30] He was considerably depressed. It was a blow to a great deal else as well. On 10 May, the North Mexico's brokers cancelled their agreement to underwrite the shares "owing to a variety of circumstances", as Frank Alder, one partner, enigmatically put it, "of which the death of King Edward was by no means the least".[31]

With Edward VII passed away the figure holding back the floodgates. His successor, George V, was altogether more pallid, insular, and hardly in control of events. The change of reign increased the mood of apprehension in the country. Confidence wilted, and when Shackleton returned to England in the middle of June, it was to find the North Mexico Land and Timber Company stillborn. The company, formed to work forests in Mexico was, in Alder's opinion, "a sound, honest concern".[32] He ought to have known; he was not only one of the company's brokers, but a director too. Frank Shackleton, said Alder, "had worked very hard", and the company "certainly looked like being successful".

This was, in fact, Frank's one genuine promotion. For him it was either make or break. In the event, within three months, he had been made a bankrupt, and the subsequent litigation brought deplorable exposures. One judge even dragged in the theft of the Irish crown jewels. "No one was ever prosecuted," his Lordship heavily remarked, "but Mr. Shackleton . . . shortly after set up in Park Lane."[33] Very likely, it was the hand of King Edward that had been shielding Frank for so long. Now his drift down to disaster had begun.

For Ernest Shackleton, a little more than yet another dream of instant fortune had crumbled in the dust. He had believed his brother might yet be his "minister of finance"; instead, he was left to carry on alone.

Shackleton was now without a home. Frank's flat in Bayswater had only been a temporary expedient. In any case, it had disappeared into the maws of the Receiver. Now, in the summer of 1910, probably because the Dorman family used to go there, Shackleton took a furnished house at Sheringham, in Norfolk.

Emily at first thought it was a well-earned seaside holiday. Summer, however, turned to autumn; autumn to winter, and still there was no sign of a move. To Emily's distress, Sheringham had become a port of call while her husband waited for something to turn up. Not that Ernest Shackleton was actually passive, but his life was dissolving into uncertainty and lack of aim. He was an opportunist in search of opportunity; a leader looking for a cause.

Scott's expedition, meanwhile, was now afoot. At the beginning of June his ship, *Terra Nova*, sailed. On 16 July Scott himself followed by mailboat from Southampton. Shackleton went down to see him off on the boat train at Waterloo station.

It was not exactly due to a change of heart. Shackleton, as he strode on to the platform, felt a wry twinge of jealousy. Scott was on his way, and with a government grant of £20,000 into the bargain; *he* would not have to wait for official help until he came back. Scott, however, had swallowed his feelings to meet Shackleton on his return, so Shackleton could hardly fail to return the gesture now.

The small group on the platform was very much Scott's coterie. Scott Keltie, smooth and bearded, was there. So too was Sir Edgar Speyer, the German-born banker, dark, moustachio'd, top-hatted and opulent, who was treasurer of Scott's organising committee. Scott's wife, Kathleen, travelling out with him, showed, in her domineering and possessive way, that Shackleton's presence was undesired.

Decorum was otherwise preserved. Shackleton, conventionally bowler-hatted, went up to Scott, like most naval officers in mufti, bare-headed. Both were noticeably stouter than they used to be. There, under the cavernous, soot-stained glass roof, while the waiting locomotive hissed and set up expectant wraiths of steam and smoke, the two rivals faced each other guardedly in farewell. As the train pulled out, "Sir Ernest Shackleton," in the words of *The Times* reporter,

> called for "three cheers for Captain Scott." These were given with enthusiasm, together with cheers for Mrs. Scott.[34]

"See you at the South Pole",[35] Scott called out of the carriage window; not, however, to Shackleton, but to a substantial figure over six feet tall. This was Herr Oberleutnant Wilhelm Filchner – as a child called "Vee Villie Vinkie", he used to reveal with glee – and he was the leader of a new German Antarctic expedition.

Filchner was an officer on the German General Staff in Berlin. A Bavarian, he had "one fault of character", as he whimsically put it. He could not "suppress laughter, especially in serious matters".[36] Restless, energetic, wayward, and hardly to be pigeon-holed, he was in some ways what Shackleton, in other circumstances, might have been. In 1900, at the age of twenty-three, he had become famous for a ride over the Pamirs in the border regions where Russia, China and Afghanistan met. Three years later, he led an expedition to Tibet. Now he was proposing to cross Antarctica.

It was like the beating of a distant drum. Shackleton had already met Filchner in Berlin and talked of crossing the Antarctic continent some day himself. Filchner had come over to consult Shackleton, as he had consulted every polar authority he could find, and he had also come to placate Scott. He proposed starting in the Weddell Sea, and crossing to the Ross Sea, where Scott would be based, and which, as he well knew, Scott considered peculiarly his own. Filchner suggested cooperation. They might, for example, meet somewhere along the way. In that case, they agreed, as Filchner put it, that "some of Scott's people would go with me towards the Ross Sea, and some of my people with Scott towards the Weddell Sea".[37] Hence Scott's seemingly flippant farewell from the train. Shackleton came away from Waterloo, and went down to Emily at Sheringham with the terrifying, forlorn sense of being trapped and left behind.

It was from this period that a story became attached to Shackleton. According to one of Emily's nephews who spent the summer at Sheringham,

> he said he must go to London on business and might be away a day or two. That same afternoon, an unkempt, odd-looking, shabbily dressed man appeared at the door of the Shackletons' house, asking for Lady Shackleton. He asked the maid to inform Lady Shackleton that he was Sir Ernest's uncle from Ireland. My aunt greeted him politely, but was rather taken aback by the old man's appearance, though nothing really surprised her about her husband's contacts and associates.
>
> She made polite small talk, until finally she recognized the twinkle in the old man's eye, and knew who it was. My uncle Ernest was a great practical joker.[38]

Like Filchner, now on his way to the Antarctic, he was unable to "suppress laughter, especially in serious matters".

XXIX

"A bit of a floating gent"

On 4 October, Shackleton was asked by the press to comment on the news from Amundsen. His feeling of unrest was intensified.

Amundsen had revealed finally that he was really heading south. Like everyone else, Shackleton was taken completely by surprise. "Amundsen", he had lamely told the *St James Gazette*, "was going to take the Arctic drift . . . that is, of course, round Cape Horn and up the Pacific coast of America to the Bering Strait." Even with hindsight, the encounter in Christiania offered him no clues.

The announcement of Amundsen's sensational switch had been brought back to Norway by his brother Leon from Madeira, *Fram*'s last port of call. By the time the news was released, Amundsen himself was, designedly, well on his way; in the trade winds and out of reach.

Meanwhile in Australia Mawson was "very much in the dark", as he put it. Shackleton "did not write and failed to answer . . . my enquiries regarding money matters".[1] Early in December, "in desperation", as he said, Mawson finally cabled Shackleton asking if he really was going to lead the expedition. Mawson was not the only one among Shackleton's men expecting him to take them south again. Raymond Priestley, now out in Sydney working on the *Nimrod* geological results, was waiting patiently too. At the end of November, he was asked to go with Scott. He cabled Shackleton for permission, and received the laconic answer "certainly".

> Thank you for your generous permission [Priestley then wrote]. I am afraid you will think that I have been showing want of faith in the inception of your 1911 expedition. That is not so, however.[2]

But it was. Scott's offer was the only opportunity Priestley could now see of going south again. The price, as Priestley put it, was "giving up my connection with Shackleton".[3] Under any circumstances, Shackleton regarded contact with Scott as desertion, and Priestley himself was plagued by a sense of guilt.

Shackleton in any case soon cabled Mawson to say that he would not, after all, be going south with him. Exploring a segment of icebound coast seemed inexpressibly hollow while Amundsen and Scott, not to mention Filchner, were racing, between them, for the South Pole and the first crossing of Antarctica. Those were the last great terrestrial journeys left. To Shackleton, they alone seemed worthwhile. He wanted to wait and see if anything remained for him. Besides, his finances were still in spectacular disarray. Talk of going south had been a surrogate for action; a way of maintaining his public image.

The expeditions under way produced a revival of Antarctic interest, and Shackleton exploited the opportunity with an extra lecture tour. This took him to Germany, Austria, Poland and Switzerland. Emily was understandably depressed at being left behind at Sheringham, while Shackleton, for his part, found lecturing no longer fun. Nonetheless, he wrote to Emily from Freiburg in November, "I ought to continue . . . as much as possible as it will be dead [in] 1912". That was when news from the Antarctic was due, and Shackleton could expect to be eclipsed. Meanwhile, "even at the rate of £30 a night", as he told Emily, "it means more money than one could earn in any ordinary way".[4]

This did not stop Shackleton lecturing free, with Filchner, for charity, in Berlin during January. Campbell Mackellar and Sir Philip Brocklehurst came over for the occasion. Mackellar tried to interest the Countess von Gröben, the rich young patroness of the lecture, in Filchner and his expedition:

> She sent Filchner a pair of gloves! But she was greatly interested in Shackleton, wrote to him, [and] had a book-plate engraved . . . for him.[5]

Germany, however, had changed since Shackleton's first visit. The mood had become bitterly anti-British. Filchner, dining after the lecture with Mackellar and some German officers, argued, in Mackellar's words,

> whether war would not be *now* & prevent him leaving: the others said no, not till Spring [1912] as the Coronation [of George V] was to be allowed to take place![6]

Filchner virtuously wrote to Hugh Robert Mill:

> Science being . . . international property, has nothing to do with politics; But even here the relation between England and Germany will always get better. In this way we are assisted a good deal by great men like Sir Ernest Shackleton who shows much understanding for Germany.[7]

On his first tour, Shackleton had delivered his lecture once or twice in German. To Herbert Dorman, Mackellar said he had not known that Shackleton understood German well enough to lecture in it.

"'Neither did I,' [Dorman replied], 'but if they ask him to lecture in Chinese, he'll do it.'

"I happened to repeat this to Shackleton.

"'But I do know some Chinese,' he said, 'I could lecture in it!'"[8]

Shackleton had simply read the words phonetically. He did, however, have an affinity for things German and now, on his second tour, he decided to learn the language properly. He took along a German-speaking Pole from Posen (Poznan) called Franks. Franks had been Shackleton's barber in Edinburgh, and combined the duties of German teacher with those of valet and secretary.

"My German," Shackleton wrote breathlessly to Emily after a fortnight or so,

> is all right now and I also speak it generally so that now I can consider that I know the language a bit, and it will be useful for Hungary: I will not let them think that I know the language at all so I can hear their conversations.[9]

Hungarian gold was still Shackleton's El Dorado. After Mawson's encouraging report from Nagybanya, he had thrown himself ardently into the project. It was not simply the prospect of money, it was the enticement of the financial world. "I am really thinking of going in for the Bar as soon as things are fixed up", he told Emily. "I am never going South again . . . my place is at home now I can see it quite clearly."[10]

On returning from America, in June 1910, Shackleton had started floating a company to develop the mines at Nagybanya. He tried his luck, once more, with Lord Iveagh. If Lord Iveagh, Shackleton disarmingly wrote, would not "go so far" as actually to buy shares in the company, "a favourable letter to me saying he would like to be interested in it . . . would be . . . sufficient":

You quite clearly understand [added Shackleton], that it is my own venture, and that I get no commission whatever, but I will get shares in the Company when it is formed for all the work that has been done.[11]

"This is an insult to my intelligence", Alfred Harmsworth, by then Lord Northcliffe, under similar circumstances, brusquely was to say.

If I wanted to go into this affair I should go to an expert . . . not an amateur. Someone is using you, Shackleton. I advise you to stick to things you understand.[12]

Lord Iveagh merely said he never invested in mining. Both he and Lord Northcliffe were Anglo-Irish too, and no doubt understood Shackleton all too well.

Shackleton drove on, undeterred. What he called the "Syndicate" was floated. Herbert Dorman, anxious for Emily's sake about his brother-in-law's affairs, agreed to act as solicitor. The managing director was a City financier called John William Taylor, indirectly involved in Frank Shackleton's affairs. A respectable City firm of engineers was asked to send someone out to continue Mawson's work and investigate the mines at Nagybanya. John King Davis was still at a loose end, so Shackleton again sent him along to help.

The most attractive mine, called Lipot, belonged to a local peasant proprietor, Mr Pokol. He lived some way out of town in a large, brightly painted mansion, the interior of which might have come straight out of a comic opera. Mawson found that some of the ore from Mr Pokol's mine was yielding four ounces to the ton, so Mr Pokol was sitting pretty, and he knew it. He might, so he hinted, be prepared to sell; but at what price? As Davis put it,

Mr Pokol had given a different answer on each occasion we had seen him. We would be ushered into one of [his] large reception rooms, jammed full with rococo furniture, and a servant would wheel in an American cocktail cabinet that was its owner's special pride. We would be offered numerous drinks and, as a special compliment, enormous cigars from a box having on its lid a portrait of King Edward . . . But at each successive interview, conducted in a mixture of broken English, German and Hungarian, he raised the price. Our negotiations, therefore, were somewhat protracted. Mr Pokol was a downy bird. He managed always to send us away . . . with the vague feeling that on the next occasion he would come to terms.[13]

Towards the end of Shackleton's lecture tour, Davis met him at Karlsruhe to report. "I found him living in the most luxuriously appointed suite of rooms in the best hotel", said Davis.

> Fresh from my modest lodgings at Nagybanya, I expressed astonishment at the unnecessary size and magnificence of the arrangements. "Why take all these rooms when there's noone to occupy them?" Shackleton replied, "You don't understand. We're showing the flag! I'm making pots of money – full houses all over Germany! . . . it would never do to put up here in any other style".[14]

Meanwhile, Shackleton was scraping up a few Swiss francs or Reichsmarks where he could for Emily to pay off small creditors. "If Hungary comes off all right," he reassured her, "well all our worries are quickly at an end."[15]

Mawson, in the meantime, had decided to lead the Antarctic expedition he and Shackleton had planned. At the end of February, he was back in London raising funds. On his previous visit, he had helped persuade a certain Gerald Lysaght to give £10,000.

Shackleton had known Lysaght since his days with the Union Castle Line. They had first met in 1899, when Lysaght was a passenger on the *Tantallon Castle* and Shackleton the Fourth Officer. "I was attracted by [Shackleton's] personality, which showed an unusual character – power and determination",[16] Lysaght afterwards explained. A wealthy steelmaker from Scunthorpe, he had helped to finance the *Nimrod* expedition.

Mawson understood Lysaght's support for the new expedition to stand, whoever was in command. "Lysaght definite",[17] had been Shackleton's reply when he cabled from Adelaide to confirm.

"I now learned", as Mawson put it after landing in England, "that Lysaght's £10,000 was *not* available. [He] had given [Shackleton] the money and it was invested in other ways."[18] Exactly how was lost in the confusion of Shackleton's affairs. Emily, at least, saw through the breezy talk of contacts, meetings, rushing round to appointments, and imminent decisions. One of her husband's eclectic associates told her he had "such a wonderful way of getting things going – but that," as she put it, "is not exactly being businesslike – I never heard anyone else say he was good at business."[19]

In the middle of February, meanwhile, Lord Ronald Sutherland-Gower was sued by his stockbrokers, Rowe and Pitman, for £10,000 owing on some shares. Frank Shackleton, albeit off stage, played the leading role. Having become Lord Ronald's financial adviser, he had palmed him off with worthless shares. Lord Ronald, as a result, was ruined. Revelations in court included interception of Lord Ronald's mail by Frank when he was staying with Lord Ronald at his home at Penshurst in Kent. "If 'foozle' meant getting all of some one else's property for oneself," said the Judge, referring to Lord Ronald's nickname for Shackleton, "Mr Shackleton deserved the title."[20] The case ended with a feeling in the air that Frank Shackleton, some time, would find himself in the dock.

"My brother," Ernest Shackleton charitably said, "has been more of a fool than anything else, it has struck my business as you can imagine."[21] The upshot was that, at the end of 1910, Shackleton had to borrow £2,000 from Sir Philip Brocklehurst. Sir Philip was the only member of the *Nimrod* expedition with whom he had kept regular contact; he was also the wealthiest. As security for the loan, Shackleton sent shares in his Hungarian company, explaining disingenuously, "Of course as yet they are not of value but when the company goes they will be valuable. This will be a great help for me old man I know you will keep it quiet", he went on, hopefully repeating what had become his *cri de coeur*, "it will enable me to pull through and square up this coming year."[22]

When Mawson arrived in England, Shackleton was back in Budapest, grappling with Mr Pokol and his gold mine. "Just now I am passing through a critical time," he wrote to Emily,

> I am homesick now and tired and want you much . . . somehow my expressions will not come out and I cannot put them on paper.[23]

"It was not a good sign," as Emily by now was beginning to understand, "when my beloved wanted me so much!" It meant, as she put it, "that he was feeling ill – or extra worried".[24]

Perhaps Shackleton was affected by the mood of Budapest. "I cannot understand," he wrote, "how it is that I am more lonely here than in any other town." The Irishman in him understood all too well the elusiveness behind the compulsive charm. The men with the power or the money were always somewhere else; or ready only next day, next week, next month, any other time but not now. Not even a useful friendship with Sandor Hegedüs, brother of the Hungarian Minister of Finance, could help. Shackleton wrote to Emily,

> I almost wish I had not gone South but stayed at home and lived a quiet life. Still that would not have been so good after all: I just long to wake up in the morning without any worry or anxiety: But that restful time [he ended, optimistically as usual], will soon come I hope.[25]

Shackleton left Budapest with the mine at Nagybanya still not settled.

His return to London brought something more unsettling yet. Late on the night of 27 March 1911 he was telephoned by the *Daily Mail* to be told that *Terra Nova* had just put in at Stewart Island, off New Zealand, with news of Scott.

The memories came flooding back. It was two years almost to the day that *Nimrod* reached the self-same place, and Shackleton had sent the cable telling of his Furthest South. *Terra Nova* now brought news that Scott and his followers were settling down at McMurdo Sound, under Erebus, and the other only too vividly remembered landmarks. Worse still, *Terra Nova* had cruised along the Ross Ice Shelf and, to quote the official cable, "we made the discovery that . . . Balloon Bight had broken away . . . merging . . . into the Bay of Whales".[26]

"This very discovery," Shackleton acidly wrote in the *Daily Mail*, having once more been asked for his opinions, "was made by me in 1908."[27] At the other end of the world, he sensed Scott's jealous obsession to deprive him of credit for his work. It undoubtedly tempered his reaction to *Terra Nova*'s really startling news. At the Bay of Whales Amundsen had been found established.

Hitherto, Amundsen's challenge had not been taken seriously in Britain. Now, it was dramatically brought home that, as he himself at the time had announced, he was "to take part in the fight for the South Pole".[28] Having imagined an unopposed parade, Scott was confronted with a race. Moral indignation was abroad; at least among leader writers and in the geographical establishment. Shackleton was more ambivalent.

Like others, Shackleton had believed that Amundsen was heading for the Weddell Sea; but now Amundsen had invaded Scott's self-appointed domain, in the words of the *Daily Mail*, by a "stolen march".[29] That was not the point. Amundsen had promised nothing. It was Shackleton who had promised Scott not to poach on his preserves. Shackleton was haunted by the memory of the fateful day when he retreated from the supposed dangers of the Bay of Whales and headed for McMurdo Sound, the broken promise to Scott like the albatross around his neck. Amundsen had dared where he had not.

"Who will reach the Pole first?" Shackleton asked in the *Daily Mail*. "I for one," he blandly said, "consider it a moot question."

> I personally want to see the British flag flying on the spot towards which we struggled in 1909 for so many weary months, frost-bitten, cold and hungry.[30]

Patriotism, however, was not all. Shackleton did not actually say that he wanted Scott to plant the flag. Like the Emperor Franz Josef, Shackleton seemed to be asking "is he a patriot for *me*?" From Filchner, Shackleton had just heard that "old Markham", as he put it, "had told him all about my row with Scott and had shown my letters to Scott etc. Filchner said it had nothing to do with him".[31]

"Captain Scott", Shackleton told *Daily Mail* readers with a gentle barb, "will undoubtedly follow my route . . . surveyed . . . to within 97 geographical miles of the South Pole." Amundsen, on the other hand, "starts from a point eighty miles further south". Amundsen's strength, Shackleton went on, with a flash of seemingly belated insight, was the "hereditary knowledge of skiing and handling of dogs that the Norwegian possesses".[32] Shackleton seemed almost not to mind if Amundsen did win the race.

"When it comes to the moral side of things," Mawson said after learning that Lysaght's money was diverted, "S. and I part brass rags."[33] Lysaght, on the other hand, shrugged off the transaction by saying that "I helped him at one time financially", and never wavered from the view that Shackleton "inspired confidence".[34] Shackleton's relations with both, as with so many others, were thoroughly ambivalent.

Without Lysaght's money, Mawson's whole enterprise was threatened. He urgently needed £12,000 for a ship. Shackleton, however, had promised to help and, since Mawson was still in London, on his doorstep, that is what he did. He introduced Mawson to Lord Northcliffe.

Northcliffe was prepared to let the *Daily Mail* sponsor an appeal for funds, but only if success were guaranteed, since on no account did he wish to be contaminated by failure. Shackleton offered to make the appeal. On 8 May, it was printed. One result was what the *Daily Mail* called an "unmannerly intervention" by Sir Clements Markham and Sir Edgar Speyer, treasurer of Scott's expedition. "The great explorer", as they put it, was still in need of money,

> and his needs ought to be considered . . . before . . . any appeal from promoters of any other scheme . . . intended to divert support.[35]

The antagonism gnawing the partisans of Shackleton and Scott worked in many ways. "Shackleton," wrote Reginald Skelton, his old shipmate from *Discovery*, to Scott, with all the news, "still keeps his name very much to the front, but I doubt if the credit attached to it is quite so good as it used to be."[36] The public, however, decides who are its favourites. Shackleton's name in the *Daily Mail* was good enough to bring in the money that Mawson needed. Mawson bought his ship – the *Aurora* – a sealer from Newfoundland. "Shackleton", as Mawson said, "double-crossed me",[37] but it was Shackleton who nonetheless had got his expedition under way. It was ironic that Shackleton's own affairs seemed mysteriously blighted, but whenever he turned to helping others he had a magic touch.

Down at Sheringham, alone in temporary lodgings with her children, and a weekend husband at best, Emily had been growing more forlorn. Shackleton had written to her in March from Budapest,

> I seem to realize what a strenuous life I have pulled you into, and how well you did your share. I just long to see you settled in your own home with your own things around you.[38]

Shackleton could no longer put this off. In May, he moved into No 7 Heathview Gardens, Putney Heath – "My settled address, we have a house at last", he wrote to Leonard Tripp, in New Zealand. "I do not myself feel settled at all."

Tripp was a Wellington lawyer whom Shackleton had known since *Discovery* days. When they first met, Tripp, in his own words, had "straightaway formed a very high opinion"[39] of Shackleton. To Shackleton, Tripp was now a conveniently distant confidant to whom he might reveal what he scarcely dared admit nearer home.

The news from Amundsen and Scott was still disturbingly fresh. Now Filchner had sailed from Hamburg, ironically in the well-remembered *Bjørn*, now renamed *Deutschland*. There was even a Japanese expedition, under Lieutenant Shirase, on its way to King Edward VII Land, sworn to reach the South Pole or die. Mawson was about to depart, taking John King Davis and Frank Wild, both having loyally waited for Shackleton as long as they could. "At present I must keep quiet," Shackleton told Tripp,

> as the missus is going to have another baby in July and I must not talk of going away. I long for the unbeaten trail again.[40]

Putney Heath was then a smart address, chosen by Shackleton also because it was convenient for the centre of London. The move nonetheless opened what Emily later called "the least happy years of his life. They certainly were of mine".[41]

Cosy, leafy, suburban, and slightly claustrophobic, Putney Heath was hardly congenial for anyone fretting to get out. Things were not made easier by the fact that it was Emily's income which ran the household, or that her sister Daisy moved in, partly, no doubt, for companionship, but partly also to help with the finances. The arrival of the third baby Edward Alexander (who later became Lord Shackleton), on 15 July, also played a part. Emily was now forty-three, and her pregnancies, coming comparatively late in life, had had a permanent effect. It was observed that Shackleton rarely entertained at home, and when he went visiting, it was without his wife.

One weekend, he was down at a country house near Crawley, in Sussex, where George Buckley, having come over from New Zealand, was now living. There, Shackleton was attacked by severe pains in the chest. It was like the day he collapsed during the southern journey on *Discovery*, eight years before. He called it acute rheumatism. Mawson happened to be present, and later described how Buckley

> had to send [Shackleton] home post haste . . . in his motor . . . The perspiration simply streamed out of S.'s face with the pain – it seemed to me . . . a very unusual form of rheumatism . . . in all probability [it was] heart . . . it must have been angina.[42]

Exactly what ailed Shackleton remained a mystery, since he, as usual, would not allow a doctor to examine him. He was not leading a healthy life. He was undoubtedly smoking and drinking too much, besides over-eating, and taking too little exercise. He was troubled by a persistent cough.

In a way that Emily had never seen before, Shackleton was now restless, moody and frustrated. Even more did he feel a marked man, obsessed with the desire to achieve ambition before it was too late. His immediate aim was the elusive fortune, with which to seize opportunity, when it came. Hungarian gold still seemed the answer. All summer, Shackleton continued the pursuit in more trips across the continent to Budapest and elsewhere.

The summer of 1911, as Skelton wrote to Scott, summarising events for when his isolation should be broken, was the "summer of the century . . . temperatures higher than anything since accurate temperatures have been taken".[43] It was coronation summer: George V was crowned in June; there were golden days for the Henley Regatta, the Eton and Harrow match at Lord's, and every one of the season's rites. Spirits were high, and determinedly extravagant. That summer too, as Skelton put it,

> We have been on the brink of war . . . all [naval] leave was stopped, ships were ordered to their war stations.

The cause, in Skelton's words, was "a sort of raid by Germany on Morocco";[44] the arrival of a gunboat at the port of Agadir, in fact, to enforce German commercial claims on France.

To the international crisis that ensued Shackleton, like many another, was serenely oblivious. His Hungarian associates, however, were even more evasive than before. By the autumn, Skelton could tell Scott, the crisis had "quieted down", but also that "Shackleton is in a bad way financially". The mine at Nagybanya had joined the Russian soldiers, *Potentia*, North Mexico, and all the rest in his limbo of faded hopes. Agadir crisis or not, Emily was by now hardly surprised. "The darling boy," as she tolerantly put it, "had always some new scheme which was going to bring in a fortune!"[45]

At the end of October, Frank Shackleton went through his examination for bankruptcy. For Ernest Shackleton, too, it was an inauspicious occasion.

It was not only that Frank had debts of nearly £85,000. From the proceedings it became only too obvious that he had defrauded Lord Ronald Sutherland-Gower. Lord Ronald himself was too ill to attend the dismal court in Carey Street. His close companion, Frank Hird, was there instead. They had lived together for thirteen years and, to regularise their relationship, Lord Ronald had taken the unusual step of legally adopting Hird as his son.

In the street after the hearing Hird, plump, moon-faced and normally inoffensive, went up to Frank Shackleton and called him a "thief". The outburst was understandable. Hird, too, had been defrauded and, during the proceedings, Frank Shackleton, after giving evidence, had deliberately gone to where he was sitting, and grinned at him. Hird then sent Ernest Shackleton a postcard with wild accusations that he and one of his sisters had aided and abetted their brother. Hird challenged Ernest to sue him for libel.

That is exactly what Ernest did. The prospect greatly intrigued Sir Arthur Vicars, waiting in the wings. What Sir Arthur called "my affair" was "bound to come up", as he wrote in a letter to a friend. Hird had told Sir Arthur so. This, of course, meant the theft of the crown jewels. Hird, as Sir Arthur Vicars informed his correspondent, "will help me as far as possible. He promises revelations . . . unless E. S. funks an exposure".[46]

In the event, it was Hird who evaded the issue. He backed down and apologised. "I am now satisfied that the statements I made with regard to you are unfounded," he wrote to Ernest Shackleton. "I undertake that there shall be no repetition."[47]

Ernest Shackleton was, in fact, vaguely involved in the bankruptcy. He had had dealings in some of his brother's shares.

He would probably have gone bankrupt himself by now, if his brother-in-law, Herbert Dorman, as his lawyer, had not kept him in check. Herbert, incidentally, charged Shackleton no fees. Moreover, he had laid out money of his own to make sure that *Nimrod* sailed on Shackleton's relief – "we Dormans stick together",[48] as he had expressed it to Emily – and had never pressed for repayment.

Even so, Shackleton persuaded Herbert to buy shares for £3,000 with him in Maxim's, the Paris restaurant. Maxim's happened to be one of Frank Shackleton's promotions, a gamble unwittingly financed by Lord Ronald.

"I have . . . been paying out for things that really were not my personal affairs," Shackleton wrote darkly to a creditor early in 1912, "only for the sake of my father's position and of course mine in a way."[49] On borrowed money, Shackleton was doing his best to help Frank, and Frank quietly went abroad. "Had I *only known* [Ernest] was borrowing from the Bank," Emily later ruefully said, "of course I would have [practised] close economy . . . I blame myself, but that does not do any good."[50]

After a long lapse, Shackleton's desultory participation in Freemasonry had now revived. In November 1911 he appeared at the Guild of Freemen Masonic Lodge, and was passed to the Second Degree. It was more than ten years since his initiation, an unusually long interval.

Housed in the Great Eastern Hotel, next to Liverpool Street Station, this Lodge was convenient for Shackleton's forays into the City. Undoubtedly he hoped that mending his Masonic connections would help him in business. There was something beyond that. Shackleton possessed the religious temperament, but had long since turned his back on churches and on priests. Freemasonry, which allowed each man to worship his God in his own way, met a pressing need in him of comfort.

Furthermore, the hint of ancient mysteries appealed to Shackleton. Freemasonry, in the words of its own ritual, bears "a near affinity to . . . the ancient Egyptians. Their philosophers, unwilling to expose their mysteries to vulgar eyes, couched their . . . learning . . . under signs and hieroglyphical figures".[51] The Masonic use of the six pointed star, Hebrew letters, geometrical patterns on the floor, references to the building of Solomon's temple, hint at cabbalistic influence. At this point, Shackleton was actually being drawn to the occult. It coincided with an almost overpowering sense of frustration.

"I wish I could get another Expedition, and be away from all business worries", he wrote to Tripp in January 1912. "All the troubles of the South are nothing to day after day of business", he added. "I suppose we shall soon hear of Scott."[52]

There lay the core of his unrest. In the Antarctic, meanwhile, an ironic little scene was being played out. Scott was floundering in Shackleton's footsteps up the Beardmore Glacier. At a certain point, he reached some unnamed ice falls. These, "Teddy" Evans, "with Scott's consent", as he blandly put it, immediately "called 'The Shackleton Ice Falls' ".[53] The pinprick was deliberate. Lieutenant E. R. G. R. Evans was Scott's naval second-in-command whom Scott's mental bullying had estranged. He had first met Shackleton when, as an officer on the *Morning*, he had sailed on the *Discovery* relief that brought Shackleton home. Evans had divined Scott's jealousy of Shackleton.

In London, Shackleton only knew that he was coming to the end of his temporary triumph. It was at this time that he went to lunch with George Bernard Shaw. Charles Sarolea, Shackleton's brother-in-law, made the introduction. It was a memorable afternoon. In temperament, background, outlook and character, Shaw and Shackleton were worlds apart. Both, however, were Anglo-Irishmen. Shaw's sardonic chuckle was soon mixing with Shackleton's uninhibited laughter. As the repartee flowed, Shackleton was observed to be almost a match for Mephistopheles. Afterwards, Shackleton received a typical letter from Shaw:

> The announcement that I am going to Budapest is untrue, like all the other announcements about me. I am much more likely to go to the South Pole . . .
>
> Have you recovered sufficiently from your previous visit to contemplate another with fortitude? If so, I have only to give Charlotte [Mrs Shaw] half a hint, and you are done for.[54]

This sort of thing could only momentarily drive from Shackleton the thought of being supplanted by Scott. *That* was hardly to be borne. "I am inclined to think we will hear from Amundsen first," Shackleton told Tripp in January. "I am looking forward to news."

On 17 May, the Norwegian national day, as it happened, the *Daily Mirror* provided one kind of answer. Across the whole front page was splashed a single picture, with the self-explanatory caption: "CAPTAIN AMUNDSEN PLANTS THE NORWEGIAN FLAG AT THE SOUTH POLE AND PHOTOGRAPHS A MEMBER OF HIS EXPEDITION STANDING BESIDE IT".

It was the first, historic picture; for the wirephoto did not yet exist. The news had actually arrived on 7 March, the day Amundsen returned to civilisation at Hobart, Tasmania. He had reached the Pole on 14 December, 1911. Amundsen indeed had won the race, and got through first with the news.

The newsbills blared; the headlines flew across the page. The last of the great geographical goals had been achieved.

Three weeks later, *Terra Nova* reached New Zealand, without Scott, but with Teddy Evans who, commanding the last support party, had left him on 5 January, still 150 miles from the Pole, and thus brought proof that Scott had lost. "The explanation," declared *The Times*, with the peculiar brand of magisterial complacency on which its readers fed, "probably lies in the much more favourable route which the Norwegian chanced to take." Amundsen, moreover, "succeeded . . . through . . . British forerunners, Captain Scott himself among them".[55]

"Shackleton is behaving in a thoroughly Shackletonian fashion", Kathleen Scott recorded. "I think he is delighted at the turn things have taken – I would willingly assist at that man's assassination."[56] He was conspicuous by his refusal to join in such churlish pooh-poohing of Amundsen's achievement. "Heartiest congratulations magnificent achievement",[57] he cabled Amundsen when the news came through. In the *Daily Chronicle* he wrote,

> The same endurance, the same skill and the same meed of endeavour must be granted to Amundsen, as the Norwegian people would grant to Scott if the positions [were] reversed.[58]

"Amundsen", he wrote even more emphatically in the *Daily Mail*, "is perhaps the greatest Polar explorer of today." There was the "thoroughness of [his] preparations", as he put it, cataloguing the reasons, "the rapidity [of] the journey . . . The outstanding feature", Shackleton summed up, "is that Amundsen made for himself an entirely new route".[59]

Shackleton was not entirely alone in his opinion. Even Kathleen Scott was driven to admit that it "was a very fine feat . . . & in spite of one's irritation one has to admire it".[60] Amundsen, as John King Davis put it, "has taught most people . . . a lesson".[61] Davis was then in Hobart, captain of *Aurora*, Mawson's ship. He had just returned from taking Mawson to the west of Cape Adare. It was the first landing on that part of the Antarctic coast, called Adélie Land, and discovered in 1840 by a Frenchman, Admiral Jules Sebastien César Dumont D'Urville.*

In Hobart, Davis found Amundsen in his ship *Fram*. Soon after his arrival, Davis visited *Fram* "to convey to Captain Amundsen

* Who brought the Venus de Milo to France.

the warm congratulations of the Australasian Antarctic Expedition", as Mawson's enterprise was called. Partly this was a reaction to the poor sportsmanship evinced in the messages coming out of England. Amundsen and Davis, as Davis in after years recalled,

> had many talks and I found that [Amundsen] was a most interesting personality. One look at his face was enough to assure one of his great strength of character, but it was rewarding to find that those stern features were capable of breaking into a ready and charming smile. His restless, active mind was attracted to every aspect of the many problems affecting polar exploration . . . "Had Shackleton landed at the Bay of Whales in 1908" . . . he told me . . . "he would have reached the South Pole. As it was, starting from McMurdo Sound, he was only ninety-seven miles short of it." Who knows, but he may have been right? He was a great man.[62]

"I . . . really would be sorry for Scott," Davis said, "if I did not know how utterly empty and personal the whole business is with him."[63] Hugh Robert Mill found "nothing to praise" in Scott's own report. That was as far as 87°30′, on 4 January, clear of the Beardmore Glacier, up on the plateau. Scott, in Mill's words,

> had done nothing new . . . He kept so close to Shackleton's track that he could discover nothing unless Shackleton had never been there; but by reference to Shackleton's names he evidently found everything as set down.[64]

After Scott's attempt to discredit Shackleton's discoveries, that was sweet vindication. These, however, were the private utterances of an exclusive coterie. Shackleton spoke in public; and his feelings were personal. His record had been beaten; he had lost his primacy, but gratitude, not resentment, was uppermost. Amundsen had saved Shackleton the sight of Scott staring smugly from the page. That a foreigner thereby had taken the game seemed by comparison a very small price to pay.

When *The Times*, quoting a letter from Scott, virtuously declared that he "never had any intention of racing Captain Amundsen to the Pole",[65] Shackleton recognised the familiar voice of high-minded humbug. It was to be heard in the person of Sir Clements Markham at a meeting of the British Association at Dundee in September. Sir Clements announced that Scott and his men would reach the Pole "dragging their own provisions . . . This is the true British way".[66] He also contrived to give a résumé of Antarctic exploration without mentioning Shackleton or Amundsen. Shackleton himself was not present, but Eric Marshall, now back from New Guinea, had been sent there to watch the interests of the *Nimrod* expedition. He entered a bitter protest.

Under whichever flag, someone else nonetheless had won. Scott had lost the race. He had paid for demanding the promise to keep away from McMurdo Sound that he had forced out of Shackleton, and which Shackleton had been forced to break. That, for Shackleton, was what counted. The person had overcome the patriot. Amundsen could not wipe out the stain of a broken promise, but he had wrought the ultimate revenge.

After a few months, Shackleton was able to repay his debt in part. In the middle of November, Amundsen arrived in England on a lecture tour. His first appearance, at the Queen's Hall in London, was under the not too willing aegis of the RGS, and Shackleton made it his business to be on the platform. "No other polar man," Sir Clements Markham wrote gleefully to Scott, "countenanced it."[67] The geographical establishment in fact boycotted the event.

That Shackleton was practically alone on the platform was perhaps why the public was reasonably friendly. Shackleton had made up for the surly snub. It was "by efficiency, not only by good luck" that Amundsen succeeded, Shackleton pointedly said, moving the vote of thanks. "We all here no doubt wish it had been a British expedition that had got there first," he went on, ostentatiously eschewing reference to Scott,

> but none the less we are proud of Amundsen having got there, and we can all recognise that not only has he done the work well, but was supported by loyal comrades . . . Throughout the lecture . . . I never heard the word "I" mentioned; [Shackleton went on to say] it was always "we". I think that is the way in which Amundsen got his men to work along with him, and it brought the thing to a successful conclusion.[68]

That, more or less, was Shackleton's own philosophy. When first he heard the news from Amundsen, he had already analysed the lessons to be learned. Compared with himself, Amundsen was "not seriously inconvenienced".[69] Shackleton was no puritan. He saw no virtue in suffering. Without resentment, he acknowledged Amundsen as his technical master. Amundsen did not have to man-haul, "and in this", Shackleton baldly commented, "he . . . was fortunate" because he was "able to take sufficient provisions throughout his journey".[70]

> Amundsen's equipment, though not so large as Scott's [Shackleton summed up] has peculiar advantages . . . The Norwegians . . . are accustomed to . . . driving . . . dogs and are born ski runners. The . . . plateau and the level stretches on the barrier surface would be excellent for skiing. The dogs will keep up the rapid pace [of] ski runners . . . and this is naturally faster than the slow-plodding foot movements of the ponies.[71]

That hid, perhaps, a strand of wry enjoyment. Scott had slavishly copied Shackleton's ponies, as he had copied everything else, and had therefore fallen into the same trap. Shackleton, at any rate, was now cured of his bizarre trust in ponies for the snow. Amundsen had vindicated the use of dogs. Shackleton had learned his lesson, but too late.

A few months later, Shackleton found himself in the gloomy ambience of a hall in Buckingham Gate giving evidence before the *Titanic* enquiry. *Titanic* sank in the North Atlantic on 15 April 1912, after colliding with an iceberg during her maiden voyage from Southampton to New York.

At much the same time, in the Antarctic, at McMurdo Sound, all hope for Scott and the polar party was finally being abandoned, but for ten more months the world would only know about the fate of the ship. In those years before 1914, waiting for Armageddon, as it were, that was enough to be going on with. "What an awful disaster the 'Titanic' is", Shackleton wrote from Cologne to a friend, "One can hardly realise it yet".[72] Over fifteen hundred souls had been lost.

More than mere coincidence seems to link the loss of the *Titanic* with the Scott débâcle. Both were exercises in unnecessary heroism. They were technical failures, eminently preventable. A morbid myth arose to cloak each sorry tale. In the case of the *Titanic* it was the inevitable "Women and children first", and gallant gentlemen who stayed behind because there was no room in the lifeboats.

Titanic was billed as the biggest, most powerful, and most luxurious liner in the world; the pride of the British merchant fleet, and absolutely unsinkable. She carried lifeboats for less than half her complement. There had been no boat drill. No stations were allotted to passengers, no crews assigned to boats. Abandoning ship, therefore, was a matter of improvisation and unnecessary sacrifice. What boats there were got away only half full. In a dead calm, with ideal weather, exactly 651 out of 2,340 people were saved.

Shackleton was called to the official enquiry as an authority on ice navigation. In his evidence he was tactless enough to suggest that *Titanic* went down because she was sailing too fast for the conditions: it was night, and speed, he suggested, ought to be reduced at night or in poor visibility as soon as icebergs were known to be about. The reason that *Titanic* was sailing too fast, Shackleton also suggested, was because the owners were on board. "When the owner is on board," as he put it, "you *go*." He added,

> There is a general feeling among people at sea, that you have to make your passage. If you do not make your passage it is not so good for you.[73]

In that lay an uncomfortable point. The captain of the *Titanic* had gone down with his ship. J. Bruce Ismay, managing director of the White Star Line, *Titanic*'s owners, had got away. The episode, in Shackleton's words, opened the "very wide question of relationship between owners and captains . . . But in view of the fact that there is wireless now, I think any accident could be avoided".[74]

That showed considerable temerity. Shackleton was still hoping for the goodwill of wealthy men, some of them shipowners. This was hardly the way to ingratiate himself with them. He had touched on a taboo. But in cross-examination, he was browbeaten by Sir Robert Finlay, an accomplished barrister representing *Titanic*'s owners. Sir Robert's brief, largely successful, was to exonerate his clients of any blame. Shackleton, in the process, found his standing as a sailor and an ice navigator impugned. Somehow, he did not shine in a formal, legalistic ambience.

Appearances were against him, too, for Shackleton gave an impression of being burned out. In Skelton's words, he had "deteriorated rapidly"[75] since returning from the *Nimrod*. He was smoking and drinking noticeably more. "A bit of a floating gent",[76] one of his cronies called him. The collapse of his various schemes, the uncanny bafflement every way he turned, had begun to tell. He was harsher, brusquer, obviously on edge. Nothing seemed to go quite right. "My wife and 3 children are well," he wrote to Tripp in New Zealand. "I see little of them though."[77] Emily remained content to immerse herself in home life. The effect on Shackleton was to afflict him with a sense of suffocation. His children, he regarded with erratic bouts of fondness and irritation. Perversely, he was irked by Emily's submissive devotion to himself.

Emily had never really fitted into Shackleton's social life. She was too conventional to approve of his eclectic circle of associates. Now moving in a hard drinking set on the fringes of the stage, he spent less and less time at home. Although hardly clubbable, he was more frequently to be found at the Marlborough Club.

This was no ordinary London club. The Marlborough had been founded by Edward VII, while Prince of Wales, as a refuge for his friends. It lay in Pall Mall, conveniently close to Marlborough House, where Edward lived before coming to the throne.

There congregated rakes and bloods, gamblers, men of letters, foreign magnates, self-made tycoons, Jewish financiers, stockbrokers by the drove. The Marlborough was, designedly, a haven for those of Edward's companions blackballed at older, grander, and more respectable clubs. It existed to create the raffish, cheerful, cosmopolitan, money-laden atmosphere in which Edward thrived. Nobody could become a member without his assent, and Shackleton was elected in the heady days after his return from the *Nimrod*.

Now that Edward VII had gone, the Marlborough Club had become a fading harkback to the Edwardian heyday. For Shackleton, it seemed faintly appropriate. He was in any case unlikely to have been admitted to any other club. In his rootless existence it served him as a base, providing a necessary mailing address, with an armchair when he fleetingly felt the need.

This unrest stemmed largely from a love affair. In the days when Frank Shackleton was living in Park Lane, one of his neighbours, at No 32, was a Mrs Chetwynd. Ernest Shackleton could hardly fail to make her acquaintance.

Mrs Chetwynd was an American, born Rosalind Secor, daughter of a New York lawyer. In search of a title, or not, she had come to London and married Guy Chetwynd, heir to a baronetcy, but by 1909, as Shackleton was returning from the *Nimrod* expedition, she was divorced.

To women of all ages, from girls who (more or less) innocently loved his teasing, Shackleton was attractive. This, however, was something different. Rosalind Chetwynd was the kind of woman for whom Ernest Shackleton hankered. Big and dark haired, she was beautiful in her way, and ten years younger than himself. She was passing rich, she had a forceful personality, and the stately sexuality of the Edwardians. Not easily approachable, she nonetheless possessed charm, and she was loyal to her friends. She radiated an uninhibited affection. In the background lurked something maternal, protective, sisterly perhaps. With her, Shackleton now fell in love.

Rosalind, meanwhile, had become attached to Jack Barnato Joel, a well-known South African financier and, incidentally, a Freemason too. It was Joel who years before had bought for her the house in Park Lane, and ever since supported her financially. They were devoted to each other. Rosalind, however, found Shackleton –

the little boy, in some ways, who never grew up – hard to resist. The elegant little house in Park Lane became a furtive ménage à trois.

Shackleton was also fitfully pining for Elspeth Beardmore. She, however, was estranged because of the unrepaid loan and the unforgiving hostility of her husband towards Shackleton.

None of this helped Shackleton's peace of mind. Sometimes he would hire a taxi by the day, and dash from one unannounced visit to the next, pacing nervously up and down drawing-room or office, a cigarette continuously dangling from his lips, and making jerky conversation before rushing off. It was as if he had to release uncontrollable bouts of restlessness, even by make-believe activity. His moods were more pronounced. "The one I liked him least in," said Campbell Mackellar, who now knew him well, "was when he became frivolously boyish."[78] At home, when he was there, Shackleton was irritable, abrupt, impatient, and remorseful by turns; and playing practical jokes when the spirit moved him. It was hardly the picture of a man at peace with himself. Also, he was not well; in May he had what *The Times* called "blood poisoning". Shackleton, to the irritation of his enemies, was still considered a prominent invalid, whose health was news.

At the end of November, there came comfort of a kind when Amundsen's book *The South Pole* appeared in English. Thirty-four pages were devoted to what he owed Shackleton:

> Sir Ernest Shackleton! [Amundsen wrote] That name has a fresh ring. It has only to be mentioned for us to see before us a man glowing with invincible will-power and boundless courage. He has shown us what one man's will and energy can accomplish.[79]

This generosity intensified Shackleton's unrest. "The discovery of the South Pole," he had written when the news of Amundsen first came through, "will not be the end of Antarctic exploration. The next work," as he put it, was "a transcontinental journey from sea to sea, crossing the Pole."[80]

That was the way his thoughts were now seriously pointing. "Another Expedition unless it crosses the continent is not much,"[81] he had already told Emily, when explaining that he was not joining Mawson. To go down in history as the precursor, even of someone like Amundsen, that man of "indomitable will", as Shackleton put it, would not suffice.

There was no certainty yet that the crossing of Antarctica was actually left for Shackleton to do. To be sure that he had not been forestalled, he had still to wait for news from Filchner and Scott.

Meanwhile, to use a favourite phrase of his, Shackleton once more tried to "square up" his affairs. "I have now after 3 years work paid off the £20,000 liability on my [*Nimrod*]", he wrote to Nansen in September 1912, "and am starting business to keep the pot boiling." Lysaght's £10,000 had obviously played a part. He continued to Nansen,

> I am writing to ask if you could give me your help, as I know you have a great deal of influence in high quarters.
>
> I own a tobacco company all my own . . . and I want to extend its scope to the [United] States of America. There if I could say that I had the warrants as suppliers to European royalties it would make a great difference . . . I want Norway also.

"If you would use your power and ask the King," Shackleton explained, coming to the point, "then the thing would be settled."[82] His firm, Shackleton explained, almost as an afterthought, was called the Tabard Cigarette Co.

Tabard was not really all his own. The story went back to the far-off, hopeful days before he sailed on *Discovery*, when Shackleton was working at the expedition offices in Burlington Gardens. Down the street, at the entrance to Albany, was a tobacconist's where he bought his cigarettes. The proprietor was a cigarette manufacturer called Forbes Lugard Smith. Shackleton, of course, soon struck up an acquaintance. Smith took a liking to this talkative and entertaining customer with the engaging touch of the brogue.

Smith was a bit of a mystery. Despite his name, he was thought not really to be English, partly because at home he went round in pyjamas! At any rate, he owned tobacco plantations in Turkey, he was rich and, it seemed, philanthropic. In the end, he joined Gerald Lysaght, Elizabeth Dawson-Lambton, Lord Iveagh, and others who had mountains in the Antarctic named after them by Shackleton in gratitude for financial aid given to the *Nimrod* expedition. What Smith gave him was a secret; he was one of those people who really liked doing good by stealth. After *Discovery*, when Shackleton moved to Edinburgh, Smith set him up in Tabard as his Scottish outlet. Smith, incidentally, was a Freemason who no doubt took seriously his obligation of charity to a brother Mason.

Shackleton saw Tabard – probably named by himself, influenced by his brother Frank, after the embroidered tunic of a herald – not as another path to instant fortune, but as a hopeful sideline. It was the one business with which he persevered, although it was no more than a glorified shop in Lynedoch Place. After the *Nimrod* expedition, it followed him from Edinburgh to London where it was housed in Smith's depot in Foubert's place, behind Regent Street.

Shackleton was in the hands of Smith, and an associate called James Aloysius Cook, who really ran Tabard. His approach to Nansen was part of a plan to use Shackleton's connections in floating Tabard as a public company. Sir Philip Brocklehurst was persuaded to take shares for £2,000. In December 1912, however, when Shackleton sailed for New York to promote Tabard in America, it was without the Norwegian or any other royal warrant to help in his campaign.

Away at Benguela in Portuguese West Africa, at the same time, Frank Shackleton was boarding another ship in the company of Detective Sergeant Cooper of Scotland Yard. The sergeant, an extraordinary figure with bulbous eyes and a heavy, curled moustache, had travelled five thousand miles to arrest Frank and bring him back for trial.

On 7 January 1913, Wilhelm Filchner arrived at Buenos Aires, bearing the news for which Shackleton, now in New York, was waiting. Filchner's base, on a grounded iceberg, had floated out into the Weddell Sea and he never penetrated beyond the coast. Whatever had happened to Scott, it was now clear that the first crossing of Antarctica still remained for someone else to do. The news from Frank was not quite so reassuring.

From the mystery of the crown jewels on, there was a selection of crimes for which Frank could have been arraigned. The charge for which he was actually arrested was fraudulent conversion of a cheque for £1,000 from a certain Miss Mary Josephine Browne.

So it was that although Ernest Shackleton – somehow – found the £1,000 for Frank's bail when Frank was charged at Bow Street on 10 January, he used their father as a proxy in court. Ernest did not want his name to figure publicly in the case, in any way. Whatever the pretext, it was convenient not to be in England when his brother landed.

James Cook from Tabard was also in New York now; but Tabard business did not exclusively occupy Shackleton's time. Emily had stayed at home; she no longer travelled with him, and he plunged into a fairly exhausting social round. But he was raking over the embers of his triumph now. On 16 January Amundsen, on tour in America, lectured in Philadelphia. Peary was there, "to have the discoverer of the North Pole", as one of the organisers put it, "introduce the discoverer of the South Pole".[83] Shackleton too was asked to speak. Amundsen, he declared, was "good enough to say that I blazed the way for him . . . Perhaps I will try again to go south".[84] It was, however, as a local journalist underlined the obvious, "distinctly an Amundsen affair, with Peary and Shackleton as side attractions",[85] but they made an historic trio on the platform. Even so, it was all rather desultory. Shackleton seemed to be waiting for something. On 17 February, he unexpectedly sailed for England.

A week before, *Terra Nova* had reached New Zealand with the news that Scott and his companions had perished on the way back from the Pole. A year earlier, when a member of Scott's expedition returned to New Zealand after the first season, he was met by the taunt: "Why didn't you get back sooner? Amundsen got the Pole in a sardine tin."[86] Since then, Scott had gradually been written off as the man who came second. Now, in the charged atmosphere of the last year before the outbreak of the Great War, the loss of five explorers was a sensation to supplant the *Titanic* in the pantheon of heroic disaster. One of Emily Shackleton's cousins remembered discussing the event with a friend at Queen's College, Harley Street, where she was at school:

> The silly part . . . was . . . We were coming down the broad stairs in the College and I was saying: "And it's not as if he slipped down a crevasse – " At that, I missed my footing, and I slipped down the stairs![87]

When Shackleton landed at Plymouth on 24 February from New York, the only comment he made was that "curiously he was the only survivor of the three who made the dash South on the previous expedition – Scott, Wilson and himself", as one journalist reported. "All the time he was the one, too, who was so seriously ill."[88]

Shackleton resented the fuss made about Scott's end. The situation was tinged with irony. Shackleton had not yet lost a man. Scott had lost in one season as many men as all the Antarctic expeditions for the past fifteen years together. Put another way, he had lost more than twice as many as the Norwegian explorers for the past quarter of a century, and *their* work ranged from the first crossing of Greenland to the conquest of the South Pole. By any standards, Scott had been notably incompetent and prodigal with life. Yet now Shackleton had to watch while his detested rival posthumously reaped the glory, as the country seemed to revel in the romanticising of failure.

"Henceforth proficiency with skis will be an indispensable qualification of every candidate for Polar exploration",[89] wrote the *Daily Mail* nonetheless. As in other fields, it took disaster to bring people to their senses. The flood of comment, however, was overwhelmingly on the subject of glorifying what was not strictly heroism but mindless bravado. It was an orgy of expiating national chagrin at having failed to be first at either the North or South

Pole. Scott, the *Daily Mail* also remarked, had proved "that the metal of our race still rings true upon the touchstone of death".[90] This was a way of begging the awkward question of why the expedition failed. It was a way of salving national self-esteem and hiding from the truth. None of this exactly appealed to Shackleton. Amundsen came closer to his thoughts when he told a journalist that "Shackleton . . . nearly met the same fate" four years before on the *Nimrod* expedition. "He turned back just in time."[91]

It was his brother's affairs rather than the news about Scott that had brought Shackleton home. Amazingly protracted committal proceedings were required to unravel Frank's tortuous affairs. Miss Mary Josephine Browne's cheque was not the only topic to be broached in open court. Frank was charged also with defrauding Lord Ronald Sutherland-Gower, and it was remembered that Ernest originally introduced them. There was another link in Frank's company promotions. These necessarily were ventilated too. As secretary or director, a certain Frederick William White was involved; and he happened to be Tabard's secretary too. Also there was the question of how and why in the first place Frank had left the country. Had Ernest now stayed away, he might have been mildly suspect himself. Before Frank was actually committed for trial, he had to return and talk to the authorities.

The reunion of the brothers was hardly edifying. Frank had rapidly decayed; financial ruin was the expression of a personal flaw. It was hard to recognise in the seedy figure on bail the erstwhile dandified flâneur on the verge of a fortune. It was uncomfortably like seeing a reflection of himself in a tarnished mirror. It was with obvious relief that, on 21 March, Ernest Shackleton boarded the RMS *Mauretania* to return to New York.

Before doing so, as if it were a signal officially dissociating him from his brother, Shackleton was commanded to Buckingham Palace for an interview with King George V. "He is," the King noted in his diary, "thinking of going to the South Pole."[92] The King promised to present the expedition with a flag, and inspect the ship at Cowes before she sailed. There was of course no expedition yet and much, much less a ship.

For another month, Shackleton remained in New York; this time out of the public eye. On 9 May, he was back in England; buoyed up, but not so wildly as before, with hopes of a fortune from Tabard in America. But the hopes once more faded away.

"One of his greatest qualities", Emily used to say of her husband, "was that he never . . . railed at bad luck."[93] Shackleton was by now nonetheless resigned to the melancholy insight that some flaw within himself remorselessly brought bafflement in its train. Marshall was possibly right in harping on his theme that "from the moment that Shackleton broke his word to Scott . . . by using his old Base . . . he was suspect' ";[94] perhaps blighted.

"I have had some hard knocks," Shackleton wrote to Elspeth Beardmore, with whom he was keeping up a fitful correspondence, "but I let the past rest, and am now looking forward to carrying out the last big thing to be done in the South."[95] In the crossing of Antarctica, Shackleton now despairingly saw the last remaining chance of fulfilling himself.

In starting his preparations, Shackleton had not waited for news from Filchner and Scott. Everything, of course, began with money. Since Amundsen, in the words of a companion, "came home with the South Pole in his pocket",[96] Shackleton had been on the old familiar begging round. An expedition leader, he said in a bout of special pleading, "ought not . . . to have the anxiety of collecting funds; his energy should be entirely devoted . . . to organization".[97]

Although as a polar explorer he was in eclipse, Shackleton remained a public figure, always good for a quote on some issue of the day. The Channel Tunnel was one. "I think it deserves support on the two grounds of a better relationship between foreign powers and also for purely commercial reasons," he told the *Daily Graphic.*

> I can see absolutely no reason – sentimental or otherwise – against the scheme. The old, comfortable theory of our "tight little island" is obsolete.[98]

Despite his fame, Shackleton shied away from a public appeal on his own account. "It causes endless book-keeping worries,"[99] as he neatly put it. His metier was private cajoling of individuals.

Scott's followers, meanwhile, were now drifting back to London from New Zealand. One was Tryggve Gran, the Norwegian who had been taken as a ski expert. He had travelled via North America, and was now staying at the Piccadilly Hotel. On the morning of Sunday, 18 May, as Gran told the tale, he was hauled out of bed. It was the day after his arrival, and he was tired. Shackleton, however, in Gran's words, was downstairs and "urgently wanted to talk to me".

They had met four years before, in Norway, when Shackleton had come to lecture on his Furthest South. Gran had actually jumped on to his train at the Swedish border and posed as a journalist in order to meet him. After being with Scott, and hearing all about Amundsen, Gran considered Shackleton's "the greatest deed in the whole of Antarctic exploration". Shackleton, Gran now observed,

> was the same as before, youthful and embarrassingly boyish. "Have you lost the taste for Antarctic exploration," he said suddenly, lighting a half-smoked cigar. "Why?" I asked, somewhat surprised. "I heard that you had plans for flying," Shackleton continued.

Shackleton had been told this by one of Gran's fellow passengers on the crossing from New York. He happened to be a certain Archibald Dexter, one of Shackleton's wealthy American acquaintances.

Gran asked Shackleton, half seriously, whether flying and polar exploration could not be combined.

> "Of course", Shackleton burst out. "Of course it can, and that is precisely why I came here. I propose . . . to attempt the crossing of the Antarctic continent. It is a difficult task, and I must use every possible aid, including aeroplanes. The question is: will you join my expedition?"

Hooded eyes enigmatically gleaming over high cheekbones, Gran considered the question. Shackleton, as Gran divined, was interested in publicity; also in the fact that he, Gran, was rich. In any case, Gran had only developed a serious interest in flying on the trans-Atlantic crossing. There, he had met Robert Lorraine, one of the early pioneers who, the year before, had been the first man to fly across the Irish Sea. Gran had decided he would buy an aeroplane, take flying lessons, and become the first man to fly across the North Sea. He preferred not to reveal this. He gave an evasive answer to Shackleton's invitation. Shackleton, as Gran told the tale, then brushed the matter aside, explaining that in any case it was

> "desirable that this evening you . . . do me the favour of attending a little function at the Savoy. Our mutual friend Mr. Dexter is the host. He is a polar enthusiast, and I hope that his enthusiasm can be increased yet more, so that tonight he will secure the financial side of my project.

Gran agreed. At the Savoy, in his own words,

> Mr . . . Dexter, and his rich friend, Jack Morgan, received the guests, who were exclusively veterans of Scott's and Shackleton's expeditions . . . the table was luxuriously and imaginatively decorated . . . Plates and glasses were filled . . . finally the atmosphere was decidedly elevated. Then Sir Ernest tapped his glass, rose to his feet, and started a speech which, in pure artistic terms, was a masterpiece. There was not one of

us who had not been transported by his words to the desolate icefields of the Antarctic. Even the two American millionaires were affected. They literally stared at the mighty mountains that Shackleton conjured out of his listener's imagination. The end of the speech I will never forget. "What will we call the land we have just discovered?" said Sir Ernest, patting my shoulder with his left hand.

I rose to my feet and shouted:

"We'll call it Archibald Dexters Land."

"And that heavenly peak which has just appeared out of the mist?"

"Mount Jack Morgan", I answered.

Whereupon, said Gran, "the band struck up the 'Stars and Stripes'. Everyone stood to attention."[100] It was all of no avail, however. Neither Dexter nor Morgan offered to finance the expedition. Shackleton had to continue looking elsewhere.

He tried Lord Rosebery, for example. Lord Rosebery was married to a Rothschild, a Scottish peer, a triple Derby winner, a former Prime Minister and a Liberal. "Apart from your personality", he brusquely told Shackleton, "I have never been able to care one farthing about the Poles." Rosebery also refused Shackleton's disingenuous request for an introduction to Sir Ernest Cassel, Edward VII's financial adviser. It would, in his words, put, "you and me in a false position", because it meant "asking people to interest themselves in a plan in which I take no interest myself".[101]

One of those with whom Shackleton had dealt since returning from *Nimrod*, was Ernest Perris, of the *Daily Chronicle*. Perris now helped by arranging contacts with potential benefactors. For one thing, he sensed a story ahead. In any case, Shackleton to him was more than just a newsworthy object. Perris, like Rosebery, was fascinated, as others were repelled, by Shackleton's personality; and it was through Perris that Shackleton was led to William Dederich.

Dederich was a German businessman settled in London. He was successful, rich, and happened to be a polar enthusiast as well. A Rhinelander from Cologne, dapper, jovial and outgoing, he was also taken by Shackleton's personality. Shackleton soon became a regular visitor at Dederich's offices near St Paul's. Dederich would take him out to lunch, often at the Cheshire Cheese, and always foot the bill.

To the office staff, used to sizing up clients, Shackleton bore the tell-tale marks of someone in financial straits. He was never a dandy; but now, to quote one of Dederich's clerks, he looked "as though he had been poured into his clothes".[102] His suits were a shade too well worn. When he strode through the office with his slow, heavy, measured tread, like an officer pacing the bridge, he was noticeably worried, brusque, humourless, preoccupied and irritable. He looked directly at people, but smiled only on first being introduced. His hands were incongruously tiny. What was even more noticeable, he did not shake hands. He seemed to shrink from being touched. These aspects of the famous man did not appreciably dim the general hero worship. The office boy paid him the wry compliment – behind his back – of guying what he called the "Shackleton stance"; hands in pockets, shoulders hunched up towards his ears.

Dederich promised money for the new expedition, and looked for others to do likewise. He was befriending Shackleton in what was perhaps his worst crisis so far: he had been deserted by his old net of wealthy contacts. Lord Rosebery was too typical, alas.

Frank Shackleton was, largely, the blight on his brother. Ernest had been unable to keep out of the way until the trouble blew over. When he returned from America in May, Frank's committal proceedings were still dragging on. They continued all through that summer of 1913. Frank's trial finally opened at the Old Bailey on 20 October.

The case was extensively reported. The man in the dock, the public were invited to recall, was the brother of Sir Ernest Shackleton. Among those who saw in Frank's prosecution a surrogate trial for the theft of the Irish crown jewels was Sir Arthur Vicars, who had been dismissed from his post as Ulster King at Arms.

Of the charges on Frank's indictment, the prosecution had elected to press only those of fraudulently converting to his own use money entrusted to him by Miss Mary Josephine Browne.

Miss Browne, a maiden lady of ripe years, seems to have been a kind of universal aunt. Frank Shackleton met her through Frank Hird in 1907, and was soon visiting her at her home at Tavistock, in Devon. Frank Shackleton soon so ingratiated himself with her that she felt for him as a mother for her son. "He suggested it," she told the court, "and I said yes it was. I was very fond of him." A letter from her to Frank was read out in court: "Dear little Francis",[103] it began. Not surprisingly, she made Frank her financial adviser, and soon he had control of her affairs.

In the dock with Frank was Thomas Jehu Garlick, and for Ernest Shackleton nothing more acutely embarrassing could have been contrived.

From the Russian soldiers on, he had had sporadic dealings with Garlick. Much, much worse, Frank, in defrauding Miss Browne of, as it turned out, nearly all her money, had used the now clearly suspect Celtic Investment Trust. That was the same company whose shares had figured in starting the *Nimrod* expedition. All this and more was ventilated in the theatre of the open court. It included the cheque from Miss Browne for £1,000 that Frank had misappropriated. He had actually passed it to Ernest for the expedition in place of the money earlier taken from Elizabeth Dawson-Lambton. The judge, however, Emily afterwards recalled, "knew E. had nothing to do with it . . . and he would not allow it to appear in the papers."[104]

What did appear was, for Ernest Shackleton, unfortunate enough. It was not as if Frank was a monster of criminality. He had financially ruined Miss Browne but when he told the court that his advice to her "was partly in her own interest", and partly rooted in his anxiety "to get shareholders for the two companies in which [I] was interested, and which [I] believed to be very good concerns",[105] he was probably telling the truth. It was what less unlucky financial advisers did as well. Frank wanted to make his own fortune but, as interest for their involuntary loan, also to make money for his friends.

Even in the dock, Frank was manifestly plausible. Seedy and broken down though he was, he still showed glimpses of the power of ingratiation that had compelled confidence against misgivings. It was unbridled optimism and the absence of the winning touch that betrayed Frank in the end. It was only too easy to recognise in the wilting figure in court the man who might have been Ernest Shackleton.

On 24 October, meanwhile, Frank was found guilty of defrauding Miss Browne. He was sentenced to fifteen months hard labour, and departed into the shades. He had, the Judge severely said, "violated all the rules of commercial morality"[106] but, with a little bit of luck, he might have found the fortune to which he had aspired. Failure was Frank Shackleton's real crime. One cannot help being struck by the abiding pity of it all.

A fortnight after the trial, Ernest Shackleton had to sustain yet more irritation: *Scott's Last Expedition* was published. This, containing the diaries of Scott throughout his second expedition, undoubtedly helped to perpetuate the heroic legend. Even though Shackleton resented that, he no doubt found a wry satisfaction in discovering that he had been Scott's ghostly pacemaker. The Beardmore Glacier, and all the other names that Shackleton gave, alone were goads to Scott: "We must be getting a much better view of the southern side of the main glacier than Shackleton got, and consequently have observed a number of peaks which he did not notice."[107] Even Scott's remark about "geological specimens carried at Wilson's special request"[108] had echoes of Shackleton's own published diary entry for 9 February 1909: "still hanging on to geological specimens".[109]

Scott's Last Expedition, however, was a mean contrast to Amundsen's *The South Pole*. Although Scott had followed in Shackleton's footsteps, he denigrated his work, and belittled the man. There was, for example, the entry for 18 January 1912, about the discovery of Amundsen's tent at the Pole: "It looks as though the Norwegian party expected colder weather . . . than they got; it could scarcely be otherwise from Shackleton's account." Shackleton was not to know that the last phrase actually read "Shackleton's overdrawn account" in the original, but the sneer even so was obvious.

The book purported to be Scott's unexpurgated diaries. In fact, Kathleen Scott, with the connivance of Sir Clements Markham, and Reginald Smith, the publisher, had censored the text. Excisions numbered seventy at least. They were dishonestly concealed. "As we advance," Scott had written on 17 December 1911, climbing up the Beardmore Glacier,

> we see that there is great & increasing error in the charting of the various points. Shackletons watch must have greatly altered its rate which throws everything out including his variation – If we can keep up this pace we gain on him.[110]

"If we can keep up this pace we gain on him" was all that actually appeared. The cuts all concerned Scott's denigration of his predecessors, brutal attacks on his companions, and admissions of incompetence. The aim was to prettify Scott's image, conceal blunders and project the myth of a perfect martyred hero.

One of the few to question the official version of events was Mrs Caroline Oates, the mother of Captain L. E. G. Oates, the man who walked out of the tent into the snow. Oates was presented as a devoted follower of Scott who had sacrificed himself to give his companions a chance; a supporting role, as it were, in a burgeoning heroic myth. Mrs Oates found that unconvincing. She declined to join in the national hysteria. Letters from her son convinced her that his life had been thrown away by Scott. She refused to go to Buckingham Palace to receive from the King the polar medal awarded posthumously to her son.

When her son's diary finally made its way into Mrs Oates' hands, she found inside perhaps the last letter written by Dr Wilson, one of the dead polar party. Her son, he explained, had asked him

> to see you and to give you this diary of his . . . Now I am in the same can and I can no longer hope to see either you or my beloved wife . . . your son died like a man and a soldier without a word of complaint except that he hadn't written to you at the last.[111]

It was a moving letter; and it raised too many unanswered questions. Why had the party been lost? If Oates only wished to save his companions, why had he persevered so long? What did Wilson mean when he wrote that "I have never seen or heard of such courage as he showed from first to last with his feet both badly frostbitten", or: "Our whole journey's record is clean and though disastrous – has no shadow over it"? Mrs Oates' doubt was intensified when she called on Kathleen Scott, to find her "not at her ease, and evidently embarrassed. Perhaps quite natural",[112] as she put it.

Mrs Oates was determined to elicit the truth. Now, at her flat in South Kensington, during the spring of 1913, she interviewed survivors of the expedition over lunch, painstakingly keeping notes. Among those she met was Dr Edward Atkinson, one of the naval surgeons in the South, and leader of the search party that found the victims in the tent.

In public, Atkinson subscribed to the legend. Mrs Oates, however, was a formidable lady, from whom it was hard to conceal anything of substance. To her, Atkinson was driven to admit, probably with relief, that "Captain Scott would be very rude and not behave well and then be very friendly and try to make it up", as Mrs Oates recorded.

> Laurie [her son] was a good deal worried about the way things were done . . . Neither Dr. Atkinson nor Laurie had ever been accustomed to such treatment from their superior officers . . . I asked Dr Atkinson point blank if he thought Laurie had ever regretted going on the expedition. He hesitated before answering and said that there were times when Laurie did.[113]

Cecil Meares, Scott's dog driver, told her that there used to be

> great trouble and unhappiness. Captain Scott would swear all day at [Teddy] Evans and the others. He said it was shocking – and the worst was it was not possible to get away from the rows.[114]

Too many interviews were in this vein. The expedition had evidently been in a state of demoralisation, not to say incipient mutiny. Mrs Oates had satisfied herself that Scott, by his apparent mental instability and incompetent leadership, was indeed responsible for the death of her son. Blaming the weather and bad luck was begging the issue.

Mrs Oates, meanwhile, befriended Emily Shackleton, eventually helping to pay her children's school fees. Mostly, perhaps, this was due to Oates himself. In his diary for 4 December 1911, at the approaches to the Beardmore Glacier, he wrote:

> And now one is here one can realise what a wonderful journey his [Shackleton's] was and the daring which prompted him to strike up the glacier instead of following the coastline.[115]

Having settled everything to her private satisfaction, Mrs Oates nonetheless kept silence too, respecting the custom of not causing public scandal. This went deep. One of Scott's followers was an Australian called Frank Debenham, who perjured himself to the extent of extolling the expedition as one in perfect harmony.

Such was the ambience as Shackleton tried once more to organise an expedition. As *Scott's Last Expedition* was being published, Debenham happened to meet Sir Clements Markham at Cambridge, where he was visiting the Master of Gonville and Caius College. Sir Clements "had no good word for [Ernest] Shackleton, but many bad ones", Debenham reported. "He is sure Shackleton is not going again. 'Worn-out' was the phrase he used. I fancy I agree."[116]

Frank Shackleton's conviction, however, seemed to have cleared the air. Early in December, David Lloyd George, Chancellor of the Exchequer, promised Ernest Shackleton a government grant of £10,000. Thereupon, on Christmas Eve, Shackleton wrote to Lord Stamfordham, the King's Equerry, that he would be "able to start shortly on the new South Polar Expedition":

> Now that the Expedition is about to organize, His Majesty . . . might like to hear the full plans.
>
> The Expedition will be called "The Imperial Transantarctic Expedition" and the sledge journey, if successful, will be the longest ever made . . . no one has crossed the South Polar Continent.[117]

Shackleton followed this on 29 December with his public announcement, which took the form of a letter to *The Times*. It was a paraphrase of the letter to the King. There was one difference, however. In *The Times*, Shackleton declared that he was being financed by an unnamed friend. To the King, he gave the friend a name. It was "a Mr. Alfred Harvey", who does not want his name to appear and is only helping the Expedition as he thinks it good for our country.

In neither case did Shackleton mention the promised government grant. It was, after all, still only a politician's promise. Besides, Lloyd George had stipulated that Shackleton "personally undertake to find the balance . . . from other sources".[118] That was not calculated to encourage benefactors, to whom Lloyd George was anathema because of his "soak-the-rich" campaign. What is certain is that when Shackleton made his announcement, he had no money yet. It was not unlike his brother Frank trying to float companies on thin air, but Ernest nonetheless had the aura of someone who could make things happen. Business, qua business, as he had every occasion to demonstrate, was beyond him. In quest of money as a means to achieve his ends, he was a very different proposition.

In the air of hustle and crisis, created by himself, Shackleton, as usual, came into his own. He had the Irishman's instinctive theatricality on which to lean. No longer was he the somewhat seedy amateur financier. Behind an expansive, guileless manner, Shackleton reverted to the watchful, calculating, ruthless and utterly professional promoter of his own designs. But not quite.

"I feel much older and a bit weary," Shackleton, now at the age of thirty-nine, wrote to Elspeth Beardmore, "but perhaps the Antarctic will make me young again."[119]

XXX

Endurance

"Enough life and money has been spent on this sterile quest," Winston Churchill, who had recently become First Lord of the Admiralty, scrawled across the page. "The Pole has already been discovered. What is the use of another expedition?"[1]

"Though the Expedition has been promised a government Grant," Shackleton had written, rather more frankly than to the public or the King, "the funds at my disposal are still limited." Shackleton wanted his expedition ship – when he finally managed to obtain one – "fitted out in a Admiralty dockyard"; failing this, would my Lords of the Admiralty give him "the Stores for the equipment of the ship?"[2]

They would not. "These polar expeditions," Churchill sharply minuted, "are becoming an industry."[3]

In her own way, Emily Shackleton felt the same. "He always said each expedition would be his last," she plaintively wrote of her husband, "can you wonder that I believed it?"[4] Her feelings were sadly torn. She dreaded the parting; on the other hand the preparations signalled a happier interlude in what had become a fitful and fading marriage. With the prospect of escape, Shackleton shed most of his irritation with domesticity. Driving himself to the limit, he needed the comfort of wife and children around him. "Ernest has to go," Emily would say, "and so the only thing to do is to make it as easy for him as possible."[5] At her suggestion, perhaps, they took a house at 11, Vicarage Gate, South Kensington, to be closer in and have more time together. It meant double rent, but it all came out of her money.

From the expedition's birth, two tales have been handed down. One was that a merchant officer called Frank Worsley joined because, in his own words,

> One night I dreamed that Burlington Street was full of ice blocks and that I was navigating a ship along it . . . next morning I hurried like mad into my togs, and down Burlington Street I went . . . a sign on a doorpost caught my eye. It bore the words "Imperial Trans-Antarctic Expedition" . . . I turned into the building.[6]

The other tale is that Shackleton put this advertisement in the press:

> Men wanted for Hazardous Journey. Small wages, bitter cold, long months of complete darkness, constant danger, safe return doubtful. Honour and recognition in case of success.[7]

The first is more likely than the second. There was a man called Worsley. He did join Shackleton. The expedition headquarters were at No 4, New Burlington Street.

Shackleton, on the other hand, had no need to advertise. In his sly support, Lloyd George had been politically shrewd. "This expedition," as Shackleton wrote to an old friend, "calls for . . . more responsibility than when I went out last without the eyes of the British nation upon me."[8]

Sir Ernest Shackleton was a popular hero yet. His new expedition was hailed by the press with a deluge of delight; and "no wonder", as the *Montreal Star* percipiently remarked. "No matter what splendid compensations there were in the story of Capt. Scott's journey to the South Pole, his failure to be first there was a sore blow to British pride."[9] Overnight, journalists and applications from hopeful volunteers descended on 4, New Burlington Street. A small, drab block among the cloth merchants off Regent Street, it now happened to be the Tabard address too, and the Tabard secretary, F. W. White, quondam director of the Celtic Investment Trust, doubled as expedition secretary. Already installed behind plain desks to run the office were two old *Nimrod* men, Frank Wild and George Marston.

They were the first to join the new expedition. Ever since *Nimrod*, Wild had been waiting to follow Shackleton again. Meanwhile, he had been south with Mawson, and cut his teeth as second-in-command. Marston, too, was devoted to Shackleton. Staying in England as an art teacher, he had kept in touch, and satisfied Shackleton's need for people always around in support. With Wild and Marston, as the office opened, was Shackleton, waving a telegram from Amundsen; just possibly solicited: "My warmest wishes for your magnificent undertaking."[10]

In aiming for the first crossing of Antarctica, the "ambition of Sir

Ernest Shackleton", explained *The Times*, was to "re-establish the prestige of Great Britain in . . . Polar exploration".[11] That was no doubt true, but Shackleton knew exactly how to use the press. He was "one more proof of the dogged nature of British courage",[12] and therefore, as *The Times*, put it, the announcement was published "with a satisfaction which will be universally shared".[13] That, more or less, was what the other papers said.

But others, besides Winston Churchill, were less than enthusiastic. To the Secretary of the Admiralty, Evan MacGregor, for example, Shackleton was "this adventurer".[14] Sir Clements Markham, eighty-four years old, and as scurrilous as ever, was "astounded at the absurdity of Shackleton's plan", as he railed in a letter to Scott Keltie; it was "designed solely for self-advertisement".[15]

Shackleton planned to start from the Weddell Sea coast and cross the continent via the South Pole to the Ross Sea. He proposed following in Filchner's tracks. An under-rated explorer, Filchner had come back with perhaps the most important Antarctic discovery since James Clark Ross. He had found the southern limit of the Weddell Sea, hence filling in a vital gap in the continental coastline, and defining the journey overland towards the Pole. He had discovered the ice shelf which now bears his name, and also a new coast which he called Prince Regent Luitpold Land, after the Regent of Bavaria. At the junction of the two, he found a possible landing place at what he called Vahsel Bay. That was named after the not wholly sympathetic captain of the *Deutschland*, who had died of a heart complaint on the voyage.

From the Pole onwards, Shackleton at first considered following Amundsen's route down the Axel Heiberg Glacier to the Bay of Whales. That would have saved a hundred miles on the polar plateau. Amundsen's mountain crossing, however, was technically too demanding. His charting was sketchy. Without one of Amundsen's party as a guide, therefore, Shackleton would have been hard put to it to find his way. In the end, therefore, he decided to use his old route down the Beardmore Glacier to McMurdo Sound. He knew it all too well, and he had a reasonable map.

Early in the southern summer, Shackleton intended to land at Vahsel Bay, and start immediately on his continental crossing. His ship, meanwhile, would sail half-way round Antarctica to pick him up on the other side. Carrying all his supplies, and doing without depots, he blithely hoped to accomplish the journey in one season without wintering at all. *In case* there was a hitch, a whaler would be landed, and he would finish off with his old ambition of a great open-boat journey.

This plan owed much to W. S. Bruce, for whom Shackleton had organised a welcome after Bruce's Antarctic expedition at the same time as *Discovery*. In 1908, Bruce had published a plan to cross Antarctica, using one ship. Indeed, he announced his start for 1911. Money was the stumbling block; his idea was stillborn and without the least *arrière pensée*, he let Shackleton adopt his scheme. They had the greatest possible respect for each other.

At some point, Shackleton was persuaded to adopt a saner plan. He would take two ships. One would sail out with him to the Weddell Sea; the other make for the Ross Sea and bring him home. The latter would also land a support party to lay depots along the route. Shackleton offered Eric Marshall command of the Ross Sea party, but in Marshall's words, "Shackleton [knew] that he was physically incapable of severe strain at 11,000 ft."[16]

> I [therefore] considered the chances of crossing the Antarctic plateau were too remote to be considered seriously, and . . . any work I put in for that object was a waste of time.[17]

Since *Nimrod*, Marshall had been turning against Shackleton, but even Hugh Robert Mill, Shackleton's staunchest friend, had doubts. "I want you to be on my side as you have always been," Shackleton pleaded:

> I desperately want to have one more go . . . I know you do not believe in tempting Fortune in this particular sphere too often, but I feel that I would make good.[18]

Mill, however, was unshakeable. He refused his support, in private or in public. It was, he said, "the nearest thing to a break in our friendship, but the friendship did not break".[19] That said much for Mill's character. To Shackleton, under normal circumstances, those who were not for him, were against him.

To Mill, the enterprise was clouded from the start. The trans-antarctic crossing was about 1,500 miles. Shackleton optimistically counted on covering the distance in 100 days. That meant fifteen miles a day, without any allowance for delays. Even Amundsen, by now demonstrably the finest polar traveller of his generation, had only managed just over sixteen miles a day on his great southern journey. Besides, nobody had been that way before. From the Weddell Sea to the Pole, the terrain was uncharted and unknown.

Even before he reached land, Shackleton's enterprise was over-laid with doubt. Vahsel Bay offered no proven landing. The

Weddell Sea was still only sketchily known. "No two voyagers," said Mill, "had found similar conditions."[20] Unlike the Ross Sea, with its open water to the south, the Weddell Sea was a slow, sinister maelstrom of ice. The three expeditions since the turn of the century did not promise well. Bruce's *Scotia* had had to turn away. The wreck of Nordenskjöld's *Antarctic* was a warning. Filchner's *Deutschland* was a warning too. She was caught in the pack, drifted for nine months, and narrowly escaped *Antarctic*'s fate.

In all this the RGS, as usual, played an equivocal role. Shackleton expected no help because, as he put it, "they are hidebound and narrow," and he was not a "particular pet . . . of theirs."[21] On 12 January 1914, nonetheless, the RGS gave Shackleton £1,000, unasked. It was in fact the first definite gift to the expedition.

The RGS did, however, have second thoughts. Shackleton's was not the only Antarctic expedition in prospect: Otto Nordenskjöld was planning to go to Graham Land; a certain J. Foster Stackhouse was aiming, amongst other things, at King Edward VII Land; and Dr Felix König, an Austrian, proposed going to Vahsel Bay. Each, in his own way, appealed to the RGS more than Shackleton.

Nordenskjöld wanted to establish a joint Swedish-British scientific station for five years near his old base off Graham Land. "This," Keltie told him, "is the kind of exploration I think we now want in the Antarctic."[22] Stackhouse, a Quaker, claimed his expedition to be "a duty laid upon me [by] my friend, the late Captain Scott", and that it called for "the finest qualities of British endurance".[23] Dr König, having been with Filchner when he discovered Vahsel Bay, claimed priority over Shackleton, and accused him of poaching. "It was very undesirable," the RGS resolved, undoubtedly pointing at Amundsen, "that there should be brought against an English explorer . . . charges similar to those . . . in other and recent cases."[24] A citadel of appeasement, self-appointed keeper of the world's geographical conscience, the RGS deprecated Shackleton's blunt response: "I do not recognize Dr König's claim,"[25] as he told *The Times*. "I cannot alter plans long since formulated," he wrote to Dr König. "I suggest that you should make some other base";[26] and took care to have that also published in the press.

Even the RGS, however, had not been able to resist the momentum and credibility Shackleton had built up. Warned by the applause for *Nimrod*, as it were, they bought with their £1,000 a share in his success but they were also troubled by his hazy plans. They summoned Shackleton on 4 March to a committee of enquiry. The chairman was the RGS President; Lord Curzon himself, tall sleek, high-minded, preposterously dignified, ex-Viceroy of India, very much the imperial grandee.

The Committee of Enquiry, by definition, was not to enquire, but to evade responsibility in case of failure. Shackleton, of course, grasped this very well. Beyond his intention to sail for the Weddell Sea in August via Buenos Aires and South Georgia, his plans were vague. Nor would his finances bear scrutiny. On the other hand, for the sheen of responsibility it lent to his complicated manoeuvring, Shackleton urgently needed to retain the endorsement of the RGS. "I was only too glad to come," he sweetly explained, "because I like to be taken seriously. I am perfectly aware that a lot of people do not take me seriously."[27] One committee man said afterwards,

> I well remember the impossibility of getting any clear answers out of Shackleton. He always answered two or three questions together, or one question in two or three different pieces.[28]

To Curzon, after his seven years as Viceroy, steeped in the guile and evasiveness of India, all this was childishly transparent. On balance, he sympathised with Shackleton. They shared a keen sense of the ridiculous. Both were entirely out of place among the worthy RGS committee-men. In Shackleton, Curzon no doubt recognised the extraordinary Anglo-Irishmen who had been so eminent in the conquest of India, such as John Nicholson of the Punjab, whose "name cowed whole provinces".[29] The committee, on the other hand, reminded him too depressingly of the incorruptible dullness of the Indian civil service. Shackleton, meanwhile, with a grand gesture announced that he would require only £500 of the £1,000 granted by the RGS.

In the midst of all this, the actual preparations were comparatively straightforward. At the office in New Burlington Street, Wild and Marston culled the blend of drifters, adventurers, escapists, idealists, that had become familiar with every succeeding polar expedition – five thousand of them. One visitor at the end of February, though not to join, was Roald Amundsen.

Amundsen, as someone who was present put it, was "frank and outspoken".[30] He quietly elaborated on his spectacular vindication of dogs and ski; at least he had cured Shackleton of his bizarre fixation with horses. Shackleton was going to cross Antarctica with dogs, and had ordered a hundred from the Hudson's Bay Company in Canada.

Amundsen regarded Shackleton with a mixture of awe and disbelief. Two years after returning from the Antarctic, he himself seemed further than ever from continuing his Arctic drift, while

Shackleton somehow had contrived to conjure up opportunity. Shackleton's gale of improvisation, on the other hand, was not the methodical preparation in which Amundsen believed. It suited Shackleton, however. If he gave others – or himself – time to think, he was lost. In similar fashion his ship, so to speak, fell into his hands.

A rising young Norwegian shipowner called Lars Christensen had formed a partnership with Adrien de Gerlache to run what they called "polar safaris" to Spitsbergen and East Greenland. It was a project of Shackletonian optimism. A special ship was ordered, a wooden barquentine of 300 tons, called *Polaris*. She was built at Sandefjord, the Norwegian whaling port and Christensen's home town.

When *Polaris* was completed, in the summer of 1913, de Gerlache was unable to pay his share, and the scheme collapsed. *Polaris* was put on the market. Her builders, the Framnaes yard, were famous for their polar ships, and she was reputedly one of the strongest ships ever built for the ice. Nonetheless, she turned out to be something of a white elephant. With ten cabins, a darkroom for amateur photographers, and no cargo space, she was useless for sealing. Nor was she luxurious enough for a yacht. *Polaris* rode dismally at anchor in the fjord outside the yard, idle and unwanted.

Late in 1913, Stackhouse appeared as a prospective buyer, but *Polaris* was less than an ideal expedition ship, and he withdrew. When, therefore, Shackleton told de Gerlache in January 1914 that he was looking for a ship, he appeared like a fairy godmother. *Polaris* was pressed on him, and he bought her for 225,000 kroner (£11,600). He did not actually have the money; but he did not have to pay for some months yet. Christensen was only too pleased to help by laying out the deposit himself.

Shackleton changed her name from *Polaris* to *Endurance*, which he had wanted to do in the case of *Nimrod*. As captain, he wanted John King Davis; but Davis thought the whole enterprise foredoomed, and refused. So, as on *Nimrod*, Shackleton had to make do with a second choice, and put Frank Worsley in command.

Endurance was going to the Weddell Sea. For the Ross Sea, Shackleton turned to Douglas Mawson. Mawson had never forgiven Shackleton for his "crooked dealing" over Lysaght's money. However, *Aurora*, Mawson's expedition ship, now back from the Antarctic, was lying idle at Hobart. "Upon a cable," as Mawson eloquently put it, "I let [Shackleton] have the *Aurora* and Stores for £3,200."[31]

Shackleton, meanwhile, wanted to man *Aurora* with a naval crew. He wrote to the Admiralty, urging upon them "the Imperial character of the Expedition and the fact that it will be the last great British expedition that can hope to discover large tracts of land".

> I have received a large number of applications from men and officers in H.M. Navy . . . Naturally my inclination . . . would be to have some of these men . . . for the good of the Expedition . . . and for the moral good I feel will result for a happy combination of the premier service with our mercantile marine . . . as an old merchant officer, I feel deeply the compliment that these men pay me in asking to serve under me . . . tried men and good comrades would mean for me the easing of a load of responsibility.[32]

There was more in this than mere flattery. *Aurora* would be far away, out of his control. He had to depend utterly on her party; and naval men, he knew, could be trusted to carry out orders. However, he had half promised command of *Aurora* to Æneas Mackintosh from *Nimrod*. This was a sentimental gesture after Mackintosh had lost his eye. He was, however, as Shackleton well knew, too impetuous, and not exactly a dependable leader. With a naval crew, Mackintosh could decently be left behind, or taken as a subordinate.

The First Sea Lord, Prince Louis of Battenberg, was severely discouraging when Shackleton came to see him. For one thing, Shackleton had stirred up the complex emotions between the Navy and the merchant service. For another, war with Germany now seemed inevitable. As the Second Sea Lord, Vice Admiral Sir John Jellicoe, put it, there was a "shortage of officers and men",[33] but to Shackleton, this was hardly the final answer. At the end of February, he appealed directly to the First Lord, Winston Churchill, and took him out to lunch.

It was a strange encounter. At the age of thirty-nine, Churchill already ruled the greatest Navy in the world. Shackleton was one year older and mysteriously baffled. Yet they had something in common. Churchill's slightly pudgy, pugnacious face with its shadow of a frown, suggested a fellow combative soul and man of action.

"Do please look favourably upon . . . our talk," Shackleton wrote to Churchill the following day:

> I will return the men safe and undamaged, as far as God wills it . . . the majority of the men will never be out of touch with civilisation for more than three months . . . so that if you want [them] back for war purposes they could . . . return to England, and I would have the ship manned with a scratch crew.

"You know from our talk yesterday that I am trying to do good and serious work," Shackleton continued, using one of his catch phrases,

> Death is a very little thing, and Knowledge very great. You yourself, for the sake of science and country, are often taking risks aloft in the pioneer science of aviation . . . and really Regent Street holds out more dangers on a busy day than the five million square miles that constitute the Antarctic Continent.

"If I go on this Expedition without the Senior Service being represented," Shackleton continued,

> it will be the first time in the history of Polar exploration, which . . . has brought forth for the last three hundred years the best qualities of the seaman and has been the brightest page in the history of our sea story . . . It means much to the country, and it means a great deal to me.[34]

"I have some sympathy with these views," Sir John Jellicoe minuted, but Churchill was the last person to be overcome by rhetoric. Shackleton was allowed to take one officer and no more. He turned out to be an idiosyncratic Anglo-Irishman, Captain Thomas Hans Orde-Lees, of the Royal Marines.

Orde-Lees was a public schoolboy, from Marlborough. His father was a formidable Victorian eccentric, who had been Chief Constable of Northamptonshire, and designed a chief constable's dress uniform. Tall, dark, with the enigmatic ghost of a constant private smile, Orde-Lees had served in China during the Boxer Rebellion. It was on hearing Nansen lecture in 1897 after his return from the drift of the *Fram* that Orde Lees "came to the conclusion", as he put it, that he "would go polar exploring one day".[35] He tried unsuccessfully to join Scott's second expedition. When he approached Shackleton, Orde-Lees was Superintendent of Physical Training at the Royal Marine Depot school at Deal. There, he had become the first to introduce Swedish drill to the armed services. What persuaded Shackleton to take Orde-Lees, however, was that he was a skier and climber. In addition, he was a motoring pioneer, and was experimenting with motor sledges.

As Orde-Lees told the tale, he rode up from Deal to London on his motorcycle for his first interview with Shackleton "to give him some idea that I had a practical knowledge of internal combustion engines". Shackleton, in what was becoming a familiar pattern, instantly, and to Orde-Lees' amazement, accepted him. The Admiralty at first refused to let him go, but told him he could retire, if he liked. "That I could not afford to do", as Orde-Lees put it.

> I passed word to Shackleton. "Come up and see me again", he wired.
>
> I went up. We got into a taxi and drove to the Admiralty . . . Straight into Mr Churchill's office we walked. He greeted Shackleton warmly, but . . . seemed taken aback when Shackleton said "I want you, if possible, to release this man for my expedition" . . . Churchill, addressing me, said, "Very well you can go if you're willing to lose time and pay". I was at once in a dilemma, reflecting on my encumbrances, wife and child. I turned to Shackleton for help and advice. With only a fraction of a twinkle in his eye and a simulation nod on his part, I turned to Mr Churchill and said "Ay, ay Sir" at which I thought he gave a faint smile. To my intense relief Shackleton then said "I'll see to that, Mr Churchill", and he did.
>
> The moment we got outside he told me that he had decided to give me £300 a year . . . more than I was getting as a captain of Marines, and would, together with my small private means, keep my "belongings" in modest comfort until I returned.[36]

As a special concession Shackleton was also allowed to take any seamen who had been with Scott and, as the Admiralty put it, were "near the end of their engagements".[37] Consequently, Shackleton was, after all, compelled to make Æneas Mackintosh captain of *Aurora* and commander of the Ross Sea party.

The War Office was more tolerant than the Admiralty. That was chiefly because the War Minister, Colonel Seely, a dashing cavalryman, found Shackleton notably sympathetic. So Lieutenant F. Dobbs, of the Royal Dublin Fusiliers, and Lieutenant Courtney Brocklehurst, of the 10th Hussars, Sir Philip Brocklehurst's brother, were allowed to join the expedition.

The War Office helped in another way. Colonel Wilfred Beveridge, the Army nutrition expert, was a pioneer of modern dietetics and already a recognised authority. Shackleton was led to him by an astonishing capacity for grasping essential technical developments. Malnutrition, Shackleton knew from Scott's men, had killed Scott. Beveridge was impressed when Shackleton consulted him, for Scott had not. Shackleton asked Beveridge to work out sledging rations; the first time a British polar explorer actually commissioned a specialist to do so.*

Partly because of Shackleton's personality, "a breezy sailor", as he put it, Beveridge dropped his ordinary work to do the job

* Nansen, on the first crossing of Greenland, 1888 to 1889, was probably the first polar explorer to do this. Amundsen followed suit.

quickly. Scurvy was the foe that Shackleton feared. Beveridge proposed to prevent it with the newly discovered "vitamines"; the word itself was hardly two years old. This was one of the first occasions when vitamins were actually specified in a diet.

Also ahead of his time in another field, Shackleton wanted dehydrated food to save weight on the march. The technique was then being pioneered by the German chemical industry, in which William Dederich had interests. Dederich proposed to supply the transcontinental party with the new products. "Five professors in Germany," he had told reporters, were "testing and improving their quality."[38]

Early in the spring, Shackleton's shadowy backer, Alfred Harvey, "made such impossible conditions", as Shackleton told the King's Secretary, "that I could not continue with him".[39] Shackleton, however, had persuaded Lloyd George to promise the government grant only because Harvey – if he existed – made that a condition of his own gift. Lloyd George, for his part, would only make the grant when he was certain that the balance would be found elsewhere. Shackleton concealed Harvey's defection, and hurried round to replace his promised gift before the Treasury found out.

As the *London Mail*, a weekly journal of gossip* put it,

> The mercenary side of a Polar "stunt" is absorbing. Any day you may see Sir Ernest – always alone – taxi-ing from one newspaper office to another. He is trying to arrange the best terms and it is going to be a battle royal both for the news and pictorial rights.[40]

In the end it was the *Daily Chronicle* that bought the rights. That, however, was hardly enough.

With all his chequered financial dealings, the taint of a brother in prison, the yet unpublished *Nimrod* accounts, and William Beardmore's hostility, Ernest Shackleton did not exactly invite trust. He nonetheless maintained the outward show of confidence.

"Would greatly value favourable opinion from you on my plans for publication at once in private circular I am sending out," Shackleton cabled Nansen urgently in the middle of April, "reply paid 100 words."[41] "The crossing," Nansen obliged by replying, "I consider most important, and an Expedition of the highest value, which will bring great results."[42] The circular, soliciting subscriptions, was sent to several hundred wealthy people.

As a result, or otherwise, Shackleton extracted from Dudley

* Very much concerned with the theft of the Irish crown jewels. It practically accused Frank Shackleton of benefiting from the proceeds.

Docker, of the BSA company in Birmingham, a gift of £10,000 to pay for *Endurance*. Lord Iveagh, once more, guaranteed a loan, this time for £5,000. Finally, an Australian banker living in London, Sir Robert Lucas-Tooth, guaranteed another £5,000. It was enough to save the government grant, which was officially announced on 4 May. Only half was to be paid that year, however. The remaining £5,000 had to wait until 1915. Various benefactors obliged with small donations. Neville Chamberlain, for example, then an alderman of Birmingham, gave £5. Elizabeth Dawson-Lambton, faithful still, produced money for Shackleton yet again. The big donors hung back; but at this point Shackleton approached a wealthy spinster called Janet Stancomb-Wills.

Miss Stancomb-Wills was the adopted daughter of Sir W. H. Wills (later Lord Winterstoke), a tobacco millionaire. She lived at Ramsgate, in a large house called East Court, which overlooked the sea. A town councillor and philanthropist, she was, in the words of someone who, as a child, knew her,

> a formidable head of an impressive household . . . She was extremely well built – had an upright carriage and an ample chest which showed off jewellery to good effect.[43]

Shackleton was led to Janet Stancomb-Wills through Ernest Perris, of the *Daily Chronicle*. Like many older women, she fell quietly in love with Shackleton. "Into my life you flashed, like a meteor out of the dark," began a poem she wrote to him, "Flooding its peaceful dullness with a splendour of glowing light."[44] Shackleton, for his part, knew how to play up to such feelings. Miss Stancomb-Wills gave generously to the expedition; although how much, was carefully concealed.

Early in June, *Endurance* arrived from Norway in the Thames. Amongst other things Shackleton, to increase her steaming range, had ordered her conversion to burn oil as well as coal. De Gerlache, in the uneasy dual role of Christensen's partner and Shackleton's agent, had supervised the work at Sandefjord. He was also captain for the crossing. Seventeen years before, almost to the day, de Gerlache had departed in *Belgica* on the voyage that opened modern Antarctic exploration. Now Shackleton, like himself, was still short of money. Who, at the eleventh hour, would play the deus ex machina?

On Monday, 29 June, the *Daily Graphic*, like most of Fleet Street, reported "SCOTS MILLIONAIRE'S GIFT TO SIR E. SHACKLETON". The adjacent headline, incidentally, was "PLOTS AGAINST THE ARCHDUKE, ADVISED NOT TO

MAKE THE TRIP TO BOSNIA". "The Archduke" was Franz Ferdinand, the heir to the Austrian throne. The day before, he had been assassinated at the obscure town of Sarajevo."WHERE IT IS COOL", ran another *Daily Graphic* headline on the following Friday. That was over a front page picture showing Shackleton in Norway, in the snow. The strange, hot summer of 1914 was under way.

It was actually in the middle of May that Shackleton had visited Norway to test his equipment and also to fetch *Endurance*, but when he reached Sandefjord, he found de Gerlache acutely embarrassed. *Endurance* was not ready. She would be a month delayed.

In any case it was to Finse, with its glacier, at the summit of the Christiania-Bergen railway, that Shackleton went for a rehearsal in the snow. "I am rather tired," he scribbled in a note to Emily, "but really splendidly fit." Eleven years after he had staggered back to *Discovery* from the south, Shackleton was trying to ski again. It was, as he put it, "rather hard after my sedentary life at the office",[45] but Amundsen had convinced him that his prejudice against ski had probably cost him the Pole in 1908; and that without them, he was unlikely to cross Antarctica alive.

At Finse, Shackleton was mainly testing equipment. That included two motor sledges, Heath Robinson contraptions, driven by propellers, designed by Orde-Lees. Shackleton also tried out new dome tents, designed by Marston and himself for reduced wind resistance and ease of pitching. They were well ahead of their time.

Shackleton really believed that a few days' hasty work could solve complex technical problems. He was, however, still desperately trying to raise funds, and the visit to Finse had been for publicity too. Perhaps that was what had influenced the "Scots millionaire". He was Sir James Key Caird, Bart, a Dundee jute magnate and a friend of Winston Churchill. Grey, goatee'd, austere, a linguist and well travelled, Sir James was a widower whose only child had died. He was a compulsive philanthropist. He had, for example, given £10,000 to propagandise Free Trade. In the middle of June, he asked Shackleton to visit him.

Sir James was not exactly interested in polar exploration. He had, however, heard various tales of Shackleton's personality. He was impressed by his determination in the face of financial setbacks. Shackleton, it emerged, had pledged to Lord Iveagh and Sir Robert Lucas-Tooth, as security for their guarantees the income from his book and lectures on the expedition. Sir James did not approve. Did Shackleton think they would release him from his obligations, if he were to tell them that there was a man in Scotland who would find the money still required? Nothing quite like this had happened to Shackleton before. He kept his self-possession. A few days later, he received from Sir James a note to say that

> I have pleasure in giving you my cheque for £24,000, without any conditions, in the hope that others may make their gifts for this Imperial journey also free of all conditions.[46]

"This magnificent gift," Shackleton told the *Morning Post*, "relieves me of all anxiety."[47] Even then, however, an echo from his brother's trial was haunting him. He was being sued by Miss Mary Josephine Browne.

Under her feathered hat, behind her plump, homely face, Miss Browne, when she left the courtroom after Frank Shackleton's conviction, nursed implacable bitterness. Punishment of the culprit would not bring back her money. What rankled was the £1,000 taken from her to replace Elizabeth Dawson-Lambton's misappropriated donation to the *Nimrod* expedition. Miss Browne (or her lawyers) decided she could recover this at least from Ernest Shackleton instead. Because of his impending departure, Miss Browne asked the High Court on 14 July to expedite the case.

Two days later, Shackleton received Queen Alexandra when, at her own desire, she inspected *Endurance* at the London docks, and showered him with gifts and good wishes. Vividly she remembered him from the *Nimrod* expedition, and the last days of her much missed husband, Edward VII. The atmosphere was very different now. With her was her sister, another melancholy royal widow, the Dowager Empress Maria Feodorovna of Russia, oppressed by the thunderclouds gathering over Europe. Both were clearly fascinated by Shackleton. Also on board, in one of her rare public appearances, was Emily Shackleton; unhappy now, and somehow apart from her husband.

Sir Philip Brocklehurst, meanwhile, was pressing for the repayment of the loan of £2,000 he had guaranteed. Shackleton had actually asked him to sail down as far as the ice "to renew old times",[48] as he put it; but Sir Philip (he said) was being harried by the bank. Perhaps his bankers, too, were worried by the prospect of Shackleton's imminent disappearance into the ice.

Shackleton somehow temporised. More or less according to plan, therefore, on Saturday 1 August, 1914, *Endurance* sailed. To be absolutely sure there would be no last-minute hitch, Shackleton had settled with Miss Browne out of court, by paying the money claimed in full.

*

There was an air of unreality as *Endurance*, gleaming in white and gilt under a cloudless sky, nosed out of the West India Docks into the muddy stream. On a dilapidated wharf, a crowd raggedly cheered. Bunting hung limply in the summer heat. The cacophony of ships' sirens tolled *Endurance* down the Thames from London to the sea. The skirl of a solitary bagpipe played her off. "In delicate allusion to the fact that there are . . . Irishmen in the expedition, including the leader," as the *Manchester Guardian* reported, "the piper struck up 'The Wearing o' the Green'."[49] It seemed a variation of *Discovery*'s and *Nimrod*'s departure for the south; but the day before, the Stock Exchange had closed.

The previous Monday, Shackleton had received a telegram from Tryggve Gran. By now a qualified pilot, Gran was definitely not sailing on *Endurance*. "Flying," as he put it, "was not yet suited for polar activities."[50] Gran, in any case, was now at Cruden Bay, near Aberdeen, waiting to fly over the North Sea. When he went to telegraph Shackleton, Gran, to his "great horror saw a notice that, because of the threatening situation, all civil flying over Britain was forbidden after 6 p.m. on the 30th July".[51] So, a few hours before the ban came into force, Gran, leather-helmeted and be-goggled, took off. He came down safely near Stavanger, in Norway, after four hours in the open cockpit of a flimsy contraption of wood and silk. Until the Atlantic was crossed, it was the longest flight out of sight of land. Gran also carried the world's first airmail with him, but in the gathering crisis, he was half ignored.

On the Tuesday, Austria-Hungary had declared war on Serbia. It was all part of the drama opened by the shot at Sarajevo. Churchill, and Shackleton's other high acquaintances, were playing what seemed like preordained roles. On the Friday the Tsar ordered Russian mobilisation. Next day, the Kaiser declared war on Russia. "Everybody is preparing swiftly for war," Churchill wrote to his wife from the Admiralty, "and at any moment now the stroke may fall."[52]

Even so, on the Saturday, when *Endurance* left her dock, no frontiers had actually been crossed. Like most Britons, Shackleton was persuaded by a century of isolation from Europe that a continental war would not affect him. As he sailed down the Thames, however, events developed with bewildering rapidity. By the Monday morning, when *Endurance* was anchored off Margate, Germany had invaded Luxembourg, and demanded free passage for her troops through Belgium. When Shackleton went ashore he found that the Navy had been mobilised.

Back on board *Endurance*, he was faced with an almost demoralising restlessness. Dobbs and Courtney Brocklehurst had already left to rejoin their regiments. Although Britain was still technically neutral, warships were belching smoke up and down the Channel. Frank Worsley, the captain of *Endurance*, in his own words, "indicated desire to fight . . . before proceeding on expedition".[53]

Shackleton was plunged into a dilemma. Would the clash of arms really break the fulfilment of ambition? But Shackleton's solution was characteristic. He mustered the crew, announced that everyone was free to leave and then, with Worsley's acquiescence, telegraphed the Admiralty offering to place

> ship staff stores and provisions at your disposal recognising the claims of my country before all other considerations respectfully submitting that if required the expedition be used as one unit. If not required I propose continuing voyage forthwith as any delay would prevent expedition getting through the pack ice this year.[54]

"Expect Expedition will be postponed," he telegraphed to Emily. A few hours later, the Admiralty declined the offer, allowing the expedition to proceed. Shackleton interpreted this as an order, which was a comfort for his conscience. *Endurance* therefore sailed on down Channel, while Germany declared war on France, and the crisis moved to its culmination.

Late on the Saturday night the author H. H. Munro, "Saki", together with a friend, had passed a London club where a dinner was apparently being given in honour of Shackleton. Saki, according to his companion,

> was keenly sorry for [Shackleton] who was leaving England and civilization, where communication of current events could not reach him. It seemed so tragic to him. Then the excitement watching the changing posters of the newsboys and the motley cries and loud opinions of the passers-by.[55]

Stopping at Eastbourne to put Shackleton ashore, *Endurance* continued to Plymouth, her last port of call. Emily had moved to Eastbourne with the children, but that was not exactly why Shackleton had landed. It was Tuesday, 4 August, and he had to be in touch with events. Britain had sent Germany an ultimatum to respect the neutrality of Belgium. At midnight, Berlin time, the ultimatum expired, but from Berlin, no answer came.

Too late, in London, as Big Ben chimed the hour, the Liberal ministers lamely grasped that British moral disapproval was not an efficacious deterrent, and their ultimatum had led inexorably to war. At 10, Downing Street, Churchill "dashed into the [Cabinet] room, radiant, his face bright, his manner keen", as Lloyd George recalled,

> one word pouring on another how he was going to send telegrams to the Mediterranean, the North Sea, and God knows where. You could see he was a really happy man.[56]

Under similar circumstances, this could be Shackleton himself. He, too, was living in a spate of telegrams. "Dobbs Brocklehurst . . . called up for service they must go," he wired Emily from London on 5 August, the first day of the war.

> King sent for me this morning spent twenty minutes there wished the expedition godspeed and gave me silk union jack.[57]

When *Endurance* put into Plymouth, however, Worsley, and D. G. Jeffrey, the Chief Officer, "Went to R.N. Barracks to see if any chance of getting into scrap," as Worsley put it, "but Commodores Sec[retary] told us no chance just then as not the whole of the Reserve had been called out."[58] Jeffrey, nonetheless, felt he could not sail now that war had been declared. At forty-eight hours' notice another merchant officer, Lionel Greenstreet, signed on in his stead. Greenstreet had also tried for a naval commission, but on being told to wait until "things settled down", decided that in the meanwhile, he might as well go south. Orde-Lees, after some heart-searching, also decided to sail.

At noon on 8 August, *Endurance* sailed from Plymouth and left the shores of England. On 21 August, following the now familiar route of ships Antarctic bound, she reached Madeira, which was still a neutral port. Anchored next to *Endurance* was SS *Hochfeld*, a German ship, which swung foul of her during the night. Next morning Worsley, captain as he was, boarded the *Hochfeld* with some of his crew and, as he wrote in his diary, "captured their 2nd & 3rd Engineers & Carpr. & put them on to repairing our jibboom where they had fouled it".[59]

Luckily for Worsley, Shackleton was not there to see him. As with the *Nimrod* expedition, much still remained to be cleared up at home. Now there was the complication of a war. Shackleton had stayed behind, to follow on by mailboat and overtake *Endurance* at Buenos Aires.

Despite Admiralty permission and royal support, Shackleton still was uncertain about proceeding. Dr König, his Austrian rival, had not been allowed the luxury of choice, and he and the members of his expedition were all forcibly turned into soldiers. His ship,

Deutschland, acquired from Filchner, was commandeered by the Austro-Hungarian Navy, and eventually sunk in the Adriatic. Such was the ironical conclusion of Wilhelm Filchner's words to Hugh Robert Mill that "science being an international property has nothing to do with politics".[60] Filchner himself, back in uniform, was now leading his company in the German march on Paris. As for Shackleton, who had shown "much understanding for Germany", as Filchner once said, he now told Emily, "I cannot think of the damned Germans without being furious I hope they will get smashed up."[61] On the other hand, "I do not particularly dislike the Germans," a friend wrote to Lady Diana Cooper, expressing a rarer, more prophetic point of view,

> my chief European preoccupation is the ultimate hegemony of the Russians, which it seems to me we are fighting to achieve.[62]

At least Shackleton now had the Antarctic continent to himself; but that only made the dilemma harder to resolve. The country was possessed by an eerie blend of war fever and "business as usual". In search of advice, Shackleton naturally gravitated to the top. He saw Lord Kitchener, whom he had met originally in New York. Kitchener, now War Minister, hinted, not too hopefully, at conscription, which would solve Shackleton's problem. Until then, it would be voluntary service. But Shackleton, at the age of forty, Kitchener would have explained, was too old and difficult to place. Ironically, Kitchener at this point was appealing for half a million recruits. His hooded eyes, over drooping moustaches, stared down from countless walls out of a famous recruiting poster: "Your country needs YOU".

It was Sir James Caird who finally settled the matter. "Now I see that the only thing for me is to go south," Shackleton told Emily after specially visiting Dundee to seek Sir James' advice.

> There are hundreds of thousands of young men who could go to the war and there are not any I think who could do my job.[63]

Charles Sarolea, Shackleton's Belgian brother-in-law, now a war correspondent "at £30 a week and his expenses", as Shackleton told Emily, "says . . . that the war will be over in 4 months not by battles but by starvation and internal revolution".[64] Ernest Perris at the *Daily Chronicle*, on the other hand, was "very much afraid that it is going to be a long business this war".[65] Either way, it argued for going on. If the war was short, there would be no chance to fight; if long, there would be plenty of time afterwards. Besides, there was the old doubt about his health. Would he be passed fit for military service?

So, as the British Army opened its first continental campaign since Waterloo and while the Germans annihilated the Russians at the Battle of Tannenberg, and the French stopped the Germans at the gates of Paris in the Battle of the Marne, Shackleton finished his preparations for the crossing of Antarctica as best he could.

"All these people here are chasing after their bills," he wrote to Emily from the office in New Burlington Street, "so I am having a fine time of it."[66] Early in September, Mackintosh was packed off to Australia in a hurry to prepare the ground for the Ross Sea party.

There were rushed visits to Janet Stancomb-Wills at Ramsgate. Shackleton "would pace up & down, pouring out plans and hopes and ideals",[67] as she recalled. The eye, as usual, was watching what the heart was saying. Occasionally, through the window, came the distant roll of the guns in Flanders. Miss Stancomb-Wills comforted him with the promise that, while he was away, she would support his family. He could depart with a reasonably clear conscience.

Finally, on 19 September, according to the press, Shackleton left Liverpool on the Houlder Bros. liner, SS *La Negra* to join *Endurance* at Buenos Aires. "The popular view," wrote the *Manchester Guardian*, would be that Shackleton was "going on a service fully as dangerous as that of active service."[68] "When he returns," as the *Irish Times* put it, "he may find that the whole political aspect of Europe, perhaps of the world, is changed."[69]

Shackleton was not actually on board *La Negra* when she sailed. He departed quietly one week later on another Houlder ship, *Urugayo*. "Family reasons," explained a Spanish newspaper when *Urugayo* touched at Vigo, "prevented him from sailing on *La Negra*."[70] Shackleton had quarrelled with Emily as they parted. He had turned back to try and make his peace. Also, at the last moment, Frank Shackleton had been released from prison, and that required attention too.

XXXI

South Georgia

"We are leaving now to carry on our white warfare," Shackleton, using one of his catch phrases, cabled from Buenos Aires, "and our farewell message to our country is that we will do our best to make good." It was 26 October, 1914. In the middle of the morning, *Endurance* sailed. The British community was down at the docks in force to see her off. Shackleton's farewell went on,

> Our thoughts and prayers will be with our brothers fighting at the front.
>
> We hope in our small way to add victories in science and discovery to that certain victory which our nation will achieve in the cause of honour and liberty.[1]

In England this, when it appeared, was generally taken as moral uplift. In calling it, waspishly, "A lost opportunity", when "Sir Ernest Shackleton decided to go not to the front but to the South Pole,"[2] the *Bystander* (a Society journal subsequently taken over by *The Tatler*) typified what criticism there was. Concern for *Endurance* centred on German raiders but, in the pious words of the *Evening Standard*, "being a vessel entirely devoted to exploration and non-combatant work, she is immune from seizure."[3] As *Endurance*, now repainted black, sailed down the wide, muddy reaches of the River Plate, dropped the pilot, and nosed into the South Atlantic, it was unmistakably the old world she was leaving astern.

On the third day out, a stowaway was found hiding in a locker in the fo'c'sle. He was a nineteen-year-old Welsh sailor called Percy Blackborrow, who had tried unsuccessfully to join at Buenos Aires. Shackleton appeared, together with Frank Wild. Blackborrow tried to stand to attention, but he was weak from seasickness and hunger. Shackleton ordered him to sit down, and then proceeded to bawl him out in a fit of what appeared to be ungovernable rage.

The sailors standing by were connoisseurs of seamanlike tongue-lashing; but even they were impressed by Shackleton's comprehensive tirade. That was partly the intention, since Blackborrow obviously must have had accomplices on board. The eye, as usual, was watching for effect. There were two certain culprits. One was a Canadian called William Bakewell, who had joined at Buenos Aires. The other was Walter How, a sailmaker, an East Ender from Bermondsey, who had spent five years in Arctic waters off Labrador. They had helped Blackborrow, because they feared that *Endurance* was short-handed. Of that, Shackleton was undoubtedly aware. Suddenly he bent down, put his face close to Blackborrow's and, as Wild recalled the scene, bellowed:

> Do you know that on these expeditions we often get very hungry, and if there is a stowaway available he is the first to be eaten?
>
> Shackleton was . . . fairly heavily built, and the boy looked him over and said, "They'd get a lot more meat off you, sir!"
>
> The Boss turned away to hide a grin and told me to turn the lad over to the bo'sun, but added, "Introduce him to the cook first". Blackborrow turned out to be a good sailor . . . and was duly signed on.[4]

It was not really so very different from Shackleton's method of choosing most others on the ship.

There was, for example, the chief surgeon, Dr Alexander Macklin, a doctor's son and, incidentally, of Ulster Protestant descent. Tall, thick-set, with a precise dark moustache set in a wide, placid face he seemed older than his twenty-four years, and gave a misleading impression of stolidity. In fact, underneath the surface, he suppressed considerable emotion. As a doctor, he had to do so, as a defence, in order to preserve his mental balance and practise his profession. Also, he concealed a restless streak. Between school and university, he went to sea before the mast. By his own account, like Orde-Lees, it was Nansen who inspired him with the desire for polar exploration, but in his case it was through discovering by chance the two volumes of *Furthest North* while he was a medical student at Manchester University.

When the *Endurance* expedition was announced, Macklin wrote a letter of application. Receiving no reply, he simply presented himself early one morning at the office in New Burlington Street, to meet what he called "a living avalanche" tearing down the stairs,

"Shackleton himself, obviously going out". Macklin blurted out his errand. Shackleton told him to go up and wait. In the afternoon, Shackleton finally returned, still in a tremendous hurry. The interview, in Macklin's words,

> was very brief –
> "Why do you want to go?"
> "I don't know, I just want to."
> "You look fit enough are you perfectly healthy . . . ?"
> "Perfectly fit."
> "What is wrong with your eyes?"
> "Nothing." [Macklin was short-sighted.]
> At this I could have kicked myself for not removing my spectacles before going in to see him. I scarcely knew what to say, but replied almost without thinking, "Many a wise face would look foolish without specs." At this he laughed, then seemed to be thinking of something else for he remained silent for several minutes. "All right, I'll take you," he said and with that pushed me out of his office.[5]

Wild had something to do with Macklin's persistence. They had met that day and, in Macklin's own words, "I was at once struck by the quiet, neat, bearded small man, with the kind blue eyes and air of general efficiency". Waiting for Shackleton, they went out to lunch when Macklin "particularly [took] stock of Wild. I determined that somehow I would find a way to go South with [him]".[6]

Dr James McIlroy, slightly built, handsome in a vaguely Mephistophelian way, and "a sardonic, sarcastic blighter",[7] as Greenstreet, the new Chief Officer who had signed on at Plymouth, put it, was very different from the self-contained, quiet-spoken Macklin. McIlroy had started by being miserable in an office, and then read medicine at Birmingham University. As he told the tale, he heard by chance at his club, the Devonshire, that Shackleton wanted a second surgeon. He had only just returned after years practising in Malaya, Egypt and Japan but a month or two of London had reminded him that "having been abroad in so many places, I couldn't have settled down in England". He telephoned the Expedition office. Shackleton immediately saw him, and seemed most concerned with the fact that McIlroy was shaking. "I'm a bit nervous in front of you", said McIlroy; for Shackleton, in McIlroy's own words, "could be a very frightening kind of individual."[8] McIlroy, however, was actually on sick leave, suffering from malaria. Both facts he was doing his best to conceal. Shackleton, rather crossly, told him to be medically examined. McIlroy somehow got a friendly physician to pass him fit, whereupon he was immediately accepted for the expedition. That no other surgeon had applied may have had something to do with the case. That McIlroy also was Irish, albeit an Ulsterman, probably counted too.

Exactly how Shackleton chose his men, he never explicitly revealed. A theatrical manager who once lunched with him in London, however, described how he

> was fascinated when I described the formation of a repertory company, and how character and temperament mattered quite as much as acting ability; just *his* problem, he said – *he* had to balance his types too, and their science or seamanship weighed little against the kind of chaps they were.[9]

As *Endurance* rolled her way over the South Atlantic swell the men on board discovered that "Shackleton afloat," as one of them said, was "a more likeable character than Shackleton ashore."[10] Greenstreet, on the other hand, by his own account easy-going, found Shackleton "a queer bird, a man of moods & I dont know whether I like him or not".[11]

Endurance had not started out a happy ship. At Buenos Aires, the crew were disloyal, insubordinate, and drunk. "This," said Orde-Lees, "shows something wrong somewhere, but," he went on, "it will all be put right when Sir Ernest arrives, thank goodness."[12] When Shackleton landed from England on 17 October, things rapidly changed. The worst seamen were discharged. "Port authorities", wrote Reginald William James, the expedition physicist,

> were pacified & all facilities granted all as a result of personal interviews. Shackleton was a great believer in the . . . personal interview & indeed I think he could persuade anyone to do almost anything if he could only talk to him. There was a mixture of personal magnetism bluff and blarney that could be irresistable.[13]

It was, in Orde-Lees' words, "splendid having Sir Ernest on board. Everything works like clockwork & one knows just where one is".

It was here that a revealing incident occurred. While manoeuvring the ship, Greenstreet fouled the propeller with a hawser, and Shackleton happened to be on the scene. It was a very nasty incident, Greenstreet's own fault, and he expected a dressing down. Instead, Shackleton quietly turned to, helped him out of the scrape, and never referred to the matter again. Shackleton never forgot, but he never recriminated. The past, as his men were to learn, to him was the past. He always looked ahead, trying to undo mistakes.

Not that Shackleton, with the mark of true leadership, appeared to do anything most of the time. It was Frank Wild – small, wiry, swift, apparently everywhere at once, worshipping Shackleton "almost like a spaniel",[14] as someone put it, the perfect second-in-command, who actually carried out the work. Wild had also joined *Endurance* at Buenos Aires. He had brought out from England the sledge dogs, who were now howling, grumbling, squabbling, fouling the decks, and generally being the most perplexing passengers.

Shackleton still seemed a corsair sailing out in search of fame and fortune. Neither Wild nor anyone else on board guessed what Shackleton, as he stalked the deck, was concealing behind the outer shell of invincible self-confidence.

"I am just good as an explorer, and nothing else," he had written to Emily. Partly it was his usual reaction to worry and overwork, but this outburst betrayed an unfamiliar note of melancholy and self-searching. "It seems a hard thing to say but," he went on, "I am just glad to . . . get out to my work and my own life."[15] This was not a cloak for self-destructiveness:

> If I can possibly get through this season you may rely on my doing so I dont want to delay neither do I want to lose my life down there.

Even after the last-minute turnabout, it was not as a happy man that Shackleton had parted from his wife. They had still quarrelled just as he was going. His farewell letters were a wild blend of reconciliation and remorse:

> I dont want you to say or think that you have been to blame for all the rows that arose [he wrote from the *Urugayo*, in the Bay of Biscay]. I think I am solely to be blamed: I expect I have a peculiar nature that the years have hardened.

Emily had by now felt a revival of her feelings for Sir Sidney Boulton, the man whom she originally had intended to marry, and the Lloyd's underwriter with whom Shackleton had dealt.

> I dont pay very much heed to the things you said about him, for I know that you are not the type of woman to be carried away especially with your eyes open and after all the children are an asset and an anchor to you.[16]

At Buenos Aires, the sombre mood of self-reproach persisted. "I know full well that I am wanting in many ways domestically," Shackleton wrote on the day *Endurance* sailed, that for some time past we have not seen eye to eye and that the fault lies with me that is the trouble and tragedy of life that one never stands still but always moves one way or the other. I wonder if you know me really: I am not worth much consideration if I were really known and I have shown you that or rather tried to show it to you only you think differently dont you?

I hardly know how to write only I dont want you to be all the time I am away worrying about me I am not worth your doing that: I have on the way out done a lot of thinking [he went on], and all to no purpose . . . I go round and round in a circle you have sometimes asked me to pretend and simulate feelings but I would be worse than I am if I did so; that deep down in your heart you know; and yet I am not without feelings as you know on the day I left London for this voyage I am a curious mixture with something feminine in me as well as being a man, and I had an uncomfortable weak feeling at leaving which according to the plan on which I am supposed by myself to be working out my life: should not exist; any how you cannot say that I am not honest and I know that you are fond of me but that at times I upset you.

"I have a curious nature," he said, revealing for a moment an inner darkness that is recognisably Irish, "and I have tried to analyse [it] without much success."

I have committed all sorts of crimes in thought if not always in action and dont worry much about it, yet I hate to see a child suffer or to be false in any way . . . I am hard also, and damnably persistent when I want anything: altogether a generally unpleasing character: I love the fight and when things [are] easy I hate it though when things are wrong I get worried. I am not going to write more in this strain I am a bit tired . . . and just wandering along.[17]

Shackleton was also ill. After leaving Buenos Aires, he suffered what he called "suppressed influenza". This was a highly personal concept, unknown in medical terminology. It stood for some recurrent trouble, a new and undefined shadow on his health. Of determinable illness, he had enlarged tonsils, and a horrible boil on his neck, pointing to some infection, possibly streptococcal. But still he refused to allow any doctor to approach him with a stethoscope. It was as if the one fear he knew was what might be discovered in his heart.

Shackleton, in any case – apart from the boil, which was only too plain – concealed his illness from his men. His diary, beyond perfunctory references, also hid anything physical that ailed him. His apparent concern was for the slow passage of *Endurance* labouring against the elements: "We need the brave west winds", he quoted on 1 November, "that sweep the sea floors white".

At Cape Coronel, that same day, off the coast of Chile, "it was not very pleasant waiting for the [Germans] to open fire", a British naval officer wrote. The Great War was reaching far out into the southern hemisphere. It was the first general engagement fought by the Royal Navy since Trafalgar. "We all knew it was hopeless," the officer continued, "and I was thinking how devilish cold the water would be and hoping a shell would get me first as being the pleasantest way out."

> The blowing up of the GOOD HOPE was an awful sight and I shall never forget it till I die.[18]

Almost a whole British squadron commanded by Admiral Cradock was sunk by a German force under Admiral von Spee. Now von Spee was headed around Cape Horn.

Of this, Shackleton was unaware. He had a wireless receiver, but it was not yet working. On the morning of 5 November, the savage, ice-clad peaks of South Georgia, like half-drowned Alps, loomed out of the mist. *Endurance*, having had a placid voyage, anchored outside the whaling station of Grytviken, at the end of a steep-sided fjord.

The whalers were surprised to see her. Originally, Shackleton had proposed sailing via Port Stanley, in the Falklands. At the last moment, over dinner at the Palace Hotel in Buenos Aires, he had announced his change of mind. He pleaded financial necessity. In reality, it was due to fear in the Falklands, cabled to the Colonial Office, and relayed by the British Ambassador, that von Spee might "evade Cradock's squadron and appear in the waters of the Colony".[19]

Also at Buenos Aires Shackleton had revealed another change of plan. After putting the landing party ashore, *Endurance* was supposed to return to civilisation for the winter. Now, as Walter How wrote to his wife, Ellen,

> The Ship will remain in the Ice . . . so you must cheer up & hope for the best . . . you need not worry as she is very strong & we have plenty of food & clothes & also we have had our wages rose to £7 [from £4] a month.[20]

Shackleton, meanwhile, in a long, melancholy letter, was explaining to Emily that "I do not trust Worsley enough to be sure he would be certain to get to the station next season to bring out the remainder of the shore party."[21]

Worsley was a New Zealander. He claimed to be part Maori, and probably was. Captain of *Endurance* all the way out to Buenos Aires, he had turned out to be wild, erratic and impulsive. He was unable to keep discipline. It was probably his appointment that made Greenstreet remark that Shackleton was "easily gulled over by talk . . . If you could . . . put a good story across, he'd fall for it."[22] Worsley, as Shackleton now wrote to Ernest Perris, was "not the type to hold men well together he is of a rather curious tactless nature so I am glad I will have the whole show under my own eyes."[23]

Shackleton himself, meanwhile, was investing South Georgia with Utopian attractions. It was an island more remote. It had no cablehead, nor wireless station yet. That meant no risk of an eleventh hour recall.

Besides, Shackleton was already thinking of life after the expedition. From Lars Christensen at Sandefjord, when buying *Endurance*, he had heard of the vast fortunes to be made from whaling and sealing. Before leaving England, he had obtained a sealing concession on the Falklands. At Buenos Aires, after visiting the Compania Argentina de Pesca, the company financing Grytviken, Shackleton decided that the money lay in whaling and in South Georgia.

The company was Argentinian in form alone. "Although the island is a British possession," Reginald James noted in his diary on arrival at South Georgia, "one might imagine oneself in Norway."[24] The place-names and the people told the story: Grytviken was a Norwegian outpost, and the staff mostly Norwegians. So were almost all South Georgia's summer population of two thousand souls. Whaling had brought them there. Norwegians then had a virtual monopoly of the whaling skills. As too often was the case the British, when they had an empire, were content with mere title to their territory; others took the trouble to reap the fruit.

Grytviken was the first of the whaling stations that had sprung up in South Georgia. Ten years before, South Georgia was an uninhabited, sub-Antarctic island. But in 1902, with the Nordenskjöld expedition, came C. A. Larsen. Larsen gave Grytviken its name, from *gryte*, Norwegian for a cauldron, and *vik*, a creek or inlet. He did so on finding blubber cauldrons strewn about the abandoned camps of sealers who had long since deserted the island after the virtual extermination of the southern fur seal.

After his open-boat journey and escape from shipwreck on Paulet Island Larsen, so the story goes, had been fêted as a hero at a banquet in Buenos Aires. In his after-dinner speech, he explained that he had been impressed with the number and size of the whales that he had seen. Despite all he had been through, he longed only to return to Grytviken and start whaling. Capital was not to be obtained in his native Norway; but he did find it in Buenos Aires, largely from expatriate financiers. By the time *Endurance* sailed up to Grytviken, it was a small township of wooden houses with a little wooden church, clinging to a narrow, snow-strewn strand between mountain, glacier and fjord. Until a few months before Shackleton arrived, Larsen had been general manager. Now, it was Larsen's son-in-law, Fridthjof Jacobsen.

Shackleton had originally intended staying at Grytviken only a few days, but it was a bad year for ice. The pack was further north than any of the whalers could recall, and Shackleton was advised to wait until the southern summer was well under way. The days turned into weeks, and still *Endurance* remained anchored in the fjord. Shackleton seemed oddly content, and in no hurry to depart.

"I felt a pride in reflecting on what a far-flung profession mine was," Macklin wrote on seeing the grave of an English doctor in the whalers' cemetery, "sending its sons everywhere, even to this out of the way island of the South Atlantic."[25]

"The people who go whaling," said Kristen Løken, a Norwegian priest on South Georgia, "are a motley race." Their work, he went on, was of "a depraving nature":

> Some have seen better days, like former noblemen and other fallen creatures who now flense, strip blubber, or render oil . . . Many, if not most . . . are ruined individuals . . . There are former criminals and runaway seamen who are at odds with life.[26]

"It is not because [we] want to come down here," one of the "fallen creatures" once said in his best English, and in his cups, when trying to explain what drove him and his kind.

> It is because [we] want get away from up there . . . us whalemen . . . not fit up there . . . and people up there not want queer folk around like . . . whalemen. And we no can write poetry or paint pictures or get away from silly world which want no part of us, same like artists do. So we come here because we not at home – *and* we no damn use – anywhere else.[27]

That curiously echoed Shackleton writing to his wife:

> This I know is my Ishmaelite life and the one thing that I am suited for.[28]

For the first time in his life, perhaps, he found himself among totally sympathetic characters, an outcast among outcasts no longer out of place.

Whaling brought squalor in its train. At Grytviken, the stupendous mountain backdrop was veiled by a characteristic stench of decomposition. The fjord was brown with blood, floating gut, grease and the disintegrating carcasses of whales discarded after being flensed by swarms of men with curved knives and hooks. Only the blubber was taken, and then rendered down to oil.

For such diverse processes as tempering armourplate or lubricating watches, there was as yet no substitute for whale oil. It also came in handy for making soap and margarine. "When I get back," Shackleton wrote to Perris, "I will make a company for whaling here, on a capital of £50,000 one can make for certain 50 to 100 thousand pounds a year net profit it is a gold mine only very few people know of it."[29]

Yet money was not quite all. Behind industrial necessity lay the mystique of the hunt. The whale was the world's biggest game. Brutal was the chase, through stormy seas; but for that very reason encrusted with a rich harvest of literature and lore. The Norwegian whalers were heirs to an ancient tradition. Even though the invention, by a Norwegian, of the whaling gun with its explosive harpoon, now stacked the odds against the whale, it still had not quite robbed whaling of its danger, excitement, and atavistic blood lust.

The whaling stations of South Georgia, lit by hydro-electric power, were only superficially modern. At heart, they remained primitive hunting communities. The managers, like Jacobsen, were deceptively mild. Underneath, they possessed the despotic power of chieftains. It was vital, given the temperamental and hierarchical communities over which they ruled. Their men ranged from the Myrmidons who rendered the blubber – the "only dangerous animals on this island",[30] as someone said – to the harpooners, the aristocrats of whaling who, Orde-Lees succinctly observed, "are like the Spanish matadors".[31]

The whalers were most hospitable and the expedition members, in their several ways, suitably uplifted by their run ashore. The dogs, released from their confinement on board, had halcyon days, gorging themselves on whale meat. Shackleton was taken in *Den Lille Kari*, a decrepit old steam whalecatcher, to visit the various station managers.

Behind the conviviality, Shackleton was watching how his men behaved. Frank Wild, for example, not to mention Worsley, and the not exactly loveable trawler hands who manned *Endurance*, allowed themselves to be plied with drink. That usually meant moonshine or, in whalers' argot, *plonk*; for the whaling companies had made the island dry.

Reginald James, meanwhile, on his own initiative, staked out on a hillside a true meridian for the whalecatchers to swing compasses. His assistant was Hubert Hudson, the Second Officer of *Endurance*. It was an unlikely combination. James, bespectacled, abstracted, intellectual, living in a private world of crystals and atomic structure, was a characteristic product of Cambridge and the Cavendish Laboratory. He dismissed Hudson – obscurely nicknamed "Buddha" – as a "typical English Phillistine [who] cannot appreciate anything not quite plain and literal".[32] James saw the university as an island of civilisation in the outer darkness.

Ever on the prowl was Frank Hurley, the expedition photographer. Hurley was an Australian; "the ungrownup Australian," said Macklin, expressing a common English attitude, "who always had to be patted on the back."[33]

The whole enterprise, in fact, partly owed its existence to Hurley. He had already been south with Mawson, and there, indeed, he had made his name. Mawson's expedition had produced another heroic disaster. In a traverse of the hinterland of what was named King George V Land, Mawson lost both his companions. Lieutenant Belgrave Ninnis was killed by falling into a crevasse when walking without ski. Dr Xavier Mertz, a Swiss, died from what was probably vitamin A poisoning caused by eating dog livers. Mawson himself carried on alone, and got through in what became one of the great sagas of survival. It was that expedition, although not that journey, that Hurley had recorded.

A few months before sailing, Shackleton had formed the ITA [Imperial Trans Antarctic] Film Syndicate Ltd. It was little more than a paper company. Its purpose was to exploit Hurley's work. The few shareholders included Ernest Perris and (for respectability) John Scott Keltie. Hurley was being used as a bait for the expedition's backers. Rights to his work on *Endurance*, or so they thought, would guarantee an adequate financial return.

"I would certainly never have advised you, man to man, to go with Shackleton," Mawson had written to Hurley in June. Mawson was then in London, arranging for the publication of *The Home of the Blizzard*, the book of his expedition.* Hurley, meanwhile, was out in the Australian bush, when he ought to have been preparing the photographs.

A swaggering character with a shock of dark, curly hair, and an uneasy cast to his face, Hurley was a compulsive roamer. As a boy,

* And aptly named. Mawson had found himself in the stormiest part of the Antarctic continent. By a freak of topography, at his base at Commonwealth Bay, he was in the path of winds sweeping down from the interior of the continent like an invisible waterfall, sometimes at speeds over a hundred miles per hour.

he had run away from home. He came to photography by chance. Now, almost having crossed Australia, he was the centre of a flurry of cables to and from Burketown, an outpost in the tropic wastes of Northern Queensland. "I gave you my advice as to what to do with regard to Shackleton's Expedition," wrote Mawson, summarising the exchange in a letter, "and you decided otherwise."

> I wired you further, reiterating . . . that you should not go with Shackleton unless paid a percentage on the profits . . . I did this all with . . . a good eye to your future . . . Had you put more belief in my statements you . . . would not have risked your life as you do in the present case . . .[34]

So deeply by now did Mawson mistrust Shackleton.

Despite this, Hurley joined *Endurance*, at six weeks' notice, in Buenos Aires. From Grytviken, he wrote to Mawson that he had made "satisfactory financial arrangements". Nonetheless, Hurley, too, had twinges of concern. "I am rather surprised at the physique of the party," he went on, "which I consider quite below our own." Tall and eminently tough, Hurley had the usual Australian's dismay at first being confronted by the average undersized Englishman of the time.

> Further I think the members are not up to ours in their various departments. From what I can see Sir E. cares very little for the scientific work but is eyeing the expdn. more in the light of a commercial venture. It will be hard to keep up that harmony of working & contentment so noticeable in the Austn. Expn [Mawson's expedition].[35]

Hurley, as Greenstreet put it, more perceptively than Macklin, was "a warrior with his camera & would go anywhere or do anything to get a picture":

> I gave him a hand to lug a whole plate camera & 40 lbs of gear & accoutrements & by gum we had some lovely places to go up, like a fly crawling up a wall . . . He did get some beauties though from the top, well worth the exertion of getting up there.[36]

One result was a telling picture of *Endurance* as a speck far down below in the bay of Grytviken, dwarfed by the ice-clad mountain amphitheatre encircling the anchorage. It was uncannily like a picture of *Antarctic* eleven years before in the self-same place, just as she was starting on her doomed voyage to the Weddell Sea.

Orde-Lees, with climbing in his blood, naturally wished to mark his stay by the first ascent of Mount Paget, the highest peak on South Georgia. It bore a striking resemblance to Mont Blanc, and if Shackleton's poetical instincts had directed him to Shelley, instead of Browning, he might have quoted a poem to that mountain, where

> . . . unearthly forms
> Pile around it, ice and rock; broad vales between
> Of frozen floods, unfathomable deeps . . .[37]

With an altitude of 9,000 feet, the ascent of Mount Paget promised, amongst other things, a view over the terrain. Captain James Cook had made the first recorded landing on the island in 1775, calling it South Georgia after King George III. Since then South Georgia, a crescent tangle of ice clad peak and glacier, encircled by grey waters, had remained an enigma. One hundred miles from end to end, and twenty miles at the widest, only the coast was charted. The interior was mostly unknown. Shackleton, however, believing Orde-Lees too impetuous, forbade him to make his climb. So Orde-Lees contented himself with skiing alone on the snow lying round the bay and testing the Håkonson motor sledge. This was an early snow scooter, made in Sweden.

The whalers, in Orde-Lees' words, were "tremendously interested in our project, as all Norwegians of course would be", but, he went on, they were astonished "when . . . told . . . that only three or four members of the expedition had ever been on ski."[38] When Shackleton ordered the dogs from the Hudson's Bay Company, he asked for a driver too. That turned out to be virtually impossible. "It is not a question of wages," the Company reported, after trying round Lake Winnipeg – Shackleton was offering at least $1,000 a year – "but they seem afraid to engage in such a venture."[39] In the end, a certain Dr George M. Ross actually arrived in London. Shackleton, however, refused to pay the premium on the life insurance which had been agreed. It may have been a superstitious fear of giving a hostage to fortune. It may also have been because Ross now turned out to have had difficulties with drink, and Shackleton wished tactfully to get rid of him. Whatever the explanation, Ross declined to continue, and returned to Canada.

By then it was late in September. Meanwhile F. H. Gjertsen, a ship's officer who had been with Amundsen, volunteered. He gave Nansen as a reference. "I have only a few days to decide," Shackleton characteristically telegraphed to Nansen hardly a week before leaving England, "wire me immediately."[40] "Believe

Gjertsen good man," replied Nansen, "but doubt experience dog driver."[41] Gjertsen was not taken, and so Shackleton set off to cross the Antarctic continent without a trained dog driver.

All in all, the whalers on South Georgia were perplexed by Shackleton's haphazard preparations. Many of them felt that under any circumstances Shackleton was rash to try conclusions with the Weddell Sea. The memory of *Antarctic*'s loss, and of Filchner's near-disaster was too fresh. *Endurance* would never get through the ice in one piece. That at least was Jacobsen's opinion.

Shackleton had, partly, been drawn to South Georgia by hopes of completing his equipment. At Buenos Aires, he had run out of money. Here, without cables or wireless, he was safe from financial enquiry, and could more easily get credit. But when he raised the question of acquiring material from their stores, the whaling managers were at first noticeably unwilling and reserved. Shackleton, however, backed his own particular brand of ingratiating charm with a very Irish hint of ruthlessness behind.

The whaling managers understood force of character for it was by force of character, after all, that they themselves ruled. So Shackleton acquired the sugar, flour, tinned butter, extra coal and good, rough, cold weather clothing that he lacked. The bills which he sent, hopefully, back to Perris, totalled over £400. "I have written a letter of thanks to all the people who have subscribed £10 and over," Shackleton explained. It was Orde-Lees, in fact, who had hurriedly written the letters; ninety of them in all. "If you require more money," Shackleton told Perris,

> you might easily write to them . . . could they send a little more. I wrote each a nice letter but did not mention that there might be a need for more money.[42]

Before these even left the island, Shackleton knew he would be hidden in the ice for two years at least, for by now he had given up his original hope of crossing the continent in one season.

On 5 December, *Endurance* finally sailed. Behind, at Grytviken, remained Sir Daniel Gooch, Bart, one of Shackleton's curious circle of friends, and a member of the crew. "Curly", as Sir Daniel was called on board, had sailed as far as South Georgia to help tend the dogs. He had signed on before the mast. Now he had to go home, because his country house was being converted to a war hospital, and he wished to supervise it himself. "There never was a better disciplined A.B. afloat than Sir Daniel Gooch," as Wild put it. "He obeyed all orders promptly & . . . was possessed of a keen sense of humour."[43]

The departure of *Endurance* was decidedly subdued. The war was preoccupying those on board more than they cared to admit publicly. Shackleton had waited for a boat expected soon with the last news before he finally headed for the ice, but he now felt he could delay no longer. Orde-Lees wrote in his diary,

> What thoughts are ours, setting out at such a time, with no chance of news from our dear ones at home who are passing through the greatest national crisis of modern times.
>
> What may we expect to learn on our return? The map of Europe may be greatly altered but God grant that England may stand where she is this day & that all those dear to us may be spared from any privations or sufferings.[44]

The feeling of unease on board also had its roots in apprehension of what lay ahead. "The Weddell Sea & shores are repellant", wrote Sir Joseph Hooker, who had been there seventy years before with Sir James Clark Ross, "the Victorian [Ross Sea] full of charm, glacial though they be".[45]

In what he called his "last letter . . . before I go South into the unknown", Shackleton, still in a mood of remorse, wrote to Emily that "I have not much that I can say . . . as I suppose I am a domestic failure . . . I find it hard to explain things in writing and I must leave it to time to settle the rights and wrongs of it all . . . I do hope", he continued, "that the price of living will not rise too high for you." With a twinge of conscience, he was remembering that while he was away Emily would only have her own £700 a year and Janet Stancomb-Wills' charity.

Among the forward hands, Walter How was hoping that his wife could get an extra £5 from the Expedition office. He was a reformed rogue or, as he had written to her, "I am a very good boy & keeping quite straight". He had left her with a six-month-old baby and, like Shackleton, was feeling twinges of regret. How wrote to his wife suggesting she approach F. W. White, the Expedition secretary: "They tell me that he is a very nice man & will do all he can to assist the dependants of the crew".

> I sometimes wish that I had never come here but there I suppose that if I had stayed at home I should have been out of work or else gone to the war . . . of course it is always the poor that have to suffer . . . I am thankful Bert is assisting you or else I dont know how you would get on . . . I hope that the Expedition is successful & then we can say that we shall have a good time & sing that little song "We'll go to Sea no More".[46]

Shackleton, meanwhile, was finishing his letter to Emily: "I have not written to Aberdeen House". That was his parents' home at Sydenham. "I have no inclination to do so and have too much to think of here."[47] He had long since found his own family a burden and a drag. For his penurious father and his mother, a professional invalid, he had little respect. For his brother Frank, he had at least arranged a job with William Dederich. There Frank, now assuming the surname Mellor, concealed his stay in prison by pretending to have returned from "some islands" abroad. The staff teased him, "but never about the rumoured theft of the Dublin crown jewels," as one of them put it, "we were too tactful."[48]

All that, Ernest Shackleton was glad at last to leave astern. Bathed in the eerie morning light *Endurance* drew away from Grytviken and, in the tracks of *Antarctic*, moved down the fjord. Like a ghost ship, she was swallowed by the mist and rain swirling down from the sombre mountains that rose straight out of the sea. To sum up what he felt at the moment of departure, Shackleton chose, with his own misquotations, a poem called *The Ship of Fools* by an Oxford don called St John Lucas:

We were the fools who could not rest in the dull earth we left behind.
But burned with passion for the South.
And drank strange frenzy from the wind.
The world where wise men sit at ease,
Fades from my unregretful eyes
And blind across uncharted seas
We stagger on our enterprise.[49]

"It was strange," added Macklin, "that the last sight of civilisation we had was a drunken man."[50]

XXXII

Pack ice at 59° 28′

On 8 December the first pack ice appeared. *Endurance* had not yet crossed the 57th parallel. The whalers had been right; it was a spectacularly bad season. Even so Shackleton was still surprised to find the pack so far north.

Worsley, although captain of the ship, was more concerned with immediate impressions. "Sea which had been a sea green colour," he jotted in his diary, "suddenly changed to an Indigo or Reeves French blue."[1] Now, as *Endurance* probed the pack,

> The scene was very fine, huge bergs with the heavy S.W. swell dashing against & leaping right onto the top of their icy cliffs : . . Add to this the booming of the sea running into ice caverns.[2]

It was like the sound of distant guns heard by German sailors that day off the Falkland Islands, as British battle cruisers opened fire. The Royal Navy was about to exact revenge for the defeat at Coronel. Shackleton's instincts in avoiding the Falklands had been right. *Endurance* might well have run into the German fleet. Now it was only the ice with which she had to contend.

The pack was only a narrow belt, which *Endurance* soon managed to circumvent. She ran into open water with all sail set; "wonderfully easy for rough sea," as Worsley put it, "& behaving very well."[3]

On the other hand, "This ship," Shackleton had written to Emily from Buenos Aires, "is not as strong as the Nimrod constructionally." He explained:

> This I have seen from her way of behaving when in a gale pressing against the dock wall though there is nothing to be scared of as I think

she will go through the ice all right only I would exchange her for the old Nimrod any day now except for comfort.[4]

The contours and behaviour of the Weddell Sea were still only vaguely known. The sum of experience, however, and the whalers' advice, was to hug the eastern shore. The reason was that the prevailing winds were south-easterly, which ought to have kept the pack in the offing, and left a reasonably clear lead. So Shackleton headed well over to the east.

As *Endurance* hauled to the wind and went round on the other tack, the crew were ordered to the sheets or sent scurrying aloft by the squeaky voice of the Third Officer, Alfred Cheetham, one of the Antarctic familiars. Cheetham normally was a staid North Sea sailor. Born in Liverpool, living in Hull, he was bosun of the *Montebello*, the mailboat, shuttling contentedly across to Norway and back, twice a week. Periodically, however, he left home, family and billet for the Antarctic, and had spent six of the past twelve years sailing south. He had first gone on *Morning*, on the *Discovery* relief, where Shackleton had met him going home. Then Cheetham had served under Shackleton on *Nimrod*, under Scott on *Terra Nova*, and now was back with Shackleton as Third Officer on *Endurance*. Small, wiry, quizzical, Cheetham somehow had a commanding presence on deck. His great virtue was that he understood the Hull trawlermen, a special breed, by whom *Endurance* was largely manned.

On 11 December, *Endurance* again found the pack. This time it could not be turned. The ship was put straight in. Once more, Shackleton was in the half world, neither land nor sea, where ice floes, like giant gleaming shields, swarmed over grey waters. Once more, he saw seal and penguins spread over the ice, whales blowing in the leads, and strange Antarctic birds swooping overhead. To the ordinary ship's sounds of water-squelch, creak of timbers, thrum of rigging, squeak of halyards easing through tackle and the flap-flap of sails filling to the wind, was added the rasp of ice against wood and the throb of engines as steam was raised to pick a way ahead through zigzag channels.

Hurley, at least, found it all drama to record. He was, said Worsley,

a marvel – with cheerful Australian profanity he perambulates alone aloft & everywhere, in the most dangerous & slippery places he can find, content & happy at all times but cursing so if he can get a good or novel picture. Stands bare & hair waving in the wind, where we are gloved & helmeted, he snaps his snap or winds his handle turning out curses of delight & pictures of Life by the fathom.[5]

The fact remained that *Endurance* entered the pack a good six hundred miles short of the nearest Antarctic coastline, along Dronning Maud Land. Shackleton could not know this, because it would only be discovered fifteen years later by a Norwegian expedition privately financed, as it happened, by the selfsame Lars Christensen to whom *Endurance* was due. Shackleton did know, however, that to Vahsel Bay it was over a thousand miles, and the pack ice stretched all the way to the horizon with no sign whatsoever of a break.

Now utterly beyond recall, Shackleton at last was released from his shore-going self. He was once more a seaman on his ship, without the cares of a world he did not really understand. He seemed in good health again, as if his illness on the way to South Georgia had only been the final reaction to all the strain of preparation and escape at last from uncongenial outer circumstances.

Now at least he had the peace of mind really to take the measure of his shipmates. The transcontinental party he had already chosen. Besides himself, Hurley, Macklin, Wild, Marston and Crean would go.

Tom Crean was an Irishman from County Kerry, and a Royal Naval petty officer. Macklin told a story of how, when Queen Alexandra inspected *Endurance* in the London docks, one of the ladies in her entourage

> laying a small delicate finger on Crean's massive chest opposite [a] white ribbon asked, "And what might that be for?" Tom replied, "That is the Polar Medal." "O" said the lady, "I thought it was for innocence." One had to be familiar with Tom's hard bitten dial to really appreciate this piece of irony.[6]

Crean was undeniably tough, determined and experienced. He had been to the Antarctic on *Discovery*, and again with Scott on his second expedition.

Crean was not entirely sympathetic. Disrated once or twice for drink and unbecoming behaviour, he had received from the Navy a less than satisfactory character. Nonetheless, in the débâcle of Scott's second expedition, Crean had been involved in the one truly heroic episode. On the return from supporting the polar party, Lieutenant Teddy Evans had collapsed with scurvy.* Crean, with another naval rating, William Lashly, saved his life by dragging him home on a sledge for the last fifty miles. It was Crean who made the final dash for safety by walking twenty hours at a

* The appearance of scurvy was obscured in the official accounts.

stretch – without ski – to bring help from Hut Point at McMurdo Sound. Crean therefore came to Shackleton on Evans' warmest recommendation. Whatever his failings, Crean was manifestly a man for a tight corner, and he mustered as second officer on *Endurance*.

It was now, as *Endurance* headed into the Weddell Sea, that Shackleton first learned how to handle Worsley. Released from the ultimate burden of leadership, Worsley was altogether more at ease. He was lost when in command himself. In carrying out orders, he was a model of determination. He was always on the alert for orders to obey. He turned out to be a more than gifted navigator.

On *Endurance*, presented by a well-wisher, was a comprehensive polar library, which included *Antarctic*, Otto Nordenskjöld's book of his expedition. That was then the most comprehensive published guide to the waters for which *Endurance* was headed. Greenstreet was the only one on board so far to have read it thoroughly. In his diary he noted that "mid Feb. 'Antarctic' crushed & sank 64°22′S. 23m. from Paulet Id. Boats 12 days to land."[7]

Greenstreet, also alone on board, had systematically tried to learn from those who had been before. He had collated the ice reports from the whalers on South Georgia. He had consulted the records of previous expeditions and of a meteorological station in the South Orkneys. He only had the years since Nordenskjöld and Bruce in 1902 to go by, but he observed that in "a close season", as he put it in his diary, "Ice line 59° S". Nordenskjöld, he noted, "met pack 59°30′". *Endurance* had found the pack at 59°28′. Greenstreet knew better than to point this out to Shackleton. Shackleton, as he had learned by now, would brusquely dismiss him as a "pessimist". Shackleton, as usual, wanted only "optimists" around him.

One at least who fulfilled that requirement was Leonard Hussey. The smallest man on the expedition, determinedly cheery to the point of egregiousness, he was something of a toady towards Shackleton. His selection, too, seemed aimless. Hussey had been reading medicine at King's College, London. In 1913, however, he interrupted his studies to join an archaeological dig, at Jebel Moya, in the Sudan. Organised by Henry (later Sir Henry) Wellcome, the dig dealt with the history of medicine. One day at Jebel Moya Hussey happened to be reading an old newspaper, and noticed an article about the *Endurance* expedition. "The idea," as he put it, "gripped me."[8] So he wrote to Shackleton, received a reply telling him to make contact on returning to London and, in July 1914, he presented himself at the office. There followed the usual short, puzzling interview, with Shackleton apparently taking no interest in the replies to his questions, and the sudden, brusque acceptance. As Hussey put it,

> My luck was explained later . . . by Shackleton, who said he was greatly amused to [receive an] application . . . from the heart of Africa, [and also] as he . . . confessed: "I thought you looked funny!"[9]

So, as *Endurance* butted and pushed through the pack, Hussey's slightly giggling laugh pealed regularly from main truck down to coal bunkers.

The pack was a shattered field of ice in all its forms; thick, thin, brittle, hard; small fragments, huge floes, and flat-topped bergs. Like an animal, driven by wind and tide, it had its moods. Sometimes frankly malevolent, it was closed and impenetrable; then cunning and deceptively friendly, it would slacken. From the crow's nest the view was spectacular. A white field stretched round the horizon, stabbed astern by the dark slash of the ship's wake, dissolving in the distance as the ice closed up again.

Shackleton, said Macklin, was on the bridge "always . . . especially when things were difficult or dangerous".

> Each watch had its characteristics. Worsley specialised in ramming, and I have a sneaking suspicion that he often went out of his way to find a nice piece of floe at which he could drive at full speed and cut in two; he loved to feel the shock, the riding up, and the sensation, as the ice gave and we drove through.

Wild, on the other hand, in Macklin's words,

> was always calm, cool or collected, in open lanes or in tight corners he was just the same; but when he did tell a man to jump, that man jumped pretty quick. He possessed that rare knack of being one with all of us, and yet maintained his authority as second-in-command. We had no "Worsley" thrills in Wild's watch.[10]

It was Worsley who, one day, passing a crowd of Adelie penguins on a floe, decided that they all knew Robert Selbie Clark, the expedition biologist:

> when he was at the wheel [they] rushed along as fast as their legs could carry them yelling out "Clark! Clark!" & apparently very indignant & perturbed that he never . . . even answered them, tho' we often called his attention to the fact that they all knew him.[11]

Together with Reginald James, the physicist, and a geologist, James Mann Wordie, Clark made up the scientific staff. There was no one on board with whom, as a class, Shackleton was less sympathetic. "You have got to surround your expedition with a scientific halo," A. E. W. Mason made his explorer hero say in *The Turnstile*. "It gets you money, and official support and the countenance of the learned societies."[12] With that, Shackleton wryly agreed. Since *Nimrod* his feeling had grown that science on an expedition of his kind was regrettably necessary humbug. Scientists, therefore, were to him so much ballast. Their selection, if possible, was even more cursory than others.

Clark came because W. S. Bruce sent him. Wordie also came on simple recommendation. Both were proverbial "dour Aberdonians". Clark redeemed himself by physical strength, by willingness to work outside his speciality, and by glimpses of a pawky humour. Wordie, nicknamed "Jock", small, dry, bespectacled and reserved, came from St John's College, Cambridge. So did Reginald James, "Gentle Jimmy",[13] as Worsley compassionately called him. That James joined the expedition was, in his own words, "almost a matter of chance":

> I was about to leave Cambridge, when I was hailed from a window in a street that I had never passed through before in my whole five years at Cambridge, by a fellow research student at the Cavendish Laboratory with the words, "Hi James, do you want to go to the Antarctic?" I said "No, not particularly. Why?"[14]

Shackleton, it turned out, was still looking for a physicist. At Cambridge, James had got to know Charles Wright and Raymond Priestley, both of whom had been with Scott. "This," said James, "had interested me in Antarctic matters, but I had no . . . ambition to take part in an expedition." Shackleton's enterprise, as James put it, "was talked of at Cambridge". Moreover, James was a friend of Wordie's, and knew that he was going. Somehow there soon came the usual, puzzling five minute interview with Shackleton at the office in London. James gave up a promising research post to which he had just been appointed, and now found himself on the deck of *Endurance* as, between the floes, she made her way into the Weddell Sea.

On 18 December when, in its slow, irregular pulsation, the pack tightened, "three penguins visited us", the ship's carpenter wrote in his diary. "Mr. Hussy [*sic*]," he continued in his idiosyncratic style, "gave them a selection of musics." The instrument was a banjo. It was Hussey's most cherished possession. With it, he had charmed cannibals in the Sudan, he said, but now, the carpenter continued, as Hussey "started on a scotch selection [the penguins] got disgusted & walked away".[15]

The carpenter was himself Scots. A hardened and argumentative old salt from Dundee called Harry McNeish, he was the antithesis of Hussey. In the way of many sailors, McNeish was afflicted in turn by drink and remorse. He was, as someone on another ship said,

> neither sweet-tempered nor tolerant and his Scots voice could rasp like frayed wire cable. He had no use whatever for a gangling first-tripper who spoke, as he expressed it, "like a pimp at a whore's tea-party" . . . I loved him not . . . Yet in the course of [a] few weeks I discovered [McNeish] to be one of the most courageous and skilful men I have ever met. My enthusiastic loathing of him gave way to respect. Finally . . . I found in place of a tormentor a good shipmate with a shrewd wit and a power of describing men and high adventure that was admirable.[16]

To Shackleton, on the other hand, McNeish was "the only man I am not dead certain of". He was

> a very good workman and shipwright, but of a dour disposition yet does nothing I can get hold of.[17]

McNeish in his way was quite well read. He had certainly prepared himself by reading *The Voyage of the Scotia*, the book about Bruce's expedition to those waters at the same time as *Discovery*. He almost seemed to have been there himself.

In any case, McNeish was making comparisons. Now, on *Endurance*, when Christmas Eve arrived, he thought that "we are drawing near the end of the pack as it is fine & open."[18] They were actually at about 64° South. In the fortnight since entering the pack, *Endurance* had only made three hundred miles southing. Once more to be sailing along at a comfortable seven knots was the finest imaginable Christmas present.

> Had my usual evening walk & smoke, as I am better of the piles but I have been thinking of my loved ones all day I hope there is nothing wrong & that You will enjoy Yourselves tomorrow X Mass.[19]

The same day, at Hobart, Tasmania, *Aurora* finally sailed for McMurdo Sound to lay depots for the transcontinental party.

When Æneas Mackintosh left England to take command of *Aurora*, he was told by Shackleton that he would absolutely have to economise. This hardly prepared him, however, for the circumstances he found when he arrived at Hobart in the middle of October. Beyond the purchase of *Aurora*, virtually nothing had been done.

Before she could safely sail, *Aurora* needed a complete refit. Shackleton had only budgeted for this (amongst other things) by assuming local help. Mackintosh found he had been left to fend for himself. He was brave and enterprising. Between *Nimrod* and *Aurora*, he had gone hunting (unsuccessfully) for buried treasure on Coco Island, off the coast of Panama. But, cold in character and lacking insight, he did not have the personality to cope with the present crisis. What he did was to engage a scratch crew, and take *Aurora* to Sydney. There, as instructed by Shackleton, he approached Edgeworth David.

Since the *Nimrod* expedition, David had kept his regard for Shackleton. As of old, he once more used his influence to ask the Australian government for help. The response was at first a blunt refusal. For one thing, the war was monopolising resources; for another, it was felt that Shackleton had tried to trap the government into helping.

Official goodwill was hardly encouraged by Shackleton's manifest dependence on last-minute improvisation. His intentions were vague. He might, as he had announced, make the transantarctic crossing this season; or he might be compelled to wait a year. Either way, he had now been swallowed by the South Atlantic, and was out of touch. David was able to explain that, without help, Shackleton would be left in the lurch. Grudgingly, the government allowed *Aurora* to be refitted at public expense in the Cockatoo naval yard at Sydney. Nor was that all.

As a result of what Orde-Lees, Royal Marine as he was, called "this damnably conceived war",[20] various contributions had not been paid. Shackleton had found himself even more than usually hard pressed. "You know I wish you well," Sir James Caird had written when he received Shackleton's inevitable supplementary appeal, "but war cancels Contracts".[21] The upshot was that Shackleton appropriated all possible money for *Endurance*. He had promised Mackintosh at least £2,000; but only half was actually sent. When Mackintosh cabled to London for the rest, it was to be told that money there was none.

Money had somehow to be found, and the only way was by mortgaging *Aurora*. That caused yet more trouble. The ship was not insured; the transfer from Mawson turned out to be incomplete. Meanwhile, the cables flew back and forth. Mackintosh only knew that Shackleton's life probably depended on him, and time was running out. Edgeworth David went back to the government, and managed to obtain a guarantee of a loan of £1,000. A few local donors now began helping with equipment. At the last moment £700 arrived from London, raised by Shackleton's solicitors somehow on the expectation of *Aurora*'s mortgage.

To add to the confusion, when the rest of the Ross Sea party arrived from England, it was found to be thoroughly ill-assorted, and riddled with dissension. Several members were discharged, partly due to drink. Mackintosh had to make up the numbers by hasty local recruiting. Eventually, he returned to Hobart to embark his sledge dogs, waiting in quarantine after being sent out from England.

Aurora was six weeks delayed. When she finally sailed down the river from Hobart for the south, it was, in the words of R. W. Richards, one of the recently joined Australians, "difficult to imagine a state of greater confusion".[22] Because of the war, no doctor could be found. The sailors were surly and discontented. *Aurora*, her engines, and her sails, despite overhaul, looked so decrepit that experienced seamen had shied off, and the crew had been impossible to complete. Even *Aurora*'s departure seemed inauspicious. She was inspected by Sir William Ellison Macartney, the Governor of Tasmania, and Lady Macartney. She, a sister of Captain Scott, innocently presented the ship with a portrait of her brother.

Aurora sailed without ship's papers. "The circumstances," said someone on board, were "disgraceful, and the less said about them the better."[23] Hardly anyone was on the wharf to see them off. Mackintosh, well meaning but gauche, did not know how to deal with the public or the press. In Australia, the expedition was more or less ignored.

Aurora's voyage south was uneventful, but under Mackintosh she was not a happy ship. On 9 January she reached Cape Crozier, at the junction of Ross Island and the Ross Ice Barrier. She was almost at her destination. Suddenly, as she was closing land, a thick fog came down. "We knew we were heading towards the Barrier," in the words of Leslie Thomson, the Second Officer,

> but did not think we were so close until the ice cliffs showed up right ahead. The engines were put astern but refused to answer and the ship crashed up against the ice cliffs and broke the jibboom off short.[24]

"This is the anniversary of Shackleton's farthest South," McNeish, the carpenter, meanwhile was writing the same day on *Endurance*, two thousand miles away in the Weddell Sea, "& everything looks much better."[25] Since 4 January, *Endurance* had been jammed in the pack. Having crossed the Antarctic Circle on New Year's Eve she was now, by the noon sight on 9 January, at 69°47′S, two miles further north than a week before. But the pack was opening up. "We are under way again," in McNeish's words. "We had Sweethearts & Wifes [*sic*] as usual" – the traditional sailor's toast on Saturdays.

Next day, 10 January, the first land was sighted. This was the undulating ice front of Coats Land, discovered by Bruce in 1902. The day's run was 136 miles; the noon latitude 72°2′S. The mood on board lifted. *Endurance* coasted along the land, dodging occasional icebergs and zigzagging through loose belts of pack. Snow showers intermittently hissed through the sails; then the weather lifted and, through air like crystal, the details of the ice front stood out. There was also much mirage. "Everything," as Worsley put it, "wears an air of unreality . . . Everything on the horizon appears drawn up & distorted . . . icebergs hang upside down in the sky . . . The tops of some of the bergs appear to boil up & rise & fall & spread themselves . . . in the quaintest way. Inshore appears a beautiful dazzling city of Cathedral spires, domes & minarets."[26] Vahsel Bay at any rate was in the offing. The crew were bagging coal for landing. Journey's end was near, and Orde-Lees became philosophical:

> I do so wish sometimes, that I could just pop home for an hour or two as easily in the flesh as in the spirit. No doubt the explorers of 2015, if there is anything left to explore, will not only carry their pocket wireless telephones fitted with wireless telescopes but will also receive their nourishment & warmth by wireless . . . and also their power to drive their motor sledges, but, of course, there will be an aerial daily excursion to both poles then, & it will be the bottom of the Atlantic, if not the centre of the earth that will form the goal in those days.[27]

On 12 January, *Endurance* reached a bay in the ice front which McNeish realised was the end of Coats Land and Bruce's Furthest South. The noon latitude was 74°1′S. "From today onwards to Luitpold Land," wrote Worsley, "we are . . . discovering absolutely new land & connecting [with] Filchner's discoveries."[28] This new land Shackleton named the Caird Coast, in honour of Sir James Caird.

Southwards the way was now barred by the ice front, which swung violently from south-west to north-west. All night, *Endurance* coasted along. In the eerie rays of the midnight sun, Worsley observed that "in one place the barrier comes with an easy sweep to the sea & it would be an easy matter to land stores in such a place".[29] He suggested that they change plans and make their base there. Shackleton disagreed. It would add two hundred miles to the overland journey, they were still 3° north of Vahsel Bay, and every mile would count.

For three days, *Endurance* crawled along the coast against ever-tightening pack. Part of the time she was caught in the ice and drifted with the floes. The wind backed west. Worsley feared that, despite what the whalers had told him on South Georgia, the pack would drive hard on to the coast, and jam *Endurance*, as had very nearly happened to *Nimrod* off King Edward Land in the Ross Sea almost exactly seven years before. It eventually became clear that *Endurance* was following an immense blunt promontory, which Shackleton, fairly appropriately, named Stancomb Wills.

After all the fitful movement in the pack, "Dame Fortune, Sir Ernest's old & constant friend," as Orde-Lees put it, "again favoured us".[30] On 15 January, as *Endurance* rounded the Stancomb Wills Promontory, open water suddenly appeared. Shackleton was repeating Filchner's experience in *Deutschland*, three years before. With all sail crowded on, and engines beating hard, *Endurance* made her best speed. In the next twenty-four hours, she covered 120 miles to the south-west. It was practically the best run of the whole voyage. Shackleton was sure he now had a clear run to Vahsel Bay.

About two in the afternoon, large herds of Crabeater seals appeared, swimming out from the ice front in sight to port. They made for *Endurance*, diving, blowing, curvetting like porpoises, making the water boil and then, wave after wave, disappeared to the north. It seemed the departure of migratory animals fleeing an early winter. They appeared deliberately to have visited *Endurance* in ironic farewell, and left behind them a vague feeling of unease. *Endurance*, meanwhile, persevered in the opposite direction. With her fore-and-aft sails spread like wings, she almost seemed a dragon-fly skimming the water in its last flight.

Early in the morning of 16 January, *Endurance* crossed the sinister crevassed tongue of a huge glacial outflow from the ice cap, which Shackleton called the Dawson-Lambton Glacier. The next day, a Sunday, *Endurance* was brought up once more by the pack. She also faced a heavy gale, and hove to in the lee of a large iceberg. Ominously, the wind was from the ENE, driving the ice on to the southern coast of the Weddell Sea.

The following day, the weather eased. *Endurance* was faced with a belt of heavy brash. Worsley took her through under fore topsail alone, stopping the propeller to avoid damage from one of the bobbing lumps of ice. Then came open water once more. After sailing twenty miles roughly south west, the ship was brought up yet again by ice. It was the confused outlier of more pack. *Endurance* headed in. Soon it was clear she could not push through, except at the cost of much coal. After a few miles, Worsley hove to, and waited for the ice to open.

"It is now seven weeks since we first entered the pack ice," Hurley observed, "& since then it has been almost an incessant battle."

> It is gratifying to feel we are only 80 miles from . . . Vahsel Bay [he continued]. We are all keen to reach it as the monotony is telling on some of us.[31]

Next day, the pack had closed in round *Endurance*. It was Tuesday 19 January, 1915; the position, 76°30′S, 31°30′W.

A week later, *Endurance* was still stuck. There was a strange chill in the air. In what should have been high Antarctic summer, the sea already had congealed. From the crow's nest, an unrelieved white plain of ice stretched round the horizon, with no hint of open water. To pass the time, Shackleton played poker in the wardroom with Wild, Crean, Worsley, McIlroy and McNeish.

On South Georgia, an admiring whaling skipper had presented Shackleton with a walking stick he himself had made out of hundreds of little whalebone washers threaded on an iron rod. It was a typical piece of whaler's scrimshaw; decorative, eccentric and impractical. Shackleton now got it out and, in Orde-Lees' words,

> with his usual eye for utility, disassembled the structure and now has as many counters as he is likely to need for this trip, at any rate.[32]

But there was something uneasily different in the way *Endurance* was behaving now. It was not only that she had ceased her southing, and now was gyrating confusedly, as if caught on the sinister slow outermost whorl of a vortex. Instead of the crash of ice being battered by the bows, or the grinding of the pack piling round the hull, there was an eerie silence broken only by the faint creak of the ship's timbers. *Endurance* was frozen solid in a floe. This, Orde-Lees wrote on 29 January,

> has happened . . . to both Bruce and Filchner. The former just managed to escape . . . Filchner got stuck [and] in nine months drifted nearly 600

> miles north . . . It certainly seems not improbable that we may [also] remain . . . incarcerated [and] drift North, emerging about this time next year near South Georgia.[33]

Shackleton, meanwhile, staring at his hand in yet another game, tried to divine what the cards before him had to say. But the cards stared back mute and inscrutable, mocking his hopes.

XXXIII

Two helpless hulks

"Blizzard!" wrote another hand that day on the opposite side of the continent. "The only thing to do is to lie in bed and wait. You can't see more than 20 yards all round: the dogs are almost covered in, and the sledge, very lopsided, is disappearing slowly."[1]

The writer was the Rev. Arnold Spencer-Smith. He came from *Aurora*, now, after many setbacks, anchored in McMurdo Sound. He was in a party moving over the Ross Ice Shelf to lay depots for Shackleton. It was that same day, 29 January, that they started out from Hut Point.

The men from *Aurora* were using the hut at Cape Evans where Scott had wintered on his second expedition. They did so, because they had neither the time nor the money to bring a finished hut of their own. They had brought building material, but the trouble of construction was too great. There was a frisson of morbid curiosity when they landed, swept away the snow, and prised open the door to the place where their ill-starred predecessors had lived. Now, under the loom of Mount Erebus, the depot party were following the same trail to the South.

"The work is cruel," wrote Spencer-Smith with relish in his diary, "but it's all in the game . . . and soon our appetites will outstrip the food supply. John 4.48.", he went on to quote, "'Except ye see signs and wonders, ye will not believe.'"

Spencer-Smith was the first ordained clergyman to set foot on the Antarctic continent; and it seemed entirely in keeping with British polar exploration that he was an Anglican cleric afflicted by doubt. He had begun by studying law, then turned to theology. He had come on the expedition in search of suffering, his way to resolve what he called "all the old questionings".[2] Tall, well built, with clean looks and an earnest but unintellectual expression on his face, Spencer-Smith was a characteristic product of Queen's College, Cambridge, the image of what was called a "muscular" Christian. His diary read like a biblical exegesis.

Spencer-Smith was on *Aurora* by default. When war broke out, he wanted to enlist but, being a clergyman, was debarred from doing so as a combatant. He did the next best thing – or so the story goes – which was to volunteer as a substitute for one of Shackleton's men who had left on active service.

Shackleton did not like clergymen; he called them "sky pilots". In truth he was not irreligious, but he had developed an aversion to the forms of organised religion. He was a kind of theist. It was one of the tales of the expedition that he only accepted Spencer-Smith because Spencer-Smith, a bachelor, happened to open an attaché case, from which a woman's silk stocking and a champagne cork rolled out. In any case, Spencer-Smith did not obtrude his religion, and joined *Aurora* as photographer. Now, struggling over the Antarctic snows, he had nightmares about the preparatory school in Edinburgh where he was teaching when war broke out. "It's curious," he wrote in his diary, "how long the depression of such lasts."[3]

Ernest Joyce, Shackleton's old companion, bearded and loquacious as ever, was also in the party heading south. Joyce had been appalled to find that, excepting Mackintosh, he alone of the twenty-eight members of the expedition had any sledging experience; and Mackintosh's qualification was a short, farcical interlude during the *Nimrod* expedition when he nearly killed himself and a companion.

Joyce, as he constantly reminded himself, was the man who, in 1909, in this very place had put out the depot that saved Shackleton on his return from the Furthest South. It was on that that Shackleton had played when he appealed to Joyce to join the new expedition. Joyce was living in Australia at the time and, to sail with *Aurora*, had left a good job with the Sydney Harbour Board.

By his letter of appointment from Shackleton, Joyce understood that he was to be in charge of all snow travel. This, Joyce discovered, had been "practically annulled" by Shackleton himself through discretionary powers given to Mackintosh. By then it was too late. *Aurora* had already put to sea.

So it was Mackintosh, tall, one-eyed like Wotan, erratic and accident prone, who had taken command of the depot-laying party. As he led the way slowly south, he showed a talent for complicating things. The dissension which had started on the voyage out from England had turned into chronic confusion and discontent. It was mostly, but not entirely Mackintosh's fault.

A motor sledge sent out from England had very quickly failed. Meanwhile Joyce, in his own words, had been

> led to believe all sledging equipment . . . was shipped [but] there was only sufficient for 10 men instead of 28. This being my department . . . I am somewhat perturbed.[4]

Even essentials were short. Hardly any sledging food had been provided, and of pemmican there was none. The party now trudging south were making do with what had been left behind on *Aurora* by Mawson, and at Cape Evans by Scott.

On 11 February, after a fortnight's depressing struggle, Mackintosh, Joyce, Spencer-Smith, and three companions reached the Bluff, the promontory jutting out into the Barrier that had been a beacon to all previous expeditions.

They had taken twelve days for a mere forty miles. "Shacks' relief getting worrysome", Mackintosh wrote in his diary when tentbound by a blizzard. "What on earth am I doing here?" he asked plaintively next day,

> That's what I ask myself, and such thoughts rush me back at home to the dear ones waiting impatiently.[5]

After much agonising, Mackintosh decided to send Spencer-Smith back: "much to my disappointment," as Spencer-Smith put it, "tho' the skipper [Mackintosh] says that there's a chance next summer of getting out to Scott's tent."[6] With him, Spencer-Smith had Irvine Gaze (a cousin), and A. Keith Jack, both Australians who had joined the expedition at the last moment. They had already passed relics of Scott's camps still showing through the snow.

Mackintosh, taking Joyce, Ernest Wild, and the best dogs, went on. Ernest was Frank Wild's brother. He joined *Aurora* from the Navy, more or less inspired by Frank. Now he half expected any moment to see his brother appear over the snow from the south. On 20 February, in any case, they reached 80°S. They had taken three weeks to cover 150 miles and were thoroughly cold, exhausted, and uncomfortable. The dogs were collapsing, because they were being worked too hard too soon after landing. To save them for the next season, Joyce had tried to persuade Mackintosh not to take them further than the Bluff. Mackintosh, as Joyce put it, "decided otherwise":

> I quite see his point of view, that Shackleton may get across this year, and expect to find the depot.[7]

At least, in a lesson learned from Amundsen, they laid out transverse cairns to guide Shackleton to the depot. In matters of survival, Amundsen by now was the proven master, even at McMurdo Sound.

Storms delayed the work. Finally, on 24 February, Mackintosh and his companions started back. They had exactly ten days' food. Next day, "trekking out of the question", as Joyce put it:

> The blizzard – fury. We are now on half rations. My heart aches for the dogs . . . Our sleeping bags are soaked; clothes in a similar condition.[8]

"Sir Ernest considers that it is . . . improbable we shall require to erect the hut," Orde-Lees wrote the following day, 26 February, on *Endurance* in the Weddell Sea:

> He has appropriated a certain portion [for] the construction of the cubicles we are to occupy in the hold.[9]

This was to prepare for the long, dark winter ahead, since the hold was warmer than the cabins. The day before, all hands had been put off ship's routine. *Endurance* was a helpless hulk, firmly frozen in.

Was this the moment when Shackleton saw the death of all his hopes? Or was it three weeks later, on 16 March, which Orde-Lees saw as the day which "virtually marks Sir Ernest's acceptance of the inevitable". By then their northward drift was clear. That day, Shackleton ordered the fires to be drawn, and boilers blown down.

From her berth in the Thames *Endurance* had sailed 12,000 miles on her maiden voyage, crossed the Roaring Forties, fought the pack for 1,000 miles, and had then been trapped 60 miles from her destination. "It was more than tantalising," wrote Macklin, "it was maddening":

> Shackleton at this time showed one of his sparks of real greatness. He did not rage at all, or show outwardly the slightest sign of disappointment; he told us simply and calmly that we must winter in the Pack; explained its dangers and possibilities; never lost his optimism, and prepared for Winter.[10]

"It is a great disappointment to us of the shore party," as Orde-Lees put it, "but what it all means to Sir Ernest it is difficult for anyone who does not know him intimately to realize."

> The disruption of his plans is a catastrophe which hardly bears thinking of from either a sentimental or a financial point of view.[11]

By an odd little irony, on the very day that Mackintosh, on his side of the continent, reached 80°S, *Endurance* was swept past the longitude of Vahsel Bay. Dimly to the south, the land above the longed for base could be tantalisingly glimpsed.

The day before, in Orde-Lees' words, had marked "a step in my career". Charles Green, the cook, had succumbed, "appropriately enough", Orde-Lees recorded in his diary, "to housemaid's knee, and Sir Ernest, having too credulously heeded my infernal swanking on culinary matters has [appointed] me cook during the indisposition of Mr. Green. Thus it came to pass":

> *Someone*: "Oh Colonel (that's me) the Boss (that's Sir E.) wants to see you."
> *Me* (Soliloq.) "What asinine thing have I done in the last 24 hours?"
>
> I proceed with desultory knock kneedness to the boss's cabin . . . On arrival I stumble over the threshold . . . and make a clumsy entrance . . . Sir E. hates clumsiness & is liable to be adversely prejudiced thereby but as he is washing his hands & has his back to me he fails to perceive my approach. Instead of the expected reprimand he merely says "you can cook can't you Lees." "No I can't," I gurgle inarticulately to myself, but he mistakes my confusion for a bashful affirmative & my fate is sealed.
>
> Oh why oh why did I let my lying tongue run riot . . . If I ever did really boast that I could cook I merely meant . . . camp cookery for one or two people, but that I could cook a three course dinner for a whole ships company of 28 men – no I never said I could do that & moreover I can't & won't do it. I'll either starve them or poison them.

"I'm not sure that it's not all a deep laid snare," Orde-Lees went on darkly, "to show me up as I now see I well deserve to be." Green who, incidentally had joined at Buenos Aires in search of adventure, was inoffensive and hard-working. Nonetheless, proceeding "dolefully to the galley . . . the place where they cook, & I don't," Orde-Lees decided that Green, "the varlet," as he put it, "malingers",

> but the doctor thinks otherwise. It is inconceivable that a doctor could connive with a cook to bring about my downfall, but the fact that the cook has been giving the doctor boiling water these last few days is more circumstantial than extenuating.

"In great desperation & yearning to share my troubles with everyone," Orde-Lees went on,

I find Blackborrow – our stowaway who is now acting as pantry boy & is really a most excellent . . . young fellow. I soon find that he knows quite a lot about cooking & I confide in him that I know nothing & that I rely upon him to pull me through. He'll have a good deal of pulling to do I'm thinking.[12]

In fact, when Green returned to duty on 6 March, Orde-Lees retired from the galley, having done "jolly well", as Reginald James put it. He had actually managed to fight the peculiar habits of the British seaman. "I have that to be indebted to my wife," said Orde-Lees, "for besides many other blessings . . . she has insisted on my learning & has taught me to cook."[13]

When fresh seal meat was served, Walter How complained that it was "a ---- cheap way of running the expedition," as Orde-Lees recorded.

I pointed out to him that . . . Sir Ernest . . . was so keen on our having seal meat . . . on account of its antiscorbutic properties but I could see he was unconvinced and he merely expressed the sentiments of every one of the sailors on board.

They were, Orde-Lees said, "an extraordinary & prejudiced lot of men". One, a Scot called Thomas McLeod, refused to eat penguin because he believed the souls of dead fishermen lived in penguins. All the seamen, Orde-Lees with astonishment discovered, showed "a preference for tinned meats".[14] It was he who broke down their prejudice; "the red letter day of my Antarctic life", as he put it.

I cooked up an extra savoury roast with lots of onions. The whole ship was permeated with the savoury odour. Meanwhile, I warmed up four . . . tins of boiled rabbit . . . when the duty man from the fo'c'sle appeared I proceeded to "get busy" with the tinned rabbit. "But what's that we smelt cooking . . ." he said. "Oh, only some seal . . . for the wardroom" I replied.

"Well if the ward room can have it we can cant we" he grumbled putting down the unopened tins of rabbit . . . "Which would you rather have then, the seal or the rabbit," I said in fear and trembling lest he should realise that he was in a trap . . . but the ruse was successful, they had seal of their own free will in preference to [tinned] rabbit and now they cannot go back to it again.[15]

Shackleton had previously attempted to free *Endurance*. A few hundred yards away was an open lead, and he ordered everyone out with saws to cut up the ice and form a channel through which the ship could batter her way out. He gave up on 15 February, his birthday. At one point he had also considered marching over the pack ice to the nearest land. This was Prince Regent Luitpold Land, to the west, only twenty miles away, the unknown coast sighted in 1912 by Filchner.

The ice was broken and hummocked. Even with all their dogs it would, as Orde-Lees put it, be "out of the question to get the hut and all our provisions ashore, some fifty tons . . . at a minimum".

> To transport the motors . . . would be impossible. The surface is precisely similar to a ruined city made of ice.[16]

It was hard to convince Shackleton of the motor sledge's limitations because, as Orde-Lees put it, he had "little mechanical sympathy. With him, the thing is all right if it goes & all wrong if it doesn't."[17] In any case Shackleton, said Orde-Lees, was "the last to admit defeat but what use is it to continue fighting against such overwhelming odds." It was

> enough to drive any leader to despair, but Sir Ernest keeps his spirits up, outwardly at least.[18]

McNeish was one, at least, who saw through Shackleton's outward optimism. "I have been insolating [*sic*] the boss's cabin," he wrote on 8 March,

> as he is going to stay in it during the winter we are drifting away from the land so I don't think there will be any chance of a landing next spring.[19]

Shackleton was still pretending that next season the transantarctic crossing could begin. He was, in Worsley's words, "the cheery, happy chief, who was leading his men in a great adventure".[20] The fact remained that, after reaching 76°58′S on 21 February *Endurance*, embedded in the pack, had started inexorably drifting north.

For almost two months Worsley, climbing every day to the crow's nest, was able to report tantalising glimpses of land on the southern horizon. These were the ice cliffs and mountain hinterland of the Filchner ice shelf. Sometimes they were miraged up, a hundred miles away. It was the start of the transantarctic crossing. Finally, as *Endurance* slowly drifted away, even the mirage dissolved. Shackleton did not go up into the crow's nest. It was as if he could not bear, for the second time, a taunting glimpse of the might-have-been.

Meanwhile, the pack was revolving, and *Endurance* followed obediently with slow, aimless, intermittent oscillations. That, more than anything else, gave a sense of helplessness before the gathering forces.

"No outside work," McNeish recorded one all too typical day in the middle of March, "only arguments about the war we are getting very anchious [*sic*] to get news of some kind".[21]

James, meanwhile, was trying to make the wireless work. Every month, the transmitter on the Falkland Islands had arranged to send a bulletin. Through the cumbersome array of condensers, spark gaps and coils the size of half gallon jars, not a single dot or dash of Morse code was heard. All that came through the earphones was the everlasting crackling and atmospherics. At a thousand miles the range at those latitudes, with such primitive apparatus, was too great.

"We are only anchious for the war news," McNeish repeated a month later. "We unanimously hope that the war God," as he picturesquely called the German Kaiser, "has been crushed without any further loss of life & we are all sorry we have no hand in the hanging of Him but," McNeish went on, in his highly idiosyncratic spelling,

> we all sincerely hope the Russians will capture him for if Briton do they will set him up in a palace for the ratepayers to keep.[22]

"Celebrated Empire Day," Worsley recorded on 24 May. It had been founded a decade before by the Earl of Meath, "to be spent by children in exercises of a patriotic and agreeable character".[23] Now, on *Endurance*, the day was marked, as Worsley put it, "by patriotic songs in the Ritz [the hold which had been turned into sleeping quarters],

> but not with liquor, tho' our hopes & wishes for Old England in her present struggle are none the less heartfelt for that.[24]

"It is all very well to talk of honour and glory," wrote Captain A. D. Talbot, of the Lancashire Fusiliers, to his fiancée that very same Empire day on the other side of the world, at Gallipoli,

> But there is another side to war; this place is nothing but a mass of dead . . . which fell on [April] 25th . . . and the worst part is neither the Turks or we want to fight each other . . . I am still very keen, but such slaughter as is going on these days seems to be wrong absolutely to me.

> Why must we throw so many noble lives away as if they were dirt. Well, cheer up; I am quite fit and cheery really but the stench round the place is starting to get on my nerves.[25]

"We drank the health of the Empire Day," Leslie Thomson, second officer of *Aurora*, was also writing that day in the Ross Sea, "and also gave the crew a tot."[26] Neither for them was it a wholly auspicious occasion. *Aurora*, under bare poles, black and weatherbeaten, was beset. On each side of the continent, both of Shackleton's ships were now helpless hulks, drifting with the ice.

Aurora had gone south with explicit orders from Shackleton that she was *not* under any circumstances to anchor in McMurdo Sound south of Glacier Tongue. Shackleton did not want the ship to suffer the fate of *Discovery*, and be frozen in. He was unwise to fetter the commander of the ship. He had in effect deprived those responsible for her safety of the only secure harbours on Ross Island. J. R. Stenhouse, Chief Officer, and in command while Mackintosh was away sledging, made the best of a bad job by mooring at Cape Evans. On 6 May, a south-easterly gale blew up. As gales go, it was not exceptionally strong, but it was from a quarter against which the anchorage was totally unprotected. *Aurora*'s moorings parted, and she was blown out to sea.

In the hut, four men were left marooned. On 2 June, the depot party returned. Mackintosh and his companions had arrived back at Hut Point on 25 March, after their journey to 80°S., very much the worse for wear. Since then they had been waiting for the sea to freeze so that they could cross to Cape Evans.

It had been a disastrous journey. Very little had been accomplished. Then Mackintosh had taken an unnecessary risk in not waiting until the ice was absolutely safe before crossing from Hut Point to Cape Evans. It was uncannily like Scott's preliminary débâcle on his depot journey in 1911.

In any case, Mackintosh was concerned to get the depots out next season as far as the Beardmore Glacier. "Most of us," as R. W. Richards put it, "were confident that [Shackleton] would cross the continent and . . . his party would [be] utterly dependent on our food depôts for their survival."[27]

XXXIV

"The secret of our unanimity"

"We are still gradually going north", Orde-Lees wrote on *Endurance* on 3 June, "but not nearly fast enough . . . to get out early enough to repeat the trans-antarctic attempt in time next year."[1] During the four and a half months since being beset, in whorls and zigzags, she had drifted nearly 650 miles, made 132 miles to the north, and now reached 74°45′ south latitude. "The Lord be thanked," wrote McNeish on 8 June, when the ship spurted five miles "nearer home", as he put it. "I am about sick of the whole thing."[2] This about summed up the feelings on board. All that could be hoped for was a safe and early escape from the ice.

"The depressing subject of conversation," in Orde-Lees' words, "is our unsatisfactory northward drift." The average was a mile a day. "We are 240 miles south of where Filsener [*sic*] the german was at this time," wrote McNeish, knowledgeably, at the end of June, "& he did not get out before Dec. 11th so I expect it will be Jan. at the earliest [*sic*] before we get to civilisation again."[3]

It was not so much of Filchner that Shackleton was thinking; nor even of Larsen in his doomed *Antarctic*. It was *Belgica*, like *Endurance*, that had been adrift on an unknown sea. From the moment that the land, or ice, behind Vahsel Bay disappeared from sight, they were in a blank on the map. The nearest known land was six hundred miles away to the north-west, at the tip of Alexander Island. What lay between was what anyone cared to think. There might have been an open channel to the west. That would threaten to lead *Endurance* into the uncharted waters of the Bellingshausen Sea, where *Belgica* was caught.

Other comparisons with *Belgica* were there to haunt Shackleton. It was *Belgica*, like *Endurance*, that had gathered a heterogeneous crew and *Belgica* eventually was riddled with ennui, insanity and dissidence. Not the geographical unknown, nor even the ice was Shackleton's real adversary: it was the human factor.

"We seem to be a wonderfully happy family," Orde-Lees recorded at the start of the drift, "but I think Sir Ernest is the real secret of our unanimity. Considering our divergent aims and difference of station it is surprising how few differences of opinion occur."[4] That was an understatement. Under normal conditions for example, Leonard Hussey (the smallest man on board) everlastingly cheerful and gregarious, would scarcely have associated with James Wordie, introverted and dignified; the man interested in people against someone concerned with things. Clark, the dedicated Aberdonian biologist, was worlds away from James, the equally dedicated Cambridge physicist. All would undoubtedly have kept away from Crean, or even George Marston, for that matter: to them, seamen and artists were equally reprobate. The permutations of incompatibility were endless. To add to the tension, there was the depressing sense of being at the mercy of outside forces. That all this was kept at bay was largely due, as Worsley remarked, to "the cheery happiness & bonhomie of Wild".[5]

Shackleton, said Macklin, "leant upon Frank Wild, and I always regarded . . . Wild as a . . . sort of foreman":

> Wild was a sort of intermediary too. Very often when we wanted things, instead of going to Shackleton we went to Wild – it was a sort of instinctive thing that you did. Wild was such a tremendously approachable fellow, and always so outstandingly ready to help in every possible way.[6]

Macklin nonetheless felt that Shackleton did not have "any cronies",[7] as he put it. Even towards Wild and Worsley, Shackleton contrived to avoid the appearance of favouritism. This was vital to avert resentment and fragmentation into cliques.

Shackleton was haunted by what he had learnt about *Belgica*. He became a stickler for routine. Punctuality at table was an inflexible requirement. "Breakfast," to quote Hurley, "was at 9 a.m. sharp else woe betide! Sir E's Humor in the mornings . . . being erratic."[8]

Although his men were left very much alone during working hours, Shackleton insisted on everyone gathering in the wardroom every day after dinner. He did not impose formal debates, as he so vividly remembered from *Discovery*, nor lectures, as Crean recounted from Scott's second expedition. The purpose was to preserve a necessary minimum of social intercourse, and prevent moral collapse. Entertainment and discussion were seemingly spontaneous. Nonetheless, in Macklin's words, Shackleton would

> nevertheless almost automatically "boss" anything that he was at the moment connected with. For example, he would even take charge of any little sing-songs we had, tell one of the party to sing this or that, and even in the course of the singing say "not so loud" etc.[9]

Sometimes Greenstreet would "fool around", as he put it, and get "a roar of laughter".

> Next time there was anything on [Shackleton would] say "Go on do your stuff" and I'd say "Well, sir, it was done on the spur of the moment, it wouldn't go over now . . ." "Oh, go on, do it." And I'd say "No, it won't go over." He was very annoyed with me for not doing it, because he wanted it. But he had a poor sense of timing for that sort of thing.[10]

Greenstreet felt that Shackleton "liked people to play up to him. If he said anything, he liked you to throw the ball back, to say 'You know best' and all that sort of thing."[11]

Behind it all, Shackleton, as usual, was very carefully watching for effect. This was no longer like *Nimrod*, with a clear and undisputed goal.

Endurance was in a kind of limbo. The only visible movement was in the alternation of wind and calm sweeping through the cold and the dark. Otherwise, *Endurance* seemed encased in a static landscape of ice. Only the occasional drift of a sounding wire, the change of altitude of the stars, detected by Worsley and James through the theodolite but too fine to be seen by the naked eye, revealed that the ship was actually moving.

As the winter dragged on, ennui nonetheless descended. For Shackleton, the choice was disintegration, or domination, even in little things. At one point he was worried about long hair on his companions. It seemed a warning signal from *Belgica*. He made everyone crop each other's hair; providing himself, incidentally, as the first victim. "We do look a lot of convicts," McNeish remarked, "& we are not much short of that life at present but still hoping to get to civilisation some day."[12]

Shackleton did, however, keep the worst dissension at bay. The one serious incident was in the fo'c'sle early in July. "Several hands," in Hurley's words, "complaining of the Bosun having called them evil names & struck them."[13] The bosun was an unsympathetic trawler hand called Vincent, a blustering bully promoted on the principle, perhaps, of poacher turning gamekeeper. He was a familiar mess-deck type. "Harmony & goodwill being imperative amongst 9 men confined . . . to a single room for a long indefinite period,"[14] as Worsley put it, Vincent was swiftly disrated. As a nickname, "Bosun" stuck.

Shackleton, said Orde-Lees, meanwhile, was "one of the greatest optimists living".[15] Orde-Lees was also driven to jot down in his diary that "Optimism is synonymous w. improvidence or at least promotes it & almost always leads to disappointment."[16] For the moment, however, he was content to observe that Shackleton's "unfailing cheeriness means a lot to a band of disappointed explorers like ourselves".

> As most of our number are prone to regulate their demeanour by his, perhaps it is just as well that he is able to conceal his disappointment . . . so splendidly.[17]

Orde-Lees was the right man to make this kind of observation, for he was the born outsider, and often it is the outsider who has the insight.

Orde-Lees sometimes took a bicycle out on to the pack ice and, in his words, "ventured on a little trick riding with some little success". Around midwinter, he got lost in the process, had to be fetched by a search party, and was ordered henceforth not to leave the ship alone. "No one," he plaintively said, "knows what it means to me to have a bicycle and a place to ride it, however rough & heavy the going."[18]

To call Orde-Lees eccentric would be too simple. He was somehow at odds with his surroundings. He even managed to quarrel with Wild, which took some doing. Wild was the ideal second-in-command, able to get on with all kinds of men.

Orde-Lees, however, was the one regular officer on *Endurance*. The conflict building up between himself and the rest "of course", as he himself put it baldly, was because "I cannot get out of 'service' ways".[19] Once, for example, to appease grumbling on the lower deck, Shackleton told him to give the seamen a quarter of every case of delicacies opened. The first time, Orde-Lees demanded from a sailor, in best Service style, a receipt for, as it happened, "½ doz. bottles of Heinz's chutnee". The sailor was offended, and complained. Shackleton, as Orde-Lees recorded in his diary,

> said that it was contrary to the spirit of . . . the Merchant service . . . he was very nice about it . . . but I could see he was displeased . . . It seems

> such a trifle yet I would have given a lot for it not to have happened . . . In the "service" it would have been far more serious to have omitted to have obtained a receipt.
>
> Thus do we sometimes err in striving to do right.[20]

Orde-Lees, in fact, had been made storekeeper and messman at his own request. He proceeded, in his own words, to restow "everything to my own satisfaction".

> My relatives who read this [as he put it] will appreciate what I mean, knowing, as they do, my diabolical propensity for packing things.[21]

Orde-Lees kept a subtly different diary from any other on *Endurance*. Although obviously intended to be read, it was chatty, informative, self-revealing, unfettered by unctuous "good taste" or fear of what others might think. It was an interior dialogue; almost a "stream of consciousness".

As *Endurance* had entered the pack, Orde-Lees was writing how "it fell to my unwilling lot to go down on my knees and scrub the passages":

> I am able to put aside pride of caste in most things but I must say that I think scrubbing floors is not fair work for people who have been brought up in refinement.
>
> On the other hand I think that under the present circumstances it has a desirable purpose as a disciplinary measure it humbles one & knocks out of one any last remnants of false pride . . . & for this reason I do it voluntarily and without being asked but always with mingled feelings of revulsion and self abnegation.[22]

"These soliloquies," as he put it, "are not of much interest but appreciative ravings about the pack are likely to become monotonous as the pack itself."[23]

The monotony was so great that at times the wardroom was reduced to parlour games. Shackleton displayed an uncanny gift for "animal, vegetable or mineral". With a few shrewd questions, he was able to arrive at the answer. That too made an impression on his companions.

"A favourite form of amusement," Orde-Lees recorded, "is mutual impersonations." He was himself, he confessed in his diary on 7 June, "inclined to be a little over anxious to please Sir Ernest at times". The night before, McIlroy, Orde-Lees himself noted, took him off "cleverly as follows":

"Yes sir, oh yes certainly sir, sardines sir, yes sir here they are (dashes to pantry and back) and bread sir, oh yes sir, bread sir . . ." (Another dash to pantry and much grovelling effusion . . .) "And may I black your boots sir," and so on.

Orde-Lees, as he explained, was in "disfavour" just then, because he had "stopped the supply of bread . . . at night and given biscuits instead. Still all said and done, there's no smoke without fire." Perhaps, he considered, the "broad hint" would do him good. "Better to be called a toad than a toady."[24] His obsequiousness before Shackleton was, paradoxically, consistent with his distaste for authority. It was the superior personality that he recognised. Threaded through his diary was an essay or commentary on Shackleton.

"To serve such a leader," Orde-Lees wrote as they were still sailing south, "is one of the greatest pleasures of the whole trip; he expects his orders to be literally & promptly obeyed but he knows one's limitations better than one does oneself and he invariably allows for them, he never expects one to do more than one is capable of, he trusts one implicitly and he always appears to be pleased with what one has done."

Thus he gets the very best . . . out of all his staff. His adaptability to each of our own views . . . & his tactful way of reconciling our views with his whilst giving us the impression that he is modifying his schemes to suit ours are amongst his most salient characteristics.[25]

Shackleton was also "splendid where intoxicants are concerned",

he gauges exactly how much is suitable to the occasion & necessary to satisfy without permitting . . . objectionable indulgence, & he allows to be issued just so much and no more.[26]

Shackleton had "brilliant resource . . . Although he is expert at nothing in particular he is easily master of everything."[27] Also, said Orde-Lees, Shackleton "combines intrepidity with caution in an extraordinary degree". That was written on 20 January, just as *Endurance* was being beset. Shackleton, Orde-Lees continued,

always seems to realise his responsibility to us & to his patrons & is ceaseless in his endeavours to save us from the remotest anxiety, without being in the least demonstrative about it.[28]

Shackleton's companions had begun to feel that although they might not trust him with their money, they would implicitly trust him with their lives.

Fear, Shackleton could charm away. Ennui was a more intractable foe. "How dreary the frozen captivity of our life," said Hurley, "but for the dogs."[29] The sixty or so who had survived fights, disease and parasites; who, snarling, playing, malingering, howling at the moon, caricatured their masters, provided entertaining companionship. Early in the drift of the *Endurance*, the dogs had been moved from the deck to the floe. There, they lived in kennels made by McNeish, and fanciful igloos concocted by others out of plates of ice. It was like a little township to break the crenellated desolation of the pack. "No animal life", was now, in winter, a frequent remark in Worsley's diary.

Idleness, as every explorer had discovered, was the pitfall of the polar night. To try and keep everybody occupied, Shackleton at first arranged a general rota of dog-minding. He then discovered that not all men are doggy, and most dogs are particular about their masters. In April, he divided the dogs into six teams, each with its regular driver. He himself was not one. The drivers were Wild, McIlroy, Hurley, Macklin, Crean and Marston; "only those", said James, "who will do the big journey".[30] Shackleton was still implying that next season, somehow, the continental crossing would be carried through; and his men, for the first time, seriously set about learning to drive dogs.

As a practice load, a passenger was often taken on the sledge. Macklin frequently took Cheetham, "a cheery little fellow", as he put it, "who had a strange outlook on life and wonderful views of his own for reforming various social evils":

> Some days we used to set off in the lovely long sunsets [said Macklin before winter clamped down] and return by moonlight. On these occasions he used to remain very silent and pensive, occasionally breaking remark:
>
> "I say, Doctor, don't you think we are better off than the King?"
>
> "I don't know, Cheetham."
>
> "Well, I'm happy, Doctor, and you're happy, and here we are sitting on a sledge driving smoothly home and looking at the wonders of the World; it goes into your soul, like, don't it, Doctor? – the King with all his might and with all his power couldn't come here and enjoy what I'm enjoying, for one thing he wouldn't be allowed to . . ."
>
> Again long silences and then a snatch of song:
>
> "Justice in England that fine and happy land
> Justice in England I cannot understand.

> Justice for the rich and poor it tells a different tale,
> For the rich man always seems to get the balance of the scale"
>
> Sometimes I took out Green . . . it was a great treat for him after the galley, and he was like a schoolboy, and thoroughly enjoyed being tumbled into snowdrifts – but then it did not happen often to him![31]

The regular patter of paws, the scrape of sledge runner on ice crystals, the drivers crying "Mush!" "Gee!" "Whoa!", created the illusion that the transantarctic crossing was still ahead. It showed how Amundsen had "got the Pole". It also, perhaps, gave Shackleton another taunting glimpse of the might-have-been. On the floe, drifting north over the Weddell Sea, his drivers were making all the beginners' mistakes they otherwise might already have made in the mysterious hinterland to the south of Vahsel Bay.

Today we know that hinterland to be a short mountain crossing and then a fairly gentle rise over the inland ice to the South Pole. Topographically, it is not nearly as difficult as the climb from the other side, nonetheless it is no place to learn as you go. Nor, with crevasses and uncertain weather, was it terrain where Shackleton was likely to have accomplished the fifteen miles day after day upon which he had based his plan. He had acted like a gambler. Orde-Lees was beginning to be "grateful to providence", as he put it, "that 'God blew with his wind' ",[32] and swept them away from landing.

To quell, perhaps, any lurking sense of apprehension, dog races were occasionally held. On 15 June, the "Dog Derby" was run. In fine, cold midwinter weather, during the faint, midday twilight, it was a festive day out on the floe.

> Everyone [said Worsley] wagers all available chocolates & cigarettes . . . the current coin . . . the betting fever rises high – finally . . . sovereigns . . . take . . . the place of chocolates and cigarettes. I get my modest "quid" on Wild . . . but Sir Ernest goes in in his usual whole-hearted style & soon has a fiver on Wild, some at 2 to 1 on.

Wild duly won – although just by a whisker ahead of Hurley, who fancied himself and his team. Shackleton displayed all the unconcerned delight of what Worsley called a "Rale Ould Irish sporting gentleman".[33]

"One wonders," it took Orde-Lees to say, "what he really does think with so much anxiety concealed beneath so calm an exterior."[34] Each man in turn got a hint during the night watches. One of the watchman's duties was to tend Shackleton's stove.

It was necessary to keep an "equable temperature", in Hurley's words,

> a difficult job as the Boss's room is but a small cabin. The temperature within is either 90° or freezing according to the . . . wind . . . Sir E's temper reciprocates with the room temperature.[35]

"One seldom found him asleep," as James put it, "he would invariably ask some question about the wind or the state of the ice."[36] Perhaps it was these glimpses of the tension Shackleton was controlling that partly explained his gift of inspiring those around him.

The movement of the ice on the Weddell Sea remained an enigma. It might well sweep *Endurance* clear. To judge by the age of some of the floes, it might equally circle round and never release its grip. Perhaps Shackleton was haunted by a tale told by Amundsen about *Belgica* when she was beset in the Bellingshausen Sea. Hopping from iceberg to iceberg, and island to island, Amundsen seriously thought of making for civilisation in a kayak. "It would naturally take several years," he had written at the time, "but there is no doubt, it would be possible."[37]

Shackleton also had the two green volumes of Nordenskjöld's *Antarctic* to haunt him with other echoes of the past. Nordenskjöld, being a Swede, was a moralistic man. One of his aims now, as the citizen of a neutral state, was to prevent future wars by rewriting school textbooks to encourage peace. On the other hand, as Shackleton knew from personal acquaintance, he was intellectually honest. Nordenskjöld had not cheated with his own experience in order to present a heroic vision. *Antarctic* was no simple schoolboy tale of derring-do; it was a rich guide to a vital store of other men's experience.

Nor was Nordenskjöld a selfish man. He had let his men tell their own tales. His book contained Larsen's own record of how *Antarctic* fared in the selfsame Weddell Sea. With the bare bones of the tale, of course, Shackleton was familiar. *Antarctic* had sunk. Her crew had escaped. It was in the manner of the deed, the way of leadership, that the lesson lay. "A seaman who loses his sense of humour and courage in the hour of need," Larsen had written in his diary as he watched *Antarctic* slowly being crushed by the ice, "ought really not to go to sea."[38]

On 12 February, 1903, *Antarctic* finally foundered. "Farewell to all illusions," wrote Larsen, "of a quick return home."[39] When everything possible had been salvaged Larsen wrote in his movingly childlike unpunctuated style,

> We improvised a tent of some salvaged sails here coffee was served after all our work there was nothing more to be done for the moment. The ship is sinking more and more at 12.45 every man stood still and watched the ship sink it was an extremely solemn moment . . . and desolate it was for us who now stood out here on the drifting ice thousands of miles from any helping hand to take us home again to our dear ones.[40]

From the start Larsen soberly proposed to get everyone home safe and sound. First, he had to get his men ashore. For sixteen days he led them in open lifeboats. "Gypsies of the drift ice," as he put it, "drifting here and there with wind and current."[41] But he got his men safely off the ice.

On the last day of February, Larsen finally reached Paulet Island, in Erebus and Terror Gulf. Paulet Island was a providential haven; but it was merely an arid cone of rock. Nobody knew where they were. They would have to save themselves. In Larsen's own words,

> Neither moaning nor groaning will help, only courage and energy here one must fight one's way forward against the elements, which do not show a pleasant side but usually are sour and perverse and try to harm us – we've seen enough of that but we will see who wins – the ice or we![42]

Early in June, one of the Norwegian sailors, Christian Wennersgaard, died from approximately the same symptoms Shackleton had shown on the southern journey on *Discovery*.

The survivors had to pin their hopes on reaching Nordenskjöld at Snow Hill Island, on the other side of Erebus and Terror Gulf, almost a hundred miles off. The outside world at least knew where Nordenskjöld was. Larsen's only means of escape, however, lay in lifeboats saved from *Antarctic*. To reach Nordenskjöld, therefore, meant an open boat journey in the spring. The outcome was by no means certain. All winter, it was the overhanging thought.

> It must not arouse too great surprise [in the words of one of Larsen's men], if now and then under the influence of hunger, darkness and cold the sense of desertion grew great, and expressed itself in a grain of despair.[43]

It was on 31 October 1903 that Larsen, with three companions, finally set off in his open boat to fetch help from Nordenskjöld. It was a dangerous and difficult voyage. Larsen had to row all the way, in the teeth of southerly storms, heaving the heavy whaler up on to a floe when threatened by the pack ice. For three nights in succession, Larsen did not sleep. In the end, of course, he did get through. As his simple words revealed, he was every inch a survivor. He had shown that even in the Antarctic, shipwreck need not necessarily mean the end. It was a notably inspiring tale to read and recall as *Endurance* creaked to the pressure of the ice.

Even Larsen's tale, however, could not help Shackleton control his craving for action. For that, Worsley was a much needed outlet: "Sir E. & I have just been projecting a voyage to the S. Pacific," he had recorded, typically, back on 12 May, "by way of reaction against our present forced inactivity."[44]

Shackleton was fascinated by buried treasure. He quite seriously wanted to look for pirate hoards on desert islands. The treasure of Captain Kidd was one of his private quests. In Worsley, Shackleton had found someone wholly congenial with whom to discuss such plans. Worsley, "Skipper" now to Shackleton, "Wuzzles" to everyone else, in any case had a yen for fabulous pearl beds in tropic lagoons. He was the man to agree even with the more outlandish schemes.

It was Wild who, gently, would deflate their plans for instant wealth. He, Shackleton and Worsley had developed into a kind of triumvirate, but it was Wild, calm and patient, who was the pillar of the little community. He was, in Greenstreet's words, a "wonderful foil to Shackleton . . . with his Irish temperament".[45] Even now Shackleton, without exception, was seen as an Irishman.

For Shackleton it must almost have come as a relief when, as McNeish recorded on 14 July,

> All hands is standing bye we had a slight shock last night . . . there was a noise under the bottom aft the same as if the ice had broken up . . . the Boss thinks it was a whale but I thinks different.[46]

"She's pretty near her end," Shackleton actually said, according to Worsley, when *Endurance* quivered to the shock. Shackleton happened to be in his own cabin, talking to Wild and Worsley at the time. As Worsley put it,

> The wind howled in the rigging and I couldn't help thinking it was making just the sort of sound you would expect a human being to utter if they were in fear of being murdered . . . Still I couldn't believe that the *Endurance* would have to go . . . "The ship can't live in this, Skipper," . . . Shackleton . . . said at length, pausing in his restless

march up and down the tiny cabin. "You had better make up your mind that it is only a matter of time . . . What the ice gets, the ice keeps."[47]

With another ship, Shackleton might have spoken in a different vein. *Endurance*, as he had come to realise, was no *Fram*. Her bilges were not round enough; her sides had too much tumble home. She was safe just as long as she was frozen in her floe. When that broke, she would be at the mercy of the ice. She would hardly rise to the inevitable squeeze, and would almost certainly be nipped. Shackleton had been warned about this before he bought *Endurance*, and so would have only himself to blame. "I admired his self-control," said Worsley, who was not exactly admired for self-control himself. But outside the cabin, no one knew what had been said.

Nobody, however, could hide the fact that the ice, after three months of quiescence was, like a volcano, showing signs of life. The tremor in the ice coincided with a spurt in its movement. *Endurance* had been drifting at about five miles a day. She was now swept northwards over the 74th parallel at twice that speed. Also she was hugging a fairly constant longitude around the 49th meridian west. The ice was actually moving parallel to what is now called the Lassiter Coast of the Antarctic Peninsular, as yet undiscovered and unknown. Shackleton understood, however, that after moving west for several months, a circular current was pressing the ice up against land. It was not a pleasant thought.

Still, there was nothing to be done but wait and see. There were, meanwhile, other difficulties with which Shackleton had to cope. When *Endurance* ceased to be a ship and became a hulk beset, her officers lost their authority. Only Cheetham, being in charge of the fo'c'sle hands, still had a function. Worsley, Hudson and Greenstreet felt dispossessed and noticeably ill at ease.

Greenstreet, in any case, was under a slight cloud. When first he joined *Endurance* he happened to mention that his father knew Joseph Kinsey, Shackleton's erstwhile agent in New Zealand. Shackleton, however, had quarrelled with Kinsey and, in Greenstreet's words, "If you were a pal of somebody he didn't much care for, he sort of classed you with him."[48]

One Saturday early in the winter, Worsley "for a change," as he put it, "ran out on the floe in a state of nature & had a brief – a very brief – snow bath" when the temperature was 29°F below freezing:

> Poor Crean who was taking his pups for their morning constitutional on catching sight of me naked in the snow nearly fainted – thinking I'd "gone wrong in the napper". Now everyone except myself, is sorry for me & say its a pity to see one so young go wrong![49]

Behind his restless and erratic buffoonery Worsley – who was physically of medium height, raw-boned, with a slightly twisted face and a suspicion of a fixed grin – hid, in the way of the sea, a surprising sensitivity and capacity for observation. Just before the sun had disappeared for the winter, for instance, he described a dog sledge excursion over the ice:

> The scenery returning is exquisitely beautiful . . . we come to . . . smooth young ice like a huge snow covered lawn with a few dark lines where it has cracked . . . the only other mark being our trail winding . . . ahead till it comes to a heavy . . . line of . . . rafted ice silhouetted against a lovely flaming crimson & golden glow in the N.W. where we can see three tiny faint black splinters standing up – our little ship solitary in a wilderness of ice, but calling us comfortably home.[50]

As winter came down he wrote, "To a seaman it sounds strange to . . . feel a fresh gale with hard squalls, & to feel absolutely no motion . . . in the ship. She is held rigid as a rock by the . . . ice frozen round her to a depth of two or three feet or more."[51] In the winter dark, on a "brilliantly clear moonlit night", as he put it, around 75° south, there was "abnormally heavy rime on deck [and] aloft. Ship looks like a Xmas cake."[52] Of this Hurley, irrepressible and indefatigable as ever, made one of his best photographs.

Even routine navigation took on an extra quality for Worsley. On 25 June, with James' help, he took an occultation for chronometer correction:

> The telescope . . . gave a magnificent sight of the moon . . . It is fascinating to watch the large brilliant glowing silver sphere sweeping steadily along direct for the star, which is eclipsed behind the thin dark invisible segment of the moon with such suddenness that it can be timed with ease to half a second.[53]

Worsley recorded how it was Crean who made himself "foster father" to the pups born along the way. They had also, said Worsley, adopted "Amundsen".

> They tyrannise him most unmercifully. It is a common sight to see him, the biggest dog in the pack, sitting out in the cold with an air of philosophic resignation, while a corpulent pup occupies the entrance to his igloo. At "Hoosh Time" Crean has to stand by Am's food otherwise these villainous young scoundrels will eat the big dog's whack, while he stands back to give them fair play . . . It is a fine sight to see the big dog

> play with them, seizing them by the throat, beck or "whatnot" in what looks like a fierce fashion while really quite gentle with them, & all the time teaching them how to hold their own & putting them up to all "the tricks of the trade".[54]

Around midwinter, when the ice stirred, the noise, to Worsley, was

> like an enormous train with squeaky axles being shunted with much bumping & clattering. Mingled with this were the sound of steamer whistles starting to blow . . . & underfoot moans & groans of damned souls in torment. A constant undertone as of a heavy distant surf is heard when the louder noises . . . cease.

The disturbance was some way off. Worsley went off to investigate. "The ship," he said, "was quite invisible, and one had to 'steer home' by the stars:

> It is impressive to stand on the blocks of heavy rafting ice & feel the irresistible forces of Nature working under your very feet . . . The ice . . . tents & domes upwards, breaks rafts in huge blocks . . . that travel forward at a steady rate of 3 feet a minute. Occasionally a thud is heard as a block topples over. Suddenly sound & motion cease, renew for a moment, then all is still again – the current has deflected or the floe has yielded to pressure.[55]

And intermittently, as a sort of backdrop to this drama, would come the display of the Aurora Australis, the Southern Lights. Like curtains in the sky, shivering and dissolving in pale unearthly colours, they glowed and died away and glowed again for hours on end, in an eerie, yet strangely uplifting display of natural forces.

To the outside, Worsley still remained erratic, a man of mad impulse, and a bit suspect. So did Orde-Lees. With him the problem had begun months before, at the start of the drift.

Seal and penguin then were plentiful, but hinting at migration. "I did venture to suggest," Orde-Lees wrote, "that we ought to lay in a . . . store . . . as we had none left, but", he went on darkly, "other considerations overruled this."[56] One of these was a simple aspect of the national character, which seems to find precautions repugnant and somehow unmanly. On the lower deck, this was magnified. To Shackleton, however, it seemed like a suspicion of defeat and a reflection on his leadership. Nor did it help that Orde-Lees cited the experience of de Gerlache on *Belgica* or Larsen on *Antarctic*, still less, perhaps, that he turned out to be right. The great herds disappeared. There was a struggle to find enough seals and penguins day by day and build up a reserve.

It was Orde-Lees who did the hunting; "always alone"; as he put it, "on ski". Once, however, Shackleton accompanied him "on foot",

> to see how I was despatching the unfortunate creatures. Satisfied that my method . . . was . . . humane . . . he helped to remove the . . . inedible parts and then gave me a hand to drag the useful portion home. On the way I had the temerity to ask him how it was that . . . he had come to select me. "Well," he replied, "you may remember that I sent you a wire telling you to come up to see me on Tuesday or Friday, whichever was the more suitable." "Oh yes," I intervened, "and of course I came up on the Tuesday." "You did," he soliloquised. "How often have I wished since that you had postponed it to Friday."

"I held my peace," as Orde-Lees put it, "but refrained from telling him that . . . he had played the identical trick on Marston in his first expedition."[57] Marston was also losing favour with Shackleton. This was chiefly because Marston's mobile, rubbery face was showing all too clearly signs of the worry within. Like Orde-Lees, for that matter, Marston had left a wife and family behind.

Orde-Lees, however, did not allow Shackleton's very Irish shaft to hurt him. Indeed, in a peculiar way, the incident seemed to enhance Orde-Lees' respect for Shackleton.

Such were the usual psychological hazards of an isolated community. Cliques, quarrels and tension hung in the background. There was the irritation of all too familiar faces, and no hope of escape. The long winter night was as usual a strain of its own. It was a combination that had all but broken de Gerlache on *Belgica*. Above all, however, it was essential to believe in the leader, and Shackleton possessed the power of forestalling trouble without actually appearing to do anything. Of that, the dig at Orde-Lees was one aspect. Macklin saw another, when he described how Shackleton

> had a nice way of every now and then, when he came across you by yourself, getting into conversation and talking to you in an intimate sort of way . . . Asking you little things about yourself, how you were getting on . . . and all that sort of thing . . . Sometimes when you felt he'd been perhaps a bit ruthless, pushing you round a bit hard, he seemed to have the knack of undoing any bad effect . . . with these little intimate talks.[58]

This, Shackleton could do both fore and aft. Doctor, stoker, sea lawyer, fo'c'sle malcontent; each would feel, for the moment, that Shackleton was his especial friend.

Not that the barriers between upper and lower deck had absolutely broken down. Officers and men still messed separately and led their separate lives. Shackleton, however, insisted on equality of treatment. "He was an amazing man," said Macklin, "he could meet *anybody* on their own ground."[59]

Shackleton grasped the ritual use of scapegoats in diverting aggression and avoiding conflict. Orde-Lees, the "Colonel", filled the bill. "He made no friends", in Macklin's words.

> Most of us grew to regard [him] as a generally . . . odd sort of person, different from the rest of the crowd. Lees . . . became the butt of everybody's bad temper; and as he was curiously receptive of abuse and rarely reacted violently, this served as a useful safety valve.[60]

It was the scientists, however, that Shackleton most deliberately baited. Under the dark beams in the wardroom, his deep voice with its faint hint of brogue, took on a dangerous mildness. Reginald James, in his own words, was "of course very green being quite fresh from Cambridge & had mixed mainly with the academic type". Shackleton was a "pretty different sort of proposition. He had little patience with the academic type of mind & would openly ridicule it". He had also, said James, "a wide general knowledge",

> But one soon found that it was not as good as he thought & also that it was wiser not to make corrections. He was given to "accurate inaccuracies" . . . giving great detail & thus creating the impression of very accurate knowlege, but often making considerable errors of larger facts. This I think was unconscious . . .
>
> [Shackleton] loved "leg pulling" & practical jokes & I was pretty easy game. One would be led on to give one's opinion . . . quite seriously only to have it turned into ridicule. Consequently at first . . . he was certainly hard to get on with [and] I never quite knew where I was.[61]

"Jimmy," in Macklin's words, was "something of a jest. He was . . . from the academic point of view quite brilliant, but from the practical point of view he was the most stupid, useless and clumsy man you could possibly imagine."[62] In Orde-Lees' words, "Jimmy does not think science compatible with humour."[63] Greenstreet agreed that James was clumsy but,

I . . . take my hat off to him. He'd led a very sheltered life, been brought up by two maiden aunts. He'd never roughed it in the world at all, but he stood up to it very well indeed . . . I went along one day . . . to . . . the meteorological station [aft] and James was in there playing around with various glass things . . . his fingers seemed to me all thumbs, and he crashed glass tubes right and left . . . and the language that he was turning out, you'd think he was a sailor! Where he'd picked up the words I wouldn't know – not from his maiden aunts anyway! He looked round and he blushed like a girl and dropped another test tube.[64]

At the midwinter celebration (one of the few organised entertainments), James, however, in Worsley's words, was the "gem of the evening" with

a Dissertation on The Calorie by Herr Prof. von Schopenbaum . . . very witty & truly unintelligible, as it is intended to be & his humour is keen but kindly. He . . . acts to perfection the part of the short-sighted kindly old German Professor, & there is a tiny touch of pathos in his humour . . . James could be [a] great actor.[65]

Behind his round spectacles, and a bland, academic exterior, James actually hid a shrewd interest in human nature. He had soon, for example, grasped Shackleton's failings, the first of which he listed as impulsiveness. Also he perceived the "mixture of personal magnetism bluff & blarney that could be irresistible". Possibly what united those on *Endurance* was that they had all succumbed to this.

James, in a sense, was lucky. He was helping Worsley with the delicate astronomical observations, or was himself out on the floe, oblivious of the cold, squinting into the eyepiece of a magnetometer to measure terrestrial magnetism. But everyone else was just waiting.

To that, Shackleton himself was particularly ill suited. Although he managed to preserve what Orde-Lees called his "inscrutable composure",[66] he did let slip through the mask sometimes a hint of all the worries behind. Then, on 1 August, McNeish recorded, "Blowing a gale of southerly wind

& the floe we were in has all broken up we got the dogs on board at 10-30 & every one got our warm clothes put up in as small a bundle as possible ready to get on to the floe it was noon before we had the boats & everything ready we have had a start out of our monotiny if ever any one had one for the ice has all broken up & the worst part of it was it broke right through the middle of the ship one half going one way &

one another it almost broke us in two halfs this hung on for about 20 minutes when the piece that was catching our bows split the other way one piece going under our bows which rectified us for a time but we are still in a precarious position it is 7 p.m. & there is no sign of a lull . . . I have placed my Loved ones fotos inside my Bible we got presented with from Queen Alexandra & put them in my bag.[67]

XXXV

Death agony of *Endurance*

There was an "oncoming tide of ice", said Frank Hurley, taking up the tale:

> Close against starboard we had the unique observation of a pressure ridge forming . . . huge blocks some 15 to 20 feet high slid off . . . When we are all in a delightful uncertainty . . . the pressure stopped & all assumed the Antarctic quiet once more. If we had been but 15 feet ahead of our present position . . . I think we would have had to abandon ship.[1]

As it was, *Endurance* had a list to port. Her beams had buckled, her rudder was damaged. From the masthead the pack, said Worsley, appeared in a "state of chaos".[2] After months as a solid plain, pressure ridges now ran in all directions. Around the ship the ice was shattered and hummocked. It was like the aftermath of an earthquake.

At least "Old Jamaica", as Worsley put it in sailor's slang, had returned. That was on 26 July. It was only the top edge of the sun, for a minute or so at noon, but after an absence of seventy-nine days "it means a lot to us", as McNeish put it.[3]

For good or ill, the monotony and the waiting had been relieved. In a sterile landscape there was movement. Icebergs which, all winter, were fixed landmarks, had drifted astern or borne up ahead. In three days *Endurance* made thirty-seven miles to the north and, on 3 August, she was carried over the 72nd parallel. She had covered four degrees of latitude in six months.

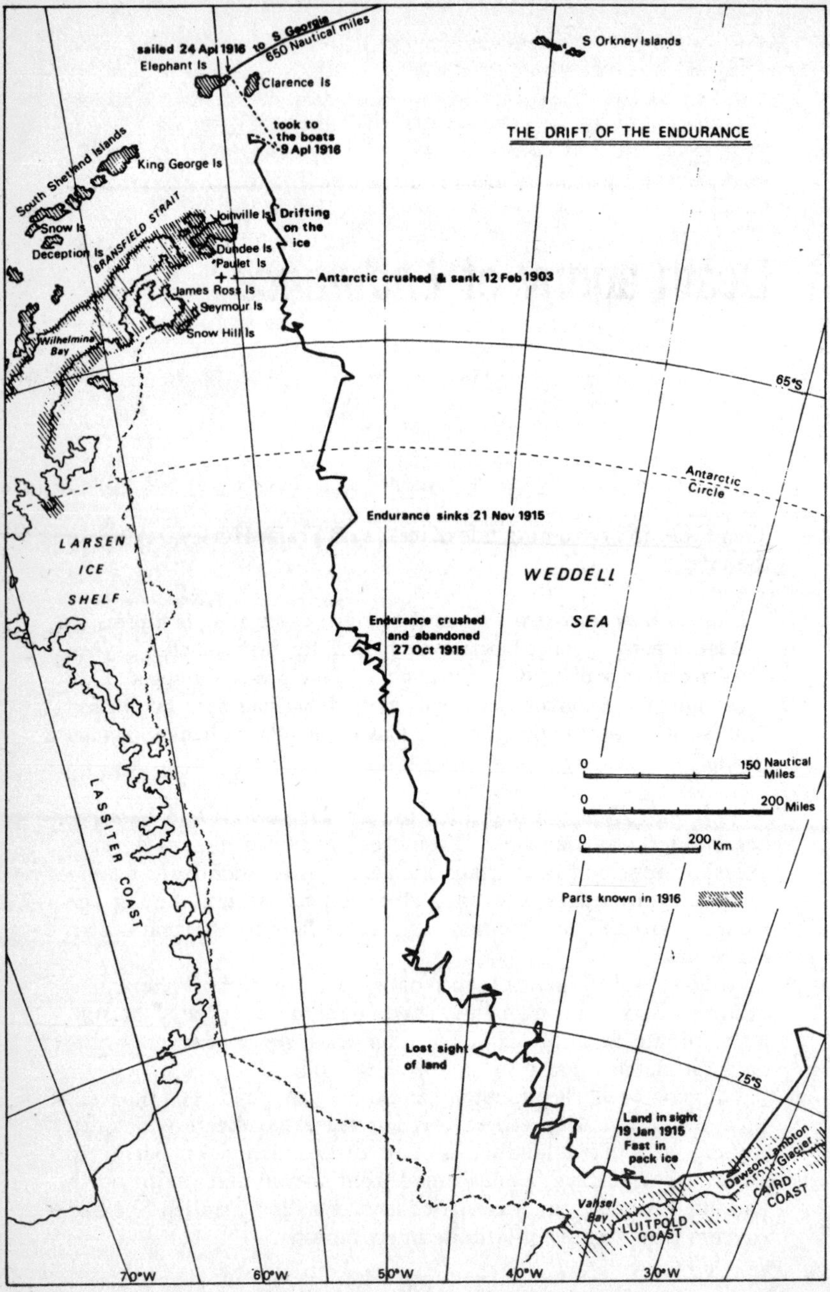
THE DRIFT OF THE ENDURANCE
sailed 24 Apl 1916 to S Georgia
650 Nautical miles
Elephant Is
Clarence Is
S Orkney Islands
took to the boats 9 Apl 1916
South Shetland Islands
King George Is
Snow Is
Deception Is
BRANSFIELD STRAIT
Joinville Is
Drifting on the ice
Dundee Is
Paulet Is
Antarctic crushed & sank 12 Feb 1903
James Ross Is
Seymour Is
Snow Hill Is
Wilhelmina Bay
65°S
Antarctic Circle
Endurance sinks 21 Nov 1915
LARSEN ICE SHELF
WEDDELL SEA
Endurance crushed and abandoned 27 Oct 1915
0 150 Nautical Miles
0 200 Miles
0 200 Km
Parts known in 1916
LASSITER COAST
Lost sight of land
75°S
Land in sight 19 Jan 1915
Fast in pack ice
Dawson-Lambton Glacier
CAIRD COAST
Vahsel Bay
LUITPOLD COAST
70°W
60°W
50°W
40°W
30°W

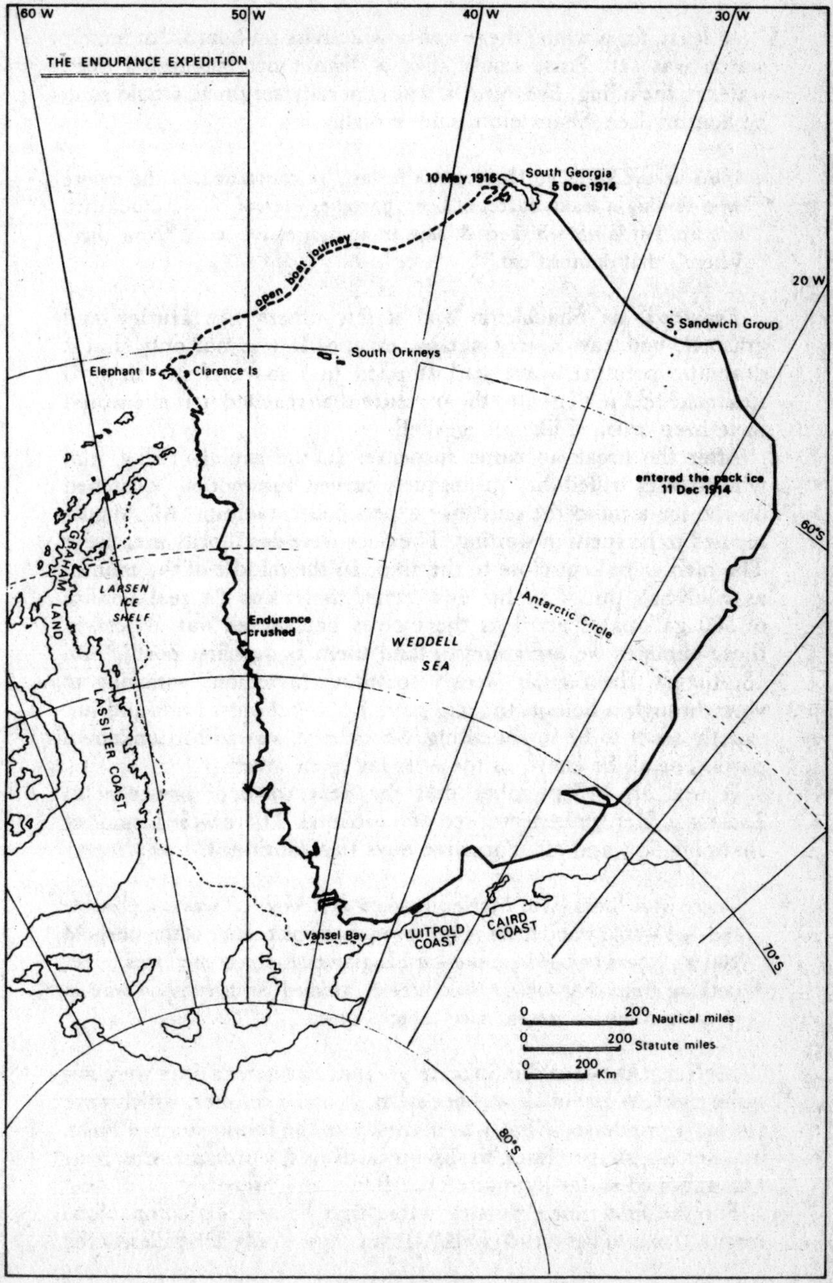

THE ENDURANCE EXPEDITION
60 W
50 W
40 W
30 W
20 W
10 May 1916
South Georgia
5 Dec 1914
open boat journey
S Sandwich Group
South Orkneys
Elephant Is
Clarence Is
entered the pack ice
11 Dec 1914
60°S
GRAHAM LAND
LARSEN ICE SHELF
Antarctic Circle
Endurance crushed
WEDDELL SEA
LASSITER COAST
Vahsel Bay
LUITPOLD COAST
CAIRD COAST
70°S
0 200 Nautical miles
0 200 Statute miles
0 200 Km
80°S

At least, for a while, there was now activity on board. An hourly watch was set. Frost smoke, like a distant fire, suggested open water in the offing. *Endurance*, it was generally assumed, would soon be floating free. Shackleton, said Worsley,

> spins us the yarn, no chestnut as far as I'm concerned, of the mouse who finding a leaky barrel of beer, partakes thereof till he's full, then sits up, twirls his whiskers & says in an aggressive tone, "Now then, where's that damned cat."[4]

Endurance, as Shackleton and a few others like Hurley had grasped, had had a very narrow escape. It was not only that a dramatic pressure wave had stopped just short of the ship. If *Endurance* had not risen to the pressure that reached her, she would have been crushed like an eggshell.

After the break-up came suspense. In the rapidly rising sun, what Hurley called the "grotesquely carved hummocks"[5] glistened on the ice around the ship like a petrified cataclysm. All August seemed to be spent in waiting. The dogs were desultorily exercised. The men were kept close to the ship. In the middle of the month, as McNeish put it in his own style, there was "a real bonfire of 500 gallons of petril as the motors has turned out useless in those climates we are going to land them at our first port".[6] On 13 August, the regular weekly sounding (a tedious winching of wire through a hole in the ice) gave 1,550 fathoms. Land did not exactly seem to be in the offing. Shackleton was still in unknown parts. For all he knew, to the west lay open water.

It was on 1 September that the next wave of pressure hit *Endurance*. Her timbers creaked and groaned. There were sounds of snapping fore and aft. For three days this continued.

> There were times [said McNeish] when we thought it was not possible the ship would stand it she is sprung in many places one of the stokhold plates . . . was buckled . . . she was hanging on from the mainmast aft & nothing from that forward the keel is jammed & there is no way in clearing it but at present everything is quiet.[7]

McNeish knew, as did Shackleton, that *Endurance*'s lines were not quite right. Worst of all was her stern. It had a counter, which gave the ice a purchase. What was needed was the round stern of *Fram*, and her egg-shaped lines, to slip upwards under pressure. *Endurance* had survived so far by main force alone, as it were.

For the first time, Worsley wrote that he and his companions might "have to get out & walk". It was now "only 250 miles to the nearest known land to Westd".[8] That was not much to go on. The "nearest known land" was Svend Føyn Land, sighted twenty years before by Larsen.

The ice was increasingly unstable now. *Endurance* seemed at the mercy of wind and tide and current that grew wilder and more erratic. All through September, tremors and shocks, like the harbinger of earthquake, reached the ship. At least the oppression of the cold and dark had gone. The thermometer was creeping up into lighter degrees of frost and even, sometimes, uncomfortable thaw. The sun was rising fast, and *Endurance* was actually moving to meet it. By the middle of the month she had crossed the 70th parallel, still drifting steadily northwards. This did not stop an outburst of Worsley's about

> delirium, induced by gazing too long on this damned infernal pack that seems like Vanderdecken [The Flying Dutchman] in a less desolate sea doomed to drift to & fro till the Crack of Doom splits N. & S. E. & W. into a thousand million fragments – & the sooner the better. No animal life! – no land! – no nothing!!![9]

The sky was Worsley's consolation. He had a taste for astronomy. He was very proud, one clear night, to be able to show James Mercury, "not often seen . . . in England's hazy climate. As a matter of fact James had never seen this elusive planet before".[10] A week later Worsley took a longitude by Mercury "for swank", as he put it, "not many people can boast of having done so".[11] Next day came another outburst about the "boring monotony & ennui of this purposeless drifting".[12]

Endurance was in an eddy and had lost a mile or two. By the end of the month, however, she had returned to her steady northerly progress with the pack. On 29 September, meanwhile, her floe had cracked, leaving open water down on one side. Next day, in McNeish's words, "The ice closed again but not in the same position & one corner caught our side abrest of the fore rigging." *Endurance* was caught in a giant pair of shears which "buckled the tween deck beems like a piece of cane we realy thought she was going to pieces when the pressure stopped".[13]

This was the third and worst squeeze that *Endurance* had so far survived. Orde-Lees was now re-reading Nordenskjöld's *Antarctic* with the very closest attention, even though neither Shackleton nor Wild quite approved of such "pessimism". *Endurance* was being carried towards the waters where *Antarctic* had met her end twelve years before.

Shackleton's unease and restlessness had now disappeared. He was almost ominously calm. It was as if he fed upon the scent of danger. His unfailing mask of optimism, in any case, suggested safety in the end. He ostentatiously gave McNeish orders to build a wheelhouse out of what remained of the hut timber, so that the steerman would have an easier time when *Endurance* actually got under way. On 10 October McNeish, as he put it, had

> been working all day getting the wheelhouse finished for we may break out at any time now as there is open water everywhere & within 12 foot from our bow but it may open round the ship the first time the wind goes south we are having a selection on the gramophone at present.[14]

On 15 October, *Endurance* did in fact break completely out of her floe. She was only in a narrow lead, but open water it was. After nine months, she was once more floating free. Worsley felt a surge of inspiration. He was actually captain of his ship again. He even hoisted sail; albeit merely a spanker to try and swing into a safe position. The forward hands also cheered up, doing real ship's work again.

That was on a Friday. "We dread Sundays," Hurley wrote, "as then the pressure seems most active."[15] McNeish commented gloomily,

> I dont see how we could have better luck than we had had. We have never had a religious service since the second [Sunday] out from Plymouth, but plenty of filthy remarks there are a few who cant speak of anything else & of course they think it makes them manly instead of Blagards.[16]

On this particular Sunday, 17 October, the floes once more jostled each other, and the ice closed. This led, the following day, to the fourth squeeze suffered by *Endurance*. It was by far the most dramatic. She was heaved up, as if by a solid wave, and thrown over to starboard in a few seconds, so that it seemed as if she must keel over on to her beam ends. She stopped, however, at a list of thirty degrees. "Dinner in the Wardroom," said Worsley, "is a quaint affair – most of the diners sit on the deck, feet against a batten & plates on their knees."[17]

Surprisingly, *Endurance* soon after righted herself. The ice relaxed. Two days later, on 20 October, the boiler was filled, and steam raised. Sea watches were set in expectation of an early break out. "The only thing not ready," as James put it in his diary, "is the ice . . . We might be any time from a few days to a couple of months before breaking out. Meantime ill concealed fidget in high places." Worsley, Hudson and Greenstreet were now noticeably excitable. James continued,

> I feel tonight a great desire to get back to work, real work, not messing about as I am afraid I have inevitably done this year. Jock [Wordie] & I have been talking a lot about Cambridge today. Would I were there again! I'll be blowed if I want to see any more ice as long as I live! I expect most of us feel the same, but we manage to conceal it fairly well nevertheless.[18]

"Last night we drank the health of our Sweethearts & Wifes," McNeish was writing the next Sunday, 23 October,

> I'm afraid we wont do so much longer as we have sprung a leak I am working all night trying to stop it the pressure is getting worse.[19]

"Things looks a bit serious," he decided next day. "I have built a coffer dam in the engine room."

Violent pressure from starboard had twisted the sternpost and started the seams. Water was pouring in. With his coffer dam, McNeish hoped to hold the water aft. Fires were lit, but the steam pumps could not cope with the leak. The hand pumps were manned watch and watch. All night long, the groaning of the ice and the cracking of timbers sounded an eerie obbligato to the clickety-clack of the pumps:

> we are still managing to keep the water down [in McNeish's words]. Sir Ernest & most of the hands are packing sledges I am afraid it is all up with the ship.[20]

McNeish was more sensible, or less inhibited, in his diary than the others. Next day, 25 October, the ice did ease, but pressure ridges were ominously creeping in all directions, like waves in some white, disturbed, infernal, viscous sea.

It was by now fairly clear that because of her fatal structural defect, *Endurance* would rise to no more pressure. When the ice opened, she had dropped down into the water. Now, instead of resting in a cradle, she was gripped above the sheer of her bilges. Had she only had rounder lines . . .

Down in the bowels of the ship, Hurley helped McNeish to caulk the coffer dam, but the water nonetheless streamed over in cascades. Still, Shackleton kept his men at the pumps. "Every muscle," in Macklin's words, "ached and revolted at the unspeakable toil."[21]

At 7 p.m., the following day, 26 October, in clear bright weather, the pressure returned to the attack on the starboard quarter, "with twisting strains racking ship fore & aft & opening butts of planking 4 & 5 inches on stard. side",[22] Worsley wrote.

Except for the ice and the ship, there was an eerie silence. Unseen forces were at work. Some far-off gale, perhaps, was compressing the ice. The tide, too, played a part; but mostly it was the westerly current crowding the floes up against land.

Whatever Shackleton was feeling, he kept it relentlessly under control. Hurley, as he put it, would "ever remember vividly" that day. "The dogs . . . set up distressed wails of uneasiness & fear – Sir Ernest standing on the poop calmly surveying the movements of the ice & giving an occasional peremptory order."[23]

All hands were kept at the pumps through the night. "Every spell on was an agony," Macklin said, "at each spell off I staggered to a settee in the wardroom and would fall asleep just in time to be prodded up for my next turn."[24]

"All hope," Hurley wrote, "is not given up yet for saving the ship."[25] But boats, provisions and equipment, were now being lowered on to the ice. "A strange occurrence," Worsley recorded,

> was the sudden appearance of 8 Emperors [penguins] . . . at the instant the heavy pressure came upon the ship. They walked a little way towards the ship then halted & after a few ordinary . . . cries proceeded to sing what sounded like a dirge for the ship.[26]

This "greatly impressed all the sailor element", wrote Macklin, trying to be detached. They "saw in it an omen". McLeod, the old Scots shellback, Macklin continued,

> cheerful as usual, immediately said "do you hear that, we'll none of us get back to our homes again." I know that the Boss was impressed by it.[27]

Worsley himself was on the verge of tears. He was losing his ship. It is an experience no captain can go through unmoved.

The morning of 27 October brought spasmodically increasing pressure. *Endurance* bent like a bow. Her seams opened. Pumping now seemed futile. "I don't remember anyone telling us to stop," said Macklin, "but we just seemed to understand that we might as well give up."[28] The ship, as Hurley put it, was

> apparently the nucleus of the disturbance, for we are surrounded by a labyrinth of grinding ridges and a maze of cracks of which she is the focus.[29]

In the middle of the afternoon, what Hurley called the "ice mill", after a respite, started again. "Closer and closer approaches the pressure wave on our starboard like a huge frozen surf. Immense slabs are rafted up to its crest, which topple are overridden by a chaos of . . . fragments."[30] *Endurance* was in a vice. She was being squeezed from both sides, and from the stern as well.

Hurley, meanwhile, was recording the scene from the ice, cranking the handle of his cine-camera, and also taking stills. He jotted in his diary,

> The ship rising on the crest of a great wave was so squeezed that her beams cracked & great ice blocks were forced under her counter . . . The whole time there was an incessant creaking & groaning of timbers . . . I went down into the Ritz & . . . fearing being jammed by cracking beams returned speedily to the deck.[31]

The ship was "in her death agony", said Macklin:

> It was a pitiful sight. To all of us she seemed like a living thing – we had sworn at her and cursed her antics in a seaway, but we had learned to love her as we now realised, and it was awful to witness her torture.

"The *Endurance*," Macklin went on, "must have been built of good stuff . . . for the way she continued to resist was wonderful." He was astonished to see the floe that butted on *Endurance*, "an old thick one holding out against the pressure but . . . in the middle holes suddenly formed, the pieces flying . . . upwards like the sections of a stage trapdoor."[32]

> *Endurance* [McNeish soberly recorded], is going to pieces fast the stern post broke . . . & then the keel was torn out of her then she filled rapidly.[33]

Out of the galley chimney, meanwhile, smoke appeared. Green, the cook, was imperturbably making supper. All hands assembled in the wardroom for the last meal on board. It was eaten in silence, while, in Hurley's words, "the ominous sound of giving timbers arises from below . . . Our sadness is for the familiar scene from which we are being expelled. The clock is ticking on the wall as we take a final leaving of the cosy wardroom."[34]

"The end came at last about 5 p.m.," wrote Shackleton, laconically, for his part. It was then, as he put it, that the "pressure started again irresistibly. She was doomed: no ship built by human hands could have withstood the strain. I ordered all hands out on the floe."[35]

As they were going over the side Shackleton turned to Orde-Lees and, in Orde-Lees' words, said "Well Old Lady" – using one of Orde-Lees' many nicknames –

> "We've got it in the neck all right this time, haven't we?" "Well, no, I don't think so", I ventured, "You wouldn't have had anything to write a book about, if it hadn't been for this". "By Jove, I'm not so sure you aren't right," he remarked [at] which we both had a good laugh.[36]

XXXVI

Responsibility to Shackleton

"I think we shall just be able by a stroke of good fortune to carry out our programme," Ernest Joyce was writing on another floe, that same day at McMurdo Sound, "That is," he continued, "lay a depot at 83°30′."[1] By that, he meant at the foot of the Beardmore Glacier, in readiness for Shackleton as he came off the ice cap.

Joyce was returning from a preliminary sortie to the Bluff, taking out supplies for the main journey south. He was leading five men the last few miles through a blizzard to the *Discovery* hut. In the intervals, he was scrawling a letter to James Paton, the bosun of *Aurora*, expecting the ship to return while he was still out on the trail.

Aurora, in fact, was just then emerging from the dangerous bottleneck between the Balleny Islands and the continental coast along Oates Land. She was still frozen solid into a floe, and the pack stretched endlessly on all sides. She was now, however, at last clear of land, out in the open sea, and only wind and current remained to interrupt her northwards drift. The Antarctic Circle was in the offing, which meant that *Aurora* had come 700 miles since the night in May when she had been blown out to sea, along with practically all equipment and supplies, leaving Mackintosh and his nine companions marooned at McMurdo Sound.

"We have left at Cape Evans," ran the official narrative of the *Terra Nova* (written by Teddy Evans) when she had picked up the survivors of Scott's second expedition two years before, "an outfit and stores that would see a dozen resourceful men through one summer and winter at least."[2] By an irony that Shackleton might not fully appreciate, Mackintosh and his companions now depended on those stores.

"The Scott expedition," said R. W. Richards, after helping to take an inventory, "was very lavishly equipped and . . . some of it was luxury stuff."[3] There was, however, a stock of tinned meat and, more important, pemmican and other sledging food.

"The only clothes I had [wrote Joyce on the other hand] was a singlet shirt drawers 2 pair Socks 1 pair finscoes [*sic*] 1 cardigan what a prospect to look forward to."[4] There, Scott's supplies were of little help. Shackleton's men had been marooned more or less with what they stood up in. All they found in the hut was some cast-off underclothing "which of course," as Richards put it, "we pounced on and used".[5] Heating and cooking seemed problematical, since even coal was short. In the end, it was successfully eked out with blubber.

Unlike Shackleton beside the wreck of *Endurance* in the Weddell Sea, Mackintosh and his men could not concentrate exclusively on their own survival. Their prime responsibility was to others, not themselves. They had to get the depot to the foot of the Beardmore Glacier, ready for Shackleton coming, as they believed, overland. Meanwhile, they had to assume that some day, somehow, they would be rescued.

Before the vital next season's journey could begin, a complete outfit had to be improvised. The only source was what Scott's expedition had left behind. Luckily there were tents and sledges, although everything needed repair. Out of a large canvas tent, Joyce and Ernest Wild, the handy sailors, made trousers and jackets. From old reindeer sleeping bags, they contrived finnesko. Three primus stoves were eventually salvaged from a scrap heap. They were, however, old, worn, maltreated, and entirely without spare parts. It was not clear how long they would last; nor therefore how long there would be warm food on the sledge journeys.

Worst of all, only six of the original eighteen dogs remained. Joyce rightly blamed this on Mackintosh's ignorance and obstinacy during the disastrous depot journey the previous season. Joyce, in fact, was one of the very few sensible British polar travellers of the age. He had a touch with dogs. Unfortunately he could not impose his knowledge and experience on Mackintosh.

Richards, a raw Australian teacher, twenty-two years old and just out of training college, had a "soft spot for old Joycey", as he put it:

> Joyce was in some way a bit larger than life, a bit of a buccaneer and inclined to exaggerate. A good chap if you knew his faults . . . A kindly soul and a good pal.

Not everyone that winter was so charitable. Most, in any case, agreed in disrespect for Mackintosh. "I neither liked nor disliked him," was Richards' verdict. "He was no leader and a colourless character."[6]

Joyce, more forcefully, blamed Mackintosh for their whole predicament. Mackintosh

> had no business to leave the ship in the first place, leaving no one on board who understood the conditions of Antarctica. The wintering of the ship there was hard to fathom: especially picking out an anchorage in the roadstead of Cape Evans.
>
> Can you realize anyone with any brains laying 13 miles away leaving sledging parties stranded without provisions fuel & light? Also lying close to the Hut at Cape Evans without landing stores and equipment, spells the last word to disaster.[7]

It was Mackintosh who had arbitrarily prohibited stores from being landed. Mackintosh's combination of weak leadership and gallantry without intelligence did not increase confidence in Shackleton who appointed him.

The group was so ill-assorted that it needed firm leadership. Mackintosh's weakness caused an unhappy winter plagued by the friction of men at odds with one another. To fill the vacuum at the top, would-be substitutes were fighting for ascendancy. Joyce acted as if he ought to be in command, of which there could be no doubt if polar experience alone counted. A Petty Officer, and the product of the late Victorian Royal Navy, however, Joyce was trained to follow, not to lead. Richards felt that he could handle Joyce, and therefore that he exerted influence unseen. In a lesser degree that held also for V. G. Hayward, a nondescript twenty-five-year-old Londoner who had come as dog driver.

The nominal second-in-command "and general factotum in all unpleasant work", as he himself put it, was A. O. Stevens, the expedition geologist. A plain-spoken Clydeside Scot, he had the position thrust upon him, against his will, by Mackintosh, with the result that he incurred the odium of an intermediary between an unpopular leader and discontented followers. The others, like most people anywhere, were absorbed in their own little worlds, hoping for survival.

To the usual strain of men in isolation, there was added the uncertainty of relief. In varying degrees, that told on everyone; most obviously in the case of John Lachlan Cope. Yet another Cambridge product, from Christ's College, he had interrupted the study of science and medicine to join the expedition. At Sydney, when no doctor appeared, he had mustered as surgeon nonetheless. Already in signing ship's articles, he showed a touch of waywardness in putting "nil" in the space for home address. At Cape Evans, he became a case of "physician, heal thyself". He suffered from constant boils and, as the winter wore on, childish outbursts of temper.

Cope was isolated and the outsider; rather like Orde-Lees on the other side of the continent, in fact. For the rest, there was fragmentation into cliques. Stevens made friends with Spencer-Smith, and Spencer-Smith attached himself to Mackintosh. In the darkroom (where normally he worked as the expedition photographer) Spencer-Smith held furtive religious services, which Mackintosh was usually alone in attending. There was tension between the Australians – Richards, Gaze and Jack – and the rest of the party. Jack meanwhile admired Joyce, while Stevens found Richards incompatible. The permutations of men at odds with one another were endless. To add to it all, smokers were suffering deprivation of tobacco, for all supplies had gone out with *Aurora*.

Somehow, they got through the winter. Amidst the ennui, one man stood out, one of those unambitious souls who radiate a quality that soothes their surroundings. This was the stocky, unremarkable figure of Ernest Wild. "There are some things that have great value but no glitter," Stevens was moved to say of Wild. "Consistent . . . long-suffering, patient, industrious, good-humoured, unswervingly loyal, he made an enormous contribution to our well-being."[8]

That was a telling tribute, for Stevens was now privately disgusted with the whole expedition and especially with Shackleton for his insouciance. Their plans, as Shackleton put it, "involved some heavy sledging, but . . . I had not anticipated that the work would be extremely difficult."[9] Shackleton's optimistic reasoning was that since he had pioneered the route, it had become reasonably familiar. The Beardmore Glacier was, however, 360 miles to the south. It was, after all, the Antarctic. It was a place where bungling was a capital offence.

Nonetheless, a sense of responsiblity to Shackleton was the one thing that united them. Whatever the cost, that depot had to be laid at the foot of the Beardmore Glacier. Partly it was conscience stirring at the belief that the lives of others depended on themselves. Partly, too, it was the drive of Shackleton's personality working on those who had met him and fallen under his spell.

In August, as the sun returned after the winter, Mackintosh visited Shackleton's old hut at Cape Royds. With him went Stevens. Amongst other things, they were in search of matches.

"Over the stove in a conspicuous place," as Mackintosh put it, "we found a notice left by Scott's party that parties using the hut should leave the dishes clean."[10] That probably had been put up on Edward Wilson's visit there four years before. Wilson had gone in a spirit of censorious curiosity, for, to the end of his days, he nursed an unforgiving disapproval of Shackleton for breaking his word to Scott in 1908 and going to McMurdo Sound. This extended to Shackleton's men. Joyce, Wilson severely recorded after viewing the hut, was "a rotter".[11] They had both been on *Discovery* together.

Joyce, meanwhile, on his return in October from the sortie to the Bluff, found the end of a sledge sticking out of the snow. Digging it out, he discovered a letter written by Apsley Cherry-Garrard to Scott on 16 March 1912:

> Dear Sir, We leave here this morning with the dogs for Hut Point. We have laid no depot on the way in, having been off the course.[12]

"It was rather pathetic picking this note up," wrote Joyce, "& dated I think after Scott's death."[13] As a dismal relic of an ineffectual rescue attempt it was almost like an omen.

Joyce and his companions were hardly uplifted as, on 27 October, in the blizzard, they reached the *Discovery* hut, ill clad and worn out by man-hauling. The main depot journey loomed up ominously:

> I suppose it will be really the biggest thing ever done [Joyce wrote to Paton]. The last bath and shift of clothes I had was Jan. 20th 1915 on the ship . . . the last pipe of tobacco in April, ah well! we will make up for lost time if we get through.

Their programme, he summarised, was to place depots at 80° and 81° S,

> and then right on to 83–30. The party who goes on last will turn about the 1st week in Feb . . . practically all parties will arrive together about 7th March. If Shackleton crosses I expect we shall be back earlier.[14]

XXXVII

"So now we'll go home"

"A terrible night," James was writing on 27 October, camped on the ice as *Endurance* was abandoned,

> with the ship sullen dark against the sky & the noise of the pressure against her . . . seeming like the cries of a living creature.[1]

In Hurley's words,

> Cold & lit by the half grey midnight light, we were hemmed in by crunching pressure on all sides. 3 times we had to shift the boats & stores owing to the floe cracking beneath us. While the groaning & cracking of splintering timbers told only too vividly the awful calamity that has overtaken the ship that has been our home for over 12 months & our only means of communication with the world.[2]

Even the least impressionable were affected. To see a ship go down was one thing; to watch her slowly being tortured was another. By some curious chance, the emergency battery light on deck was automatically switched on and an intermittent flashing seemed to transmit a final message of farewell. Almost everyone was glad to snatch a few hours to sleep away their shock.

Shackleton, meanwhile, prowled around outside. He had been the last to leave the ship; he now felt he had to be on watch. In any case, he could not sleep. With him was the small figure of Wild, in attendance, calm and comforting as usual. It seemed to run in the family.

At about 5 a.m., Shackleton and Wild lit a cooker, made morning coffee, and went around the tents – there were five – to wake the inmates with a warming drink.

> Nobody [said Walter How] had the common decency to say thank you. And Frank Wild's remark was "Would any gentleman like his boots cleaned." I'll never forget it! They'd been out all night long, below zero, and we were tucked up in our bags or blankets or whatever we'd got.[3]

There were only eighteen reindeer fur sleeping bags for twenty-eight men. The remainder had to make do with woollen blanket bags. *Endurance* had not been equipped for an emergency such as this, for only the shore party had been expected to sleep out in the snow. The bags were distributed by lot. Nonetheless, in Hurley's words, the "precarious residence on the floe" was "preferable to the continuance of the anxiety we have endured the past two months on board ship".[4]

Now, as his men straggled out of the tents, Shackleton gathered them round him. A hundred yards away, like a fallen beast, *Endurance* lay limply, gripped by rafting floes, down by her head, her hull shattered, masts awry, yards inertly dangling in the air.

"It must have been a moment of bitter disappointment to Shackleton," wrote Macklin; "he [had] lost his ship, and with her any chance of crossing the Antarctic Continent,

> but he shewed it neither in word or manner. As always with him what had happened had happened: it was in the past and he looked to the future . . . without emotion, melodrama or excitement [he] said "ship and stores have gone – so now we'll go home."

"I think it would be difficult to convey just what those words meant to us," Macklin went on, "situated as we were, surrounded by jostling ice floes as far as the eye could reach, tired out with our efforts to save the ship, and with no idea as to what was likely to happen to us – 'We'll go home.' "[5]

Shackleton was trying neither to bolster his own courage nor to deceive himself. The task ahead was defined by Gunnar Isachsen, the Norwegian explorer who, in the days before *Nimrod*, had tried to persuade him to take ski and dogs. Men, said Isachsen, are social creatures, and therefore dependent on certain forms of civilisation. If they are removed from their milieu, they are deprived of their points of reference, and need mental stimulation to compensate for the loss. This was particularly true, Isachsen remarked, after his experience of four years in the Arctic, a long polar expedition. The leader, he said, had to provide the missing stimulation, and his personality was critical.

"Shackleton," said someone who knew him under other circumstances, was "a man who could look you straight in the eyes and tell you to go to hell if you stood in his path."[6] It was the obverse side of that quality that now came into play. Shackleton proceeded to instil in his men the desire to survive.

He had a motley crowd with whom to deal. On the one hand there were quiet, unremarkable characters, like Rickinson, the Chief Engineer, and Kerr (a Scot), the Second Engineer, simply waiting to be led. At the other extreme were cantankerous individualists, of whom Orde-Lees was the prime example, questioning every move. In between were varying shades of personality and intelligence. Shackleton was faced by the unpleasant fact that he had not actually chosen too well. His men were not exactly compatible; nor were most of them suited to the circumstances. His one weapon was a superiority of will, not exactly despotic, but compelling. He held both the formal and the psychological leadership, and on that depended the sanity at least of his companions.

Since being beset, ten months before, *Endurance* had drifted 1300 miles. Her position, on being abandoned, was 69°5′S, 51°30′W. Nobody had been in those waters before. The closest was Larsen in *Jason*, on his pioneering voyage in 1893. That was 180 miles to the west, and a whole degree north.

As far as 70°S, the west coast of Graham Land was known. South of 66°, however, the Weddell Sea coast was terra incognita. Everything to the shore of the Bellingshausen Sea was an enigma. Besides, Shackleton had loudly told the world that before February 1916 there would be no need to worry. Until then, he was absolutely on his own. The position was about as bad as it could possibly be; but Shackleton persuaded his men that they would get through. He simply willed them to believe that they would survive.

"A man must shape himself to a new mark directly the old one goes to ground," Shackleton wrote. Out of the ruins of one ambition, he had found another: "I pray God," as he put it, "I can manage to get the whole party to civilization."[7] That was a very private jotting in his diary.

"His first thought," Greenstreet said, "was for the men under him. He didn't care if he went without a shirt on his back so long as the men he was leading had sufficient clothing. He was a wonderful man that way; you felt that the party mattered more than anything else."[8]

To the men gathered round him on the floe, Shackleton explained, in his quiet, intimate way, how he would get them home. They would march over the pack ice to land. Which land? They would head north-west for Nordenskjöld's old base at Snow Hill. There lay a hut, well stocked with emergency stores "for the likes of us",[9] as Orde-Lees put it. That, Shackleton knew for certain. He had, after all, helped Lieutenant Irizar fit out his voyage of relief for Nordenskjöld twelve years before, and had himself suggested dumping supplies for shipwrecked mariners.

The pack gave a comforting illusion of terra firma. It required an effort of will to remember that the solid-looking surroundings were in reality a frail crust drifting on the deep. But the uncomfortable fact was that for four months the drift had been virtually due north. It if continued, the castaways would eventually be disgorged from the Weddell Sea into the open waters of the South Atlantic somewhere east of Cape Horn. By marching west, therefore, they could counteract the drift and, with luck, be carried to Snow Hill.

That, however, would only be a halt along the way. Nobody would know where they were. Any search would concentrate round their originally announced landing at Vahsel Bay. So from Snow Hill Shackleton would take a small party to cross Graham Land and fetch help from Wilhelmina Bay. That lay in the Gerlache Strait. It was a place whalers from Deception Island were known to visit. It was the nearest outpost of civilisation.

The distance to Snow Hill, as Worsley calculated, was 312 miles, as the crow flies. To Wilhelmina Bay was another 130 miles over mountainous and glaciated terrain. It was, Hurley noted, "a great undertaking with such a large . . . & inexperienced party".[10] Worsley too was worried, because of possible damage to the boats, "our ultimate salvation",[11] as he put it.

Worsley was also worried that Shackleton was taking only two lifeboats, where the absolute minimum seemed three. They were to be dragged on sledges over rough and broken ice. To Worsley this seemed a recipe for senseless exhaustion. Worsley's idea was to

> camp on the nearest flat berg . . . & await the outward drift of pack & berg to open . . . water. This would save the grave dangers we are now incurring of getting entangled in impassable pressure . . . or . . . having the floe split under us in camp as happened twice to us [last] night.[12]

Shackleton had listened, but decided otherwise. He was in a palpable hurry. It was on a Wednesday that *Endurance* was crushed. Shackleton set the start for Snow Hill on the Saturday. "All rather cold but cheerful & full of hope & general confidence in Sir E.,"[13] Orde-Lees observed on the Friday. That was despite his remark the day before that the chances of actually reaching Snow Hill were "rather doubtful. Five miles a day will be the most possible on the ice."[14] But Shackleton could still carry people along against their better judgment.

Perhaps Orde-Lees grasped that in the general state of shock, action, of any kind, was preferable to inaction. He was now among those who, on the Friday, visited *Endurance* to salvage vital gear. "Found water & ice up to Ward room stove," he remarked, "fo'c'sle head under water a terrible sight – makes ones stomach ache to see it."[15] Mangled and twisted, *Endurance* was held up only by the grip of the ice. When that relaxed, she would sink.

Meanwhile, there was great activity preparing for the journey. Two of *Endurance*'s lifeboats were rigged on sledges. Shackleton ordered the destruction of useless animals. That included McNeish's cat, Mrs Chippy, and Sirius, a favourite pup of Macklin's.

To save weight on the march, Shackleton ordered all but vital gear to be jettisoned. Much salvaged from the ship was left behind. Each man was allowed only 2 lbs of personal possessions, in addition to the barest minimum of clothing. Everything else had to be abandoned. Shackleton set the example by demonstratively flinging a handful of sovereigns on the floe; very possibly the last cash in the world that he actually possessed. This was one place on earth where gold, at least theoretically, was dross. As an act of faith perhaps, Macklin kept two sovereigns sewn into his belt. For the coming journey, he had fitted a pocket to the front of his jersey for toilet paper and other necessities. It was closed by a cumbersome arrangement of four safety pins; one, incidentally, gold.

Finally, at three o'clock on the Saturday afternoon, 30 October, the journey started. It was a long and straggling caravan. First went a pioneer sledge, man-hauled by Shackleton, Wordie, Hussey and Hudson, carrying picks and shovels. They had to find a way across working cracks, and hack a path through an inferno of ice ridges, blocks, pinnacles, and seracs ominously poised ready to fall and crush anything beneath them.

Then came seven dog teams, relaying twice, because the loads were too great. After that, Wild and Marston went back yet again to haul the smaller lifeboat. Fifteen men, meanwhile, yoked to the sledge carrying the larger boat, a whaler, hauled painfully, step by step. The load was about a ton.

The whole column on the march was about half a mile from end to end. At any moment, the ice could open and cut it in two. Constant liaison between front and rear was vital. For this "simple duty", as he called it, Orde-Lees, the only reasonable skier among them, was detailed. "I had been back and forth four times," Orde-Lees recalled, when Shackleton said to me . . . "Do you know, I had no idea how quickly it was possible for a man on ski to get about. In that respect you'd have been quite useful on the trans-continental march; but that's a thing of the past."

That, said Orde-Lees, "set me wondering why he had not come to this conclusion long before and had not insisted on every man in the expedition being able at least to move on ski at a modest five miles an hour. Amundsen's rapid journey to the pole was enough to convince one of the value of skis."[16]

The men hauling the boat looked like one of the heroic engravings of nineteenth-century British naval expeditions in the Arctic. It was not an encouraging comparison. After two hours, Shackleton ordered camp for the day. After vast effort, they had hardly covered a mile. "All are in high hopes," Hurley nonetheless wrote, "& glad a start has been made from the depressing neighbourhood of the Wreck."[17]

The following day was another slow and tedious plod through mushy snow in a jumble of broken ice. "Many look on this as spree," Shackleton jotted laconically in his diary. "It is better so."[18] It was too warm. Everyone was sweating dangerously. Their clothing was too tight, with insufficient ventilation. The reward of all their moil and toil was just another mile.

Next day, Monday 1 November, Shackleton abandoned the march.

"Changes of mind," Amundsen had remarked on the North-West Passage, "easily cause discontent and are therefore tiresome",[19] and the men who had been under Scott could bear witness to that. In Shackleton, the same apparent behaviour seemed "one of his outstanding features", to quote Macklin. It showed "the rapidity with which he could adapt himself to altered circumstances and change plans to meet new situations".[20]

The clue lay in Hurley's diary:

> Sir Ernest, Wild, Worsley & Self, who comprise a directive Committee, climbed some adjacent hummocks. The prospect was frightfully rough & the surface so soft we sank to our hips – under these conditions with the boats & large party further travel is impossible. The Quorum unanimously agreed to . . . camp . . . await the breaking up of the ice.[21]

McNeish put it in similar words: "We have made up our minds to stop on this floe until the ice opens."[22]

Shackleton took his men into his confidence, or at least made it seem so. Nobody said of him, as one of Scott's men had prophetically said four years before, that "if he keeps [his] men . . . in the dark as they were on this depot trip things are likely to go wrong".[23] Shackleton contrived, by some sleight of hand, to make his orders appear the decisions of his men. It was a vital link in the trust compelled by the leader from the led.

Hurley and McNeish were difficult customers and, as it were, needed nursing. McNeish was exceedingly proud of being a shipwright. Hurley was more than just a professional photographer. He was a survivor. From a tough Australian upbringing, he had acquired all the resource of a pioneer. He was always "full of good suggestions",[24] as Shackleton bore witness.

Hurley, in fact, was a trained metal worker, ingenious and inventive. He was always making things. To cook on, for example, there was only an improvised camp stove, so he constructed a proper blubber-burning one out of the ash chute from the wreck. This was a square structure made of quarter-inch steel. Most tools had been lost. "The chipping of two holes fifteen inches in diameter with a blunt flat chisel," as Hurley put it, was "a somewhat arduous undertaking."[25]

Within two days the stove was completed, and in service. Henceforth, the whole expedition depended on it for hot meals. Hurley was justifiably proud. To some of his companions he seemed "bombastic", but he was simply an uninhibited Australian. He wanted recognition when it was his due, and why not? He was arguably the hardest and most intelligent worker of them all. It was also he who arranged to floor the tents with timber from the wreck.

The floe on which they had settled was a safe-looking oasis of flatness in the wild confusion, apparently two years old at least. It would probably be their home until they chose to move. It was named "Ocean Camp".

The third boat and all the gear were now moved up, by the dogs, from the original camp. Much more was also salvaged from *Endurance*. Her abandonment had not been sufficiently prepared. Too much had been left behind. All hatches and companion ways had collapsed to bar the way below. It was Hurley who suggested cutting through the decks to reach the stores and save what could still be saved. It was a dangerous and nerve-wracking job, floundering in flooded holds, while at any moment the wreck threatened to subside.

At all costs, Hurley was determined to retrieve his negatives which had been left behind (on Shackleton's insistence) because of weight. Hurley now broke into the refrigerator – *Endurance* actually had one – where they had been stored, and "Bared from head to waist," as he put it, he "probed in the mushy ice."

> The cases which fortunately were zinc lined & soldered & contained the negatives in soldered tins I located submerged beneath 3 feet of mushy ice & practically all were intact.[26]

Hurley then had to go through another heartbreaking experience. Since his negatives were mostly glass plates, and far too heavy, he could not expect to save them all. So he chose 150 of the best, and smashed the remainder – about 400 – on the ice to remove all chance of second thoughts. These, together with his cinema film, he packed in double tins, hermetically sealed, and proposed to carry them back home. He had to dump his equipment, keeping only a pocket camera and three rolls of film, but at least he had saved the record of his year's work.

Macklin was not so fortunate. "I wish I had realised that we were not going to make a dash for land," he wrote regretfully, "for I would have brought my Diary and my Bible, both of which I value highly."[27]

Shackleton, meanwhile, was hurrying to prepare for a second attempt to make for land. The floe was melting at the edges. "Trust that next wind will open this up,"[28] was his sanguine hope.

He was not only concerned with the act of travel. He feared the effect of waiting on morale. Shackleton and his companions were, in a sense, too civilised. They were dependent on activity, almost like a drug. They had lost the understanding that nature sometimes requires nothing but the patience to wait. In these circumstances, the Eskimo would have been the wiser man. However, Shackleton had to avert the slow insidious panic that could grow when waiting generated apathy and helplessness. He also had to cope with his own temperament which, if left unchecked, would trap him into activity for its own sake.

After a meeting of the "directive committee", Worsley recorded that Shackleton was prepared

> for the worst eventuality of having to stop on the Pack for another winter . . . On the other hand if by the end of January we have, as is probable, drifted near enough to Graham's Land, or the S. Orkneys, we may make one or the other by aid of the leads we hope to have come to . . . The third alternative is a risky but a necessary dash to the West at the end of Jan, abandoning boats but sledging the small punt the Carpenter has made. This we would only do if the drift became arrested . . . so . . . that we were fairly certain we would otherwise have spent the winter on the floe running the risk of it opening and crushing the boats some dark winters midnight.

"I do not worry about these dangers," Worsley commented, "but live comfortably & happily in the present, & can truly say that at present I am enjoying myself far more than I would in civilization."[29] In Macklin's words, "We are almost as well off as we were aboard the ship, and most of us are just as happy."[30]

Everyone, or almost everyone, indeed, was a shade too conspicuously cheerful. The one obvious exception was Orde-Lees, sternly stalking up and down, husbanding every pin, determined to eke out the food. "Belly burglar"[31] was the soubriquet he was awarded by the cook; "very good as stores officer", Shackleton, recorded on the other hand, "accurate, painstaking".[32] Hurley, having been told to count the matches, found "We had ample for 12 months," but in the same breath recorded privately

> Very anxious however to reach Snow Hill early this season so as to avoid wintering another year in the Antarctic,[33]

while Macklin wrote in a telling diary entry,

> As long as we can come out of this predicament with our lives, we shall not grumble – and please God we shall succeed . . . My thoughts often turn to those at home, but as a rule I try not to think of anything but our surroundings.[34]

Shackleton sensed the undertones. He took care to keep up a bustle of preparation. McNeish was raising the gunwhale of the big whaler. He had to make do with used nails, as new ones, with so much else, were irretrievably trapped in the wreck. His tools were there as well. "I have only a saw hammer & chisel & adze but we are managing all right",[35] he remarked with no little pride.

Hurley, in the meantime, was contriving a bilge pump for the whaler out of the Flinders bar from the ship's compass. No one else, apparently, saw the connection with the iron cylinder moving in a tube, used to correct the disturbance in a magnetic compass. It was Hurley, too, who was making crampons "from sundry bits of iron & screws", in his own words, for the crossing "as we hope"[36] of Graham Land to Wilhelmina Bay.

On 7 November, the floe at last cleared the 69th parallel. It had taken seventy days to cover one degree of latitude. Now, the ice, with an occasional hiccough, was drifting north at a steady three miles a day.

Shackleton was manifestly pleased. The dogs were restless and bellicose. A general air of expectancy pervaded the camp. "My sledge," as Macklin put it, "is . . . in perfect condition for leaving at a moment's notice."[37]

Everything turned on Shackleton's leadership and personality. "Responsibility", as Worsley put it, was "a heavy weight, but Sir E. on whom practically the whole of it falls carries it splendidly no man could carry it better under any conditions."[38] The way Shackleton constantly prowled about the camp betrayed the restlessless within. "Put footstep of courage", as he laconically jotted, "into stirrup of patience."[39]

He longed to leave the ice; yet he knew that, except to ships, the ice was at heart friendly. It gave food, shelter, drink, and something solid underfoot. It kept the waters calm. The open sea, which was the sole avenue of escape, he knew only too well, as a seaman, was ruthless, implacable and hostile.

Always, it was the condition of his men that preoccupied Shackleton. There were five tents on the floe. With him, Shackleton had Hurley, James and Hudson. These were not exactly the most turbulent characters, but each in his way could cause irritation. Not that James was offensive, but his withdrawn academic manner did not go down too well. Hudson was much more disturbing. He was generally thought to be unbalanced, and was at any rate incorrigibly argumentative. "Lack of knowledge of a subject," James caustically remarked after one episode, "rather stimulates argument in the Antarctic."[40] These people were best kept in quarantine, as it were.

Macklin incurred Shackleton's displeasure when, one morning, he was out with Greenstreet, looking for seals, "but found no seals".

> So for diversion [in Macklin's words] we got on a small piece of ice, and shoved out into the lead, paddling ourselves along with ski sticks. We were just like a couple of schoolboys doing a stupid thing just for devilment. Sir E. saw us, and I personally had the feeling of a schoolboy caught stealing apples.[41]

Shackleton, as he brutally made clear, did not approve of unnecessary risks. "Cautious Jack", he had started to call himself; and he liked to be called it because he had to convince everyone that he would not risk anyone's life in vain.

In their sleeping bags, to which they often fled to escape the raw, creeping dampness of spring in the pack, Shackleton, as he had been doing since his *Hoghton Tower* days, determinedly quoted Browning. Despite this, Hurley expressed "great admiration for the boss – who is ever considerate & kindly disposed – an excellent comrade",[42] and retaliated by reading Keats out loud.

To himself, Shackleton was reading Kinglake's *Eothen*, one of the motley volumes salvaged from the ship; "a charming book",[43] as he put it. An ice floe, drifting like a colossal raft over uncharted waters, was an odd background for a famous Victorian chronicle of Middle Eastern travel. Helpless in a gale, Shackleton could get an ironic satisfaction out of Kinglake's Turkish Pasha chanting "whiz! whiz! all by steam!"[44] in admiration of English technical mastery over nature.

Through shifting fog and clear air, Shackleton was wistfully watching the remnants of *Endurance*, a few miles off. On 21 November, "at 4.50," in his own words, "saw the funnel dip behind a hummock suddenly: ran up the lookout". This was a wooden tower, containing the ship's standard compass, put up as observation post and navigating bridge. "She's going, boys," Shackleton called out.

"We are not sorry to see the last of the wreck," wrote Hurley, harping on a theme, for it was "an object of depression to all who turned their eyes in that direction."[45] Shackleton himself, however, recorded very privately,

> At 5 p.m. she went down by the head: the stern the cause of all the trouble was the last to go under water. I cannot write about it.[46]

XXXVIII

From Ocean Camp to Patience Camp

Derelict as she was, *Endurance* had symbolised the connection with the outside world. Now that she was gone, it was like the umbilical cord being cut. When a party visited where she had lain, the ice had closed over, and it was if she had never been. The aftermath was a forlorn blend of desolation and of relief at no longer clinging to a wreck.

Worsley tellingly remarked in his diary,

> I don't think we have a genuine pessimist amongst us. Certainly a good deal of our cheerfulness is due to the order & routine which Sir E. establishes wherever he settles down. The regular daily task & matter of fact groove into which everything settles inspires confidence in itself & the Leader's state of mind is naturally reflected in the whole party.[1]

This was true, but tainted by self-censorship. After the expedition all diaries, by contract, were to be handed over to Shackleton. Worsley was particularly exposed, for Shackleton was self-confessedly keeping only the sketchiest of journals, and would depend on Worsley's record for the expedition narrative.

Worsley was also inhibited by a gnawing fear of succumbing to despair. At the beginning of December, he betrayed a whiff of this when he wrote

> Sir E. optimistically discusses an expedition to the Lands N. of Canada. We . . . wax enthusiastic about our next trip before we can definitely settle how the devil we are going to get out of this one.[2]

Shackleton was remorseless in his determination to avoid a

breakdown of morale. One device at least, on abandoning *Endurance*, was to pretend that they would be home by the year's end. Perhaps Shackleton half believed it himself. "I got myself into pretty hot water with the Boss," Orde-Lees recorded, "for expressing myself too freely on the point."

> He happened to be passing our tent . . . and heard me say, "It's all bunk to say we shall be in England by Xmas this year." Himself an irrepressible optimist, I think he never quite forgave me.[3]

For similar reasons, Shackleton had already turned against Marston, and he was uneasy with the unsmiling expressions of James and Wordie. Shackleton did not understand the inner world of the contemplative man, in which he could find solace. Nonetheless, when *Endurance* sank, there were unmistakable signs of depression all round.

Partly it was due to the squalor of the camp. Absorption of the sun's rays by the refuse strewn around had thawed the snow into a dun and dingy quagmire. Every other step meant sinking to the knee. On 1 December, Shackleton shifted camp about fifty yards to firm, clean snow.

Even more than surroundings, Shackleton believed that the seat of the emotions lay in the stomach. He raised the food allowance too. The depression, mostly, lifted. Shackleton by no means felt the ease he was taking care to display. Scurvy remained his abiding fear. It worried him more than the direction of the drift. Depression, as he knew, was an early symptom of the disease.

Macklin's thoughts, too, were "clouded by the fear of scurvy". Before leaving England, he had "assimilated all the available literature", as he put it, but was "left with a mass of conflicting evidence – I did not know the cause of scurvy".[4] McIlroy, a thoroughly conventional physician, was very little help. Macklin, for his part, had discussed

> the new "vitamine" theory with a number of . . . prominent medical men . . . Most of them were very sceptical.

So Macklin, in his turn, was "unwilling to forego the older conception," and accepted, *faute de mieux*, that "scurvy was really the result of a gastro-intestinal infection".[5]

Shackleton, on the other hand, "who was rather an amazing man in the way he had made himself au fait with all the latest developments . . . and who had [also] collected all the latest information as regards scurvy," as Macklin put it, "was very enthusiastic [about] the idea of the vitamin." During endless discussions on *Endurance* Shackleton, "used to say to me, 'Surely you have here the perfect explanation for all that has been puzzling you?' ".[6]

Now that *Endurance* had sunk beneath the ice, Shackleton did not want the word "scurvy" even mentioned. He was not burying his head in the sand, he was simply afraid of the effect on morale. The very name of scurvy, its cause not yet settled, still had the power to strike fear into the heart. Tacitly Shackleton decreed the vitamin theory. He decided that fresh meat would supply the vitamin or vitamins that prevented scurvy. The camp on the ice floe still above the Antarctic Circle was probably the only place in the world where the vitamin theory, as it were, had become official orthodoxy. At least it was one uncertainty removed.

Macklin, nonetheless, in his own words, "discussed the problem very earnestly" with his tent mates, "a conglomerate lot",[7] as he put it, who included Worsley, Clark and Orde-Lees:

> Someone asked why seals and penguins did not get scurvy and suggested that as they did not and humans did there must be something in their make up which prevented it. This gave us the idea that if we ate all of the seal and the penguin including brain, heart, liver, kidney and sweetbread. . . this might help to avoid scurvy.[8]

They had stumbled on the truth: the brain, heart and kidneys of the seal are potent sources of vitamin C. Although it would only be scientifically demonstrated after another quarter of a century, the polar Eskimos, who have never suffered from scurvy, understood it instinctively.

Shackleton, however, "did not think much of the idea", said Macklin. "Because in order to feed the dogs we had to kill . . . a large number of [seals] the choicest pieces only were eaten by the men and the rest by the dogs."

To secure the bonds of leadership, Shackleton was now doubly careful to consult his companions. On his rounds one day Shackleton asked Greenstreet whether there was "anything we might be doing that we aren't doing". Greenstreet was just then re-reading Nordenskjöld's *Antarctic*.* What impressed Greenstreet about Larsen's tale of the wreck of the *Antarctic* was that, when Larsen got his crew ashore on Paulet Island, his first concern was to gather food for the winter. Looking around him, Greenstreet saw that only

* One of the books rescued from *Endurance*. Others included the first seven volumes of the *Encyclopedia Britannica*, Carlyle's *French Revolution*, Tolstoy's *Anna Karenina*, and Walter Scott's *Guy Mannering*.

enough seals and penguins were being hunted for the day. He remembered how they had disappeared before. He knew that from *Endurance* only about three months' food remained. In his own words, he said to Shackleton,

> "Well, sir, I don't think it would be a bad idea if every seal and every penguin that came up we killed and depoted . . ." "Oh," he said, "you're a bloody pessimist. That would put the wind up the fo'c'sle crowd, they'd think we were never going to get out."[9]

This was true, of course. Larsen had been dealing with men whose whole tradition, in a harsh climate, was of putting food by for the winter. Shackleton, on the other hand, was faced with the improvidence of British working-class men who did not look beyond the day. Stocking up food, to them, would be an admission of disaster. Looking round the fo'c'sle hands – Green, Blackborrow, Vincent, How, McLeod, Stephenson, Holness – Shackleton recognised the limited intelligence, the disorientation of a seaman without his ship. Wrongly handled, they might easily break down. Starvation was, perhaps, preferable to insanity.

In any case, on 5 December Shackleton declared a holiday, to celebrate the anniversary of the departure from South Georgia. McNeish was in his sleeping bag, reading McLintock's *The Voyage of the "Fox"*, which was all about the

> search of Franklin sent by Lady Franklin when the British government – curse them – refused her appeal to send a ship.[10]

Was this a hint of their own predicament? For a fortnight before *Endurance* sank, the floe had been almost stationary; now it had made a spurt of fifty miles, and the 68th parallel was left behind. But now the drift had turned just east of north.

This was what Shackleton had been fearing all along. So far the drift, heading roughly NNW, had promised a reasonable chance of reaching Snow Hill. Now he would have to aim, in Larsen's wake, for Paulet Island instead. There lay the hut that Larsen and his men had built fourteen years before. There, too, a food depot had been left, made up of supplies Shackleton had ordered when helping to fit out Irizar's relief expedition. It would, in Shackleton's own words, be "a strange turn of fate if the very cases . . . I had . . . sent out so many years before, were now to support us".[11]

At all events, going to Paulet Island would involve an open-boat journey at least to the tip of Graham Land on the way to fetch help at Wilhelmina Bay. That was the least unpleasant possibility. The eastward trend, if it continued, would sweep them out through the gap between the South Shetland and the South Orkney Islands, and into the ocean.

They had now come almost two-thirds of the way up Graham Land. Paulet Island and the mouth of the Weddell Sea were just over 250 miles away. Shackleton urgently wanted to strike out again for land, but he knew he had to wait. Hiding his impatience under a mask of genial good humour, he took care nevertheless to maintain the impetus of preparation. On 27 November the three lifeboats had been christened. The large whaler was called *James Caird*; the smaller cutters *Dudley Docker* and *Stancomb Wills* – in Hurley's words, "What names!"[12] The boats, he went on, "only await an opening of the ice".[13] On 8 December, the *James Caird* was tried in the water. She proved to be crank when empty, but quite stable with eleven men and about a ton of stores.

Meanwhile there were, as Hurley put it, "discussions & calculations re weights for Cross Country Sledging [to fetch help at Wilhelmina Bay]".[14] Out of an ash bucket from *Endurance*, he made a portable blubber stove for the boats. "Great success," he recorded, "boiled 2 1/2 Galls water from ice 1/2 hour."[15]

In the tent, one day, after tea, Shackleton told Hurley and Hudson the story of his southern journey in 1908–9. He seemed to be reliving his one great triumph, and his greatest disappointment. "I have," Hurley thereupon recorded, "great affection for the Chief, who is one of the finest characters I have met."[16]

For the first fortnight in December, Shackleton was intermittently laid up with what he called "sciatica"; and also a mysterious "cold" which no one else seemed to share. It was his first recorded allusion to ill-health since the "suppressed influenza" on the way to South Georgia, fourteen months before. He allowed the doctors to examine him, but only so far, no further. His heart was still forbidden territory. Once more he seemed a driven man, yearning for achievement before it was too late.

At the same time a blend of ennui and expectancy settled on the camp. It was, said Macklin on 8 December, with the floe steadily drifting north-east into danger,

> an anxious time . . . but everybody is cheerful . . . We are getting a good allowance of food, and we have adapted ourselves pretty well to this tent life. I feel just as happy here as I did in hospital with all its comforts . . . If we come through alive and safe it will be a great experience to look back on.[17]

In the middle of the month Macklin, probably inspired by Amundsen in *The South Pole* but also, no doubt, secretly oppressed by the general uneventfulness, described in his diary what a visitor from outside would see. If he arrived at midnight, wrote Macklin,

> he would notice that . . . it was still light, the sun never setting at this time of year in this latitude. He would have to pass a line of dogs tethered in teams to wires . . . secured at one end to their own loaded sledges and at the other to an iron stanchion driven deeply in the snow. The sledge trace is in position and the harnesses all secured in place and ready to be put on the dogs . . . The sledges are loaded . . . and . . . lashed . . . everything ready to be moved at a moment's notice.

At sight of the visitor, Macklin continued, the dogs set up a furious barking . . . The night watchman . . . greets the visitor, and shows him the general arrangement of the camp:

> The gallery, so called, is a canvas structure made from the ship's sails and spars. Inside . . . is the stove . . . In the same "galley" is the little library . . . saved from the ship. Here also Marston does his cobbling, Hurley makes his self-devised apparatus etc. etc. There is also in here a chronometer giving the local time, and of all things in the world, a looking glass.

Orde-Lees, a member of Macklin's tent, "prefers to sleep among his stores at the back end of the galley".

> At about 7.0 a.m. people begin to appear from the various tents, and make their way to the galley, most . . . in search of water to clean their teeth, and some even try to get water for washing, though that is a luxury for the privileged few . . . at 7.45 the night watchman goes the round of the tents singing out . . . "Lash up and stow." If the visitor now returns to the galley he will find . . . 5 men . . . coming in . . . one from each tent . . . each carrying two pots . . . These are the tent "Peggies" and have come for the breakfast. This is served promptly at 8.0 a.m., and consists every other day of seal steak, at other times of something else, tinned fish, porridge or pemmican . . .
>
> After breakfast [everyone] goes to different jobs . . . Clark and Greenstreet take a small sledge to an ice hummock and bring in ice for melting into water.

Old sea ice, in fact, is naturally leached of salt, and provides unlimited fresh water. "The visitor" – Macklin pursues his fantasy – "will notice other men walking off in pairs to look for seals, while the dog drivers are harnessing up their teams for exercise . . . The dogs . . . are excited . . . their tails high in the air, and barking with desire to be off.

Wild [Macklin continues] goes round giving out the special work for the day. Worsley, Hudson, Wild and Sir E. compare their chronometers at 9.0 a.m. daily.

The floe is completely surrounded by water except at one or two points, and so exercise, where risks are unnecessary, is limited to running round and round the floe . . .

We return to our tent . . . for . . . lunch . . . Generally the . . . afternoon is spent as the individual likes . . .

At 5.0 p.m. there is a shout of "Dog wallahs", followed by a terrific barking by the dogs. It is feeding time . . . Often there is fighting, and the driver has to freely use his whip, or feet or fists, to prevent their damaging each other, for when these animals get to grips they shew no mercy to each other . . .

At 5.30 supper, and again the same routine.

After supper the Peggy clears away superflous gear, and after a smoke most members settle down for the night. Some may have a game of cards . . . The next few hours are spent in reading, talking . . . or writing up diaries. About 10 p.m. all have finally turned in, and the whole camp is asleep, except for the night watchman, and possibly a few restless dogs . . .

. . . It is No. 5's night watch [No. 5 tent, Macklin's], and one by one the members go out to keep the hour's watch. This is not too unpleasant on good evenings, but in bad weather with a lot of driving snow one looks eagerly for the relief. Under these conditions . . . it is difficult to keep snow from the tent, and the returning night watchman has to be very careful to dust and clean carefully his clothes and boots from snow.[18]

About this time, too, Worsley recorded a view from another perspective. On 17 December, he and Wordie walked a mile or two to what he called the "Stained Berg". They climbed it; a height of about 120 feet.

The view from the top, was splendid. The Pack to the horizon all around lay spread out below us – a wide plain traversed & corrugated by hedgerow masses of pressure ice broken here & there by icy looking pools & leads where the impersonal Ocean showed through to the North it lay glistening & silvery in lines & patches where the sun was shining thro' the lattice like bands of soft-grey cumulo-stratus clouds. The floes bounded by the "hedgerows" looked like smooth fields covered with snow. A few low bergs dotted the pack, but most of them fairly evenly divided into barrier bergs & lay waiting all round the horizon. Our floe [is] the only solid heavy one near. The Camp on it looks like a collection of Indian wigwams.[19]

What neither Macklin nor Worsley mentioned was the not entirely euphonious twang of a banjo rising from the tents. Leonard Hussey had originally left the instrument on *Endurance*, but Shackleton retrieved it:

> "It's rather heavy," I said, dubiously. "Do you think we ought to take it?"
>
> "Yes, certainly," was the Chief's prompt answer. "It's vital mental medicine, and we shall need it."[20]

So Hussey went the round of the tents, accompanying sing-songs on his banjo. "We had a merry evening," wrote Macklin on a typical occasion, "though it is difficult to find songs that we have not heard many times before."[21]

One day Hussey was called out by Shackleton to act as his ADC. Shackleton had donned Worsley's RNR full-dress uniform tunic and cocked hat, which had somehow survived the wreck of the *Endurance*. Hussey shouldered a spade like a rifle and, tied together by a rope round their waists, they walked round the camp parodying a naval inspection.

Behind pranks like these which relieved the monotony, Shackleton was growing more impatient, tensed, and worried. "Hope we may keep going another 60 miles," he wrote on 16 December, "& we will be in waters more than once navigated by ships." He meant *Antarctic*; also the earlier forays by *Jason* and other whalers in 1893. "All cheerful," he jotted, "banjo goes every night."[22]

At that point the floe had been heading uninterruptedly north for almost a month. Next day, the 67th parallel was touched. In seventeen days a whole degree of latitude had been put behind. Then, in two days, a foul wind forced the floe back again ten miles to the south. "Such things must happen," Shackleton wrote. "All cheerful",[23] he reiterated, his philosophy slightly strained.

For a week, the floe had been drifting ominously to the east, but now it was distinctly moving west towards safety again. On 19 December, though losing ground to the north, it was back over the 52nd meridian of west longitude.

"Discussion re marching," Hurley recorded. This was partly out of a desire to seize the moment before the floe turned east again perhaps towards the mouth of the Weddell Sea and danger again. It was also, wrote Hurley,

> brought about by the apparent improved surface & abundance of seals – which renders it possible to feed our dogs without carrying extra weight.

"Sir E.," concluded Hurley, "is favourably inclined."[24]

Apart from the broad suggestion of a clockwise drift sweeping up the coast of Graham Land, the currents of the Weddell Sea were virtually unknown. Later observation suggests that just about where Ocean Camp now floated, like a lily on a pond, the current divided. One branch swept north-east towards the South Atlantic and oblivion. The other continued just west of north towards Paulet Island and a chance of safety. The swing of the floe south and west suggested it was caught in a dangerous eddy at the boundary of the two. That was enough to rouse Shackleton's premonitions once again.

Increasingly he was worried about morale. He discussed privately with Wild – as he discussed everything else – the idea that another bout of sledge travel might cure what Greenstreet called "organized dissatisfaction"[25] among the forward hands. This stemmed from a belief that, since the ship had sunk, they were now without pay. Marooned on an ice floe in an unknown sea, a strike would be suicidal. Vincent, the disrated bosun with an obtuse mentality, was probably the ringleader. Wild "agreed . . . that a spell of hard work would do everybody good".[26]

So, after intense scouting, Shackleton announced on 21 December that they would start "the day after tomorrow. Told all hands at 5. Everyone seems pleased."[27] To Macklin who hid fretfulness at inaction beneath a phlegmatic exterior, it was a "red-letter day".[28] He immediately took his dogs for an extra practice run.

On 22 December they celebrated Christmas Day. Shackleton allowed everyone as much food as they desired. Was this to quell disaffection through full bellies and indigestion? Or not to interrupt the march?

At 4.30 a.m., after a peculiar, damp misty start, they set off from Ocean Camp. Again, the boats were man-hauled, on sledges, in exhausting relays. Again, the dog drivers shuttled back and forth ferrying supplies. Again, to Worsley's barely veiled concern, only two boats – the *James Caird* and *Dudley Docker* – were taken and the third, the *Stancomb Wills,* was left behind.

In two months they had drifted two degrees further north, and at that latitude, at midsummer, the sun was still above the horizon all round the clock. It was uncomfortably warm.

The going was not exactly what Shackleton had foreseen. Since the original reconnaissance, more leads had opened. The pack had moved. Icebergs had shifted among the floes like pieces on a chess board. Pressure ridges had appeared. A road for the boats had to be hacked between the hummocks. Although Shackleton marched at night, for a harder surface, the going was abominable.

The outcome of eight hours' labour was exactly one and a quarter miles.

Next day, Christmas Eve, open leads stopped all travel. Christmas Day was foggy, dreary, wet, with slushy falling snow, and the peculiar raw and bitter feeling of the summer pack. The surface was atrociously soft. After much struggle, three miles was achieved. "Curious Christmas," Shackleton tersely jotted down. "Home thoughts."[29] The dogs, everyone agreed, were "marvels".

Boxing Day was merely repetition of the drudgery. Ten men had to hack a way through the pressure ridges for the boats. The road, in Worsley's words, had to be

> at least 5 feet broad to take the runners with safety & 7 to 8 ft. [broad] higher up to prevent smashing the sides of the boats when passing between high blocks of ice.

Worsley also described the passage of the sledge with the blubber stove "in charge of Potash & Perlmutter [Lees & the Cook]". It got under way "amidst storms of laughter & volleys of . . . Antarctic wit":

> The "Colonel" really deserves a V.C. for the gallant way in which he has taken charge of & stuck to the culinary Dept. under the most adverse condition. He wears a furry cap, snow goggles, & a beard, which however is hardly distinguishable from the soot & blubber that covers the rest of his face. He is the living breathing GOLLIWOG himself.

But nobody was clean any longer exactly. "His Lieutenant de Cuisine, the Chef, is equally black, indefatigable and good natured,"[30] Worsley continued in his diary.

One and three quarter miles was the outcome of the day. Everybody except "Potash & Perlmutter" had to relay, thus covering at least three times the distance.

At the end of the day Orde-Lees ski'd off to shoot one of the seals basking at the edge of the floe, and bring it in for food. On the way, he passed a tilted iceberg, in his words, "affording ski slope",[31] and stopped for a quick downhill run. Despite all the snow and ice around, he was a little nostalgic for Davos and the Swiss Alps, which he knew so well.

From the top of the same berg Shackleton, Wild, Crean and Hurley later surveyed the route ahead. Next day Shackleton, as usual, went out with Wild to pioneer the road. He returned to find the sledges stopped and a group awkwardly standing around. The centre of the tableau was Worsley facing McNeish; the one in a state of considerable agitation, the other mulish and obstinate.

McNeish had suddenly stopped work. He refused to obey Worsley's orders. He declined to go on.

The snow was appalling. The men were sinking to their knees. The labour of hauling the boats was inhuman. To McNeish, because of his piles, every step was agony. He was also a drinker deprived of drink. Something seemed to snap.

McNeish thought the whole idea of marching over the ice misguided. He was nursing considerable resentment. In the middle of November, he had decided that, from the remnants of *Endurance*, with the help of all hands, he could have built a sloop to carry everyone to safety. Then, it would have simply been a matter of waiting for the ice to break up. Shackleton had brusquely decided against it.

"The plan," as Macklin guardedly put it at the time, "was fascinating . . . However it is foolish to seriously discuss the decisions of experienced men."[32]

The trouble was that Worsley really agreed with McNeish. The whole party was divided over the wisdom of marching at all and the position was exacerbated by antagonism between Worsley and McNeish. The nub of the matter, however, was that McNeish had disobeyed an officer.

Shackleton was faced with the first real threat to his authority. It had to be crushed before mutiny and demoralisation followed. With the stark background of tumbled ice, the drama unfolded. The sole outside spectator was a solitary petrel swooping overhead.

In his sharp, Dundee accents, McNeish was stolidly arguing that *Endurance* was lost and, therefore, according to law Ship's Articles had lapsed. Consequently, he was no longer obliged to obey orders. McNeish was a big man; physically as strong as anyone else; as tough mentally as Shackleton himself.

Shackleton said not a word. He went away, and returned with the crew list of *Endurance*. He called all hands. From the front page of the document, he slowly began to read out Ship's Articles. In his characteristic quiet, intimate way, yet with unmistakable menace behind the Irish inflexion in his voice, he intoned the clauses engraved on every seaman's heart:

> And the Crew agree to conduct themselves in an orderly, faithful, honest and sober manner, and to be at all times diligent in their respective Duties, and to be obedient to the lawful commands of the said Master, or of any Person who shall lawfully succeed him . . . whether on board, in boats or on shore . . .
>
> . . . disobedience to lawful commands will be legally punishable.[33]

Shackleton stopped. At Buenos Aires, he announced, he had signed on as Master. Worsley became Sailing Master. That was not exactly true. It was, however, what Shackleton had hurriedly improvised with Worsley. It was what he now authoritatively explained, with every sign of conviction in his voice. He remained, therefore, not only leader of the expedition, but lawful Master too. Thus, he implied, he exercised both moral and legal authority.

In any case, he declared, Ship's Articles had *not* been terminated by the loss of the *Endurance*. A special clause ensured that. This, too, was specious. Shackleton wound up by explaining that neither had wages ceased, as under ordinary articles. They would continue until return to port. That also was contrived on the spur of the moment, and it was good enough for the crew. It lifted the worry that had been gnawing at them since the ship went down. It removed the cause of discontent.

It was an impressive performance. At a stroke, McNeish had been isolated.

Shackleton took him on one side and spoke with brutal directness. McNeish was obdurate. Shackleton hinted that he would be shot if he persisted with his insubordination. This was not the excitable scene, eight years before, on the *Nimrod* expedition, when Shackleton had wildly threatened to shoot Mackay. Behind his words, it seemed that Shackleton meant exactly what he said. When the caravan started up again, McNeish was at his post. In his diary, he mentioned the incident by not a single word.

Shackleton had crushed the one challenge to his leadership, but he was also deeply hurt. "I shall never forget him", he wrote in his diary of McNeish, "in this time of strain & stress."[34] These were not empty words. Loyalty, to Shackleton, was the cardinal virtue; its absence, more than a vice, was a personal affront.

McNeish, however, was no ordinary mutineer. "He never," in the words of a shipmate on another voyage,

> seemed to feel surprise. He never stood just watching something happen. He was always doing something about it while it was still happening. He could work seemingly endless hours, and if he ever knew fear, not a suspicion of it showed on the solid, graven brickwork of his face.[35]

McNeish's defiance had its roots in a too obvious belief that he knew better than Shackleton how to save them all. That, to Shackleton, was probably the greatest insubordination.

This was a case where Shackleton's casual methods of selection had not exactly worked. He wanted his men to believe implicitly in him, although he did not expect them supinely to wait to be saved. Wild and Crean, he now felt, were the only men he could absolutely trust.

The next stage, the night 27-28 December, was a disappointment. With much effort and some danger they made two and a half miles. In places the ice was so thin that the sledges broke through to the sea water underneath. Shackleton, when he went to prospect, saw from a height ice disintegrating and ominously swirling. At 7 a.m., he arrived back in camp and "turned in", as he put it, "but did not sleep".

> Thought the whole matter over & decided to retreat to more secure ice: it is the only safe thing to do . . . I do not like retreating but prudence demands this course.[36]

So next day they withdrew half a mile to an old and solid-seeming floe. There, Shackleton announced, they would wait until the ice broke up, or a practicable path appeared. Meanwhile, among the fracturing field of hummocked ice, like a giant furrowed field, there was no way ahead. McNeish, after all, had been right. Macklin, for his part, wrote,

> I am sorry that we are stuck for I infinitely prefer the work, pretty hard though it be, to the lounging that follows upon camp life.[37]

He spoke for a minority. Worsley, for one, was relieved. They were hardly ten miles from Ocean Camp. Often he turned his binoculars longingly in that direction, hoping to see the boat they had left behind. Shackleton, meanwhile, was preparing for an early break-up of the ice, "Lees," he wrote, once more, was "invaluable for checking stores."[38] McNeish was refastening and caulking the *Dudley Docker* "as she has all opened up", he noted, confirming his and Worsley's fears, "going over the hummocks of ice".[39] Back at his trade, McNeish was calm again.

"I am rather tired," wrote Shackleton on 30 December, "I suppose it is the strain." Next day, New Year's Eve, was the depressing festival of concealed regret it is anywhere on earth.

In Shackleton's tent, four individuals who otherwise would never have dreamt of associating with each other, were lying cheek by jowl. Crowded in the half gloom of their tent, they snuggled down into their sleeping bags, to celebrate as best they might. Hurley caught the mood in his diary:

> Our present position one cannot altogether regard as sweet – Drifting about on an ice floe 189 miles from nearest known land. Still to apply our old sledging motto; It might be much worse.

Hurley was one of the few overtly interested in the characters of his companions:

> Inside the tent [he continued] all is comfortable. Sir E. is Thinking, Buddha [Hudson] Day dreaming & Jimmy [James] solving magic squares.

"The last day of the old year," Shackleton was writing,

> May the new one bring us good fortune & a safe deliverance from this anxious time & all good things to those we love so far away . . . Thinking much [he said] makes one not desirous of writing much.[40]

There were, as Hurley put it, no New Year resolutions to make,

> as there is nothing to make them for – unless it be to keep our hoosh pots & faces cleaner. I am now appointed to the official post of fire kindler – my motto being 1 match 1 meal.[41]

A week later, Shackleton was reading Nordenskjöld's *Antarctic*. He was now 130 miles from where *Antarctic* had been crushed in the ice and, like C. A. Larsen, perhaps, Shackleton and his castaways would have to row for safety too.

"Anniversary of our Furthest South last Expedition," he remembered to write two days later, 9 January,1916. "What a change in fortune." But was it?

Wild had brought with him his diary from that southern journey. It was only by chance that it had been rescued from *Endurance*. "We have decided to shorten our march," he could, had he wished, have read in a poignant entry before reaching the Furthest South.

> We are therefore going on only three more days, which should put us within 100 miles of the Pole. It seems hard we cannot do the remainder, but as it is absolutely certain we should all die if we did, it would not do us or the world much good, and we have anyhow made a splendid record.[42]

It was a difference in bafflement only to a degree. Neither Wild nor Shackleton really had any desire to reminisce, although they had been companions then. "I am," as Shackleton put it, "growing anxious now with all this party."[43]

From 16 to 22 January a continuous southerly gale drove them a whole degree and a half north. On 21 January, they crossed the Antarctic Circle into waters sailed before. To the west lay, at last, the certainty of known land. There, just over the horizon, was the Larsen ice shelf, and the tip of Graham Land seen at least from afar.

"Better & better," wrote Shackleton as the observations told the tale of driving north by twenty miles a day. Then the wind dropped, sea fog rolled over, and the floe swung east. "Lees & Worsley are the only pessimistic ones," Shackleton remarked, but there was a reaction all round. "No news," was all Shackleton could write on 26 January, surveying the lonely cluster of tents and boats huddled on the floe. He called it Patience Camp.

"Waiting.
Waiting.
Waiting."[44]

XXXIX

Escape by a hair's breadth

On the Beardmore Glacier that day, a dark patch was being examined by R. W. Richards "very minutely for signs of life":

> It was some miles away and its shape resembled that of one of the tents carried by Shackleton. I was optimistic enough to think that it may have been the transcontinental party camped there on the way across.[1]

Richards, Joyce, Hayward, Mackintosh and Ernest Wild had just attained their goal. It was, in Wild's words, "just 12 months since we left the ship. It's the longest time I've been off a ship for over 20 years".[2]

Wan, wasted figures, somehow marked by disease, they were standing on the Gateway at the foot of the Beardmore staring down at the scene that Shackleton, eight years before, had been the first to find. There, Joyce now laid the depot that Shackleton had ordered. It contained a fortnight's food and fuel for six men, the expected size of the transcontinental party. "I picked a place," said Joyce, "which could not be missed by anyone coming from the S."[3] It was marked, ironically, by two sledges left behind by Scott, which they had found sticking out of the snow. "Wrote a letter to Frank,"[4] Ernest Wild recorded, and posted it in the depot for his brother to find.

Under a clear sky the Beardmore, glistening below and snaking endlessly to the South, Joyce found "a wonderful sight. In fact it was worth all the trouble".

Since finally leaving Hut Point on 13 December for what Joyce in his diary called "the biggest job of my life, that is to get to 83°S and if possible relieve Shackleton",[5] they had had to fight for every yard. It was not that the snow or weather was particularly bad, but they had to contend with improvised equipment and inherently defective technique.

Where unity was vital, Mackintosh and Joyce had quarrelled. Joyce had succumbed to pent-up resentment over Mackintosh's obstinate incompetence which, the season before, had destroyed most of the dogs. Only four remained. They had pulled all the way, but they were too few. The men had to haul as well. Also one of the only two primus stoves had failed, but there was no question of one party turning back, which common sense required. Mackintosh and Joyce were irrevocably condemned to each other's company.

"Mackintosh," as Joyce put it when the depot was laid, "acknowledged our work the first acknowledgment we have had from him since we started sledging." But now Joyce had a broken leader on his hands. Mackintosh had bleeding gums, swollen knees, black bruised limbs. He was weak and intermittently rambling, but Joyce, after his experience on *Discovery*, needed no medical practitioner to identify scurvy.

Joyce had long since assumed command. Richards believed that it was only his own private urging that stopped Joyce turning back and persuaded him to carry on to Mount Hope. That reflected the strains within the party. Joyce was tacitly accepted as temporary leader, and he undoubtedly *felt* the responsibility. "As lives depended on us, we did not want any bungling," he had said. "Now the biggest thing is to get back to Hut Point. Our only hope is the dogs."

Spencer-Smith had been left behind thirty miles from Mount Hope, sick and weak. Mackintosh had refused to stay and nurse him, so Spencer-Smith had to wait alone.

Scarcely able to crawl out of the tent, Spencer-Smith claimed to be "all right bar loneliness and disappointment (probably merited!)", as he put it in his diary. "Dreamt that we met Sir Ernest and Frank Wild with one motor and one dog sledge," he wrote on 23 January, "both clean and neat, and F.W. wearing a very much gold-laced cap! Sir E. clean-shaven."[6] Two days earlier, Spencer-Smith had dreamt "that the war was over – 'that all German rivers are now English rivers'".[7] On 29 January, after a week he spent "half sleeping, half waking", as he put it, his companions returned. "Laus Deo! [Praise the Lord!]" he wrote, feelingly. "It is strange but cheery to hear men and dogs again."[8]

By now, Spencer-Smith's limbs were black; his gums swollen. He was unable to move. This too was a clear case of scurvy, with unknown complications. Four years before, Captain L. E. G. Oates was in a similar state on that self-same route, but not nearly so far out. "He . . . must know that he can never get through. [He] is the greatest handicap",[9] Captain Scott wrote then, and Oates of course crawled out of the tent, never to be seen again. Spencer-Smith was three hundred miles from home. Without discussion, he was packed on one of the sledges in a dry sleeping bag, and his companions, with their four faithful dogs, started the long haul to drag him back. Joyce wrote,

> Well, we have got to make the best of it, longer hours & distances. This is one of the Trials of the Antarctic, & one must expect these things.[10]

For weeks, his ailing companions hauled Spencer-Smith on a sledge. They none of them had ski, repeating the old prejudice of British polar explorers. After a few days, Mackintosh and Hayward were just staggering along. Only Joyce, Richards and Ernest Wild, weakening with scurvy, were left to pull, yoked next to the dogs. Somehow Joyce had mastered the art of making dogs haul side by side with their masters. Or were man and dog bound by their common instinct for survival? In any case, the men knew that without the dogs they were lost. These were their characters, at least seen with human eyes:

> Con [in Richards' words] one of Mawson's dogs, a Samyoed . . . A "good living" dog and the others hated his guts for being good living. Oscar, a big surly dog . . . a bad living dog, and hated by the others because he was continually trying to shag them. [He was] named after Oscar Wild [*sic*]. Gunner, a gentleman, part Newfoundland, and Towser, smaller than the [rest was] a bit of a butt for them.[11]

Through arid drift like quicksand, in the teeth of blizzards that had stopped Scott, this motley phalanx of men and dogs drove on day after day. On 11 February, they staggered into the depot at 80°S. For two hundred miles, Spencer-Smith had been hauled on the sledge. He would have to be hauled the remaining one hundred miles as well. There was not the slightest question of leaving him to his fate.

They were running short of supplies. Joyce nonetheless stinted himself. "I am leaving just on 4 weeks food for Shackleton," as he put it, "which ought to see him through."

Spencer-Smith now seemed to be wandering. He was nonetheless keeping up his diary, and showed how he was in a twilight world "hovering round Gray's Inn", as he wrote one day or delivering "very bourgeois discourses on 'Self as Sin' and 'The Wages of Sin' (man a social animal develops self alone – consequently cannot pass on to a further social state)."[12] In lucid moments, Spencer-Smith had fierce arguments with Wild, his devoted nurse; on the White Man in Africa, for example, or rhyming in the English language.

Spencer-Smith was now unable to leave his sleeping bag. He had to be manhandled on and off the sledge. Mackintosh and Hayward at least could perform their natural functions in the snow. Wild had to remove Spencer-Smith's night soil from his bag. They were running short of fuel yet, without hot water, Wild somehow managed to keep his patient clean. He also sang to keep his spirits up.

Scurvy now afflicted them all. The cause was clear. Circumstances had protracted their travel far beyond the safety point. Since the preliminary journeys in the spring, these men had been away from fresh food and hence the source of vitamin C for nearly five months. As a result, their vitamin C reserves had long since drained away. Joyce, Richards, Wild, were still hauling with the dogs. Mackintosh was in such a pitiable state, limbs swollen, moving along by sheer willpower, that Joyce had long since ceased to reproach him for their plight.

On 18 February, a southerly blizzard blew up and kept them tent bound. It might have been a blessing in disguise. For days the going had been abominable. On fine drift snow the sledge, overloaded and distorted, slid hardly at all, and the men, without ski, were sinking up to their knees. "Poor dogs & selves," Joyce had written on 15 February, "practically done up . . . it seems we are pulling over 300 lbs per man instead of about 130 lbs. I suppose we are getting a bit shaken up & want some fresh meat."[13]

After somehow marching between eight and twelve miles a day for weeks on end, a rest was in order. They were only ten miles from the Bluff depot. Safety was within reach. But the days passed. "The wind," wrote Spencer-Smith, "almost carries a note of personal animus."[14] By 22 February, having been weatherbound continuously for five days, they were running out of food. Joyce, "after a talk with Richards & Hayward," as he put it, "decided we would get under way tomorrow in any case."[15] In Richards' words, it was "the lesser of two evils".[16] Otherwise, said Joyce, "we shall share the same fate as Captain Scott & his party." They were not far off the place where Scott gave in. They were almost exactly the same distance from their depot.

Next day, the storm still raged unabated. Joyce and his companions nonetheless started on their way. After a few hundred yards, Mackintosh collapsed. Now in an advanced stage of scurvy, he was delirious and for weeks had been bleeding from the bowels.

Joyce pitched one of the tents. In it he put Mackintosh and Spencer-Smith, with Wild, reluctantly, as nurse. Taking Richards, Hayward and the dogs, he set off for the Bluff depot to fetch food. It was, they all knew, a forlorn hope. Richards said,

> Conditions were impossible. Wind was of hurricane force and extremely gusty making it difficult to retain our feet. We could only see a few yards and even the sky was no different in appearance to anywhere else. There appeared to be no up or down.[17]

It was at least a following wind. The difficulty was steering. They had lost their line of cairns, and had to steer by the angle of the trace to the wind. To save weight, they had long since jettisoned their sledgemeter. They estimated their progress at three-quarters of a mile an hour.

On 24 February, they managed to struggle on for five hours. Then the blizzard became too much, and they camped. Next day, the storm was still raging. Nonetheless, at 4 a.m., they forced themselves to get under way. In twenty-four hours they had had two cups of lukewarm tea and scrapings of dog food. They had left the primus behind with Wild, and they themselves had only a little methylated spirits in a dish for cooking. The dogs had not eaten for two days.

Short of breath from scurvy and exposure, they were stopping every quarter of an hour. The tearing of the wind was wearing them down. After each halt the men alone were unable to break the sledge out. The dogs too were losing heart but, in the crisis, it was the hated Oscar who saved the day. As Richards wrote, he

> just lowered his massive head and pulled as he never did when things were going well. He even at times got a bit of a run on the sledge and tried to bite the heels of the dog ahead to make him work . . . It seemed to us that Oscar was aware that we were looking for something that would give him a full meal once more.[18]

Time seemed to lose its meaning. "We often talk about Captain Scott & party & the blizzard that finished him," Joyce wrote in his diary,

> If we had stayed in our tent another day I am certain we should never have got under way & shared the same fate.

There was something uncanny in the way that Joyce and his companions were repeating the experience of things past.

From the *Discovery* onwards every return on the polar route, except Amundsen's, had been a crisis. Joyce now continued as if determined not to follow Scott's example:

> If the worst comes, we have made up our minds to carry on & die in harness on the track; if anyone were to see us, they would be surprised 4 dogs & 3 men staggering on with practically an empty sledge, & just crawling along. Our clothes are in tatters & finnesko worn right through. The worst part is our tent torn right down the front. We are afraid to camp on that account. It is too cold to mend the tent the temperature being about −30°.[19]

Nonetheless they did camp twice, because of the blizzard. At 1 a.m. on 26 February, there was a lull. They hurried to get away. Soon after starting Richards sighted the depot straight ahead. "It was a fluke," in his words, "that I doubt could be repeated."[20] They had been camped within three-quarters of a mile of it.

The sight of the depot inspired the dogs. "They started to run," as Joyce put it:

> Ricky [Richards] & I could only just crawl & I fell down being so weak so brought the dogs to a standstill again. It took us over 2 hours to reach the Depot . . . arriving . . . in an exhausted condition. Then came the struggle to put the tent up which took over an hour, in ordinary circumstances [taking] under . . . 5 minutes . . . If we had not sighted the depot today we would never have pitched the tent again.[21]

Even so Richards felt "gloomy" because there was "no sign of a party here from the ship".[22]

After two days' feeding and recuperation, Joyce turned south again, into the teeth of the gale. On 29 February somehow Richards saw the tent they had left behind; another "fluke", as he put it. Wild meanwhile had heard the dogs.

> He crawled from the tent [in Richards' words], and unemotionally reached for his harness and staggered to meet us to help us in. We had had three days' food by then while he had been out of food for six days. Several of us broke down and cried at his action.[23]

It was now the twelfth continuous day of the blizzard; but then it began to drop. Hayward, meanwhile, broke down mentally as scurvy advanced.

Joyce had brought two sledges back from the depot. Spencer-Smith was put on the one; Mackintosh on the other. Hayward was tied to the front one like a broken down horse. With better snow, a following wind, and "bursting with thankfulness and food",[24] as Spencer-Smith put it in the diary he somehow still managed to keep, they now marched north as hard as they could. "Erebus and Terror have been visible all day," he wrote on 1 March, "for the first time for many weeks . . . it is homely to see the old place again."[25]

A week later, Hayward collapsed physically. Even on Joyce, Wild and Richards, black limbs and swelling gums told the tale of scurvy advancing on them all. To haul three invalids was beyond their powers, so Mackintosh was put in a tent alone with three weeks' food, to wait while the rest went on to Hut Point for fresh meat and the means to stop scurvy. Apathetic, Mackintosh accepted his fate.

Two days later Spencer-Smith was dead. It had been a "very bad night", as Joyce wrote. "Temperature down to about −30°." Spencer-Smith had been suffering from stomach pain. About 4.30 a.m., as they were preparing to get up, he complained of his heart. By six o'clock he had gone. "We have pulled him helpless for 40 days, over a distance of 300 miles,"[26] Richards summarised. Joyce added

> Poor chap, his sleeping bag was wet through all that time & we had no sun for drying & the jolting of the sledge on a weak heart must have been agony for him.[27]

Two days later, after much struggle, they reached Hut Point and the *Discovery* hut, which Joyce, as he remarked, had helped to build fourteen years before. By then, even the dogs were failing. For three days, they rested, killing seal and gorging themselves on fresh meat. The scurvy began to recede.

On 14 March, leaving Hayward behind alone, Joyce, Wild and Richards turned south again to fetch Mackintosh. The dogs were pathetically reluctant. The men's clothes, said Joyce, were "in tatters & past mending, our faces as black as niggers a sort of crowd to run away from".

They found Mackintosh withdrawn and apathetic. He did not react, even when told about Spencer-Smith's death and the absence of news about *Aurora*. At least, he was alive. On 18 March, they were all back at Hut Point, effectively marooned until the freezing of the sea. But they were safe, with nothing to do except wait and get well.

> We have been [out] over 200 days [Joyce recorded], laying the Depôt & suffered hardships that I did not think was possible for man to exist under the same conditions, I think the irony of fate was poor Smith going under a day before we arrived in.[28]

Scott was much on his mind. Joyce, after all, had been following in his footsteps, and escaped his fate by a hair's breadth. He had been out almost twice as long in conditions just as bad. Why had he got through when Scott had not? The easy explanation is that Scott had failed. Amundsen, after all, had beaten him to the Pole. Joyce and his companions, two legged and four, on the other hand, had done exactly what they had set out to do; the only measure of success. They were among the very few explorers who could say as much, and for generations, the only British ones to do so.

But it was not as simple as that. Mackintosh aside, there was something inherently more stable mentally about this party. Joyce and his companions were free of the heroic delusion; and nobody had morbid expectations of self sacrifice for anybody's benefit. They had shown devotion and loyalty which outshone anything their predecessors had done. For themselves, they were simply glad to be alive.

When they reached Hut Point, Joyce wrote:

> As there is no news of the ship, & we cannot see her, we surmise she has gone down with all hands. If the war is still on I should have thought America would have sent down a ship?

"I wonder", he continued, "how Shackleton is faring?"

> On our struggling in with our companions I very often looked wistfully to the South to see if by any chance Shackleton was coming up.[29]

XL

"We can only wait and see"

"Fancy that ridiculous Shackleton & his South Pole – in the crash of the world,"[1] Winston Churchill was writing to his wife on 28 March. For some days, the London papers, which were regularly delivered to the front, had been hoisting headlines like "SHACKLETON'S PLIGHT" or "BAD NEWS FROM THE ANTARCTIC".[2]

Churchill, of course, had originally been responsible for allowing Shackleton to proceed. He was, however, no longer First Lord of the Admiralty, having resigned over the failure of the Dardanelles campaign. He had joined the Army, and was now a Lieutenant-Colonel, in command of the 6th Royal Scots Fusiliers. He was in the trenches at Ploegstreet, in Flanders, in the Ypres Salient, one of the bloodiest battlefields of the Western Front.

On 24 March, a wireless message from *Aurora* had been picked up in Australia:

> Hull severely strained. Ship released from ice March 14th . . . drift 500 miles . . . Wireless appeals for relief ship sent during winter no acknowledgment. Ship proceeding Port Chalmers, New Zealand. Jury rudder no anchors short of fuel.[3]

This was signed "Stenhouse", the First Mate. It was the first news of Shackleton's expedition, either branch, since its departure in 1914. To start with, there was no one to whom the telegram could be delivered. The expedition offices in New Burlington Street had for some time been closed. F. W. White, the sometime secretary, had disappeared.

Eventually a "meeting [was] held . . . at the offices of Messrs.

Hutchison and Cuff, solicitors to the expedition," *The Times* reported. "Lady Shackleton and Mrs. Mackintosh present."

Shackleton was assumed to have crossed the continent and reached McMurdo Sound. In the words of the *Daily Chronicle*, Lady Shackleton feared he "would be in need of great rest and recuperation."[4] "It was decided," said *The Times*, "that steps must be taken immediately to organize a relief expedition to the Ross Sea."[5]

"When all the sick & wounded have been tended," Churchill continued to his wife from Flanders,

> when all their impoverished & broken hearted homes have been restored, when every hospital is gorged with money, & every charitable subscription is closed, then & not till then wd I concern myself with those penguins. I suppose however something will have to be done.[6]

Like Churchill, Shackleton was now going through a profound personal crisis. He too was fighting to redeem bafflement and failure.

For three long months Shackleton had been stuck at Patience Camp. Meanwhile, it had remorselessly been drifting northwards with the pack. Now it had reached a position opposite the archipelago at the tip of Graham Land. The end of the Weddell Sea was in sight.

Wind and current would decide whether Shackleton was to be swirled to safety on solid earth or whether, after all, he would be swept out into the South Atlantic and the nightmare prospect of oblivion. He was approaching the point of no return. There was nothing to do but wait.

Shackleton was not made to be the prisoner of circumstance. He tried to contain his frustration, but he was visibly moody and morose; no longer the old Shackleton they all had known. Nonetheless, he had contrived to dispel a sense of paralysing helplessness, and somehow generated a feeling that ultimately they would all be masters of their own fate.

In the meantime, he was compelled to cut down food. "The 'old man'," Macklin remarked, "seems to be getting a bit scared about the lack of game." Macklin took care to write in a private code. "I think," he went on, "the Boss was a bit improvident in not getting in all the food possible whilst the going was good." Orde-Lees alone had dared to raise the subject openly with Shackleton. "Boss," in Macklin's words, "rather snapped at him, saying 'It will do some of those people good to go hungry, their bloody appetites are too big!' "[7]

Shackleton's attitude, as usual, was complex and contradictory. "Cautious Jack" or "Old Cautious" were what he still wanted to be called. On the other hand, stocking up with food, as he had long ago told Greenstreet, "would put the wind up the fo'c'sle crowd". By now some of them had "started going crackers", as Green phrased it. "One man put copper wire round his belly; thought he was going to walk home."[8] Green himself, buried in an unfamiliar sense of humour, seemed intermittently unbalanced himself.

Shackleton thought he detected suicidal tendencies. Most of the seamen had signed on for a voyage, not an expedition. They were trained for the sea, not the ice. They were in alien surroundings. Total mental collapse could probably only be forestalled by letting the future take care of itself.

Not only the seamen preferred living from day to day. Wild, for instance, was uncomfortable in the face of what he considered excessive precaution. Shackleton had his own streak of improvidence which needed to be nursed. Also, as the summer wore on and the pack began to thaw, the risks of hunting outweighed, in his mind, the benefits of extra food.

From the start, at Patience Camp, food had been a source of dissension. Orde-Lees, independent to a fault, accepted any risk to lay in stocks. One day, after roaming far, he "gets it in the neck", as Worsley put it. "I am promoted to be Lees' shepherd!" he noted soon after. "His foolhardiness, altho in pursuit of seals, has been considered beyond bounds."[9] But, he added with irony, "Fancy me!" A thief, as it were, set to catch a thief.

Ten days later, however, in the middle of February, "owing to my letting [Lees] get 200 yards away from my charge, altho across a solid unbroken floe," in Worsley's words, "we are both stopped from going out again. It is far more important," he added, with an oblique dig at Shackleton, "that the letter of the law be obeyed than that food & blubber be obtained."[10]

Not that Shackleton cared for Orde-Lees in particular. "I am . . . anxious," as he wrote, "to get all out safely."[11] It was a telling repetition of what he had said when *Endurance* was abandoned.* Shackleton had never lost a man under his own command. To keep that record was the last ambition, as it were, to be salvaged from disaster.

It was no use Orde-Lees protesting that, on ski, he was comparatively safe. In fact, Shackleton remained remarkably estranged from the world in which he was immersed. Had he learned from the Eskimos, he would have taken the precaution of

*See p. 456.

bringing a few kayaks, and men trained to use them. A kayak was light enough for one man to haul over the ice. It would have enabled Shackleton to scout ahead. There would have been no trouble hunting.

In the middle of January, Shackleton had most of the dogs shot. Only Greenstreet's and Macklin's teams were left. That caused distress, since the dogs had become friends and, to men suffering from sexual deprivation, surrogate objects of affection. Shackleton's reason was shortage of food. The dogs needed a seal a day; but one seal would last all 28 men three days.

Worsley strongly disagreed, although not on sentimental grounds. He wanted to keep the dogs "for as long as we cd. feed them,"[12] and make another dash towards land before the ice broke up.

It was the third boat, however, that really continued to perturb Worsley. Since the last move, he had not ceased to urge on Shackleton the necessity of fetching it. Now, by the gyrations of the pack, it was only six miles off. Finally, on 1 February, Worsley was "very glad to say Sir E. has decided to send to Ocean Camp for the 'Stancomb Wills'".[13] Next day, Wild took eighteen men and hauled the *Stancomb Wills* back to Patience Camp. "The Boss," in James' words, "met us about a mile out with a sledge with a hoosh pot full of tea, the most welcome tea I ever had."[14]

"A good day's work," said Macklin, "and may yet prove our salvation. One has to be destitute of work," he continued darkly, "to know what a pleasure it is."[15] Fetching the *Stancomb Wills* was the last active effort left to ensure escape. Now it was up to the ice. "We can only sit," wrote Macklin "and, like Mr. Asquith, 'wait and see'."[16]

An awful ennui settled on the camp. It affected all the different kinds of men locked into the little community. "There is nothing for it," wrote McNeish on one notably damp, depressing day, "but to get into our sleeping bags. And smoke away the hunger, what loyde george [*sic*: Lloyd George] calls a luxury for working men. I wish to God," McNeish went on vindictively, "he was here"; the worst fate he could wish on anyone. McNeish was brooding over Lloyd George as Chancellor of the Exchequer before the war; that shrill demagogic Welshman, with his "people's budget".

> I expect [McNeish bitterly predicted], we will have to submit to have about £2 S10 abducted from our wages after being out of the world for 2 years & received no benefits, & then They will say Briton is a free Country This is where him & his fellow ministers should be for any good *They* ever done a working man or woman.[17]

"The worst thing," wrote James, "is having to kill time. It seems such a waste, yet there is nothing else to do. I don't find any theoretical work which I might do possible in the present environment. Fear my work is getting horribly rusty."[18]

Green, in a sense, was the least affected of them all. He was practising his trade. Early and late, weatherworn and smoke-begrimed, he was slaving over his sooty blubber stove. His job was to cook hot meals for his companions. Come what may, he proposed to do his job. One day, as he told the tale, he was cooking

> on the floe. It was a bitter day . . . I was crying my eyes out. I was absolutely done . . . the Boss turned up, asked me how I was getting on. "Oh, all right" I said. He said "What are you going to do with all the money when you get home?" I said "I'm coming on another expedition with you if I can." He turned to the Captain he said "Would you believe it, he hasn't had enough, he wants to come again." I thought he'd go to the Bering Straits to beat Amundsen's cook.[19]

Green was thinking of Adolf Henrik Lindstrøm, who had been with Amundsen, both in the Arctic and Antarctic.

Sometimes the only break in the monotony was the ghostly wheeze of whales blowing in a lead. "We find ourselves getting more taciturn daily," as James put it on 10 March. That applied even to Worsley, whom Macklin now called downright "morose". Hussey, with McIlroy and Wild, was among the few to keep chattering and cheerful, but he had ceased to play his banjo. That may have been because "his 6 tunes", as McNeish rather brutally put it, "is heartbreaking."[20]

They now were confined to a single floe, around which they trudged a dreary path for exercise. A sense of frustration pervaded the atmosphere. In an outburst at the beginning of March, Worsley wanted soon to be

> "up & doing" something however little to aid our escape from this white interminable prison where the minds energies & abilities of all are atrophying & where we are rusting & wasting our lives away, while the whole world is at War & we know nothing of how it goes.[21]

Shackleton, incidentally, thought that the war had been over for a year at least.

Worsley tried to escape from his depression by burying himself in polar history, in particular Amundsen's *North West Passage*; as he put it, "a well written most modest account of a well conceived enterprise".[22] Even that hammered home the lesson of laying in plentiful stocks of food.

Crammed in crowded tents, individuals' personal habits could become a kind of mental torture. Clark, with a constant sniff, and Orde-Lees who, as Worsley put it, "makes night hideous with a star turn on his nasal trombone",[23] drove their companions to distraction.

Strange dreams would disturb troubled sleep. Worsley, for example, dreamed "that the Daily Mail had the heading about us, 'Compulsory Trans Antarctic Expedition'".[24] Hurley recorded dreaming that he tried "to drown multicoloured hounds of the Dachsund (German sausage) breed. My endeavours were not fraught with great success, for the Dachshunds after assuming the form of seals, eyed me complacently with gummy eyes."

> Then so burning are our desires for liberation [Hurley continued] that we all more or less dream of sailing from the pack in the luxuriant comfort of an ocean liner.[25]

There were bouts of quarrelling; usually centred round Orde-Lees. Partly it was explained by the weather. Rain, damp and fog constantly rolled down in a grey miasma. Together with rotting ice, it was a peculiarly depressing and irritating combination.

Partly too, physical causes had a hand. By now, they were eating almost exclusively seal meat. Their remaining flour had been left at Ocean Camp. They had hardly any carbohydrates or fibre left at all. Worsley had read in the *Encyclopaedia Britannica* how Nansen and Johansen had lived for months healthily on bear and walrus meat, Eskimo fashion. "This is very reassuring to us," wrote Worsley, but he observed also that "Dr. Macklin says we have no evidence of how civilized man can stand a diet of little or no carbohydrates."[26] Chronic constipation seemed to be the main result. It was enough in itself to explain snappish tempers.

Two obsessions now reigned. One was food. Green, the cook, had aroused obloquy by the very human habit of giving larger portions to the seats of power, that is, to Shackleton's and Wild's tents. (This caused Macklin to comment waspishly that McIlroy had made Wild "a great buddy . . . from the very start. McIlroy had a certain cleverness, you know, and I think he felt that if he was well in with Wild things would be all right for him."[27]) To avert a minor mutiny, Shackleton told Wild to share out the food.

"We also suffer from 'Anemomania'",* as James put it.

> This disease [he wrote with his old undergraduate humour] may be exhibited in two forms, either one is morbidly anxious about the wind direction & gibbers continually about it, or else a sort of lunacy is produced by listening to other Anemomaniacs.

*From the Greek ἄνεμος, wind.

Tension rose, as they approached the point where the ice might be expected to break up. Nonetheless, ever the rational physicist, James deprecated the constant theorising on their ultimate destination, because it was based

> sometimes on what we see around us . . . but more often . . . on nothing at all. Can't help thinking of "Theory of Relativity". Anyhow we have only an horizon for a few miles and the Weddell Sea is roughly 200,000* square miles. A bug on a single molecule of oxygen in a gale of wind would have about the same chance of predicting where he was likely to finish up.[28]

With the shell of the introvert and insulated by his powerful inner life, James was probably the most successful of them all in coping with the pressures of uncertainty. Unlike everyone else, his demeanour had not changed from the day he joined the expedition. Nonetheless, he kept his thoughts for his diary, for anything approaching fatalism infuriated Shackleton.

Physical disease, at least, was kept at bay. Kerr and Greenstreet had rheumatism, McNeish his piles. That was virtually all. Shackleton showed no sign of whatever it was that periodically ailed him. Of scurvy Macklin, ever on the alert, found no recognisable symptoms.

In late March, meanwhile, Hussey complained of "a severe lassitude and inability to work", as Macklin put it. Hussey was not the only sufferer. "A beef steak, large and juicy," Macklin remarked, "is the treatment indicated . . . but alas it was not in my power to give it."[29] In modern terms, Macklin saw the spectre of protein deficiency. Malnutrition was obvious. For one thing, because game was scarce, and there were no reserves, they were quite simply not getting enough food. Macklin worked out that they were getting 1800 calories a day, less than a clerk at home. In any case, Macklin now realised that they were not strong enough both to attempt a journey over the ice *and* row the boats to safety. Perhaps Shackleton had, after all, been right to stay on the floe.

The months of stagnation at Patience Camp had taken their toll. Shackleton was moodier than anyone could remember having seen him yet. His strange, compelling personal magnetism, however, still kept fear at bay. No one seemed to doubt that Shackleton would save them all; and for him it was a responsibility on which he still seemed to thrive. It was almost as if he lived on a sense of being needed by other people. "Frequently . . . at night," in Hurley's

*Actually closer to 500,000.

words, Shackleton would "start up as if from some ugly nightmare. He would then wake me up and relate some imaginary happening for which his plans had not been set."[30]

The constant danger had ever been of the floe cracking beneath their feet. Even at Ocean Camp, Shackleton had devised a drill to cope with that emergency. Now that the danger was manifestly increasing, he responded by heightening preparedness. Everyone had to sleep fully clothed, with finnesko on, ready to be out in thirty seconds.

It was a display of forethought that considerably helped morale. Nonetheless, in Worsley's words, there was "always the knowledge that your efforts will probably have to give way before some upheaval of Nature . . . that you cannot provide for beforehand."[31] For example, one day at dawn two icebergs, as Worsley related, suddenly accelerated

> and came charging towards us, ploughing through the . . . pack ice as though this had been tissue-paper. Huge floes were lifted and flung aside by the cliff-like fronts of these monsters . . . For miles behind them there was a wake of chaos, floe piled on floe and crashing in all directions. Our camp was straight in their path and it seemed as though destruction was inevitable. Shackleton, clinging to what then seemed a forlorn hope, had ordered all preparations to be made to try to move out of their track, although this would necessitate leaving our supplies, since it would have been an impossibility to transport them in the time. Nearer and nearer the mountains of ice approached. We stood together watching them, Shackleton waiting to give the word which would send us scrambling over the heaving ice-floes – on which we should have had small chance of escaping starvation. He was quite cool, and smoking a cigarette.[32]

At the last moment, the bergs sheered off on another course. That danger was over. Shackleton always managed to give the impression of never being taken unawares. Through all the strain and disappointment, he still preserved the force of unshakeable optimism. His moods still hardly spoiled the mask, because they were plainly rooted not in depression but in impatience.

It was, however, Frank Wild, patient, unambitious, modest and unobtrusive, who did most to keep up morale. He was fulfilling exactly the role of his brother on the other side of the continent, as if there were some mysterious family bond or shared trait. Both knew how to wait, but by some obscure paradox Frank almost wished to prolong the crisis, for both he and Shackleton knew that some lurking flaw was waiting to confound them in civilisation.

The general mood swung literally with wind and weather. Macklin, outwardly unemotional, could write one day: "How I hate this 'Pack'.

> The water is drip-dripping from the tent roof . . . I pray God to give us dry weather soon, for this is misery. I have never seen such depression of spirits as there is in the tent.[33]

"On the few occasions when we have . . . bright sunshine," he could also write,

> things are different – the ice shows up in its purest, shadows relieve the white monotony, and the air is often warm and pleasant. *That* is the real Antarctic weather.[34]

Worsley's spirits too occasionally rose. "In all directions," he wrote one day, "we hear Adelie [penguins] making quaint noises – like men talking in deep tones – dogs barking – sheep bleating & a variety of quaint sounds of their own."[35]

Shackleton showed how the welfare of his men was still his first concern. "If he had half a pipe of tobacco," said Walter How, echoing Greenstreet, "he'd give you half of it, if there was no other to share out."[36]

Shackleton continued to walk alone. He seemed to have no favourite. It was not exactly an illusion. He had some inner core which he kept inaccessible and locked. He remained somehow apart, though not aloof, the unifying link. Cliques had built up because of constantly being crammed up together in the same tents, but the party showed no sign yet of disintegrating.

Shackleton explained all his decisions. By little acts, he contrived to preserve a kind of normalcy. "Hurley & Boss play religiously . . . six games of poker patience every afternoon," James recorded. "I think each regards it as a duty."[37]

As the floe zigzagged its way fitfully north, the castaways pinned all their hopes on Paulet Island, and Larsen's hut. Then one day, Orde-Lees woke up "suffering from nausea", as he told the tale. It might have been indigestion, from too many hoarded bits of blubber, but he insisted that he had

> always been susceptible to sea-sickness [and] was immediately convinced that the only cause . . . must be . . . heaving of our floe during the night. When I told Sir Ernest this he was delighted and told me to let him know what I felt the following night.[38]

Soon after indeed, on 9 March, movement was distinctly felt. The pack was creaking rhythmically. Loose pieces of ice were running slightly to and fro. Big floes, as Worsley meticulously observed, were rising and falling by about an inch. It was not much; but it was an undoubted swell. Open water could not be far off.

For more than a year, the castaways had not felt the surge of the sea. By the faces around him, said Worsley, it was easy to see that "life had lost its zest".[39] But the slight surge beneath their feet seemed to pierce the apathy. "We realised that our present existence was only a phase," as Worsley expressed it. Thoughts turned again outwards to the world. A flush of hope was rekindled.

Shackleton, however, was still a model of caution. "Trust [the swell] will not increase," he remarked, "until leads form."[40] Floes jostling and crashing up against each other would combine all the perils of ice and water, without defence from either.

The boats were given their final trial stowage, and prepared for sea. But next day, the swell had disappeared. It had only been a tantalising interlude.

Although Shackleton was suffering unbearably from bafflement and inaction, he did not lose the gift of separating emotion and judgment. What he feared now was a collapse from anti-climax. "People seem to be feeling the enforced idleness," he jotted in his sketchy diary, "as no one can leave the floe owing to looseness of the pack."[41]

On 11 March, the pack suddenly opened in a surge. It was the biggest stretch of open water they had seen for a year. Shackleton prepared to launch the boats and make for Paulet Island, eighty-five miles to the westward, virtually the closest land. Then something made him change his mind. He decided to stay on the floe. Soon after, the ice closed up again.

"I don't suppose there is much chance of us seeing Paulet Island," McNeish thereupon remarked. "It will be the South Shetlands or Orkney. I am positive," he repeated, that "we lost our chance."

> But we dare not say so as we are more like Prisoners than anything else & a darned sight worse off.[42]

On 17 March, Shackleton was still hoping for a change of wind that would break up the pack and allow him to "make the desired haven". It was, he noted in his diary, "St. Patricks Day", a date which, along with his own, Emily's and his children's birthdays and the anniversary of his Furthest South, he always remarked.

He was now prowling restlessly about on the look-out, ever climbing hummocks for a better view. But, except that a large segment had cracked off the floe, nothing had altered the bleak prospect of jumbled ice when 22 March, and the autumnal equinox, arrived. That day, as Shackleton set winter watches, the spectre rose up before them of another year in the pack.

The following day, Thursday 23 March, "a day to remember", as Shackleton tersely put it, "I saw the land at 7.30 a black island. Long looked for." He called the others to confirm what he had seen. Hurley recorded,

> General rejoicing! Our first glimpse of land for just 16 months & the 139th day of our life on the floe since the ship's destruction.[43]

It was only a shadow glimpsed through fog between stranded bergs, but, Hurley repeated, it was "land – Land that we have been watching & dreaming of for 5 months".

It was probably one of the Danger Islands at the entrance to Erebus and Terror Gulf. During the afternoon, the air cleared. Above a bank of clouds, a row of ice-clad peaks glistened like mountains floating in the sky. This was Joinville Island, the furthest tip of Graham Land. Paulet Island lay hidden in its lee.

"Cheered all up the sight of land", Shackleton noted, for his part. "Please God we will soon get ashore."[44]

It was the last entry in his diary. Bafflement was perhaps too great. The land was scarcely forty miles off or, in Hurley's words: "One days row in the boats".[45] There was, however, as Worsley admitted ruefully,

> no prospect that we can get . . . across to Paulet now as we would probably drift North as fast as we could travel. The ice does not *appear* solid enough to sledge across . . . nor open enough to launch the boats.[46]

Was this what Shackleton all along had feared? Perhaps that had made him stick to the floe. It is hard in any case to say exactly why. Perhaps he had been influenced by reading about Larsen's boat journey in Nordenskjöld's *Antarctic*. In those waters, Larsen had found the ice at the mercy of a vicious tidal race. Even now Patience Camp on its floe was being crowded ever northwards by the pack crushed up against the land.

Shackleton had once more undergone the conflict of judgment and desire. Staying on the ice in sight of land was an epic moment of decision. It was like 9 January 1909, when he had turned with the Pole within his grasp. He was tormented yet again by the tantalising glimpse of the might-have-been.

McNeish, in any case, had been vindicated. By 28 March, Joinville Island was receding to the south. The floe, after all, had been swept out of the Weddell Sea.

There would be no haven in the wake of Larsen; no comfort of Nordenskjöld's base at Snow Hill, no overland crossing to Wilhelmina Bay. Shackleton and his men were now irrevocably committed on a disintegrating floe to the mercy of the sea.

The sight of the Promised Land, fading out of their grasp as it were, after they had drifted nearly 2,000 miles, was almost too much for some of the men. Shackleton's decision, as Worsley put it, was "received with silent disappointment":

> Any struggle, however desperate seemed preferable to inactivity, and the glimpse of land had raised their hopes high. Only their loyalty to Shackleton and their absolute conviction that whatever he did was for the best made them control their feelings.[47]

"We are all very silent & absorbed," wrote James, describing life in Shackleton's tent, and a view of Shackleton behind the mask. "There is an air of expectancy about which causes much preoccupation."[48] Whatever the destination, it had been clear for some time that soon they would have to take to the boats.

Like a vast jigsaw puzzle slowly being shuffled by a giant hand, the pack opened, to display tantalising dark water lanes of escape, and then closed up again. The boats were loaded on and off their sledges. Even the big floes, insidiously weakened by thaws and constant strain, were beginning to break up.

Fear and tension rose among the men; but with the approach of physical danger, Shackleton appeared to drop his moods. He more obviously seemed to exert authority and stretch out a soothing hand.

But as March drew to a close, conditions grew notably miserable. Now there was almost twelve hours' darkness. Winter was not far off. Seals obstinately kept away. Not only food was dismally short now; blubber, and hence fuel was too. To eke out supplies, there were only two warm meals a day.

After six months without a bath, a sense of dirt had atrophied. Macklin nonetheless got out his last, hoarded tube of toothpaste, "and what a pleasant thing it was to have a fresh feeling in one's mouth again", he said. "Before this I have been using galley-soot and snow, and this does not have a very stimulating effect."[49]

"Pack weather," as James commented, "is nearly always dull &

cloudy"; the air was "raw and chilling." Sleet and drizzle came down in waves. James wanted to stay in his sleeping bag. Everyone, however, was becoming "fidgety", with "much anxiety in high quarters" and, James plaintively recorded, Worsley and he were "hauled out at least glimpse of sunlight",[50] to get sights, and discover where they were. The boats, Worsley noted for his part, were hauled about

> till ice & frozen snow is cleared off runners turn all other sledges over scrape ice off runners. This is absolutely necessary after all this rain and then hard frost, otherwise the sledges are almost immovable.[51]

Even the surviving dogs were miserable, but in any case their days were numbered. On 30 March, they were shot. Macklin, to whom most of them belonged, had mixed feelings at the end. On the one hand, he was sorry to lose them for, like most dog drivers, he had come to regard them as friends. On the other hand, they seemed to have no further use.

Almost immediately the dogs were cooked and served. "They were faithful hardworking servants," wrote Macklin, "and would have done good work had the Trans-Continental journey been started on."[52] That did not stop his devouring with the rest the cutlets of his sometime friends. But, as Hurley recorded,

> A casual observer, might think the Explorer a frozen hearted individual, especially if he noticed the mouths watering when tears ought to be expected. Hunger brings us all to the level of other species, and our Saying "that sledge dogs are born for work & bred for food" is but the rationale of experience.[53]

That day the floe had cracked again. The break-up could not be longer delayed. By now, the floe was at the mercy of the tidal race and unknown eddies of the Bransfield Strait. Shackleton turned his thoughts to Clarence or Elephant Island, the outliers of the South Shetlands, one hundred miles due north.

> This with any luck appears possible [Hurley remarked], though any terra firma that would alleviate our incessant anxiety of drift & insecurity would be welcomed as Arcady. Such a life ages one.[54]

At least the depressing rain and damp had lifted. April opened with a cold snap followed by mild, clear weather. Also, the seals had returned. Food was plentiful once more. Shackleton abandoned rationing and told his men to eat all they could. Perhaps he remembered the advice of Otto Sverdrup in the Arctic: "Before a great action or a difficult decision, eat your fill – otherwise it won't be any use!"[55]

By 4 April, the floe had shrunk to a small remnant, just big enough for the camp. That day McLeod, the old Scottish seaman, was standing at the edge of the floe flapping his arms to keep warm, when a sea leopard suddenly leaped out of the water on to the floe at his feet. The sea leopard is a large predatory seal with a vicious set of fangs, and McLeod gracefully retired. The sea leopard humped along menacingly behind, and stopped after a few yards to take stock with jaws agape. It was a comic tableau although not, of course, for McLeod. Wild eventually fetched a rifle and shot the beast. It supplied a large and well-timed quantity of blubber.

Entirely surrounded by water, the floe was swinging back and forth and rocking like a raft in a seaway. Water was lapping over the edges. The encircling ice was pulsating to and fro. "Altho' it will be a nasty dangerous job being out in a heavy swell on a dirty cold winters night," wrote Worsley, "it still gives us a pleasant glow of hope to think it may be soon." Behind his volatile exterior, Worsley was a very shrewd seaman. He still wanted to delay getting into open boats. "I think it would be a good plan to get on a flat berg if one comes within reach," he said.[56]

Despite the sudden flood of food, the craving for carbohydrates remained a very real irritation. Shackleton nonetheless was now overflowing with all his old carefree optimism. After a lapse of time, he returned to his treasure-hunting passion, and talked seriously about finding Alaric's treasure, or retrieving King John's train from the Wash. He even recommenced plying his tent mates with what Hurley called "poetic outpourings".

The ice had now begun heaving with a rapid and uneasy movement. No longer was there the comforting illusion of something solid underfoot. The swell was all too plain. The floe was disintegrating. Fingers of grey water, flecked with brash like blobs of cotton wool, were thinning out the pack. The critical decision now was when to launch the boats and take to the sea. In the end, Shackleton's mind was more or less made up for him.

On 9 April, the pack had closed again. It was undulating in a heavy swell. Leads had been reduced to working cracks. Floes were riding up and down, ice grinding against ice; the most dangerous conditions of all. Twice in less than twenty-four hours Shackleton's floe had split.

Late in the morning, an opening reappeared.

At 1 p.m., Shackleton ordered all boats into the water. Among the heavy floes they were not easy to load. The *Dudley Docker* and

Stancomb Wills had to stand off with skeleton crews while all hands launched the *James Caird*, biggest and heaviest of the three.

In the midst of it all, as if caught by the ebb of the tide, the pack, with a sinister rushing sound, suddenly began to close. Shackleton was just about to order all boats on the floe again, when the ice opened once more. He seized the moment.

"We said goodbye to all that was left of Patience Camp," Macklin wrote. "Well it deserved its name, and no sorrow was felt on leaving it." At 1.30 the little flotilla rowed out into open water. After five long months on the ice and more than a year since *Endurance* was beset, "it felt fine to be under way and off", said Macklin, "doing some good for oneself".[57]

XLI

Into the open sea

Standing up at the stern of the leading boat, a south-east wind blowing at his back, stood Shackleton, with a characteristic scowl, peering ahead. A school of whales followed blowing, as if in salute. Overhead, petrels swooped and dived causing, in Macklin's words, "annoyance of dropped excreta".[1] It was like an escort in derisory farewell.

Since losing *Endurance*, they had covered seven degrees of latitude. It was now the sixth month of their journey. James wrote in his diary, no doubt echoing Shackleton,

> Certainly it is one of the most remarkable man was fated to make. We look forward earnestly to at least a temporary ending & breather on the land. After that we have our rescue to think about for we are making for an island where no one is likely to look for us & which since the extermination of the Southern fur seal is not visited. There are two alternatives. One for a picket boat party to make Deception Island 180 miles WSW of us or second South Georgia 630 ENE. The advantage of the latter is that it is directly to leeward . . . However first we must get the main party to land.[2]

So far Shackleton had brought all his men unscathed, physically at least, through a drift of two thousand miles. Did he think, meanwhile, of *Nimrod*, and how *that* was to end in a great open-boat journey across "the sea on the other side"?[3] Now his prayers were being answered although, as usual, not exactly in the way the supplicant imagines.

For Shackleton, the auguries were enigmatic. In his scanty

personal belongings was a page from the Book of Job with the verses (38, 29-30):

> Out of whose womb came the ice? and the hoary frost of heaven, who hath gendered it?
> The waters are hid as with a stone, and the face of the deep is frozen.

This he had torn from the Bible presented by Queen Alexandra to *Endurance*. He had also kept the page with the 23rd Psalm, "The Lord is my shepherd"; and the flyleaf inscribed by Queen Alexandra:

> May the Lord help you to do your deeds guide you through all dangers by land and Sea.
> "May you see the Works of the Lord & all His wonders in the Deep."

Because of the weight, Shackleton had abandoned the rest of the volume when *Endurance* had foundered. What he did not know was that McLeod, the old Scottish shellback, had secretly retrieved it. To him, throwing a Bible away would bring bad luck.

One of the few books knowingly brought with them was Nordenskjöld's *Antarctic*, for it held the tale of Larsen's voyage from Paulet Island to Snow Hill. That distance was about a hundred miles, longer than the crossing of Bransfield Strait to Clarence or Elephant Island, where Shackleton was now heading.

In 1892, a Norwegian ship's captain called Magnus Andersen had crossed the North Atlantic, solo, in a ship's lifeboat to show it could be done. It was the new "navigable double ender", conceived by Colin Archer, on which the *James Caird* was based. But nobody had ever attempted, or at least survived, an open-boat journey in the Southern Ocean.

In any case, as Shackleton started down the wind-flecked channel between the floes, he was threatened once more by the pack advancing on his starboard side. He escaped being crushed by a spectacularly small margin. After that, thin ice impeded rowing, and the boats had heavy work forcing belts of brash. "Skilful ice navigation by Sir E.," as Macklin put it,[4] meant winding in roughly the right direction through the pack. "We were only stopped by dark," said Macklin, "from going ahead."[5]

The boats were hauled up on a floe, and camp made for the night. "We . . . went to sleep," said James, "well satisfied with our progress."[6] However, an "intangible feeling of uneasiness," as Shackleton related, "made me leave my tent about 11 p.m."[7] The floe was a long one. When they landed, it was at right angles to a heavy swell rolling in from the north-west. Now it had swung round until it was end on. Shackleton, in his own words,

> started to walk across the floe to warn the watchman to look carefully for cracks when the floe lifted on the crest of a swell and cracked under my feet as I was passing the men's tent. [It] was one of the dome . . . tents, and it began to stretch apart as the ice opened . . . I rushed forward, helped some men to come out from under the canvas . . .
>
> The crack had widened to about 4 feet and . . . I saw a whitish object floating in the water. It was a sleeping bag with a man inside. I was able to grasp it, and, with a heave, lifted man and bag on the floe. A few seconds later the ice-edges came together again with tremendous force.

The bag contained Holness, one of the Hull trawler hands who, as Shackleton put it, was "wet but otherwise unscathed".[8] By now the whole camp was aroused. It was, said Hurley, "a night of tension & anxiety – on a par with the night of the ship's destruction".

The *James Caird* and Shackleton's tent were separated by the crack from the rest. "Party reassembled with difficulty,"[9] Hurley noted. At one point, Shackleton found himself marooned, alone, on a fragment of the floe steadily drifting away. On the other side, the *Stancomb Wills* was hurriedly launched. "The few minutes that it took to fetch Shackleton," said Worsley, "were among the most anxious I have ever known."[10] The force of the currents and a tidal rip, as well he knew, could have swept Shackleton off into the darkness. The loss of their leader did not bear thinking about.

Tents were struck now, "& all spend rest of the dismal night shivering and waiting for morning,"[11] as Hurley put it. Macklin, on the other hand, used to summing up moods and feelings, wrote that

> We were so elated at our escape from Patience Camp that nothing could depress us, and the irrepressible Hussey with his (feeble) jokes . . . made us laugh, and helped to pass the long hours of darkness.[12]

In the small hours Shackleton who, as Macklin put it, "is extremely thoughtful on these occasions . . . had some [dried] milk warmed up . . . crowded round the little stove with its smoky flickering blubber flames [we] looked like hobgoblins."[13] Holness' shipmates meanwhile "kept him on the run all night long", as How put it, because there was no change of clothes, and it was the only way to get him dry. "Every movement he made [was] just a crackle of icy clothes."[14]

The seamen indeed were in notably good spirits. Even if it was only an overloaded cockleshell, they each had a ship again. The officers once more felt the comfort of command. Worsley especially now came into his own. Launching the boats next morning, and manoeuvring through the heavy running swell, he was superb. Handling open boats turned out to be his real metier. He had after all grown up with them in New Zealand. He knew how to cope with surf and breakers, backwash, rip tides, blind rollers, and all the different snares where the untramelled ocean rages against the land.

Worsley commanded the *Dudley Docker*. His crew were the same men who, though liking "Wuzzles", in Macklin's words, had so far mistrusted him as "a rather wild, excitable, hare-brained, half grown up, kind of customer quite incapable of responsible action". From now on, however, said Macklin, Worsley "assumed new stature".[15]

Shackleton had taken command of the *James Caird*. In the far-off days on the *Hoghton Tower* at Iquique, he too had learned how to handle open boats in the Pacific surf.

In the *Stancomb Wills* Hudson, for the sake of hierarchy and morale, was nominally in charge. Back at sea, as it were, he seemed to have regained his bearings somewhat. Still, there was the feeling that he hovered between dullness and a touch of quiet insanity. Crean, the Second Mate on *Endurance* and also accustomed to small boats, was effectively in command. Neither Shackleton nor Crean, however, had Worsley's flair.

There was a chill east wind on the morning of 10 April, as the boats left the broken floe. Along shifting lanes, they rowed through the pack, making as much northing as they could, but were pulled over to the west. When the floes thinned, sail was set and at 11 a.m., the little squadron ran out into ice-free water, "a great sight", as Macklin put it, "after all these months in our Pack prison".[16] There is, however, nothing quite as frightening and exposed as an open boat in a seaway, even for a person like Macklin, who had grown up in boats among the treacherous waters of the Scilly Isles.

A nasty, choppy sea was tumbling about. The *James Caird*, bumping heavily, was nonetheless happy under sail. The other boats were making leeway, but when the wind backed northerly the *Dudley Docker* and *Stancomb Wills* could not come across. Overloaded, and ill-trimmed, all three heaved and dropped sluggishly in the troughs. Freezing spray was shipped with every sea. Men and boats were caked with sheaths of ice. It was too much. Worsley was preparing to jettison food for safety, when Shackleton gave the signal to turn and run back for shelter in the pack.

As before, the boats were drawn up and camp made at dusk on a floe. This time, however, it was a solid-seeming floe-berg with a hummock high enough for a look-out. "Pray to God," in Hurley's words, "it will remain entire throughout the night."

> No sleep for 48 hours. All wet Cold & miserable with a N.E. Blizzard raging. Sympathetic with Sir E. for whom I have greater admiration than ever – with an eye to everything, so considerate to the party as to neglect himself.

"No sight of land," Hurley dismally continued, "& pray for cessation of these wild conditions & fine weather, given which we can make Land."

Hurley, who belonged to the *James Caird* under Shackleton, was forthright and uninhibited in a way the others were not. But he, Shackleton and Wild had just "narrowly escaped immersion",[17] when the overhanging edge of the floe collapsed under them as they were unloading the boats.

Tired, soaked, frozen, everyone tumbled as they were into damp sleeping bags. Nonetheless, with the comfort of a hot meal, cooked by the devoted Green, they "got in a splendid sleep". The floe did not split but "Morning showed that we had been sleeping in a fool's paradise," James said, "for the floe was rapidly decaying round the edges."[18]

James had not begun the day well. True to his reputation of the absentminded academic, he woke Macklin by mistake instead of Kerr at 3 a.m. for the morning watch. "I was," said Macklin, "not complimentary":

> Not being able to get to sleep again I lay and listened to the surge of water against the sides of the berglet. It seemed to me to have increased considerably since we turned in, floes were girning and grinding together all round us, and every now and again the berg received a heavy jolt.

"Never shall I forget the sight that met my eyes in the early dawn light," he continued when, eventually he was called at 5 a.m., the proper time for his watch.

> Ice had surrounded the berg . . . and the whole mass, made up of all sizes and shapes, and little bergs like our own, was rising and falling on enormous waves which rolled in from the North-West. It was a magnificent and awe-inspiring sight.[19]

Shackleton was called. Observing, in Macklin's words, that "we were quite helpless to help ourselves", he ordered everyone back to their sleeping bags to get all the sleep they could. The cook was not to be called until after eight o'clock.

When eventually the camp was roused, the ice still surrounded the berg. Breakfast was a rushed affair of quarter of a pound of dog pemmican and thin, but warm powdered milk. Afterwards, the boats were dragged to the edge of the berg, ready for launching.

The ice clung obstinately round the berg. White hills of ice-clad sea bore down out of a mist. Dark streaks of water showed between the floes, undulating venomously on remorseless rollers. This was the treacherous border between ice and sea. Survival was no more than a matter of chance.

In the middle of the morning the berg split in two without, this time, dividing the party. What remained of the berg, about the size of a tennis court, was steadily being eaten away and undermined by the hissing and soughing surf. There was no chance to relax. Periodically all gear had to be hauled to safety, while the ice-clad waves clattered and surged. No opening of the floes appeared; no chance of launching the boat. They were trapped.

Shackleton, outwardly impassive, jaw thrust out, and with his familiar frown, paced up and down, no more or less restlessly than usual. Now and then he clambered the few yards to the summit of the berg to survey the ice. His men followed his every move, like dogs watching their master. "Shackleton had that personality," as Greenstreet put it, "that imbued you with trust – you felt that if he led you everything was going to be all right."[20]

About midday, the ice around the remaining fragment of the berg eased to form an open pool. The chance seemed slim, but Shackleton now launched the boats. They were hurled, pell-mell, into the water, luckily without being stove in. The pool turned into a lead and, as James put it, "We were able to get away much relieved in mind to be off that piece of floe." Shackleton, he said, was "determined never to camp on another".[21]

So when darkness fell, they tied up to a floe, just long enough to land Green and his stove from the *James Caird* for a warm meal, and as soon as possible cast off again. They spent the night rowing desultorily to keep station. "Happy to be, as we said, on the first leg of our way home," as Orde-Lees, in the *Dudley Docker*, put it, "we spent a rotten time." It was fairly calm, but wet snow showers soaked them, and they were miserably cold. There was very little chance of sleep for anybody, except Orde-Lees and Worsley. *They* had an irritating capacity for catnaps under any circumstances. To Macklin, there was one compensation: "living on the [ice] we had developed tent cliques", and the new distribution meant "a pleasant change".[22]

During the night, they were joined by a school of killer whales. Most of the men were afraid that any moment one of the leviathans would foul the painters tying the boats together, or deliberately capsize them all. But the killer whale is not the ogre that has often been depicted. Rather it is a kind of giant dolphin, and frighteningly intelligent. One of them lay close alongside the *Dudley Docket* for hours, as if giving, or seeking lee. Macklin found their presence "companionable and rather comforting"; their groaning and exhaling was at least as bearable as the snoring of Orde-Lees![23]

Around midnight, everyone was roused from a frozen stupor by Hudson calling that he saw a light away down on the north-west horizon. "Though 'Buddha' stuck to his guns," as Macklin put it, "we realized, after a momentary intense reaction, that this could only have been a delusion." At dawn, James recorded,

> clear & bright. Sun rose brilliantly in a clear sky. Never was he more welcome to mortal man.[24]

It was the first glimpse of the sun since setting sail, three long days before. Worsley, clinging with one hand to the mast to steady himself against the rocking of the boat, somehow juggled with the sextant to get a shot of the sun. On a carefully hoarded handkerchief, Macklin found a rare non-greasy area with which to remove the fog from the eyepiece.

Crouching down on the thwarts, Worsley flipped over the damp pages of his navigational tables and, with a stump of pencil, did his sums. He could work fast and accurately under almost any conditions. "A terrible disappt.,"[25] he jotted down eloquently when the result was clear.

The *James Caird* came alongside, and Shackleton went aboard to examine the calculations. They were some sixty miles east and twenty miles south of their dead reckoning position. They were actually ten miles south and about thirty miles east of Patience Camp. They were further from their goal than before. All their work had been for nought. "Whatever Shackleton may have felt," said Macklin, "he did not show it . . . finding . . . Worsley's figures . . . correct [he] observed almost casually 'this must be due to the current running out of Bransfield Strait'."[26]

Shackleton returned to the *James Caird* and, after talking to Wild, ordered a change of course. The wind was from the north-west and foul for the South Shetlands. They would run south-west instead for Hope Bay, at the tip of Graham Land, where some of Nordenskjöld's men had involuntarily wintered in 1903–04.

It was now 12 April. The day before, Shackleton, believing he was running west, had changed destination from Clarence to Elephant or King George Island. He had to change plans with the wind because the *Stancomb Wills* could not beat to windward. "Our spirits," said James at the change of plan, "were much dampened."[27] He was probably thinking of Wordie, taciturn and dour as always, in the *James Caird* with him; but the others took heart at following the wind and chasing a new objective.

For the second night running, they lay to in the boats. Around 8 p.m., the wind suddenly backed right round to south-west. That made the floes, under which they had sought shelter, a "lee shore", the seaman's nightmare. Shackleton ordered his little fleet to cast loose and tie up to each other stem to stern.

The *Dudley Docker*, in the lead, was told to row through the night in order to keep her head to wind. Her crew took a grumbling satisfaction in seeing this as a compliment to their superior seamanship. They were probably right. Worsley was notably proud of Cheetham and McLeod, "The latter a typical old Scotch deep sea salt . . . the former a pirate to his fingertips."[28]

It was another miserable night, with no sleep; but at least it was reasonably calm. The boats were iced up, with encrustation like armour plating on the hulls. About a quarter of a ton had accumulated on each and as most of it was forward, they were all down by the bows. They had to draw up alongside each other, while someone from another boat hacked the ice away.

By running for Hope Bay Shackleton had shown what Orde-Lees, with hindsight, called "an almost uncanny intuition".[29] He had made far enough to the west now to use the south-westerly wind, otherwise they would probably have been driven out into the Atlantic by now. As it was, after pestering Worsley frequently about navigation, Shackleton now ordered yet another change of destination. At first light, the boats put about, and ran before the wind for Elephant Island.

It was Thursday, 13 April, and their fifth day in the boats. Shackleton was now seriously worried that exposure was beginning to tell. He refused to stop any longer to cook on a floe. Food was to be gnawed cold, under way.

Carefully, they sailed between the floes, occasionally, to Shackleton's unconcealed annoyance, bumping into bits of ice. "Our boats' dark sails show up in contrast to the masses of white pack," Worsley wrote. "We look like a fleet of exploring or mauruading Vikings."[30]

Shackleton, standing up in *James Caird*, so as to be seen, indeed had something of the archetypal chieftain about him. "Practically ever since we had first started," Orde-Lees remarked,

> Sir Ernest has been standing erect day and night on the stern-counter of the Caird, only holding on to one of the stays of the little mizzen mast conning our course the whole time the boats were under way.[31]

It was Shackleton's style of leadership not only to be in command, but to be seen to be in command. "How he stood the incessant vigil," Orde-Lees went on, "is marvellous, but he is a wonderful man . . . He simply never spares himself if, by his individual toil, he can possibly benefit anyone else."

At one point, Hurley lost his mittens. As Orde-Lees related, Shackleton,

> at once divested himself of his own, and in spite of the fact that he was standing up in the most exposed position all the while he insisted upon Hurley's acceptance of the mits, and on the latter's protesting Sir Ernest was on the point of throwing them overboard rather than wear them when one of his subordinates had to go without; as a consequence Sir Ernest had one finger rather severely frostbitten.[32]

In the middle of the morning, after an hour or two working through brash and freezing water, they suddenly broke clear of the pack. Into an open sea they went, and ran before the wind. Curling breakers caught the boats, and hurled them forward with a surge. It was wild and exhilarating. For once the men could relax and let the wind do the work. Elephant Island was not visible, but, as Macklin wrote, the sense of speeding towards their goal was uplifting:

> It was for me, and I expect for all of us, an unforgettable day – the wind torn cloudy sky, great banks of cumulus with shafts of sunlight breaking through, the vast ocean with curling white horses . . . the Caird leaping away ahead and behind us the gallant little [Stancomb] Wills at one moment outlined against the sky on the top of a crest, and the next falling into the trough so that we could only see the top of her mast.[33]

"The problem," James recorded, "was what to do at night."[34] Worsley, in a state of great excitement, was all for pushing on. Shackleton, however, was afraid of their being scattered in the dark. He ordered all three boats to lie to, tied up once more stem to stern. To ride out the hours of darkness the *Dudley Docker* ("Always," wrote Macklin, "it was the Docker for these jobs") laid a sea anchor improvised out of two oars lashed together.

"On the Caird," said James, "we were fairly comfortable & took no water, but we could see things were pretty critical with the other boats." The waves were throwing up spray that froze as it fell. The *Stancomb Wills* was shipping so many seas, she was soon encrusted again with ice. To stop her foundering, it had continually to be hacked off.

The *Dudley Docker* did not have a pleasant time. A heavy swell continued to run, but the wind fell off, so that she could not be kept headed into the seas, and continually swung across the breakers. Between the sea anchor and the two boats astern, she suffered a jerky, violent motion, like a cradle rocked by some drunken termagant. It was too much for even the strongest stomachs. Everyone on board the *Dudley Docker* was seasick. Also, because of the uncooked dog pemmican they had been eating, they had violent diarrhoea. To relieve themselves, they had to "sit on the gunwhales, holding on by the wire stay or supported by a comrade", as Macklin graphically recorded,

> whilst the seas swept up and wetted not only our exposed parts but our clothing as well. To clean ourselves we had only little pieces of ice.[35]

They were also tormented by thirst, aggravated by the loss of fluid through the diarrhoea. Their water supply had failed because they had run into the open sea so suddenly they had not thought to collect fresh water ice.

A tent cloth had been spread over the *Dudley Docker* for some protection. "Never," wrote Macklin, "will I forget the writhing mass of humanity which tried to snatch a few moments sleep under it. Men cursed each other, the sea, the boat, and everything cursable."[36]

Especially did they curse Orde-Lees. He had declined to row, because it was too rough, too cold, or he was a "rotten oarsman". Orde-Lees also appropriated the one set of oilskins, refused to give it up, and lay down like a passenger under the thwarts. He now absolutely declined to make room under the tent cloth for his neighbours. Either he was stupendously insensitive or, having been miserably nauseous from seasickness from the start, he was past caring. It was Marston who saved the situation. Emerging with a stream of profanity, he went to the stern, where he sat, for hours it seemed, singing songs. "One which stuck in my head," said Macklin, "had a chorus which went 'Twankedillo, twankedillo, and my roaring pair of bagpipes made from the green willow.' "[37] It was the only way Marston could relieve his feelings, and it probably saved a suicidal fight.

Marston's singing was carried down wind to the other boats. In the morning Shackleton congratulated him on his efforts to keep up morale. By then, Orde-Lees had partially redeemed himself. When the boat started shipping too many seas, he jumped up and, singlehanded, bailed her dry. Secondly, in the small hours, Greenstreet's feet had become frostbitten; more seriously than anyone else's, that is. It was Orde-Lees who put them between his stomach and his jersey where, in his own words, he "nursed [them] for an hour while [Greenstreet] suffered great pain and I cursed myself for a Samaritan".[38]

The day, once more, was a reward for the inferno of the night. It was cold, the boats were iced up, but the waves had eased, and the wind fallen off. "A truly magnificent sunrise," in Orde-Lees' words, "reveals Clarence Island looming up ahead . . . then Elephant Island becomes visible & being nearer we make for it."[39] After all their misery, they had really worked closer to their goal.

Worsley preened himself on the fact that the islands were

> both exactly on the bearings I had said they would be; & Sir Ernest congratulates me on the accuracy of my navigation under circumstances of some difficulty & after 2 days of Dead Reckoning, while working in & out amongst pack ice with no very accurate means of taking Compass courses & lying to for 2 nights at the mercy of the winds & currents.[40]

This more or less confirmed the crew of the *Dudley Docker* in their by now almost blind faith in Worsley as a navigator.

Physically and mentally, however, they were all worn. It was 14 April, the sixth day of their voyage. For three nights they had had no sleep. When the boats closed for the morning conference Shackleton, in Macklin's words, "was looking haggard, and his usually strong voice had become husky. He seemed . . . a bit edgy and short of temper."[41]

In an otherwise open sea now gently rolling with an even swell, a small iceberg had earlier appeared. The *Dudley Docker*, being ahead, had sheered off to it in order to quarry ice for drinking. The *James Caird*, meanwhile, had drawn abreast, Shackleton bawling at them to leave the ice alone and join him. "We were a little chagrined," said Macklin, "when on coming alongside he remarked 'You people in the Docker seem to think of nothing but your stomachs. Don't you want to get to land?'"[42] Since they had to wait twenty minutes for the *Stancomb Wills* to catch up with them, they could have got all the ice they needed without loss of time.

Shackleton, however, fearing for the lives of his men, wanted them ashore without delay. As it was, from the *Stancomb Wills* came the news that Hudson had collapsed. Shackleton told Worsley to push on and make land before night. Worsley said it was impossible and, in Macklin's words, "had his head bitten off by the Boss, who thought he had been careless in his answer".[43] What Shackleton meant was that the others had overheard. He wanted them to believe they would arrive before nightfall. That was partly why he had stopped the *Dudley Docker* collecting ice for drinking water, for it would have implied they were preparing for another day afloat.

The day was fine, but Shackleton had destroyed any pleasure by condemning them to the torment of thirst. When Worsley saw some tempting pieces of glacier ice floating near, he left them alone for fear of risking a second outburst of Shackleton's temper. In the end, they all had to make do by sucking a few scattered bits of ice, and pieces of frozen seal meat.

Chafed buttocks from rowing continually on hard seats, and suppurating sea water boils added to their misery. Although the peaks of Elephant Island grew plainly nearer through the day, there was very little talk in the boats. It was hope without enjoyment.

Shackleton, now worried that the *Stancomb Wills* was holding them back, ordered the three boats to tie up together, hoping thereby to tow her and make better speed. In the middle of the afternoon, a nasty head wind blew up. It then backed to southwest, and soon rose to a gale, with a dangerous lumpy sea running. Worsley urgently suggested separating. Shackleton agreed. The *James Caird* kept the *Stancomb Wills* in tow, while the *Dudley Docker* sheered off on her own.

Fog and drifting cloud blotted out all sign of land. Only filtered moonlight gave a faint blink ahead which was assumed to be the glaciers of Elephant Island. It was in any case an uncertain sea mark. For the first time an inkling of terror settled on the fleet. They were quite possibly on the verge of realising the nightmare haunting them since they left Patience Camp. At the last moment, wind and current might yet sweep them past their landfall out into the waters where there was no hope. It seemed almost the final battle with the cruel, impersonal sea.

Shackleton had told Worsley to keep in sight. At the best of times, it would have been hard. Since they had no navigation lights Shackleton shone the compass lantern on the *James Caird*'s mainsail to show Worsley where he was,. Soon, however, visibility was blotted out by snow squalls. The boats lost sight of each other and it became, in Orde-Lees' words, "a case of sauve-qui-peut".[44]

On the *Dudley Docker* Worsley was soon fighting to keep the boat from being swamped. First, he struck sails, and kept head to wind by rowing, but he soon saw that his crew were too exhausted to keep going. As he himself was also on the point of exhaustion, he set sail again, the lesser of two evils.

Superb boatman though he was, Worsley could not keep the *Dudley Docker* dry. With her lugsail, she could not come far enough up into the wind, and so drove broadside on. So he trimmed her to leeward; a frightening manoeuvre, getting men to shift down over a rolling boat against all their instincts, with the fear of being tossed overboard. The idea was to raise the weather freeboard from the normal miserable few inches and stop water being shipped. It worked, up to a point. Then water started coming in over the lee gunwale.

It was in this final emergency that Orde-Lees really came into his own. Without orders, he started bailing like one possessed, and continued hour after hour, keeping the water down. He was about the only man with the strength or, indeed, the will to do so. His gymnastic training undoubtedly came to his aid, but it was almost as if some obscure instinct had made him avoid other effort to save himself for this moment. Cheetham helped, but Worsley was convinced that Orde-Lees, singlehanded, stopped them from foundering that night.

That was only half of Worsley's concern, however. He also had to keep them from being swept past the land. The boat's compass had been smashed, so he could only claw up to windward as hard as he could, and hope for the best. About 2 a.m., the dismal hour, the wind appeared to have veered to north-west. "Think we are getting out to sea & lost,"[45] as Orde-Lees laconically put it. Somehow, in between bailing, he contrived to keep his diary as a running log.

Macklin and Greenstreet, meanwhile, had found a pocket compass. Crawling under a canvas cover at the bottom of the boat, they tried to read the dial with a match, but squalls wormed their way even there and blew out several matches before they could get a glimpse. The wind, after all, turned out still to be south-west, and they were heading north-west. Unless they were making stupendous leeway, they still had a chance.

"Cheetham thinks he hears boat cracking in centre," Orde-Lees recorded about 5 a.m. "All shift aft & so get no protection. Much irritability. Dawn at last & find ourselves bang in front of land."[46]

It was 15 April, and the seventh day of the journey. Worsley, despite his gift for catnaps, was now uncontrollably overcome with fatigue. After fifty hours continuously on watch, he was falling asleep at the tiller. Macklin took his place, handing over to Greenstreet as soon as he could be roused.

There was no respite yet. The land was not exactly a haven.

Perpendicular stone cliffs and glaciers shaped a hostile shore. There was no question of a landing. They were evidently in the south-eastern bight of Elephant Island.

For a while, the wind dropped. The sea had had its say. Now it was the turn of the land. Venomous offshore gusts, rolling down from the ice-clad summits of the overhanging peaks, roared across the waves to shake and toss the *Dudley Docker* like some beast playing with its prey.

Greenstreet lowered sail, kept head to wind by rowing. It was desperately hard work for exhausted men. Then a particularly violent squall bore down, driving before it in the early morning light a grey-green sea that, to eyes dancing with fatigue, appeared like a tidal bore, a tidal wave perhaps.

Greenstreet was a competent ship's officer, but a boatman he was not. With this sluggish open, overloaded cockshell, he quite simply did not know what to do. "Wake Worsley!" He spoke everybody's thoughts.

It was easier said than done. Worsley was in a state of profound slumber on some packing cases at the bottom of the boat. McLeod gave him one or two kicks. Worsley started to grumble about being wakened but, becoming aware of the danger, he was up in a second, put the boat about, ordered sail up, and ran off before the wall of water that was now almost on top of them.

There was no time to get way on the boat. The first wave pooped the *Dudley Docker*. Again, it was Orde-Lees who baled her out, and once more probably saved them all. But it was the end of their terror; as if sea and land had spent their venom. The *Dudley Docker* surged on the swell along the coast looking for a landing.

When the boats had separated, Shackleton in the *James Caird* had the burden of the *Stancomb Wills* on his mind. She could not survive the seas on her own. If the tow parted, she was lost. In the dark, only a glimpse of the white froth of waves breaking on the *Stancomb Wills* revealed whether she was still afloat. Wild, meanwhile, had "early discovered," as he put it, "that I had no-one . . . except Shackleton who could be trusted at the tiller, and he was fully occupied by the general supervision of the fleet. I was at the tiller the whole time we were moving."[47]

By the time the *Dudley Docker* had disappeared in the dark, several of those in the *James Caird* were "insane". As Wild added, they were

> fortunately not violent, simply helpless and hopeless. Again Shackleton's marvellous unselfishness and consideration for others were shown . . . he looked after those helpless men just as though they were babes in arms.[48]

At least on the *James Caird* there was not the tension of the *Dudley Docker*. Also, since the *James Caird* was a better sailer Shackleton was at least relieved of the worry of keeping up into the wind. Even so, she took green seas aboard, repeatedly soaking men who could ill stand the strain. Spume spouted as the bows ploughed into the waves. The snarl of a cutting wind and the hiss of a running sea did not help deranged minds. Even to Wild, still calm and imperturbable at the helm, that night was "the worst I have ever known".

He too was worried about being swept irrevocably to leeward and lost in the ocean:

> About 3 a.m., Shackleton was attending to one of the semi-conscious men and asked me some question. Peering ahead through my sore and bloodshot eyes, I had just at that moment caught a glimpse of a moonlit glacier on Elephant Island, and instead of replying to the question I said as plainly as I was able with swollen and aching tongue and throat, "I can see it! I can see it!" By the time Shackleton turned the island was obscured and he afterwards told me he had a momentary dread that "poor old Wild's gone off his head."[49]

Soon after Wild felt the need to rest his eyes, if nothing else. In a lull, he told McNeish, who was at the sheet, to take the tiller. Almost immediately the boat broached to. A huge ice cold sea swept aboard. By a miracle, the *James Caird* escaped foundering. McNeish collapsed, probably from thirst and exposure. Shackleton had another patient. Wild had to spring to the tiller again.

Shortly before dawn, the wind seemed to reach a crescendo of malevolence, screaming and tearing at the boat. It then eased off slightly. "Wild," said James, "had been steering now for something like 30 hours continuously & said he thought we were still within striking distance of land." The sky was just beginning to get light when suddenly land appeared on the port bow.

> We . . . seemed to be right on top of it. We at once put about, but found we are not quite as close as we thought, still quite close enough, not more than a quarter of a mile. The morning was misty & we could only see [a] great black headland bearing up in the fog. Wild gave it as his opinion, which subsequently proved to be correct that it was the extreme Eastern end of the island which we had just managed to grasp as the storm drove us past.[50]

They weathered the point, and at last found the lee of the island. They put about, and started sailing along the northern coast in search of a landing but "the land," as James put it, "was of a most uncompromising type. The cliffs were absolutely sheer . . . Dominican gulls were swarming around the cliffs but," he added whimsically, "we cannot lodge where they can".

After about a mile they rounded a bleak promontory called Cape Valentine, and found a beach in a sheltered bay behind a line of rocks. Shackleton decided to land there. Calling up the *Stancomb Wills*, he used her as a tender to investigate the shore first.

Shackleton, however, was seriously concerned about the *Dudley Docker*. She had not been seen since 10 p.m. the night before. On the *Dudley Docker*, the same worries reigned. Worsley had finally collapsed from a combination of fatigue and thirst. Greenstreet took the boat along the coast looking for a landing. "Round a point," in the words of Orde-Lees' diary jotting, "looks suitable & there see other two boats. Joyful reunion."[51]

Shackleton had actually just arrived. The *Dudley Docker* was able to help with the landing. She got stuck on a bar going in, but was undamaged. About half a dozen men were still fit for work, but weak. Somehow they dragged the three boats on shore to what seemed like safety. It was the first known landing on Elephant Island since American sealers were there in 1830.

It was not exactly a hospitable place; only a narrow shingly beach clinging to a hostile shore. But, as Hurley expressed it,

> Conceive our joy on setting foot on solid earth after 170 days of life on a drifting ice floe each day filled with anxiety patience & watching & being driven whither to an obscure destination.[52]

Exposure and mental strain had told on them. Some staggered about; others seemed in a daze; a few were shaking as if with palsy. Almost the whole crew of the *Stancomb Wills* was incapacitated. Hudson, as McNeish put it, "has gone of [*sic*] his head".[53]

Thirst had played a part in what had gone before. The joy of landing meant also unlimited fresh water ice to slake its torments. Shackleton had not got his men ashore a moment too soon.

On the boat, Orde-Lees had "risked the consequences", as he maintained, "whatever they might be, of drinking salt water":

> Some say that one goes mad. Maybe I am or was, but I did not hesitate to drink with discretion small quantities of sea-water, and I do not think I suffered in the aftermath any more.[54]

"Shackleton himself," said Macklin, "looked gaunt and haggard and could scarcely speak above a whisper. Little Frankie Wild . . . alone of all the party looked something like his normal self."[55]

One other person at least displayed a touch of normalcy. Green, the cook, who had collapsed on the boat, was soon bending as usual over his smoking blubber stove on the beach, although robbed of his habitual smile. In Hurley's words, a toast to "our phenomenal escape was drunk in hot steaming milk".

"Most of us," James wrote in his diary, "hardly knew whether to laugh or cry. We did not know until it was released, what a strain the last few days had been. We took childish joy in looking at the black rocks & picking up the stones, for we had stepped on no land since Dec. 5 1914."[56]

XLII

Half-way house

"Now that the party are established at an immovable base," Hurley soon was writing, "I review their general behaviour during the memorable escape from the floe. This success

> is due to the admirable & able direction of Sir E. who never for a moment allowed a boat out of sight, did all possible to ameliorate the privations & took no risks.

This more or less echoed the feelings of the men still dazed upon the beach. "It is regrettable to state," Hurley nonetheless went on,

> that many conducted themselves in a manner unworthy of gentlemen & British sailors. Some whom it was anticipated would be the bulwarks of the party "stove in".
>
> In the majority of cases those suffering from severe frostbites could be traced to negligence, whilst the numerous cases of temporary aberration are excusable under the plea of intense privation & suffering.

"Amongst those that stand meritorious," Hurley went on,

> Sir E. has mentioned: Wild – a tower of strength who appeared as well as ever after 32 hours at the tiller in frozen clothes, Crean who . . . piloted the Wills, McNeish (Carpenter) Vincent (AB) McCarthy (AB) Marston (Dudley Docker) & [Hurley recorded without false modesty] self.

Was this a way of making sure that Shackleton remembered? Hurley knew that by contract his diary would be open to inspection. "A fair proportion of the remainder," he continued, "I am convinced they would starve or freeze if left to their own resources on this island,"

> for there is such improvident disregard for their equipment, as to allow it to be buried in snow or carried off by the winds. Those who shirk duties, or lack a fair sense of practicability [*sic*] should not be in these parts. These are harsh places where it takes all one's time & energies to attend to the individual, & so make himself as effective & useful a unit as possible.[1]

Shackleton might interpret that as criticism of his choice of men; but Hurley was also saying that, given such unpromising material, his leadership stood out even more.

"Thank God I haven't killed one of my men!" That, according to Worsley, was what Shackleton said in a "confidential talk" soon after landing:

> Shackleton had always insisted that the ultimate responsibility for anything that befell us was his and his only. But until then I had not understood the painful seriousness with which he viewed his relation to us. My view was that we were all grown men, going of our own free wills on this expedition, and that it was up to us to bear whatever was coming to us. Not so Shackleton. His idea was that we had trusted him, that we had placed ourselves in his hands, and that should anything happen to us, he was morally responsible. His attitude was almost patriarchal.

It was in any case contractual. In return for unquestioning devotion, he would give absolute care. An outcast he might be, but Shackleton fulfilled a primitive need. As Worsley told him,

> "Whatever happens, we all know that you have worked superhumanly to look after us." . . . "Superhuman effort" . . . he retorted, rather gruffly . . . "isn't worth a damn unless it achieves results."[2]

There undoubtedly rang the true voice of Shackleton. He was the man still in search of his destiny, whom Destiny somehow had not touched. That was his private tragedy. Even now he felt time running out.

The landing hardly justified euphoria. Elephant Island was terra firma, but it was truly a desert island; a bleak and inaccessible patch of rock and ice twenty miles from end to end.

The beach was in fact a death trap. Tide marks and other signs proved that it was periodically awash. Scattered boulders hinted at rock falls from the cliff behind. To discover whether there was a refuge higher up, Shackleton sent the only climbers in the party, Wordie and Orde-Lees.

> We may have ascended five hundred feet [said Orde-Lees], but finding neither a ledge nor any likelihood of one further up, we came down and reported "nothing doing". In fit condition we would have considered it an easy climb; weak as we were, we found it almost beyond our remaining strength, and were glad not to be asked to try it again.[3]

The day after their arrival, therefore, Shackleton sent Wild out in the *Dudley Docker* with a boat's party to find a safer beach. Late in the evening, Wild returned with the news that along a uniformly bleak and hostile coast, "no possible abiding place was seen"[4] until about seven miles to the west. Next day, 17 April, the whole party loaded up the boats and started rowing there. At first some of the men refused to forsake dry land for another boat journey. Their instincts turned out to be sound.

The weather since the arrival at Elephant Island had been fair. Soon after setting out, they ran into a storm blowing in squalls off the land. Drift snow pouring down gulleys in the cliffs mingled with the spume to lash the boats with a nasty, freezing foam. Those few miles seemed worse than the whole long way from Patience Camp.

About half-way to the new refuge, there was a large rock about a quarter of a mile off shore. The *James Caird* and *Stancomb Wills* passed to landwards. Worsley took the *Dudley Docker* round to seawards. Macklin called it one of his "incalculable impulses".[5] It was in fact quite understandable. Worsley knew that along steep high shores under coastal mountains there blew treacherous winds. They are simply currents of air plunging down from the heights like waterfalls to spill out over the sea. Also, steep shores mean dangerous choppy waves. Worsley thought he would escape all this by sheering off from land.

Elephant Island, however, is really just a half-submerged mountain massif with an ice sheet on its back. It has its own climate, featuring the worst aspects of the sea, the mountain world, and high latitudes. Worsley had failed to allow for the sheer height of the cliffs and glacier fronts. Thrusting a thousand feet or more straight out of the water, they formed a kind of lee under the falling air. That meant it might be sensible to hug the coast. Worsley found himself in the vicious disturbance where the falling wind hit the water. He was nearly blown out to sea, but somehow weathered the headland. Along the way, he lost an oar, and having only three oars left scarcely improved matters.

It was night by the time they all arrived. In the storm and the dark the new haven "did not look half so hospitable," in Wild's words, "as when I had seen it in bright sunshine the day before".[6] It was in fact no more than a spit of land, perhaps two hundred yards long, jutting out from a sheer rock and ice face. To seaward it ended in a flat-topped rock. To the west was a bay with a glacier dropping into the sea; to the east another bay backed by more gloomy weather-scoured rock and ice. It was not much, but the storm showed that it was unlikely to be swamped, it was solid earth and, by comparison with what they had left, it seemed broadly habitable. Cape Wild, it was dubbed; Cape Bloody Wild, the seamen said.

It was at least a place where one could survive. Disease there was none. From the glacier ice there was unlimited drinking water. The headland at the end of the spit was a penguin rookery. That, together with seals and various sea birds, would provide food and fuel.

The day after arriving at the new beach, Shackleton took Worsley and Wild aside to discuss his plans. They agreed that there was little hope of rescue. No search expedition would look for them on Elephant Island although, if Otto Nordenskjöld were involved, he might just do so. Because of reefs, half-tide rocks, pack ice, grounded bergs, and other devilment, passing whalers would not come in close enough to sight them. In any case, winter was near. Logically, the thing to do was to wait on the island, and escape when summer came. But "Some of the party," as Wild put it, "had become despondent, and were in a 'What's the use' sort of mood and had to be driven to work, none too gently either."[7] Worsley added,

> We were, in a world of our own, we had only ourselves to look to, and the world was as completely cut off from us as though we had come from another planet. I have experienced a good many strange things in my time, but this sensation of detachment from the living world was one of the most memorable.[8]

It was a sensation that few of them had the capacity to endure. Escape was vital, and the sooner the better.

The only practicable goal, as everyone knew by now, was South Georgia. Cape Horn or the Falkland Islands were much closer, but reaching either would require beating up against the prevailing winds. South Georgia was over seven hundred miles away, but it was to leeward, directly in the path of the Westerlies storming round the globe at those latitudes. "We all agreed", wrote Wild, "that an attempt to take the whole party would certainly mean the loss of all hands."[9] In Shackleton's own words therefore,

> The conclusion was forced upon me, that a boat journey in search of relief was necessary . . . The hazards . . . were obvious, but I calculated that at worst this venture would add nothing to the risks of the men left on the island . . . Worsley and Wild realised that the attempt must be made and asked to be allowed to accompany me on the voyage.
>
> I had at once, to tell Wild that he must stay behind, for I relied upon him to hold the party together while I was away, and, should our attempt . . . end in failure, to make the best of his way to Deception Island in the spring. I determined to take Worsley with me as I had a very high opinion of his accuracy and quickness as a navigator.[10]

On 19 April, two days after arriving at Cape Wild, Shackleton announced that he was going off immediately to fetch help. He asked for volunteers. It was a telling scene.

Gathered around Shackleton, grizzled and weatherworn, was a group of ragged, unkempt creatures, with dirty faces from which the eyeballs shone unnaturally white against the dark grime of ingrained blubber soot. To hear what he said, they were forced to strain their ears against the roar of the gale that had been blowing remorselessly since they landed on the beach. During the night, one of the tents had been ripped by a gust. The inmates had sought shelter in a boat. No one had slept much. To the north a patchwork of floes and icebergs graphically illustrated the dilemma of men caught between land and sea. Many of them wished never to get into a boat again. Shackleton's plan "struck me as the forlornest forlorn hope conceivable", Orde-Lees frankly admitted. "I decided to excuse myself."[11]

Macklin and McIlroy, on the other hand, earnestly volunteered. They, however, as doctors, were needed on the island. During the journey from Patience Camp, Blackborrow's toes had been frostbitten. It had happened to others, but in his case, the circulation could not be restored. Gangrene was setting in. An operation was necessary. Shackleton fleetingly considered taking him to South Georgia but an open boat was hardly the place for an invalid.

For medical reasons, the operation could not take place for about six weeks. By then, Shackleton confidently hoped to have his men back in civilisation. In case of accidents, however, Blackborrow would have to have the operation on the island, for which both doctors would then be needed; one to operate, one to give the anaesthetic.

McNeish was also one of the few wholeheartedly to volunteer. "I don't think there will be many survivors", as he put it, if they had "to put in a winter here."[12] He too preferred the perils of the sea.

Despite McNeish's "mutiny" on the ice five months before, Shackleton took him. In the first place, on any wooden craft, a skilled carpenter might mean the difference between foundering or not. Besides, in the strain of being left behind, McNeish would potentially be a trouble-maker.

For the same reason, Shackleton chose Vincent, the bosun disrated for bullying. Vincent was a good sailor, of the kind only troublesome ashore. Shackleton also took a seaman called Timothy McCarthy, probably because he was Irish. Finally, he made up the crew with Crean, partly because Crean begged so hard to go, perhaps also because he was Irish too.

The journey from Patience Camp had shown that the *James Caird*, besides being the largest of the boats, was also the most seaworthy. Before she could sail, however, she had to be decked in and made ready for sea. That needed a shipwright. Everything therefore now turned on McNeish.

McNeish was not only an accomplished shipwright. His cantankerousness was the dark side of perseverance and ingenuity. On the ice, he had already raised the freeboard of the *James Caird* by ten inches with wood salvaged from *Endurance*. He had also covered her fo'c'sle. There remained the rest of an open hull.

The *James Caird* was 22 feet long and 6½ feet in the beam, but a thousand miles from the nearest tree, this meant an unimaginable area. The beach was absolutely barren, nor was there any driftwood. The wood McNeish had at his disposal consisted of a sledge and some packing case lids. Also he dismantled the extra freeboard he had built on the *Dudley Docker*. It was too little by far for a deck, but it was enough for a framework. The covering had to be improvised from canvas, a bolt of which had luckily been brought along.

"There are 5 on the sick list," McNeish found time to note, "some heart trouble some frostbite & 1 dilly [Hudson]."[13] Most of the remainder were helping with the work. Some were making up rations from what remained of the sledging food. Some were sewing bags out of blankets to hold shingle for the ballast. Marston and McLeod were caulking the seams, improvising with lamp wick and Marston's oil paints.

"Cheatham," as McNeish spelt it, "& McCarthy have been busy trying to stitch the canvas for the deck. They had rather a job as it was frozen stiff. They had to pull the needle through with a pair of pinchers."[14]

Being swamped was only one of the dangers ahead. In heavy seas the boat might break her back. McNeish took the mast out of the *Stancomb Wills*, and laid it along the inside of the *James Caird* as a hog's back to reinforce her keel.

Bitter winds, meanwhile, continued incessantly to sweep down from the heights and rake the beach. To almost everyone, these days were the most depressing so far on the whole expedition. McNeish was proof against it all as, with his scanty tools and frostbitten hands, he sawed, chipped and hammered in the blast as imperturbably as if he had been in a boatyard at home. On 22 April however, even he was defeated by a south-east blizzard, with gusts of around 60 m.p.h. "All day . . . there has been nothing doing," as he phrased it, "but lay in our wet bags & have our rations passed in."[15]

The pack ice hovered menacingly off shore. Every hour might count in what had become a race to get the *James Caird* away before it was too late. With his one ambition to get every one of his men out alive, Shackleton could only hope that the doctors would be able to save Blackborrow; but his constant fear was that "if things went wrong," as he said to Worsley, he would be accused of abandoning his men. They, on the other hand, had no doubts at all. For one thing, as Macklin phrased it,

> Shackleton sitting still and doing nothing wasn't Shackleton at all, We'd had all that at Patience Camp.[16]

Also, there was fairly general relief that someone else was willing to take the necessary risks. Besides, they had a mystic faith by now that, if anyone could get through, it was the Boss.

On Monday 24 April, "a fine morning," in McNeish's words,

> I started on the boat at daybreak & finished it at 10 a.m. Then all hands were mustered & we launched her & as we were getting her off the beach a heavy surf came up & owing to us being unable to get her bow off the beach she almost capsised as it was she emptyed myself & Vincent overboard.[17]

The boat had started to fill with water. Worsley, crawling into the bilges, discovered that the bottom plug had been left out. He quickly found the cork, and put it in the hole; but the *James Caird* then had to be baled out before she had even started on her voyage. Orde-Lees described the scene:

> The carpenter came ashore, rather moistly, and swearing.
>
> Volunteers were called for to change clothes with the wet men. The carpenter, however, declined to change with anyone and as only his

> legs were wet perhaps he had no special reason to decline . . . but Vincent was wet through to the neck and his refusal to change anything except drawers and trousers which he did with How naturally called forth some unfavourable comment as to the reason and it was freely stated that he had a good deal of other people's property concealed about his person.

How, being without a change of clothing, had to withdraw into his sleeping bag while Vincent's garments dried. "Under the existing conditions," Orde-Lees drily wrote, "this might be a long time."[18]

The *James Caird* was now anchored about a hundred yards offshore. She had been launched light and now, with the *Stancomb Wills* as tender, she was loaded up for sea. Nineteen bags of ballast had to be ferried from the beach, and much gear besides. It took four trips.

As soon as Shackleton and the last of the cargo were on board, the *James Caird* set sail. It was 12.30 in the afternoon. "With a final wave of the hand, and three squawky cheers from us and the penguins, Sir Ernest and his crew set off on their perilous journey. . . . The wind they started with could not have been better both in strength & direction," Orde-Lees continued, "being S.W.":

> They made surprising speed for such a small craft. We watched them until they were out of sight; which was not long, for such a tiny boat was soon lost to sight on that great heaving ocean; as she dipped into the trough of each wave she disappeared completely sail & all.[19]

"Great confidence," wrote Hurley, summing up the feelings of all those left behind, "is reposed in [the] crew":

> six proven veterans, seasoned by the salt & experience of the Sea. The distance to . . . South Georgia is 700 miles, 700 miles of wintry sea, the most tempestuous zone of the oceans. The Caird is an excellent sailer, & guided by providence, should make Sth. Georgia in 14 days. It is intended to commission the "Undine" of the Grytviken Whaling Coy, & rescue this party immediately. How we shall count the days.[20]

XLIII

Tension on Elephant Island

"Loud reports in glacier," Orde-Lees was writing on Elephant Island on 12 June, "at first mistaken for relief ship firing."[1]

Wild, as Orde-Lees recorded the day that the *James Caird* sailed, was "confident that Sir Ernest will be here with a relief ship in less than a fortnight."[2] That would have been about 7 May. Orde-Lees, meanwhile, in his own words, had heard Wild "say with respect to one of his rash prognostications that if it does not 'come off', the man who reminds him of it ought to be ashamed of himself."[3]

Orde-Lees admitted that there was "an estrangement between Wild & myself which . . . remains unreconciled."[4] The quarrel with Wild, however, had deeper roots, for as soon as the *James Caird* sailed, Orde-Lees told Wild, just as he had told Shackleton, when *Endurance* was first beset, that they ought immediately to start building up a food reserve.

Elephant Island originally got its name from the sea elephants supposed to throng its shores. Of these, however, there was no sign. Seals also seemed ominously few. Of penguins, on the other hand, there were plenty, both Adelie and Gentoo. Orde-Lees wanted a slaughter of all the game that could be found until there was a stock of meat large enough to last the winter. He argued that Shackleton might not return as soon as expected. He also maintained that both seals and penguins might easily migrate. In support, he could quote W. S. Bruce's experience in the South Orkneys on the *Scotia* expedition.

"To my surprise," said Orde-Lees, "Mr. Wild . . . ridiculed the idea that penguins might not come up in such large quantities during the winter . . . he asserted that what happened at the South Orkneys was no guide as to what was going to happen here.

> I think he considered I was exceeding my prerogative in discussing the matter at all and judging from what he then said I suppose that he considered that if people observed that he was laying in a stock of meat for the winter it might convey to them the impression that he expected to have to remain for the winter & so cause people to become despondent.

"There is no doubt something to be said for this optimistic policy," Orde-Lees continued, "but I certainly have no use for it."[5]

Orde-Lees was inevitably the odd man out. Nor did it help that he was usually right. From the start, for example, he maintained that the pack ice would delay relief, and the day after the *James Caird* sailed, the pack did indeed close round. Shackleton had got away just in time. Since then, with short intervals, floes and bergs had blocked the approaches far out to sea. "Installing ourselves for the winter," Hurley was already recording on 23 May, "little hope being entertained of immediate relief."

Then the seals in fact did disappear, and the numbers of penguins began rapidly to decline. Even so, Wild only took enough for the day, more or less. "He's a keen humanitarian,"[6] Orde-Lees ironically commented. The trouble was that, faced with what he called "fatuous optimism",[7] Orde-Lees had to be so insistent and extreme as to appear suspect. He was the man who disturbed a comforting complacency by mentioning the unmentionable. He was guilty of the one unforgivable sin: refusing to conceal awkward facts. For example, he referred to one Arctic exploration when, in 1879, an American, Lieutenant Adolphus Greely wintered "at Cape Sabine with only a small quantity of stores in much the same way as we are here and when eighteen of his men died of starvation".[8]

Sometimes, however, Orde-Lees did speak for others:

> Living . . . piled close upon one another as we are, we have been given to understand that we are all on an equal footing and of course, the sailors, like most people of their class . . . become objectionably familiar & have revolting habits.

"There is one brilliant exception," Orde-Lees admitted; "Bakewell, a Canadian of some refinement, who is always respectful as well as being self-respectful."[9] Hurley agreed:

> Our sailors are a very meagre set ignorant & illiterate & of [a] complaining disposition . . . incapable of discoursing on even the most

> commonplace subjects. Even as regards endurance, [he went on] the genteel born has proved himself far more capable of sustaining prolonged exertion under arduous circumstances & hardship.[10]

James took the same view. But even James enjoyed the spectacle on 3 June when "Pessimistic Lees", as he put it, "loses 3 bets"[11] about the numbers of penguins walking up the beach. Orde-Lees had attracted a blend of resentment and amusement over his inveterate betting. He used it to acquire other people's Nut Food. This was a much prized remnant of the sledging rations carefully doled out. It was a tiny variation of an exclusively meat diet from which Orde-Lees suffered much. "I commute bet with Blackborrow of 1 [Nut Food] due at end of month," he wrote on 11 June, "for 3/4 N.F. due today." That was not only greed. Blackborrow was about to have his operation.

The doctors were growing quietly restless at the delay in the relief. Whatever the reasons, they were concerned about the effect on their patient. It was necessary, with gangrene, to wait for what was called a "line of demarcation". That was to make sure where the healthy tissues began, and it appears about six weeks after the gangrene has set in. That time had now elapsed. There could no longer be a delay. If Shackleton did not return by 15 June, McIlroy decided he would operate then.

They were, according to Orde-Lees, "living in awful squalor".[12] Macklin was more precise. They were

> living in a smoky, dirty, ramshackle little hut with only just sufficient room to cram us all in: drinking out of a common pot with people suffering from dental caries etc., and lying in close proximity to a man [Hudson] with a large discharging abscess.[13]

To begin with, the energy of the party had been devoted to getting the *James Caird* away. It was only after her departure that they could take stock and concentrate on finding shelter for themselves.

The upper reaches of the island offer reasonable space on glacier and snowfield. From where they were, however, even accomplished mountaineers would be hard put to find a way out. Precipices and glaciers rising sheer out of the water effectively confined them to their bay, clinging to a habitable rim.

Their barren little spit of land was notably exposed. From the sea in front came gale after gale. From the land behind, sudden small whirlwinds swept down bewilderingly from the heights. "Williwaws", Bakewell called them, using a seaman's term from the Straits of Magellan; and the name has stuck.

In finding shelter, there were the same obstacles as in fitting out the *James Caird*. The only building material, more or less, was what they had managed to bring. Against the williwaws, and the rest of the inhospitable climate, the remaining tattered tents could not long survive. Natural shelter there was none. On the wind-scoured beach there was not enough snow to make igloos. Of wood, too, there was practically none. Sealskins would have been useful, but none had been collected.

At first, the castaways tried excavating a cave in a glacier snout facing the beach. That rapidly turned out to be cold, dripping, and probably dangerous. Everybody was cold, miserable, and continuously wet, with no hope of drying their clothes. On 27 April, three days after Shackleton sailed, Wild called a halt. "So all our labours," as Hurley put it, "have gone for nil."[14]

Marston and Greenstreet now suggested building a hut with the two upturned boats as roof. Wild agreed. He chose a site with the only scrap of protection. It was near the end of the spit, in the lee of the rock to the north.

Two walls, four feet high, were constructed nineteen feet apart. Rocks for building material had to be collected from all over the spit. Everybody by now was manifestly weakened perhaps, as Hurley believed, from a practically unrelieved meat diet. Orde-Lees thought they had "modified, incipient scurvy". Whatever the explanation, building took long, and was unexpectedly exhausting.

On top of the stone walls, the two boats were up-ended, resting at stem and stern. The long sides were then draped with an assortment of canvas remnants and tent walls. "All work," as Orde-Lees put it, "was very hard on our frost-bitten fingers . . . we were almost destitute of materials . . . The only nails available were the boot-making nails & this meant enroaching upon our small supply of boot-repairing gear."[15]

On 29 April, after two days' work, it was ready for occupation. The interior was dark. It reeked from guano, since the foundation was an old penguin rookery. It was impossible to stand upright inside. Into this, twenty-two men would be crammed with a floor space of only about 19 feet by 10 feet.

To Hurley and James the prospect was so uninviting that they preferred to stay in their tent. It was Shackleton's old tent, the only whole one surviving. "Miss Sir E. very much," Hurley recorded, "our admirable tent mate, with whom the time fair flew by, with cigarette & discourse. We expect relief in about a fortnight."[16]

Another stormy night, however, drove Hurley and James next

day into the hut. "We pray that Caird may reach Sth. Georgia safely and bring relief without delay," as Hurley wrote. "Life here without a hut & equipment is almost beyond endurance."[17]

What Hurley and James had so unwillingly moved into, was a mixture of a hell-ship's fo'c'sle and some unsavoury slum. The penetration of snow-drift through cracks and crevices, though uncomfortable, was at least a whiff of cleansing. When that was finally stopped, the dirt and overcrowding were unrelieved. Rapidly, the most refined sense of smell adjusted to the blend of foetid, unventilated room, rancid blubber, bodies unwashed and clothes unchanged for six months, and guano slowly thawing underfoot to make up the distinctive aroma of the place.

The sailors, plus Greenstreet, Clark and Hussey, slept in an "upper storey" contrived from the thwarts of the upturned boats. That at least made the congestion on the floor just bearable. At night, in the dim rays of the blubber night light it was, said Hurley,

> a catacomb like scene of objects resembling mummies. These objects are us in reindeer sleeping bags mingling our snores with the roar of the blizzard.[18]

Hairs from moulting reindeer sleeping bags filled the atmosphere and gravitated to the food. From the roof came a steady drip of water, part leak, part condensation. Even with a window improvised from a piece of celluloid sewn into a canvas wall, the interior was dark, but at least it masked the thickening cake of greasy soot deposited everywhere by the blubber stove. A chimney had been contrived out of a biscuit tin, but acrid smoke still seeped out into the hut. Only a chance gleam of light revealed that liquid from dirty drying socks, together with a stream from the nose of Green, the cook, was frequently discharging into the cooking pot.

This was the space at the disposal of the doctors as they prepared for the operation on Blackborrow which could not be long delayed. As yet there was little open talk of Shackleton's fate but, as Hurley had put it on 12 June, "all anxiously & longingly await relief. Today is the seventh week since the departure of the Caird."[19]

On the glacier snout at the back of the spit, a flagstaff had been rigged. From it, as a signal to any approaching ship, flew the burgee of the Royal Thames Yacht Club, with which *Endurance* had been registered. "Every morning," as Macklin put it, he went up to the flagpost, "and in spite of everything I cannot help hoping to see a ship coming to our relief."[20] On 14 June, he saw, as usual, an empty horizon. He and McIlroy decided to operate on Blackborrow next day.

McIlroy operated; Macklin was anaesthetist. "Never, perhaps," as Hurley phrased it, "was anaesthetic administered under more extraordinary circumstances.

> The operating table was built from a number of nutfood boxes covered with blankets, the temperature of the "Theatre" (our murky interior) being maintained at +79° [F] by ardently stoking the bogie [stove] with penguin skins.[21]

This was necessary to vaporise the chloroform; too cold, and it would not work. Only a few ounces had survived the various moves. Luckily it was enough to put Blackborrow under.

There were no disinfectants, let alone operating gowns. The doctors simply stripped to their vests. The instruments were sterilised by boiling them over a primus stove in a cooking pot.

The doctors turned almost everyone out of the hut. Hurley was allowed to stay as "stoker". Wild was asked to assist at the operation. Greenstreet and Hudson, being invalids, were also allowed to stay. Hudson, besides his discharging abscess, was still, in Orde-Lees' words,

> suffering from what is generally described as "nervous breakdown." [His] breakdown is remarkable for a man of such a fine physique; but it is often the case that powerfully built men do not endure hardship & exposure very well.[22]

Hudson was upset by the surgeon's work, and kept his face averted. Greenstreet, on the other hand, lay in his place on the thwarts and, as Macklin put it, "took a lively interest in the proceedings". Greenstreet was recovering from a frostbitten foot, and might have been on the operating table himself. In preparation for his Extra Master's Certificate, to be taken on his returning home, he was also being given lessons by Macklin on first aid to the injured. He described the operation:

> Blackborrow had . . . all the toes of his left foot taken off about 1/4″ stumps being left . . . The poor beggar behaved splendidly & it went thro' without a hitch . . . Time from start to finish 55 minutes. When Blackborrow came to he was as cheerful as anything & started joking directly.[23]

After the operation Macklin found that some hot water was left, and so, with a carefully hoarded towel and cake of soap, he had his first wash for eight months.

The operation at least was a break in what Macklin called "the deadly monotony".[24] Each day was very much like the rest. "The cook & his firekeeper for the day turn out between 6 & 7 & light the bogie with penguin skins," James wrote in his diary. Breakfast, of penguin steaks, "was not usually ready till 9 or 10 according to the temper of the fire, or the ability of the fireman":

> Those whose beds are against the stove, roused out by heat & blubber utilise the time for drying gear. When things are cooked, Wild rouses all hands with a lusty "Lash up & stow!" The sleepers on the floor roll up their bags & blankets & stow them in the boat overhead. The two seat placers for the day bring the boxes of stores which during the night have formed a bedstead for the cook & place them in a wide ring round the stove for seats. We then take our places, moving on one place at each meal so that all may get a fair share of the heat in due course.[25]

"With the welcome cry of 'Hoosh oh,'" wrote Hurley, taking up the tale,

> the "peggy" from each mess (there are four) takes his pot to the galley, where Wild officiates in the "Whacking out." The . . . "grub" is divided into individual portions as accurately as possible & "Whosed." This method of [sharing was] instituted by Sir E.

"After the grub has been measured out by the mess 'peggy'," Hurley went on,

> one of the members turns his back & in reply to "Whose," announces the name of the person for whom he intends the ration. His announcement is final. After breakfast . . . Wild allots various occupations.[26]

There was "not much to do as a rule", James wrote. Lunch was at 12.30. Unless there were penguins to be caught, the afternoons were usually free and "spent round the fire talking . . . & doing personal jobs. It gets dark too early to do much." At 4.30, came the evening meal and, afterwards, the blubber lamp was lit. It was, in Hurley's words,

> a weird sight. The light thrown up by the lamp illuminates the smoke colored faces like stage footlights. The sparkling eyes & glint on the aluminium mugs, the stream of flickering light thrown out from the open [stove] door, making weird dancing shadows on the inside of the boats makes me think of a council of brigands . . . after an escape in a chimney or a coalmine.

"Conversation," said Hurley, "generally wanders back to the civilised world . . . To what we intend doing . . . on returning – Things not likely to be done & orgies physically impossible."

> After Smoke o the decks are again cleared by stowing the "box seats" to form the Cooks bunk, the tenants of the attic bunks swing into [them] with monkey-like agility & the "ground plan" is spread with sleeping bags into which the owners retreat.

There, he went on, "[We] spend a broken night & so each day passes wearily & monotonously . . . Each day, we scout the horizon for a mast & daily discuss relief – may it come soon." He wrote also of a "mental & physical coma" caused by "this indolent life & enervating climate".

> One feels a disinclination to perform even the small necessaries of life requiring exertion & only feels in a fit state to lie in ones bag & idly ponder.[27]

Worst of all, in Macklin's words, was "this waiting in uncertainty," which he found "almost unendurable."[28]

Wild countered this by an unfailing cheerfulness. He was, Macklin recorded in his diary, "a magnificent leader here, scrupulously fair in everything, and popular and respected by everyone".[29]

Morale was Wild's concern. His outstanding achievement, perhaps, was the control of sanitation. The dismal overcrowding under the boats was a temptation for laziness and dirt. Wild set an example, and enforced a very high standard of hygiene among a group of men with differing standards of decency.

Wild had a lack of imagination, a calm demeanour, and a total faith in Shackleton. He had a doggedness, an inborn defensiveness, a capacity to wait and suffer and hold the fort. These were essentially British qualities, and exactly what was needed here to check the clash of character and keep mental collapse at bay. Even Orde-Lees, who admitted to "fits of depression & hopelessness" and continued thoroughly to disapprove of Wild's house-keeping, wrote that

> Wild is a fine fellow to keep one's spirits up. He is as great an optimist as Sir Ernest himself & that is saying a good deal.

Wild, for his part, found Orde-Lees "a horrible pessimist," and a danger to morale. In Wild's own words, "I had to threaten to shoot him to make him keep his tongue between his teeth".[30]

"But of course," Orde-Lees, undeterred, wrote in his diary,

"some of [Wild's] remarks dont bear much analysis and he ought not to try & dupe me over the meat supplies for . . . it is truly a case of 'telling it to the marines'."[31] That was on 30 June. The *James Caird* had been gone more than two months, but in Orde-Lees' words, "the subject is practically taboo".

> Everyone keeps their own counsel . . . and it is quite obvious that no one really dare say what they really think.[32]

"No penguins," Orde-Lees now frequently had to record. The seals had not returned. "I know that our food reserve is critical," he wrote on 7 July. "I cannot reconcile myself to the happy go lucky hand to mouth style of saying 'Oh it will be all right.'"

Orde-Lees had now found a like-minded ally in Wordie. At the midwinter celebration on 22 June, Wordie had charitably shared with the sailors some of his carefully saved tobacco. Within a day or so they had smoked it all up which, as Orde-Lees recorded on 9 July, "makes them very irritable & impertinent. They sit about moping & cursing." Wild gave them each a small piece of tobacco

> which [in Orde-Lees' words] they immediately consume. Wild tells me that they have been very improvident but . . . it is hardly to be wondered at . . . as they are always being told [by him] that "the ship" will be here tomorrow . . . It's the right spirit but it is so easily liable to abuse that it wants handling with care. The roughest mental calculation reveals the absurdity of some of his hopeful predictions and even the sailors who used to swallow it & hang hopes on much of what he said have lately become incredulous.[33]

Inside the hut, Orde-Lees had erected over himself a private canopy made out of a piece of tent cloth. This was to protect himself against the objects drizzling down from those living in the thwarts on to the men lying below. It was eminently practical, but served only to enhance his reputation for oddness. Orde-Lees, in fact, personified the eccentric; that version of the outsider which once was prominent in building up the British Empire.

Orde-Lees had always been the outsider. To his own family he was an embarrassment; climbing a drainpipe, for example, to go upstairs. When he was newly commissioned into the Royal Marines, there was a regulation prohibiting officers in uniform from carrying parcels. He responded by having the buttons of his tunic reinforced so that he could hang his shopping down his front. Also, he allowed himself to be pictured in a magazine demonstrating trick cycling. This was deemed conduct unbecoming to an officer and gentleman. His brother officers, so the story goes, were so incensed that they tied

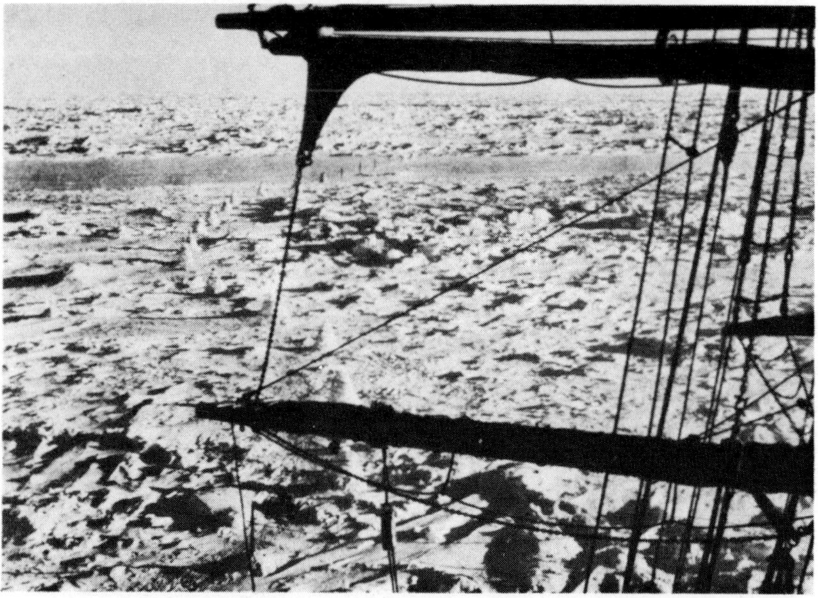

Two famous photographs by Frank Hurley. *Top, Endurance* caught in the ice; *below,* a view from the truck of the main mast, showing (to the left) the cairns on the ice that were used as a guide for those going to and from the ship for exercise or hunting. Most of Hurley's photographs were left behind in the ice, but Shackleton insisted the best be preserved.

Frank Wild.

Reginald William James, physicist.

Leonard Hussey, meteorologist.

Dr Alec Macklin, chief surgeon.

"The Ritz", the messroom on board *Endurance,* during the winter of 1915.

Endurance, a week before she was crushed. Shackleton on board.

Endurance, crushed and sinking.

Dragging *James Caird* across the ice on the march to the mainland.

Ocean Camp, 1915.

Top, the party marooned on Elephant Island. *Below*, the upturned boats on Elephant Island which formed the hut.

Preparing *James Caird* for the 700-mile journey from Elephant Island to South Georgia. *Below left,* Frank Worsley, "the skipper" and navigator and, *right,* Tom Crean who also took part in the open-boat journey and the crossing of South Georgia.

Top, Shackleton photographed at Port Stanley in the Falkland Islands after the failure of his first attempt to rescue his men from Elephant Island. Captain Ingvar Thom is on the far right.

Most of the Elephant Island party reunited with Shackleton on their arrival at Punta Arenas in the Straits of Magellan in September 1916. From left to right: Hussey, Hurley, Kerr, James, Wordie, Crean, Worsley, Wild, Shackleton, Captain Pardo of *Yelcho,* Orde-Lees, Marston, How, Holness, Stephenson, Bakewell, Green, McLeod, Greenstreet and Cheetham.

Shackleton photographed in the United States, 1917.

a rope round his waist and threw him overboard from a moving destroyer, and he spent six weeks in hospital as a result.

Here, among the castaways, Orde-Lees was still playing the familiar and necessary role of scapegoat. He diverted resentment that otherwise would have been vented on the leader. But behind the eccentricity Orde-Lees was undergoing a religious crisis. He had been brought up a Protestant. Before sailing on *Endurance*, he had started turning to Catholicism. At Buenos Aires, he had actually bought Catholic medallions, as he hoped, to carry on the Transantarctic journey. Now, on Elephant Island, his conversion was taking place. Because it was a secret process, and there was none with whom he could discuss it, Orde-Lees was probably the most isolated of anyone on Elephant Island.

In this community of unkempt, soot-begrimed tramps, Orde-Lees' tall, rangy figure, with an emaciated face wearing always the suspicion of a private smile, must have seemed like a living reproach to his companions, and in particular to Wild.

On Douglas Mawson's expedition, four years before, Wild had already commanded men marooned in uncertainty. He was then in charge of the Western party on Queen Mary Land. When *Aurora* vanished over the horizon, driven by an offshore gale, their fate was unclear for, in the not unlikely event of her foundering, no one would know where they were.

By his own account, the first time Mawson met Wild, in New Zealand, during the *Nimrod* expedition, Wild was being carried drunk out of a hotel. Since the Antarctic was virtually dry, Mawson reasoned that there, Wild would be absolutely reliable. In the event his judgement was vindicated. After a year, when *Aurora* eventually did return, it was observed that his companions regarded Wild with something between affection and worship. Quiet and unremarkable, his leadership had been inspired. That no doubt was why Shackleton had chosen to leave him in command on Elephant Island.

On Queen Mary Land, Wild had under him seven Australian university graduates, all Antarctic tyros. They were tough, reasonably homogeneous and compatible. Now, he was faced with an ill-assorted crowd of doubtful resilience.

A seaman whose roots lay in sailing ships, Wild was used to motley crews cooped up together for months in isolation. The hut on Elephant Island, after all, bore many similarities to the fo'c'sle of a square rigger caught in the doldrums. For men growing heartily sick of the same faces around them, bizarre, lurking conflict was a part of daily life.

Macklin, for example, was challenged to a duel by Orde-Lees;

weapons, broken oars on the beach at dawn. Green wished to fight Marston because, as he put it, "He started to come a bit rough."[34] Everybody at some time wrangled with neighbours in the hut about encroachment on their floor space. Wild would allow them all to let off steam and then, just when they appeared on the verge of blows, would defuse the situation with sweet arbitration.

> Frank Wild [said Macklin] was a placid little man whom nothing ever upset . . . we always called him Frankie, or Frank, nobody ever called him anything else, the lower deck always called him Mr. Wild. They were never required to but they did automatically. He was a man who exercised a wonderful control without any outward sign of authority.[35]

Wild, indeed, was almost the perfect lieutenant. In another age, under different circumstances, he might have been the hero of a sea story. But there was one flaw. In contriving to maintain a rhythm to the weeks, every Saturday he served tots all round for the traditional sailors' "sweethearts and wives". This was a drink he improvised out of the methylated spirits used for starting the primus stoves.

It was variously mixed with sugar and water or dried milk. It was a horrible concoction, which some people, notably Greenstreet, McIlroy, Green, Hurley and Orde-Lees, did not hesitate to drink. Wild, however, was noticeably an addict. The sailors, too, unconcernedly swigged the methylated spirits. Under its influence, they were observed to become almost congenial.

One Saturday, in Green's words, "Wild said, 'If the Boss turned up now, tonight, he wouldn't take us off.' He said we were too happy. [The] wood alcohol . . . was making us drunk as fiddles, we were singing and Hussey was playing the banjo."[36]

Somehow, Hussey had brought his instrument unscathed all the way from *Endurance*. No longer was his limited repertoire the subject of groaning derision. "Hussey's banjo," as Hurley now admitted, "is indispensable."[37] "It really does, as Sir Ernest said, supply brain food,"[38] Orde-Lees added.

Hussey was asked, not so much for solos, as accompaniments to topical songs. For Midwinter Day James, still to his companions the dry academic, surprised them all with a ballad to the tune of "Solomon Levi". The chorus ran:

> My name is Franky Wild-o and my hut's on Elephant Isle.
> The wall's without a single brick and the roof's without a tile.
> Yet, nevertheless, you must confess by many and many a mile,
> It's the most palatial dwelling place you'll find on Elephant Isle.[39]

Orde-Lees was the subject of many "topicals", as they were called; too many, in his view, which, as he put it, "I hope to . . . forget . . . as soon [as] possible." Orde-Lees used to prowl about the beach savouring the weather. Elephant Island lies just north of the cold current of the Weddell Sea. It is also just out of the main tracks of the depressions circling Antarctica. Its winter climate therefore is relatively mild. Temperatures hover around five degrees of frost. Winds are stormy but intermittent.

Occasionally there was the kind of day which sent Orde-Lees to his diary (kept, eccentrically, in bank pass books) to describe

> Magnificent golden sunset, sun as a great pale greenish yellow disc settling in a mass of golden fire later the crescent moon shows up & sets in the midst of a crescent sunset. Venus close to the moon. Many huge bergs appear pale violet & pink, sea a deep indigo & snow peaks behind first golden then aglow with alpengluh.

Mostly, he was not so content. Nine days out of ten, the pack was jammed close in, excluding all possibility of rescue. Storms raked the camp, lifting packing cases like matchboxes, driving shingle like hailstones. Sometimes williwaws brought a bombardment of mysterious ice plates as big as saucers. Occasionally a bitter blizzard coated the whole spit with an armourplate of frozen sea spray. The offshore rocks were covered with mushroom hats of ice. Then it would soon dissolve in fog and damp and green ice floes pressing on the shore.

Periodically, they were reminded that their lives hung upon a thread. On 15 July, a huge fall from a hanging glacier to the west caused a monster of a wave. But for loose brash floating in the bay, it would have overwhelmed the spit.

Next day, Hurley went for his "Sunday promenade", as he put it, "the well beaten 100 yards track on the Spit".

> This one would not tire of provided we knew Sir E. & the crew of the "Caird" were safe & when relief could be definitely expected.

On 27 July, "9 months since the ships crushing", as Hurley recorded, there was another warm respite, with almost open sea, and hope therefore of relief.

> Engage in slight diversion of cricket . . . the bat being a small piece of sledge runner, the balls pebbles from the strand – We are sadly out of practice.

Food, meanwhile, was clearly running out. Orde-Lees, appalled by Wild's persistent refusal to build up stocks, grew more gloomy. He was yet more resentful when, early in June, he was stopped from reading Nordenskjöld's *Antarctic*. This was the most topical book in their small library but one "which for some reason Wild does not seem to care to have circulated".[40]

No doubt the work made subversive reading on Elephant Island. In chapter 28 Larsen described the start of his sojourn on Paulet Island with his shipwrecked companions:

> We were forced to feed ourselves mainly by seals and penguins. Already during the first few days of our stay on the island, we were lucky enough to kill [enough] not only for our immediate needs but also for a winter supply. Thus, on the 11 March [1903] 184 penguins were killed, 326 on the 12th, 508 on the 13th and so on.[41]

Wild's reluctance did not, however, stop Hurley eventually reading Nordenskjöld. "So similar to our position is his narrative," as Hurley put it,

> that I became so interested & absorbed that I actually felt it was our party that was being rescued by the "Uruguay."[42]

"A wonderful day," Nordenskjöld wrote of the event. After two years marooned at Snow Hill, he saw men from the *Uruguay* walking across the ice:

> We were faced with one of those moments when one's whole mind seems to dissolve into a mist before the intense emotion of something completely unexpected that drags us into its vortex.[43]

That was 8 November 1903. Hurley read this on 1 August 1916. A terrible ennui was now settling down that even Wild, for all his cheerful optimism, could not dispel. Until now, the war had not been much discussed, but Orde-Lees began to feel "a little ashamed", as he put it, "of having run away".

> Most, though by no means all of us think it must be over by now. I . . . think the contrary. If it is over it must have ended in a draw, and Britain would never tolerate that.[44]

Meanwhile, as he wrote on 3 August, "Indifference as to what is going to happen has been very marked lately; probably this is merely due to want of sunshine and Sir Ernest's long absence."

> Sir Ernest's non-return is now openly discussed. No one likes to think that he could possibly have failed to reach South Georgia, and yet Wild has given orders that every scrap of cord & wood and all nails are to be carefully kept in view of the possibility of his having to make a boat journey to Deception Island in the spring.[45]

The pack ice was so dense that not only did relief seem impossible, but no penguins were coming ashore. Food was now running out. There were no reserves. "Everyone is concerned about it," wrote Orde-Lees on 23 August, with the melancholy satisfaction of the prophet vindicated.

To stave off starvation, limpets had hurriedly to be collected. That was something of a forlorn hope. "Food is life and life is too serious a matter to risk needlessly," Orde-Lees wrote. "Strange to say, now that there really is a shortage the imperturbable pessimists are apparently quite unconcerned . . . It is not unusual that pessimism and equanimity are counterparts."

> The fatuous optimists [he went on] exhibit their fears [by] assuming that the pessimists are now thoroughly scared and therefore making mocking remarks such as . . . "We shall have to eat the one who dies first" and so on, which has actually occurred before now when people have been in only very slightly worse straits than we are now. There's many a true word said in jest.[46]

If Hussey is to be believed, Wild and he quite seriously discussed who was to be sacrificed if all the food gave out, and Orde-Lees was first choice. It was a revealing indication of their state of mind.

XLIV

Relief preparations

"The *Endurance*," said John King Davis, "was full of . . . people without any qualification . . . just pushed in there because they thought it was an adventure".[1]

Davis was in London, at the headquarters of the Royal Geographical Society overlooking Kensington Gardens, being interviewed about an expedition to rescue Shackleton. It was 10 April 1916. In the Weddell Sea that day, Shackleton was dealing with the floe that cracked under his camp on the way to Elephant Island from Patience Camp.

No longer was there Sir Clements Markham to rail against Shackleton. Sir Clements had been burned to death at the end of January that year, when the candle he habitually used as a bedside reading lamp fell over when he dozed and set the bedclothes alight.

Official ill-will towards Shackleton anyway hardly needed fanning. Late in March, when the news of *Aurora*'s arrival in New Zealand came through, bringing intimations of disaster, the RGS virtuously announced that it was "not responsible for the equipment of any Relief Expedition".[2] The RGS had not been

> consulted in any way as to [the] practical organisation [of the *Endurance* expedition]. Its connection was limited to that of a subscriber. Nor was [the RGS] consulted as to its proposed abandonment on the outbreak of war.[3]

"We should firmly decline further contributions to the Antarctic," declared Douglas Freshfield, the RGS President and a celebrated mountaineer. "The speculative syndicate who are running S's project must find the funds [for his relief] – and will."[4]

The "speculative syndicate", however, hardly existed. Sir James Caird and Sir Robert Lucas-Tooth had died. F. W. White, the expedition's erstwhile secretary, had quietly withdrawn. His one tenuous connection with Shackleton remained as a director of the Tabard Cigarette Company, now reconstituted after going into liquidation.

The expedition, in fact, had no organisation at all. Shackleton had blithely sailed away, leaving everything behind him to the charity of individuals; first, perhaps, his womenfolk.

Down at Eastbourne was the ever-patient Emily, constantly wearing her "Southern Cross" brooch, a memento now of the lost world before the war, the happy aftermath of the *Nimrod*, and the last time before she lost her hold on her husband.

Janet Stancomb-Wills was also waiting; and so was Elizabeth Dawson-Lambton. In London, Rosalind Chetwynd was waiting for Ernest Shackleton too. William Dederich, meanwhile, had kept his promise to Ernest Shackleton, and given Frank a job when he came out of the shades.

The expedition's interests were being cared for by Hutchison & Cuff, Shackleton's solicitors. Ernest Perris, on the *Daily Chronicle*, was also involved. Who had the main responsibility was not exactly clear. In any case, it was little Alfred Hutchison, precise, dark-suited, wing-collared, nursing behind his pince-nez a concern for Shackleton beyond that of solicitor for his client, who alerted the authorities. (Shackleton had gone to Hutchison, when domestic tensions made it awkward to continue using Emily's brother as his solicitor.)

Early in 1914, when the RGS had granted Shackleton £1,000 he, in a grand gesture, called only on £500.[5] On 24 January 1916, Hutchison, after all, had to ask for the second instalment. "Money which was promised to the Expedition," he told the RGS, "was not paid owing to the War, and we have had considerable difficulty on this account."[6] Amongst other things, after the end of March, the seamen's allotments to their families could no longer be paid.

Someone would clearly have to organise a rescue. Davis, when April came with no news of *Endurance*, was certain she had foundered, and approached the RGS. He was undoubtedly relieved to have refused command of *Endurance*; but now he felt he had to try and rescue Shackleton.

Hutchison and Perris had also appealed to Herbert Asquith, the Prime Minister. The upshot was that the Admiralty agreed to rescue Shackleton. The RGS could wash its hands of the whole affair, although, said Freshfield, "We shall be very likely to have another catastrophe – one has no confidence left in any official plans and management."[7]

That was understandable. The war was now in its second year. A series of British follies from the refusal to give the soldiers steel helmets (the fault of the generals), to a present suicidal shell shortage (the result of trade union obstruction in the munition factories), had sapped faith in the official mind, wherever it might be. The war had long since drifted into deadlock. Along the Western Front, the armies were trapped among the trenches in a state of semi-siege warfare.

From all this, England was curiously insulated. "London," said Robert Graves, when he came home on leave from the trenches, "seemed unreally itself. Despite the number of uniforms in the streets, the general indifference to, and ignorance about, the war surprised me . . . The universal catchword was 'Business as usual'."[8] People appeared sunk in their own little world, waiting for rescue. The mood, in fact, was not so very different from that forced upon the castaways on Elephant Island.

These were the circumstances in which the news from the *Aurora* burst upon the world, and the Admiralty took up the work of Shackleton's relief.

The Royal Navy so far had had a strangely unsatisfactory war. The great, decisive battle, Trafalgar repeated, as it were, had somehow failed to materialise. In the grand and sober building in the shadow of Admiralty Arch, Admiral Parry, the Hydrographer, was Shackleton's one friend. It was Parry who had pushed forward the necessity of relief.

A committee was formed. From unexpected places sprang a desire to help. In Norway, Nansen offered the use of the *Fram*, although she was now worm-eaten and needed an extensive refit. From the Western Front, Eric Marshall, a RAMC Captain with the Rifle Brigade, volunteered to sail, although his admiration for Shackleton had decidedly cooled. Tryggve Gran, the Norwegian who had been with Scott, also volunteered. He was now a pilot with the RFC, and *his* admiration for Shackleton was undimmed. Even Lady Scott, who once said she would "gladly assist at that man's annihilation,"[9] now discussed over lunch "the necessity of a relief expedition for Shackleton in the Weddell Sea and," she noted, "its possible commanders".[10]

At the Admiralty, there was understandably much hindsight and irritation. "I sincerely hope," one hand minuted, "that we shall never again assist or encourage such enterprises."[11] That was on 26 April. "My opinion is and always has been," another minute ran next day, "that this expedition should never have been permitted to start."[12]

In Dublin, on 24 April, following the old nationalist creed that

England's misfortune was Ireland's chance, the sombre outlook was clouded by the Easter Rising. It was Easter Monday. The centre of the city was soon in flames. The insurgents were said to have marched, singing "The wearin' O' the Green." Away in the Antarctic, by some twist of fate, this was the day that Shackleton left Elephant Island in the *James Caird* to sail in search of help.

XLV

The open-boat journey

On the *James Caird*, Crean, as Worsley put it, was making "noises at the helm that we found by a Sherlock Holmes system of deduction, represented The Wearin' O' the Green."[1]

Half the crew was Irish, in fact. Besides Crean and Shackleton there was Tim McCarthy, "the most irrepressible optimist," said Worsley, "I've ever met":

> [Once when] I relieved him at the helm, seas pouring down our necks, one came right over us & I felt like swearing but just kept it back & he informed me with a cheerful grin "It's a foine day, sorr".
>
> As a rule when a sea wets a sailor through he swears at it comprehensively, and impartially curses everything in sight beginning with the ship & "the old man" – if he's not within hearing, but on this trip we said nothing when a sea hit us in the face. It was grin & bear it, for it was Sir Ernest's theory that by keeping our tempers . . . we each helped to keep one another up. We all lived up to this to the best of our ability, but McCarthy was a marvel.[2]

Between Shackleton and Crean, in Worsley's words, "a quaint sort of mimic bickering arose".

> It was partly chaff & partly a comic revolt against the conditions . . . As they turned in, a kind of wordless rumbling, muttering, growling noise could be heard issuing from the dark & gloomy lair in the bows, sometimes directed at one another, sometimes at things in general, & sometimes at nothing at all. At times they were so full of quaint conceits & Crean's remarks were so Irish that I ran risk of explosion by suppressed laughter. "Go to sleep Crean & don't be clucking like an old

hen". "Boss I can't eat those reindeer hairs. I'll have an inside on me like a billygoats neck. Let's give 'em to the Skipper & McCarthy. They never know what they're eatin'." & so on.[3]

The departure from Cape Wild had promised well. With a fair offshore wind, "We cut the painter," as Shackleton phrased it, "and moved away to the north-east. The men who were staying behind made a pathetic little group on the beach."[4]

From the look-out on land, a belt of ice had been observed a few miles offshore, but also a promising gap over what was clearly a shoal. In two hours Worsley brought the *James Caird* to the gap. "We managed to get through in about an hour," as McNeish put it. "Then we were in the open sea wet through but happy through it all."[5] The passage of the pack was not quite as easy as McNeish had suggested. At one point, to avoid damaging the boat, they had had to lower sails and row.

The last few hours before departure, Worsley talked about the "black forbidding cliffs & blue menacing glacier fronts . . . of Elephant Island".[6] With sails filling to the wind, however, with sparkling sea, sun shining in a lightly clouded sky "our spirits were high" and Elephant Island, "opening out astern", now seemed

> in majesty of glittering snowy peaks & uplands fronted by glacier walls & towering cliffs the haunt . . . of the . . . cheery little Cape Pigeon.[7]

Not for a moment did the absurdity of the enterprise occur to him. A seaman's place, after all, is on the sea, and his view of land from a vessel under way.

They were setting out to cross the stormiest seas on earth in a cockleshell that was like an insect swimming in a tidal wave. They had all seen lifeboats like their own smashed on the decks of ships by storms in the ocean they were now proceeding to challenge. Nonetheless, as Elephant Island dipped below the horizon, leaving them alone, encircled by the sea, it hardly seemed a forlorn hope.

In civilisation, it was said of Shackleton that he was puerile, childish, had never grown up. Now, sitting in the cockpit of the *James Caird*, hunched up more than usual, he seemed prematurely to have aged. That was merely the superficial imprint of events. Shackleton, at the age of forty-two, had preserved all the hopes and illusions of youth.

It was not only sleight of hand that made him give the impression that they were starting on an adventure. He quite genuinely believed it. Neither despair nor cynicism were part of his birthright; as they were not of the world he had left behind in 1914.

He was, after all, setting out on the great open-boat journey that had lain at the core of his ambition.

Nosing out of the ice, the *James Caird* dipped into the swell, and ran northwards before a fair fresh breeze. Shackleton ordered the four sailors below to get some warmth and sleep while the going was good. Meanwhile, with Worsley, he stayed up without relief through the night. "We snuggled close together for warmth," Worsley recorded, "for by midnight the sea was rising & every other wave that hit came over & wet us through and through."[8]

The cockpit was merely a square hatch about four feet by two feet in the canvas deck framed with bits of wood. Oilskins had disappeared long ago when *Endurance* was abandoned. All they had were threadbare sledging garments and reindeer finnesko on their feet. These were intended for dry cold, not the sea. They soaked up water and held it like clinging, clammy, greasy washcloths.

> Cold and clear with the Southern Cross high overhead [wrote Worsley] we held her North by the stars that swept in glittering procession over the Atlantic towards the Pacific, looking straight down on lucky souls swizzling cool drinks in the tropics.[9]

They were heading north, first because Shackleton wanted to get well clear of the ice as quickly as he could. Also, he wanted to reach the westerlies so that he could put South Georgia to leeward and run down along the line.

As usual Shackleton was the leader on board, but he left someone else to be the captain of the ship. It was the kind of divided command which had caused such trouble on *Nimrod*, and which might have affected the fate of *Endurance*. Here the circumstances were different – or were they? In any case Worsley was considered skipper by the seamen and by Shackleton called Skipper and nothing else.

In that first spell at the helm Shackleton, in Worsley's words, suddenly said

> "Do you know I know nothing about boat sailing?" I laughed. My reply "Allright Boss I do. This is my *3rd* boat journey" slightly ruffled him & he said "I'm telling you that I don't."

To Worsley, this was where Shackleton's "courage shone most". Worsley himself was "used to boat work, surf landings & every kind of craft that sailed the sea". To Shackleton, however, "who had gradually drifted from the sea & become . . . a land explorer", what he now faced must have been "menacing, perhaps even appalling".[10]

> While I steered we discussed plans & yarned in low tones, his arm thrown over my shoulder. We smoked all night & he rolled cigarettes for us both at which I was unhandy.[11]

Worsley was not quite as content as he made out. In the first place, he disliked the boat's rig. On Elephant Island, a short mizzen mast had been added. The boat was now carrying a jib and standing lugsail on the mainmast, and a small gaff sail on the mizzen. With enough canvas, Worsley would have preferred one mast with jib and standing lug only. "A 3*d.* sail," as he put it, would be "a 3*d.* source of misery." Besides, ship's boats, as he well knew, especially having designed this one, were built to float, not sail. They would always gripe to windwards. The mizzen kept the *James Caird* so much into the wind that the rudder was always dragging across her. Besides, the boom was in the way, preventing the use of a tiller. The rudder had to be worked with a yoke and yoke lines. The helmsman was forced to crouch uncomfortably.

Of more concern, the *James Caird* had over a ton of ballast. Worsley believed it was quarter of a ton too much. He had pleaded in vain with Shackleton to reduce weight. Knowing the danger of under-ballasting Shackleton, as Worsley phrased it, "went to the other extreme":

> If a . . . boat is overweighted, she jerks, will not sail fast & does not heel away from the wind & so constantly takes seas over her & is at all times wet . . . If ballast . . . is too low . . . it makes . . . vessels . . . stiff & they roll . . . heavily & jerkily . . . Again if it is spread all along the bottom as in the "Caird" instead of being piled up in the centre, it makes her pitch very heavily.[12]

Most of this, as soon as the boat dipped into the seaway, Worsley could sadly confirm. From the first moderate swell, spume continually spurted up like a geyser to drench the deck.

The ice at least had been left behind. All through the night, Shackleton talked. They had been hard at it since 6 a.m., but Shackleton appeared not to notice.

> As the sky paled in the East [said Worsley], I nodded, yawned, nodded again & [Shackleton] slightly annoyed, said "You're sleepy – turn in" & steered while I slept 2 hours.[13]

By the morning of Tuesday, 25 April, one day out, they had made about 45 miles from Elephant Island. Worsley refrained from telling Shackleton that if they had ballasted as he wanted, it might have been somewhat more.

By dawn, the ocean's truce was over. The wind swung dead ahead to north, forcing the boat back for a few hours, before coming round to WSW. A cross sea was running. The waves were at least twenty feet from crest to trough. A nice strong gale was blowing, force 9, that is to say about forty-five knots, with "dense streaks of foam along the direction of the wind", to quote the sober language of the Beaufort Wind Scale, "crests of waves begin to topple, tumble and roll over".[14] The *James Caird* was tossed about with a hard jerky motion. Everybody except McCarthy and Worsley was seasick.

A ship is all routine. Sea watches were now set. Worsley took one with McCarthy and Vincent; Shackleton, the other, with Crean and McNeish. They went watch and watch, four hours on and four hours off; one man at the helm, one at the sails and one baling as hard as he could. They were suspended between the sky and the bottom of the sea.

Worsley talked about the "men marooned on Elephant Island":

> We knew that a disaster to us would in all likelihood be fatal to them. One night, between the drunken lurches of the boat, Shackleton said to me: "Skipper, if anything happens to me while those fellows are waiting for me, I shall feel like a murderer!"[15]

Yet seaworthiness, as each of them knew, was not the same as size. In some ways the *James Caird*, tossing about like a toy, was preferable to a square rigger. She was stable, her ballast would not shift, she righted herself quickly (an uncomfortable boat is a safe boat), and, above all, there was no going aloft.

Navigation is an art, of which Worsley had shown himself a master on the voyage from Patience Camp to Elephant Island. That in a sense had been a worse ordeal. The boats were open, ill-stowed, and unstable. The *James Caird* was properly trimmed and, although water was running down into her bilges with every sea, she did have decking of a kind. His shipmates were sure that Worsley would get them through.

Worsley himself was not so sure. Almost everything turned on the accuracy of his chronometer. It was on the very day of departure from Elephant Island that the sun finally appeared with a horizon clear enough for him to get a check. Even that was uncertain, since the longitude of Cape Wild was not exactly known. In compensation, Worsley assumed the chronometer to be about one minute slower than it seemed. He could only hope that he was right.

Three days out, there appeared two small pieces of wreckage

heaving on a wave, "the remains probably", as Shackleton put it, "of some unfortunate vessel that had failed to weather the strong gales south of Cape Horn".[16] Since *Endurance* entered the ice, it was the first message from the outside world. It was a kind of comfort, like footprints in the snow.

It was on this day, 26 April, that Worsley got his first observation. "Boat pitching rolling & jerking heavily all the time," he said, "making it an almost impossible matter." He had to kneel on the forepart of the cockpit, while McCarthy and Vincent clung to him, to steady him and also to prevent him pitching overboard, sextant and all. Worsley, in his own words, then caught the sun "as the boat rose her highest on the crest of a sea & allowing the 'height of eye' accordingly".[17] In the troughs, the horizon was cut off. Shackleton, meanwhile, crouched below decks, "booked" the sight and read off the chronometer.

Did Shackleton remember telling Emily, in the distant days of 1914 that he did not quite trust Worsley as captain of *Endurace*? In the meantime, Worsley had revealed an almost uncanny gift for getting sights under all conditions, so that now Shackleton had a blind faith in him as navigator of the *James Caird*.

Worsley's calculations put them at 59°46′S, 52°18′W. His dead reckoning, as he expected "was wide of the mark".[18] They were now 128 miles from Elephant Island, and had covered two degrees of latitude. That included a day hove to in a northerly gale. They had made enough northing to be out of the danger zone of ice. The boat was now turned towards the north-east, and headed straight for South Georgia. They had passed their first milestone along the way.

Worsley, however, could not be certain of the course. For one thing, he did not know exactly how much leeway the *James Caird* made; for another, he could only guess the set of sea and current. He was haunted by the knowledge that South Georgia was a rather small patch in a very big ocean six hundred miles to leeward. A little inaccuracy would make him miss his goal, and then they would be irrevocably lost, with no chance of beating back into the wind.

The possibilities of error were frighteningly compounded. It was not only the hazard of lining up the sun and horizon in the sextant on a tumbling boat, Worsley had to guess the right allowance for "height of eye" from the crest of a wave. He did have a sextant in reserve, but only one chronometer. He could only hope that it would not change its rate or break down.

Even the one compass was an uncertain aid. It was a small, crude, prismatic model, erratically influenced by the iron in the pump. Also, it had to be shielded below deck, so that the helmsman could not see it all the time. At night, it could not be used, because there was no binnacle lamp, and the one stump of candle on board was being saved by Worsley for the landfall. So the helmsman reverted to the age-old method of steering by the wind and the sea. Once a night, a flaming lifeboat match would be lit to check the course against the compass. Occasionally, the interminable storm clouds would be torn aside and the helmsman could steer by the stars, especially, as Worsley put it, by "an old friend called Antares – the Scorpion's red eye".[19]

The sea at least is no desert. There is life in the waters. Penguins at intervals swam around the boat, and since leaving Elephant Island she had been followed by an albatross.

The ancestors of that albatross "followed the Maoris", Worsley wrote, "discovering New Zealand two hundred years before Columbus discovered America".[20] Perhaps Worsley felt that he had in some mysterious way inherited the gifts of his Polynesian ancestors roaming the Pacific in their war canoes.

Shackleton, on the other hand, was driven by all the old sea tales of lifeboats found floating empty or with their occupants dead. Neither missing his landfall nor the foundering of the boat was his main concern; it was the survival of his men.

Turning in after each watch meant creeping into the bows. The sleeping compartment was there because it was decked in with wood, and therefore the least soaked part of the boat. It was seven feet long and five feet wide, tapering to nothing at the bows. Here, three men had to pack themselves, in bulky reindeer sleeping bags, on top of food cases, besides bags of shingle and sharp rocks making up the ballast. To reach this place meant crawling through a narrow space between ballast and store below and the thwart above. As Worsley put it,

> What a crawl! The southern Ocean draining out of your . . . clothing . . . you brace yourself up – or rather down . . . wriggling on chest [and] stomach . . . feeling half suffocated . . . you insinuate yourself [through] the gloomy entrance to a dungeon cell.[21]

It was only a short crawl, but it was a nightmare. Not only was one watch trying to get in; the other was creeping out. Shackleton himself directed the procedure, managing the queue, and calling out the order of entering and vacating the sleeping bags.

This was a practical necessity, which would have evolved by other means. By doing it himself, Shackleton was seen to be in command in little things. He ran the whole routine of the boat. He arranged meal times, and "whacked out" stores.

Crean was the cook, but it required three men to fight the violent movement of the boat. This is what every morsel of hot food required. The only cooker was an ordinary primus stove, used on sledging journeys. First, Crean lit it. He was bent double, since there was not only no head room; there was hardly space to sit up properly. The burner was susceptible to choking by dirt and reindeer hairs from the sleeping bags. It had to be regularly cleaned. This meant pushing a thin wire pricker into a tiny hole, a subtle form of tantalisation in a small boat lurching about in a seaway.

Worsley and Crean would then put their backs against each side of the boat, and extend their feet towards each other, with the primus jammed in the middle. This position saved the pot from being dislodged when the boat threatened to stand on its head.

Worsley, playing "scullion", as he put it, or rather human gimbals, to Crean's "chef",

> held the aluminium [pot] that was to receive the sacred HOOSH & my duty . . . was to swiftly but reverently raise it on high whenever the boat gave a madder leap than usual & so save the precious contents from spilling.[22]

McCarthy meanwhile broke in pieces of ice brought for cooking, and Crean stirred in the food. It was the sledging ration originally brought for the transantarctic journey; a form of dehydrated meat protein. There was half a pound a man. "All eyes, except the helmsman's", said Worsley, "were fastened on the cooker. [Mugs] & spoons were ready."

> As soon as it boiled Crean shouted "Hoosh" & blew out the Primus. All [mugs] were held out, Crean rapidly filling them in turn. We took it down scalding hot . . . The first man to finish his hoosh jumped outside & relieved the helmsman for his while still hot.[23]

His narrow escapes on the *Discovery* and *Nimrod* expeditions had underlined for Shackleton how food, sleep and warmth were necessary for life. It was possible to survive without two, but not without all three. His only choice on the *James Caird* was to depend on food. He gave his men all they wanted to eat. There were two hot meals a day. With each he allowed nut food, a sledging biscuit each, and four lumps of sugar. In between meals, every four hours, he had a drink of hot dried milk served all round. At that rate there was enough food for a month.

"The worst feature of meals," said Worsley, "was that there was not enough headroom to sit upright. One has no idea before making the experiment how . . . distressing this is. The chest is pressed down on the stomach, one swallows with difficulty & the food appears to have no room to go down."

Day after day, the *James Caird* heaved along on her erratic course. She was now where the huge rollers of the Southern Ocean, without obstruction, sweep round the globe like Leviathan chasing its tail. Up to a mile apart, on a front of hundreds of miles, the waves incessantly sweep on from west to east. When storms roar down, it is simply to superimpose a local, and sometimes contrary disturbance on the underlying surge.

"High were the hills when we perched momentarily on the tops of giant combers", as Shackleton put it.

> Nearly always there were gales. So small was our boat and so great were the seas that often our sail flapped idly in the calm between the crests of two waves. Then we would climb the next slope and catch the full fury of the gale where the wool-like whiteness of the breaking water surged around us.[24]

It is not the size of a wave that troubles a seaman; it is fear of the deep. It is the knowledge that all that lies between him and the void below is the frail skin of his boat. This is the fear that has to be mastered in coming to terms with the sea. Thus it was not the towering combers that made the *James Caird* and all in her seem so tiny and insignificant. It was the sense that what was seen was only the tip of a monstrous rhythmic disturbance welling up from the deep. The wave heaving up high over the mast top, went down far below the surface of the sea. If it hit a bank, it would surge up, no longer a wave, but a solid wall of water capsizing and crushing anything in its path.

Everything was grey. There was no touch of colour in relief. Sky, sea and cloud seemed to merge into one another. Time almost lost its meaning. Days ran into each other. Ears were dinned by the roar of the wind, the agonised creak of timbers, the boiling surge of the sea, and the slosh of water running up and down the bilges. Existence dissolved into a twilight succession of eating, steering, working sails, freeing iced-up gear, baling, pumping, and trying to sleep, of which Worsley said,

> We were lifted up & hurled down, & our bodies were whipped . . . flailed & stamped . . . And yet [he went on] I believe her motion was better than some small vessels; but we were in the bows & she was overweighted.[25]

Worse was the constant wet and chill. The canvas that formed the deck was leaking. The only nails McNeish could find to fix it to the hull came from the sledges, and they were too short. The movement of the boat worked them loose, and water washed down in cascades with every sea. In the bows, the damp, sickly smell of moulding reindeer pelt was overpowering. In that confined and twisting, stagnant dungeon the air was bad. They had a sense of lying awake. In fact, they did manage spells of restless sleep broken by spasms of suffocation. "More than once," said Worsley, "when I woke suddenly I . . . had the ghastly fear that I was buried alive."[26]

One thing of which they could not be deprived was a (mostly) following wind. "She steers like a Dutch galliot," was the stock phrase of the helmsman; but every lurch meant that much closer to the distant shore. There were even moments when thoughts were forced outwards from sheer survival to the terrible beauty of the sea. Shackleton, grizzled, hunched, with watchful eyes, peering round him in the gloom below decks, and squinting ahead at the helm, radiated a kind of satisfaction. It was almost as if he only came alive when he was fighting, whether it was men or the sea.

On 29 April, Worsley found something in the middle watch to fix in his memory:

> We rolled & plunged along in the dark . . . Dark hills of water reared suddenly . . . ahead & astern capped by pale gleams of breaking seas. A hiss of water at the bows as she ran heeling down a long sea. Dark shapes of sails overhead & forward bellied to leeward. Drenched through again & again there was yet a certain satisfaction in holding her to her course.[27]

It was, said, Worsley, "a glorious run", 92 miles all told. That day, the sixth day out, he glimpsed the sun for the second time, and was able to get an observation. It placed them (he hoped) at 58°38'S, 50° W. For the first time he noted in his log the distance to his landfall: 458 miles. They had already come 238 miles, almost one-third of the way.

Next day the terrible sea, mother and murderess of men, counter-attacked. For the best part of a week a gale had continuously blown, but the waves had been long and regular. Now the sea became lumpy and confused. The *James Caird* was yawing and steering wildly. She was shipping heavy seas. The water in the bilges was ominously swilling about. Shackleton could drive men and boat no more. At about midday, he hove to.

The need continuously to pump ship was alone an intolerable strain. The pump that Hurley had contrived in the now faraway days on the ice, could only work with the water below a certain level. First the boat had to be bailed. That meant frantic work with cooking pots and contortions to fling out the contents through the hatch. The pump was like a large syringe. One man had to hold the inlet down, by main force, while the other worked the plunger. Every few minutes, they had to change positions, because the water was ice cold, and hands rapidly were numbed.

Hove to, the boat still surged up and down on the waves, but now took on less water. A sea anchor was put out. This is a cone-shaped canvas bag attached by a line at its mouth to the bows. The apex, which has a small hole, points away from the ship, and the effect is to act as a drag in the water, around which the vessel swings to keep head to wind. This is essential for a small boat to survive in a seaway.

Shackleton could take a crumb of comfort from the fact that they were now in the region of the great easterly drift. This is the current revolving round the globe between the fiftieth and sixtieth parallels of latitude. Even when hove to, the *James Caird* would be driven thirty miles or more every day towards her goal. In that sense, nature was on her side.

But the cold became intense. It seemed colder than at any time since the voyage began. It was a reminder that, after all, it was nearly winter in the sub-Antarctic seas. The cold at first merely compounded the misery of Shackleton and his men. They lay contorted in the dark hole that served as their saloon, while water as usual seeped in cascades through the canvas deck. After an hour or two, however, that eased, and eventually stopped.

The explanation was that the spray was now freezing on the canvas as it fell. Amongst other things, that made it waterproof. "We could hardly believe," said Worsley, "that anything so wonderful had happened."[28] For the first time since the voyage began they were not getting drenched.

For the first time, too, there was no need to bail and pump continuously. To stop them freezing up, the sails had already been taken down and somehow stowed in the already confined space below decks. Shackleton now lashed the helm and ordered everyone below, including himself, to snatch some sleep.

It was taking a risk, of course, but it would have taken a greater risk not to seize the opportunity for rest. Seven days' keeping watch and watch had worn them out. Constantly being wet had made their limbs numb and swollen. Shackleton was bent double with another bout of his sciatica. He "grinned", according to Worsley, "at my chestnut of Mick's query to Pat who came home & found his wife in bed with sciatica. 'Did ye kill the Oitalian divvle?' "[29]

> Even when cracked lips and swollen mouths checked the outward and visible signs of amusement [said Shackleton, for his part] we could see a joke of the primitive kind. Man's sense of humour is most easily stirred by the petty misfortunes of his neighbours, and I shall never forget Worsley's efforts on one occasion to place the hot aluminium stand on top of the Primus stove after it had fallen off in an extra heavy roll. With his frost-bitten fingers he picked it up, dropped it, picked it up again, and toyed with it gingerly as though it were some fragile article of lady's wear. We laughed, or rather gurgled with laughter.[30]

Gratefully, they turned in, and slept something like five hours. It was the longest stretch since leaving land.

Towards three in the morning of 1 May, however, they all woke up. "A feeling of uneasiness," Worsley wrote, "seemed to have communicated itself to every man aboard."[31] The boat was moving in a sinister, laboured, unfamiliar fashion. Shackleton, putting his head above the hatch found, in the dark, that the boat was iced over. A layer of frozen spume, almost a foot thick in places, was clinging to the deck and sides. The *James Caird* was not only top heavy and threatening to capsize. She was slowly foundering by the sheer accumulation of weight.

"Something," said Worsley, "had to be done & quickly."

> so we all took it in turns to crawl out with an axe & chop it off. What a job! The boat leaping & kicking like a mad mule & a great fifteen inch thick slippery casing of ice over her like a turtle back with slush all over where the last sea was freezing. First you chopped a handhold, then a kneehold & then went on chopping ice for dear life while an occasional sea leapt over you. After four or five minutes you slid back into the boat – fed up or frostbitten & the next man took up the work, in doing which it was "One hand for yourself & one for the King" because if a man had gone overboard then it would have been goodbye.[32]

All that day and night, the cold gale whined down, the lumpy sea persisted, and the *James Caird* had to stay hove to. Twice more, the men had to take their lives in their hands and remove the ice. The boat's antics were malevolent and erratic. Worsley found it almost impossible to jot down the bare necessity of figures in his log. When it was time to turn in, "you had serious doubts", he said, "as to whether it was worth while", because entering the sleeping bag was like "getting between freezing rawhide".[33]

There was not much conversation. What each man was thinking, he kept to himself. Perhaps Worsley now and then considered that had he had his way with the ballast, they would be riding more easily. Or had Shackleton's excess ballasting saved them when the boat iced over? McNeish possibly was hoping that his work would hold; for upon that, as much as Worsley's seamanship, all their lives depended. Was the hog's back strong enough or would the *James Caird* yet break in two? Would the nails that fixed the canvas decking stay in? Or was McNeish thinking that had he had his way and built his sloop long ago on the ice, they would all have been in safety by now?

As the *James Caird* wallowed in the icy sea, hove to, Shackleton sensed that now was perhaps the crisis of the voyage. He believed that the sanity and the survival of his shipmates hinged on a sense of being cared for. This he had taken pains to provide. There was something almost feminine in the concern that he displayed. He was like a nurse. Shackleton, said Worsley in a telling passage, "keeps us going with hot food or milk":

> He always, as it were, has his finger on our pulse & at the psychological moment orders a hot feed. This . . . saves any bad effects & possibly our lives.[34]

McNeish was beginning to show signs of exposure. When he, or anyone else, seemed to need special nourishment, Shackleton ordered an extra drink of hot milk all round, so as not to disturb them with a hint that they were seen as invalids.

On the morning of 2 May, the painter snapped, and the sea anchor carried away. This seemed an unmitigated disaster. A heavy sea almost immediately struck the boat. Her bows fell off into the wind, and she broached to. When the remnant of the painter was hauled on board, it was found to have been frayed by an encrustation of ice.

By now the gale had eased. The ice was beaten out of the canvas, and sail was set once more. After nearly forty-eight hours hove to, the *James Caird* ran drunkenly before the wind under reefed lugsail and mizzen.

> In steering a small boat before a heavy gale, dont look back [Worsley wrote], it may disconcert you. Fix your eye with a glassy glare on a cloud or breaking sea right ahead & keep her straight, if you can. When you hear a roaring Bull of Bashan with a wet nose galloping up behind you, keep your head well forward & your shoulders hunched up to your ears – till you get it.[35]

Next day, 3 May, the wind dropped. It was fine and clear with passing clouds. For once in a while the *James Caird* took no water on board. It was as if, for the moment, the sea had tired of trying to batter this little intruder into submission. It was their tenth day out, and the best day of the voyage so far.

Shackleton, to use a favourite phrase of his on land too, took the opportunity to "square things up". He jettisoned two of the worst reindeer sleeping bags, which were irredeemably soaked, and therefore unnecessary top weight. "The boat," he said, "must have presented a strange appearance." Deck and rigging were festooned with sleeping bags and clothes being reduced, as Worsley put it, "from wet to damp".[36] After ten days imprisoned underneath the canvas decking, the men were basking in the fitful sunshine. They could almost forget that their knees were raw from crawling over the stones that were part of the ballast, and their thighs sore and inflamed from constant chafing by wet clothes.

Men can adapt to almost anything. Shackleton, in his own words,

> had not realised until the sunlight came how small our boat really was. There was some influence in the light and warmth, some hint of happier days, that made us revive memories of other voyages, when we had stout decks beneath out feet, unlimited food at our command and pleasant cabins for our use. Now we clung to a battered little boat . . . So low in the water were we that each succeeding swell cut off our view of the sky-line. We were a tiny speck in the vast vista of the sea – the ocean that is . . . pitiless always to weakness. For a moment the consciousness of the forces arrayed against us would be overwhelming. Then hope and confidence would rise again as our boat rose to a wave and tossed aside the crest in a sparkling shower like the play of prismatic colours at the foot of a waterfall.[37]

The tableau was completed by an albatross hovering overhead. It was the same one, or another, that had followed them intermittently all the way from Elephant Island. Shackleton had a gun aboard. For fresh meat, he "might have shot [the] albatross", as he put it, "but the wandering king of the ocean aroused in us something of the feeling that inspired, too late, the Ancient Mariner".[38]

For the first time since the voyage began the sun was now visible long and clearly enough for Worsley to take proper observations. Still the *James Caird*, all 22 feet of her, was dwarfed by the swell. As before, Worsley had to time his shots as the boat's upward leap culminated on the crest of a sea. Now, at least, he managed it all "while cuddling the mast with arm & swinging fore & aft & round the mast sextant & all".[39]

The navigational tables were a sodden mass of pulp. Worsley had carefully to prise each page apart. In the end, he made their position 56°13′S, 45°38′W. They had come 444 miles. Allowing for all reasonable errors, they had passed the halfway mark. Nobody, however, quite believed it until the following day when Worsley got another set of observations. That put them at 55°31′S, 44°43′W. It was their eleventh day at sea. They were 496 miles from Elephant Island, and only 250 miles from the nearest point of South Georgia.

For the second day in succession, the sea was kind. The *James Caird* drove before a pleasant southerly breeze, Force 4. Small as she was, she rode up on the long backs of the swells and swooped down on the rolling fronts. She was safer and more comfortable than in the short choppy waves of a narrow sea. "We felt very uppish indeed," as Worsley put it, "& thought with pity of our unfortunate pals on Elephant Id.; 333 miles farther South than we were."[40]

But next day, 5 May and the twelfth day out, it was back to the old misery. As night drew on, the wind hauled to the north-west and was blowing a moderate gale on the beam. Once more came the lumpy cross sea on top of the underlying swell. Once more the boat was shipping seas one after the other. Snow squalls added to the misery. Everything was wet again. There was something indefinably unpleasant about the conflict of wind and water in this particular cross sea, but that by now seemed all in the day's work. Then, around midnight Shackleton, as he put it,

> was at the tiller and suddenly noticed a line of clear sky between the south and south-west. I called to the other men that the sky was clearing, and then a moment later I realized that what I had seen was not a rift in the clouds but the white crest of an enormous wave. During twenty-six years' experience of the ocean in all its moods I had not encountered a wave so gigantic. It was a mighty upheaval of the ocean, a thing quite apart from the white-capped seas that had been our tireless enemies for many days. I shouted "For God's sake, hold on! It's got us!" Then came a moment of suspense that seemed drawn out into hours. White surged the foam of the breaking sea around us. We felt our boat lifted and flung forward like a cork in a breaking surf. We were in a seething chaos of tortured water, but somehow the boat lived through it, half-full of water, sagging to the dead weight and shuddering under the blow. We bailed with the energy of men fighting for life, flinging the water over the sides with every receptacle that came to our

> hands, and after ten minutes of uncertainty we felt the boat renew her life beneath us. She floated again and ceased to lurch drunkenly as though dazed by the attack of the sea.[41]

The wind backed north and blew a gale before the beam. By dawn, the sea was "too heavy to carry on, – Tho I wanted to," as Worsley eloquently jotted in his log, "Sir E. Said no,"[42] and the rest of the day they were hove to under reefed jib. Without a sea anchor, the boat bobbed and squirmed and shipped plenty of green water. The compass glass was broken, but repaired with sticking plaster from the medicine chest.

The worst that wind and sea could do, could not now quash a sense of journey's end. It was the thirteenth day of the voyage, 6 May. At this point, said Worsley, "a small bobtailed bird flew & fussed around us with terrific energy". It might have been the sign of land for which everyone was looking. Nonetheless,

> the only time I heard Sir Ernest swear on this passage was when this little fellow buzzed around. It faintly annoyed us all, but for some reason it irritated him, tho he may have sworn at it to amuse us, thinking "anything for a laugh or to buck things up."[43]

Worsley's calculations put them 657 miles from Elephant Island. The South Georgian coast could only be about 115 miles off. It was, however, only dead reckoning. For two days in a row, thick cloud had obscured the sun and prevented an astronomical fix.

Whether the men survived or not still depended, however, on Shackleton's ability to inspire them. In the case of Vincent, the instinct of self-preservation seemed to have failed. After the first few days, he had mentally collapsed, and ceased to be an active member of the crew. Shackleton, as he put it, "could not easily account for his collapse". McNeish, almost twice Vincent's age, "was suffering particularly, but he showed grit and spirit". Physically, Shackleton went on, Vincent

> was one of the strongest men in the boat. He was a young man, he had served on North Sea trawlers, and he should have been able to bear hardships better than McCarthy, who, not so strong, was always happy.[44]

That was a revealing comment. It said much for his view of human beings. In another form, he expressed it about Crean, who

> always sang while he was steering, and nobody ever discovered what the song was. It was devoid of tune and monotonous as the chanting of a Buddhist monk at his prayers; yet somehow it was cheerful.[45]

In any case, Vincent was now a passenger, and how much longer McNeish would be able to work was uncertain. The burden of survival rested on the remaining four: three Irishmen, as perhaps Shackleton reflected, and a New Zealander. But how much more could even McCarthy endure?

Outwardly, Shackleton nonetheless gave the impression, in his own words, that "It looked as if we were going to get through."[46] However, said Worsley,

> Sir E. discussed with me what we would do if thro' lack of . . . observations or a heavy series of Sly gales blowing us off course, we missed S. Georgia. The prospect was not attractive. Our water, we knew, would [soon] be finished . . . Our food would have lasted a fortnight, but that didn't alter the problem, if we had no water so we dropped the discussion as it was futile.[47]

XLVI

A slight change of course

Everything depended on Worsley. He absolutely had to find his position. There was no other navigator of that calibre on board; not even Shackleton. He did not have much leeway.

In the small hours of 7 May, when the wind dropped enough for them to get under way again, they were less than one hundred miles from land, and making perhaps two knots.

A fresh NNW gale was blowing. The night sky was clear. At six in the morning, as dawn was beginning to approach, it clouded over, and banks of fog rolled down. "Most unfabl. conditions of Obs.," as Worsley blandly jotted in his sketchy log. He needed two sights; one in the morning for longitude and one for latitude at noon.

As the sun rose, it gleamed through the haze but, for the morning sight, the horizon was blurred by the mist, and at noon, it was the turn of the Sun's "limb". This is the nautical term for the edge of the sun or moon. Calculations depend on the centre of the disc, but that is hard to find by eye. Instead, the procedure is to line up the "limb" with the horizon in the sextant mirror, and then work out the altitude of the centre with a mathematical correction.

That is the ideal. In other cases, "You bring, by guesswork the centre of the glow behind the clouds that represents the sun down to the horizon," as Worsley put it. "By practice & taking a series of 'sights' you can get a mean that has no bigger error than one minute of arc."

Worsley was further hindered in this delicate proceeding by a broken northerly sea in which "the boat was jumping like a flea, & shipping seas all over her."[1] He made the position 54°26′S, 40°44′W.

They now appeared to be ninety miles from Willis Island, the western end of South Georgia. It was for this point that Worsley had been making since leaving Elephant Island, fourteen long days before. He now wanted to hold his course, and then round Willis Island to make for the whaling stations on the northern coast. Shackleton, however, in Worsley's words, asked

> "Can you be positive of your position?" I said "Not to 10 [miles] but can easily allow for that".[2]

Shackleton was not so sure. He felt there was a very good chance that a shift of wind would sweep them north of the point and irrevocably out to sea. He insisted on a change of course slightly to the east, to bring them inside Willis Island.

At dusk, they saw a piece of kelp heaving on a wave, their first sign of land. Privately, Worsley recorded that it might have been borne by the current from the Shag Rocks, well to the west but, to his shipmates, he did not press the point. All night, "shipping seas fast & merrily as usual", they held on an ENE course with a light NNW gale on the beam. Worsley was not in fact as devil-may-care as he wished to make out. He dearly wanted another navigational fix. He had obtained exactly four the whole fourteen days at sea.

> I looked after dawn in vain for the sun & felt anxious, for my navigation had, perforce, been so extraordinarily crude that we might make a bad landfall. The sky was overcast & the weather misty & foggy . . . Heavy cross swells from N. & W. & a heavy confused lumpy sea did not make matters pleasant, but we felt happy & excited for we were "making the land" & even hoped by dark to be on good solid earth once more & to have beautiful clear water gurgling down our parched throats.[3]

Two days earlier, they had finished their first cask of drinking water. When they broached the second and last, salt water was found to have got into it. It had happened long before, as they were leaving Elephant Island, on the last trip out to the *James Caird* in the *Stancomb Wills*. McLeod, McIlroy and Macklin were at the oars. They had to negotiate a nasty passage in a reef with a heavy running surf and, in Macklin's words, "We had learned exactly how to do it." Shackleton was on board

> and [said Macklin] he insisted on giving instructions "easy starboard, pull port" etc. Before we knew what had happened we were right in the wash and had the devil's own job to get clear without being swamped.[4]

The *Stancomb Wills* had been towing a cask of drinking water for the voyage. One consequence of the confusion was that the cask got adrift. It was finally retrieved, but only after being bumped by the swell against a rock. Clearly it had then been damaged enough to let in the sea.

The water had been laboriously obtained by thawing glacier ice over the blubber stove in the far-off camp on the beach at Cape Wild. Now, brackish, and spoiled, it was unpleasant, and only seemed to make the drinker thirsty. Moreover, it was full of reindeer hairs and sediment. Every drop had to be strained. It was in any case desperately short, and each man was down to a quarter of a pint daily. Two days' supply was left. The end of the voyage was bedevilled by the agonies of thirst.

Early in the morning more seaweed appeared. Birds began to crowd around the boat. Among them was the little bobtailed kind that had so annoyed Shackleton before. Then at around eight o'clock, the first shag appeared. "The sight of these birds," as Worsley put it, "is a guarantee that you are within 15 miles of the land."[5]

All morning the men crowded to the weather side of their lurching craft to see what they could see. By noon, the fog had cleared, but heavy, ragged clouds were driving hard across from the north-west. Low, misty squalls of hail were obscuring the view. Worsley was now intensely worried because still nothing had been seen.

> "Land!" McCarthy suddenly called out. & there right ahead [wrote Worsley] through a rift in the flying scud our glad but salt rimmed eyes saw a towering black . . . crag with a lacework of snow around its flanks. One glimpse & it was gone again.

The time was 12.30 in the afternoon of 8 May, their fifteenth day at sea.

> We looked at one another with cheerful foolish grins of joy, The feelings uppermost were "We've done it."[6]

Not even the torment of thirst could quite dim the joy of that moment.

XLVII

The line that divides success from failure

The land, Worsley guessed, was Cape Demidov, at the entrance to King Haakon Bay. An hour later, the weather lifted, the coast strung out to port and starboard, and he was sure that he was right. His navigation had been better than he had dared to hope. But they had missed the tip of South Georgia, and were heading for the south coast.

Captain James Cook, when he first saw South Georgia from the deck of the *Resolution* a hundred and forty years before, called it

> savage and horrible . . . the very sides and craggy summits of the lofty Mountains were cased with snow and ice, but the quantity which lay in the Vallies is incredible.[1]

This was inspired by the north coast. The south coast was even more savage and desolate. The first navigator to survey it had been Thadeus Bellingshausen, an Estonian admiral in Russian service, on a voyage of circumnavigation in 1819. That, incidentally, explained the Russian place names on a British island. Cape Demidov was named after one of Bellingshausen's officers. So too was a sinister offshore island called Annenkov. Less expressive than Cook, Bellingshausen contented himself by saying blandly that on the south coast,

> only the steep rocks on which snow and ice cannot lie show a dark colour . . . An extremely heavy surf . . . thundered against the cliffs . . . To wait . . . for better weather . . . to survey the land, frozen and, so to say, dead as it was, seemed . . . useless.[2]

For the men on the *James Caird*, the south coast was nonetheless their haven. Even now, it was uninhabited. All along Worsley had been aiming for the north coast and its whaling stations. Had he been allowed to hold his course the day before, he would have succeeded, and they would already have been close to human habitation. Yet, as so often with Shackleton, Worsley suspected that Shackleton had somehow saved him in spite of himself. For Worsley now discovered that although the latitude of his last sight had been correct to within two miles, he had been astern in his longitude by about twenty miles. Given the circumstances he was fighting, after some 700 miles, it was an astonishing performance. Nonetheless, had Shackleton not insisted on the eastward change of course, the error was enough to have sent them well past the tip of South Georgia and out into the Atlantic.

Every sailor knows that more ships have been wrecked making a landfall than ever were lost out to sea. Heading for an imperfectly known coast, Worsley and Shackleton were now both considerably more worried about the last few miles than they had been the whole long way from Elephant Island. By the middle of the afternoon, to add to their preoccupation, something about the clouds, the tint of the land, the way the boat heaved to an awkward sea, made Worsley sense "dirty weather ahead".[3]

They were at the mouth of what Worsley insisted was King Haakon Bay. He wanted to stand on and seek shelter as quickly as he could. Shackleton disagreed. As they drew inshore, they skirted on their starboard hand a patch of dark, "blind" whalebacked rollers, where the sea swept over an uncharted shoal. These "blind" rollers are far more dangerous than waves out to sea. They do not lift a ship like even combers in a storm. Shallow, fast, turbulent and powerful, they will grab a ship and fling her remorselessly to destruction.

Ahead, meanwhile, sudden great spouts of white and roaring breakers showed where the everlasting westerly swell battered against a reef. The short winter's day was coming to an end. Among such dangers, to attempt a landing in the dark was, in Shackleton's opinion, an unacceptable risk. Devoured by thirst though they all were, and with all the fresh water they could want within reach, he nonetheless ordered Worsley to stand off for the night.

A stiff breeze was blowing, north by east. At 6 p.m., the wind hauled round the WNW and rose to Force 10, which is a storm, and one notch harder than they had experienced even during the worst days of the voyage. Now, however, there was no sea room. Worsley hauled off on the starboard tack to make a safe offing for the night, and after a few hours hove to.

The sea was in a tumult. It was the natural inferno of shoaling waters and making land. In turn, the *James Caird* was flung about by waves that seemed to come from all directions at once. Sometimes she shipped seas to port and starboard. All night she had to be bailed and pumped; and in the dark it was impossible to see where she was drifting.

At daybreak, the boat was wallowing in a frightful, heavy cross sea. Thick driving misty squalls obscured the view. The land only occasionally broke through, but by the sound of the breakers, it was gradually coming nearer. A mountainous westerly swell was helping the wind to set the *James Caird* in towards the coast. Before her was the old sailors' nightmare, a lee shore. At its closest, to port, the land was hardly five miles off. Would they not have done better, after all, to run into King Haakon Bay?

All day, the boat was stormed at in turns by rain, hail, sleet and snow. By noon, the gale rose to hurricane force, hauled to south-west, and drove the *James Caird* harder than ever towards the rock-bound coast.

As the boat was lifted on each swell, the men on board anxiously peered to leeward, looking for the tell-tale break of the coast or an uncharted reef. It was hopeless trying to keep a tally of position because in that part of the coast, tide and currents were unrecorded. All that could be done was to remain hove to.

Early in the afternoon, through a sudden rift in the storm-driven clouds, there appeared on the lee quarter two high jagged peaked crags and a stark line of cliffs and glaciers. The *James Caird* was being literally blown ashore.

Shackleton seemed impassive. The crew had become automata, pumping and bailing literally for life. Even Vincent, still mentally collapsed, displayed the stirrings of self-preservation through his dulled mind, and turned to.

In the crisis, Worsley showed his true stature. It was not only that he displayed no fear. He became possessed of a fierce detachment out of which he was able to apply his knowledge of boats and experience of the sea. A sense of being above the battle was the quality he concealed under the adolescent wildness of himself ashore or on bigger ships.

Worsley identified the land glimpsed through the clouds as the coast between King Haakon Bay and Annenkov Island. It was the most dangerous and least known part of the South Georgia shore.

It was an infernal, awe-inspiring scene. The sky was torn with flying scud. The sea to windward was like surf on a shelving beach. One great line of breakers roared behind the other until lost in spume, spindrift, and the fierce squalls feeding the seas. Mist, from the flying tops of the seas cut off by the wind, filled the great hollows between the swells. The water was everywhere covered with a gauzy tracery of foam, and long parallel lines of yeasty froth or broken by boiling white masses of breaking seas that left their temporary mark.

On each succeeding sea the boat swept upward till she heeled before the screeching fury of the hurricane, and then fell into the hollow till she was almost becalmed. Each sea swept her closer in and, with rising fury, galloped past towards the land until, after a few minutes, it was thundering on the shore beneath rock cliffs and glaciers. The boat, and all in her, seemed doomed.

What Worsley now did was this. The boat was under a reefed jib on the mainmast. He got it shifted right forward. He then set a reefed lug on the mainmast, and the mizzen. The idea was to exploit every ounce of the boat's capacity to gripe to windward. In the screaming wind, it took an hour to change the sails, while the roar of the surf against the shore grew closer.

A larger craft would by now have been doomed, but Worsley, even in the screaming of the hurricane, knew the strength of what he had. Because the *James Caird* was so low in the water, the wind could get no purchase on her sides. The scraps of sail it was safe to set could do their work.

Slowly, the boat began to claw offshore. Then, as she gathered way, she started to crash against the on-rushing seas. The impact put an immense strain on the mast. The crew could only pray that the backstays would hold. Once before they had carried away.

Meeting each wave was like striking a stone wall. The force was such that as the boat halted, trembling, before leaping forward again, the bow planks opened and water squirted in through every seam. As the seams opened and closed with every wave, the *James Caird* started to fill with water. At the same time, the huge seas threatened to swamp her. Incessantly bailing and pumping, thirst almost forgotten, six men were fighting for their lives.

After two hours the shore, as if by a miracle, started to recede. Inch by inch, they were gaining precious sea room. Then danger threatened from another quarter.

They were drawing away from the main coast; but the sea and their own leeway was now driving them on towards the western point of Annenkov Island. They had to keep to windward, because to sheer off to leeward would fling them back on the inshore reefs along South Georgia which they were desperately trying to avoid. They could not even lie to in the lee of the island, because the waters were completely uncharted.

The pale snow-capped peak of Annenkov Island gleamed spectrally aloft, while the *James Caird* heaved and tossed and rolled in the breakers driven past by the hurricane to roar against the cliffs so close that the pounding of the water could almost be felt. The boat drove into the frothing backwash of the surf. The suction of the next sea must fling them on the rocks.

Then, as Shackleton put it, with his favourite echo of Browning, "just when things looked their worst, they changed for the best; so thin is the line which divides success from failure".[4]

Some eddy drove them clear. In Worsley's own words,

> Sir Ernest had just been relieved at the helm, & . . . we bailed together peering under the clew of the lugsail . . . The Island was now so close that we had to crane our necks to look up at the peak. Inch by inch we staggered & lurched drunkenly past the . . . black fangs of the rocky point. The moments became so tense that we feared even to speak – just held our breath or baled for life.
>
> By [nightfall] we knew we were safe. High, almost overhead it seemed, the great peak loomed mysteriously through the darkness. Right abeam long pale fingers from the surf reached back threateningly for us, but they held no terrors then; every moment the clamorous roar of the surf on the rocky point became more faint with distance on the lee quarter.[5]

By some uncanny coincidence, as soon as the boat was out of danger, the wind rapidly began to drop. For four hours, as Worsley put it, "We had fought the hurricane at its height [and] by the grace of God . . . pulled thro' . . . in a 22 ft. boat."[6]

His thoughts, when all seemed lost, he remembered clearly.

> I said to myself: What a pity. We have made this great boat journey and nobody will ever know. We might just as well have foundered immediately after leaving Elephant Island. Then I thought how annoying it was that my precious diary, which I had been at such pains to preserve, should be lost too. I don't think that any of us were conscious of actual fear of death. I know that I did have, however, a very disagreeable, cold sort of feeling, quite different from the physical chill that I suffered. It was a sort of mental coldness. I felt, too, a sharp resentment that we should all be going in such a way, and in sight of our goal.[7]

After the storm, they were able to work the boat again and get some sleep. Worsley had the morning watch. He headed back for Willis Island to round the tip of South Georgia on to the north coast so that he could make one of the whaling stations.

But he found it a nearly impossible task. The interminable

western swell continued to roll past. The wind had all but dropped, and now came ahead from the north-west. Against this, the *James Caird*, all reefs out, could make little headway.

As Crean was crawling out from the bows, he struck the thwart with his shoulder. The slight shock knocked out the pin that held the mast clamp in place. The clamp swung open, and the mast started to fall back, but McCarthy caught it and secured it again. The pin must have worked loose during the hurricane, until the point alone held it. "Had it fallen out in the hurricane," as Worsley remarked, "the mast would have snapped like a carrot, and no power on earth could have saved us. Providence had certainly held us in the hollow of His hand."[8]

When Shackleton emerged from his sleeping bag at dawn, he had to remind Worsley that the nearest whaling station, Prince Olav Harbour, was nearly one hundred miles away by sea. Fresh water was their first concern. Theirs had all gone by now. They had not drunk anything for more than forty-eight hours. Their tongues were swollen, and they could hardly eat.

Worsley, however, seemed to feel thirst less than anyone else on board. He was consumed by the desire to reach civilisation as quickly as he could. He did not quite grasp other people's limitations; but Shackleton did. He was sure that they were all on the verge of collapse, Worsley included. He feared particularly for Vincent and McNeish, and, even more after their miraculous deliverance, he was consumed by the ambition to bring all his men back alive.

Worsley suggested putting into a bay called Wilson Harbour. This was on the way to Willis Island, and was known to have fresh water. To Shackleton, that was too far. They had by now beaten back almost to the mouth of what Worsley had identified as King Haakon Bay and there, Shackleton said, they would put in.

Even so, nature still seemed to bear him a grudge. As the *James Caird* wore round to run into King Haakon Sound, a wind, falling from the snow-clad uplands, blew out of the fjord to drive her back. The tide helped the wind. Now, the one friend of the men on board was the everlasting swell rolling in from the west which, as it broke on the reefs, spouted what Worsley called "white beacon warnings".[9] Close up in the fitful sunlight, he could see how narrow and dangerous was the passage. Shackleton had indeed been right to sheer off when he did.

For four hours, the *James Caird* tacked back and forth across the entrance, trying vainly to beat up into the fjord. Worsley did everything he could. He tried rowing to windward to help the sails. The boat made no headway. Without a shift of wind, she could not get into the fjord. Perhaps they would not land that day, either. Half-ringed by glaciers though they were, they could find not a morsel of ice with which to slake their now almost unendurable thirst.

Nowhere along the rock-bound coast did there appear a temporary haven. Then, as dusk was gathering, Worsley noticed a little cove just inside the southern headland of the fjord. By now, it was apparent that some of them might not survive another day at sea. So, as a last resort, they hauled to the wind, ran on the port tack, and made for the entrance of the cove.

In about an hour they arrived. It was just light enough to make out the passage of the reef between high cliffs. The entrance was so narrow that they had to lower sails and row, but the oars fouled the kelp on either side. "I stood in the bows," wrote Shackleton, "and directed the steering."[10]

In a few minutes, the *James Caird* was through the entrance and, borne on a swell, grounded on a beach at the head of the little cove. Shackleton was the first ashore, and held on to the painter as the boat was sucked out on the backward surge. When she came in again, others jumped out and took over the painter.

Shackleton meanwhile clambered up some rocks with a line to find a proper mooring. Stiff and awkward after being cramped so long in the boat he slipped and, in his own words, "nearly closed my part of the story".[11] He fell a little way, and bruised himself but that, luckily, was all. He made the line fast, and then they were all safe on the beach, with the boat floating just off the shore.

By now it was dark. Through the noise of the surging sea they could hear a little gurgling sound. Almost exactly where they had landed was a tiny stream of fresh water. They fell on their knees, "drinking the pure, ice-cold water in long draughts which put new life into us", in Shackleton's words. "It was a splendid moment."[12]

Such was the end of the boat journey. The date was Wednesday 10 May, 1916. It was their seventeenth day since leaving Elephant Island.

XLVIII

King Haakon Bay

After the ordeal, the temptation in the dark was to leave things until the morning. Shackleton, however, immediately had all food and gear unloaded and brought to safety. He then dumped the ballast to lighten the boat so that she could be beached. "But," as McNeish put it,

> we were all about done in [so] we left her rolling in the surf . . . with 1 man on watch. The Boss found a cave & drove us into it for the night.[1]

The "cave" was merely the undercut face of a cliff, with long icicles, like daggers hanging down in front, and sloping shingle as a floor. It was shelter, however, and it was on dry land.

Shackleton took the first watch. Partly it was to hide the restlessness which overlaid even the aftermath of the voyage. Also, his first care was always for his men.

One certainty, as Shackleton huddled under a rock, listening to the surge of the swell, was that his men could not be driven any more. Not even the thought of the castaways left behind on Elephant Island could overcome that. From exposure and lack of exercise, they had partly lost the use of their limbs. The way they stumbled about showed how weak they were.

Shackleton genuinely felt the others needed the rest more, and he took a double watch to let Worsley, who was to have relieved him, get some extra sleep. That was more than consideration; it was a gesture of gratitude. Shackleton understood that it was Worsley's superb seamanship that had got them through.

In clothes still soaked from the sea, it was in any case hard to sleep. Worsley, as he put it, was "disturbed by the grinding &

bumping of the boat on the stony beach", and feared that "she [would] be hopelessly damaged before morning".

> We were called out at 3 a.m. [said McNeish] as the painter had carried away. We tryed then to turn the boat over to roll her up the beach but it was too much for us so we had a good hot hush & stood by until day light.

McNeish and McCarthy then cut deck and topsides off the boat. They were all so weak, it was the only way of lightening her enough to be hauled up on land. It was noon before she was finally brought clear of the surf.

The *James Caird* had paid for her epic voyage. Her timbers were strained. As Worsley feared, she had been damaged during the night. Some of her strakes had been ground dangerously thin. Almost at the moment of arrival, she had lost her rudder in a swell, and it had floated out of sight. With men and boat in the condition they were, however, Shackleton had no intention of putting to sea again. McNeish and Vincent at least would be unlikely to survive. Instead of sailing round the coast, Shackleton intended to make for a whaling station overland.

Worsley suggested Prince Olav Harbour. It was still the closest whaling station. The route lay between the head of King Haakon Bay and Possession Bay. It was where South Georgia tapered off to its westernmost point. The actual mountain crossing was only about seven miles. Shackleton, however, doubted whether Prince Olav Harbour was manned in winter, but he knew for certain that Husvik was open all year round. He decided therefore to make for Husvik, although the mountain crossing would be twenty miles at least. Norwegian whalers had probably crossed South Georgia at various points on ski, but nobody had traversed this particular route before.

Almost against his will, Shackleton now felt a suspension of his impatience. He understood that, if they were to survive, they first would need rest. He decided to stay in the cove for a while and recover from the voyage.

On the second day, Worsley took a noon sight. The result was 54°10′S which, as he pointedly put it, "proved we were where I had said – King Haakon [Bay]".[2] The coast was imperfectly charted, and they had no way of exactly identifying their surroundings by appearance.

The cove, in any case, seemed unbelievably hospitable. There was tussock grass which, strewn on the floor of the cave, made a dry and comfortable carpet on which to lie. There was driftwood for fuel. There were nesting albatrosses for food. The men took some of the chicks. "The first time," said Worsley, "I felt like a murderer [but] after that I just thought what . . . a glorious feed the first had been."[3] So, gorging themselves on fresh food, they let time drift by. As Worsley wrote,

> The Boss and I discussed making enough money to start another expedition by taking . . . baby albatross and selling them to the epicures . . . of Europe and New York at £50 a piece, quite ignoring the fact that there is a regulation, forbidding the killing of these chicks . . . We were then a law unto ourselves, and looked it.[4]

On the third day ashore there was a kind of retribution when Crean found his eyes inflamed from the wood smoke while cooking. By then they had got themselves and their belongings dry. Although only four of them had reindeer sleeping bags, and the others had to make do with blankets, that night they had their first proper rest for weeks:

> We slept comfortably for about ten hours [said Worsley], except when disturbed by Crean's twisting and muffled groans from the pain of his eyes.
>
> [Shackleton] lost more sleep than we did, as he attended to Crean and put some [drops] – into his eyes. It sounded very quaint to hear Crean demurring like a fractious child, and Sir Ernest, like a worried parent, reproving him until he got him off to sleep.

That night, too, in Worsley's words, Shackleton

> suddenly . . . awoke us all by loudly shouting: "Look out, boys, look out! Hold on!" At the same moment he clutched me by the shoulder in his excitement. I sat up, looked around, and, seeing nothing of note, said: "What is it, Boss?" He said: "Look! It's just going to break on us," pointing to the black wall of cliff opposite, white-crested with snow, which he, dreaming of the boat journey, and waking suddenly, imagined to be the great sea that broke over us.[5]

In the morning, the cove was filled with ice. It was now 13 May, and the fourth day ashore. Shackleton felt that they had fed and rested enough. It was time to continue on their way. After breakfast, he took Worsley, and tramped off along the coast to find the route.

After a mile or two, they were brought up by a glacier dropping right down into the water. "The long bay," as Shackleton put it, was

> a magnificent sight, even to eyes which had dwelt long enough on grandeur and were hungry for the familiar things of every-day life. Its green-blue waters were being beaten to fury by the gale. The mountains peered through the mists, and between them huge glaciers poured down the great ice-slopes which lay behind.[6]

Shackleton and Worsley were sitting side by side on some tussock grass overlooking King Haakon Bay. After eighteen months in the ice, they had still not quite got used again to the sight of vegetation.

On the other side of the fjord, they counted twelve glaciers coming down to the water. Shackleton, said Worsley, then and there, "named some of them, the first after myself".[7] By some historical quirk, the hospitable promontory which had given them a haven was already called Cape Rosa; and Rosa was what Shackleton's mistress, Rosalind Chetwynd, called herself.

Their first move, at least, had been settled for them. From the sea, they had observed a saddle at the head of the fjord which seemed the only way to start the crossing of South Georgia, but clearly it was accessible by boat alone.

Shackleton then explained that he and Worsley, together with Crean, alone would make the crossing of South Georgia. The others were too weak, so they would have to stay behind.

On their way back to the cave, Shackleton and Worsley came across a sea elephant. They stunned it with a stone, and then with their knives killed and carved it. Carrying as much flesh and blubber as they could, they continued on their way. Approaching their companions, Shackleton, as Worsley told the tale,

> with his usual love of leg-pulling, said with a twinkle in his eye, "We'll hide this stuff, go in and tell 'em you saved my life from a sea-elephant that tore your blouse off and badly wounded you – to account for the blood." . . . Of course our tale was not believed.[8]

The ice, meanwhile, had now gone out of the cove with the tide. Shackleton decided to sail next day to the head of the fjord.

In the morning, however, a gale was blowing, with squalls of rain, and departure was postponed. During the afternoon, when the wind dropped, McNeish, in his own words,

> went on top of the hill & had a lay on the grass, & it put me in mind of old times at *Home* sitting on the hillside looking down at the sea.[9]

Vincent, meanwhile, was lying apathetically in the cave before the fire. Mentally, he had not yet recovered. Physically, there was something indefinably wrong.

McCarthy, walking idly along the beach, suddenly found the boat's rudder floating in on the tide. Shackleton saw this as an exhilarating confirmation of the lucky star under which he believed he had been born. The rudder, "with all the broad Atlantic to sail in", as he put it, had come "bobbing back into our cove".[10]

Early next morning, 15 May, they loaded all their belongings into their cut-down boat, and set off. "We felt really happy and excited", Worsley wrote:

> The weather was fine, the prospects looked good . . . and ahead of us was action – action always doubly inspiriting after enforced inactivity.[11]

Nonetheless, there was a tinge of regret as they pulled out through the narrow entrance, set sail up the bay, and watched the cove fade astern. For five days, it had been their haven.

"We were a curious looking party," said Shackleton, "but we were feeling happy. We even broke into song, and, but for our Robinson Crusoe appearance, a casual observer might have taken us for a picnic party in a Norwegian fiord."[12] The wind blew fresh, and the *James Caird* sailed over deep waters ruffled by white horses sparkling in the sun. Bleak shores cloven through ice-clad mountain peaks, stretched on either side. The pitted fronts of glaciers broken with séracs* pushed out into the bay. Clumps of ice like puffballs floated by. Through the splash of the waves, the distant, coughing roar of sea elephants was borne on the wind.

Around midday, after a run of about thirty miles, Shackleton found a sloping shingle beach on the northern shore. It lay close to the head of the bay, just under what all along had appeared the pass into the interior. As it seemed the right starting point for their journey, they put in there.

Lowering sail, they took to the oars and, pulling through a small surf, beached the boat. There was a strange finality as the *James Caird*'s keel grated on the shore.

Close by was an enormous pile of driftwood. Like a graveyard of the seas, some freak of wind and current had thrown up there the wreckage of sunken ships. It was there too that Shackleton first saw exactly what he had achieved. The flotsam strewn about the shingle told the tale of all those who had gone down in the waters where he had survived.

Once more, the *James Caird* was unloaded, and everything carried above high water mark. There was no hospitable cave here so, as on Elephant Island, a hut was contrived by beaching the boat and turning it upside down.

* Ice towers formed by the intersection of crevasses. South Georgia has 163 glaciers.

After their rest in the cove under Cape Rosa, work was no longer so enervating. The upturned boat was placed against a rocky outcrop breaking through the snow, with walls built out of rocks and tussock grass and the mainsail for a door. With driftwood, a "second storey" was built on the thwarts of the boat. It was finished by being covered with tussock and moss until, in Worsley's words, "It looked like an Irish turfed hut".[13] They called it "Peggotty Camp", after the house made out of a boat that belonged to Peggotty in Dickens' *David Copperfield*.

It was at all events shelter in the cold while sea elephants, lolling in droves around the beach, promised food and fuel without end. It was a tempting place in which to wait for spring, but that, of course, was unthinkable.

Shackleton not only now proposed to cross an unknown mountain range on a sub-Antarctic island, but he had to do so when winter was well under way. At all times, the weather on South Georgia was notoriously unstable, and his one hope was to rush across in a safe interlude. He would have to travel day and night; but the nights were long and dark, and it required a combination of moonlight and fine weather.

It was now, as it happened, full moon. Wind, mist and sleet continued, however, to sweep down from the uplands. Twice, Shackleton and Worsley set off to scout the start of the journey, and each time, the weather drove them back. They had first to find a way round a glacier snout that thrust out over the beach into the bay and barred the way.

On the second occasion, after plodding through soft snow for three hours, they reached the mountain saddle that promised a path into the interior. The view was obscured by driving misty squalls. Since landing at Cape Rosa, more than a week before, there had not been a single day fine enough for the crossing safely to begin.

"Some day, Skipper," Shackleton, according to Worsley, had said when first he saw the pile of driftwood on the beach, "you and I will come and dig here for old treasure or perhaps," he added, "sleep quietly with the other old seamen."[14]

That was an unfamiliar note. By 18 May, still unable to start, Shackleton, said Worsley, was "more discouraged, worried and nearer to depression than I had ever seen him".[15]

It was not only bafflement or the thought of the men left on Elephant Island. An unpleasant Föhn* storm was blowing down from the mountains. Like any Föhn anywhere, it made everyone nervous and depressed, with the slight suggestion of a headache.

* A warm, dry unseasonal wind.

To the eerie muffled roar of a glacier calving across the bay, Shackleton nursed his thoughts, then suddenly "Skipper," he burst out, according to Worsley, "I'll never make another expedition."[16]

Worsley scented change from the Föhn. All that day he

> tried to get indications of what was to come, by observing the height and formation of the cloud-mists that swathed the upper mountain tops. Shackleton asked me repeatedly, "What do you think of the weather?" and "What is to-night going to be?"

By dusk the signs were good. For the first time since their landing, fair weather seemed in the offing. "The change in Shackleton as soon as he realised this," said Worsley, "was remarkable. He seemed to tauten and gain strength":

> [He] was vigorous and excited and talked of how soon we should be able to get the men off Elephant Island. He was the old Shackleton again.[17]

But not quite. Somewhere along the open-boat journey Shackleton had crossed an invisible line. Spirit, determination, hope, optimism, he still possessed but, belatedly perhaps, he had left his youth behind and passed into the twilight world that divides it from maturity.

They went to bed early under their upturned boat. Consumed by anxiety, Shackleton could hardly sleep. Twice during the night he got up to look at the weather. The second time, he met Worsley. "To our joy," said Worsley, "the moon was shining, and, as . . . sailors say, 'scoffing up the clouds'."[18]

By two in the morning, the weather was fine, clear, and calm, the moon shining brilliantly. Shackleton ordered a start. An hour later they had eaten breakfast and were on their way.

McNeish and McCarthy went along to see them off. Vincent, still ill and apathetic, stayed behind in the hut. At the glacier front that barred the way ahead, they parted. Shackleton and his companions had to cross the ice front where it met the waters of the fjord. They did so by dodging around projecting snouts as each swell receded. They soon disappeared into the shadows, and McNeish and McCarthy were left to walk back to camp.

"I am about to try and reach Husvik . . . for relief for our party," Shackleton had scribbled in McNeish's diary. "I am leaving you in charge." This was psychologically correct, although McNeish was physically weakened, and McCarthy was the strongest of those staying behind.

"You will remain here until relief arrives," Shackleton continued in his instructions to McNeish. "You have ample seal food which you can supplement with birds & fish according to your skill." Even with survival hanging by a thread, Shackleton preserved a shrewd corner of himself to be prepared for civilisation. Already he was anticipating charges of abandoning his men. "You are left with a double barrelled gun," he itemised,

> 50 cartridges – 40 to 50 Bovril sledging rations, 25 to 30 biscuits: 40 Streimer Nutfood. You also have all the necessary equipment to support life for an indefinite period. In the event of my non-return you had better after the winter try and sail round to the [North] Coast.
>
> I trust to have returned in a few days.[19]

XLIX

The crossing of South Georgia

Shackleton, Worsley, Crean – they were like strange beings plodding up the slope towards the pass, ingrained blubber smoke and dirt giving to their faces, in the moonlight, the pallid tinge of an unearthly mask.

Since the *Endurance* was crushed, Shackleton had come fifteen hundred miles. To Husvik, it was only twenty miles more. That, of course, was the nub. The last mile is always the worst. What lay ahead was not objectively difficult. It was an extended tramp over snowfields through mountains nowhere above 3,000 feet in height although, at the time, this was concealed from Shackleton. Everything was unknown, except what could be seen from the shore.

The weather, however, was recognisably the main hazard. Shackleton was invading a country that combined all the menace of the mountain world, the sea, and the polar regions in an unholy, fickle blend. It would have been a trial for fit men properly clad, but these men were neither. They were castaways with worn and threadbare clothes. Their heavy gait said everything about the fatigue and exposure which had been their lot.

Out of driftwood McNeish, the indefatigable craftsman, had made a sledge for the crossing but, at the outset, Shackleton had abandoned it as too heavy and cumbrous. With the same materials, McNeish might have made rudimentary snowshoes, which would have saved Shackleton the effort wasted as he sank up to his ankles in the snow. As it was, he had to make do with smooth-soled boots, although McNeish had given them some grip with screws taken from the *James Caird*.

Shackleton had decided to cut weight to the bone. He put his faith in speed. He left the sleeping bags* behind so that the crossing would have to be done at one stretch. As food, Shackleton took some of the biscuits and the concentrated sledging ration left over from the boat journey. Each man carried three days' supply. There was also a primus stove with a full tank, but no extra fuel, and a small saucepan.

When the *James Caird* reached the head of King Haakon Bay, only two boxes of matches remained; one full, the other partly used. Shackleton had left the full one behind with the men at Peggotty Camp. With him, for survival, he had exactly forty-eight matches.

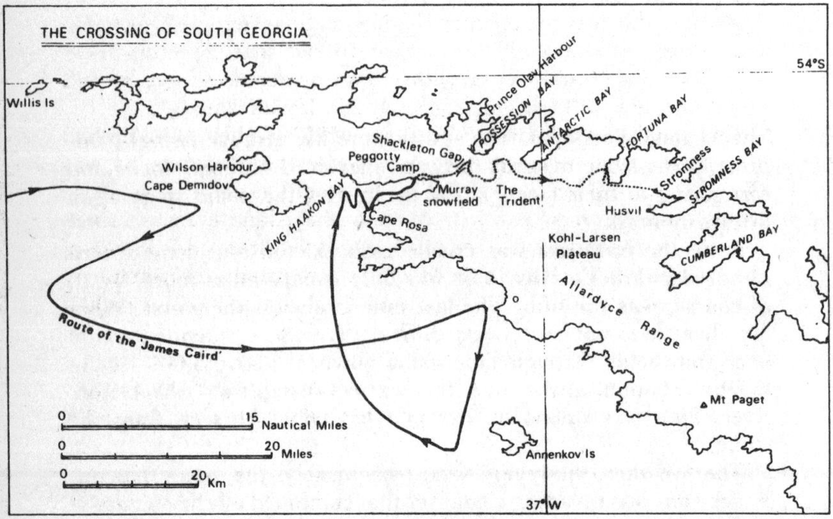

Shackleton's equipment was grossly inadequate. He had no rucksacks. To carry their loads, he and his companions were hung about with parcels like tramps. Each man carried his food in a canvas boot tied around his neck with lamp wick. "I was half-strangled with four cords and straps around my neck before I coiled the Alpine rope on top of all," said Worsley. "We had to leave our arms clear to use our 'alpenstocks'."[1] These were laths from the decking of the *James Caird*, and originally part of the sledges intended for the transantarctic crossing. McNeish's adze, his last remaining tool, had also been brought along as an ice axe.

* A reindeer fur sleeping bag weighed 10lbs. The modern equivalent, made of nylon, with duck down filling, weighs about 2½lbs.

They were all three weakened by privation and exposure, but they were by now professional survivors. Shackleton and Crean had more than three thousand miles of sledge travel behind them. What lay ahead could not, for example, compare with Shackleton's first ascent of the Beardmore Glacier. Crean, one of the last men to see Scott alive four years before, had turned back, with Teddy Evans on the inland ice 150 miles from the Pole. Both he and Shackleton were, however, seamen at heart, and the voyage from Elephant Island probably seemed to them less alien than what was in store. Worsley, on the other hand, was used to mountains, both in New Zealand and the Alps. He was exactly the amalgam of seaman and mountaineer now needed.

Against this was the obscure shadow on Shackleton's health. He was unable to shake off the inchoate dread that something was awry with his heart. Despite all he had overcome so far, he still could not be sure he was fit for what still lay ahead.

"As usual," said Worsley, "I navigated."[2] To help him, he had a sketchy chart of South Georgia. With ironic aptness, it was German, having been prepared by Filchner's expedition in 1911, while waiting to go south. Although the island was a British possession, the British authorities had not yet mapped it. Some of the coastline on the chart depended on the running survey made by James Cook when he sailed along the island almost a century and a half before.

The chart was a blueprint – that is to say, it was like a photographic negative, with faint white lines breaking a mottled ground of blue. It had been roughly reproduced in the workshops at Grytviken, and was in any case only an outline of the coast. The interior was an absolute blank.

Worsley had two compasses. One was a heavy, sledging model; the other, a small silver one given to him five years before in Switzerland. "My procedure," he wrote,

> was at first to lay the "chart" and sledging compass on the snow together and take a bearing of a peak or bluff near our course, and then steer by it. This compass was a nuisance to read, caused us to stop and delayed us . . . I soon found that, holding my little compass in my hand, tilting it when near the proper bearing to stop it swinging, and standing still for two seconds, I could instantly read the bearing and go on.[3]

To start with, they followed the unnamed pass that later was called the Shackleton Gap. From King Haakon Bay, it ran almost directly east, which was the course for Husvik. "After two hours' steady climbing," as Shackleton put it, "we were 2,500 ft. above sea level." That spoke for his state of mind, and the distortion of travel by night. The summit of the gap is only about 1,000 feet, and they had not yet reached the top. In Shackleton's own words,

> The bright moonlight, showed us that the interior was tremendously broken. High peaks, impassable cliffs, steep snow-slopes, and sharply descending glaciers could be seen in all directions, with stretches of snow-plain overlaying the ice-sheet of the interior.[4]

Meanwhile, at about 5 a.m., a mist began to rise. They passed close to a large oval pit at least one hundred feet deep, facing uphill, so that they only saw it at the last moment. They then stopped to rope up to avoid accidents, for now it appeared that they were not on a snowfield but a glacier. Shackleton led and kept a course set by Worsley, coming last, calling out the direction by lining up the rope against the compass. The rope was only about fifty feet long, frayed, weathered and worn, and whether it would actually hold if anybody fell, was problematic.

Steadily they tramped through the mist, making short halts every quarter of an hour. That, Shackleton believed, was the best way to prevent exhaustion. By 6 a.m. they had crossed the saddle, and the mist was beginning to clear.

Down below they saw what seemed to be a frozen lake, exactly on their course. Its level surface, gleaming like a medal in the moonlight, beckoned with promise of better going. Since there seemed an easy way down, they started to descend, although the further shore was still shrouded in the mist and the end of the slope was hidden from their view.

After an hour, crevasses showed that they were still on a glacier. Shackleton stopped and ordered what Worsley called "a cold snack of pemmican and biscuit, with two lumps of sugar and a handful of snow for a drink". Meanwhile, day dawned.

> Soon [said Worsley] the rosy clouds of mist were lifting, and the lake lengthening. Presently we saw it stretching to the horizon. It was in fact no lake, but an arm of the sea – Possession Bay.[5]

It was now about 8 a.m. on Saturday 20 May, and they had reached the northern coast. After about six hours they had actually crossed the narrow isthmus of South Georgia. It had not in fact done them much good. The coast, as they well knew, was impassable, and the only way was over the mountains. They had no alternative but to retrace their steps.

Worsley ascribed the mistake to "chart error" and perhaps local disturbance of the compass. Filchner's chart, in fact, was astonishingly accurate, as far as it went. It clearly indicated Possession Bay. Moreover, in that part, no magnetic disturbance has yet been found. The incident revealed their almost hallucinatory state of mental exhaustion. They had broken the cardinal rule of travel in unknown terrain by deserting the high ground before being sure of their surroundings.

At least the weather continued, inexplicably, fine. In a region where the westerlies rage, there was that morning hardly a breath of wind. The sun shone from a clear and almost cloudless sky. The sensations of the mountain world triumphed, at least for Worsley, and the prospect of what was later called the Allardyce Range moved him to write of the

> sunshine on the snow valleys and uplands with black upthrusting crags, and peak beyond peak . . . snow clad and majestic glittering like armed monarchs in the morning sun.[6]

But Worsley was soon jerked back to reality by the depressing exercise of regaining lost height. They swung left from their downward tracks to turn east towards their destination. Athwart their course lay a curving mountain ridge, from which protruded five pinnacles, like sentries in a row, barring the way ahead. It was the northern spur of a massif today known as the Trident.

There was an easy way round, but it meant skirting the Trident to the south, and making a high and circuitous detour over the agreeable expanses of the Kohl-Larsen plateau. But Shackleton was not to know this. The plateau had not yet been discovered, much less named. He decided to drive straight on, although in the mountains, the direct route is rarely the quickest. He had no alternative. He had neither time nor energy to scout around; and mentally it was vital to drive on without a check. They were balanced on a knife edge, and the least delay, the merest hint of confusion, could make the party crack. Shackleton decided to force the ridge stabbing the bleak wintry sunlit sky ahead.

Between the pinnacles, there appeared four distinct passes to the hinterland. At a certain point, Worsley suggested, and Shackleton agreed, that they try the southernmost, and what seemed the lowest gap. They were now making their way over the undulating surface of what later was called the Murray Snowfield. Worsley said,

> The only sounds were the crunch of our feet through the snow, the soft swish of the rope – we were roped now, ready for crevasses – and an occasional alarming sudden hiss as . . . the snow around fell about eight

inches with us. Every step we took we sank half-way to our knees . . . At each quarter of an hour, when we halted for a minute, we threw ourselves flat on our backs, spread-eagled, and, drawing in great daughts of air, took the most complete rest in the shortest possible time.[7]

They were invading territory that demanded men on snowshoes or on ski. After about an hour, and perhaps a third of the way up, Shackleton ordered the first hot meal. It was now 9 a.m., and they had been on the march for seven hours. They dug a hole in the slope for protection because although "there was no wind at the moment", in Shackleton's words, "a gust might come suddenly".[8] Crean, as he had been all the way from Elephant Island, was cook. Automatically almost, he lit the primus stove and boiled up pemmican hoosh.

Just before midday, they reached the crest of the pass. For the last fifty feet or so, steps had to be cut. The slope was not exactly steep, but to men on the brink of exhaustion it posed untold danger, and with boot soles now virtually worn smooth, there was ever the danger of a slip. Even cutting the steps was an awkward process, because all they had was the carpenter's adze, with too short a handle for the purpose.

At the top, "the outlook", as Shackleton put it, "was disappointing":

I looked down a sheer precipice to a chaos of crumpled ice 1,500 feet below. There was no way down for us.[9]

Shackleton led off on a traverse, cutting steps round a dolomite pillar to the left, hoping for better things on the other side. He found the same precipice again.

The only alternative was to try the next gap along the ridge to the north. There was what Worsley called "the sickening retreat of our hard-won climb". Skirting the base of the mountain, they were checked by a "great chasm", as he put it,

cut down into the snow and ice by the . . . gales . . . blowing round the flank of the next peak. We approached the edge gingerly, and, lying down on the cornice . . . we peered . . . into a gloomy gulf about 200 feet deep and broad and 2,000 feet long. Two battleships could have been hidden in it; but what impressed us most was the fearful force of the elements that had . . . chiselled it out, while we knew that, if a gale came on, we could live but an hour or so on these wind-threshed . . . uplands.[10]

Circumventing this "windscoop", as modern terminology has it, they stopped for their next meal. The weather was still calm, but Worsley thought his feet were frostbitten, "as their feeling", he said, "was not yet normal after the boat journey". Taking off his boots, he found his feet in a reasonable state, but wet and cold. His boots, amongst other things, were torn and leaking.

He wrung out his dripping socks. Alone, he had brought along a spare pair, which he carried as shoulder pads for his loads. He now put them on, replacing them with the wet pair – "to Shackleton's amused admiration", as he put it. Shackleton, said Worsley, "took his usual paternal interest and praised my foresight".

Worsley and Crean were wearing what Worsley called "Shackleton boots". They were really copies of the boot Amundsen designed for his journey to the South Pole, with stiff soles and soft uppers of leather and canvas. Worsley, once he had bound the uppers so that no snow got in from the top, had wet feet no more.

Shackleton himself was wearing leather ski boots. "How [he] avoided frost-bite," as Worsley put it, was "a bit of a mystery. With his usual self-sacrifice he had given his own [Amundsen] boots to one of the men in the boat."[11]

After what Shackleton called "another weary climb" they reached the third gap. They had to cut steps as they moved in zigzags across a hard snow slope leaning at about forty-five degrees. The summit turned out to be a thin layer of loose snow over blue ice. The descent on the far side "might or might not have been possible", said Worsley:

> I wanted to try it, but Sir Ernest, with his usual caution, said "No," and very likely he was right; but we all felt "fed up" with our wearying search up and down, up and down, for a road through.[12]

It was by now late afternoon. The sun all day had loosened the snow. The going was treacherous. Now another menace appeared, in the shape of a sea fog stealthily creeping up from below. Trying not to hurry too much, Shackleton led the way down and then up again towards the fourth gap. They reached the top as dusk was beginning to fall.

This gap was a sharp ice ridge which they all three straddled while they debated what to do. The fog had stolen up behind them and completely obscured the country they had crossed. As they sat there, thin wisps of the fog actually passed between them. In Worsley's words,

> Crean said, quaintly, "You won't be able to do much navigating in this, Skipper;" but Shackleton, who was usually amused by his remarks, did

not smile. He said tersely, "I don't like our position at all. We must get out of it somehow; we shall freeze if we wait here till the moon rises."[13]

It was impossible in the fading light to see the whole descent. From the third gap along the ridge, however, it had appeared as if there might be a way down. As Worsley put it,

Darkness in front, fog behind – there was not much choice . . . finally "Shacks" said: "We'll try it." Cutting every step with the adze and keeping the rope taut between us, he led down for about 200 yards.[14]

"Although," said Worsley, "Crean and I had several times asked him to let us take the lead for a while, he would not, but led the whole [way], though it was certainly more exhausting breaking the trail, and I thought I could see it telling on him."[15]

The slope was now easing a little. Shackleton halted, Worsley and Crean working their way down to join him on a little ledge he had cut. In the gathering darkness it was impossible to see whether the slope dropped away to a precipice or eased out on to the level that seemed so frighteningly dim and far below. In any case, to climb down, cutting steps, would take too long. When would the weather break? How much longer could their failing strength last? Time was running out. They had wasted almost the whole day trying to find a way over the ridge.

Crean had been through it all before. On 13 January, 1912 he, Teddy Evans, and William Lashly, in coming off the island ice had blundered to the top of the Shackleton Ice Falls. The Beardmore Glacier was hundreds of feet below. They too had been racing against time. It would have taken three days to go round. Instead they tobogganed through the falls, and survived.

Shackleton now decided to copy the performance. "It's a devil of a risk," he said, according to Worsley, "but we've got to take it." Not having a sledge each man sat on his portion of the alpine rope coiled up as a rudimentary toboggan. Shackleton as usual was in front. Worsley straddled behind him, holding his shoulder, and Crean did the same to Worsley. As Worsley tells it,

We seemed to shoot into space. For a moment my hair fairly stood on end. Then quite suddenly I was grinning! I was actually enjoying it . . . I yelled with excitement, and found that Shackleton and Crean were yelling too.

The sharp slope eased out towards the level runout below and they knew that they were safe.

Little by little, our speed slackened, and we finished up at the bottom in a bank of snow. We picked ourselves up and solemnly shook hands all round.

"It's not good to do that kind of thing too often," said Shackleton slowly, ". . . the risk was justified this time."[16]

The whole slide had taken about three minutes. Worsley judged that they had dropped about 3,000 feet, but in fact it was nearer 1,500 feet. Worsley's trousers had been badly torn by the glissade. "Shackleton," as he put it, "laughed, but when I pointed out . . . that his own were in equally bad case his laugh eased up a bit."

In retrospect, the greatest risk seemed that of starting an avalanche. Briskly they moved out of harm's way, and then stopped for another meal. Looking back, they saw on the ridge they had just left, what Shackleton called "grey fingers of fog . . . as though reaching out after the intruders . . . but we had escaped".[17]

It was now dark, and a piercing, cold wind had started to blow down from the heights. Crean had greater difficulty than usual in cooking, and had to shield the primus from eddying gusts. "We awaited impatiently the verdict of our chef," as Worsley put it. "She's biling, bhoys!" They then crouched round and dipped their spoons in turn into the saucepan. They had no mugs, and this was the only equitable way of sharing out:

Shackleton [said Worsley], chaffingly accused Crean of having the biggest spoon, and he replied: "Holy smoke, look at the Skipper's mouth!" So I took advantage of the discussion to take another spoonful.[18]

Behind the banter was the wearing stress of unknown terrain and a sense of failing strength. It was now about 6 p.m. Since leaving King Haakon Bay, they had been on the march for fifteen hours. They had come about ten miles, and were not yet half-way to their destination. There was no question of camping for the night. They had neither sleeping bag nor tent; but apart from anything else, they were driven by the haunting fear of time running out. The moon had not yet risen but, as soon as they had finished eating, they roped up and plodded on trustingly in the dark.

By observing from the heights in daylight they knew roughly the lie of the land. They had to keep to a terrace in the ice sheet above the outfall to the northern coast. At one point two rocky bluffs projecting from a jagged ridge on their right forced them over to the left, but not enough to bring them into danger. One certain landmark they had. To their left they could faintly make out Antarctic Bay.

The moon rose, just in time, as it happened, to guide them through a menacing patch of crevasses and minor ice falls. They now plodded up a gently sloping snowfield on what is now called the Crean glacier, with a domed *nunatak* ahead as a guide. The wind dropped and the temperature sank. They did not mind the cold, because it froze the surface of the snow, and as the night wore on, they found themselves walking on hard crust. "Sometimes," said Worsley, "we would go along for a hundred yards without sinking in at all, and laughed and shouted for joy."[19]

"I do not like to set any bounds to the limit of human endurance,"[20] Shackleton had once said in the days when Amundsen was making for the South Pole. Now it was almost as if fate required him to put his own words to the test. It was the end of the long trail of disappointment that began fifteen months before, when *Endurance* was beset. They were moving almost like automata. Midnight came and went. Shackleton somehow kept a rhythm of short regular rests and a hot meal every four hours. They had no way of gauging distance. Shackleton's one fear was overshooting Stromness Bay, which would have been fatal.

In any case, they had passed the domed *nunatak*. The snow now sloped enticingly down and lured them on. The freer striding chafed the inside of their thighs, and reopened the wounds caused by salt and wetting on the boat journey. They were soon raw and bleeding, but it hardly mattered. In their near hallucinatory state of fatigue they believed they were on the last lap descending to Stromness Bay.

Soon after they started to descend, a thin bitter wind began to blow. It penetrated into their very bones, for they had now been on the march for over twenty hours, halting only for occasional meals. As Shackleton put it,

> I suppose our desires were giving wings to our fancies, for we pointed out . . . various landmarks revealed by the now vagrant light of the moon, whose friendly face was cloud-swept. Our high hopes were soon shattered. Crevasses warned us that we were on another glacier.[21]

There was no glacier at Stromness. They had turned too soon, and were moving down the Fortuna Glacier towards the open sea, away from their goal. "Wearily and mechanically," said Worsley, they climbed up again. There was, he said, a "hopeless feeling at having to retrace our steps and climb again to previously hard-won heights".

The rope, meanwhile, was periodically so slack that Worsley, in his own words,

> had difficulty to avoid treading on it, and once . . . did so. This is irritating to . . . others in ordinary mountaineering, but with fatigued men it is almost more than they can bear . . . following the example of our leader, we did our utmost to . . . avoid any cause of annoyance . . . responding to Shackleton's unselfishness.

"In normal times," as Worsley wonderingly put it, Shackleton could be "irritable, but never when things were going badly and we were up against it."[22]

It was a long, distressing climb, up a slope that seemed inhumanly steep. It was in just such a situation that the wrong party, wrongly handled, could break down, but somehow they regained their lost height and resumed their proper course. They were making for what Shackleton called a "jagged line of peaks with a gap like a broken tooth" that barred the way ahead.

At about 5 a.m. they reached the base of the rocks. They had now been travelling for twenty-two hours without sleep. The wind was stinging them with snow drift, and driving through their tattered clothes.

Behind them, a mysterious tragedy was being played out. While they were still crossing the ocean in the *James Caird*, an auxiliary sailing vessel called *Argos* left Buenos Aires for South Georgia. She never arrived. After the winter, when Prince Olav Harbour was reopened, a shed was found to have been broken open, and inside were seven rough beds. Near the station, a dead man was found. Some of *Argos*' cargo was afterwards discovered at King Haakon Bay. Had she foundered off South Georgia, and had some of her crew survived to cross the island via the Shackleton Gap but, finding Prince Olav Harbour closed, perished while trying to reach human habitation?

Shackleton, Worsley and Crean were now near the end of their tether. It was not physical exhaustion precisely, for by regular and frequent food, Shackleton had kept them going past the rational limits of endurance. The one great lack, which Shackleton could not know about, was lack of liquid. In any case, there had not been enough fuel to melt the snow in order to prevent that. They were therefore suffering from dehydration, and that was pushing them over into the half world where physical and mental phenomena meet. Their nerves were on edge. Delusion hovered in the air. Shadows seemed like ghosts. They imagined unseen companions by their side.

At all costs, Shackleton now decided they must have rest. So they sought shelter behind a rock, laid their alpenstocks and adze on the snow as a seat, snuggled up to each other, and fell asleep. That is to say Worsley and Crean did. Shackleton somehow kept awake. It would, as he put it,

> be disastrous if we all slumbered together, for sleep under such conditions merges into death. After five minutes shook them into consciousness again, told them they had slept for half an hour, and gave the word for a fresh start.[23]

After another steep climb of about an hour, they surmounted the ridge and went through the gap between the peaks. In Shackleton's words: "If the further slope had proved impassable our situation would have been almost desperate but", he said, turning once more to Browning, "the worst was turning to the best for us".[24]

They hardly noticed the icy wind that met them as they passed through the gap, but in any case, it died away on the other side. It was a clear, calm morning. The moon was paling in the west. At their altitude (Worsley estimated 4,000 feet; in fact it was about 2,000 feet) the dawn was coming early.

Like a stage set as the lights go up, a panorama softly materialised at their feet. Down below lay the dark waters of Fortuna Bay. Straight ahead, beyond the mountains on the other side, Shackleton recognised a peculiar twisted formation like a "Z" in a rock face above Stromness Bay. They were within sight of journey's end. For the first time since starting off, twenty-seven hours before, they had got their bearings.

Even so, they received a check. They had emerged above an eastern indentation of Fortuna Bay well out towards the sea. Their way was round the head. In any case, straight down, the slope fell away to what, from their position, seemed a precipice. To the right, however, was an apparently easy descent across the slope. It seemed almost too good to be true.

Shackleton ordered breakfast. While Worsley and Crean busied themselves with the primus, Shackleton climbed up, cutting steps in wind-packed snow, to get a better view.

There was something else. At 6.30 a.m. he thought he heard a steam whistle. He could not be certain, but he seemed to remember that the men at the whaling stations were woken at about that time. He descended to his companions, and asked Worsley to get out the chronometer. Worsley was carrying it round his neck, next to his skin to keep it warm. He drew it out from beneath his ragged, grease-caked garments and, as Shackleton recorded,

> in intense excitement we watched the chronometer for seven o'clock when the whalers would be summoned to work. Right to the minute

> the steam-whistle came to us, borne clearly on the wind across the intervening miles of rock and snow. Never had any one of us heard sweeter music. It was the first sound created by outside human agency that had come to our ears since we left [Grytviken] in December 1914.

They had come full circle; only *Endurance* was at the bottom of the sea.

That piping echo of a factory, in any case, was the first proof positive of their position. For the first time since leaving King Haakon Bay twenty-seven hours before, they were free of the gnawing sense of being lost.

"It was," said Shackleton, "a moment hard to describe. Pain and ache, boat journeys, marches, hunger and fatigue seemed to belong to the limbo of forgotten things, and there remained only the perfect contentment that comes of work accomplished."[25]

They solemnly shook hands again. Worsley, by his own account, found himself "yelling 'Yoicks! Tally-Ho!' "[26]

Shackleton, for his part, grasped that the inspiration was bound to pass. The danger was that they felt the journey to be as good as done. Several miles of unfamiliar terrain still remained. It was almost an invitation for a fatal slip just as they were reaching safety. This was especially true since, in their condition, anti-climax must follow soon. It was essential to ride on the surge of the moment.

Shackleton now explained what he had seen from higher up. The fjord seemed directly underneath, as if rippling against a precipice,

> "but perhaps there is no precipice [he said]. If we don't go down we shall have to make a detour of at least five miles before we reach level going. What shall it be?" They both replied at once, "Try the slope."[27]

So they abandoned the primus, which was now empty, and struck out diagonally to the right across the slope, heading south towards the head of Fortuna Bay. For perhaps half a mile, the going was tiring, but not difficult. It meant plodding through deep snow on a not too steep slope.

Then they came to a *mauvais pas*. The slope steepened, and turned to blue ice. Worsley baulked. For one thing, the screws on their boots had now practically worn away, so that they had virtually no grip. Worsley proposed turning back and, after all, finding a better way down.

Shackleton very firmly declined. Either his own impatience, or an instinct that to turn back now would be fatal, made him drive on, despite Worsley's reluctance. Shackleton's solution to the problem was to cut steps vertically downwards on the ice, while

Worsley and Crean secured him on the rope from above. It was merely an illusion of safety. Neither had any form of belay. A single slip would have meant the end of all three. Then they followed, much more frightened than they cared to admit, and joined Shackleton where he had cut a small ledge.

It was a passage that would have tested a practised mountaineer and none of them was that. But Shackleton had no desire to presume on his good fortune any longer. For at least thirty hours they had enjoyed frighteningly ideal weather. At any moment it could break, and in their condition there would be no chance of survival. Shackleton wanted to get off the heights as quickly as he could. He chipped away at the slope with controlled desperation, placing his feet gingerly in each step as it was cut. The only sounds were his own laboured breathing, the dull impact of the adze, and the subdued tinkle of the ice chips running down the slope. Between his legs, when he dared to look, was the dark, rippled water of the fjord which seemed thousands of feet below.

If they could have trusted themselves and, equally important, the rope, they could probably have abseiled down in a few minutes. As it was, they spent two hours laboriously cutting steps down two or three hundred feet. At a certain point, Shackleton noticed the ice chips disappearing with a little bound into space very close below. He sheered off to the left, where protruding rocks offered an escape. Somehow, they scrambled down another steep pitch, backs to the slope, kicking steps with their heels, not daring to look down. Fleetingly the ice slope was revealed in profile, and they saw that, just below the point that they traversed, it dropped away into a short, vertical wall. Zigzagging underneath, they turned it, and the worst suddenly was over.

They were now perhaps still five hundred feet up, but the slope was levelling out. Half stumbling, they ploughed their way diagonally downwards to the right through loose, wet snow; next they reached patches of tussock grass; and then, almost before they knew it, they were on the strip of beach between a glacier front and the water at the head of Fortuna Bay.

The gravelly flats were almost like quicksand, and they sank sometimes half-way to their knees. Gentoo penguins appeared; also what Shackleton called "the first evidence of the proximity of man":[28] dead seal with bullet wounds and mysterious tracks which, eventually, he placed by recalling how the whalers had introduced reindeer from Norway.

It all passed as if in a dream. It was the last agonising few miles, with the driving fear that everything, somehow, could still crumble in disaster.

One more range of mountains still lay between them and the whaling stations in Stromness Bay. They had a choice of three: Leith Harbour to the north, Stromness straight ahead, and Husvik to the south. Shackleton chose Stromness.

As fast as their failing strength allowed, they crossed the beach, and started the climb up on the other side, where they were faced with what even to them was a gentle, easy col. To Worsley it was "too good to be true".[29] Without mishap they reached the summit between two peaks, and then trudged on through clinging snow along the flat saddle of the col, Shackleton still leading, followed by Crean, with Worsley bringing up the rear.

They were crossing a frozen mountain tarn when Crean fell through up to his waist. He was pulled out and, walking delicately, they reached rising ground and safety after about two hundred yards. It was now about 11 a.m. They stopped, ate a little cold food, and went on in silence except for the squelch of wet snow beneath their feet, and the sinister moan of a rising wind. The tramp, to their jaded sense, seemed never to come to an end.

Suddenly, beneath their feet, black waters appeared. They were looking down on Stromness Bay. Two whale-catchers, like insects on a pond, were steaming far below. They could also see part of the whaling station.

Such was their first glimpse of civilisation since December 1914. It was 1.30 p.m., 20 May, 1916. Worsley, in his own words, "yelled and waved against the skyline but, of course, no one saw or heard".[30] Then, yet again, they solemnly shook hands.

The journey was not over yet, however. Still they had to get down what seemed like 3,000 feet of vertical drop, but was only half. It was enough.

The way ahead seemed much too steep to try. Instead Shackleton, against Worsley's insistent pleas, bore over to the left to follow what seemed an easier path. In exhaustion, however, he had had another lapse of judgment. He was following an unknown water-course, and soon had to pay for his mistake. The valley along which they were stumbling grew steeper, narrower, and turned into a ravine. In the end they were forced into the stream. To Worsley, "It seemed a great hardship to be doing the last lap in this beastly cold water."[31]

In the end, they came to the point where the stream flowed out over the ravine down a half-frozen waterfall. There was in fact a practicable way of escape up the sides of the ravine but to Shackleton and his companions, however, it seemed absolutely impassable. They would have to retrace their steps and find a better way. That, however, said Shackleton, "was scarcely thinkable in our utterly wearied condition".[32] So they decided to go down the waterfall. The drop was about thirty feet. They would have to abseil down the alpine rope. There was no obvious belay, so Worsley suggested that as he was the lightest, he should hold the rope while the others went down, and they could catch him if he slipped.

So first Shackleton, then Crean, slid down on the rope, getting drenched in the cascade. Worsley then bunched up the end of the rope, stamped it into a hollow in a rock, eased himself over the edge, and then, sailor-fashion, slid rapidly down so as to put no strain on the rope until just before he reached his companions' outstretched hands. He then checked hard, expecting the rope to come with him as they caught him:

> To my surprise, it held, and then a strange thing happened. The three of us tugged and hauled on that rope, but could not dislodge it, though it only lay over the rock . . . It might have been frozen; anyway we left it there.[33]

At least they were now standing on dry land. They picked up the objects they had thrown down from the top of the waterfall – McNeish's adze; and Worsley's log, the only record of the expedition they had brought all the way from Elephant Island. Less logically, they had also preserved their saucepan, wrapped in one of their shirts. Except for the wet clothes they stood up in, that was all that they brought with them out of the Antarctic.

Even the last mile was an obstacle. After some snow-covered hills, they reached frozen marshy flats, covered with ice. On this, the now smooth soles of their boots got no grip. In Worsley's words,

> we slipped about, and, being tired, fell heavily several times, which shook us up badly and annoyed us very much, as we considered our troubles should be over.[34]

L

A trio of scarecrows

At 4 p.m. Shackleton, Worsley and Crean reached the whaling station. They had travelled continuously for thirty-six hours, stopping only for meals. They were wet and cold with the penetrating chill that comes from physical exhaustion. They did not care. They had got through. They were hungering only for fresh faces and the sound of another voice.

They were so keyed up that it was almost inevitable the moment should dissolve into low comedy.

The first outside human beings they had seen for over eighteen months turned out to be two boys who bolted at the sight of them. That made them look at each other with different eyes. "We were," said Worsley, "a terrible looking trio of scarecrows but had become so used to ourselves, that we did not mind."[1]

They went on, through the "digesting house", a dark, smoke-stained cavernous shed, lined with boilers for extracting oil from the blubber. Someone wheeling a barrow stared as Shackleton tried to talk to him, and passed on with a grunt. They carried on until they reached the quay, where some men were carrying gear off a whale catcher. Shackleton went up to the man who seemed to be in charge.

He was in fact the station foreman, a Norwegian called Matthias Andersen, although he did not then trouble to introduce himself. He had been at sea for many years before being appointed to his post. *He* was hardly disconcerted by the three figures that had so unexpectedly materialised. As far as he was concerned, the blood-shot eyes, which came from lack of sleep might have come from an overdose of semi-poisonous plonk. Likewise, the wild, drawn look on haggard faces dark with exposure, wind, frostbite and accumulated blubber soot, might simply have been the product of a monumental hangover.

Shackleton, Worsley and Crean were indescribably ragged and filthy. For three months they had been unwashed; for six months they had had no change of clothes. Hair and beards were long, matted, and impregnated with grease. Nor did it help that Worsley had three large safety pins distributed about his person to mend his rags, but which only drew attention to his deficiencies. "We were," he said, "perhaps more terrifying than primitive savages."[2] Andersen, however, was used to "whalers, group VIII" – the lowest of the low.

When Shackleton, in a strained and slightly unreal voice began speaking English, Andersen took it in his stride. He spoke the language as well. He did not know these men, but when Shackleton asked for his namesake, Captain Anton Andersen, it placed him in a way, for Anton Andersen had until recently been the Stromness winter manager.

Now whoever this weird figure really was, he clearly knew someone identifiable. Andersen courteously escorted them the hundred yards or so to the manager's house at the southern end of the station. When they arrived at the neat, white-painted timber building, Andersen left the mysterious strangers outside while he went in to announce their arrival.

The present manager was called Thoralf Sørlle, who now was in charge all year round. There were, Andersen explained, three "funny-looking men" outside, and he gave the gist of a little cross-examination he had conducted on the way. The question of identity they had ignored, but they appeared to know Sørlle. They said they had lost their ship and crossed the island.

In the expressive Norwegian idiom, "one has to hear much before one's ears fall off". Sørlle, a dark-haired, moustachio'd, substantial and authoritative figure,

> came to the door [as Shackleton related] and said,
> "Well?"
> "Don't you know me?" I said.
> "I know your voice," he replied doubtfully.

In fact, when Shackleton had passed through South Georgia in 1914, he had made friends particularly with Sørlle. Sørlle was from Sandefjord, and knew all about *Endurance*. He had actually been on board at Grytviken as Shackleton's guest. Sørlle had known the Weddell Sea since 1892, when he first sailed there with Larsen in *Jason*. He was one of those who in 1914 had firmly predicted that

Endurance would never leave the ice in one piece. In Shackleton's own words, Sørlle went on,

> "You're the mate of the *Daisy*,
> "My name is Shackleton," I said.
> Immediately he put out his hand and said, "Come in. Come in."
> "Tell me, when was the war over?" I asked.
> "The war is not over," he answered, "Millions are being killed. Europe is mad. The world is mad."[3]

Shackleton's immediate reply, according to Worsley was:

> "I'm afraid we smell." But [Sørlle] replied: "That doesn't matter, we're used to it on a whaling station.!"[4]

Shackleton asked Sørlle to take their pictures. Unfortunately he had no film so, as Worsley put it, "The world lost a picture of its three dirtiest men."

Sørlle sent his steward to prepare hot baths. Then he sat the three men down at table. They were dirty, but they had been given up for lost, and they were his guests. Therefore they had to eat. They were plied with coffee, scones, cakes and bread. Sørlle guessed, no doubt, that they would be hungering for farinacious food. Meanwhile he summarised the war for what Worsley called "three Rip Van Winkles, who listened in amazement to what had happened".[5]

In his calm, deliberate manner, and heavy accent, Sørlle talked on, and Shackleton for once played the listener. Shackleton let the words roll over him, drinking in the sound of another human voice, allowing isolation to be broken. In any case Shackleton could not really grasp what Sørlle was saying. Sørlle himself had a puzzled look as if he were recounting some incomprehensible saga.

Most modern polar expeditions had returned to be jolted by the pace of change but, as Shackleton put it, "I suppose our experience was unique."[6] They had truly stepped out of the past. When they left civilisation, the war had still been an old-fashioned one of movement, with comprehensible casualties. Now they had to grapple with the alien concept of a deadlocked war of position, with futile static battles that cost more lives than whole wars past. The sheer scale of slaughter passed their understanding.

Harder yet to grasp was the technical innovation. There was the German use of poison gas for the first time on 22 April, 1915, at Ypres. There was submarine warfare. There was, above all, the war in the air. It was all too much like once-derided futuristic novels come true.

Sørlle could only give the bare bones of events. He could not convey the atmosphere or, indeed, the idea of total war. He was not a belligerent, he was the citizen of a neutral country. To him, both sides seemed equally unbalanced. Besides, South Georgia, although it was British soil, seemed somehow a neutral haven. It was all so unreal and far away.

Sørlle, however, was able to relate the *Aurora*'s misadventures. Even that seemed somehow remote. For what counted now was to fetch the men at King Haakon Bay and then rescue those left behind on Elephant Island.

But first, after coffee, they shed their rags, one by one, and went into the bath. "I don't think I have ever appreciated anything so much as that hot bath," said Worsley. ". . . it was . . . worth all that we had been through to get it":

> Before bathing, I saw myself in the mirror . . . three days before . . . living under the boat – I had attempted to wash my face with snow [but] had . . . merely rubbed soot and blubber into a sort of polished paste. The result was awful.

Slowly the accumulated grime of months dissolved. Yet somehow, it was "clean dirt". There was none of the depressing filth of cities. "After the bath," Worsley continued, "came the somewhat difficult operation of shaving."[7] The steward, meanwhile, had fetched new clothes from the station stores. Within an hour or two, "We had ceased to be savages," said Shackleton, "and had become civilized men again."[8]

Then came a vast meal. The steward "looked after us like a hen with three chicks", as Worsley put it, "and evidently considered us his own peculiar property".[9] Late that night, when Shackleton and Crean were lying in the first proper beds they had known for months, unable to sleep from the tumult of impressions, the steward again tended them, with tea, bread and butter and more cakes.

Sørlle, for his part, had seemed almost as glad as his guests to see new faces. When he got the gist of Shackleton's tale, he immediately ordered a whale-catcher called *Samson* to raise steam and fetch the men from King Haakon Bay. By the time Shackleton and Crean were being served their late snack in bed, Worsley had gone on board.

Worsley did not feel at all resentful. He was merely sailing as a passenger to show the way to the camp. As *Samson* drew away from the gloomy mountains, and steamed out of Stromness Bay, Worsley lay down to sleep, "in a comfortable bunk", as he put it, "with clean sheets":

> The last sound I heard was a rising S.E. gale, which blew all night, beginning five or six hours after we had got through. Had we been crossing that night nothing could have saved us.[10]

Shackleton had stayed behind to start the rescue of his men on Elephant Island. It was almost a month since he had sailed away. Every hour now seemed a reproach.

Shackleton feared that perhaps there had been a hitch in settling the accounts from his visit on the way south in 1914. If there were, Sørlle was too tactful to mention it. First thing on Sunday morning, with deep snow blanketing the land after the blizzard of the night, he took Shackleton by motor boat to Husvik in order to find a ship.

On South Georgia there was no cablehead or wireless yet. Admittedly that meant Shackleton was still cut off from home, but by the same token the outside could not instantly obtrude. That made the island a kind of limbo in which to cushion the shock of meeting an unfamiliar world. Also, it postponed the dismal necessity of coping once more with finance. For all its hardships, the Antarctic was a place where money did not count. Above all, Shackleton could rescue his own men himself.

At Husvik, a large steam whaler called the *Southern Sky* happened to be laid up for the winter. She was the best available ship for the rescue, but she belonged to an English company. There, too, isolation was a blessing. No time need be wasted in cabling her owners; or, for that matter, enquiring after Shackleton's finances. He was instantly lent the ship, and given all necessary stores.

Nor was there any trouble in getting a crew. The whole whaling station appeared to volunteer. That included Ingvar Thom, a Norwegian captain whom Shackleton had met on South Georgia in 1914, and who happened to be in Husvik commanding a transport ship called *Orwell*. A large, solid figure, with drooping moustaches, high cheekbones, pointed head and piercing eyes, Thom looked like a medieval sculpture of a Viking. He offered to sail with Shackleton in any capacity. Shackleton made him captain of the *Southern Sky*.

On Sunday afternoon, work was started on getting her ready for sea. Next day, Worsley returned on *Samson*. Because of the gales, he was delayed, but he did have with him McNeish, McCarthy and

Vincent. When he landed at King Haakon Sound Worsley, in his own words,

> heard McCarthy say disappointedly: "Well, we thought the Skipper would have come back, anyway." I said: "Well, I'm here," and they stared . . . They had been in my presence daily for [almost] two years, but failed to recognize me after a bath, a shave, and a change of clothing.[11]

At King Haakon Bay, there had been a lull in the weather, as if especially timed, so that Worsley could easily find the camp. The whole boat party had survived, and the first part of the rescue had succeeded. Understandably by now Worsley felt that "Providence had been with us".[12]

With him, Worsley also brought back the *James Caird*. The Norwegian whalers, in his own words,

> would not let us put a hand to her, and every man on the place claimed the honour of helping to haul her up to the wharf. I think Shackleton must have felt it was one of his proudest moments. The [gesture] was so spontaneous . . . that it was quite affecting.[13]

That evening, Captain Thom gave a little reception on board *Orwell* for Shackleton and his companions. They went into a saloon "full of captains and mates and sailors", as Worsley put it, "and hazy with tobacco smoke". Shackleton talked about his journey from Elephant Island.

Afterwards, three or four of what Worsley called "white haired veterans of the sea came forward":

> one spoke in Norse, and the manager translated. He said he had been at sea over forty years; that he knew this stormy Southern Ocean intimately . . . and that never had he heard of such a wonderful feat of daring seamanship as bringing the 22-foot open boat from Elephant Island to South Georgia, and then to crown it, tramping across the ice and snow and rocky heights of the interior, and that he felt it an honour to meet and shake hands with Sir Ernest and his comrades. He finished with a dramatic gesture:
>
> "These are Men!"
>
> All the seamen present then came forward and solemnly shook hands with us in turn. Coming from brother seamen, men of our own cloth and members of a great seafaring race like the Norwegians, this was a wonderful tribute, and one of which we all felt proud.[14]

Shackleton recorded the scene in another way:

> I do not wish to belittle our success with the pride that apes humility. Under Providence we had overcome great difficulties and dangers, and it was pleasant to tell the tale to men who knew those sullen and treacherous southern seas.[15]

On Tuesday morning, Shackleton sailed off in the *Southern Sky* for Elephant Island. It was 23 May, almost exactly a month since he had set sail on the *James Caird*, and three days since he had stumbled into Stromness. Shackleton, even more than before, radiated the indefinable force of someone who made things happen. It was exactly the quality that the whalers understood.

With him Shackleton had Crean and Worsley. For McNeish, Vincent and McCarthy, he had arranged passages back to England directly from South Georgia. From McNeish and, especially, Vincent, they parted without regret. McCarthy, on the other hand, Worsley gratefully remembered as a "big, brave, smiling, golden-hearted Merchant Service Jack".[16]

> After being on short rations for so long [said Worsley] we had developed a positive passion for food . . . we had five good meals a day, and at least as many snacks. The Norwegians seemed to think that they could make up for all that we had gone through if they could only persuade us to eat continuously, and they did their best.[17]

LI

"Urgent need immediate rescue"

Just before midnight on 31 May, the Admiralty in London received a cable from Port Stanley in the Falkland Islands: "Sir Ernest Shackleton arrived today".[1] It was only one of many signals that night flooding through the sober building at the entrance to the Mall. Shackleton had made contact with the outside world on the very day that the Battle of Jutland, the last fleet action ever to be fought by the Royal Navy, was taking place. It was an uncanny coincidence.

At dawn on 1 June, as a second cable about Shackleton reached the Admiralty from the Falklands, an eighteen-year-old midshipman on HMS *Royal Oak* noted in his diary: "Decided to return to England . . . with I am afraid our mission hardly successful."[2] It was a melancholy end to the previous afternoon when, in his own hopeful words,

> we all went to General Action Stations. Our Silk [battle] Ensign was hoisted . . . Gunfire increases. Can see the flashes. Had a slight interval for tea & then closed up again.[3]

It was hardly the morning after Trafalgar. Despite a crushing numerical superiority, Admiral Sir John Jellicoe had been fought to a depressing stalemate by the German commander, Vice-Admiral Reinhard Scheer. Because German shells were better than British shells and German armour-plate better than British armour-plate, three British battle cruisers were blown out of the water.

The Admiralty was not alone in hearing from Shackleton that fateful night. It so happened that Campbell Mackellar, loquacious as ever, was dining with Emily Shackleton at her home in Vicarage

Gate. With him was Tryggve Gran, still offering to join a relief expedition. After dinner, as Mackellar related,

> we sat . . . discussing all the pros and cons of Shackleton's chances . . . and we talked about him the whole evening, till I noticed it was twelve o'clock and we rose at once to go. Lady Shackleton came out into the hall with us while Allan her Scottish maid with her for so many years, stood at the open door to intercept any passing cab for us. She hailed one successfully, and as she did so the telephone bell rang. We bade a hasty goodnight as Lady Shackleton went to the telephone and it being raining we ran down the steps and jumped into the cab. They tried to stop us, Allan even running after the cab, but we were gone. It was the news of Shackleton.[4]

It had come from Ernest Perris at the *Daily Chronicle.* He had just received a cable from Shackleton. Next morning, the headline splashed across the front page: "SAFE ARRIVAL OF SIR ERNEST SHACKLETON AT FALKLAND ISLANDS".

Even in the midst of war, Shackleton was news. He was above the battle. The Berlin press also reported his arrival. Reprinting an interview with Emily in a French newspaper, which arrived via a neutral country, the *Vossische Zeitung* admiringly commented on the "character and perseverance of her husband".[5] In London, another kind of enemy was overwhelmed, in spite of herself. "Shackleton or no Shackleton," Kathleen, Scott's widow was moved to say, "I think it one of the most wonderful adventures I ever read of, magnificent."[6]

From the newsprint, Shackleton's half scowling portrait stared out. He had something in common with Vice-Admiral Sir David Beatty, a fellow Anglo-Irishman, the luckless commander of the battle cruisers at Jutland. Despite his setback, Beatty remained, with his jaunty air and cap aslant, the darling of the public. Both Shackleton and he, oddly enough, had an actor's face.

Of Jutland, there was nothing in the papers for two days. Shackleton made a welcome diversion from the British Army bogged down in a dreary war of attrition, and the murderous deadlock on the Western Front that the Navy was to break. "FIFTEEN MONTHS ADVENTURES IN THE GREAT FROZEN SOUTH"[7] ran the banner headline on 2 June, "103rd day of Verdun Battle" ran the smaller cross head underneath, hinting at the slaughter of French and Germans trying to bleed each other to death. Column after column, however, was devoted to Shackleton, and the long cable he had sent detailing his adventures. It was only the following day, 3 June, that Shackleton was dethroned from the front page by the first report of Jutland. Even so, he shared the leader page, at least in the *Daily Chronicle*. "The spirit of the British Navy," ran one leading article stoutly, "will not be impaired by a check due to the great superiority of the enemy in ships and guns at a given place and given time." The other leading article more cheerfully said, "Send help quickly to the Antarctic."[8]

In his cable to the *Daily Chronicle*, Shackleton had succinctly summarised his rescue voyage:

> 26th [May] enter large area pancake ice owing unprotected condition [*Southern Sky*] stood north. 27th renewed attempt . . . found streams of packed [ice] 28th made final attempt ice too formidable for eighty ton unprotected whaler . . . also view shortage coal reluctantly decided turn north for assistance Falklands this decision caused great disappointment generous Norwegian friends.[9]

As well it might. Captain Thom, no more than Shackleton, relished the idea of outside help. In any case, as a Norwegian, part of the national character would make him sympathise entirely with anyone forced to turn back with an unaccomplished errand. He parted from Shackleton, and sailed back to South Georgia with regret.

Among the whalers, Shackleton had left behind the sort of memory out of which legend is born. At least, on South Georgia, he felt he had been among friends. He had only made for Port Stanley now because, from where he was stopped by ice, seventy miles short of Elephant Island, it was considerably closer than South Georgia, and because it was also the nearest cablehead.

According to *John Bull*, this was Shackleton's reception at Port Stanley:

> On May 31st, a solitary whaler made its way into Port Stanley and dropped anchor. A bearded figure, with curly hair falling to his shoulders, endeavoured to go immediately ashore. He was stopped by the customs officers, but refused to reveal his identity. At length, however, finding matters too warm for him, and possibly afraid of being taken for a German spy, he swore the two officers to secrecy, and thus landed.

Shackleton wished to arrive incognito, because he was under contract to the *Daily Chronicle* and had to make certain that his report was exclusive. "After a somewhat hurried visit to Government House," *John Bull* continued, Shackleton

> fled to the cable office and sent off a 2,000 word Press telegram. Having waited till about 11 o'clock next morning, he condescended to reveal himself – but not a soul in Stanley seemed to care one scrap! Not a single flag was flown . . . And why? An old kelper [Falkland Islander] remarked, "'E ought ter 'ave been at the war long ago instead of messing about on icebergs."[10]

Well might Shackleton wish himself back among the whalers of South Georgia. *John Bull*, to quote someone who knew Port Stanley, "clearly expressed [the] point of view taken by the Falkland Islands of the Imperial Trans-Antarctic Expedition in general and Sir Ernest Shackleton in particular".[11]

The governor, Douglas Young, nonetheless, was civil. An amiable, minor administrator of Empire, he had Shackleton to stay with him in the largish villa that here was the ubiquitous Government House of British rule. What Young could not do, however, was immediately to find Shackleton a ship.

To Shackleton, this was an almost unbearable check. He had assumed that on the Falklands, at the edge of the Antarctic, there must be some vessel that could be used. He deeply regretted having sent Captain Thom away so soon. The days dissolved into a nightmare of waiting. Luckily, he still had with him Worsley and Crean.

The Admiralty had arrangements for a search expedition well in hand. Shackleton's arrival at Port Stanley simplified the task. But Shackleton fretted as the cables came and went. He expected help from the Admiralty, but at the same time he was humiliated by having to depend on them for the rescue of his men. He did not yet understand the world to which he had returned. It was a world in which, for the first time in modern history, the British had enforced conscription. Britain was involved in total war, and in total war only an official body had the resources to look for lost explorers.

Even that had limitations. HMS *Avoca*, a British armed merchant cruiser at Port Stanley, might have taken Shackleton to Punta Arenas in the Straits of Magellan. Someone at the Admiralty, however, sharply minuted that *Avoca*

> cannot remain waiting on Shackleton's convenience . . . men o'war cannot be delayed in war time for matters not connected with the war.[12]

At least in one way Shackleton himself had not changed since 1914. "I . . . can tell you," he wrote to Emily, "when I get back money will be all right":

> I have had a year and a half of hell, and am older of course, but no lives have been lost, though we have been through what no other Polar expedition has done. It was Nature against us all the time the cable [to the *Daily Chronicle*] but barely describes a little of what it was. Wild and Crean were splendid throughout.[13]

Even allowing for Shackleton's constitutional dislike of writing, there was something curiously perfunctory about this first letter after eighteen months in the ice. The one real touch of warmth was when he asked to be remembered to Elizabeth Dawson-Lambton. That expressed the genuine sense of debt he felt towards his earliest benefactor.

Rosalind Chetwynd was still much in Shackleton's mind. In the first flush of return, however, he did feel a twinge of remorse at the memory of the quarrel with which he and Emily had parted.

Emily, for her part, was realistically accepting the position – or was she pathetically clinging to a hope? She received, unexpectedly, a letter from Douglas Mawson, who was in England doing war work.

"The news of the return of Sir Ernest heralded in a week of intense excitement did it not – " wrote Douglas Mawson, "though perhaps the North Sea fight [Battle of Jutland] – Kitchener's death* fell flat on you after the news of Sir Ernest."[14] Mawson felt he had to write something, if only for Emily's sake. She, meanwhile, wrote to Hugh Robert Mill:

> The news was indeed a wonderful & glad surprise, & I can hardly realize it yet, having tried to school myself to another year's suspense.

Perhaps Emily and her husband, behind the façade, both understood that their marriage could not be revived. Regret, pity, and other surrogate emotions remained but love, alas, was dead. Even so, Shackleton still clung to Emily as his sheet anchor.

"I am so thankful," Emily added to Mill, "he rescued his men so far . . . instead of being *fetched*!!"[15] That was the heart of the matter. Shackleton had averted the ultimate disgrace. It was working for him in a way that, in his barely controlled agitation at Port Stanley, he perhaps divined.

When the news of *Southern Sky*'s failure arrived, with Shackleton's terse appeal: "urgent need immediate rescue",[16] the Admiralty had acted. For the relief of Elephant Island, the old *Discovery* had already been obtained from the Hudson's Bay Company, but

* Field Marshal Lord Kitchener, Secretary of State for War, was killed on 5 June when the cruiser HMS *Hampshire* mysteriously sank while carrying him on a mission to Russia.

it would be at least three months before she could actually sail. Under the British flag, no other ice-strengthened ship was immediately available. Within a few hours, therefore, the Admiralty had requested the Foreign Office to ask the governments of Argentina, Chile and Uruguay "whether a suitable vessel can be obtained and promptly despatched".[17]

From Port Stanley the governor had suggested to the Colonial Office that the Argentine be asked to send the *Uruguay*, in a repeat, as it were, of the Nordenskjöld rescue thirteen years before. Nothing came of this, but in Buenos Aires, the managers of Grytviken, the Societa Argentina de Pesca, offered to rescue Shackleton's men themselves. C. A. Larsen, they hoped, would be in command. Other South American offers reached Shackleton at Port Stanley. Finally, he accepted one from Montevideo, not because the ship was necessarily the best, but because it would be the first to start. It was a steam trawler, *Instituto de Pesca No 1*, belonging to the Uruguayan fisheries research institute. The Uruguayan government provided the ship, her commander, Lieutenant Ruperto Elichiribehety, and her crew, immediately, free of charge. Exactly why was hard to say. Partly, perhaps, it was because, as one Uruguayan put it: "The world was following with anguish the results of the drama being undergone by the men abandoned on a desolate island, and the desperate attempts of their leader to save them." Possibly it also had something to do with the ambivalent attitude to Britain that the Uruguayans shared with most Latin Americans. It would decidedly be a feather in their cap were they to succeed where the British Empire, with all its might, could not. Perhaps again the clue lay in calling Shackleton "*el héroe irlandés*" [the Irish hero].[18] Ever since Irish mercenaries had led the uprisings against Spanish colonial rule, there had been an affinity between the South Americans and the Irish,

In any case, the *Instituto de Pesca No 1* left Montevideo for Port Stanley on 9 June. Three days earlier, the Admiralty in London had cabled to the British minister in Montevideo that

> In view of inexperience of commander [of *Instituto de Pesca No 1*], could you arrange that Captain [C. A.] Larsen, experienced seaman who knows Elephant Island should join trawler. For particulars of Captain Larsen, apply to His Majesty's representative in Buenos Aires.[19]

Larsen, in fact, had been back in Norway for two years farming, more or less, in retirement. He was restless now, and longing to return to sea. He strenuously denied, however, that he was going on the relief expedition. For one thing, Larsen was reputed to have had a brush with the Royal Navy. In 1904, when he landed in South Georgia to found Grytviken, he had apparently raised the Argentine flag. That was because of the nationality of the Compania Argentina de Pesca, but when the news reached Port Stanley, it was not well received. As it was, the Argentine laid claim to the Falklands, and this could only encourage demands for South Georgia too. A British warship apparently was despatched to Grytviken and compelled Larsen to haul down the Argentinian flag.[20]

Nor had Larsen any desire to make his comeback with an Antarctic voyage in midwinter. Because of his own experience on Paulet Island Larsen, *The Times* reported, "believes that Sir E. Shackleton's people will be able to capture sufficient supplies of seals and penguins even without firearms".[21] In other words, they could last the winter, and when the summer came, a relief ship could go down with no risk.

Larsen, however, assumed that Wild and his companions would have laid in a stock of food before winter came down. He made no allowance for the difference in national psychology while Shackleton would have understood only too well that his men depended on luck and the last moment. After all, his mind worked the same way. Difficult as Larsen would find it to believe, the party on Elephant Island would be on the verge of starvation. They had to be rescued soon.

On 16 June, the *Instituto de Pesca No 1* reached Port Stanley. Her engines were faulty, her bottom was foul. She was neither fast nor safe enough for the task. The crew of twenty-six nonetheless appeared "to think they are out for a picnic", as Worsley put it, "ordered 200 botts. spirits . . . squashed by E.H.S.".[22] Next day, after coaling, the *Instituto de Pesca No 1* sailed for Elephant Island with Shackleton, and also Worsley and Crean. In Worsley's words, they were "thankful to step aboard . . . for the time we had spent in kicking our heels about the cable office . . . had got on our nerves, and Shackleton himself was in a fever of impatience".[23]

Also on board was Lieutenant Ryan, of HMS *Macedonia*. He had sailed from Montevideo as official British representative. *Macedonia*, an armed merchant cruiser, had been stationed half-way between the Falklands and Montevideo to transmit radio messages.

The *Instituto de Pesca No 1* had stormy weather all the way. On the third day out, at dawn, Elephant Island hove into view. It was now the middle of the southern winter. Twenty miles offshore, a solid field of pack ice barred the way ahead. With Worsley's prompting, Lieutenant Elichiribehety tried to push on between the floes. It was soon all too clear that, unless the trawler got out quickly she would be beset herself and, since she was not built for the ice, she would have gone down immediately she was pinched. On top of it all, coal was running short. "Therefore," as Worsley put it, "although Shackleton was nearly heart-broken, we were compelled to return." He added,

> It was a dreadful experience to get within so short a distance of our marooned shipmates and then fail to reach them. At one time we were actually facing the camp, and had it not been for a . . . low-lying mist they would have seen us. With each mile that we put between the island and ourselves our spirits sank lower, and we were not altogether sorry when a gale sprang up and took our minds from the waiting men.[24]

The *Instituto de Pesca No 1* reached Port Stanley again on 25 June, with bunkers nearly empty, and engines ominously knocking. The Uruguayan government offered to have her dry-docked and made ready for another attempt; but that, Shackleton felt, would take too long, so he sent the trawler back with thanks.

HMS *Glasgow*, a light cruiser of the Royal Navy, was at Port Stanley when Shackleton returned. On board was Commodore John Luce, Senior Naval Officer, South-East Coast of South America. Luce was wholly sympathetic to Shackleton in his bafflement and distress. He coaled and repaired the *Instituto de Pesca No 1* for her return to Montevideo. He also had Worsley to stay on board, lending him his cabin. Shackleton, as before, was the guest of the governor.

Luce's job was to patrol up and down offshore and keep German merchant ships bottled up in the neutral South American ports. It was all very quiet. *Glasgow* was a veteran of the Battle of the Falklands. Since then, she had seen no action, and Luce was getting rather bored. On 29 June, he cabled the Admiralty for permission to try and rescue Shackleton's men "on the possibility", as he phrased it, "of gales having driven ice away since last attempt. Every care will be taken not to allow 'Glasgow' to get amongst ice."[25]

"Your telegram not approved," came back the austere reply next day. The possibilities at Port Stanley were exhausted, but the mailship *Orita*, meanwhile, opportunely put in. On 1 July, Shackleton and his companions sailed with her to try their luck at Punta Arenas.

Punta Arenas, part of Chile, one of the most southerly towns in the world, the capital of Patagonia, and the main port of the Straits of Magellan. With its low wooden buildings clustered along wide streets, it looked like a gold rush town. It had the air of a temporary settlement built for nomads. It was neutral, but generally pro-German. The harbour was dotted with German merchantmen laid up because of the war. Nonetheless, for Shackleton it was more congenial than Port Stanley. For one thing, it was larger. It was a frontier town and colonial outpost and thoroughly cosmopolitan, also less parochial and censorious. It was receptive to Shackleton's personality in a way that Port Stanley was not. To quote a local newspaper,

> With face much wind-burned, square of chin, with heavy brow overarching deep-set grey-blue eyes telling a tale of strain and constant care, but brightening not seldom with joviality and good humour; solid, forceful and infinitely determined, – such is Sir Ernest Shackleton.[26]

Punta Arenas was the centre of a large and prosperous British colony living around the Straits of Magellan. That for Shackleton had undoubtedly been one of its attractions and there Allan Macdonald took care of him.

Macdonald was the vice president of the British Club. Through the club, which included wealthy sheep farmers, he raised £1,500 for Shackleton almost literally overnight. With this he chartered a rakish, oak-built schooner of 75 tons called the *Emma*, a well known seal poacher laid up for the winter. Punta Arenas, an outpost also of the Latin world, believed in live and let live.

Not only the British colony rallied round. A rich Chilean called Francisco Campos made a handsome contribution too. Shackleton's appeal still cut across class and nationality. He undoubtedly charmed the governor of the territory, Don Fernando Edwards, and the naval commander, Admiral Lopez. On 12 July, Shackleton sailed from Punta Arenas on his third attempt to rescue his men. It was little more than a week after he had arrived. He found himself provided, free of charge, with a naval vessel called the *Yelcho* to tow him part of the way. *Yelcho* was forced to turn back south of Staten Island, and *Emma* was left to carry on alone.

Shackleton was Master for the voyage; Worsley, First Mate, and Crean, Second Mate. A scratch crew of six had been signed on: "Barbados nigger cook," Worsley enumerated, "American engineer, two Norwegian ABs, one Chilian AB & the Andorran Republic AB."[27] One of the sailors had been twelve months in jail for seal poaching in the self-same ship but, as Worsley put it, "This did not worry us as we found him a good and cheery seaman".

Worsley had commanded schooners in the South Pacific and, in his own words, "rather looked forward to the voyage. I soon found, however, that this was a very different proposition. In a seventy foot schooner far south of Cape Horn in the depth of winter you can have quite a lively time. We did."[28]

Emma had an auxiliary diesel motor. The marine diesel of those days, however, needed skilled attention. Of that, the engineer was incapable. *Emma* had to make her way mostly under sail alone through almost constant gales. She careered violently against the waves like a wild horse, the temperature steadily dropped, and rigging and canvas started to ice up. Some of the crew collapsed under the strain. The upshot was that about a hundred miles short of Elephant Island they were stopped by a solid belt of pack ice.

Wooden ship though she was, *Emma* was not strong enough to be forced through; so, for the third time Shackleton had to turn back. "So deep were his emotions," said Worsley, "that, in contradistinction to his behaviour after the first two attempts, he did not even speak of the men on the island now." Worsley went on,

> I dreaded the landing, for I knew that to return to port would be so very different from all that Shackleton had hoped, and that to step ashore without having accomplished our object would be like rubbing salt into an open wound.

Emma had to beat up to Cape Horn against the prevailing westerlies. It was virtually one continuous gale all the way. "The wear and tear of this period was dreadful," as Worsley put it. "To Shackleton it was little less than maddening . . . he was . . . human enough to become irritable with me and to treat me rather as though I could have prevented the gale had I so chosen. So far from minding this," Worsley loyally said, "I was glad that he should have some little outlet for his misery."[29]

To unburden himself, Shackleton sat down in the cabin to write a letter, not to Emily or Rosalind Chetwynd, or even Elspeth Beardmore; but to his daughter Cecily:

> I am very anxious about . . . our men for they must have so little to eat now . . . We are very short of water, and have not been able to wash since we left South America . . . but that is nothing for I had no wash from October last year until 25th May this year . . .
>
> I will have many stories to tell you . . . when I return, but I cannot write them. I just hate writing letters but I want you to get this to know I am thinking of you my little daughter.[30]

Finally, on 3 August, after three weeks at sea, *Emma* beat up into Port Stanley. She arrived just after dark.

> Shackleton [said Worsley] was taking his disappointment very badly. As I had feared, the sight of the land to which he had counted on

> bringing his men . . . cast him into the depths of despair. For the first time in three years I saw him take a glass of whiskey. He was unaccustomed to it and it affected him at once.[31]

"Conditions this winter evidently extremely severe,"[32] he told Perris in a spate of cables when he landed. *Emma* was too weak for another attempt. "Wooden steam whaler or the Discovery or sea going ice breaker only suitable vessels," Shackleton informed the Admiralty:

> Urge . . . immediate dispatch of ice breaker or Discovery. Breakers operating in White Sea either Russian or Canadian should now be free failing this how long would it take sending Discovery Falklands.[33]

To this there was no immediate reply. *Discovery*, however, was known to be leaving England soon. The governor urged Shackleton to settle down at Port Stanley and wait. Shackleton found it hard to agree. The main street of Port Stanley, as he put it,

> has the slaughter-house at one end and the graveyard at the other. The chief distraction is to walk from the slaughter-house to the graveyard. For a change one may walk from the graveyard to the slaughter-house.

"Ellaline Terriss," Shackleton went on, mentioning the celebrated Edwardian actress, the wife of Sir Seymour Hicks, "was born at Port Stanley – a fact not forgotten by the residents, but," he waspishly concluded, "she has not lived there much since."[34]

In any case Shackleton could not settle down to wait so long as his men might be on the verge of starvation. He was "deeply affected by the delay", in the words of one report, "and his friends are worried by reason of the effect on his health which his anxiety and depression may cause."[35]

At least Shackleton could use the necessity of returning the *Emma* to her owners as a pretext to escape from Port Stanley. He cabled the British Association at Punta Arenas for a tug; and through them the Chilean government obliged with the *Yelcho* again. She arrived on 9 August; departed next day with the *Emma* in tow, and on 14 August reached Punta Arenas. Shackleton had to be helped ashore, mysteriously incapacitated.

At home, meanwhile, Shackleton's enemies were having their say. A Scottish newspaper, the *Strathspey Herald*, almost certainly inspired by William Beardmore, asked why Shackleton

> was allowed to go playing the giddy goat at the South Pole in the interests of nobody and nothing but himself, why was he allowed to take away useful men whose services might have been utilised in war . . . there are men on Elephant Island who might have been more useful and quite as much entertained in Flanders and Salonika. We have very little use for Sir E. Shackleton.[36]

Of this, and other attacks, Shackleton was not aware, but all along he had sensed hostility in the messages coming out of London. At Punta Arenas, he now received from the Admiralty a cable saying that the *Discovery* would arrive about 20 September. "Captain has instructions to embark you at Port Stanley," it ran, "Letter sent you . . . through Governor Falklands, copy by Captain Discovery."[37] At this, Shackleton decidedly smelt a rat. "Have you instructed . . . Captain Discovery . . . place himself under my orders," he peremptorily cabled back on the 17th August, "Please reply here immediately."[38]

To Ernest Perris, meanwhile, Shackleton urgently cabled, asking him to obtain the Admiralty's instruction. Perris cabled back,

> Impossible to reply to your question except to say unsympathetic attitude to your material welfare on part of Mawson and [Admiral Sir Lewis] Beaumont and customary attitude of Navy to Mercantile Marine which it seems resulted from desire of Admiralty to boom its own relief Expedition.[39]

This message, as Perris well knew it would be, was intercepted by the Admiralty through the wartime censorship. "Strongly advise patience until you know details," he ostentatiously ended, "then exercise skill and tact in getting round difficult but not insuperable position."[40]

The Admiralty orders were already on their way out in *Discovery*. Perris now tried to discover what they were, so that he could cable them to Shackleton. As a newspaper editor, however, Perris was an equivocal figure to the Admiralty. The chief censor minuted,

> If these orders *are* cabled out, Sir Ernest Shackleton (who will not like them) will spend some more cash in cabling back to this country to try and get the decision . . . rescinded . . . if Admiralty orders . . . are to be cabled by anybody it should not be any outside party but by the Admiralty itself, and I see no necessity for the latter.[41]

The chief censor was Captain Sir Douglas Brownrigg. Emily Shackleton, lobbying for her husband as best she could, found him "narrow". Sir Douglas, in fact, had been a naval friend of Scott's. For that reason, or some other, he did not favour Shackleton. On 24 August, Sir Douglas met Perris at the Admiralty and

> told him we had decided to wait till Sir E.S. cabled Admiralty direct: [as he put it] also I told him we thought his wire to Sir E.S. describing attitude of Admiralty very unfair: he did not agree & said "it was his view" & that was all.

All Perris could now do, knowing that Sir Douglas would read every word he sent, was to cable Shackleton guardedly to ask the Admiralty himself.

Shackleton had still not received a reply to his cable of 17 August. "Your . . . silence," he now cabled the Admiralty, "leads me suppose supreme command invested Commander Discovery. Trust this is not so." The Admiralty replied,

> Captain of Discovery to embark you and carry out as far as possible measures you advise for rescue of men, Command of vessel and all on board and responsiblity for action remains in his hands.[42]

By now, however, Shackleton was no longer in Punta Arenas. As the messages came out of the cable office, he had grown angrier and more humiliated. With him almost always now was Crean who, in the words of a local resident, "seemed to be his bodyguard . . . and would watch over him, even to the extent of warning him not to have another drink."[43] However, the *Magellan Times*, the organ of the British colony, reviewing his experience so far, said,

> Sir Ernest showed a courage no less than the best of our race have shown in the battlefields of France, Gallipoli and Mesopotamia.[44]

The local Chileans now unreservedly admired Shackleton too. They entirely sympathised when he expressed a fierce desire to rescue his own men, not caring who helped him, as long as it was not the British Admiralty. It was a point of honour which they, as Latins, perfectly understood. Shackleton therefore asked the naval commander at Punta Arenas to lend him the *Yelcho* for one more attempt to reach Elephant Island. After a rapid exchange of telegrams, the naval headquarters in Santiago agreed.

It was, in every sense, a forlorn hope. The *Yelcho* was a steel lighthouse tender of about 150 tons, originally built as an ocean-going tug. Even properly maintained, she could not survive the pack. As it was, paint had long since disappeared from her hull. Plates were dented. Rust was flaking off. Her engines and boiler were suspect.

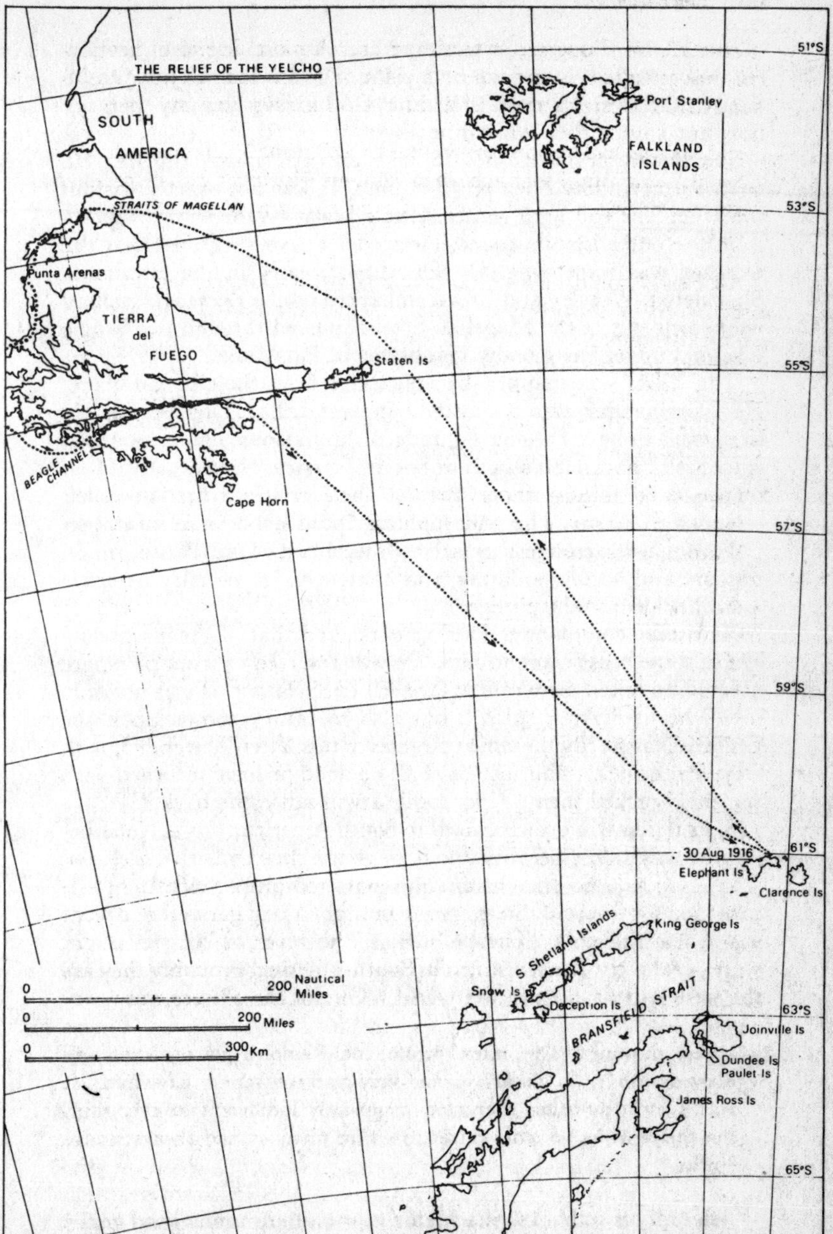

THE RELIEF OF THE YELCHO
SOUTH AMERICA
Port Stanley
FALKLAND ISLANDS
STRAITS OF MAGELLAN
Punta Arenas
TIERRA del FUEGO
Staten Is
BEAGLE CHANNEL
Cape Horn
30 Aug 1916
Elephant Is
Clarence Is
King George Is
S Shetland Islands
Snow Is
Deception Is
BRANSFIELD STRAIT
Joinville Is
Dundee Is
Paulet Is
James Ross Is
0 200 Nautical Miles
0 200 Miles
0 300 Km
51°S
53°S
55°S
57°S
59°S
61°S
63°S
65°S
76°W
74°W
72°W
70°W
68°W
66°W
64°W
62°W
60°W
58°W
56°W
54°W

Shackleton, however, was desperate. Almost any risk, he now felt, was justified. It was not only pride. The *Discovery* as he wrote to Emily, had been "a devil of a time. God knows how my men are now but I hope they will all be alive."[45]

Shackleton promised not to take the *Yelcho* into the ice. He counted on finding open sea this time. It was not exactly wishful thinking. The southern winter, after all, was on the wane. Reports from the outer islands round Tierra del Fuego suggested that the weather was improving. On 25 August, early in the afternoon, Shackleton, Worsley and Crean embarked on the *Yelcho* and, sailing westwards out of the Magellan Straits, passed through the Beagle Channel under the gloomy mountains of Patagonia.

The *Yelcho* was manned by volunteers from the Chilean Navy. Her commander was a naval lieutenant called Luis Pardo. He happened to be a Freemason, indeed the Masonic connection had smoothed Shackleton's path in South America. Shackleton had no objection to sailing under Pardo. Their relations had been left refreshingly vague. The philosophical Spanish motto, *Se las arreglar* ("Things will arrange themselves") summed it up. Pardo, quiet, obscure and accommodating, was content to let Worsley navigate and Shackleton take charge.

As titular commander Pardo understood that, if there was any glory, some must come to him. He was resolved to triumph where others had failed, he wrote in farewell to his father. It was not only in a "humanitarian spirit", but also to bring renown upon the Chilean Navy. "By the time you receive this letter," he ended, with a typical quixotic flourish, "I shall be dead or have returned with the shipwrecked men . . . for alone I will not come back."[46]

Shackleton was growing used to South American ways. Nonetheless, he was mildly perplexed to observe the crew embark *a la chilena.* That is to say, no one (justifiably) expected proper clothing to be provided for the cold. So everyone brought along garments to wear *under* their uniforms. "These Chileans," however, as Worsley put it, were "by far the finest seamen in South America. Probably they are the best Latin sailors in the world." One of the officers was

> a very dashing little Chilean lieutenant, Ramon Aguirre, who came aboard with . . . a guitar . . . and very glad we were to have him. He was a most amusing character, completely indifferent to everything but the pleasure he could extract from the moment, and always in high spirits.[47]

After all his setbacks, Shackleton now had uncannily good going. South of Cape Horn, the weather was fine and clear; the sea almost smooth. "Shackleton," as Worsley put it, "was a different man – vigorous and alert, urging the engineers to drive the little ship hell-for-leather."[48]

By the evening of 29 August, the *Yelcho* was sixty miles from Elephant Island, in open water still. Winds or currents or both had driven the pack off. *Yelcho* had her chance to slip through.

Around midnight a thick fog came down. Shackleton dared not wait for this to lift. He was afraid of the pack closing in. Taking command of the ship, he closed the island, blind.

Again, Worsley, with his mysterious talent, made an exact landfall. About 10 a.m. he saw through the fog the spume of waves on the North-West Breaker. This was a reef that marked the point of Elephant Island. A little later he sighted Seal Rocks. He had got his bearings, and he set a course eastwards along the coast. Soon the *Yelcho* was threading her way through bergs grounded on the shoals. The fog was lifting, and out of the dissolving wraiths appeared the glaciers and peaks of Elephant Island. A few patches of drifting ice threatened the advent of the pack. It was now manifestly a race against time.

By about 1 p.m. the *Yelcho* was close inshore in what to Shackleton, Worsley and Crean seemed familiar surroundings. They were perplexed at not yet seeing the spit. It was Worsley who glanced back and grasped that they had overshot the mark. Without a proper chart, they could only navigate from memory. They had approached Cape Wild from the west, and they had never seen that side before from seawards. It was only when they had gone past, and its eastern profile opened up, that they were able to recognise what was indeed that same view which they vividly remembered fading astern on the day they had sailed away on the *James Caird.*

LII

Cape Wild

"Things dont look too well now for our getting relief from the Cairds party," Greenstreet meanwhile was writing at Cape Wild on 28 August,

> as it is now over 126 days since they left & even if they had been waiting for the Aurora to come round they should have been down here by now. I shall give them till about Sept. 10th & after that I shall think that something has happened to them & that we shall have to rely on getting to Deception Island & getting relief from there.[1]

Most of the men on Elephant Island were near the end of their tether. It was not only that they were running out of food. About this time, Orde-Lees recorded Hurley saying "I believe in eat & drink then snuff out."[2] Hope was starting to fade. It was not clear how much longer Wild could keep the threat of mental disintegration at bay.

On 30 August, everyone was out along the foreshore gathering limpets which was now virtually their sole source of food. Lunch that day was a stew made of old seal bones. Hurley described what happened next:

> Whilst the party were in [the hut] at lunch Marston & I were without shelling limpets, when I called Marston's attention to a curious piece of ice on the horizon, which bore a striking resemblance to a ship. Whilst we were so engaged a ship rounded the [point]! We immediately called out Ship O, which was instantly followed by a general exodus of cheering & semi hysterical . . . inmates.[3]

Blackborrow could not yet walk. Orde-Lees and Hudson stayed behind to carry him outside so that he should not miss what Orde-Lees called "the thrilling sight". The ship, however, appeared to be going past. In Hussey's words, "We . . . had the fear that those on board . . . might not have seen us. The terrible thought crept into our minds that we would then be left on Elephant Island to die, for by this time we could not have held out for more than a few days."[4]

Marston, for one, kept his head. Ought they not, he suggested, to make a smoke signal? There was a stampede to make a fire with blubber, sennegrass and a can of paraffin. "Much blaze & explosion of can," as Orde-Lees put it, "but little smoke."

Every morning for months, Wild had ordered everything packed and ready to leave, in case rescue came that day. Originally, it was to keep up morale. Now it bore fruit. As the ship turned, and headed for the spit, the baggage was brought down to the beach. Among the motley bundles, were Hurley's three precious tins with his films and plates. Somehow, he had brought them safely all the way from Patience Camp in the boats. Greenstreet too, in the best traditions of the sea, had saved the log of the *Endurance*.

The mysterious ship meanwhile approached to within 150 yards of the shore. "We saw she was an iron tug or whaler with Chile ensign (naval)," Orde-Lees noted in his diary. "This puzzled us." She was

> not at all the wooden polar ice-breaking craft we expected to see . . . Whether she was here by accident or design was still a mystery.[5]
>
> Now that the end was in sight [he later wrote in retrospect], we all realized the debt of gratitude we owed to our splendid capable leader Wild . . .
>
> Every man is prone to make errors of judgement at times . . . but if ever a man worked hard and conscientiously to keep up the spirits and maintain the general peace & welfare of a community containing one or two "difficile" members that man was Frank Wild who . . . by his buoyant optimism, dogged determination . . . and calm demeanour had pulled us through these trying months of waiting.[6]

The ship now stopped. A boat was lowered, and started pulling for the shore. Almost the whole party was down on the beach, waving and feebly cheering. The square-set figure of Shackleton was soon recognised standing up in the boat. Crean was there too. "I felt jolly near blubbing for a bit," as Wild put it, "& could not speak for several minutes."[7] As soon as he was within hailing distance, Shackleton called out to ask whether all were well. There was a tense note of anxiety in his voice.

When the ship had first appeared round the point, Macklin ran to the mast above the entrance to the cave and hoisted an old Burberry shirt as a flag. The halyard, however, jammed, so that it was flying at half mast. Shackleton immediately jumped to the conclusion that some of his men had died. His relief when the little figure of Wild standing on a rock answered that all were well, was indescribable. Orde-Lees painted the scene in his diary.

> At last someone shouted out to Sir Ernest "are you all well . . ." to which he laughingly replied "Don't we look all right now that we've washed" for evidently our filthy condition had not failed to attract his notice and then we burst into a hearty laugh which was followed . . . by the rowers as soon as they saw what he was laughing at, then like silly school-girls, we all started giggling and looking at each other's black faces.[8]

The bay was free of ice. The water was practically calmer than it had yet been. Nonetheless an awkward sea was running, and Wild directed the boat to a safe landing among the rocks.

As soon as the boat was alongside, Shackleton urgently ordered instant embarkation. A change of wind might bring the ice back at any time. He was desperately anxious to get away from this "Godforsaken spot", as he put it, as quickly as he could. Within a few minutes, the boat was on its way back to the *Yelcho* with half the party and all the baggage on board.

Wild, Orde-Lees, Clark and Greenstreet returned to the hut to clear up. Orde-Lees stayed behind after the others "to show Sir Ernest over the premises", as he put it, for the hut had been built since Shackleton sailed away, and therefore he had not yet seen it. Nor, as it turned out, did he have any intention of seeing it. It would have wasted precious time. Besides, he even had a superstitious disinclination of setting foot on Elephant Island again. He stayed in the boat, and, when he returned for the second load, he waited just long enough to embark the remainder of the party. With the boat well on its way back to the ship Orde-Lees, as he himself whimsically told the tale,

> was seen running frantically along the beach waving his arms and screaming with alarm for fear of being left behind. It would have served old "always last" right if he had been left like Ben Gunn on Treasure Island but Sir Ernest took undeserved compassion on him and headed the boat once more for [land] and the last man to leave the accursed

> spot took a flying header into the boat where he arrived with a grateful . . . flop inflicting minor injuries on . . . Chilean sailors amongst whom he fell.
>
> Sir Ernest rather sarcastically congratulated him both on his punctuality and his aerial manoeuvres cautioning him to be more careful in future, but it was not the time for strafing worn out maroons and Sir Ernest, appreciating the humour of the situation, let the culprit off more lightly than he has done in the past for many a less offence.[9]

As soon as the boat was alongside, Shackleton told Pardo to get under way. The *Yelcho* had reached the spit just after 1 p.m.; it was now only 2 p.m., and she was heading out to sea as fast as her engines could turn.

With twenty-two extra men on board, the *Yelcho* was uncomfortably cramped, but nobody minded. As Hurley put it,

> I am not very susceptible to emotion, but this happy reunion with our comrades, whom we had almost given up as lost & our happy release, with the lonely peaks like mute sentinels witnessing our departure has left an indelible impression . . . Oh! the bliss of once more feeling the motion of the sea, the music of fresh though foreign voices and to sense at last that our anxieties & privations are ended.

Excitement on that first night did not allow much sleep. Hurley

> lay on the floor wrapped in a blanket meditating & thinking how ineffably more pleasing to be kept awake by the throb of the engines that are hurrying us back to life, than like smouldering logs on Elephant Isle, hearking to the stentorious snores that ebbed away our existence.[10]

Now it was the turn of the men from Elephant Island to adjust to the outside world. Shackleton had thoughtfully brought down a collection of London newspapers and periodicals. The latest were at least a month old, but even the events of eighteen months before were new to those just breaking isolation. "It seems that the world has altered much," James wrote soberly. "Feel rather like 'Wells' sleeper."[11] In the words of Orde-Lees,

> We fairly wallowed in the papers and naturally found the war news thrilling. The whole world is at war . . . Germany has put up a wonderful fight but the tide is just beginning to turn against her. Three million men have been killed already.

Orde-Lees was the one man on board to articulate the glimmerings of culture shock. "People think nothing of being killed," he went on, "nowadays it is looked on as an honour. Opinions have changed on all sorts of subjects. They call it the Roll of Honour now instead of the casualty list . . . Maybe one or two of us congratulated ourselves on our luck in still being in time to do our bit."

Orde-Lees noted other things: "The theatres and the changes in women's attire were the most interesting. We noted very little change in motor car construction but enormous strides in aviation."[12]

But in the isolation of a small ship heaving her way alone through an indifferent ocean, events seemed even more unreal than they had appeared to Shackleton on South Georgia. There was a touch of immediacy in a copy of the *Daily Mail* with a picture of *Endurance*. It was Shackleton's tale of the rescue that really affected his men. To them, it was astonishing that in the course of four months he had not only carried out an open-boat journey, but then organised what amounted to four separate expeditions. "Good old Boss!" said Hurley.

> We all admire . . . his indefatigable pertinacity, determination & enduring hopes & honor him accordingly. [He] had the supreme satisfaction in rescuing us by his individual efforts.

It was, Hurley considered, all due to Shackleton's "powerful personality, which I believe would coax St. Peter into letting him pass the golden gate." Hurley also found it

> intensely gratifying to observe that though the world is so much engrossed in the business of warfare . . . there still exists practical manifestations of Humanity. For here we have nations entirely foreign to us, manning & equipping expeditions for our relief. Surely this is evidence of the goodwill existing between them & the Empire.[13]

Orde-Lees, for his part, admired the Chilean officers and crew

> for their courage in coming down into the . . . Antarctic without any previous experience, with practically no equipment, at a moment's notice.[14]

Between Shackleton and the Chileans on board, there was an air of conspiracy. They all were notably pleased that the *Discovery*, now three weeks out from England, would not be required.

Late in the evening of 2 September, *Yelcho* entered the Straits of Magellan and, early next morning, anchored off a cold storage plant at Rio Seco, about five miles from Punta Arenas. Shackleton went ashore, and the works foreman, in the words of the manager, ran down the jetty to greet him and, getting things a bit muddled, said, "Welcome, Captain Scott", to which Shackleton replied, "Captain Scott be so-and-soed! He's been dead for years!"[15]

Shackleton was too good a showman to arrive unannounced. He had stopped at Rio Seco to telephone ahead; and then waited a few hours before going on. When *Yelcho* reached Punta Arenas, what appeared to be the whole population was cramming the waterfront to welcome her. As she steamed past, the ships in the roadstead blew their sirens. When the noise subsided, cheer upon cheer rose from the crowd ashore. "This," said Orde-Lees, "was no mean home coming."[16]

Then the men from Elephant Island landed on the wharf, and marched through the town to the music of a brass band. Shackleton had told them not to shave or cut their hair before landing, so that they could appear in their wild, romantic state, as it were. They were still in their original, filthy Elephant Island clothes. "The welcome we got," said James, "was wonderfully spontaneous & genuine not only from the numerous English colony . . . but from Chileans: Even the Germans & Austrians had their flags out."[17]

They first went to a hotel where, as James put it, "a barber attacked us". Then they were distributed among the British colony for their first baths for ten months. They were made to feel absolutely at home.

Shackleton, meanwhile, belatedly received the Admiralty cable with the orders for the captain of *Discovery*. "Command," it said, "remains in his hands."[18] Shackleton hurried on board a mailboat about to sail, and dashed off a letter to Emily:

> I have done it. Damn the Admiralty: I wonder who is responsible for their attitude to me. Not a life lost and we have been through Hell. Soon I will be home and then I will rest.[19]

LIII

Aurora and the end of the expedition

Hudson was the only one actually to hurry home. Released from the confinement of Elephant Island, his mysterious ills, mental and physical, cleared up. "He felt," in Orde-Lees' words, "that his country had need of him and couldn't wait another minute."[1]

The others remained at Punta Arenas to rest and enjoy their fame. Shackleton was certainly enjoying his. The Falklands he completely ignored. He let the governor learn of his success through an intercepted wireless message from Punta Arenas.

" 'No one seemed to care a cuss about him,' are the words which describe Shackleton's arrival in Port Stanley," the *Magellan Times* indignantly recalled.

> What a reception to a man who . . . had risked death a hundred times to save his fellow men left on Elephant Island. They did not seem to care a "cuss" about the men marooned on Elephant Island either, for if it had been left to the people of the Falkland Islands, Frank Wild and his gallant little party would still be fighting against the gaunt spectre of starvation.[2]

Soon after landing at Punta Arenas, Shackleton cabled the Foreign Office in London suggesting that he visit Santiago, personally to thank the government of Chile for their help. The proposal, Viscount Grey, the Foreign Secretary, cabled back, "seems very suitable".[3]

It was not only that Shackleton wished to extend the season of acclaim. "As from the dead we came back to find the world gone mad,"[4] he told one journalist, but he was beginning to sense the burden of the distant war. He felt the urge to serve. He could be a British propaganda weapon in the campaign against German influence in Chile, and perhaps help to bring Chile into the war on the side of the Allies.

On 15 September Shackleton left Punta Arenas for Valparaiso in the *Yelcho* with most of his men. Nobody actually wished to sail in the *Yelcho*. The Chilean authorities, however, wanted it, because it would make a national demonstration.

At Valparaiso, and then at Santiago, the reception was as sensational as at Punta Arenas. Huge crowds came down to the quayside, and lined the streets. By his personal magic, Shackleton appeared as the right kind of hero.

The expedition, of course, had been an unmitigated failure. On the other hand, as he wrote to Emily, "I have been the means under Providence of carrying out the biggest saving out of disaster that has ever been done in the Polar regions North or South."[5] From that Shackleton had, consciously or otherwise, squeezed out a phenomenal personal success.

"The British Army failed . . . at Mons," added Orde-Lees, making comparisons with a defeat early in the war,

> and carried out a retreat of unparalleled masterfulness, which was nothing but glorious . . .
>
> The retreat of Sir Ernest Shackleton against overwhelming odds was none the less honourable and equally as successful in its own little sphere.[6]

Shackleton undoubtedly had the sleight of hand to create the illusion of victory out of defeat. It was in one way yet another version of the British taste for the glorious failure. To that, however, Shackleton added something very much his own. He radiated the magic of the survivor, which undoubtedly spoke to a Latin. He had made himself something more than merely the victor in defeat. He was a hero flawed only by the absence of the winning touch. It was the kind of pathos that appealed. Shackleton never showed the flaccid face of complacent mediocrity. Single-handed he repaired some of the damage done to British prestige by the Battle of Jutland. His journey through Chile became a triumphal progress.

On 3 October, Shackleton left Santiago by train across the Andes for Buenos Aires. At the town of Los Andes, not far from the Argentine border, the train was stopped, at midnight, for a civic reception.

> SHACKLETON is the crystallization of Human Endeavour triumphing over the Forces of Nature [ran a welcoming leaflet] Hosanna!
>
> WILD shows us how a man of Character and Faith can arrive at the most perfect abnegation. Hosanna!
>
> Both make, together, the symbol of those lofty sentiments of Love

for the Truth, of ones's Country, of Science and of Humanity, which bear Mankind onwards with ardour towards its ideal, which places men above suffering, above destiny, which makes them heroes . . . Hosanna![7]

The reception in Buenos Aires was not so effusive, for it was only the British colony that really took notice. However Shackleton went on to Montevideo to thank the President personally for Uruguayan help with the second relief voyage. On 7 October he returned to Buenos Aires. His plans by then had been changed.

From Punta Arenas, Shackleton had sent eight of his men, under Cheetham, directly to Buenos Aires. There, they were all to meet again for the journey home. Afterwards, Shackleton would travel out to New Zealand to take command, as he assumed, of the *Aurora* and rescue the Ross Sea party. But at Santiago, from the stream of cables trailing in his wake, Shackleton had learned that obstacles were being raised.

The Australian, New Zealand and British governments had agreed jointly to organise and pay for the relief. The Australians were "prepared to rescue the men of the expedition but want to have nothing to do with Shackleton," Douglas Mawson wrote to Edgeworth David, in an echo of the past. "His crooked dealings have brought it on himself."[8] Both he and David were disenchanted with Shackleton over publication of the *Nimrod* scientific results. After seven years, it was still not complete; "what a chapter of accidents", in David's words. Shackleton , he went on, was "not the helpless 'ingenue' in finance that he would have us believe". David agreed that the Australian and New Zealand governments "do not wish to deal with Shackleton".[9]

Of this, Shackleton was unaware, but what he did know was that the Australians, with the agreement of the New Zealand and the British governments, had appointed John King Davis to command the *Aurora*.

Davis, after all, had been on the *Nimrod*; and he and Shackleton had been cronies over the gold mines at Nagybanya before the war. Davis, however, was no longer exactly Shackleton's man. Had he not refused command of *Endurance*?

Shackleton wanted Stenhouse as captain of *Aurora*. He had been her original Chief Mate, and brought her back to New Zealand. There was, however, complete mistrust of Stenhouse. The drift of the *Aurora* and the plight of the party at McMurdo Sound were felt to be his fault. To make the whole affair thoroughly galling, Davis had been placed in absolute, overall command of the whole expedition.

Shackleton was certain there was a plot to let *Aurora* sail without him. If he now went to England, he might not be able to get away in time if, perhaps, at all. At Buenos Aires, therefore, he decided to turn while the going was good. Early one morning he took the international express back over the Andes to Chile once again.

Thus it was that the *Endurance* expedition ended, with an anticlimax, on a platform of the Retiro railway station in Buenos Aires. At 7 a.m. on Sunday 8 October, all Shackleton's men came down to say goodbye. "We have properly broken up," Macklin remarked. Mostly they were going home, as he put it, "to take a part in this awful war." Bakewell, the Canadian, however, decided to go sheep farming in Patagonia. "All things have an end," Macklin wistfully recorded, "we shall each go our different ways. It would be nice if some day we could all meet again."[10]

Shackleton took Worsley with him; both for company on his travels and, if necessary, to command *Aurora*. "We both felt a bit down," in Worsley's words, when the train drew out, leaving all their companions behind.

By his abrupt change of course, Shackleton had disconcerted the authorities. "As the vessel [*Aurora*] belongs to Shackleton," Lord Liverpool, the governor of New Zealand, cabled to the Colonial Secretary, "difficult situation is being developed."[11]

Originally, Shackleton intended heading straight for Sydney to deal with the Australian government. As he sailed up the Pacific coast from Valparaiso, however, cables overtook him to make it plain that he was not officially wanted in Australia. He then decided it would be tactically better to make for New Zealand instead, and intercept *Aurora* at her point of departure.

It was not only pride in personally saving all his men that had sent Shackleton back across the Andes. The return to civilisation also meant grappling with finance, and, as usual, Shackleton had no money. He believed that he could "get certain assistance America",[12] as he cabled to Perris, and went on through the Panama Canal, across to New Orleans, and thence by train to San Francisco.

> As usual Sir E. travels free [Worsley wrote in his diary]. Everything opens before him. Royalty wd. not be treated better – if as well. Kings & Presidents compete for the honour of entertaining him & he pays for nothing except his cablegrams & an occasional Hotel bill.[13]

Yet from San Francisco, Shackleton had to tell Emily, "I have simply been up to my eyes in work trying to get money here but it has been no go." It had been "beastly work". He did not want to write too much because "the censor seems right at my side".[14] Because of the war, of course, the mails in and out of the United Kingdom were heavily censored.

"Put embargo on departure Aurora if attempts sail before arrival."[15] Shackleton cabled his old friend, Leonard Tripp, in Wellington. On 10 November, Shackleton then embarked on a small steamer called *Moana*, and sailed out of the Golden Gate, with three weeks to brood on his predicament as he crossed the Pacific.

"I am deadly tired of it all," Shackleton wrote on board to Janet Stancomb-Wills. To her he was writing at least as intensively as to Emily. "I . . . cannot understand why they are so set against my trying to rescue my own men."[16]

When Shackleton turned, he had cabled to Emily that if there had not been a war, he would have brought her out to meet him. In some ways, perhaps, both of them preferred to postpone their reunion. At a distance Shackleton, protesting always that he "hated" writing letters, found it easier to unburden himself:

> I did think that at last I was going to get home after all these last two years of strain and anxiety: but it cannot be helped: I can see that [it] is absolutely necessary that I should carry through this show as Leader of the Expedition but once it is over there will be rest I hope.

"I am old and tired," he went on, brooding still over the official attitude to the relief of Elephant Island. "Anyhow I beat them on their own ground." He went on in his jerky, inconsequential style,

> There is not much I can say here in this letter: I am longing to see you . . . and to see *my our* children once more . . . I want you to see Wild, McIlroy and Crean see Crean separately: Wild and Mick are men of the world and will tell you the whole story of the expedition . . . I am not a good hand at telling about the show . . . only I want you to know that I have been having a tough time of it from the day we left South Georgia.

"You must not mind [being] older," Shackleton told Emily in answer to a melancholy letter:

> We all are that: I am quite grey at the temples and threads throughout: but de rien it is all in the day's work. Anyhow you & I have the children who live our lives over again and that should help a good bit.

"It was and still is such an awful shock," Shackleton wrote about Daisy Dorman, who had died while he was away:

> You must if you believe in the future at all realize that you will see her again I have no doubt at all about the future and I have been near it lots of times.

"Don't worry about this trip," Shackleton said, making an old, familiar point. "I am really very cautious." It was quite true, as usual. Emily was reminded to "keep in with Miss Stancomb-Wills she is absolutely charming". But, said Shackleton, Emily was not to let Elizabeth Dawson-Lambton "get jealous of her so dont say too much about her financial help". Even now, Janet Stancomb-Wills was virtually paying for the upkeep of Emily and the children. "Dear Elizabeth," said Shackleton, "has done all she could."[17]

Another, different Shackleton faced Worsley as they sailed over the Pacific. He was moody, and obsessed with all the official opposition to himself. Worsley, who by now regarded Shackleton with almost uncritical hero-worship, was correspondingly angry and irritated.

When Shackleton reached Wellington on 2 December he was met by Leonard Tripp. Tripp had known Shackleton since 1903, and they had last met in 1909 when Tripp visited England. A quiet, unremarkable man, Tripp considered himself a "personal friend of Shackleton's"[18] and had obviously fallen under Shackleton's spell. That had not stopped his understanding Shackleton's character. He took the precaution of going out to meet Shackleton in the stream.

As Tripp expected, Shackleton was defiant and belligerent. "I was much amused," said Tripp, with his lawyer's detached appraisal of a difficult client, "because he evidently loves a fight."[19] By hook or crook, Shackleton proposed to have Davis removed, and sail on *Aurora* in command himself. When Worsley suggested pirating *Aurora* Shackleton was in such a state of mind that he even half seriously considered the idea.

Tripp was not a prominent citizen, but in the informal manner of a small country, he did have access to politicians. Straight from the boat, he took Shackleton to see Dr Robert McNab, the New Zealand Minister of Marine. Between them they tried to placate Shackleton, but only partially succeeded. Shackleton was in his truculent mood; his speech emerging in staccato bursts, all the Irish coming to the top. McNab nonetheless took an instant liking to him.

McNab asked Davis, who was then in Dunedin preparing *Aurora* for sea, to visit Wellington and talk to Shackleton. Davis was shocked at the change in his old leader. Shackleton had aged. He was now bitter, resentful, and full of self-pity. This was not the Shackleton who had introduced him to the Grand Duke of Baden in Germany before the war by announcing

> "And this, sir is Davis . . . He is descended from the Irish Kings, forty of whom were killed in one battle." The Grand Duke seemed rather taken aback by this piece of information and so, to tell the truth, was I![20]

In 1914, when Shackleton had tried to make him captain of *Endurance*, Davis called him

> an Irishman of great persuasive power whom few people could resist, [but] he was addressing another Irishman who had already made up his mind.[21]

From the same point of view Davis now decided to tell Shackleton some "unpleasant truths", as he phrased it, "so that he might . . . appreciate the nature of the ground he was treading on".

Almost alone, Davis grasped that Shackleton had not yet adjusted to the strange embattled world to which he had returned. He still had the pre-war attitudes. To him, the lives of a few men marooned in the Antarctic were of supreme importance; yet against the carnage of the battlefields, they scarcely counted. Davis told Shackleton that he

> seemed unable to realize, yet, that the war was engrossing the thoughts and emotions of the majority of civilized man and that, consequently, people were apt to be impatient with polar exploration. And, when every man in uniform was either a real, or at least a potential hero, people were also a little impatient of polar explorers in general . . .

All this Davis, tall, thin and deadly serious, delivered coldly and directly, with no attempt to save Shackleton's feelings:

> I also pointed out to him that the three governments [of Britain, Australia and New Zealand] engaged in making war on a scale hitherto unimagined, had nevertheless agreed to . . . make the relief of his men possible, solely on humanitarian grounds.

If, said Davis, Shackleton felt that the Australian authorities were against him, he had only himself to blame. The Ross Sea party had been sent off without enough money. Australians, private or official, had been casually expected to make up the deficit. This was quite enough to rouse the deep resentment of the "pommie". Shackleton had touched a very raw part of the Australian character.

The Australian government, Davis explained, had not wished to help *Aurora* sail in 1914. They had been morally bullied into doing so by the realisation that unless the depots were laid from the Ross Sea side, the transantarctic party would perish. An enquiry had then revealed the criminal incompetence and slipshod organisation of this side of the expedition. "Under these circumstances," Davis, in his own words, told Shackleton, "it was inevitable that he, as leader, would be blamed for this state of affairs."

Finally, Davis reminded Shackleton that "on the return of the *Aurora* in a desperate condition . . . the [three] governments had been obliged, in war time, to take over a bankrupt enterprise". They had, said Davis,

> spent in the vicinity of £20,000 of public money and I put it to him that, under the circumstances, it did not seem unreasonable that they should appoint their own officer to command what was, after all, their own enterprise.[22]

The upshot was that Shackleton accepted Davis as commander of the expedition. At that, there was more than relief. "His nature was such," as Davis put it, "that it was easy for people to admire him, and I had always been one of his admirers."[23]

The intention was that Shackleton should sail down as a passenger, or rather the owner. He, on his own volition, proposed to sign on under Davis. In Tripp's words, "this came as a bombshell to McNab". It shocked Tripp and Davis too. What Shackleton had not yet been told was that the Australian committee had independently insisted on his signing on as a condition of his going. Tripp recalled,

> McNab . . . said – ". . . I am quite satisfied now that the Australian committee . . . is trying to humble you, and I don't want you to sign on." Shackleton said, "I don't care whether I am being humbled or otherwise; no one knows better than I that you cannot have two masters on one ship, and if we get into trouble in the ice, and it is not known that I have signed on, many of the crew may come to me for advice, and so I am very sorry, but my mind is absolutely made up, and I am going to sign on."[24]

Eventually, Shackleton signed on as supernumerary officer. For this, he was much admired as it was undoubtedly a big gesture to make. However Davis had shown him that his position was decidedly weak, and Shackleton, still the shrewd survivor, recognised that it was the only practicable alternative. He also had the art of doing things with good grace.

Years later, there appeared at the Ambassadors Theatre in London a play called *After My Fashion*. It was about an Antarctic explorer called Starcross, whose expeditions were "fakes", because they were organised for his own personal ambition. Eric Marshall saw it, and in Starcross saw Shackleton. Marshall, still brooding over the uncertainty of the Furthest South in 1909, was now sure that Shackleton had organised the *Endurance* expedition "solely", as he put it, "to prove that he was a great 'leader' ".[25]

There was something in that view, but Shackleton did not want others to suffer for his ambition. He felt an intense and very personal responsibility for anyone who served under him. For his own satisfaction, he felt he had to be present at any attempt to rescue his men, if they were still alive to be rescued.

In any case, Shackleton was able to exploit the situation. Knowing that the antagonism to himself came mostly from Australia, he played on the New Zealander's suspicion of the Australian. He emphasised how the South Americans had helped him unreservedly, and that, now he was among his "own" people, he was treated with resentment. He played also on the irony that he was going to sail as a subordinate in what was legally his own ship.

Davis did not exactly see the irony but, in his own words, "my faith in him was vindicated. The man I had known eight years before had returned."[26] The Australians had urged him to sneak off without Shackleton. So, too, in New Zealand, had Joseph Kinsey, now to be numbered among Shackleton's enemies. Davis had, in fact, been loyal.

At last, on 18 December, Shackleton left Wellington to join *Aurora* at the well-remembered Port Chalmers. With him were Worsley and Stenhouse. They, however, were only coming to see him off. Davis had refused to have either on the ship. That offended Shackleton's sense of loyalty, of course, and it was only under pressure from Tripp and McNab that he agreed.

Shackleton's personality had soon begun to take effect. Those under its spell, now including Davis, were willing to forgive him his failings. "The more I see of him," Tripp told McNab soon after Shackleton had landed at Wellington, "the more I like him especially the way he fights any of his troubles."[27] McNab, for his part, had made himself Shackleton's devoted ally. He arranged for the New Zealand government to pay Worsley's and Stenhouse's salaries as long as necessary, and give them first class passages to England. It was a way both of saving Shackleton some financial burden and of easing his conscience.

"It has been the most trying time of all my life," Shackleton wrote to Emily a few hours before sailing. "Give my dear love to the children and . . . Prospice,"[28] he added, with the old code from Browning, which meant

> "For sudden the worst turns the best to the brave,
> The black minute's at an end."

The day after he landed at Wellington from San Francisco, Shackleton had received a cable from England that £5,000 was required at once to pay the wages of the *Endurance* party. Shackleton wrote to Emily,

> I cannot understand the attitude of those men whom I saved being in such an urgent hurry to get more than their legal amount of money, and not even waiting for that for a little time.[29]

On his way through the Americas, Shackleton had cabled Perris to discontinue the pay of most of the *Endurance* crew. Perris was to explain that "legal position directly Endurance abandoned pay ceased".[30] Nonetheless, Shackleton, as he well knew, had promised on the ice to continue paying his men, and that promise now had to be redeemed. He also had the salaries of the shore party to pay, virtually since the start. That, incidentally, included £30 per month to Dr G. M. Ross, the Canadian dog driver whom Shackleton had not taken, but whom he was obliged to pay for two years because he had broken the contract. Dr Ross had the Hudson's Bay Company behind him.

Tripp immediately started raising a loan for Shackleton among his business friends. As he expressed it, Shackleton was

> perfectly candid saying that if anyone lent him money, the prospects of ever getting it back depended on his health and his not being killed in the war. He let them know definitely that he was going to get to the Front as soon as ever he could.[31]

Within a week Tripp had found the whole £5,000. McNab, moreover, had persuaded the New Zealand government to waive all claims on Shackleton for the money spent on *Aurora*. They in turn persuaded the Australians and, with a little trouble, the British government, to do the same.

"We in New Zealand have always admired Shackleton, because we have felt that he has paddled his own canoe," Tripp wrote pointedly to Sir Harry Wilson, Secretary of the Royal Colonial Institute in London. Shackleton, Tripp said,

> was a leading Antarctic Explorer, who had been honoured by others, being treated with the cold shoulder by the English Government. We

did not want this aspect to present itself; we knew there would be a howl against the British Government in our press and it is most important in these times that there should be nothing to cause friction between ourselves and England.[32]

Tripp had been to Trinity Hall, Cambridge. He visited England from time to time, and understood some of the pressures on Shackleton. He saw the baleful influence of the Little Englanders or, to put it in his own words, it was necessary to look at Shackleton "from an Imperial point of view".

So once more, on 20 December 1916, Shackleton sailed south, "with an easy mind", as said, or at least spared the burden of an extra debt.

"Never before," in Davis' words, "had it felt so good to be at sea." He too had had his share of frustration and provocation in the long months of getting ready to sail:

As the high land of the Otago Peninsular dropped out of sight astern, and the old fashioned jib-boom, decorated with the traditional tail of a shark, rose and fell in wide, unhurried arcs across the southern sky, I experienced a sensation of profound relief.

Aboard *Aurora*, the radio crackled with the morse code of Admiralty messages to shipping, so that despite empty horizons, the war could not quite be forgotten:

But the old, accustomed sounds – the hiss of the seas, the muffled thud of the engines . . . the chirping of a block, the music of that invisible orchestra in the rigging, the old accustomed scents – coal smoke, steam and whiffs from the galley mingled with the smell of tar and paint and the strong but indefinable tang of the ocean; the old accustomed harmony of the routine life of a small ship on passage – these things together created the illusion that we were leaving the war behind us.

Davis had been the captain of an Australian troopship for two years when he joined *Aurora*. "As we retraced our steps over this old familiar road to the South," he said wistfully, "we seemed to have embarked upon a voyage where . . . we were receding into the past. In no one was this seeming reversal of the time-space equation more marked than in . . . Shackleton." As *Aurora* put the miles behind her Shackleton, said Davis tellingly, became "more and more the man I had admired so much in 1907."[33]

Freed from the bonds of life ashore, Shackleton's personality began once more to assert itself. Without meaning to, perhaps, he took the psychological leadership, as he had done before. Davis grasped this; but he still was the captain in command. It was clear now that Shackleton had shown profound insight in acting as he had.

He was in any case unnaturally subdued. "I am anxious more and more," as he wrote in his sketchy diary, "to see our 10 men safe and well then will I rest."[34] On New Year's Day, 1917, he came on deck to find that *Aurora* had got through the pack in a few hours during the night. Going to his cabin he returned with a worn sheet of paper which he handed to Davis. It was, said Shackleton, a New Year's card. Davis deserved it because they were in open water so quickly, and would soon be at McMurdo Sound. It was a printed copy of Rudyard Kipling's *If*, with certain couplets bracketed in heavy lead pencil:

> If you can force your heart and nerve and sinew
> To serve your turn long after they are gone,
> And so hold on when there is nothing in you
> Except the Will that says to them, "Hold on!"

"My dear Davis", Shackleton had written on the back,

> These lines hung in my cabin throughout the *Endurance*'s voyage and were with me on the floe. I now hand them to you on this the first day of a New year which I trust may be of certainty successful as its dawn promises.

"The gift," as Davis soberly put it, "was a characteristic gesture."

On 9 January, the familiar cone of Mount Erebus once more appeared over the horizon, its faint plume of steam rising in a cloudless sky. "Time," as Davis philosophically noted, with memories of *Nimrod*, "is a cunning thief."[35]

It was the anniversary of Shackleton's Furthest South eight years before. And it was the self-same scene that met Shackleton after turning from the Bay of Whales and making for McMurdo Sound, burdened with the broken promise to Scott. Did he remember what he had written to Emily then, nine years ago?

> . . . my heart was heavy within me . . . if I had not promised Scott that I would not use "his" place, I would then have gone on to McMurdo Sound but I had promised and I felt each mile that I went to the West was a horror to me.[36]

If Scott had paid for putting Shackleton in that terrible predicament, the broken promise, like nemesis, had hounded Shackleton all those years, and was implacably hounding him still.

On 10 January, *Aurora* entered McMurdo Sound. The ice was loose enough for unimpeded sailing. First the ship hove to off Cape Royds. Shackleton went ashore to see his old hut, and came back in a subdued mood. Going back to places is a melancholy exercise, and in this case nobody was there. The only trace of the party was an undated note to say they were at Cape Evans.

Off Cape Evans, figures could be seen coming across the sea ice. Shackleton left the ship and went out towards them. With him was Morton Moyes, an Australian who had been on the Mawson expedition, and Dr F. G. Middleton, another Australian. With exquisite tact, Davis had stayed behind, so that Shackleton would be seen to be in command ashore. Slowly the two parties converged. Behind, as backdrop to the scene, was the broad flank of Mount Erebus sweeping up to the heights.

It was a poignant meeting. To the men who had raggedly trudged out from shore, it was the first contact with the outside world for over two years, since December 1914.

Shackleton was profoundly shocked by what he saw. These men were in an even worse state than those had been on Elephant Island. They too were filthy, ragged, and unkempt. Bloodshot eyes stared out from pallid faces. Hair was matted and uncut. Beards were impregnated with grease and blubber soot. This was understandable, given the fact that *Aurora* had been driven off to leave them in the lurch. But beyond that, a wandering expression on their faces, and their unmodulated speech hinted at the lurking mental strain.

With an effort, Shackleton recognised Ernest Joyce. There was a short conversation. Then, to the astonishment of the men from Cape Evans, the three from the ship lay down on the ice. It was, Shackleton explained, a prearranged signal to tell Davis how many of the original party were missing.

What Shackleton had just heard was the futile aftermath of an ironical tale.

In the middle of March, 1916, when Æneas Mackintosh and his companions reached Hut Point after the southern journey to the Beardmore Glacier, they knew they would have to wait until the sea had frozen sufficiently for them to cross to Cape Evans. Early in May, they were still waiting. At breakfast on 8 May, Mackintosh announced that he was leaving that day.

> "Now look sir [Joyce said, as R. W. Richards recalled the scene], you may call me Old Cautious . . . but I wouldn't go to Cape Evans today for all the tea in China."[37]

That was a reasonably direct hint that Mackintosh could not

order anyone to follow him. Hayward, however, had volunteered to go as well. The others were upset, because these were the men who had ridden on the sledges all the way from the south.

> After dragging them back from death [as Joyce put it], they seem to think they can court it again. Ah well! Such is life & what fools we have to put up with.[38]

The ice was thin and dangerous. All previous experience suggested that it would not be safe for another month at least. Besides, a blizzard was clearly threatening. To cap it all, neither Mackintosh nor Hayward had yet quite recovered from scurvy. It was thirteen miles to Cape Evans. They proposed to do the distance at one stretch, even though they had hardly managed to walk two miles uninterrupted since starting to convalesce. Nothing, however, could dissuade Mackintosh from setting out.

Mackintosh could not exactly be classified as a fool, but why he was determined to go was hard to say. Perhaps he had simply grown tired of the primitive conditions of the *Discovery* hut, with blubber the only light and fuel, and the walls hardly windproof. Cape Evans by comparison was a palace.

"As I stood watching the figures . . . disappearing into the gloom of midday," said Richards, "there was a tinge of bitterness in my thoughts at the tremendous effort we had made to get those two back."[39]

Half an hour after Mackintosh and Hayward left, the expected blizzard arrived. "I don't know why these people are so anxious to risk their lives again," Joyce moodily wrote in his diary, "but it seems they are that way inclined."

For two days the blizzard blew. Afterwards, the ice was seen to have gone out to the north. "We are quite happy here," said Joyce, "and do not intend to leave until [the ice is] safe. There is no need to risk one's life without a cause."[40]

It was not in fact until 15 July that they finally reached Cape Evans. It was ten months since they had left. As they approached the hut, the inmates, alerted by the barking of the dogs, came out to meet them. Cope, the so-called medical officer, in Richards' words, said "Hello Ricky . . . I'm not good, I've got appendicitis – I'm shitting nanny-goats turds."

> The other fellows . . . told me that he was not quite normal [as Richards put it]. He'd stay in his bunk all day and wouldn't eat . . . and eat something when everyone else was in bed . . . He was quite irrational.[41]

A few months later, Richards himself collapsed mentally and physically. The strain of the southern journey had been too much. Besides, there was the uncertainty of rescue. Richards was placed in Scott's old cubicle as an improvised sick bay.

Of Mackintosh and Hayward there was no sign. They had obviously been killed when the ice went out. Joyce remarked that "an experience Mack had previously on the sea-ice should have proved a warning".[42] That had been on the return of the *Nimrod* in January 1909. She was stuck in the ice off Cape Bird. Mackintosh had decided to cross over to Shackleton's hut at Cape Royds with the mails. The ice had unexpectedly started breaking up, and Mackintosh was very nearly lost, together with the sailor accompanying him.

Very likely, Richards' collapse also had something to do with the fact that all his agony had been in vain. Spencer-Smith's death, within sight of safety, had been ironic, but truly tragic. Mackintosh, however, had thrown the lives of himself and his companion away. Above all, it was clear by then that Shackleton was not going to get through from the south. All the effort of putting out the depot at the Beardmore glacier had been for nought.

Understandably, Richards went on board *Aurora* straight from meeting Shackleton on the ice, and refused to go on land again. Shackleton, for his part, barely consented to visit the hut, heavy with its memories of Scott.

Shackleton clung to a faint hope that Mackintosh and Hayward might have survived to spend the winter on the other side of McMurdo Sound, but after ten days' search, not a trace was found and, on 25 January, *Aurora* finally headed north again.

By this time, the maroons had practically regained normalcy. Richards in any case had merely been suffering from acute depression. The arrival of Shackleton had in a way been the cure.

All the time in the Antarctic, Joyce and his companions had in different degrees blamed Shackleton, justifiably, for their predicament. There was a cleavage, however, between the British members, who had already met Shackleton, and the three Australians who had not. The Australians

> heard a lot about Shacks . . . when we were marooned [as Richards put it]. The British contingent . . . were loud in his praise but we Australians would not have a bar of this hero worship. We had heard a good deal of the muddle . . . in Sydney and we were not impressed with his choice of Mackintosh as leader.

But, said Richards,

> when we met him and were exposed to the full force of his personality we became as staunch admirers of Shackleton as the others from England.[43]

Not for the first time, Shackleton's personality had overwhelmed people, against their better judgment, perhaps.

Shackleton turned his back on McMurdo Sound with relief. It was too much a graveyard of his hopes for comfort, and he grieved for the three men who had been lost. His reaction as leader of the expedition, however, was characteristic. What he did was to write to Joyce that "I [am] Commander of the Expedition [and] though I was thousands of miles away, the responsibility still lay on my shoulders."[44]

As *Aurora* now made her way back to New Zealand, it was the turn of the men from McMurdo Sound to adjust to the world outside. They had been isolated longest of all, for over two years. Shackleton, as on the relief of Elephant Island, had brought down all the illustrated papers he could. "I still remember," Richards said years after, "the intense shock in the party. We were probably the only people in the whole world who had been completely ignorant of what had gone [on]":

> I think we were all somewhat dazed for the first few days on board. We had left with the more or less naive outlook of the early years of the century and come back to what seemed . . . a world of veritable devils . . . we were stunned, literally stunned . . . our party [went] round for a few days after reading these things . . . with a completely unbelieving and stunned look on our faces . . . We seemed to have come back to a completely different world . . . we just couldn't take it in . . . We just simply couldn't take in that war had developed into such a horrible sort of thing . . . we experienced a sense of acute shock.[45]

Still ruminating on what he had called the "seeming reversal of the time-space equation" that had so changed Shackleton, Davis called it "this strange voyage, that had seemed almost to set time at nought, and be a voyage into the past".[46] He was half regretful when it ended, on 9 February, on arrival at Wellington, New Zealand, and Shackleton as he crossed the gangway seemed to revert to his more complex, shore-going self. That, Davis did not quite understand. Nonetheless, the open-boat journey, the rescue of the men on Elephant Island, and now Shackleton's presence on the relief of the Ross Sea party, had done their work. In New Zealand, Shackleton was welcomed like a returning hero.

"I love you and am coming home soon," he wrote to Emily, patiently waiting in London, or Eastbourne. It was eight months since her husband had returned to civilisation, but Shackleton still had matters to clear up before he could start for home. Beyond that, however, he still betrayed in undertones a curious reluctance to go back just yet.

"I always feel as long as I am doing the work and getting through the fight that all is well," Shackleton, still in New Zealand, wrote to Emily at the end of February, "but I am no good at writing it all up for it seems just like going through it all again. Out here," he went on, "people do not feel the pinch of war":

> indeed the country has never been so prosperous. I have good friends who have helped me greatly; it seems to me, that it needs me personally all the time to be on the spot to clear and settle things [he added, perhaps a little naïvely], and it was a mercy that I went down to the Ross Sea for everything was in a state of chaos. Mackintosh seemed to have had no idea of discipline or organisation and it required all the tact I possessed to square things up. He had made a very bad impression in Australia by the way things were run at the start, but poor chap he is dead through his own carelessness and I wont say any more now.

"I do not think that ever again will I venture far from the homeside and your love," Shackleton went on, in an old refrain, and then, almost in the same breath, tellingly declared:

> I have battled against great odds and extraordinary conditions for now more than three years and it is true that I should have a rest from it all. I would not alter or have changed one bit of the work and all its trials for there is a feeling of power that I like.[47]

By now the inner history of the *Aurora* expedition had leaked out. New Zealand public opinion was for Shackleton. There was a corresponding reaction against Davis. The mayor of Wellington proposed not asking him to a civic reception for Shackleton. Shackleton thereupon issued an ultimatum. If there was to be any reception, it had to be for all his men. Unless the mayor had Davis on his left hand, he, Shackleton, being on the right, he would not go. The mayor acquiesced.

Soon after arrival, *Aurora* was handed over to Shackleton, free of liability, as he had been promised. Because of the war, tonnage was at a premium, and she was quickly sold, to an American firm, for £10,000.

Leonard Tripp, who combined friendliness with firmness, had

taken Shackleton's finances in hand; and Shackleton did not resist. He had at last found the kind of adviser he needed. For this period, as a result, Shackleton's affairs were swathed in exemplary order.

Originally Shackleton had promised to repay the loan that Tripp raised by lecturing in America. Instead, he now used the purchase money for *Aurora*. As a result, before he left early in March, Shackleton had repaid all his debts in New Zealand.

One member of the lending syndicate promptly returned the interest sent with the repayment, adding what he called "a little help to a brave man who has had cruel bad luck and has set us all a bright example".[48]

Shackleton cabled Emily £200. It was a way of making up for the drop in her income because of the war. It was the first money he had sent her for four years at least. He asked her to keep it private. Shackleton's affairs at home were as muddled as ever, and he did not want news of the transaction to reach his creditors. These included Emily's brothers, who, between them, had lent him £6,000, and were patiently waiting for repayment.

Tripp, meanwhile, was concerned about the book of the expedition while Shackleton, as usual, was unenthusiastic. Even more than before, he hated the mechanical business of writing. Once again Edward Saunders was brought in to ghost the book.

Tripp insisted that Shackleton have the vital parts written before leaving "in case he got killed in the war".[49]

On principle, Shackleton now refused to make any money out of the expedition as long as the war lasted. He gave lectures, starting in New Zealand, but donated the proceeds to charity. He devoted one lecture to starting a trust fund for Mackintosh's widow, for Mackintosh had left his family more or less destitute.

To confront his opponents, Shackleton crossed over to Australia before going home. Reaching Melbourne via Sydney in the middle of March, he was met at the station by the *Aurora* relief committee. Shackleton was not exactly radiating charm. He had a certain grim look on his face which his expedition companions would have recognised. He demanded a private meeting. Not very willingly, the committee agreed.

Once they were inside the room, and seated around a table, Shackleton stood up and went for them, bull-headed. Why were they against him? Why had they tried to get *Aurora* away without him? They could hardly say that they thought Shackleton was plucky but reckless. Shackleton passed into his mood of cold fury. Bluntly, he said that he had been treated unfairly. "If I have an enemy," he said, "I would like to meet him face to face and I feel I have got one in this room."[50]

It so happened that with Shackleton was Edward Saunders, sitting in a corner. Saunders had travelled as far as Australia with Shackleton to continue working on the book; and act as an informal secretary. "I received the impression," Saunders said, "that some members of the [committee] had been strongly prejudiced against Shackleton and that personal contact was forcing them to revise their estimate of the man."[51]

Shackleton finally shook hands formally, and marched out of the room, leaving behind him a fairly tense atmosphere. A few moments later, he reappeared in the doorway. The scowl on his face was replaced by a broad smile. He wanted to shake hands with them all again. That, said Professor Orme Masson, Shackleton's chief antagonist on the committee, showed the charming side of his nature. Shackleton had not wanted to quarrel. "Have had Committee on carpet," he characteristically cabled Tripp. "Now feel better and buried hatchet."[52] Not for the first time, his opponents, against their will, had succumbed to his personality, without exactly forgiving him his actions.

The upshot was that Shackleton was asked to address a recruiting meeting in Sydney before he left. Australia depended on volunteers for the armed forces and, as war weariness set in, more persuasion was needed. Because of Shackleton, what the *Sydney Morning Herald* called "the biggest recruiting meeting ever held in Sydney blocked Martin-place".

> As a man from a darkened world [Shackleton declaimed] after nearly two years unknowing, and having no understanding of all that is going on in this world today, when I arrived in civilization I realised one great thing: That was, that this war is not a question of mere patriotism, of mere duty, or of the exigencies of the situation, but it is the question of the saving of a man's own opinion of himself.

This was already archaic language. Shackleton was still speaking as a relic of the age that dissolved in August, 1914:

> Death is a very little thing [Shackleton went on, using the same phrase he had written to Winston Churchill when trying to organize the *Endurance* expedition], And I know it, because I have been face to face with it for 12 long months. All I know is that if a man can save his own soul and be true to himself and his manhood that is what counts . . .

"The blood that has been shed on the burning hills of Gallipoli," Shackleton said in a message distributed later, "and the sodden fields of Flanders calls to you."[53]

When the time came to call recruits up to the platform, "some of the enthusiasm had died down", as one reporter eloquently put it, "and the crowd that had come to hear Sir Ernest Shackleton had dwindled by some thousands".[54]

From Sydney Shackleton started home at last, via America. There, he stayed for a month en route for the lecture tour originally intended to pay off the loan in New Zealand. "Miss your advice,"[55] he tellingly announced to Tripp in one of the cables that, as usual, flagged his trail.

On the *Overland Limited*, from San Francisco to Chicago, Shackleton wrote one of his rare, expansive letters to Tripp. He had gone down well at San Francisco, net takings $2,000, and at Seattle, where he made $2,500. He liked Portland, Oregon too. At Tacoma, however, the hall was half full. Shackleton was guaranteed $500 but, in his own words,

> as it was a woman running this [lecture] I cut my guarantee down so that she would not lose on it. It was not her fault . . . There has been a mistake in the name TACOMA – the T and A should come off and it should read "COMA".[56]

Shackleton's lecture tour, meanwhile, had acquired an unforeseen dimension. On 6 April, three days before he landed at San Francisco, America had entered the war on the side of the Allies.

British stock in America was low. Partly it was due to the perennial Irish question and the aftermath of the Easter rebellion, partly to insular and lacklustre leaders. It was also due to inept propaganda. Sir Cecil Spring-Rice, the British ambassador, believed that Shackleton, with his overwhelming public personality and his Irish connection, would redress the balance. Sir Cecil set great store by Shackleton's last lecture, at the Carnegie Hall, in New York, on 28 April.

In the audience was Sir Shane Leslie, an Anglo-Irish man of letters. On him, the occasion made a vivid and lasting impression, as he later recalled:

> Shackleton was like a man who had discovered the Poles or the equator . . . we were all raised to a state of frenzy . . . you see [we] hadn't dared to send over any generals, so he represented the people who made the British Empire, the pioneers . . . You can see . . . what it meant for the American mind.[57]

Sir Shane had been invalided out of the army after being kicked by a mule. He was originally sent to America to help Sir Cecil

Spring-Rice bring America into the war. A member of the Protestant Ascendancy who had turned Catholic and become an Irish Nationalist, Sir Shane nonetheless supported Britain in the war. Dark-haired, with chubby good looks, married to an American, and in touch with all factions, the anti-British Irish Americans included, Sir Shane was felt to be more acceptable to the Americans than an orthodox Englishman.

The lecture at the Carnegie Hall, as Sir Shane put it,

> was the most exciting, tremendous meeting I ever attended in the United States . . . the emotion between [Shackleton] and his audience was such as you very seldom feel. The only other time I've ever felt it is between Winston [Churchill] and his audience . . . I've never felt the audience played on like an organ by a man talking except Winston and Shackleton, and . . . it hardly mattered what they said.[58]

Sir Shane was a cousin of Winston Churchill – their mothers were sisters – and he was a connoisseur of oratory. Shackleton he wholeheartedly admired:

> for the first time for a long time the British Anthem was heard . . . Shackleton had done his work; it was frantically effective.[59]

Shane Leslie had crossed Shackleton's tracks before. In 1911, on another visit to America, he was staying with his sister-in-law, Anne Bourke Cockran, at her house in Long Island. She showed him a globe on which Shackleton, during his first lecture tour in 1909, had drawn his journeys, past and projected. Now Sir Shane found it all wiped out.

Anne, as Sir Shane put it, was "a devastating beauty" and she and Shackleton "were both taken with each other", although Sir Shane thought that their "love affair was very innocent".

Anne was married to a celebrated Irish American lawyer called Bourke Cockran. He was twenty years older than his wife and, in Sir Shane's words, "madly jealous". It was Cockran who had removed Shackleton's drawing from the globe. Sir Shane, as he told the tale,

> got hold of the visitor's book and [Shackleton's] name . . . was wiped out. Jealousy is a terrible thing. But Anne mastered [Bourke Cockran]. She said "You've no right to be jealous. I admire him, he's a hero, and you know whether I'm a good wife or not" and then I think he fell down on his knees and cried . . . he was a very good-hearted man.[60]

Anne came to Shackleton's lecture, but Bourke Cockran did not.*

When, on 29 May, Shackleton finally landed in England, everything by comparison seemed drab, and his return was hardly noticed. It was not the homecoming he had foreseen when he departed in 1914.

His reunion with Emily dissolved into its usual, melancholy anti-climax. For a little while, nevertheless, Shackleton was pleased with a haven of domesticity. Emily had taken a small house at Eastbourne but, as she resignedly wrote to Tripp, "it would bore Ernest to be here for any length of time". She had taken a flat again at Queen Anne Mansions, in London, so that she could be with him most of the week, instead of only at weekends; for he still had the affairs of the expedition to deal with.

"Through Shackleton not returning," Frank Wild had written on coming home from Buenos Aires in November the year before,

> all the business of the expedition has fallen to me, & you cannot realise what numbers of people I have had to see, (mostly just time-wasters); & what an awful lot of correspondence there still is.[61]

When F. W. White, Shackleton's former secretary, had disappeared, he left a pile of unpaid bills and a tangle of neglected paperwork. Wild had been unable to cope, so Shackleton, when he reached London, had to deal with the aftermath. "The whole Expedition is now paid off and clear," he finally wrote to Tripp in July 1917, "and there are no liabilities."[62]

Frank Hurley, meanwhile, had visited South Georgia to finish shooting his film and take pictures for the book of the expedition. He tried to repeat Shackleton's crossing of the island, but although it was the southern summer, and he was properly equipped, he found it impossible.

Hurley then went to France as official photographer to the Australian forces. In September 1917, he wrote to Douglas Mawson, now doing war work as a transport officer in England, asking for

> a little advice re an affair of Shackleton. He owes me £530 promised faithfully twice to settle [*Endurance* salary] & I gave him certain extensions, neither obligations has he met. I wrote him from here about it but S. ignored my letter. Although we are friends, I am disgusted to think that he should have waited till I got over here to dodge paying. It's just the most contemptible thing he could have done.[63]

* According to Shane Leslie, Cockran taught Churchill "how to pull out the emotional stops".

This was the same man of whom Hurley, a bare eighteen months before, on the ice, had written:

> I especially admire . . . Sir E., on whom the entire brunt of responsibility & decisions fall . . . with an eye to everything & so considerate to the party as to neglect himself.[64]

LIV

South America and Northern Russia

"Have important war work abroad,"[1] Shackleton had exuberantly cabled to Tripp on arriving back in England in May 1917.

Shackleton was not actually obliged to fight. After eighteen months depending on volunteers, Britain had finally introduced conscription. All men aged between 18 and 41 were liable for service. At 42, Shackleton was legally exempt. Nonetheless, as he had repeatedly announced, he was going to join up.

To find more soldiers, the authorities were lowering their standards. Nonetheless, joining the Army meant a medical examination of sorts. Shackleton did not want even Army doctors to listen to his heart. Did he fear rejection? Besides, in war or peace, Shackleton had no wish to sink into the ruck.

The "important war work" of his cable to Tripp was with an American mission to Russia. As *Aurora* was returning from McMurdo Sound, the first Russian revolution had broken out. It threatened the collapse of the Eastern Front, and that meant the freeing of fresh German troops to be thrown against the Western Allies. At all costs the Russians had to be kept in the war. In an historic intervention the Americans decided to prop up a failing ally with technical assistance. Since communications were seen to be a notable Russian weakness, an American railway and transport mission was swiftly assembled to visit Russia and give advice. It was to travel via San Francisco and Vladivostok.

With his talent for meeting people in high places, perhaps through the Masonic connection, Shackleton made contact with the mission as he was passing through San Francisco. "I expect to go to Russia soon after I get home,"[2] he was already writing to Tripp on 21 April, barely a fortnight after sailing into San Francisco Bay.

"No actual news from Russia yet," Shackleton was still writing almost three months later. "Patience had to be a large part of my equipment down south," as he put it, "so I must have the same here."

> I am a little vicious that after people saying why did I ever go South when the great war was on, [I] should have to chase from pillar to post in order to get a job.[3]

Getting to the war was uncannily following the characteristic Shackleton cycle of optimism and bafflement.

Whenever he turned to helping others, Shackleton's name, as usual, was like a magic wand. Orde-Lees, for example, was having difficulties too. He had no desire to return to the Marines. From Punta Arenas he had applied to transfer to the Royal Flying Corps, the predecessor of the RAF. When returning home, Orde-Lees nonetheless found time (an Irish newspaper reported) to visit Rome for an audience with the Pope. Elephant Island had been the last stage in the process that made Orde-Lees convert to Roman Catholicism. Meanwhile, his application to join the RFC was blocked. Shackleton interceded, and the billet was obtained, almost overnight. Orde-Lees then pursued his eccentric career, fighting for the issue of parachutes to pilots. Senior officers opposed the parachute, on the grounds that it was unmanly and would spoil a pilot's fighting spirit. To publicise his ideas Orde-Lees, amongst other things, jumped from Tower Bridge, probably the lowest parachute jump ever made.

In finding a billet for himself, however, Shackleton was consistently frustrated. He was still trying to get to Russia at the end of July. "There is more scope there," as he wrote to Tripp, "even though times are troublous out there."[4] Largely because of tortuous objections by the Foreign Office, the opening with the American mission had disappeared. Instead, Shackleton was negotiating with the Russian representative in London. He wanted to go out and work in winter transport which, as he put it, without conscious irony, "is right in my line".[5] The War Office would give him military rank and pay. The Russian military attaché cabled Prince Lvov who, he said, was the Prime Minister, but the answer was a long time coming.

Shackleton's interest in Russia was not military alone. "All evidence," he told an American journalist, "is favourable to the promise of a new world after the war ends." Shackleton looked ahead to "the regeneration and the splendid freedom of an emancipated Russia". He had swallowed a common illusion. The

Tsar may have been deposed, but the Bolsheviks were lurking in the wings.

"The possibilities of Russia," Shackleton naïvely remarked, "are beyond belief . . . It is not unlikely that she will lead the world in mineral production." It was Siberia that interested him, as it did many others at the time. Only transport, as he put it, was "indeed to make the incredible resources of this immense territory available for quick development".[6] In Siberia, he saw one more chance of that elusive fortune that he always sought. Going to Russia now would be an opportunity to prospect. Shackleton saw no inconsistency in keeping an eye on peacetime business while helping to fight a war.

The summer drifted by. No answer came from Prince Lvov, or whoever was ruling in Petrograd as St Petersburg was now called. Shackleton remained baffled in London, and counted more than thirty members of his expedition, Weddell Sea and Ross Sea branches, fighting with the forces. Sadly though, McCarthy, having survived the open-boat journey, was killed at sea.

"We, his shipmates who truly learned his worth in that boat journey, are proud of his memory," wrote Worsley, himself now in the Navy as captain of an anti-submarine "Q" or "Mystery ship":

> I always felt that, no matter where we were or what exalted company we might have been in, if Timothy McCarthy passed by he must be welcomed to a place of honour and given the best of everything, as befitted a brave man and one of Nature's gentlemen.[7]

Shackleton, too, had always thought a lot of McCarthy; and now McCarthy had gone, while he was reduced to hawking himself round the smug and leaden precincts of Whitehall. With his distaste for authority, it was a very dispiriting experience.

As chaos enveloped Russia, Shackleton found his prospects there becoming unmistakably vaguer. He chose nonetheless to believe that a decision would be coming tomorrow, next week, certainly next month, or whatever he was told. Life with Emily at Eastbourne became unbearably claustrophobic. Shackleton, by choice once more a guest in his own home, went there now only to rest and keep up appearances. "He is getting restless – & is chafing to be off – " Emily wrote to Tripp, "so for his sake I shall be glad when he gets his billet."[8] Before they could quarrel, he would escape to London, from where he would affectionately telephone or, occasionally, write.

Emily saw through it all. She knew she was only one of three women in her husband's life. In London, he was seeing Rosalind Chetwynd. For years she had wanted to be an actress. As Rosa Lynd she was now, at the age of thirty-three, finally, on the stage. When Shackleton returned to England, she was finishing a run with Gerald DuMaurier in *London Pride* at Wyndham's Theatre. Shackleton was as deeply as ever in love with her. To put it another way, he clung to her because, so much younger than he, she gave the illusion of prolonging youth. She was also the woman of strong personality that he still craved, and she still had her house in Park Lane.

The third in this triumvirate was Janet Stancomb-Wills, with her own kind of hold. She was providing him with money which, as he said, he could not take, except as a loan. Already from the Falkland Islands, before rescuing his men, he had written to explain that he had seen no mountains, and so had named a boat after her:

> I have seen [on] this voyage God in his splendour [he wrote then]. I have been down in the depths yet grasped at glory and all through I have remembered and thought of those who helped me to go forth.[9]

To Miss Stancomb-Wills, with her very English combination of virtue strangling passions underneath, Shackleton meant "the opening of the gates of Romance". As she wrote,

> Life is for the most part humdrum for the majority of us, & it is something to have had glimpses through the "magic casement".

In her, Shackleton had nonetheless met his match in shrewdness. He was, as she put it, "not perfect, but intensely human & entirely lovable though," she gently remarked,

> I cannot help wondering why his (presumably) thrifty Quaker forebears did not bestow *that* gift upon him to counteract the reckless generosity of his Irish ancestry.[10]

It was to Miss Stancomb-Wills that Shackleton really turned while he was waiting. "My pen wanders on when I write to you," as he put it in one of his many letters:

> You do realize that in spite of this dusty workaday life I have ideals and far away in my own White south I open my arms to the Romance of it all and it abides with me now you and I understand each other; there is strength in what you write, I feel in you the sense of reliance that I did

with one or two of my men and yet it does not take away from the woman side and that quick sympathy that we men lack so much. I write very openly because I know you understand. I have hammered through life made but few friends and it is good to know you.[11]

By August, the Russian opening had finally petered out. Shackleton, meanwhile, was bombarding the War Office with proposals to go to France on front-line transport. He tried the Foreign Office for a mission to Italy. There was talk of the post of coordinator of food supplies to the Allies "but the question is," said Shackleton, "whether it migh in some quarters be thought that I was avoiding the active side of the war".[12] There was a futile burst of bustling around to meetings with Mr Ulick Wintour, First Secretary at the Ministry of Food, and probably a well wisher. It was all becoming a wartime version of *Potentia*, the Russian soldiers, and the North Mexico Company. Everything seemed mysteriously to dissolve in the way of Shackleton's schemes outside exploration.

It was as if unseen enemies, or worse, wary friends, lurked in high places. Shackleton was undoubtedly mistrusted; and he also now gave a distinct impression of decay. He was drinking just a little too much. It was what had been observed after the *Nimrod* expedition, but this went further yet. Somehow Shackleton seemed spent. He appeared to have aged beyond his years, and he was ill at ease.

After all that had gone before, Shackleton found it hard to accept, perhaps, that only years of anticlimax remained. He still clung to the hope that he could snatch fulfilment before it was too late. For the moment, however, he was in eclipse. He had saved all the men directly under his command – it was his greatest pride. But, unfortunately, Shackleton the heroic survivor did not match the bellicose spirit of the civilians.

In 1914, before sailing on *Endurance*, Shackleton had written that he did not "want to lose my life down there".[13] That exactly described the war-weary soldiers of 1917, but the civilians were looking for something else. Miss Stancomb-Wills was more in tune with this mood when she wrote to Shackleton this verse:

"Death is nothing" and Ease & Comfort are but dross to be cast away.
For a Man must be up & doing if he keep his manhood true.

Or, as a reviewer in *The Times Literary Supplement* aptly put it: "How vastly the spiritual gain of those who are left behind outweighs the agony and loss of those who fight and die . . . the everlasting glory and exaltation of war".[14] Heroism was established as an end in itself. In this atmosphere the witless valour of Scott exercised the greater appeal, and his reputation was being secured by the turn of mind that believed in the efficacy of British guts against the machine gun.

More than ever, Shackleton seemed to have been born out of his time. James Wordie (now on the Western Front, in the Artillery) "always pictured Shackleton as very much the Elizabethan", he once said. "I think we on the 'Endurance' could have palmed ourselves off as a very creditable 16th-century effort."[15]

Shackleton would undoubtedly have been an ornament of that age of the individual. Like many Anglo-Irishmen, however, in England he was somehow out of place. The country worshipped mediocrity, and of that, he could not be accused. Despite his talk of "ideals", he was foreign to high-mindedness. It was still easier to imagine him, for example, as one of the Spanish conquistadores of his early reading: rootless optimists carving out empires in America, "to serve God and His Majesty . . . and to grow rich, as all men desire to do,"[16] as the frankest of them, Bernal Diaz, engagingly put it. Among his other schemes, Shackleton had canvassed a propaganda mission to South America. Now, as all other prospects faded, he returned to the idea. It had originally been planted in his mind by Tripp. Upon hearing how Shackleton had captivated the Chileans after the relief of Elephant Island, Tripp thought this could be harnessed to the larger conduct of the war. It might also enable Shackleton to settle down.

Tripp was much concerned for Shackleton's welfare. It would, as he remarked in a valedictory letter, "be impossible for you to do any Exploring . . . for many years". Moreover, said Tripp, with hardly veiled reproof,

> it would be unwise for you ever to take on another Expedition unless you not only had sufficient money to pay your way if everything went on alright but you would have to have money in hand to provide for accidents.

"Even if you can get the money say in six years time," Tripp went on, "I think you will be too old."

Tripp was concerned less about money than about something else. On *Aurora* at McMurdo Sound, during the Ross Sea relief, Shackleton had collected some likely looking mud. This he hopefully sent to the government analyst in Wellington for assay, expecting to find gold. In the midst of everything, he remained his old treasure-hunting self. Tripp now had to convey the information that in the mud there was no trace of gold at all.

"My advice to you is when the War is over," said Tripp, "you should try and get some position which will suit you. I should think," he sagely added, "the position of Consul would be in your line."[17]

Tripp, meanwhile, wrote about Shackleton to political contacts in England. One of them happened to be Reginald Neville, an old Cambridge friend, and Unionist MP for Wigan. Neville showed Tripp's letters to Sir Edward Carson. Perris, to whom Tripp had written, also approached Carson. The upshot was that Carson took Shackleton under his wing.

Sir Edward Carson, an Anglo-Irishman too, was the famous barrister who, in a celebrated libel suit, had defended the Marquess of Queensberry against Oscar Wilde. That had led to Wilde's prosecution and conviction for sodomy. Carson was even more famous, however, as a politician. He was the spokesman of the Ulster Protestants. A Unionist MP, he used his great talents to keep Ulster in the United Kingdom, and out of the hands of the Catholic South when Home Rule was on the cards. He could be called the architect of the partition of Ireland.

When Shackleton swam into his ken, Carson had just become Minister without Portfolio in Lloyd George's War Cabinet, after six months as First Lord of the Admiralty. He was a thoroughly ambivalent figure. "The necessary supply of heroes must be maintained at all costs,"[18] he had recently said, in a memorable phrase. Tall, thin, sinewy, with a long jaw and piercing glance; persuasive, stormy and eloquent, with a feeling for the underdog, Carson was a powerful, subversive and very Irish figure. Shackleton he found, broadly speaking, sympathetic. For Shackleton, in any case, he found a timely use.

Carson was dissatisfied with the conduct of the war in general and propaganda in particular. In South America, the latter seemed notably inept. An inter-departmental commission was on its way. Carson wished to forestall humbug and procrastination with an independent and expendable investigator.

Shackleton filled the bill. Since Lloyd George also wanted some job for Shackleton, but preferably far away, Carson decided to send him out to Latin America.

This displeased the Foreign Office functionaries, "a stiff necked red taped lot", as Shackleton called them. "They resent me thinking I might not be tactful enough."[19] Their well-oiled machine began to turn. "The time is not suitable," one official smoothly minuted early in September, "for Sir Ernest Shackleton to engage on a tour . . . to South America."[20] But Sir Edward Carson was not the minister to be stopped by Civil Service obstructionism.

Because of the prestige abroad, Carson tried to get Shackleton naval rank. Not even Carson, however, could overcome the Admiralty. "I am sorry," he wrote to Shackleton, "but I imagine with your name & reputation it will not make much difference."[21]

"After consulting with Carson, I am not taking naval rank,"[22] was the way Shackleton put it for the benefit of Janet Stancomb-Wills. The rebuff cut deep, even although King George V had given Shackleton the royal imprimatur. On 30 May, the day after he returned to England, Shackleton had been received at Buckingham Palace. Now, he was suddenly commanded to Sandringham to lecture on the *Endurance* expedition.

It was about this time that Shackleton requested the Polar Medal for his men. In the words of an Admiralty minute, "an exploration medal in the middle of a great war would be out of place",[23] but Shackleton, with royal influence, managed to secure the award. Shackleton deliberately excluded McNeish, Vincent, Stephenson and Holness. He regarded the decoration, not as a campaign medal, but as an award for exceptional service. The four seamen did not come up to his standards. Where McNeish was concerned, his one moment of mutiny on the ice outweighed all his other virtues; even the fact that the open-boat journey had depended on his skill. Shackleton did not believe that one splendid deed could atone for an ignoble life. He was essentially Irish in his implacable creed that one slip from the path of absolute loyalty for ever damned a man.

Shackleton sailed at last for Buenos Aires, via New York; on 17 October. Not even the German U-boat offensive, now sinking 300,000 tons of British shipping every month, could subdue the relief of getting out again.

The day he sailed Shackleton sent Emily a cheque for a new coat, but "don't let Frank [Dorman] or Stancomb see it," he warned, "it does not matter anyone else with Liz [Dawson Lambton]" he suggested, "say you have had it a long time."[24] These were sensible precautions. Her brother Frank and Miss Stancomb-Wills, Emily saw only occasionally; but Elizabeth Dawson Lambton was now living nearby at Eastbourne.

Shackleton, as usual, was setting off like a privateer. When Carson had asked if he wanted a salary, "I said it did not matter," Shackleton grandly told Miss Stancomb-Wills, "but I must have a free hand."[25] He was actually sailing without pay.

Emily, meanwhile, would have to continue somehow keeping herself and her children on her own income of about seven hundred pounds a year. Shackleton was also burdened by having to help support his parents, still living at Sydenham in need. He now positively disliked them, but felt under a moral obligation. His mother remained an invalid; his father's medical practice was failing, he was unable to support himself, and he had a debt that his son had to pay. Janet Stancomb-Wills would continue to help although only, Shackleton hopefully continued to maintain, as a loan.

It was not easy, at the age of forty-three, for Shackleton to depend on charity; or even living by his wits. In any case, he would have been hard put to explain how he found the money for a new coat for his wife. He might have extracted it from official travelling expenses. It might equally have been a by-product of the still muddled expedition funds. Strictly speaking, therefore, it belonged to one of his men, still waiting patiently for payment of outstanding salary. Either way, it was sensible for benefactors not to know. But, as Shackleton told Emily, "I want to think of you with some real warmth this winter."[26]

As usual, Shackleton was setting off optimistically. With luck, he was going for the duration of the war although, in his own words to Emily, "It may be that I will get home for a little if I can make good in one place."[27]

As usual, too, parting was the signal for a stream of affectionate correspondence tinged with remorse. "I was happy really happy this time when all was right between us," Shackleton wrote on the passage from New York to Buenos Aires. "I am missing you" he said, knowing very well, and so did she, that once reunited, he would soon grow bored and irritated again. "I am," as he put it, "a funny curious sort of wanderer."[28]

There was, also, the familiar tale of the rich shipboard acquaintance who was going to solve all problems. James Dunn was this one's name: "only 42," said Shackleton, "and has built up a great fortune . . . he and I have agreed to work together after the war and it means now darling that there is no need for any future financial worry for I know I will be on my feet: so the soothsayers will be right."[29]

There was something jaded about Shackleton's optimism now. In Buenos Aires, which he reached at the end of November, he complained of being ill in the heat. Twice in succession he wrote to Emily reassuring her that now he was "an absolute teetotaller". He was having bouts of drinking. That was the flaw he feared.

"Many wonderful things have happened," wrote an English language newspaper in Buenos Aires, when Shackleton arrived, "since the 'Endurance' went down to her 'funk-hole' in the Antarctic . . . In the meantime Sir Ernest, the man who has been and seen and done things, is among us again."[30] It was not exactly like the reception after the Elephant Island rescue. But Shackleton was not trying to live on the past. He desperately wanted to succeed at something new. Sir Edward Carson's letter of instruction told him that he was to

> examine the already existing propaganda agencies [and to] suggest . . . changes . . . which appear to you desirable.[31]

As soon as he had settled in at the Plaza hotel, Shackleton plunged into his mission with typical abruptness.

Propaganda was wholly compatible with Shackleton's leanings. He was, after all, an editor manqué. He was used to putting a gloss on a situation. From the now far-off days of *Potentia*, and its persuasive begetter, Niels Grøn, Shackleton had preserved a vague belief in the use of information for beneficial ends.

"Dispatch no more propaganda literature to Argentine," Shackleton was soon peremptorily cabling back to London. He had found about twenty tons of printed matter mouldering in warehouses, long since out of date. The Argentine, as he put it, was "absolutely indifferent and unswayed by . . . lengthy publications". He wanted short, authoritative statements. He demanded "greater clarity, cohesion . . . in your weekly communiqués I suggest you . . . revise your style."[32]

All this was addressed to the Department of Information, whose head happened to be the well-known author John Buchan. After Shackleton's burst of cables, an official in London told Buchan he had "arranged for more competent men to prepare these . . . communiqués".[33]

Characteristically, Shackleton had not felt bound by the literal terms of his instructions. Exactly as, on his first halting steps in business, he had felt an instant financier, now he had a vision of himself as an accomplished diplomat, on the way to a sensational coup. "I left . . . with what I considered a clear vision of the war," as he tellingly summed up in his final report.

> Propaganda is a term proportionate to the mind that conceives it and anything that militated against the consummation of the main object the winning of the War I considered to be pertinent to my mission.[34]

After three years of war, it was the day of the nostrum for victory. Shackleton decided that his aim must be to persuade the governments of Argentina and Chile to forsake neutrality and enter the war on the side of the Allies.

> I only wish I had tons of money [he naïvely told Janet Stancomb-Wills] I would then on my own work the propaganda so that within three months the Germans would be quite exposed in South America.[35]

How he set to work, Shackleton explained in the report he wrote for Lord Robert Cecil, Under-Secretary of State for Foreign Affairs. On first arriving Shackleton "got in touch with the twenty five families who constitute best Argentine society". They were, however, "the Conservative element" as he put it, and no longer the "governing class". So, Shackleton wrote, he

> gradually dropped this section of society and cultivated relations with the Radicals and with the North American community. I left the English community practically alone as though of course patriotic and reliable, they are insular and have a limited horizon.

The President was the object of Shackleton's attention. Shackleton "got into very close touch, during the course of three and a half months", in his own words, "with the President's nearest friends", as a result of which he discovered that the President's personality was "dominating and almost sinister". The President, he went on,

> lives in four rooms over a boot-black's shop, having refused on his election to reside in Government House. In his home live his Austrian mistress and his illegitimate daughter. Neither has any influence over him.

In fact, said Shackleton, the President "would brook no interference from anyone . . . he considered himself ordained to effect the consolidation of South America through his own personality and that the Argentine through him was to be the brightest jewel in the Crown of the Continent." He added in a shrewd aside:

> For 100 years the Argentine has fought battles mainly for quixotic causes . . . as a nation and as individuals the people are not influenced by their pockets.

The Falkland Islands were not then the main trouble. It was, Shackleton reported, the so-called Black List. This was an official list of neutral firms suspected of German sympathies. To trade with them incurred British official displeasure. The Black List, in Shackleton's view,

> damages British prestige . . . and has failed entirely in its avowed objects – to cripple and kill German trade . . . Argentines . . . who have

> always been on friendly terms with England . . . have lost entirely their sympathy on account of their utter disgust of our methods.
>
> Circulars are constantly appearing from British official quarters which . . . make one believe that the commerce of [Argentina] is under the orders of England . . . the President . . . has stated that English official representatives seem to forget that they are foreigners . . . and . . . have no right to attack Argentine citizens who have the right to deal with whom they choose.

"No amount of propaganda," Shackleton properly concluded, "will have the effect of wiping out this unpopularity if things are allowed to continue as they are at present." Perhaps the tool of others, Shackleton also reported that Sir Reginald Tower, the British Minister to the Argentine, was "seriously overworked":

> The Legation is understaffed, the Minister is badly housed . . . Appearances go a good deal with the Latin-Americans, and it would be a great advantage . . . if the British Minister were able to keep up an appearance commensurate with the dignity of the Empire.[36]

It was all to little effect. An all too familiar pattern had emerged. After the first bustle of activity, Shackleton was once more beset by bafflement. His report was pigeon-holed, and he had quickly found himself at odds with most British diplomats. Besides, when Edward Carson resigned in January 1918 over Home Rule, Shackleton lost his patron. In the middle of March, he left Buenos Aires to return to London, via Santiago, Panama and the United States. When he arrived in London at the end of April, 1918, he was politely given the cold shoulder. There was no place in the official hierarchy for an amateur diplomat, especially of Shackleton's freebooting kind.

So, once more, Shackleton went the rounds, trying to enlist. The atmosphere was tense. In March, the Germans under General Ludendorff had launched the astonishing offensive that looked as if it might just conceivably defeat the Allies at the last moment. Shackleton talked of becoming a liaison officer in France between the newly formed RAF and the Americans. Almost predictably, it came to nothing.

While in Buenos Aires, Shackleton had worked with Allan Macdonald, the British businessman who had helped him at Punta Arenas with the Elephant Island relief. Macdonald was setting up a shadowy private organisation for political propaganda and, probably, intelligence. "Bitterest possible dislike [mildly] describes the . . . attitude of the British Legation towards you,"[37] Macdonald now cabled privately to Shackleton. The message was intercepted, and appeared in the Foreign Office files. The gossip was spilling out into Whitehall.

Shackleton, meanwhile, became involved in a curious undercover enterprise. A concern called the Northern Exploration Company was preparing an expedition to Spitsbergen. Shackleton was asked to be the leader in the field. Shares in the company were part of the deal. It was, as he wistfully told Emily, "a job I would have loved in peace time".[38] At first, he nonetheless hesitated. He did not, as he himself put it, want to be "side-tracked" from service in the war.

Ostensibly, the company was going to prospect and work mineral claims that they had owned since 1910. In fact, they had official backing. While Shackleton was in South America, the Bolsheviks had taken power in Russia. On 3 March, 1918, they had made a separate peace with the Germans by the treaty of Brest-Litovsk. In one of the clauses, the new Soviet government agreed to support Germany in her claims on Spitsbergen. The British government regarded this as a strategic threat, since Spitsbergen guarded the Arctic approaches to the North Atlantic.

Since 1910 the Germans had had a meteorological station at Ebeltofthaven in West Spitsbergen, which was only withdrawn at the outbreak of war. The status of Spitsbergen was delicate, not to say confused. It was administered by Norway, a neutral country; and a Norwegian company was already mining coal. A military occupation therefore would have been politically tactless. Instead, the British government proposed using the Northern Exploration Company to establish a British presence on the islands.

When convinced of official approval, Shackleton agreed to join the expedition. In any case, it was obvious that now, with the country mobilised for total war, very little could happen without at least tacit official support. To make the point, the government provided the expedition with transport, in the shape of an armed merchant ship, the *Ella*.

Shackleton was the man for this kind of privateering enterprise. Reassured by what he called "the political people" at the Foreign Office, he could with a clear conscience combine his old pursuit of instant fortune with war service. "I am very busy arranging an expedition for the Government," was the way he chose to put it in one of his erratic letters to his daughter Cecily. She was now almost twelve years old and at school at Roedean; fees paid no one quite knew how. Shackleton doted on her:

> I am looking forward . . . to see you [he wrote] also to seeing the other sweet girls. I shall be shy; so if you see my finger in my mouth and a

blush on my milk and roses complexion you will know this delicate little explorer is oh so shy.

Your loving old father . . .[39]

"Your tottering aged Daddy", was another revealing variation; "your ancient revered and highly respectable Daddy", yet one more. With a pang, Shackleton realised that Cecily, his only daughter, was growing up, and that, in turn, accentuated a sense of growing old.

The Northern Exploration Company had approached Shackleton because there was still, in spite of everything, a mystique to his name. Also, the heterogeneous workmen being collected to work in polar conditions might require leadership of the kind Shackleton had shown in the south.

As assistant, Shackleton asked for Frank Wild. Since the summer of 1917 Wild had been at Archangel, the port in northern Russia. The Allies had been bringing in supplies that way in a desperate attempt to shore up the Russian army. Wild, after a crash course in Russian, had been commissioned as a temporary lieutenant in the RNVR, and sent out as one of the naval transport officers controlling British shipping. The Admiralty now obligingly released him. Someone else from the *Endurance*, Dr McIlroy, joined Shackleton too. McIlroy had been invalided out of the Army after being severely wounded at Ypres.

By the middle of August, Shackleton had reached Tromsø, in northern Norway, on his way to Spitsbergen. It was the first time he had crossed the Arctic Circle, which satisfied an old ambition to visit the polar regions, north and south. Once more on an enterprise, he displayed his more congenial sea-going self. In the words of a seaman on the *Ella*, he was "just like a grown up kid".[40]

It was at Tromsø one day that Shackleton was suddenly taken ill. He "changed colour very badly", as McIlroy put it. He suspected a heart attack.

McIlroy found that even now Shackleton "wouldn't undress", as he put it, "and let me listen to his heart".[41] The diagnosis remained hanging in the air. Nonetheless, it was the first clear hint that Shackleton might actually be suffering from heart disease. It was almost as if his fears were being fulfilled. It was like the closing of one chapter and the opening of another.

Meanwhile, Shackleton had to turn back. On 22 July, a few days before leaving London he had been gazetted a temporary major. After more than a year he had been graciously permitted to join the Army. He had a uniform at last.

What had happened was this. The Allies in France were reeling under the blows of Ludendorff's offensive. The Germans had advanced to within sixty miles of Paris. The Treaty of Brest-Litovsk, which started the scurry to Spitsbergen, had in a broader context allowed the Germans to move fresh troops to the Western Front. The Allies hastily looked for diversions to ease the pressure. The only feasible plan appeared to be a reconstruction of the Eastern Front. That included a landing in northern Russia. Its purpose was also to prevent the Germans capturing Murmansk and using it as a submarine base.

Murmansk was the only major north Russian port ice-free all year round. From there, German submarines would be able to evade the British naval defences in the North Sea and pour into the Atlantic through the gap between Iceland and northern Norway to wreak havoc among the ships bringing American troops to Europe. Not far from Murmansk, in Finland, the Germans actually had an army 50,000 strong, under General von der Goltz, poised, or so it was thought, to attack.

By June, the British had occupied Murmansk and forestalled the Germans. The war, however, was expected to last at least another year, and it was then realised that a winter in polar conditions lay ahead. Someone was needed to organise transport and equipment. As the best available authority, the War Office turned to Shackleton.

He was told to start planning, but not actually join up until September. He would only be wanted for the winter. It was almost as if the authorities wished to keep him at a distance as long as they possibly could. The War Office however were happy for him to go to Spitsbergen and spend a few weeks there, but there were delays in Norway. The Northern Exploration Company was ineptly led. There was no time for Shackleton to go on to Spitsbergen. He still had to complete equipping the expeditionary force for winter. Everything was late. The War Office now urgently required him, and from Tromsø he was hurriedly recalled. *Ella* had to sail without him, but with Wild as leader of the expedition. Early in September, Shackleton was back in London, immersed once more in the familiar, congenial race against time, as if it were one of his own expeditions.

The northern Russia campaign, to quote one its one commanders, General Ironside, "was a side show of the Great War":

> It was a hasty improvisation conceived without much previous consideration by either political or military experts, almost in desperation, as it were, to prevent the Germans winning the war in France.[42]

Soldiers could hardly be spared, the Allies were scraping the bottom of the barrel, and the troops sent to north Russia were unfit for service elsewhere. Nobody now was going to worry about the condition of Shackleton's heart.

Early in October, Shackleton finally sailed for Murmansk, apparently content to be on active service at last. It was a "job after my own heart", as he phrased it in a letter to Leonard Tripp, "winter sledging with a fight at the end".[43] Since returning from the *Endurance*, in fact, Shackleton, as he could not conceal from himself, had been fobbed off with side shows. It intensified his sense of time running out. "If I were rich," he wrote to Janet Stancomb-Wills while still at sea, "I would do some good exploration when this is over before I grow too old, not that I feel a bit old now."[44]

But a few days later, as he crossed the Barents Sea, approaching his destination, and sensed the atmosphere of the Arctic, he wrote to her: "All is sheer beauty and keen delight":

> The very first . . . snow-squalls bring home to us the memories of our old South Lands. There is a freshness in the air, a briskness in the breeze that renews one's youth.

"This day 3 years [ago] the 'Endurance' was crushed in the ice," Shackleton wrote to his younger son, Edward, on 26 October, "and we all were . . . sleeping on rather moving about on the moving ice with no home to go to. I have been to many places since then, now it is the other end of the world."[45]

Shackleton had just landed at Murmansk. A fortnight later, on 11 November, the Armistice was signed. The war with Germany was over. Once more, somehow, Shackleton had been baffled.

War in northern Russia, however, was not yet at an end. By a complex twist of circumstances, the Allied forces now found themselves embroiled in the internal affairs of Russia, and fighting the Bolsheviks instead.

Soon after Shackleton landed, he was surprised by Macklin urgently appearing at his billet. They had not met since parting at the Retiro railway station in Buenos Aires after the *Endurance* expedition, two years before. In a brief exchange of letters during 1917, Shackleton had written hoping that

> when this war is over . . . we may all foregather . . .
>
> I always have the warmest feelings of friendship and gratitude towards you for you never failed me throughout the expedition.[46]

Since then, they had not been in touch.

On coming home, Macklin had gone to France as a doctor with

the Tanks. He volunteered for northern Russia as soon as the opportunity arose. He had been at Murmansk almost from the start. When Shackleton arrived, he was up country with Major-General Charles Maynard, the British commander. Shackleton had been sent out to join Maynard's staff. Macklin hurried round not only to welcome his old chief, but to warn him of his likely reception.

> "I've heard about this man Shackleton [Macklin had heard the General say]. He's an impossible person. He likes to run everything in his own way . . . I'm not going to have him."[47]

This was an echo of Shackleton's old quarrel with Scott. The north Russia force, in fact, had attracted various polar explorers, one of whom happened to be Captain Victor Campbell, the leader of the northern party on Scott's second expedition. (Campbell had also commanded the Northern Exploration Company's last expeditions to Spitsbergen before the war.) No doubt Maynard had been influenced by Campbell, for Macklin had actually overheard Campbell "haranguing a party", as he put it,

> and he wasn't playing the game with Shackleton at all. He was talking about this impossible, bossy, dreadful man, and enlarging upon the difference between Scott and him.[48]

The antagonism between the Shackleton and Scott factions died hard, and now it had actually reached Archangel, in the White Sea. There another branch of the north Russia expeditionary force was established. Among the medical officers were, on the one hand, Dr Edward Atkinson, from the Scott camp, and on the other Dr Eric Marshall from the *Nimrod* expedition. Atkinson had been among those who found Scott's polar party. Marshall was convinced that Atkinson was covering up the fact that scurvy killed Scott. He taxed Atkinson with the deception whenever they met and now, at Archangel, he returned to the attack.

There had been an outbreak of scurvy in the region, and one day Marshall heard Atkinson "laying off" on the disease, as he put it, to another army doctor. To Marshall, Atkinson had previously pretended ignorance of scurvy. Now Atkinson was claiming special knowledge of scurvy because of its appearance on Scott's expedition which, in Marshall's words, "he had up to then denied". Atkinson was then "forced to concede the case of Lieut. Evans", but "still denied its existence"[49] in the polar party.

There was a sequel. When Macklin met Atkinson, and attacked

him too about scurvy having probably killed Scott, Atkinson tacitly admitted it but, said Macklin, he

> made this . . . rather surprising remark that he felt it would be disloyal to Scott to say so . . . it was a reflection on his ability as an organiser to say that scurvy had developed.[50]

Both Marshall and Macklin, although otherwise they had little in common, were scandalised at this intellectual dishonesty. The whole "Scott camp" subscribed to it, in order to foster the burgeoning heroic legend. The denial was also aimed at Shackleton. Scurvy was concealed in the case of Scott, because Shackleton had manifestly conquered the disease on the expeditions that he had personally led.

In any case, Shackleton told Macklin at Murmansk that he could cope with General Maynard. It was not the old, familiar ebullient, tearaway Shackleton, that Macklin remembered, but someone subdued, quiet, amenable and effortlessly fitting in to an hierarchical military structure. His old companions found it an astonishing metamorphosis. Besides Macklin, Shackleton had Worsley and Hussey from the *Endurance* with him, together with Stenhouse from the *Aurora*. To them, it was as if Shackleton had shed one personality, to assume another.

This was not precisely the case. Shackleton had merely adapted to circumstances. He was playing a different role. It was mirrored by his handwriting, which altered with his mood. It was the old Shackleton in a different guise.

General Maynard, in Macklin's words, appeared "rather a disgruntled, unsmiling, bad-tempered customer".[51] That may have been because he had been given a thankless task with inadequate means. He had been pitchforked into an unfamiliar and repugnant half world between soldiering and politics. There were units from eight nationalities in the polyglot force under his command.

Shackleton's official designation was "Staff officer in charge of Arctic equipment". In fact he was a glorified storekeeper. Most of his work had been done in London. The outfits he had provided were doubtful; his own expeditions, after all, had been struggles against unsatisfactory equipment. The American troops in the region rapidly discarded the Shackleton clothing and boots provided by the Allied command, and reverted to their own patterns.

General Maynard's problem was to fight a winter campaign. That implied ski troops. It was Victor Campbell, not Shackleton, who was hastily put in charge of training. However, as Maynard put it: "More than a few weeks are required to convert the average British foot-soldier into a confident performer on ski,"[52] and he had to depend for cross-country work on Canadian, French, and Italian units, with a sprinkling of Serbs and Karelians.

In any case Shackleton was kept at headquarters in Murmansk, with relatively little to do. He concentrated on making himself agreeable to Maynard. Soon, in his characteristic way, Shackleton had disarmed Maynard's antagonism, and acquired a psychological ascendancy. Whatever the form in which he chose to appear, Shackleton preserved his force of personality. In Maynard's own words, Shackleton

> proved a cheerful and amusing companion, and . . . his presence did much to keep us free from gloom and depression.[53]

At the end of December, Maynard hurriedly visited London, personally to demand proper support and chiefly, as he put it, because the Treasury "think . . . that it doesn't matter how many lives are needlessly risked . . . so long as they can save a few miserable thousand pounds".[54] Shackleton went too, ostensibly because he had to attend to winter equipment. He attached himself to General Maynard as a kind of unofficial ADC. That led, incidentally, to another audience with King George V.

Shackleton had cogent reasons for the visit. "The Lord knows what I will do when this show is over," he had written to Emily. "I don't want to go lecturing all over the place."[55] There was his future to consider. He had to find a source of income against the time when he should leave the Army. Even less than before, was he interested in making a living. The sense of time running out remained to haunt him. He was still in search of instant fortune.

On the same boat, returning to Murmansk at the end of December, was a General Miller. "I cultivated him assiduously," Shackleton wrote to Emily, "and he repays keeping in with."[56]

General Miller was a Russian officer. He had escaped from the Bolsheviks who, under Lenin and Trotsky, were being attacked on all sides. To isolate the Reds, the Allies were backing various anti-Soviet movements, one of which was an independent North Russian government, centred on Archangel and Murmansk. The plan was hastily to train a local army and give the regime the strength to survive. That would enable the Allied forces honourably to withdraw. General Miller, after a tortuous journey via Rome and Paris, was on his way to Archangel as governor-general. Until further notice, he would be the effective head of the North Russian government.

General Miller revived in Shackleton the vision of northern

Russia as his new El Dorado. The general for his part, had to consider the economic survival of his territory. North Russia was poor and primitive; but there lay untold timber and mineral resources, in which Shackleton saw his chance. He would form a company to develop the territory.

Tall, slim, drooping, with a long cavalry moustache, looking as if he had stepped out of a play by Chekhov, General Miller was typical of the *ancien régime*. He was at any rate thoroughly Russian with big, broad plans, and vagueness over detail, and in him, Shackleton found someone notably compatible.

Before sailing back from Scapa Flow, Shackleton had got Emily up to Scotland for a sentimental farewell. He told her that his affair with Rosalind Chetwynd was finished. It was certainly true that for some time Rosalind had been in New York; although now she was back in London, appearing at the Lyric, Hammersmith, in a play called *Make Believe*. In any case, Shackleton had now given up all pretence of being anything but an absentee husband and father. He was suggesting to Cecily that she ought not to stay too long at school, but go home and be a companion to her mother.

To Cecily herself, Shackleton wrote from Murmansk that he might be able to

> bring a fur of some sort back to adorn you with: a white fox would suit your style of beauty.

And again:

> The children and women here are all extremely plain to say the least of it. They have not that beautiful hair that someone aged 11 or 12 has!!![57]

To the soldiers around him, Shackleton appeared a temperamental Irishman, genial to his superiors, unpredictable to his subordinates. One Army captain recalled being out with Shackleton on an excursion round the base at Murmansk when Shackleton stopped to "gaze over what to me was the abomination of monotony . . . vast expanses of snow; in the distance the gun-metal of the Kola Inlet. [He looked] at it . . . as though he wished to imprint it on his memory . . . and . . . began to declaim poetry."

> He had a beautiful speaking voice, full, & resonant. I slithered up [on ski] and remarked "said Mr. Browning". He turned to me as though in anger. "How did you know that it was Browning? I replied that, as at the time of the outbreak of [the war] I was placidly pursuing an honours course of English literature in the University of Oxford I was

entitled to raise my hat at least to Mr. Browning – even if I didn't know him well enough to call him Robert."

Mollified, but puzzled, Shackleton said "First man in . . . uniform I've met who'd even heard of Robert Browning".

On another outing Shackleton, in the same officer's words, "again declaimed".

"You don't know who said that," he affirmed.

"No. I don't know who said that."

"Well, Shackleton said it."

"That explorer-man? I asked. "He must be a man of parts. I never knew he was a poet!"

Again he turned on me. "Then why the devil did you think he became an explorer?"

I can't remember when my eyes were more completely opened.[58]

About this time, a naval officer vividly recalled Shackleton talking in a quiet moment about a "fourth presence" on the crossing of South Georgia. However "He attempted no explanation. 'In religion I am what I am' were his words."[59]

"I have not been too fit lately," Shackleton was writing meanwhile to Emily. "I am tired darling a bit and just want a little rest away from the world and you." Emily now was the mother confessor with whom he could not dispense.

I am an erratic sort of person in many ways [he went on] and cannot understand myself: Sometimes I think I am no good at anything but being away in the wilds just with men and sometimes I grow restless and feel . . . part of youth is slipping away from me and that nothing matters: I want to upset everybodys calm and peace of mind when I meet calm and contented people.[60]

The strain of a divided self was telling on Shackleton. "I am strictly on the water wagon now," he wrote, yet again to Emily, at the end of January, 1919. He had got thoroughly drunk on Christmas Day but, in his own words,

after a lot of thought I have cut it right out it does me no good and I can tell my imagination is vivid enough without alcohol it makes me extravagant in ideas and I lose balance . . . I did not upset my superiors everyone was awash only it seems to take different people different ways [he added darkly]. If I had not some strength of will I would make a first class drunkard.[61]

Shackleton had left his affairs behind in a more than usually profound state of muddle. Money, he did not actually possess. Emily had to fend for herself. Cecily was at Roedean, Ray (the eldest boy) at Harrow. Shackleton hoped to cover the school fees from, amongst other things, his Northern Exploration Company shares. He had actually given his brother Frank – to hide his past, still living under the name of Mellor – some of the shares to sell. The transaction naturally withered. Emily had to turn for help to her old love, Sir Sydney Boulton. Shackleton was "not vexed", as he wrote to Emily, "but I hate to think of you having to ask him through a breakdown on my part".[62] It was, however, preferable, he consoled her, to having to turn to Frank Mellor.

In northern Russia, there had been a mutiny among the Allied troops, and the local Bolsheviks were beginning to take the offensive. Their masters in Moscow were showing the ruthlessness of men who knew what they wanted, and were determined to rule. They had already murdered the ex-Tsar Nicholas II and his family. Brutal callousness, as Shackleton no doubt felt by now, besides insidious intrigue, seemed to be part of the Russian character. The question was whether the anti-Bolsheviks would be able to withstand the storm when the Allied forces had gone. That, the various governments had decided, would be before the next winter.

By then, the north Russian government would have to stand on its own feet, or at least have the appearance of doing so. It was there that Shackleton had his chance. Since there would not be another winter campaign, his military work was done. His scheme for a company to develop northern Russia, on the other hand, seemed suddenly important.

Shackleton had made enemies among the British officers by the way he used his military position to promote his private affairs. In a more robust age, when what was good for the individual was considered good for the country, Shackleton would have been better appreciated. At all events, he was openly in contact with the local Russian officials. In particular, he was seeing Yermoloff, the deputy-governor of Murmansk.

It is doubtful if Yermoloff was exactly taken in by Shackleton. Short, sallow-faced, with sandy hair, unremarkable features, and a morose expression, Yermoloff shunned the display usually dear to the Russian. A dispossessed small landowner from Novgorod, a refugee in his own country, he had lost all his worldly goods; part of the human flotsam of revolution and civil war. Speaking no language but his own, he had to communicate through an interpreter. A typical Russian with an innate suspicion of foreigners, he had seen optimists like Shackleton before.

A romantic Russian nineteenth-century novelist once made one of his characters talk of "the ready way in which a Russian can adapt himself to the customs of the people among whom he happens to live. I don't know whether this faculty is blameworthy or commendable, but it is a proof of our incomparable suppleness."[63] The same might have been said of Shackleton. With his fluid personality and, as his friends regretfully had to admit, an air of decay, he now resembled certain Russians of the *ancien régime* himself.

Shackleton's scheme was about the only promise of economic development in the whole region. For that reason, Yermoloff took him at his own valuation. So did General Maynard. He had Shackleton's plans officially recognised in England. Shackleton was to resign his commission in the spring, and turn himself into an entrepreneur. It was a measure of official desperation, and also of Shackleton's enduring power of persuasion, that the economic survival of a whole prospective state had in effect been entrusted to him.

It would, he wrote to Emily, "do something for . . . Britain in this country and . . . put the spoke in the French and Yankee wheels . . . also," he added, "it will be good business." It meant, as he elaborated,

> a thing that makes Spitsbergen small beside it . . . The trading alone is worth £250,000 p.a. so at last all is well: I feel very keenly all you have to put up with and the difficulties about money but . . . just hang on for 2 or 3 weeks and you will find that never again will you have to worry about finance.[64]

Emily recognised the accents only too well. Nonetheless, there was just the correct touch of reality to make her suspend disbelief, a little, yet once more.

In April, Shackleton wrote to Yermoloff sketching his plans for northern Russia. First of all the company, provided it was given the concessions required, would start by acting as a relief agency, providing emergency aid "in the form of clothes, tobacco, furniture, etc. I would then develop the region". Shackleton asked for exclusive mineral, timber, fishing, and water-power rights for five years. Also he wanted a franchise to develop the town and port of Murmansk, at present a shoddy settlement recently sprung up after the construction of a railway from Petrograd. The plan had the authentic Shackleton touch. His company, he promised, would finance "the reorganisation of the Alexandrovsky biological station", because he was "convinced that the fishing industry will greatly benefit by the efficient functioning of that institution". The company would be "a private one, composed of men well known to me, with good business and financial reputations".

It was all there: Shackleton's persuasive optimism in the prose of a company prospectus; the vague hints of all the capital he needed; the combination of business and philanthropy; the belief in applied science. His head office, he ended, would be in London. "My permanent place of domicile," however, he went on to say, "will be Murmansk, so that I shall be able to supervise all the immediate concerns of this enterprise."[65] That was genuine. Like so many of his contemporaries, Shackleton remained a displaced Edwardian. Post-war London was an alien place to him, while the country around Murmansk, as he wrote to Emily, was

> grand: I thought that it was going to be flat and uninteresting instead of which it is hilly with birch forests and wonderful lakes nestling in the valleys . . . We could be very comfy up here.[66]

By the end of March, Shackleton was back in London, and demobilised after five months in the field. His standing was enough to merit an interview in *The Times*. There was now an overwhelming public agitation for withdrawal of Allied troops, which, said Shackleton, was "simply manna" for Bolshevik propaganda. Nearly half a million people, in his words,

> threw in their lot with us . . . against the Bolshevist menace. It is thus not merely a question of saving our own troops, but a moral obligation to civilization . . .
>
> No domestic or political consideration should be allowed to interfere with steps being taken immediately to prevent anything in the nature of a reverse to our arms in these regions . . . In Murmansk, as elsewhere, the peasant is not Bolshevist . . . but without armed support he is helpless . . . do not let us be too late . . . the British people do not yet realize what Bolshevism means . . . it is . . . becoming far worse than German militarism.[67]

The chances of a North Russian government did not impress financiers. In any case, the only one with whom Shackleton was seriously in contact happened to be James Dunn, his shipboard acquaintance from the voyage out to South America in 1917. Before the winter of 1919, the Allies had withdrawn from Murmansk and Archangel. Soon after, both towns fell to the Red forces. Yermoloff refused to flee, and was duly murdered by the Bolsheviks.

In the bloodbath of a sordid revolution, Shackleton saw one more dream of fortune fade.

LV

Quest

So Shackleton was, after all, reduced to lecturing on the *Endurance*. From December 1919 until May 1920, he appeared twice daily at the Philharmonic Hall in Great Portland Street. It was drudgery and worse. He did not even have the consolation of good receipts, for often he faced half empty houses. London in the aftermath of the Great War was no place to talk about polar exploration. In any case, the burgeoning legend of Scott, encapsulating the cult of the glorious death, was more in the spirit of the times.

At the Philharmonic Hall, the feeling was intense, for Shackleton was giving a live commentary on Hurley's silent film of the expedition. "To a sailor", Shackleton had said, "his ship is more than a floating home, and in the *Endurance* I have centred ambitions . . . and desires."[1] Twice daily the image of *Endurance* being crushed in the ice flickered on the screen, and he had to live again through the death of all his hopes.

For the same reason, Shackleton was repelled by the thought of working on the book of the expedition; but finally, at the end of 1919, it appeared as *South*. Since originally dictating the text to Saunders in New Zealand and Australia early in 1917, Shackleton, by his own account, had not touched it. Saunders had to work on the book alone. Shackleton lacked the money to pay him, but this was one debt he wished instantly to clear. Long before, he had told Leonard Tripp in Wellington to sell the chronometers brought back by the Ross Sea party, and give Saunders the proceeds.

Now, at the last moment, Leonard Hussey did the final editing, without payment. During the north Russian campaign, he had been together again with Shackleton and since then attached himself to his old leader as an honorary aide. Shackleton, as Hussey explained to a correspondent,

> I say this with all diffidence – always refers to me as "one of the most cheerful and loyal ones" . . . He is one of the finest men I have ever met, and I would follow him anywhere . . . he has always been the same – always cheerful, confident and resourceful, and at his best when things looked blackest. It is to him that we owe all our lives. And what makes us admire him all the more is that he is so very human. He is a *real* man, and a white man.[2]

The critics, in general, gave *South* their praise. Among them happened to be Apsley Cherry-Garrard, who had been with Scott, and who even then was gestating his own account of the expedition, *The Worst Journey in the World*. Writing in the *Nation*, Cherry-Garrard offered in the guise of a review of *South* a comparison between Shackleton and Scott.

Cherry-Garrard was writing of two losers; although in the words of Roald Amundsen, the ultimate winner,

> Do not let it be said that Shackleton has failed . . . No man fails who sets an example of high courage, of unbroken resolution, of unshrinking endurance.[3]

"Explorers," Cherry-Garrard wrote nonetheless, "run each other down like the deuce". Yet, he added, "as I read with a critical eye Shackleton's account of the loss of the *Endurance*",

> I get the feeling that he . . . is a good man to get you out of a tight place. There is an impression, of the right thing being done without fuss or panic.

The story of how the men on Elephant Island won through "is fine", as Cherry-Garrard put it, "but the interest to me and," he added meaningly, "to some others, is the leadership."

"The Boss," Tom Crean had written to him in 1917, "is a splendid gentleman, and I done my duty towards him to the last."[4] Now, said Cherry-Garrard,

> I know why it is that every man who has served under Shackleton swears by him. I believe Shackleton has never lost a man: he must have had some doubts as to whether he would save one then. But he did, he saved them every one.

Cherry-Garrard, with his own nightmare memories of Scott in the Antarctic, went on

> Nothing is harder to a leader than to wait. The unknown is always terrible, and it is so much easier to go right ahead and get it over one way or the other than to sit and think about it. But Shackleton waited . . . and waited, it seems quite philosophically . . . Through it all one seems to see Shackleton sticking out his jaw and saying to himself that he is not going to be beaten by any conditions which were ever created.

Shackleton, in Cherry-Garrard's words, had

> always given an impression of great grip – I should watch with joy the education of a shirker who served under the Boss. A picture haunts my mind – of three boats, crammed with frost-bitten, wet, and dreadfully thirsty men who have had no proper sleep for many days and nights. Some of them are comatose, some of them are on the threshold of delirium, or worse. Darkness is coming on, the sea is heavy, it is decided to lie off the cliffs and glaciers of Elephant Island and try and find a landing with the light . . . Many would have tried to get a little rest in preparation for the coming struggle. But Shackleton is afraid the boat made fast to his own may break adrift . . . All night long he sits with his hand on the painter, which grows heavier and heavier with ice as the unseen seas surge by, and as the rope tightens and droops under his hand his thoughts are busy with future plans.[5]

It was just as well that Cherry-Garrard never actually met Shackleton at this point. Far from showing "an impression of great grip", Shackleton would have exhibited the uncomfortable self that appeared in civilisation. He was also noticeably jaded, not quite well, and he was suffering a succession of mysterious colds and back pains.

South sold well, but Shackleton earned nothing from it. So far, he had been unable to repay any of the money borrowed for *Endurance*. Most of his benefactors, making a virtue of a necessity, had written off their loans. The one exception was Sir Robert Lucas-Tooth, or rather his heirs. Sir Robert had died in 1915; both his sons had been killed in the war. His executors required from Shackleton repayment of the loan; and his only asset was *South*. In settlement, he assigned all the rights.

Meanwhile, Shackleton had been trying yet again for fortune through a company promotion. In 1919, he became a shareholder and director of the Elstree Chemical Works, which produced artificial fertilisers, outside London. His old benefactor, William Dederich, had taken over the company; and Janet Stancomb-Wills lent Shackleton money to buy his holding. General Maynard, safely back from northern Russia, became a shareholder too. Shackleton was frequently seen arriving and departing by taxi, although the railway station was nearby. Unfortunately, fertilisers were a war-time boom, and Shackleton, despite all his bustling, never actually made any money out of Elstree. The company soon failed, and the building became a film studio.

Shackleton could find no way of earning money; he was oppressed by a crushing sense of failure and still haunted by the sense of time running out. He was prepared to do almost anything quickly to justify himself.

At the end of 1919, Shackleton's name was coupled with a theatrical company that was to tour Holland, with Rosalind Chetwynd as the star. Rosalind now called herself Lady Chetwynd, although with what justification is not exactly clear. Her former husband had come into the baronetcy, but had subsequently remarried. In any case, her stage name was still Rosa Lynd. Shackleton was hanging around the company in London while it was in rehearsal. The manager told Shackleton that his name was hurting the preliminary publicity, since his sole connection seemed that of Rosalind's lover. Years afterwards, the manager recalled "the embarrassment with which I said what I had to say, and how much I respected him for the way he took it".[6]

The Dutch tour soon closed and in May 1920 – as Shackleton was finishing his lectures at the Philharmonic Hall – Rosalind took the Comedy Theatre in London for a season as actress-manager. Their affair had now permanently revived and, although Shackleton was obviously fuming at fortune, they seemed very happy together.

Shackleton was well capable of casual affairs. He was ill suited, however, to the demands of living between mistress and wife. He did not have a talent for concealment. He became too transparently shifty. He could not cope with the strains of the divided self. The outcome now was an erratic life. He sometimes returned to Emily at Eastbourne, but soon he would flee back to London, almost panic-stricken by the sense of suffocation invariably brought on by her well-meant domesticity.

To Shackleton, his family was now an emotional drain. Emily was over fifty and, though well preserved, made Shackleton conscious of having a wife rather older than himself. Even more his children haunted him with the sense of growing old. Rosalind at least was younger than Shackleton.

On Emily, the humiliation of having to accept that her husband preferred a mistress to herself; the strain of running a family alone, had begun to tell. To her children, her family and the outside, at least she maintained an air of serenity, but she could not quite conceal the unhappiness that lay behind. In any case, she had thrown herself into the Girl Guide movement.

Janet Stancomb-Wills remained faithful to Shackleton, in her fashion. Dame Janet, as she now was, honoured for wartime services, was perhaps the shrewdest of the women in Shackleton's life. She took no sides, continuing to help Emily financially, paying the children's school fees. To Shackleton she was still the female confidante of which he stood in need.

Towards Emily, he could respond only with pity and remorse. Such was the outcome of sixteen years' marriage. Divorce occurred to neither. Emily was grateful for even an occasional husband, and Shackleton needed his family as a haven now and then. More often, unremarkably dressed, with a shapeless felt hat squashed on his head, he was to be seen around Rosalind's house at 32 Chesterfield Gardens, in Mayfair, whither she had moved back from Park Lane. Frequently he would go to the barber at Selfridge's to be shaved. There he became a well known figure. It was noticed that his hands often trembled early in the morning.

Shackleton was drinking heavily again. He was also smoking and eating too much. He was putting on weight. He was constantly plagued by colds and fevers, and what he called "indigestion", which meant severe pain across the shoulder blades.

Money, as usual, Shackleton had none. Dame Janet sometimes helped; so too did Rosalind, not that he was exactly living on either. Through Rosalind, meanwhile, he had renewed his acquaintance with Jack Barnato Joel. Again they were back in the old triangle, and this brought Shackleton into a rich set, where he paid his way, as it were, by his name as an explorer, his wit, his talent as a raconteur. It soon began to pall. Shackleton's overpowering restlessness once more had him in its grip. The role of aging hanger-on was not, after all, for him.

In the spring of 1920, he began expressing a desire to see the polar regions just once more. It was not as sudden as it seemed. On and off, Shackleton had had the craving for at least a year and a half. To Emily, it came almost as a relief. If her husband had to be away, it was better in the ice than in the questionable precincts of Mayfair. She even suggested ways and means. One was to write to Teddy Evans; now Captain E. R. G. R. Evans, DSO, and a naval hero – "Evans of the Broke".* In August, 1920, Shackleton followed her advice.

* From HMS *Broke*, a destroyer in which he rammed and sank an enemy warship.

> I know [wrote Shackleton] you have always been a good friend to me; that there is not a spark of jealousy or backbiting about you, that both publicly and privately you have always boosted my work and myself, and stood by me so that I count you as a real friend. This is no balderdash or gush on my part. I *know it.*[7]

Since taking part in Scott's second expedition, Evans had bitterly disliked Scott. Almost by reaction, he had befriended Shackleton. When Shackleton had announced the *Endurance* expedition, Evans had written what amounted to a rebuttal of Scott's systematic belittling of Shackleton's achievements:

> Those of Captain Scott's followers who made . . . the ascent of the Beardmore Glacier, were amazed at Shackleton's fine performance . . . His descriptions were so easy and so careful that every landmark was recognised . . . We easily saw from the copies of his diary, which we carried along, where we might look for coal and other interesting geological specimens . . . on the plateau we met with just the conditions he had described . . . we used his splendid charts, and generally benefited by his praiseworthy pioneer work. Indeed, Shackleton and his companions set up a standard that was extremely difficult to live up to, and impossible to better.[8]

Seven years on, Shackleton now wrote to Evans:

> I want your help urgently. You know that I have done my best in the South. You know what it is to be up against it, both in the fight with the ice and the other fights. Each time I went South, I met with troubles; I tried always to turn disaster into success.

"Now," Shackleton explained, "my eyes are turned from the South to the North, and I want to lead one more Expedition. This will be the last." It would be to the Beaufort Sea, in the Canadian Arctic, and also, as Shackleton put it,

> to the North Pole . . . Amundsen, I know from the Siberian side is planning to reach the North Pole. Why should I not get there before him?[9]

What Shackleton was referring to was this. In June, 1918, Amundsen had sailed from Norway, in a specially built ship called *Maud*, to start an Arctic drift. His plan was to sail along the Siberian coast, enter the ice at a suitable point, and drift across the Arctic Ocean towards Spitsbergen with the pack. It was to be an improvement on Nansen's voyage in the *Fram* two decades before.

In July 1920, two years after setting sail, Amundsen reached Nome, in Alaska. He had never got further north than the New Siberian Islands so that, "for the time being," as Shackleton put it, "his expedition has failed".[10] Amundsen nonetheless had become the second man ever to have navigated the North-East Passage. Also, passing through the Bering Strait, he crossed the course of his North West Passage of 1903-06, "and thus" in his own words, "became the first man to carry out the circumnavigation of the Arctic Ocean. In our age of records," as he put it, in his dry, ironical way, "that may have some significance".[11] Thus effortlessly, it seemed, Amundsen had salved a kind of triumph out of failure. But his heart was not really in this enterprise. It was an act of conscience to prove that he really had been heading north when he secretly turned south in 1910 to beat Scott to the South Pole. As far as Amundsen was concerned, Shackleton was welcome to the North Pole. Since Cook and Peary claimed to have reached it ten years before, the distinction, to Amundsen, was meaningless.

Shackleton, however, as he told Evans, felt "sure that there is land in the Beaufort Sea if not practically at the Pole". Shackleton was looking for mythical lands and the Islands of the Blest, just over the horizon. More practically, he needed money:

> I cannot afford now with the children growing up [Shackleton told Evans] to ever again mortgage my book lectures and film as I have done up to now for [he repeated] this must be my last expedition.

"I am assured of a certain amount of money," Shackleton declared, in only too well worn words,

> but not nearly enough and I want you to help me with your influence, your prestige, your practical knowledge of Polar work, to enable me to obtain the full amount I require.

"Now the crux and gist of this long letter," Shackleton disingenuously explained to Evans,

> is to ask you to give me as many personal letters of introduction to any of your Cardiff or other friends whom you think might help. If you have 10 friends who might put up £3000 each I would be all right.[12]

The Canadian explorer, Vilhjalmur Stefansson, meanwhile, also wanted to explore the Beaufort Sea. Shackleton's plans, if Stefansson were to be believed, had been stolen from himself.

Of Icelandic descent, Stefansson was a flamboyant, entertaining and persuasive character. Early in 1920 he had visited London and, by his own account, was entertained by Shackleton at the Marlborough Club. There, over port, "the orthodox beverage of the gentry", as Stefansson waspishly phrased it, "to the fringe of which Shackleton claimed that he belonged",

> I sat . . . talking freely and behaving like a simpleton, lulled by the feeling that he was an Antarctic man who cared nothing for anything but outdoing Scott and Amundsen.

Stefansson, in his own words, did not

> remember a word spoken at the Marlborough Club about any serious interest that Shackleton may have had in the northern polar regions . . . I do remember, however, that I revealed to Shackleton the very plans I had so far meticulously hidden.[13]

Shackleton later talked of penetrating the "Zone of Inaccessibility". The name, said Stefansson, he had "invented in 1918" himself.

It was not wholly implausible. For over a decade, Stefansson had been exploring in the Arctic. He had become the loud-spoken prophet of a rich and profitable north. Shackleton could hardly fail to have been apprised of his opinions. In any case, Shackleton had already talked of the Canadian Arctic while he was in north Russia. Late in 1920, he asked the Canadian government to help finance his expedition. He then became involved in the obscure byways of Canadian politics.

Stefansson had alerted the government in Ottawa to the weakness of the Canadian title to the Arctic archipelago. The government proposed to establish title with a secret expedition that would establish police posts. It had to be secret, in order not to alert other contenders, notably Denmark and the United States. Stefansson wished to be the expedition leader. He was, however, a controversial and widely mistrusted figure.

While Shackleton was in the south on *Endurance*, Stefansson had been in the Canadian Arctic. He had discovered new land at the edge of the Beaufort Sea and changed the map. Unfortunately, in the process, eleven of his men were killed. Among them were two of Shackleton's companions from the *Nimrod*: James Murray, and Alistair Forbes Mackay.

When Shackleton appeared on the scene, with money, plans and, as he said, a ship, Stefansson's enemies saw him as an alternative to the original expedition. Shackleton entered into involved negotiations with the Canadian government. He plunged happily yet again into the congenial rush of preparation.

In politics, as in business, Shackleton was naïve. He believed he had obtained an unqualified promise of Canadian support. He did not understand that he was being played off against Stefansson. The Cabinet was divided. The Premier, Arthur Meighen, broadly favoured Stefansson. In March 1921, a Canadian civil servant warned that

> if any aid or recognition is given . . . Shackleton . . . either (or both) the United States and Denmark may receive advance information from Stefansson . . . because Shackleton proposes to explore the identical region that Stefansson also proposes to explore . . . the chance of putting Stefansson in the camp of our enemies is too great a one to be taken.[14]

Only in the spring of 1921, after two rushed visits to Ottawa, did Shackleton begin to comprehend. Early in May, in a typically imperious cable, he told Meighen he was "urgently awaiting your action":

> Please cable Government's definite support and amount bearing in mind the Government's Arctic Expedition would have cost approximately quarter million dollars.[15]

This was partly an attempt to out-manoeuvre Stefansson, who wished to be wholly financed by the government. Stefansson for his part alleged that Shackleton had double-crossed him by spreading rumours that he was no longer interested in exploration. By then, caught between two such persistent and turbulent characters, Meighen had decided that the best way out of the predicament would be to send no expedition at all.

Shackleton bluntly cabled that he had been told in Ottawa that the "Government would support me if I would get adequate outside help".[16] The Canadian government, Meighen cabled in reply, had

> made no definite commitment whatever . . . promise of consideration, was upon conditions that at no time to date have been complied with Stop Furthermore Government was advised recently . . . that you could not go on with your expedition this year.[17]

"Keen disappointment adverse decision," Shackleton characteristically cabled in reply,

> Cannot see where I failed to comply with conditions . . . I have held my ship waiting confirmation of Government and that is why the main expedition was postponed . . . Earnestly beg your reconsideration.[18]

To which Meighen coolly answered that he could not "give any definite promise".[19]

More even than before, Shackleton was afraid of being trapped. He had not yet finished paying for the *Endurance* expedition. He was ensnared in a lifetime's accumulation of debt. He desperately wanted to escape from an insoluble financial predicament.

Evans' introductions had not actually produced any money. Shackleton, however, had been lucky with John Quiller Rowett, an old school friend. They used to walk home together from Dulwich, and Shackleton would help Rowett with his prep. They had kept intermittent contact down the years and now Shackleton's powers of persuasion finally worked.

Rowett was conspicuously wealthy, his fortune coming mostly from rum. He was supposed actually to have cornered most of the world's supply. Stodgy and prosaic looking, he concealed a wistful desire to do something more than merely making money. He was an amateur farmer. He founded an Institute of Animal Nutrition at Aberdeen University. He endowed dental research at the Middlesex Hospital. He now followed in the footsteps of William Beardmore and Sir James Caird to finance one of Shackleton's expeditions.

Rowett at first had agreed only partly to finance Shackleton. He expected the Canadians to do the rest. Such was still Shackleton's personal magnetism, and such his self-control in the face of the emotions welling up within, that Rowett now calmly agreed to pay almost everything himself. Despite all his resolutions, Shackleton, once more, promised repayment out of future lectures, films, and a book.

It was now too late for the Arctic that year, but Shackleton somehow could not bear to wait. Like Amundsen in 1910, he swung from one hemisphere to the other. To avoid any more delay, he would use the Antarctic summer and go south instead. Rowett generously agreed.

Shackleton had three months in which to cram his preparations, whereas even for *Nimrod* and *Endurance* he had had six months at least. In one way, as of old, he was revived by the rush. Nonetheless, he seemed a driven man in a way he had not been before.

In April, had come an echo from the past. At Kilmorna, in the West of Ireland, Sir Arthur Vicars was murdered in the terror against the Anglo-Irish demesnes that accompanied the foundation of the Irish Free State. Sir Arthur was one more victim of the fate that, one by one, had enveloped those concerned in the theft of the Irish crown jewels.

After fourteen years, the mystery had never, officially, been solved. Until the day he was dragged out of bed and shot, Sir Arthur believed that the "real culprit and thief", as he put it, was "Francis R. Shackleton, (brother of the explorer who didn't reach the South Pole)".

Sir Arthur's belief was so strong that he put it in his will. He did not, in his own words, "have more to dispose of" because he had been made a "scapegoat to save other departments responsible" for the disappearance of the jewels and they, in their turn, shielded Frank. "My whole life & work," said Sir Arthur, "was ruined by this cruel misfortune."[20]

Frank himself made a final fleeting appearance in his brother's life. He arrived one day at the expedition offices in the City, near the Thames, offering to obtain cheap equipment. Shackleton by now had disowned Frank, and brusquely ordered him to keep away. For thirty years Frank, who had aspired so high, lived on under his pseudonym, never to emerge from his obscurity, and ending his days as an antique dealer near Chichester, with an interest in precious stones.

On 17 September 1921, from St Katharine's Dock, under Tower Bridge, Shackleton finally sailed. A large crowd on the riverside cheered and waved farewell. By then, Shackleton had been elected to the Royal Yacht Squadron so that, at last, he could fly the White Ensign. Also, he had his sixth audience with King George V.

Emily was not down at the docks to see her husband off, but Rosalind Chetwynd did visit the ship before she sailed. Shackleton was obviously more relaxed now with his mistress than with his wife. That did not stop him writing copiously to Emily along the way, with all the old phrases like "I miss you more than I put in words."[21] Emily, as usual, knew that if he really was missing her, all could not be well.

Shackleton had received several letters from Rowett, "a mixture of moans and friendship", as he wrote to Emily from Madeira; "moans at the expense and terms of friendship combined . . . fundamentally he is all right but he feels the parting with the money". Moreover, he warned Emily that Rowett and his wife were "very kind", but inclined to be possessive, especially Rowett himself. So, Shackleton advised,

> *dont* be too dependent on him and *dont* discuss little household things with him . . . Let him run after *you* more than you talking to him otherwise you will have no peace and Keep your independence. You can afford to whatever he has paid he has had his money's worth.[22]

That was hardly fair. Shackleton had left Emily, once more, without any means of support except her own income. £700 a year no longer went as far as it did in 1914. Janet Stancomb-Wills helped, but Rowett, out of sheer charity, came to Emily's rescue.

It was out of charity, too, that Rowett had paid for the expedition. It was not like those before. It had no dramatic scheme; there was no obvious goal. It was only too clearly a piece of improvisation, a pretext to get away.

What Shackleton proposed was a circumnavigation of the Antarctic continent, looking for "lost" or uncertain sub-Antarctic islands. He considered exploring the Enderby quadrant of the continental coastline, still incompletely known. Then he wanted to look for Captain Kidd's treasure on South Trinidad in the Atlantic, and again he thought of searching for a certain pearl lagoon in the South Seas. Oceanography was on his programme too. Also, he intended to ascertain "once for all", as he put it, "the history and methods of the Pacific natives in their navigation across the Pacific spaces hundreds of years before Columbus crossed the Atlantic".[23]

These were almost the same words as Worsley had used when soliloquising about the albatross on the open-boat journey, five years before. The item was inserted because Worsley was captain of this ship too.

The nucleus of the expedition was the "old guard" as Shackleton put it, from *Endurance*. By cable mostly, he had called for them; and they came: Macklin, Worsley, McIlroy, Wild, Hussey, McLeod, Kerr, and Green, the cook who had imperturbably produced meals under the most unlikely conditions. Some had not yet been paid all the money owed them from *Endurance*, but still they came, McIlroy and Wild all the way from Nyasaland. There, after a less than satisfactory winter in Spitsbergen with the Northern Exploration Company, they had gone to try cotton planting. It was like a reunion, or a farewell.

The vessel in which they sailed was ill-found, and uncomfortable. Shackleton had bought her on a hasty visit to Norway at the beginning of the year. She was a wooden sealer of 125 tons originally called *Foca I*. At Emily's suggestion she was aptly renamed *Quest*.

Small and straight-stemmed, *Quest* had been intended for the Arctic expedition. She was not suited to a long, oceanic voyage. With an awkward square rig on her mainmast, she wallowed in the

Atlantic rollers, and lumbered heavily in the trade winds. Her engines were too weak. Out at sea, her boiler was found to be cracked. She needed repairs at every port of call.

Against all this, Shackleton seemed to fight as he had always fought. But there was a strange undertone of regret on board. In an unguarded moment, Shackleton was heard to remark that he wished he were young enough still to cross Antarctica. "The years are mounting up," he wrote to Janet Stancomb-Wills from Rio de Janeiro, with his now constant theme,

> I am mad to get away. If I knew you less well I would not write like this but I want to open up . . . we . . . go into the ice into the life that is mine and I do pray that we will make good, it will be my last time I want to write your good name high on the map and however erratic I may seem always remember this, that I go to work secure in the trust of a few who know me and you my friend not least among them.[24]

The voyage seemed to have a beginning but, somehow, no end. The expedition geologist, Vibert Douglas, believed that Shackleton "hoped to find some mineral deposit that would get him out of his financial straits".[25] Douglas was a Canadian, intended originally for the abortive Arctic expedition. He had not sailed with Shackleton before.

Nor had an Australian on board called George (later Sir Hubert) Wilkins. A cameraman by training, and a compulsive wanderer with a mystic streak, Wilkins found solace only away from civilisation. He had been with Stefansson in the north, and was therefore used to probing the motives of explorers. He believed this was "to be a long, but not entirely selfish joy ride . . . a last expedition [Shackleton] was determined to have".[26]

In Murmansk, a brother officer had found Shackleton one of the "few men of note", as he put it, "who 'off-stage' have lived up to their stage personalities."[27] On *Quest*, except in spurts, it was hard to feel that way. Wilkins, in his own words, was "not very much impressed with Sir Ernest's leadership. He is far less competent than Stefansson & not such a big minded man. He cares only for newspaper notices & money."[28]

The presence on board of an eighteen-year-old Boy Scout called James Marr seemed partly confirmation. He was there for publicity, organised by the *Daily Mail*. He was obliged to put his name to a ghosted book, under a contract arranged by Shackleton. Marr afterwards became an explorer in his own right, but he was always considerably embarrassed by the recollection of this aspect of the voyage.

Even to his old companions, Shackleton was not the man they had known. "There is something different in him this trip as compared with the last", as Macklin put it, "which I do not understand."[29] By then, it was late December, and they were pitching and tossing out in the South Atlantic on the way to South Georgia.

Since meeting Shackleton in north Russia, Macklin had known that he would follow him on his next expedition. After a chance meeting in London, Shackleton asked him to stay by him, and help with the preliminaries. It was undoubtedly a compliment.

Macklin nonetheless was uneasy when Shackleton made his new approach. In the first place, the expedition was still no more than an idea, and Shackleton too transparently wanted a tame hanger-on; a social secretary, for he dreaded loneliness. Macklin was realistic enough to realise that it was the Shackleton of the wilds that he admired. He was not really at ease with the Shackleton of civilisation.

For that reason, Macklin declined Shackleton's pressing invitation. Instead, he went back to hospital, and then sailed as a ship's surgeon to Japan. When he returned, in the spring of 1921, Shackleton made the expedition seem a reality and so then he joined.

Even so, Macklin was still not quite at ease. Shackleton left virtually all the organisation to him. That was out of character. It was as if Shackleton were losing his vitality.

Macklin was also unable to keep clear of Shackleton's private affairs. Emily, although more or less resigned to Rosalind Chetwynd's role, persisted in questioning him about her husband's movements when they met. That aroused Macklin's resentment. In any case, he knew too much about Rosalind and said as little as he could.[30]

In April, when the Arctic was the goal, and the Canadian government was still involved, Shackleton had sent Macklin out to Canada to buy the expedition dogs without, however, revealing the uncertainties of the situation. Eventually, in a flurry of cables, Macklin was suddenly recalled. He was not entirely unprepared, for in Canada he had gradually been acquainted with the real state of affairs. Passing through New York, he found himself, at Shackleton's request, cabling the terms of Rosalind's mother's will to her in London. "Don't spare words," Shackleton had characteristically said. Rosalind, he cabled Macklin, "very grateful all you have done".[31]

Also in New York, Macklin had accidentally learned that Shackleton had left thousands of dollars lying with his American agents, perhaps out of forgetfulness, perhaps out of a desire to keep something beyond the reach of English creditors, or benefactors. In a most casual way, Macklin was told to draw upon these funds as he wished, although as a matter of fact, he was among those who had not yet been paid what they were owed from the *Endurance* expedition. It did not impair his devotion to his old chief.

Back in London, Macklin came in contact with a little company called Cargo and General, another of Shackleton's hopeful money-spinners. Its two employees had not been paid for weeks. Macklin decided that Shackleton was "unbusinesslike" and shrugged it off. His loyalty was entirely to the Boss.

As a doctor, however, Macklin was uneasy. On board *Quest*, Shackleton was manifestly ill. His broad face seemed unnaturally wan and pinched. He was, however, Macklin's leader, not exactly his patient, and he fended off all attempts at turning casual talk into a consultation.

At Rio de Janeiro, Shackleton had a massive heart attack, called for Macklin and then, as usual, refused to be examined. It was nonetheless quite clear to Macklin now that he was suffering from heart disease. Macklin could see the change in Shackleton since the *Endurance*. All the ailments, which Shackleton had done his best to conceal, now fell into a pattern. It went back at least three years to the suspected heart attack during the Spitsbergen expedition. For want of anything more precise, Macklin called it angina.

Shackleton was noticeably drinking. He took champagne in the mornings, possibly to ease pain. Sometimes, he showed flashes of his old self, but he was also displaying an unfamiliar combination of docility, peevishness and vacillation, interspersed with his old obstinacy. Against all Macklin's urgent professional advice, Shackleton insisted on staying on the bridge four nights in a row during a storm.

More than anything else, it was Shackleton's mental changes that troubled Macklin. Shackleton seemed unnaturally listless. He had no plans, and the only certainty was that they were headed for South Georgia as their first port of call after leaving Rio. Much of the time, Shackleton seemed content simply to listen to Hussey strumming his banjo; the same instrument he had on Elephant Island. It was hard to explain to the newcomers what sort of leader Shackleton had been.

Only in spells did his old personality appear to well up. He seemed to have turned towards the past. One of the men on board was James Dell, his old messdeck friend from *Discovery*, whom Shackleton impulsively took on *Quest*, after a reunion at the dockside in London. Dell sailed as a companion with whom

Shackleton could talk over old times from a fresh point of view. They were bound by a common dislike of Scott. It was to Dell that Shackleton now unburdened his feelings. After all those years, he still burned with resentment at the way Scott had made him renounce McMurdo Sound, and thus forced him to break his promise when he sailed there on *Nimrod* after all. *That* was the albatross around his neck.[32]

"The Boss," Macklin wrote on the last day of 1921, "says . . . quite frankly that he does not know what he will do after S. Georgia." It seemed almost another person. "I do not," as Macklin put it, "understand his enigmatical attitude."[33]

"Rest and calm after the storm," Shackleton wrote next day. He was always erratic in keeping a diary. This time he had ceased very early in the voyage. Now, on New Year's Day, he decided to start again.

> The year has begun kindly for us: it is curious how a certain date becomes a factor and milestone in ones life: Christmas Day in the raging gale seemed out of place . . . Anxiety [he said] has been probing deeply into me: for until the very end of the year things have gone awry: engines unreliable: furnace cracked, water short: heavy gales: all that physically can go wrong but the spirit of all on board sound & good:
> "There are two points in the adventures of the diver,
> One when a beggar he prepares to plunge,
> One when a prince he rises with his pearl."[34]

"The old familiar sight," he wrote next day, after passing the first iceberg, "aroused in me memories that the strenuous year had deadened":

> Ah me: the years that have gone since in the pride of young manhood I first went forth to the fight I grow old and tired but must always lead on.[35]

The following day, calm and clear again, Shackleton found "a difficulty in settling down to write", as he put it, "I am so much on the qui vive". Fortune, he went on,

> seems to attend us this New Year. But so anxious have I been, when things are going well I wonder what internal difficulty will be sprung on me . . . I pray that the furnace will hold out.[36]
> "Thankful that I can
> Be crossed and thwarted as a man."

Finally, next day, 4 January, *Quest* raised the mountains of South Georgia and closed the land.

"Like a pair of excitable kids", said Worsley, he and Shackleton

> were rushing around shewing everyone where we first came over the mountains on our 1916 tramp across S.G. from King Haakon [Bay] to Stromness Bay after our boat journey from Elephant Id. Finally the "Boss" called me when I was on the bridge to come & show some of the others a point he wasn't quite sure of, but I couldn't leave here at the time & came down later, but the dear old "Boss" was quite prepared for me to let the ship wander along on her own.[37]

Past the old landmarks, *Quest* sailed on: past Possession Bay, Fortuna Bay, the ridge down which Shackleton, Worsley and Crean had glissaded on the journey that seemed so long ago. "At last after 16 days of turmoil and anxiety: on a peaceful sunshiny day," as Shackleton put it, *Quest* anchored outside the whaling station of Grytviken. It was eight years since he had sailed up the selfsame fjord in *Endurance*, full of hope, on his way to the Weddell Sea.

Many of the old faces were there. Fridthjof Jacobsen was still station manager. He came out in a boat to *Quest*, and took Shackleton ashore.

"The 'Boss'", in the words of Lieutenant Jeffrey, the navigating officer, was now "more like himself than he has been so far this trip." Jeffrey, having left *Endurance* before she sailed from England, because war had broken out, had at last satisfied his ambition of serving under Shackleton. What Jeffrey now saw, as he put it, was "more like the Shacks I knew in 1914".[38]

Macklin was not so sanguine. Jacobsen, he found, had

> changed very much, is very much stouter looking & not the same pleasant man that he was last time. . . . I could not help thinking how much both of them had changed, & how much older looking they were than when I last saw them together.[39]

Shackleton was in a strange, docile mood when he returned on board. "Now we must speed all we can," he wrote in his diary that night, "but the prospect is not too bright . . ."

> The old smell of dead whale permeates everything: It is a strange and curious place . . . A wonderful evening.
>
> "In the darkening twilight I saw a lone star hover, gem like above the bay."[40]

Macklin was not really surprised when in the small hours he was called to Shackleton, and found him with another heart attack. Macklin told him, as he had told him many times before, that he would have to change his way of life. In Macklin's words:

> He replied "You're always wanting me to give up things, what is it I ought to give up." I replied "chiefly alcohol Boss I don't think it agrees with you."[41]

A few minutes later Shackleton was dead.

It was 5 January 1922.

Events, with hindsight, fell into place. Shocked and saddened, Worsley wrote:

> Shackleton being superstitious to a certain extent about some things appears to have been impressed by some fortune teller that he told us had before the last expedition told him he would die at 48. He died within 41 days of attaining that age.[42]

McIlroy never forgot that, as they were coming out of Plymouth, their last port in England,

> there was one of these bell buoys [with] rather a mournful sound and [Shackleton] turned to the . . . Harbourmaster . . . and he said "That's my death knell."[43]

Dell for his part remembered that Shackleton "never understood why they made such a fuss over Scott's death. He remarked on that to me the night practically that he died."[44] When the news got back to England, an admirer recalled that, just before sailing on *Quest*, Shackleton told him that

> he did not mean to die in Europe. He wanted some day to die away on one of his expeditions. "And," he said, "I shall go on going, old man, till one day I shall not come back."[45]

For Macklin, there was a special poignancy in something Shackleton had written not long before:

> "Never the lowered Banner
>   Never the lost Endeavour."[46]

Macklin had the awful duty of performing a post mortem on his friend. He found that Shackleton's last years at least must have been a fight against heart disease. Shackleton, in Macklin's own words, died from

> *atheroma* [fatty degeneration] *of the coronary arteries*. The condition was a long-standing one and, in my opinion was due to overstrain during a period of debility. [It] may have been produced during his own great pioneer journey towards the South Pole.

"What is remarkable," said Macklin, in quiet tribute as friend, follower and doctor, "is that in such an advanced condition he was able to carry on as he did. It shows, psychologically, a wonderful will power and an unyielding determination."

> His physical qualities [in Macklin's telling words] are well known. As a living organism he was wonderful.[47]

Shackleton's body was sent back to England for burial. With it went Hussey, who had no heart for the expedition now that the leader had gone.

When Emily heard what had happened, she decided that her husband should be buried on South Georgia. His unquiet spirit had no place in the green fields of England where, somehow, he had never been at ease. If he had a home on earth, it must be among the wild, mystic crags and glaciers of the island in the Southern Ocean which had meant so much to him. To the end, it was Emily who understood Ernest Shackleton best of all.

So from Montevideo, Hussey turned, and brought Shackleton's remains back to Grytviken. There, on 5 March, he was laid to rest in the Norwegian cemetery, along with the whalers, the outcasts of the sea, amongst whom he had felt at home.

"Life," Frank Hurley had finished his book on the *Endurance* expedition by saying, "is one long call to conflict, anyway."[48] Shackleton's whole life had been a battle. He had fought the shadow of heart disease, as he had fought the obscure bafflement that seemed to be his fate. The last voyage had been an astonishing display of determination. Where most other men would have quietly lain down in bed, he had made himself survive until he had escaped from civilisation.

Shackleton spanned the classic age of Antarctic discovery, before machines took over. His great service was to break the mould of mediocrity that bedevilled British polar exploration. He did this by bringing character and humour to a pursuit often cursed by excessive high-mindedness and lacklustre overseers. He showed what sheer power of leadership achieves. He created in England the image of the polar explorer as hero.

When he died, Shackleton left debts of £40,000, over £500,000 in today's terms. That money, however, came from people who could afford it. Shackleton never battened on the public. He never assumed the air of deserving virtue. He was one of the last examples of private enterprise in exploration.

Shackleton was ruthless and ambitious, and sought personal fulfilment. All this, however, withered before the flame of leadership which burned within him. He had the indefinable ability to make things happen. After all, with no money of his own, he somehow organised three expeditions.

Shackleton's tragedy was that he lacked the winning touch. Technical deficiency was the only bar to his success. While waiting to start for the South Pole, Amundsen put it in these words:

> I admire in the highest degree what [Shackleton] and his companions achieved with the equipment they had. Bravery, determination, strength they did not lack. A little more experience . . . would have crowned their work with success.[49]

Mental sloth was Shackleton's fatal flaw. He lacked the patience to acquire the necessary technique. He was punished by having to play the precursor. He was the man fated to go ahead, while others reaped the fruits of his work. There, too, Amundsen was the man who understood him well. "We did not pass . . . without expressing our highest admiration and recognition for the man who . . . had placed his country's flag closer to the goal than any of his predecessors", he wrote on reaching Shackleton's Furthest South on the way to the South Pole.

> Sir Ernest Shackleton's name will for evermore be engraved with letters of fire in the history of Antarctic exploration. Courage and willpower can make miracles. I know of no better example than what that man has accomplished.[50]

From another point of view, Shackleton was almost the typical British hero in the age of decline: the glorious failure. He added something of his own, however. He was a survivor.

That was an inspiring example, or ought to have been. It was the very reason, perhaps, why in England his reputation soon began to wane. Mindless heroism was more to the public taste. Besides, Shackleton was too much the frank adventurer. The English required their heroes to assume a moralistic sheen. And in the end, Shackleton lived by his personality and conversation; so that when he went, it was hard to preserve the sense of what he was.

Even as an Anglo-Irishman, Shackleton was soon half-forgotten. An Irish hero he did not become; although there was something quintessentially Irish about the strange unfulfilled nature of his life.

Behind him, Shackleton left the same extreme emotions he had always conjured up. His enemies remained his enemies. The partisans of Scott remained contemptuous and cutting. Among them, morality was commercial, and by that touchstone, Shackleton had long since been dismissed. He, however, came from a tradition where personal qualities meant more than money, and loyalty stood higher than financial rectitude.

Among his friends and followers, Shackleton left a void they found difficult to express. Rowett put it one way when he wrote that "although the [*Quest*] Expedition cost me a great deal more than I intended," – £70,000 in fact – "I shall always be grateful for the friendship we had for each other."[51]

Shackleton may have sought personal fulfilment, but he would not sacrifice his followers to his ambition. Rather, he was prepared to risk his life to save his men. That, his followers saw as his great redeeming virtue.

In the words of Leonard Hussey,

> For us he had faults but no vices . . . He had his faults & knew it, too, and he expected perfection in no man; but he was quite willing to overlook what was bad and just remembered the good in everyone. He had a way of compelling loyalty. We would have gone anywhere without question just on his order . . . Now that he has gone, there is a gap in our lives that can never be filled.[52]

In the last resort, Shackleton defied categorisation. When his old school, Dulwich, listed famous old boys by profession, he was classified simply as – Shackleton.

After Shackleton died, the *Quest* carried on, under Wild's command. Without Shackleton, however, Wild was lost. He was soon drinking heavily, something he had never done before at sea. He seemed practically an alcoholic. Eventually, sixteen years later, he died in miserable circumstances in South Africa. The voyage was not a success; but before *Quest* sailed back to England in June, Wild took her to Elephant Island. "What memories the sight . . . revives," Macklin wrote, in a strange, pensive and unaccustomed mood,

> the boat journey, the last bad night, the landing at Valentine, the row to Cape Wild, the subsequent miseries & the long sojourn on Wild spit. We have stood gazing with bincculars picking out & recognizing old familiar spots, each reminiscent of some incident which we recall by

saying "do you remember the rock we nearly got washed up on, there it is just coming into view etc." Few of us thought when we left it last that it would ever be our fate to see it again. Ah what memories what memories! – they rush to one like a great flood & bring tears to ones eyes, & as I sit & try to write a great rush of feeling comes over me & I find I cannot express myself or what I feel. Once more I see the little boat, Frankie Wild's hut, dark & dirty, but a snug little shelter all the same. Once more I see the old faces & hear the old voices – old friends scattered everywhere. But to express all I feel is impossible.[53]

Epilogue

The Fourth Presence

Shackleton's epitaph was written by a Scots doctor on South Georgia, conveying what he had heard from the whalers. While he was half-forgotten at home, Shackleton had become a legend among the whalers. "So what they do," one whaler – a composite character – was made to say, in his broken English, telling the oft-told yarn of the *Endurance*:

> So what they do? They sit down and pray to God? Or start writing dramatic diaries about all is lost, same like Captain Scott? Na-a-a-w! Shackleton just say: "O.K. boys! We go home!" – and he bring 'em all home, safe and well.[1]

"When I look back on those days," Shackleton himself had written in *South*, at the end of the chapter on the crossing of South Georgia,

> I have no doubt that Providence guided us, not only across the snowfields, but across the storm-white sea that separated Elephant island from our landing-place on South Georgia. I know that during that long and racking march of thirty-six hours over the unnamed mountains and glaciers of South Georgia it seemed to me often that we were four, not three.[2]

Leonard Tripp had actually been present when Shackleton dictated that passage to Saunders:

> I shall never forget the occasion . . . Shackleton walked up and down the room, smoking a cigarette, and I was absolutely amazed at his language. He very seldom hesitated, but every now and then he would tell Saunders . . . he had not got the right word.

I watched him, and his whole face seemed to swell – you know what a big face he had, and you could see the man was suffering. After about half-an-hour he turned to me, and with tears in his eyes he said, "Tripp, you don't know what I've been through, and I am going through it all again, and I can't do it." – I would say "But we must get it down".

"He would go on for an hour and then all of a sudden . . . walked out of the room as if he intended to go away . . . and then in about five minutes would come back and start as if nothing had happened. The same thing happened after about another half hour or so":

You could see that the man was suffering, and then he came to this mention of the fourth man . . .

At that Shackleton, in Tripp's own words, "turned round to me and said, 'Tripp, this is something I have not told you'".[3]

At the time, as Shackleton also wrote in *South*,

I said nothing to my companions on the point, but afterwards Worsley said to me, "Boss, I had a curious feeling on the march that there was another person with us." Crean confessed to the same idea. One feels "the dearth of human words, the roughness of mortal speech" in trying to describe things intangible, but a record of our journeys would be incomplete without a reference to a subject very near to our hearts.[4]

This passage was invoked in sermons, tracts, and revivalist urgings. Shackleton himself, in any case, believed he had undergone a mystical experience.

About the time that Shackleton died T. S. Eliot was completing *The Waste Land*. When he came to write the haunting lines:

Who is the third who walks always beside you?
When I count, there are only you and I together
But when I look ahead up the white road
There is always another one walking beside you
Gliding wrapt in a brown mantle, hooded
I do not know whether a man or a woman
– But who is that on the other side of you?

Eliot explained in his notes to the poem that he was

stimulated by the account of one of the Antarctic expeditions (I forget which, but I think one of Shackleton's): it was related that the party of explorers, at the extremity of their strength, had the constant delusion that there was *one more member* than could actually be counted.[5]

Thus did Shackleton's belief in the Fourth Presence on the crossing of South Georgia come to rest. He did not achieve public immortality through being the first man to reach the South Pole, which he so ardently desired. The final, poignant irony of his life is that Shackleton, the frustrated poet, found a more hidden immortality through one of the great poems of the age.

Appendices

Note on units

A short list of useful temperatures in Fahrenheit and Centigrade:

Water freezes at 32°F, which is 0°C.
Normal body temperature, 98.4°F is 37°C.
−50°F (82 degrees of frost) is −45.5°C.
−40°F (72 degrees of frost) is −40°C.
−30°F (62 degrees of frost) is −34.5°C.
−20°F (52 degrees of frost) is −29°C.
0°F (32 degrees of frost) is −18°C.

During most of Shackleton's lifetime, inflation was negligible, sterling was stable, its rate of exchange against the dollar was about 4.8, and in 1985 terms £1 was equivalent to about £27. In 1920, however, £1 was only worth approximately £14 in 1985 terms. Its dollar value was unchanged.

The historical, predecimalised pound sterling was divided into 20 shillings, each of 12 pence; usually referred to by their symbols £ s d.

The pound weight (lb) contains 16 ounces (oz), and there are 2⅕ lbs to the kilogram. The Imperial ton and metric tonne are virtually equal.

A foot is equivalent to about 30.5 cms.

The nautical, or geographical mile is one sixtieth of a degree, or one minute of latitude. It is fixed at 6,080 feet, equivalent to 1⅐ statute miles, or 1.85 kilometres.

Abbreviations

AAC Australian Archives, Canberra.

DKB Det Kongelige Bibliotek (the Royal Library), Copenhagen.

HRM H. R. Mill's notes of Ernest Shackleton's correspondence with Janet Stancomb-Wills in the archives of the Scott Polar Research Institute, Cambridge.

MFP Macklin family papers, in the possession of Mrs Jean Macklin, Aberdeen.

MI Mawson Institute for Antarctic Research, Adelaide, Australia.

ML Mitchell Library, State Library of New South Wales, Sydney, Australia.

NA National Archives and Records Service, Washington, D.C.

NMG National Maritime Museum, Greenwich.

PAC Public Archives of Canada, Ottawa.

PRO Public Record Office, Kew.

RGS Royal Geographical Society.

SPRI Scott Polar Research Institute, Cambridge.

TBL Alexander Turnbull Library, Wellington, New Zealand.

UB Universitetsbibliotek (University library), Oslo.

US University of Sydney Archives.

Notes

Prologue: "Great Shack!"
(page 3)

1 Miss Swinford Edwards, interview with author.

2 E. H. Shackleton, diary, 29 October 1908 (SPRI).

Chapter I: Anglo-Irish background
(pages 4–12)

1 Charles McCormick, *Memoirs of the Right Honourable Edmund Burke*, p. 6.
2 Terence De Vere White, *The Anglo-Irish*, p. 23.
3 Ibid., p. 24.
4 *Band of Hope Melodies*, 1873.
5 J. G. Dunlop, letters to James Fisher, 17 April, 1 May, 1959.
6 J. C. Beckett, *The Anglo Irish Tradition*, p. 59.
7 O. T. Burne, letter to H. R. Mill, 10 May 1922 (SPRI).
8 William Townend, *quoted* Benny Green, *P. G. Wodehouse—A Literary Biography*, p. 11.
9 *The Captain*, April 1910, p. 42.
10 Ibid.
11 *Boys' Own Paper*, 9 June 1889.
12 Mrs E. C. Davis, letter to Margery Fisher, 20 September 1955.
13 Nicetas Petrides, letter to H. R. Mill, 3 April 1923 (SPRI).
14 G. Wilson Knight, manuscript in Dulwich College Library.
15 *Quoted*, Sheila Hodges, *God's Gift*, p. 64.
16 *The Captain*, op. cit.
17 Ibid., p. 45.

Chapter II: Round the Horn
(pages 13–23)

1 E. H. Shackleton, letter to Nicetas Petrides, 7 January 1892 (SPRI).
2 *The Captain*, April 1910, p. 44.
3 H. R. Mill, *The Life of Sir Ernest Shackleton*, p. 33.
4 E. H. Shackleton, op. cit.
5 J. A. Hussey, letter to H. R. Mill, 18 June 1922 (SPRI).
6 E. H. Shackleton, op. cit.
7 Thomas Peers, interview with Margery Fisher (SPRI).
8 O. T. Burne, letter to H. R. Mill, 10 May 1922 (SPRI).
9 James Dunsmore, *The United Methodist*, 4 May 1922, p. 213.
10 Ibid.
11 *The Captain*, April 1910, p. 43.
12 James Dunsmore, op. cit.
13 Kathleen Shackleton, letter to Margery Fisher, 25 November 1955 (SPRI).
14 Emily Shackleton, letter to H. R. Mill, 26 June 1922 (SPRI).
15 Charles Sarolea, *Contemporary Review*, Vol. 121, 1922, p. 321.
16 E. H. Shackleton, letter to Emily Dorman, 12 August 1898 (SPRI).
17 Browning, *Paracelsus*, II, line 420.
18 E. H. Shackleton, op. cit.
19 Ibid.
20 J. A. Hussey, op. cit.
21 E. H. Shackleton, op. cit.

Chapter III: A path to fame and fortune?
(pages 24–30)

1 *The Captain*, April 1910, p. 42.
2 *Boys' Own Paper*, 4 February 1882.
3 J. A. Hussey, letter to H. R. Mill, 27 July 1922 (SPRI).
4 Ibid., 18 May 1922.
5 J. Scott Keltie, letter to E. H. Shackleton, 15 February 1900 (RGS).
6 *The Times*, 29 May 1900.
7 *Westminster Gazette*, 2 April 1900, p. 1.
8 *The Times*, op. cit.
9 Ibid.
10 *Westminster Gazette*, 4 July 1900.
11 Ibid., 2 April 1900.
12 H. R. Mill, *An Autobiography*, p. 138.
13 *Daily Chronicle*, 19 March 1899.
14 A. B. Armitage, memorandum for H. R. Mill (SPRI).
15 Ibid.
16 Sir Clements Markham, *Officers of the Discovery* (SPRI).

Chapter IV: National Antarctic Expedition
(pages 31–44)

1 *Pall Mall Gazette*, 20 May 1901.
2 J. W. Gregory, letter to Professor Poulton, 21 January 1901 (SPRI).
3 *Quoted*, Arthur Marder, *British Naval Policy: 1880–1905, The Anatomy of British Sea Power*, p. 44.
4 Sir Clements Markham, "Address to the Royal Geographical Society", 5 June 1899, *Geographical Journal*, Vol. xiv, 1899, p. 12.
5 Sir Clements Markham, diary, 23 January 1901 (RGS).
6 *Quoted*, Nowell-Smith, *Edwardian England*, p. 3.
7 *The Times*, 23 January 1901.
8 Ibid., 1 January 1901.
9 Sir Clements Markham, *Officers of the Discovery* (SPRI).
10 Sir Clements Markham, *The Starting of the Antarctic Expedition* (SPRI).
11 Sir Clements Markham, *Officers of the Discovery*.
12 *Pall Mall Gazette*, op. cit.
13 Rear Admiral Sir William Wharton, letter to Lord Walter Kerr, 1 May 1901 (PRO ADM 1/7463 B).
14 Sir Clements Markham, letter to Admiral Lord Walter Kerr, 2 April 1900 (PRO ADM 1/7463 B).
15 R. F. Scott, Service Record (PRO ADM 196/42 fol. 501).
16 Rear Admiral Sir William Wharton, op. cit.
17 Admiral Lord Walter Kerr, minute, Rear Admiral Sir William Wharton, op. cit.
18 Rear Admiral Sir William Wharton, op. cit.
19 Sir Clements Markham, letter to J. Scott Keltie, 24 July 1899 (RGS).
20 John S. Flett, "J. W. Gregory", *Nature*, 25 June 1932, p. 930.
21 J. W. Gregory, letter to Professor Poulton, op. cit.
22 Ibid., 16 January 1901.
23 George Murray, letter to H. R. Mill, 24 February 1901 (SPRI).
24 J. W. Gregory, op. cit., 16 January 1901 (SPRI).
25 Ibid., 21 January 1901.
26 Sir Clements Markham, diary, 25 April 1901 (RGS).
27 E. H. Shackleton, letter to Emily Dorman, 20 April 1901 (SPRI).
28 E. H. Shackleton, letter to Charles Dorman, 3 August 1901 (SPRI).
29 H. R. Mill, *An Autobiography*, p. 96.
30 Admiral Fitzgerald, address to United Service Institution, 10 April 1895.
31 *Morning Post*, 5 August 1901.
32 *Referee*.
33 Ibid.
34 *Daily Express*, 29 July 1901.
35 Ibid.
36 *Constitution of the Ancient Fraternity of Free and Accepted Masons*.
37 *Quoted*, Jacobs, *The Radical Enlightenment*, p. 133.
38 Mellor, *Our Separated Brethren, the Freemasons*, p. 90.
39 *The Complete Workings of Craft Freemasonry*, p. 39.
40 Charles Dorman, letter to E. H. Shackleton, 8 August 1901 (SPRI).

Chapter V: *Discovery*
(pages 45–50)

1 H. R. Mill, *An Autobiography*, p. 135.
2 Ibid.
3 *Daily News*, 1 August 1901.
4 H. R. Mill, *The Life of Sir Ernest Shackleton*, p. 61.
5 Ibid.
6 H. R. Mill, "Ernest Henry Shackleton, M.V.O.", *Travel & Exploration*, Vol. ii, No. 7, July 1909, p. 2.
7 H. R. Mill, "Lieutenant Shackleton's Achievement", *The Geographical Journal*, Vol. xxxiii, p. 570.
8 H. R. Mill, *The Life of Sir Ernest Shackleton*, p. 57.
9 E. H. Shackleton, diary, 16 August 1901 (SPRI).
10 The *Evening Standard*, 29 March 1899.
11 J. W. Gregory, letter to Mrs Edith Chapman, 29 October 1901 (SPRI).
12 E. H. Shackleton, op. cit., 25 August 1901.
13 Ibid., 1 September 1901.
14 Mrs Edith Chapman to Mrs Gregory, 10 December 1901 (SPRI).
15 C. W. Royds, diary, 25 August 1901 (SPRI).
16 E. H. Shackleton, op. cit., 24 August 1901.
17 Mrs Evelyn Forbes, interview with author.
18 James Dell, interview with James Fisher (SPRI).
19 E. A. Wilson, diary, 19 August 1901.
20 Ibid., 28 August 1901.
21 R. F. Scott, diary, 18 September 1901 (SPRI).
22 Ibid., 22 November 1901.
23 E. A. Wilson, op. cit., 28 November 1901.

Chapter VI: A protean world of ice
(pages 51–63)

1 E. H. Shackleton, diary, 1 January 1902 (SPRI).
2 Ibid., 30 December 1901.
3 R. W. Skelton, diary, 30 December 1902 (SPRI).
4 C. W. Royds, diary, 2 January 1902 (SPRI).
5 R. F. Scott, *The Voyage of the "Discovery"*, Vol. i, p. 83.
6 Nansen, *Pa Ski over Grønland*, p. 160.
7 Otto Nordenskjöld, *Antarctic*, Vol. i, p. 60.
8 R. F. Scott, diary, 8 January 1902 (SPRI).
9 C. Hare, diary, 5 January 1902 (SPRI).
10 E. H. Shackleton, op. cit., 6 January 1902.
11 E. A. Wilson, diary, 8 January 1902.
12 E. H. Shackleton, op. cit., 13 January 1902.
13 L. C. Bernacchi, *Saga of the Discovery*, p. 218.
14 R. F. Scott, op. cit.
15 E. A. Wilson, op. cit., 9 January 1902.
16 L. C. Bernacchi, diary, 1 January 1900 (SPRI).
17 R. F. Scott, letter to Mrs Scott (his mother), 24 February 1903 (SPRI).
18 E. H. Shackleton, op. cit., 11 January 1902.
19 E. A. Wilson, op. cit., 15 January 1902.
20 E. H. Shackleton, diary, 20 January 1902, *quoted*, H. R. Mill, *The Life of Sir Ernest Shackleton*, p. 64.
21 E. A. Wilson, op. cit., 28 January 1902.
22 E. H. Shackleton, op. cit., 25 January 1902.
23 C. W. Royds, op. cit., 30 January 1902.
24 E. H. Shackleton, op. cit., 1 February 1902.
25 R. F. Scott, letter to J. Scott Keltie, 7 December 1901 (RGS).
26 *Discovery* log, 1 February 1902 (RGS).
27 C. W. Royds, op. cit., 1 February 1902.
28 L. C. Bernacchi, op. cit., 17 February 1900 (SPRI).
29 R. W. Skelton, op. cit., 3 February 1902.
30 R. F. Scott, *The Voyage of the "Discovery"*, Vol. i., p. 147.
31 E. A. Wilson, op. cit., 3 February 1902.
32 R. F. Scott, *The Voyage of the "Discovery"*, Vol. i, p. 154.
33 E. H. Shackleton, op. cit., 8 February 1902.
34 Browning, *Childe Roland*, XXV.
35 R. W. Skelton, letter to R. F. Scott, 21 February 1912 (SPRI).
36 E. H. Shackleton, op. cit., 14 February 1902.
37 Ibid., 15 February 1902.

Chapter VII: Polar travel
(pages 64–69)

1 E. H. Shackleton, letter to Emily Dorman, "Friday" (SPRI).
2 Gerald Doorly, title of an article.
3 C. W. Royds, diary, 18 February 1902 (SPRI).
4 Otto Sverdrup, *Nyt Land*, Vol. i, pp. 19–20.
5 Dr George Simpson, *Athabasca Journal*, 8 February 1821.
6 William MacTavish, letter to Letitia MacTavish, 16 July 1834.
7 H. T. Ferrar, diary, 19 February 1902 (SPRI).
8 Edgeworth David, diary, 7 March 1908 (ML).
9 E. A. Wilson, diary, 19 February 1902.
10 H. T. Ferrar, op. cit., 20 February 1902.
11 E. A. Wilson, op. cit., 20 February 1902.
12 C. W. Royds, op. cit., 22 February 1902.
13 *Daily Service*, No. 69, p. 84.
14 *Dublin Express*, 15 December 1909.

Chapter VIII: Polar night
(pages 70–78)

1 R. W. Skelton, diary, 5 March 1902 (SPRI).
2 E. H. Shackleton, diary, 21 August 1901 (SPRI).
3 Ibid., 3 March 1902 (SPRI).
4 Ibid., 14 May 1902; Shakespeare, *Cymbeline*, Act IV, scene 2.
5 Ibid., 22 June 1902.
6 J. W. Gregory, letter to Professor Poulton, 21 January 1901 (SPRI).
7 E. H. Shackleton, op. cit., 12 May 1902.
8 A. B. Armitage, memorandum for H. R. Mill (SPRI).
9 E. H. Shackleton, op. cit., 23 April 1902.
10 E. H. Shackleton, *O.H.M.S.*, p. 16.
11 E. H. Shackleton, diary, 16 April 1902 (SPRI).
12 Ibid., 25 April 1902.
13 E. A. Wilson, letter to his wife, *quoted*, George Seaver, *Edward Wilson of the Antarctic*, p. 103.
14 Otto Nordenskjöld, *Antarctic*, Vol. i, p. 219.
15 Sir Clements Markham, memorandum, 1901 (Royal Society).
16 James Dell, interview with James Fisher (SPRI).
17 Ibid.
18 E. A. Wilson, diary, 30 October 1911.
19 E. H. Shackleton, op. cit., 22 May 1902.
20 T. V. Hodgson, diary, 11 May 1902 (SPRI).
21 C. H. Hare, letter to Margery Fisher (SPRI).
22 M. Barne, interview with James Fisher (SPRI).
23 R. W. Skelton, op. cit., 11 September 1902 (SPRI).
24 E. A. Wilson, letter to his wife, *quoted*, George Seaver, op. cit., p. 104.
25 L. C. Bernacchi, *Saga of the Discovery*, p. 221.
26 R. Ford, letter to Margery Fisher, 12 January 1956 (SPRI).
27 C. H. Hare, op. cit.
28 Ibid.
29 James Dell, op. cit.
30 E. H. Shackleton, op. cit., 12 June 1902.
31 R. Amundsen, diary, 21 June 1898 (UB).
32 E. H. Shackleton, op. cit., 12 June 1902.
33 E. A. Wilson, letter to his wife, *quoted*, Seaver, op. cit., p. 75.
34 Ibid., p. 107.
35 Ibid., p. 105.
36 E. A. Wilson, diary, 12 June 1902.
37 E. A. Wilson, letter to his wife, *quoted*, Seaver, op. cit., p. 106.

Chapter IX: Dogs and diet
(pages 79–87)

1 A. B. Armitage, memorandum for H. R. Mill (SPRI).
2 E. H. Shackleton, diary, 19 June 1902 (SPRI).
3 C. W. Royds, diary, 18 July 1902 (SPRI).
4 *Quoted*, James Morris, *Heaven's Command*, p. 195.

5 C. W. Royds, op. cit., 1 August 1902.
6 T. Williamson, op. cit., 22 August 1902.
7 E. H. Shackleton, op. cit., 17 September 1902.
8 Ibid., 25 September 1902.
9 Ibid., 10 September 1902.
10 E. H. Shackleton, letter to Mr Lethbridge, 20 September 1902.
11 E. H. Shackleton, diary, 3 October 1902.
12 Ibid., 4 October 1902.
13 E. A. Wilson, diary, 3 October 1902.
14 E. H. Shackleton, op. cit., 9 October 1902.
15 Ibid., 12 June 1902.
16 *Quoted*, James Morris, op. cit., p. 212.
17 *Report of the Inter-Departmental Committee on Physical Deterioration*, p. 589.
18 James Dell, interview with James Fisher (SPRI).
19 L. C. Bernacchi, diary, 2 October 1902 (SPRI).
20 R. W. Skelton, op. cit., 15 November 1902.
21 L. C. Bernacchi, op. cit., 2 October 1902.
22 E. H. Shackleton, op. cit., 6 October 1902.
23 Ibid., 14 October 1902.
24 H. T. Ferrar, diary, 6 October 1902 (SPRI).

Chapter X: The southern journey (pages 88–103)

1 E. A. Wilson, diary, 19 September 1902.
2 C. W. Royds, diary, 2 November 1902 (SPRI).
3 L. C. Bernacchi, diary, 2 November 1902 (SPRI).
4 C. H. Hare, diary, 2 November 1902 (SPRI).
5 E. H. Shackleton, diary, 2 November 1902 (SPRI).
6 E. A. Wilson, op. cit., 6 November 1902.
7 E. H. Shackleton, letter to Emily Dorman, 31 October 1902 (SPRI).
8 E. A. Wilson, op. cit., 2 November 1902.
9 E. H. Shackleton, diary, 9 November 1902 (SPRI).
10 Ibid., 5 December 1902.
11 Darwin, *Origin of Species*, p. 462.
12 E. A. Wilson, op. cit., 9 November 1902.
13 E. H. Shackleton, op. cit., 15 November 1902.
14 Ibid., 12 November 1902.
15 Ibid., 15 November 1902.
16 E. A. Wilson, op. cit., 14 November 1902.
17 James Dell, interview with James Fisher (SPRI).
18 E. H. Shackleton, op. cit., 21 November 1902.
19 Ibid.
20 Otto Nordenskjöld, *Antarctic*, Vol. i, p. 327.
21 Otto Sverdrup, *Nyt Land*, Vol. i, p. 86.
22 E. H. Shackleton, op. cit., 21 November 1902.
23 Otto Sverdrup, op. cit., Vol. ii, p. 228.
24 Fridtjof Nansen, *Fram over Polhavet*, Vol. ii, p. 19.
25 George Seaver, letter to author.
26 E. H. Shackleton, op. cit., 12 December 1902.
27 Ibid., 20 November 1902.
28 R. F. Scott, *The Voyage of the "Discovery"*, Vol. ii, p. 25.
29 A. B. Armitage, memorandum for H. R. Mill (SPRI).
30 *Origin of Species*, p. 233.
31 E. H. Shackleton, op. cit., 6 December 1902.
32 Ibid., 19 December 1902.
33 E. A. Wilson, op. cit., 15 October 1902.
34 E. H. Shackleton, op. cit., 13 December 1902.
35 Ibid., 19 December 1902.
36 Ibid., 30 November 1902.
37 Ibid., 13 December 1902.
38 Ibid., 26 December 1902.
39 Ibid.
40 E. A. Wilson, op. cit., 15 December 1902.
41 E. H. Shackleton, op. cit., 20–21 December 1902.
42 Ibid., 24 December 1902.
43 Ibid., 18 December 1902.
44 Ibid., 16–19 December 1902.
45 Ibid., 12–28 December 1902.
46 Ibid., 20 November 1902.
47 Ibid., 13 December 1902.
48 Ibid., 19 December 1902.
49 E. A. Wilson, op. cit., 1 January 1903.
50 Ibid., 30 November 1902.
51 Ibid., 24 December 1902.
52 Ibid.
53 Ibid., 29 December 1902.
54 Ibid., 28 December 1902.
55 E. A. Wilson, op. cit., 30 December 1902.
56 E. H. Shackleton, op. cit., 2 January 1903.
57 E. H. Shackleton, "Life in the Antarctic", *Pearson's Magazine*, March 1904, p. 319.

Chapter XI: Race for life
(pages 104–113)

1 E. A. Wilson, diary, 1 January 1903.
2 E. H. Shackleton, diary, 1–2 January 1903 (SPRI).
3 E. A. Wilson, op. cit., 7 January 1903.
4 E. H. Shackleton, op. cit., 9 January 1903.
5 E. A. Wilson, op. cit., 2 January 1903.
6 Nansen, *Pa Ski over Grønland*, p. 72.
7 Sir Martin Conway, *With Ski & Sledge over Arctic Glaciers*, p. 90.
8 E. H. Shackleton, op. cit., 11 January 1903.
9 E. A. Wilson, op. cit., 12 January 1903.
10 J. W. Gregory, letter to Professor Poulton, 16 January 1900 (SPRI).
11 E. H. Shackleton, op. cit., 13 January 1903.
12 Ibid., 14 January 1903.
13 E. A. Wilson, op. cit., 14 January 1903.
14 Ibid.
15 Nansen, *Fram over Polhavet*, Vol. ii, p. 190.
16 E. H. Shackleton, op. cit., 14 January 1903.
17 Ibid., 17 January 1903.
18 E. A. Wilson, op. cit., 19 January 1903.
19 E. H. Shackleton, op. cit., 21 January 1903.
20 Ibid., 22 January 1903.
21 E. A. Wilson, op. cit., 26 January 1903.
22 G. Seaver, *Edward Wilson of the Antarctic*, p. 114; letter to the author.
23 Ibid.
24 E. A. Wilson, op. cit., 22 January 1903.
25 Ibid., 24 January 1903.
26 E. H. Shackleton, op. cit., 27 January 1903.
27 E. A. Wilson, op. cit., 28 January 1903.
28 Ibid., 3 February 1903.
29 L. C. Bernacchi, diary, 3 February 1903 (SPRI).
30 R. W. Skelton, diary, 3 February 1903 (SPRI).
31 E. A. Wilson, op. cit., 3 February 1903.
32 E. H. Shackleton, op. cit., 3 February 1903.
33 R. W. Skelton, op. cit., 22 February 1902.

Chapter XII: Invalided home
(pages 114–118)

1 R. W. Skelton, diary, 3 February 1903 (SPRI).
2 T. V. Hodgson, diary, 28 February 1903 (SPRI).
3 L. C. Bernacchi, diary, 21 February 1903 (SPRI).
4 A. B. Armitage, memorandum to H. R. Mill (SPRI).
5 R. F. Scott, memorandum to R. Koettlitz, 19 February 1903 (SPRI).
6 R. Koettlitz, memorandum to R. F. Scott, 19 February 1903 (SPRI).
7 R. F. Scott, diary, 7 March 1903 (SPRI).
8 R. Koettlitz, op. cit.
9 E. H. Shackleton, diary, 16 January 1903 (SPRI).
10 R. Koettlitz, letter to J. S. Keltie, 24 February 1903 (RGS).
11 A. B. Armitage, op. cit.
12 James Dell, interview with James Fisher (SPRI).
13 R. F. Scott, certificate for E. H. Shackleton (RGS).
14 R. F. Scott, diary, 7 March 1903 (SPRI).
15 E. H. Shackleton, op. cit., 28 February 1903.
16 J. A. McIlroy, interview with James Fisher (SPRI).
17 Gilbert Scott, diary, 1 March 1903 (SPRI).
18 E. H. Shackleton, op. cit., 28 February 1903.
19 Ibid., 1 March 1903.
20 Ibid., 5 March 1903.
21 Ibid.
22 E. H. Shackleton, cable to Emily Dorman, 29 March 1903 (SPRI).

Chapter XIII: A new and better path?
(pages 119–128)

1 Admiral Wharton, telegram to E. H. Shackleton, 20 June 1903, *quoted*, Sir Clements Markham, diary, 20 June 1903 (RGS).
2 *Daily Mail*, 29 June 1903.
3 *Quoted*, Risting, *Kaptein C. A. Larsen*, p. 20.
4 A. B. Armitage, memorandum for H. R. Mill (SPRI).

5 Medical certificate, 21 July 1903 (PRO ADM 116/943).
6 Emily Shackleton, letter to Leonard Tripp, 23 March 1922 (TBL).
7 Sir Clements Markham, diary, 2 October 1903 (RGS).
8 E. H. Shackleton, letter to [J. E. Bernier], 26 September 1903 (Dulwich).
9 L. C. Bernacchi, diary, 6 January 1904 (SPRI).
10 Supplement to *The Illustrated London News*, 27 June 1903.
11 *Pearson's Magazine*, March 1904, p. 313.
12 Sir Clements Markham, letter to J. S. Keltie, 15 January 1903 (RGS).
13 Lady Constance Barne, letter to Evan MacGregor, 1 July 1903 (PRO ADM 116/944).
14 Evan MacGregor, Admiralty minute 11 April 1904 (PRO ADM 116/944).
15 Rear-Admiral Pelham Aldrich, memorandum to Rear-Admiral Wharton and Rear-Admiral Boyes, 24 July 1903 (PRO ADM 116/944).
16 E. W. Hornung, *Raffles*, p. 10.
17 Philip Gibbs, title of book.
18 A. B. Armitage, op. cit.
19 *Royal Magazine*, June 1909, p. 192; *Pearson's Weekly*, 8 April 1909, p. 818.
20 L. C. Bernacchi, diary, 1 January 1904 (SPRI).
21 Reginald Ford, letter to Margery Fisher, 22 November 1955 (SPRI).
22 A. B. Armitage, op. cit.
23 Reginald Ford, op. cit.
24 *Pearson's Weekly*, 8 April 1909, p. 818.
25 Ibid.
26 The *Royal Magazine*, November 1903, p. 82.
27 Sir Alfred Milner, *quoted*, Pearsall, *Edwardian Life and Leisure*, p. 95.
28 Joseph Chamberlain, 1902, *quoted*, Read, *Documents from Edwardian England*, p. 179.
29 Masterman, *The Condition of England*, p. 25.
30 H. G. Wells, *Tono-Bungay*, p. 89.
31 H. R. Mill, *An Autobiography*, p. 102.
32 E. H. Shackleton, letter to H. R. Mill, 15 December 1903 (SPRI).
33 Ibid.
34 H. R. Mill, testimonial for E. H. Shackleton, 20 November 1903 (SPRI).
35 J. Gunnar Andersson, in Wordenskjöld, *Antarctic*, Vol. ii, p. 350.
36 E. H. Shackleton, letters to Emily Dorman, 11–20 January 1904 (SPRI).

Chapter XIV: "An east-windy, west-endy place" (pages 129–139)

1 H. R. Mill, *The Life of Sir Ernest Shackleton*, p. 86.
2 E. H. Shackleton, letter to Emily Dorman, 20 January 1904 (SPRI).
3 Mrs Peggy Sheridan-Young, interview with author.
4 E. H. Shackleton, letter to R. F. Scott, 3 September 1904.
5 E. H. Shackleton, letter to Emily Dorman, 21 January 1904 (SPRI).
6 H. R. Mill, op. cit., p. 88.
7 Ibid., p. 98.
8 E. H. Shackleton, letter to Emily Dorman, 30 March 1904 (SPRI).
9 Ibid., 20 April 1901 (SPRI).
10 Ibid., 10 February; 30 March 1904 (SPRI).
11 Emily Shackleton, letter to H. R. Mill, 7 September 1916 (SPRI).
12 E. H. Shackleton, letter to Emily Dorman, 26 February 1904 (SPRI).
13 Ibid., 26 February 1904 (SPRI).
14 E. H. Shackleton, letters to H. R. Mill, 3 and 26 February 1904 (SPRI).
15 Ibid., 3 February 1904.
16 W. S. Bruce, letter to Sir Clements Markham, 15 April 1899 (SPRI).
17 E. H. Shackleton, letter to R. F. Scott, 3 September 1904 (SPRI).
18 H. R. Mill, letter to R. F. Scott, 8 October 1903 (SPRI).
19 *Daily Mail*, 8 November 1904.
20 The *Dundee Courier*, 16 November 1904.
21 Ibid., 9 January 1906.
22 PRO ADM 12/1392 68–5^{a}, p. 1.
23 The *Dundee Courier*, 13 January 1906.
24 J. G. Bartholomew, letter to H. R. Mill, 11 November 1904 (SPRI).
25 E. H. Shackleton, letter to R. F. Scott, 21 January 1905 (SPRI).
26 E. H. Shackleton, letter to H. R Mill, 22 February 1905.

Chapter XV: Prospects, but no work
(pages 140–157)

1 Bamford, *Vicious Circle*, p. 10.
2 Mrs Peggy Sheridan-Young, interview with author.
3 *Danmarks Biografiske Lexicon*, Vol. viii, p. 405.
4 Niels Grøn, New Year's card, 1911 (DKB).
5 E. H. Shackleton, letter to Emily Dorman, 20 January 1904 (SPRI).
6 Charles Sarolea, "Sir Ernest Shackleton", *The Contemporary Review*, Vol. 121, 1922, p. 321.
7 Niels Grøn, letter to Ludwig Bramsen, 19 March 1908 (DKB).
8 "National Antarctic Expedition: Report of the Commander", *Geographical Journal*, Vol. xxii, p. 32.
9 E. H. Shackleton, diary, 21 January 1903 (SPRI).
10 R. F. Scott, *The Voyage of the "Discovery"*, Vol. ii, p. 90.
11 E. A. Wilson, diary, 3 October 1903.
12 R. F. Scott, op. cit., pp. 67, 85, 89.
13 Ibid., p. 77.
14 Ibid., p. 42.
15 E. H. Shackleton, op. cit., 25 December 1902.
16 R. F. Scott, op. cit., p. 121.
17 *The Complete Workings of Craft Freemasonry*, p. 96.
18 E. H. Shackleton, *Plan for an Antarctic Expedition* (SPRI).
19 *The Times*, 14 November 1905.
20 The *Dundee Courier*, 8 January 1906.
21 Ibid., 3 January 1906.
22 E. H. Shackleton, letter to Emily Shackleton, 3 January 1906 (SPRI).
23 Ibid., "1906" (SPRI).
24 The *Dundee Courier*, 9 January 1906.
25 Ibid., 13 January 1906.
26 Ibid.
27 Ibid., 9 January 1906.
28 H. R. Mill, *The Life of Sir Ernest Shackleton*, p. 9.
29 *Quoted*, Barbara Tuchman, *The Proud Tower*, p. 367.
30 E. H. Shackleton, letter to Emily Shackleton, "Friday" [February 1906] (SPRI).
31 *Quoted*, Bamford, op. cit., p. 81.
32 E. H. Shackleton, letter to Emily Shackleton, 9 February 1906 (SPRI).
33 Ibid., "Friday".
34 Ibid.
35 Ibid.
36 Ibid., "Saturday".
37 Ibid., "Monday".
38 *Report of the Viceregal Commission*, p. 977.
39 E. H. Shackleton, letter to Emily Shackleton, "Sunday" (SPRI).
40 David Kirkwood, *My Life of Revolt*, p. 121.
41 A. G. McDuff, interview with James Fisher (SPRI).
42 *The Times*, 16 October 1906.
43 E. H. Shackleton, letter to H. R. Mill, 26 December 1906 (SPRI).
44 Ibid.
45 E. H. Shackleton, letter to Emily Shackleton, "Friday" [April 1906].
46 E. H. Shackleton, letter to Elspeth Beardmore, "Monday" (NMG).
47 Emily Shackleton, letters to H. R. Mill, 27 May and 16 August 1922 (SPRI).
48 *The Times*, 26 June 1913.
49 R. N. Rudmose Brown, *A Naturalist at the Poles*, p. 247.
50 H. R. Mill, "Ernest Henry Shackleton, M.V.O.", *Travel and Exploration*, July 1909, p. 1.
51 Henrik Ibsen, *Peer Gynt*, Act II.
52 A. G. McDuff, interview with James Fisher (SPRI).
53 Emily Shackleton, letter to H. R. Mill, 27 March 1922 (SPRI).

Chapter XVI: British Antarctic Expedition, 1907
(pages 158–166)

1 J. Scott Keltie, letter to R. F. Scott, 18 February 1907 (RGS).
2 Ibid.
3 *The Times*, 12 February 1907.
4 E. H. Shackleton, letter to E. A. Wilson, 12 February 1907, *quoted*, George Seaver, *Edward Wilson of the Antarctic*, p. 174.
5 Ibid., 14 February 1907, p. 174.
6 Ibid., 15 February 1907, p. 176.
7 Ibid., 14 February 1907, p. 174.
8 E. A. Wilson, letter to E. H. Shackleton, 14 February 1907 (SPRI).
9 E. H. Shackleton, letter to E. A. Wilson, 15 February 1907, Seaver, op. cit., p. 175.

10 Ibid., p. 176.
11 E. H. Shackleton, letter to E. A. Wilson, 12 February 1907, Seaver, op. cit., p. 174.
12 E. A. Wilson, letter to E. H. Shackleton, 23 February 1907 (SPRI).
13 George Mulock, letter to E. H. Shackleton, 19 February 1907 (SPRI).
14 E. H. Shackleton, letter to R. F. Scott, 27 February 1907 (SPRI).
15 *The Times*, 12 February 1907.
16 E. A. Wilson, letter to R. F. Scott, 16 February 1907 (SPRI).
17 *The Times*, loc. cit.
18 E. H. Shackleton, letter to R. F. Scott, 28 February 1907 (SPRI).
19 Ibid.
20 E. A. Wilson, letter to E. H. Shackleton, 28 February 1907 (SPRI).
21 Charles Sarolea, "Sir Ernest Shackleton", *The Contemporary Review*, Vol. 121, 1922, p. 328.
22 J. Scott Keltie, letter to R. F. Scott, 1 March 1907 (RGS).
23 R. F. Scott, letter to Sven Hedin, 25 March 1905 (Riksarkivet, Stockholm).
24 Capt. B. M. Peck, letter to Reginald Pound, 30 July 1965.
25 E. A. Wilson, letter to E. H. Shackleton, 8 March 1907 (SPRI).
26 E. H. Shackleton, letter to E. A. Wilson, 11 March 1907 (SPRI).
27 J. Scott Keltie, letter to R. F. Scott, 27 March 1907 (RGS).
28 J. Scott Keltie, letter to E. H. Shackleton, 6 March 1907 (SPRI).
29 J. Scott Keltie, letter to R. F. Scott, 18 February 1907 (RGS).
30 Ibid., 1 and 8 March 1907 (RGS).
31 Ibid., 18 February 1907 (RGS).
32 E. H. Shackleton, letter to E. A. Wilson, 11 February 1907 (SPRI).
33 A. B. Armitage, memorandum for H. R. Mill (SPRI).
34 Ibid.

Chapter XVII: Seven months to prepare (167–177)

1 E. H. Shackleton, letter to Elspeth Beardmore, 13 May 1907 (NMG).
2 J. A. McIlroy, interview with James Fisher (SPRI).
3 E. H. Shackleton, letter to Professor Arthur Schuster, 14 May 1907 (SPRI).
4 E. H. Shackleton, letter to Elspeth Beardmore, 13 May 1907 (NMG).
5 Sir Philip Brocklehurst, interview with James Fisher (SPRI).
6 E. H. Shackleton, letter to Sir Philip Brocklehurst, n.d. (Van Haeften).
7 Campbell Mackellar, *Scented Isles and Coral Gardens*, p. 199.
8 E. H. Shackleton, letter to R. W. Skelton, 13 June 1907 (SPRI).
9 *Quoted*, Tim Greve, *Nansen*, Vol. ii, p. 59.
10 *Geographical Journal*, Vol. iii, No. 1, January 1894, p. 25.
11 Fridtjof Nansen, letter to Emily Shackleton, 18 April 1909 (SPRI).
12 F. G. Jackson, diary, 21 June 1896 (SPRI).
13 E. H. Shackleton, "Life in the Antarctic", *Pearson's Magazine*, March 1904, p. 313.
14 F. G. Jackson, *The Lure of Unknown Lands*, p. 248.
15 Ibid., p. 98.
16 R. Amundsen, *Sydpolen*, Vol. i, p. 154.
17 F. G. Jackson, diary, 10 April 1897, in *1000 Days in the Arctic*, Vol. ii, p. 230.
18 F. G. Jackson, op. cit., 30 April 1895, Vol. i, p. 266.
19 F. G. Jackson, *1000 Days in the Arctic*, Vol i, p. 276; *The Lure of Unknown Lands*, p. 98.
20 E. H. Shackleton, letter to J. Scott Keltie, 24 April 1907 (RGS).
21 *Aftenposten*, 22 April 1907.
22 *The Car*, 23 October 1907.
23 The *Morning Post*, 16 April 1907.
24 *Norsk Idraettsblad*, No. 46, 1907.
25 Gunnar Isachsen, "Polarhunden", *Polar-Årboken*, 1933, p. 48.
26 Viscount Goschen, speech at Lewes, 26 February 1896, in *The Oxford Dictionary of Quotations*, p. 227.
27 E. H. Shackleton, letter to J. Scott Keltie, 24 April 1907 (RGS).
28 E. H. Shackleton, letter to Elspeth Beardmore, 13 May 1907 (NMG).
29 Gen. 9:8. Milton, *Paradise Lost*, XII, 24.
30 E. H. Shackleton, letter to William Colbeck, 27 February 1907 (SPRI).
31 J. K. Davis, *High Latitude*, p. 59.
32 E. H. Shackleton, letter to Elspeth Beardmore, 6 October 1907 (NMG).
33 E. H. Shackleton, letter to R. F. Scott, 17 May 1907 (SPRI).

Chapter XVIII: When *Nimrod* sailed
(pages 178–186)

1 Sir Clements Markham, letter to E. H. Shackleton, 10 July 1907 (Lord Iveagh).
2 E. H. Shackleton, letter to Elspeth Beardmore, 30 June 1907 (NMG).
3 E. H. Shackleton, letter to Lord Knollys, 25 July 1907 (Royal Archives).
4 E. H. Shackleton, letter to William Beardmore, 25 July [1907] (Lord Iveagh).
5 Gen. Sir Dighton Probyn to E. H. Shackleton, 29 July 1907 (Royal Archives).
6 *The Antarctic Petrel* (TBL).
7 E. H. Shackleton, letter to Elspeth Beardmore, 6 October 1907 (NMG).
8 The *Daily Mail*, 5 August 1907.
9 E. H. Shackleton, letter to Elspeth Beardmore, 13 May 1907 (NMG).
10 E. H. Shackleton, letter to William Beardmore, 15 March 1907, *quoted*, Macduff, interview with James Fisher (SPRI).
11 J. K. Davis, *High Latitude*, p. 66.
12 *The Antarctic Petrel* (TBL).
13 E. H. Shackleton, letter to Elspeth Beardmore, 6 October 1907 (NMG).
14 Ibid., 3 September 1907.
15 Duncan Mackellar, notes for H. R. Mill (SPRI).
16 *Report of Viceregal Commission*, p. 285; 2897.
17 E. H. Shackleton, letter to Elspeth Beardmore, 6 October 1907 (NMG).
18 Ibid.
19 Ibid.
20 E. H. Shackleton, letter to Emily Shackleton, 31 October 1907 (SPRI).
21 Ibid., 6 November 1907.
22 Ibid., 31 October 1907.
23 Ibid.
24 Ibid., 6 November 1907.

Chapter XIX: A broken promise
(pages 187–207)

1 E. H. Shackleton, letter to Emily Shackleton, 1 January 1908 (SPRI).
2 *The Register*, Adelaide, 2 December 1907.
3 M. Edgeworth David, *Professor David*, p. 125.
4 Sir Douglas Mawson, draft letter to Margery Fisher, n.d. (MI).
5 Ibid.
6 T. Edgeworth David, letter to Sir William Lyne, 16 December 1907 (AAC).
7 E. H. Shackleton, letter to Joseph Kinsey, 9 May 1903 (TBL).
8 Alfred Deakin, telegram to E. H. Shackleton, 27 December 1907 (AAC).
9 E. H. Shackleton, telegram to Alfred Deakin, 28 December 1907 (AAC).
10 T. Edgeworth David, telegram to Alfred Deakin, 28 December 1907 (AAC).
11 E. Barter, letter to J. J. Kinsey, 18 March 1910 (TBL).
12 E. H. Shackleton, letter to Emily Shackleton, 1 January 1908 (SPRI).
13 The *Lyttelton Times*, 2 January 1908.
14 E. H. Shackleton, letter to Emily Shackleton, 1 January 1908.
15 Ibid.
16 Ibid., 6 November 1907.
17 Ibid., 1 January 1908.
18 A. E. Harbord, diary, 1 January 1908 (Dr Derek Harbord).
19 F. P. A. Evans, narrative (SPRI).
20 A. E. Harbord, op. cit., 3 January 1908.
21 R. E. Priestley, narrative (SPRI).
22 R. E. Priestley, *Sir Jameson Boyd Adams* (SPRI).
23 J. B. Adams, interview with James Fisher (SPRI).
24 Ibid.
25 R. E. Priestley, *Prelude to Antarctic Adventure*, p. 2 (SPRI).
26 Ibid.
27 Ibid.
28 Ibid.
29 Ibid., p. 8.
30 E. H. Shackleton, "The Making of an Explorer", *Pearson's Magazine*, August 1914, p. 138.
31 A. E. Harbord, op. cit., 7 January 1908.
32 A. E. Harbord, fragment of letter to unknown correspondent (Dr Derek Harbord).
33 *Nimrod*, log, 9 January 1908 (TBL).
34 E. S. Marshall, diary, 9 January 1908 (RGS).
35 Ibid. and F. R. Wild, letter to Rupert Wild, 14 January 1908.
36 E. S. Marshall, op. cit.
37 E. H. Shackleton, letter to Emily Shackleton, 14 January 1908 (SPRI).
38 E. S. Marshall, op. cit., 11 January 1908.
39 A. E. Harbord, diary, 15 January 1908.
40 E. S. Marshall, op. cit., 20 January 1908.

41 E. H. Shackleton, op. cit., 10 January 1908.
42 Ibid.
43 Ibid., 14 January 1908 (SPRI).
44 J. K. Davis, *High Latitude*, p. 78.
45 T. Edgeworth David, "The British Antarctic Expedition, 1907", *Sydney Morning Telegraph*, 28 March 1908.
46 R. E. Priestley, diary, 23 January 1908 (SPRI).
47 E. S. Marshall, op. cit., 22 January 1908.
48 R. E. Priestley, op. cit., 23 January 1908.
49 E. S. Marshall, op. cit., 24 January 1908.
50 *Nimrod*, log, 24 January 1908.
51 R. E. Priestley, op. cit., 24 January 1908.
52 E. H. Shackleton, op. cit., 26 January 1908.
53 E. H. Shackleton, *The Heart of the Antarctic*, Vol. i, p. 76.
54 E. S. Marshall, op. cit., 24 January 1908.
55 *Nimrod*, log, 25 January 1908.
56 A. E. Harbord, op. cit., 25 January 1908.
57 R. England, letter to Jessie Turner, n.d. (Mrs Ruth Hatch).
58 E. S. Marshall, op. cit., 25 January 1908.
59 E. H. Shackleton, letter to Emily Shackleton, 26 January 1908 (SPRI).
60 *The Complete Workings of Craft Freemasonry*, p. 96.
61 E. S. Marshall, letter to J. Scott Keltie, 27 January 1908 (RGS).

Chapter XX: McMurdo Sound
(pages 208–218)

1 E. H. Shackleton, *The Heart of the Antarctic*, Vol. i, p. 85.
2 A. E. Harbord, diary, 29 January 1908 (Dr Derek Harbord).
3 R. E. Priestley, diary, 29 January 1908 (SPRI).
4 A. E. Harbord, op. cit., 1 February 1908.
5 R. E. Priestley, op. cit., 3 February 1908.
6 J. K. Davis, *High Latitude*, p. 101.
7 Ibid., p. 102.
8 E. H. Shackleton, *The Heart of the Antarctic*, Vol. i, p. 97.
9 A. E. Harbord, op. cit., 4 February 1908.
10 R. E. Priestley, op. cit., 3 February 1908.
11 Frank Wild,, letter to "Dear Fred", 18 February 1908 (SPRI).
12 A. E. Harbord, op. cit., 9 February 1908.
13 E. H. Shackleton, letter to Emily Shackleton, 14 January 1908 (SPRI).
14 E. H. Shackleton, letter to R. England, 18 January 1908 (RGS).
15 E. S. Marshall, diary, 6 February 1908.
16 H. J. L. Dunlop, letter to J. D. Morrison, 3 June 1908 (SPRI).
17 R. England, letter to Jessie Turner, 27 January 1908 (Mrs Ruth Hatch).
18 E. H. Shackleton, letter to R. England, 15 July 1909 (RGS).
19 J. K. Davis, *High Latitude*, p. 82.
20 A. E. Harbord, op. cit., 9 February 1908.
21 Ibid., 12 February 1908.
22 R. E. Priestley, op. cit., 21 February 1908.
23 J. K. Davis, *High Latitude*, p. 88.
24 Robert Browning, *Prospice*.
25 E. H. Shackleton, letter to R. England, 20 January 1908 (RGS).
26 Ibid.

Chapter XXI: The conquest of Mount Erebus
(pages 219–228)

1 E. S. Marshall, diary, 22 February 1908 (RGS).
2 Ibid.
3 Ibid.
4 E. H. Shackleton, letter to Emily Shackleton, 15 February 1908 (SPRI).
5 E. S. Marshall, op. cit., 23 February 1908.
6 Ibid., 2 March 1908.
7 Ibid., 23 February 1908.
8 Ibid.
9 J. A. McIlroy, interview with James Fisher (SPRI).
10 E. S. Marshall, op. cit., 27 February 1908.
11 T. Edgeworth David, diary, 5 March 1908 (ML).
12 T. Edgeworth David, "The Ascent of Mount Erebus", *Aurora Australis* (SPRI).
13 Ibid.

14 T. Edgeworth David, diary, 5 March 1908 (ML).
15 Douglas Mawson, letter to T. Edgeworth David, 28 September 1907 (US).
16 T. Edgeworth David, op. cit., 10 March 1908.
17 E. S. Marshall, op. cit., 11 March 1908.
18 E. H. Shackleton, letter to R. England, 20 February 1908 (RGS).
19 R. England, letter to W. Colbeck, 22 April 1908.
20 E. H. Shackleton, letter to R. England, 20 February 1908.
21 R. England, letter to W. Colbeck, 22 April 1908 (Mrs Ruth Hatch).
22 *Daily Mail*, 7 March 1908.
23 Kathleen Bruce, letter to R. F. Scott, 13 March 1908 (SPRI).
24 R. F. Scott, letter to J. Scott Keltie, 28 March 1908 (RGS).
25 J. Scott Keltie, letter to Sir Clements Markham, 31 March 1908 (RGS).
26 Sir Clements Markham, letter to Emily Shackleton, 26 May 1908 (SPRI).
27 Sir Clements Markham, letters to J. Scott Keltie, 2 April and 26 May 1908 (RGS).
28 Sir Clements Markham, letter to Emily Shackleton, 26 May 1908 (SPRI).
29 Herbert Dorman, letter to Emily Shackleton, 12 June 1908 (SPRI).
30 Ibid.
31 *Report of the Viceregal Commission*, p. 966.
32 Ibid., p. 1746.
33 *John Bull*, 4 April 1908.
34 C. D. Mackellar, letter to Emily Shackleton, April, 1908 (SPRI).
35 H. R. Mill, letter to Emily Shackleton, 22 June 1908 (SPRI).

Chapter XXII: Midwinter
(pages 229–238)

1 Dante, *Inferno*, canto xxxiv.
2 E. H. Shackleton, *The Heart of the Antarctic*, Vol. i, p. 143.
3 R. E. Priestley, *Prelude to Antarctic Adventure* (SPRI).
4 R. E. Priestley, diary, 16–24 May 1908 (SPRI).
5 Ibid.
6 Ibid., 11 March 1908.
7 Ibid., 1–4 June 1908.
8 Sir Philip Brocklehurst, interview with James Fisher (SPRI).
9 A. H. Macklin, interview with James Fisher (SPRI).
10 A. E. Harbord, interview with James Fisher (SPRI).
11 E. S. Marshall, diary, 9 January 1908 (RGS).
12 M. Edgeworth David, *Professor David*, p. 125.
13 E. S. Marshall, op. cit., 23 June 1908.
14 Ibid., 16 March 1908.
15 Ibid., 23 June 1908.
16 R. E. Priestley, op. cit., 3 August 1908.
17 E. S. Marshall, op. cit., 3 August 1908.
18 Ibid., 25 May 1908.
19 Ibid., 27 February 1908.
20 Ibid., 3 May 1908.
21 Ibid., 27 August 1908.
22 E. S. Marshall, letter to John Kendall, 22 August 1950 (SPRI).
23 E. S. Marshall, diary, 24 June 1908 (RGS).
24 E. S. Marshall, letter to John Kendall, "15 May" [1952] (SPRI).
25 E. S. Marshall, diary, 5 July 1908 (RGS).
26 Ibid., 31 March 1908.
27 Ibid., 12 August 1908.
28 Ibid., 17 April 1908.
29 Ibid., 30 July 1908.
30 Ibid., 19 July 1908.
31 Ibid.
32 E. S. Marshall, letter to John Kendall, 24 August 1950 (SPRI).
33 R. E. Priestley, op. cit., 12 April 1908.
34 E. H. Shackleton, *The Heart of the Antarctic*, Vol. i, p. 233.
35 Ibid., p. 238.
36 T. Edgeworth David, diary, 5 October 1908 (ML).
37 Douglas Mawson, diary, 8 October 1908 (MI).

Chapter XXIII: "A glorious day for our start"
(pages 239–248)

1 E. H. Shackleton, diary, 29 October 1908 (SPRI).
2 Ibid.
3 E. H. Shackleton, letter to E. S. Marshall, 21 October 1908 (SPRI).
4 James Murray, *Antarctic Days*, p. xvii.
5 E. H. Shackleton, diary, 29 October 1908 (SPRI).
6 Ibid.
7 E. S. Marshall, diary, 3 November 1908.

8 F. R. Wild, diary, 3 November 1908 (US).
9 E. H. Shackleton, op. cit., 28 February 1903.
10 Ibid., 3 November 1908.
11 E. H. Shackleton, *The Heart of the Antarctic*, Vol. i, p. 230.
12 E. H. Shackleton, op. cit., 3 November 1908.
13 F. R. Wild, op. cit., 5 November 1908.
14 E. H. Shackleton, op. cit., 6 November 1908.
15 Ibid.
16 Ibid.
17 Ibid.
18 Ibid., 7 November 1908.
19 Ibid., 8 November 1908.
20 Ibid., 7 November 1908.
21 Ibid., 9 November 1908.
22 F. R. Wild, op. cit., 9 November 1908.
23 E. S. Marshall, op. cit., 9 November 1908.
24 F. R. Wild, op. cit., ibid.
25 Douglas Mawson, diary, 9 November 1908 (MI).
26 E. H. Shackleton, letter to Mawson, 28 October 1908 (SPRI).
27 Douglas Mawson, op. cit., 29 October 1908.
28 F. R. Wild, op. cit., 10 November 1908.
29 Douglas Mawson, op. cit., 23 November 1908.
30 Ibid., 29 October 1908.
31 Ibid.
32 T. Edgeworth David, "Professor David's Narrative", in *The Heart of the Antarctic*, Vol. ii, p. 108.

Chapter XXIV: Furthest South
(pages 249–274)

1 F. R. Wild, diary, 25 November 1908 (US).
2 E. H. Shackleton, diary, 26 November 1908 (SPRI).
3 E. S. Marshall, diary, 26 November 1908 (RGS).
4 E. H. Shackleton, op. cit., 13 November 1908 (SPRI).
5 Ibid., 14 November 1908.
6 F. R. Wild, op. cit., 10 November 1908.
7 R. Amundsen, diary, 22 June 1904 (UB).
8 E. H. Shackleton, op. cit., 18 and 19 November 1908.
9 E. H. Shackleton, *The Heart of the Antarctic*, Vol. i, p. 156.
10 E. S. Marshall, op. cit., 22 November 1908.
11 E. H. Shackleton, op. cit., 13 November 1908.
12 J. B. Adams, interview with James Fisher.
13 E. H. Shackleton, 20 November 1908.
14 F. R. Wild, op. cit., 27 November 1908.
15 E. H. Shackleton, op. cit., 1 December 1908.
16 Ibid., 30 November 1908.
17 Ibid., 1 December 1908.
18 Ibid., 2 December 1908.
19 E. S. Marshall, op. cit., 1 December 1908.
20 Ibid., 24 November 1908.
21 F. R. Wild, op. cit., 27 and 28 November 1908.
22 J. B. Adams, op. cit.
23 E. S. Marshall, op. cit., 2 December 1908.
24 F. R. Wild, op. cit, 2 December 1908.
25 E. H. Shackleton, op. cit., 2 December 1908.
26 Ibid., 3 December 1908.
27 Ibid.
28 Ibid., 4 December 1908.
29 E. S. Marshall, op. cit., 3 December 1908.
30 F. R. Wild, op. cit., 3 December 1908.
31 E. S. Marshall, op. cit., 4 December 1908.
32 F. R. Wild, op. cit., ibid.
33 Ibid., 4 December 1908.
34 F. R. Wild, op. cit., 4 December 1908.
35 Ibid.
36 E. H. Shackleton, op. cit., 4 December 1908.
37 F. R. Wild, op. cit., 5 December 1908.
38 E. H. Shackleton, op. cit., 5 December 1908.
39 F. R. Wild, op. cit., 6 December 1908.
40 E. S. Marshall, op. cit., 7 December 1908.
41 Ibid.
42 Ibid., 9 December 1908.
43 E. H. Shackleton, op. cit., 12 December 1908.
44 Ibid., 11 December 1908.
45 Ibid., 17 December 1908.
46 E. S. Marshall, op. cit., 17 December 1908.
47 F. R. Wild, op. cit., 15 December 1908.
48 Ibid., 17 December 1908.

49 E. H. Shackleton, op. cit., 22 December 1908.
50 Ibid., 21 December 1908.
51 F. R. Wild, op. cit., 11 December 1908.
52 Ibid., 19 December 1908.
53 E. S. Marshall, letter to K. G. Thomson, 15 July 1952 (SPRI).
54 E. S. Marshall, op. cit., 14 December 1908.
55 Ibid., 21 December 1908.
56 Ibid., 19 December 1908.
57 Ibid., 21 December 1908.
58 F. R. Wild, op. cit., 23 December 1908.
59 Ibid., 25 December 1908.
60 E. H. Shackleton, op. cit., 29 December 1908.
61 E. S. Marshall, op. cit., 31 December 1908.
62 E. H. Shackleton, op. cit., 24 December 1908.
63 Herbert Dorman, letter to Emily Shackleton, 29 December 1908 (SPRI).
64 E. H. Shackleton, op. cit., 29 December 1908.
65 Ibid., 30 December 1908.
66 Ibid., 31 December 1908.
67 Ibid.
68 Ibid., 1 January 1909.
69 Ibid., 2 January 1909.
70 F. R. Wild, op. cit., 31 December 1908.
71 E. S. Marshall, op. cit., 29 December 1908.
72 Ibid., 1 January 1909.
73 Ibid., 2 January 1909.
74 Ibid., 1 January 1909.
75 Ibid., 3 January 1909.
76 F. R. Wild, op. cit., 3 January 1909.
77 J. B. Adams, op. cit.
78 E. H. Shackleton, op. cit., 2 January 1909.
79 Ibid., 4 January 1909.
80 Dannevig, *Fjellboka*, p. 90.
81 E. H. Shackleton, op. cit., 4 January 1909.
82 F. R. Wild, op. cit., 4 January 1909.
83 E. S. Marshall, op. cit., 4 January 1909.
84 F. R. Wild, op. cit., 4 January 1909.
85 E. H. Shackleton, op. cit., ibid.
86 F. R. Wild, op. cit., ibid.
87 Ibid., 6 January 1909.
88 E. H. Shackleton, op. cit., 6 January 1909.
89 Ibid., 7 January 1909.
90 Ibid., 8 January 1909.
91 *The Merchant of Venice*, Act III, scene 2.
92 E. H. Shackleton, op. cit., 9 January 1909.
93 F. R. Wild, op. cit., 9 January 1909.
94 E. S. Marshall, op. cit., "Epilogue".
95 E. S. Marshall, letter to John Kendall, 16 December 1952 (SPRI).
96 E. S. Marshall, diary, "Epilogue".
97 E. H. Shackleton, op. cit., 9 January 1909.
98 Ibid., 10 January 1909.
99 E. S. Marshall, op. cit., 11 January 1909.
100 E. H. Shackleton, op. cit., 13 January 1909.
101 F. R. Wild, op. cit., 16 January 1909.

Chapter XXV: March or die
(pages 275–292)

1 T. Edgeworth David, diary, 16 January 1909 (US).
2 Douglas Mawson, diary, 24 and 25 January 1909 (MI).
3 E. S. Marshall, diary, 17 January 1909 (RGS).
4 Ibid., 18 January 1909.
5 F. R. Wild, diary, 19 January 1909 (US).
6 Ibid.
7 Ibid., 20 January 1909.
8 E. H. Shackleton, diary, 20 January 1909 (SPRI).
9 F. R. Wild, op. cit., 21 January 1909.
10 E. S. Marshall, op. cit., 21 January 1909.
11 F. R. Wild, op. cit., loc. cit.
12 E. S. Marshall, op. cit., 21 January 1909.
13 F. R. Wild, op. cit., 24 January 1909.
14 Ibid., 15 January 1909.
15 *Wellcome's Medical Diary 1908*, p. 99.
16 E. H. Shackleton, op. cit., 26–27 January 1909.
17 E. S. Marshall, letter to John Kendall, 26 January 1951 (SPRI).
18 E. S. Marshall, diary, 26–27 January 1909 (RGS).
19 E. H. Shackleton, op. cit., ibid.
20 Ibid., 28 January 1909.
21 E. S. Marshall, op. cit., 29 January 1909.
22 Ibid., 28 January 1909.
23 E. H. Shackleton, op. cit., 30 January 1909.
24 F. R. Wild, op. cit., 31 January 1909.
25 E. H. Shackleton, op. cit., 3 February 1909.
26 Douglas Mawson, op. cit., 3 February 1909.

27 Ibid., 31 January 1909.
28 Ibid., 4 February 1909.
29 Ibid.
30 F. P. Evans, *Narrative of the Expedition* (SPRI).
31 Ibid.
32 J. K. Davis, *High Latitude*, p. 104.
33 Ibid., p. 107.
34 E. M. Joyce, "The Bluff Depot Journey", in *The Heart of the Antarctic*, Vol. ii, p. 60.
35 Ibid.
36 A. F. Mackay, diary, 21 February 1909 (SPRI).
37 E. S. Marshall, op. cit., 4 February 1909.
38 F. R. Wild, op. cit., 19 February 1909.
39 Ibid., 15 February 1909.
40 Ibid., 28 January 1909.
41 Ibid., 5 February 1909.
42 F. R. Wild, unpublished memoirs, p. 57 (ML).
43 F. R. Wild, diary, 22 February 1909.
44 E. H. Shackleton, op. cit., 22 February 1909.
45 F. R. Wild, op. cit., 23 February 1909.
46 E. S. Marshall, op. cit., 25 February 1909.
47 F. R. Wild, *Memoirs*, p. 52.
48 Ibid., p. 53.
49 E. H. Shackleton, *The Heart of the Antarctic*, Vol. i, p. 368.
50 Ibid.
51 F. R. Wild, op. cit., p. 53.
52 Ibid.
53 A. F. Mackay, diary, 28 February 1909 (SPRI).
54 F. P. Evans, diary, 28 February 1909 (TBL).
55 A. F. Mackay, op. cit., 25 February 1909.
56 E. H. Shackleton, letter to James Murray, 23 October 1908 (SPRI).
57 A. F. Mackay, op. cit., 25 February 1909.
58 F. R. Wild, op. cit., ibid.
59 E. H. Shackleton, op. cit., Vol. i, p. 369.
60 A. F. Mackay, op. cit., 22 February 1909.
61 R. E. Priestley, diary, 1 March 1909 (SPRI).
62 A. F. Mackay, op. cit., 25 February 1909.
63 R. E. Priestley, op. cit., ibid.
64 A. E. Harbord, diary, 5 March 1909 (Dr Derek Harbord).
65 F. R. Wild, op. cit., p. 54.
66 J. K. Davis, op. cit., p. 109.
67 E. S. Marshall, op. cit., 27 February 1909.
68 A. E. Harbord, op. cit., 5 March 1909.
69 A. F. Mackay, op. cit., 5 March 1909.
70 Ibid.
71 E. H. Shackleton, op. cit., Vol. ii, p. 227.

Chapter XXVI: National Hero
(pages 293–303)

1 *Verdens Gang*, *Aftenposten*, 16 October 1909.
2 Ibid.
3 *Pelican*, 16 June 1909.
4 The *Morning Post*, 17 June 1909.
5 E. H. Shackleton, letter to H. R. Mill, 5 May 1909 (SPRI).
6 E. H. Shackleton, *The Heart of the Antarctic*, Vol. ii, p. 232.
7 Dr Laura Mill, letter to author.
8 Emily Shackleton, letter to H. R. Mill, 27 March, [1922] (SPRI).
9 Fridtjof Nansen, letter to Emily Shackleton, 18 April 1909 (SPRI).
10 Otto Nordenskjöld, letter to J. Scott Keltie, 10 April 1909 (RGS).
11 J. Scott Keltie, letter to R. F. Scott, 25 February 1907 (RGS).
12 R. Amundsen, letter to J. Scott Keltie, 25 March 1909 (RGS).
13 Fridtjof Nansen, letter to R. Amundsen, 2 April 1913 (UB).
14 H. R. Mill, *The Life of Sir Ernest Shackleton*, p. 166.
15 F. S. Welhaven, *Protesialos*.
16 *Leeds Mercury*, 1 June 1910.
17 R. Amundsen, *Sydpolen*, Vol. i, p. 136.
18 *Daily Mail*, 27 March 1909.
19 *The Sketch*, 26 March 1909.
20 The *Daily Graphic*, 15 June 1909.
21 The *Daily Telegraph*, *The Times*, 16 June 1909.
22 The *Yorkshire Observer*, 17 June 1909.
23 *Evening Telegraph* (Dublin), 24 March 1909.
24 *The Weekly Freeman*, 27 March 1909.
25 The *Dublin Express*, 15 December 1909.
26 R. Amundsen, letter to J. Scott Keltie, 25 March 1909 (RGS).
27 Fridtjof Nansen, letter to Emily Shackleton, 18 April 1909 (SPRI).
28 E. H. Shackleton, letter to Elspeth Beardmore, 21 June 1909 (NMG).
29 Emily Shackleton, letter to H. R. Mill, 16 August 1922 (SPRI).

30 *The Bristol Times & Mirror*, 15 June 1909.
31 C. D. Mackellar, notes for H. R. Mill (SPRI).
32 *The Nottingham Express*, 16 June 1909.
33 A. B. Armitage, *From Cadet to Commodore*, p. 200.
34 The *Daily Telegraph*, 12 June 1909.
35 Kathleen Shackleton, letter to Sven Hedin, 28 September 1909 (Riko-arkivet, Stockholm).
36 A. B. Armitage, memo for H. R. Mill.
37 E. S. Marshall, letter to Dr John Kendall, 28 November 1950 (SPRI).

Chapter XXVII: Sir Ernest's debts
(pages 304–320)

1 R. F. Scott, letter to J. Scott Keltie, 28 March 1908 (RGS).
2 Sir Clements Markham, letter to E. H. Shackleton, 5 June 1909 (SPRI).
3 Sir Clements Markham, letter to J. Scott Keltie, 28 March 1909 (RGS).
4 Sir Clements Markham, letter to R. Feilden, 13 April 1909 (RGS).
5 Sir Clements Markham, letter to R. F. Scott, 22 April 1909 (SPRI).
6 E. H. Shackleton, cable to J. Scott Keltie, 31 March 1909 (RGS).
7 J. Scott Keltie, letter to E. H. Shackleton, 1 April 1909 (RGS).
8 Sir Clements Markham, letter to R. F. Scott, 22 April 1909 (SPRI).
9 King George V, diary, 28 June 1909 (Royal Archives).
10 E. H. Shackleton, letter to Emily Shackleton, 25 September 1909 (SPRI).
11 The *Observer*, 20 June 1909.
12 The *Morning Post*, 13 October 1909.
13 A. E. W. Mason, *The Turnstile*, pp. 300–3.
14 R. E. Priestley, interview with James Fisher (SPRI).
15 The *Morning Post*, 2 November 1909.
16 E. H. Shackleton, letter to Emily Shackleton, 25 April 1909 (SPRI).
17 Emily Shackleton, letter to Alexander Nansen, 16 October 1909 (UB).
18 E. H. Shackleton, letter to R. F. Scott, 6 July 1909 (SPRI).
19 E. A. Wilson, letter to E. H. Shackleton, undated (SPRI).
20 The *Saturday Review*, 11 June 1909.
21 Sir Clements Markham, letter to J. Scott Keltie, 28 March 1909 (RGS).
22 J. Scott Keltie, letter to E. H. Shackleton, 1 April 1909 (RGS).
23 E. H. Shackleton, letter to H. R. Mill, 5 May 1909 (SPRI).
24 Sir Clements Markham, letter to J. Scott Keltie, 28 March 1909 (RGS).
25 Sir Clements Markham, diary, 4 June 1909 (RGS).
26 Ibid., 13 April 1909 (RGS).
27 E. S. Marshall, letter to John Kendall, 17 August 1952 (SPRI).
28 Sir Clements Markham, letter to E. H. Shackleton, 5 June 1909 (SPRI).
29 R. F. Scott, diary, 7 January 1902 (SPRI).
30 E. A. Reeves, *Mr E. Shackleton's Observations*, 14 September 1909 (RGS).
31 Ibid.
32 E. S. Marshall, letter to John Kendall, 24 August 1950 (SPRI).
33 E. S. Marshall, diary, 4 January 1909 (RGS).
34 Ibid., 9 January 1909.
35 E. S. Marshall, letter to John Kendall, 13 October 1952 (SPRI).
36 E. H. Shackleton, letter to Elspeth Beardmore, 21 June 1909 (NMG).
37 Ibid.
38 E. H. Shackleton, letter to Emily Shackleton, 5 April 1909 (SPRI).
39 Sir Henry Lucy, *Sixty Years in the Wilderness*, p. 247.
40 Ibid., p. 248.
41 The *Cork Examiner*, 11 August 1909.
42 The *Kentish Mercury*, 14 August 1909.
43 The *Dundee Advertiser*, 10 August 1909.
44 E. H. Shackleton, letter to Emily Shackleton, 18 August 1909 (SPRI).
45 The *Morning Post*, 20 August 1909.
46 The *Bath Chronicle*, 20 August 1909.
47 E. H. Shackleton, letter to Lord Iveagh, 10 November 1909 (Lord Iveagh).
48 *Quoted*, Bamford, *Vicious Circle*, p. 164.
49 The *Daily Mirror*, 8 November 1909.
50 The *Western Morning News*, 21 August 1909.
51 J. K. Davis, *High Latitude*, p. 137.
52 R. E. Priestley, *Between Two Expeditions* (SPRI).
53 C. D. Mackellar, letter to H. R. Mill, 31 May 1922 (SPRI).
54 E. H. Shackleton, letter to Emily Shackleton, 4 March 1919.

55 E. H. Shackleton, Blue Amberol recording, 30 March 1909.
56 E. Saunders, letter to L. Tripp, 10 August 1922 (TBL).
57 The *Manchester Guardian*, 17 November 1909.
58 E. H. Shackleton, letter to J. J. Kinsey, 6 December 1909 (TBL).
59 E. Saunders, op. cit., ibid.
60 *The Times Literary Supplement*, 4 November 1909.
61 The *Observer*, 7 November 1909.
62 E. H. Shackleton, *The Heart of the Antarctic*, Vol. ii, p. 18.
63 *Quoted*, Tryggve Gran, *Fra Tjuagutt til Sydpolfarer*, p. 158.
64 *The Sphere*, 6 November 1909.
65 The *Daily Mail*, 19 October 1909.

Chapter XXVIII: Hungarian mines (pages 321–330)

1 Daisy Dorman, letter to "Dearest Con", 9 January [1910] (Mrs Sheridan-Young).
2 *Aftenposten*, 16 October 1909.
3 *Pester Lloyd*, 12 January 1910.
4 Daisy Dorman, op. cit.
5 The *Morning Leader*, 17 January 1910.
6 C. D. Mackellar, memorandum for H. R. Mill (SPRI).
7 Douglas Mawson, *Abbreviated Log* (MI).
8 Douglas Mawson, letter to Margery Fisher (draft), 7 January 1958 (MI).
9 Douglas Mawson, *Abbreviated Log* (MI).
10 E. H. Shackleton, letter to E. Barter, 8 February 1910 (TBL).
11 E. H. Shackleton, letter to Adrien de Gerlache, 17 February 1910 (Baron de Gerlache).
12 E. H. Shackleton, letter to R. F. Scott, 21 February 1910 (SPRI).
13 J. K. Davis, *High Latitude*, p. 138.
14 E. H. Shackleton, letter to Douglas Mawson, 19 March 1910 (MI).
15 The *Winning Post*, 2 April 1910.
16 The *Record* (Philadelphia), 17 April 1910.
17 Ibid.
18 *Woman at Home*, February 1910.
19 The *New York Times*, 1 May 1910.
20 Ibid., 9 April 1910.
21 The *New York Evening Sun*, 30 March 1910.
22 H. Arçtowski, letter to H. R. Mill, 8 May [1910] (SPRI).
23 The *New York World*, 3 April 1910.
24 The *Star* (Lincoln, Nebraska), 14 May 1910.
25 Ibid.
26 The *Record* (Philadelphia), 17 April 1910.
27 The *New York Sun*, 31 March 1910.
28 Douglas Mawson, draft agreement with E. H. Shackleton, Omaha, Nebraska, 16 May 1910 (MI).
29 Douglas Mawson, *Abbreviated Log* (MI).
30 The *New York Times*, 9 May 1910.
31 *The Times*, 15 April 1913.
32 Ibid., 15 April 1913.
33 Ibid., 17 February 1911.
34 Ibid., 18 July 1910.
35 Wilhelm Filchner, *Ein Forscherleben*, p. 108.
36 Ibid.
37 *Zeitschrift der Gesellschaft, Für Erdkunde Zu Berlin*, No. 7, 1910, p. 424.
38 Geoffrey Dorman, *My Uncle Ernest*, broadcast on BBC, 27 November 1969.

Chapter XXIX: "A bit of a floating gent" (pages 331–363)

1 Douglas Mawson, *Abbreviated Log* (MI).
2 R. E. Priestley, letter to EHS, n.d. (SPRI).
3 R. E. Priestley, letter to Debenham, n.d. (SPRI).
4 E. H. Shackleton, letter to Emily Shackleton, November 1910 (SPRI).
5 C. D. Mackellar, memorandum for H. R. Mill (SPRI).
6 C. D. Mackellar, letter to John Murray, 17 August 1911 (John Murray).
7 Wilhelm Filchner, letter to H. R. Mill, 15 January 1911 (SPRI).
8 C. D. Mackellar, memorandum for H. R. Mill (SPRI).
9 E. H. Shackleton, letter to Emily Shackleton, 22 November 1910 (SPRI).
10 Ibid., 27 September 1910.
11 E. H. Shackleton, letter to C. H. Bland, 20 July 1910 (Lord Iveagh).
12 Tom Clarke, *My Northcliffe Diary*, p. 222.

13 J. K. Davis, *High Latitude*, p. 139.
14 Ibid., p. 140.
15 E. H. Shackleton, letter to Emily Shackleton, November 1910 (SPRI).
16 Gerald Lysaght, letter to H. R. Mill, 21 June 1922.
17 E. H. Shackleton, cable to Douglas Mawson, [21] September 1910 (MI).
18 Douglas Mawson, op. cit.
19 Emily Shackleton, letter to H. R. Mill, 28 August 1922 (SPRI).
20 *The Times*, 17 February 1911.
21 E. H. Shackleton, letter to Leonard Tripp, 24 May 1911 (TBL).
22 E. H. Shackleton, letter to Sir Philip Brocklehurst, n.d. (Van Haeften).
23 E. H. Shackleton, letter to Emily Shackleton, 8 March 1911 (SPRI).
24 Emily Shackleton, letter to H. R. Mill, 27 March 1911 (SPRI).
25 E. H. Shackleton, letter to Emily Shackleton, 9 March 1911 (SPRI).
26 The *Daily Mail*, 28 March 1911.
27 Ibid.
28 *Morgenbladet* (Christiania), 3 October 1910.
29 The *Daily Mail*, 28 March 1911.
30 Ibid.
31 E. H. Shackleton, letter to Emily Shackleton, 4 [5] March 1911 (SPRI).
32 The *Daily Mail*, 28 March 1911.
33 Douglas Mawson, letter to H. R. Mill, 18 July 1922 (SPRI).
34 Gerald Lysaght, letter to H. R. Mill, 21 June 1922 (SPRI).
35 The *Daily Mail*, 9 May 1911.
36 R. W. Skelton, letter to R. F. Scott, 8 October 1911 (SPRI).
37 Douglas Mawson, draft letter to Margery Fisher, 7 January 1958 (MI).
38 E. H. Shackleton, letter to Emily Shackleton, 8 March 1911 (SPRI).
39 Leonard Tripp, memorandum for H. R. Mill, 1 March 1922 (TBL).
40 E. H. Shackleton, letter to Leonard Tripp, 24 May 1911 (SPRI).
41 Emily Shackleton, letter to H. R. Mill, 29 August 1922 (SPRI).
42 Douglas Mawson, letter to H. R. Mill, 18 July 1922 (SPRI).
43 R. W. Skelton, op. cit.
44 Ibid.
45 Emily Shackleton, letter to H. R. Mill, 30 May 1922 (SPRI).
46 Sir Arthur Vicars, letter to James Fuller, *quoted*, Bamford, *Vicious Circle*, p. 66.
47 *The Times*, 20 March 1911.
48 Herbert Dorman, letter to Emily Shackleton, 15 November 1908 (SPRI).
49 E. H. Shackleton, letter to F. L. Smith, 7 February [1912] (SPRI).
50 Emily Shackleton, letter to H. R. Mill, 16 August [1922] (SPRI).
51 *The Complete Workings of Craft Freemasonry*, p. 58.
52 E. H. Shackleton, letter to Leonard Tripp, 21 January 1912 (TBL).
53 E. R. Evans, *South with Scott*, p. 198.
54 G. B. Shaw, letter to E. H. Shackleton, 14 January 1912 (SPRI).
55 *The Times*, 3 April 1912.
56 *Quoted*, Huntford, *Scott and Amundsen*, p. 549.
57 E. H. Shackleton, cable to R. Amundsen, 10 March 1912 (UB).
58 The *Daily Chronicle*, 8 March 1912.
59 The *Daily Mail*, 11 March 1912.
60 Kathleen Scott, letter to R. W. Skelton, "Quarter Day" (SPRI).
61 J. K. Davis, letter to W. S. Bruce, 12 November 1912 (SPRI).
62 J. K. Davis, *High Latitude*, p. 186.
63 J. K. Davis, letter to W. S. Bruce, 18 July 1912.
64 H. R. Mill, letter to J. Scott Keltie, 7 April 1912 (RGS).
65 *The Times*, 5 April 1912.
66 *Geographical Journal*, Vol. xl, p. 544.
67 Sir Clements Markham, letter to R. F. Scott, 1 February 1913 (SPRI).
68 "The Norwegian South Polar Expedition", *Geographical Journal*, Vol. xli, No. 1, January 1913, p. 15.
69 The *Daily Chronicle*, 11 March 1912.
70 Ibid.
71 The *Daily Chronicle*, 8 March 1912.
72 E. H. Shackleton, letter to F. L. Smith, 19 April 1912 (SPRI).
73 "Minutes of Evidence", *Commission on the loss of the S.S. "Titanic"*, p. 722.
74 Ibid.
75 H. R. Mill, record of conversation with R. W. Skelton, 14 June 1925 (SPRI).
76 Sir Harry Brittain, interview with James Fisher (SPRI).
77 E. H. Shackleton, letter to Leonard Tripp, 21 January 1912 (TBL).
78 C. D. Mackellar, memorandum for H. R. Mill (SPRI).
79 R. Amundsen, *Sydpolen*, Vol. i, p. 103.
80 The *Daily Mail*, 11 March 1911.
81 E. H. Shackleton, letter to Emily Shackleton, 8 March 1911 (SPRI).
82 E. H. Shackleton, letter to Fridtjof Nansen, 28 September 1912 (UB).
83 Henry Bryant, letter to R. E. Peary, 13 December 1912 (NA).
84 The *Williamsport Sun*, 17 January 1913.

85 The *Philadelphia Record*, 17 January 1913.
86 Griffith Taylor, *With Scott: The Silver Lining*, p. 434.
87 Miss Irene Swinford Edwards, interview with author.
88 The *Illustrated Western Weekly News*, 1 March 1913.
89 *Daily Mail*, 12 February 1913.
90 Ibid.
91 The *Daily Telegraph*, 13 February 1913.
92 King George V, diary, 12 March 1913 (Royal Archives, Windsor).
93 Emily Shackleton, letter to H. R. Mill, 11 July 1922 (SPRI).
94 E. S. Marshall, letter to John Kendall, 17 July 1952 (SPRI).
95 E. H. Shackleton, letter to Elspeth Beardmore, 13 January 1914 (NMG).
96 Olaf Bjaaland, *quoted*, Odd Arnesen, *"Fram" Hele Norges Skute*, p. 216.
97 "The Imperial Trans-Antarctic Expedition", *Geographical Journal*, Vol. xliii, March 1914, p. 321.
98 The *Daily Graphic*, 21 June 1913.
99 *Report of Conference of a Committee of the Royal Geographical Society with Sir Ernest Shackleton, March 4, 1914*, p. 8 (RGS).
100 Tryggve Gran, *Slik var det*, p. 193.
101 Lord Rosebery, letter to E. H. Shackleton, 16 October 1912 (SPRI).
102 Mrs Ireland, interview with Lady Harriet Shackleton.
103 *The Times*, 21 October 1913.
104 Emily Shackleton, letter to H. R. Mill, 7 August 1922 (SPRI).
105 *The Times*, 22 October 1913.
106 Ibid., 25 October 1913.
107 *Scott's Last Expedition*, Vol. i, p. 499.
108 Ibid., p. 503.
109 E. H. Shackleton, *The Heart of the Antarctic*, Vol. i, p. 358.
110 *The Diaries of Captain Robert Scott*, 17 December 1911.
111 E. A. Wilson, letter to Mrs Oates, n.d. (SPRI).
112 Mrs Caroline Oates, notes of conversation with Kathleen Scott, 26 April 1913 (Christopher Dennistoun).
113 Mrs Caroline Oates, notes of conversation with Dr Edward Atkinson, 27 April 1913 (Christopher Dennistoun).
114 Mrs Caroline Oates, notes of conversation with Cecil Meares, 28 April 1913 (Christopher Dennistoun).
115 Captain L. E. G. Oates, diary, 4 December 1911 (Sue Limb).
116 Frank Debenham, *Note . . . on talk with Sir Clements Markham*, 14 November 1913 (SPRI).
117 E. H. Shackleton, letter to Lord Stamfordham, 24 December 1913 (Royal Archives, Windsor).
118 Lloyd George, letter to E. H. Shackleton, 2 December 1913 (RGS).
119 E. H. Shackleton, letter to Elspeth Beardmore, 13 January 1914 (NMG).

Chapter XXX: *Endurance*
pages (364–382)

1 Winston Churchill, Admiralty minute, 23 January 1914 (PRO ADM 1/8368/29).
2 E. H. Shackleton, letter to the Lords Commissioners of the Admiralty, 2 January 1914 (PRO ADM 1/8368/29).
3 Winston Churchill, Admiralty minute, 19 February 1914 (PRO ADM 1/8368/29).
4 Emily Shackleton, letter to H. R. Mill, 16 August 1922 (SPRI).
5 C. D. Mackellar, memorandum for H. R. Mill (SPRI).
6 F. A. Worsley, *Endurance*, p. 12.
7 *Quoted, The World's 100 Greatest Advertisements*.
8 E. H. Shackleton, letter to A. E. Cripps, n.d. (SPRI).
9 *Montreal Star*, 30 December 1913.
10 The *Daily Mail*, 5 January 1914.
11 *The Times*, 30 December 1913.
12 Ibid.
13 Ibid., 29 December 1913.
14 Admiralty minute, 2 February 1914 (PRO ADM 1/8368/29).
15 Sir Clements Markham, letter to J. Scott Keltie, 14 January 1914 (RGS).
16 E. S. Marshall, letter to John Kendall, 20 July 1952 (SPRI).
17 Ibid., 15 September 1950 (SPRI).
18 E. H. Shackleton, letter to H. R. Mill, 13 August 1913 (SPRI).
19 H. R. Mill, *An Autobiography*, p. 151.
20 H. R. Mill, *The Life of Sir Ernest Shackleton*, p. 194.
21 E. H. Shackleton, letter to W. S. Bruce, 20 August 1913 (SPRI).
22 J. Scott Keltie, letter to Otto Nordenskjöld, 21 April 1913 (Kungliga vetenskapsakadamien, Stockholm).
23 The *Nottingham Evening Post*, 4 November 1913.
24 Minutes, R.G.S. Council, 6 April 1914 (RGS).

25 *The Times*, 28 February 1914.
26 The *Daily Chronicle*, 4 March 1914.
27 *Report of Conference of a Committee of the Royal Geographical Society with Sir Ernest Shackleton, March 4, 1914* (RGS).
28 A. J. Hinks, letter to Douglas Freshfield, 1 May 1916 (RGS).
29 *Quoted*, James Morris, *Heaven's Command*, p. 187.
30 T. H. Orde-Lees, *Beset by Berg and Floe*, p. 1 (SPRI).
31 Douglas Mawson, letter to H. R. Mill, 18 July 1922 (SPRI).
32 E. H. Shackleton, memorandum to Admiralty, n.d. (PRO ADM 1/8368/29).
33 Admiralty memorandum, 13 February 1914 (PRO ADM 1/8368/29).
34 E. H. Shackleton, letter to Winston Churchill, 27 February 1914 (PRO ADM 1/8368/92).
35 The *Winning Post*, 8 April 1909.
36 T. H. Orde-Lees, op. cit., p. 3.
37 Admiralty memorandum, 30 January 1914 (PRO ADM 1/8368/29).
38 The *Manchester Guardian*, 30 December 1913.
39 E. H. Shackleton, letter to Lord Stamfordham, 22 June 1914 (Royal Archives, Windsor).
40 The *London Mail*, 17 January 1914.
41 E. H. Shackleton, telegram to Fridtjof Nansen, 17 April 1914 (UB).
42 *The Imperial Trans-Antarctic Expedition* (fund raising circular) (SPRI).
43 Mrs Glass, letter to author.
44 H. R. Mill's notes, correspondence between Shackleton and Janet Stancomb-Wills (SPRI).
45 E. H. Shackleton, letter to Emily Shackleton, May 1914 (SPRI).
46 Sir James Caird, letter to E. H. Shackleton, 17 June 1914 (SPRI).
47 The *Morning Post*, 29 June 1914.
48 E. H. Shackleton, letter to Sir Philip Brocklehurst, "Monday" (Van Haeften).
49 The *Manchester Guardian*, 3 August 1914.
50 Tryggve Gran, *Slik var det*, p. 214.
51 Ibid.
52 Winston Churchill, letter to his wife, 31 July 1914, Martin Gilbert, *Winston Churchill*, p. 1993.
53 F. A. Worsley, diary, 3 August 1914 (SPRI).
54 E. H. Shackleton, telegram to Admiralty, 3 August 1914 (PRO ADM 137/51, p. 455).
55 "Saki" (H. H. Munro), *The Square Egg*, p. 111.
56 *Quoted*, Martin Gilbert, op. cit., Vol. iii, p. 31.
57 E. H. Shackleton, letter to Emily Shackleton, 5 August 1914 (SPRI).
58 F. A. Worsley, op. cit., 5 August 1914 (SPRI).
59 Ibid., 22 August 1914.
60 Wilhelm Filchner, letter to H. R. Mill, 13 January 1911 (SPRI).
61 E. H. Shackleton, letter to Emily Shackleton, [August 1914] (SPRI).
62 *Quoted*, Lady Diana Cooper, *The Rainbow Comes and Goes*, p. 115.
63 E. H. Shackleton, letter to Emily Shackleton, 17 August 1914 (SPRI).
64 Ibid., 31 August 1914 (SPRI).
65 Ibid., 18 August 1914.
66 Ibid., 17 August 1914.
67 Janet Stancomb-Wills, letter to H. R. Mill, 31 October 1922 (SPRI).
68 The *Manchester Guardian*, 3 August 1914.
69 The *Irish Times*, 3 August 1914.
70 *El Liberal* (Madrid), 29 September 1914.

Chapter XXXI: South Georgia
(pages 383–398)

1 The *Daily Chronicle*, 29 October 1914.
2 The *Bystander*, 23 September 1914.
3 The *Evening Standard*, 5 August 1914.
4 F. R. Wild, unpublished memoirs, p. 159 (ML).
5 A. H. Macklin, unpublished narrative (MFP).
6 Ibid.
7 L. Greenstreet, interview with James Fisher (SPRI).
8 J. A. McIlroy, interview with James Fisher (SPRI).
9 Bridges Adams, letter to James Fisher, 31 July 1955 (SPRI).
10 R. W. James, letter to H. R. Mill, 12 May 1922 (SPRI).
11 L. Greenstreet, letter to his father, 7 November 1914 (Mrs Audrey Greenstreet).
12 T. H. Orde-Lees, diary, 13 October 1914 (TBL).
13 R. W. James, op. cit.
14 Sir Harry Brittain, interview with James Fisher (SPRI).
15 E. H. Shackleton, letter to Emily Shackleton, 26 October 1914 (SPRI).
16 Ibid., October 1914.
17 Ibid., 26 October 1914.

18 Unidentified officer, HMS *Glasgow*, eyewitness account, Battle of Coronel (Imperial War Museum).
19 Governor, Falkland Islands, cable to Colonial Office, 19 October 1914 (PRO CO 78/131).
20 Walter How, letter to his wife, 26 October 1914.
21 E. H. Shackleton, letter to Emily Shackleton, 26 October 1914 (SPRI).
22 L. Greenstreet, interview with James Fisher (SPRI).
23 E. H. Shackleton, letter to Ernest Perris, 30 November 1914 (SPRI).
24 R. W. James, diary, 5 November 1914 (SPRI).
25 A. H. Macklin, op. cit.
26 K. Løken, letter to bishop, n.d., and letter to family, 15 April 1912 (Hvalfangstmuseet, Sandefjord).
27 R. B. Robertson, *Of Whales and Men*, p. 61.
28 E. H. Shackleton, letter to Emily Shackleton, 26 October 1914 (SPRI).
29 E. H. Shackleton, letter to Ernest Perris, 30 November 1914 (SPRI).
30 R. B. Robertson, op. cit., p. 51.
31 T. H. Orde-Lees, op. cit., 10 November 1914 (TBL).
32 R. W. James, op. cit., 2 May 1915 (SPRI).
33 A. H. Macklin, op. cit.
34 Douglas Mawson, letter to Frank Hurley, 18 April 1914 (MI).
35 Frank Hurley, letter to Douglas Mawson, 19 November 1914 (MI).
36 L. Greenstreet, letter to his father, 17 November 1914 (Mrs Audrey Greenstreet).
37 Shelley, *Mont Blanc*.
38 T. H. Orde-Lees, *Beset by Berg and Floe* (SPRI).
39 Hudson's Bay Co., Winnipeg, letter to F. C. Ingram, Hudson's Bay Co., London, 27 June 1914 (Hudson's Bay Archives, A12/FT MISC/222).
40 E. H. Shackleton, telegram to Fridtjof Nansen, 18 September 1914 (UB).
41 Fridtjof Nansen, telegram to E. H. Shackleton, [18 September 1914] (UB).
42 E. H. Shackleton, letter to Ernest Perris, 30 November 1914 (SPRI).
43 F. R. Wild, op. cit., p. 206 (ML).
44 T. H. Orde-Lees, diary, 5 December 1914 (TBL).
45 Sir Joseph Hooker, letter to R. F. Scott, 1 June 1910 (SPRI).
46 Walter How, letters to his wife, August–December 1914.
47 E. H. Shackleton, letter to Emily Shackleton, 4 December 1914 (SPRI).
48 Mrs Ireland, interview with Lady Harriet Shackleton.
49 H. R. Mill, *The Life of Sir Ernest Shackleton*, p. 265.
50 A. H. Macklin, op. cit.

Chapter XXXII: Pack ice at 59° 28′
(pages 399–411)

1 F. A. Worsley, diary, 7 December 1914 (SPRI).
2 Ibid., 8 December 1914 (SPRI).
3 Ibid., 7 December 1914.
4 E. H. Shackleton, letter to Emily Shackleton, 26 October 1914 (SPRI).
5 F. A. Worsley, op. cit., 24 January 1915.
6 A. H. Macklin, unpublished narrative (MFP).
7 L. Greenstreet, diary (Mrs Audrey Greenstreet).
8 L. D. A. Hussey, *South with Shackleton*, p. 3.
9 Ibid., p. 4.
10 A. H. Macklin, op. cit.
11 F. A. Worsley, op. cit., 8 January 1915.
12 A. E. W. Mason, *The Turnstile*, p. 251.
13 F. A. Worsley, op. cit., 16 August 1915.
14 R. W. James, letter to Margery Fisher, n.d. (SPRI).
15 H. McNeish, diary, 18 December 1914 (TBL).
16 Gerald Bowman, *Men of Antarctica*, p. 72.
17 E. H. Shackleton, letter to Ernest Perris, 30 November 1914.
18 H. McNeish, op. cit., 24 December 1914.
19 Ibid.
20 T. H. Orde-Lees, diary, 25 December 1914 (TBL).
21 Sir James Caird, letter to E. H. Shackleton, 15 September 1914 (SPRI).
22 R. W. Richards, *Marooned in the Antarctic*, manuscript in possession of author.
23 A. Stevens, letter to H. R. Mill, 20 November 1928 (SPRI).
24 L. Thomson, diary, 9 January 1915 (SPRI).
25 H. McNeish, op. cit., 9 January 1915.

26 F. A. Worsley, op. cit., 23 January 1915.
27 T. H. Orde-Lees, op. cit., 10 January 1915 (TBL).
28 F. A. Worsley, op. cit., 12 January 1915.
29 Ibid., 13 January 1915.
30 T. H. Orde-Lees, op. cit., 15 January 1915.
31 Frank Hurley, diary, 18 January 1915 (ML).
32 T. H. Orde-Lees, op. cit., 2 January 1915.
33 Ibid., 29 January 1915.

Chapter XXXIII: Two helpless hulks
(pages 412–420)

1 A. Spencer-Smith, diary, 29 January 1915 (SPRI).
2 Ibid., 31 January 1915.
3 Ibid., 5 February 1915.
4 E. M. Joyce, *The South Polar Trail*, p. 49.
5 A. Mackintosh, diary, 13–14 February 1915 (RGS).
6 A. Spencer-Smith, op. cit., 11 February 1915.
7 E. M. Joyce, op. cit., p. 60.
8 E. M. Joyce, op. cit., p. 64.
9 T. H. Orde-Lees, diary, 25 February 1915 (TBL).
10 A. H. Macklin, unpublished narrative (MFP).
11 T. H. Orde-Lees, op. cit., 16 March 1915.
12 Ibid., 19 February 1915.
13 Ibid., 21 March 1915.
14 Ibid., 20 February 1915.
15 Ibid., 4 March 1915.
16 Ibid., 29 January 1915.
17 Ibid., 13 February 1915.
18 Ibid., 1 and 15 February 1915.
19 H. McNeish, diary, 8 March 1915 (TBL).
20 F. A. Worsley, *Endurance*, p. 4.
21 H. McNeish, op. cit., 16 March 1915.
22 Ibid., 10 April 1915.
23 The Earl of Meath, *Memoirs of the Twentieth Century*, p. 43.
24 F. A. Worsley, diary, 24 May 1915 (SPRI).
25 Capt. A. D. Talbot, letter to Miss Turle, 24 May 1915 (Imperial War Museum).
26 Leslie Thomson, diary, 24 May 1915 (SPRI).
27 R. W. Richards, *Marooned in the Antarctic*, p. 17.

Chapter XXXIV: "The secret of our unanimity"
(pages 421–438)

1 T. H. Orde-Lees, diary, 3 June 1915 (TBL).
2 H. McNeish, diary, 8 June 1915 (TBL).
3 Ibid., 30 June 1915.
4 T. H. Orde-Lees, op. cit., 26 January 1915.
5 F. A. Worsley, diary, 8 February 1915.
6 A. H. Macklin, interview with James Fisher (SPRI).
7 Ibid.
8 Frank Hurley, diary, 2 July 1915 (ML).
9 A. H. Macklin, op. cit.
10 L. Greenstreet, interview with James Fisher (SPRI).
11 Ibid.
12 H. McNeish, op. cit., 20 May 1915.
13 Frank Hurley, op. cit., 7 July 1915.
14 F. A. Worsley, op. cit., 7 August 1915.
15 T. H. Orde-Lees, op. cit., 30 March 1915.
16 T. H. Orde-Lees, diary, 1915–16 (SPRI).
17 T. H. Orde-Lees, diary, 30 March 1915 (TBL).
18 Ibid., 11 March 1915.
19 Ibid., 25 December 1914.
20 Ibid.
21 Ibid., 18 February 1915.
22 Ibid., 16 December 1914.
23 Ibid.
24 Ibid., 7 June 1915.
25 Ibid., 18 December 1914.
26 Ibid., 25 December 1914.
27 Ibid., 23 December 1914; 10 February 1915.
28 Ibid., 20 January 1915.

29 Frank Hurley, *Argonauts of the South*, p. 166.
30 R. W. James, diary, 4 April 1915 (SPRI).
31 A. H. Macklin, narrative (MFP).
32 T. H. Orde-Lees, *Beset by Berg and Floe* (SPRI).
33 F. A. Worsley, op. cit., 15 June 1915.
34 T. H. Orde-Lees, diary, 9 February 1915 (TBL).
35 Frank Hurley, diary, 30 June 1915 (ML).
36 R. W. James, letter to H. R. Mill, 12 May 1922 (SPRI).
37 R. Amundsen, diary on *Belgica*, 1 April 1898 (UB).
38 C. A. Larsen, diary, 1 February 1903 (B. T. Larsen).
39 Ibid., 11 February 1903.
40 Ibid., 12 February 1903.
41 Ibid., 17 February 1903.
42 Ibid., 16 February 1903.
43 C. Skottsberg in Otto Nordenskjöld, *Antarctic*, Vol. ii, p. 487.
44 F. A. Worsley, op. cit., 12 May 1915.
45 L. Greenstreet, op. cit.
46 H. McNeish, op. cit., 14 July 1915.
47 F. A. Worsley, *Endurance*, p. 4.
48 L. Greenstreet, op. cit.
49 F. A. Worsley, diary, 17 April 1915 (SPRI).
50 Ibid., 9 May 1915.
51 Ibid., 2 March 1915.
52 Ibid., 4 May 1915.
53 Ibid., 25 June 1915.
54 Ibid., 1 June 1915.
55 Ibid., 10 June 1915.
56 T. H. Orde-Lees, op. cit., 29 January 1915.
57 T. H. Orde-Lees, *Beset by Berg and Floe* (SPRI).
58 A. H. Macklin, interview with James Fisher (SPRI).
59 Ibid.
60 A. H. Macklin, letter to Alfred Lansing, 9 March 1958 (MFP).
61 R. W. James, op. cit.
62 A. H. Macklin, letter to Alfred Lansing, 20 January 1958 (MFP).
63 T. H. Orde-Lees, diary, 4 June 1915 (TBL).
64 L. Greenstreet, op. cit.
65 F. A. Worsley, op. cit., 22 June 1915.
66 T. H. Orde-Lees, op. cit., 9 February 1915.
67 H. McNeish, op. cit., 1 August 1915.

Chapter XXXV: Death agony of *Endurance*
(pages 439–448)

1 Frank Hurley, diary, 1 August 1915 (ML).
2 F. A. Worsley, diary, 3 August 1915 (SPRI).
3 H. McNeish, diary, 26 July 1915 (TBL).
4 F. A. Worsley, op. cit., 4 August 1915.
5 Frank Hurley, op. cit., 26 August 1915.
6 H. McNeish, op. cit., 12 August 1915.
7 Ibid., 4 September 1916.
8 F. A. Worsley, op. cit., 1 September 1915.
9 Ibid., 8 September 1915.
10 Ibid., 13 September 1915.
11 Ibid., 21 September 1915.
12 Ibid., 22 September 1915.
13 H. McNeish, op. cit., 30 September 1915.
14 Ibid., 10 October 1915.
15 Frank Hurley, op. cit., 17 October 1915.
16 H. McNeish, 18 July 1915.
17 F. A. Worsley, op. cit., 18 October 1915.
18 R. W. James, diary, 20 October 1915.
19 H. McNeish, op. cit., 23 October 1915.
20 Ibid., 24 October 1915.
21 A. H. Macklin, diary, 28 October 1915 (MFP).
22 F. A. Worsley, op. cit., 26 October 1915.
23 Frank Hurley, op. cit., 26 October 1915.
24 A. H. Macklin, op. cit., loc. cit.
25 Frank Hurley, op. cit., loc. cit.
26 F. A. Worsley, op. cit., loc. cit.
27 A. H. Macklin, op. cit., loc. cit.
28 Ibid.
29 Frank Hurley, op. cit., 27 October 1915.
30 Ibid.
31 Ibid.
32 A. H. Macklin, op. cit., loc. cit.
33 H. McNeish, op. cit., 27 October 1915.
34 Frank Hurley, op. cit., loc. cit.
35 E. H. Shackleton, diary, 27 October 1915.
36 T. H. Orde-Lees, *Beset by Berg and Floe* (SPRI).

Chapter XXXVI: Responsibility to Shackleton
(pages 449–453)

1 E. M. Joyce, letter to "Paton and Bhoys", 22 October 1915 (TBL).
2 E. R. G. R. Evans and H. L. L. Pennell, "Voyages of the *Terra Nova*", in *Scott's Last Expedition*, Vol. ii, p. 397.
3 R. W. Richards, interview with Lennard Bickel (ML).
4 E. M. Joyce, op. cit.
5 R. W. Richards, op. cit.
6 R. W. Richards, letter to the author, 26 August 1982.
7 E. M. Joyce, letter to Charles Royds, 7 April 1930 (SPRI).
8 A. O. Stevens, *Report of the Ross Sea Party*, p. 35.
9 E. H. Shackleton, *South*, p. 242.
10 *Quoted*, E. H. Shackleton, ibid., p. 166.
11 E. A. Wilson, diary, 22 May 1911.
12 E. M. Joyce, diary, 26 October 1915 (TBL).
13 Ibid.
14 E. M. Joyce, letter to "Paton and Bhoys", 22 October 1915.

Chapter XXXVII: "So now we'll go home"
(pages 454–464)

1 R. W. James, diary, 27 October 1915 (SPRI).
2 Frank Hurley, diary, 27 October 1915 (ML).
3 Walter How, interview with James Fisher (SPRI).
4 Frank Hurley, op. cit., 29 October 1915.
5 A. H. Macklin, *Shackleton as I knew him*, unpublished manuscript (MFP).
6 Christopher Naisbitt "I went with Shackleton", *Hampstead News and Golders Green Gazette*, 22 November 1956.
7 E. H. Shackleton, diary, 29 October 1915 (SPRI).
8 L. Greenstreet, interview with James Fisher (SPRI).
9 T. H. Orde-Lees, *Beset by Berg and Floe* (SPRI).
10 Frank Hurley, op. cit., 28 October 1915.
11 F. A. Worsley, diary, 30 October 1915 (SPRI).
12 Ibid.
13 T. H. Orde-Lees, diary, 29 October 1915 (SPRI).
14 Ibid., 28 October 1915.
15 Ibid., 29 October 1915.
16 T. H. Orde-Lees, *Beset by Berg and Floe*.
17 Frank Hurley, op. cit., 30 October 1915.
18 E. H. Shackleton, op. cit., 31 October 1915.
19 R. Amundsen, *Nordvestpassagen*, p. 134.
20 A. H. Macklin, op. cit.
21 Frank Hurley, op. cit., 1 November 1915.
22 H. McNeish, diary, 1 November 1915 (TBL).
23 Frank Debenham, diary, 18 April 1911 (SPRI).
24 E. H. Shackleton, op. cit., 30 October 1915.
25 Frank Hurley, op. cit., 5 November 1915.
26 Ibid., 2 November 1915.
27 A. H. Macklin, diary, 8 November 1915 (MFP).
28 E. H. Shackleton, op. cit., 21 November 1915.
29 F. A. Worsley, op. cit., 6 November 1915.
30 A. H. Macklin, op. cit., 14 November 1915.
31 F. A. Worsley, op. cit., 11 November 1915.
32 E. H. Shackleton, op. cit., 3, 13 November 1915.
33 Frank Hurley, op. cit., 16 November 1915.
34 A. H. Macklin, op. cit., 14 November 1915.
35 H. McNeish, op. cit., 18 November 1915.
36 Frank Hurley, op. cit., 13 November 1915.
37 A. H. Macklin, op. cit., 14 November 1915.
38 F. A. Worsley, op. cit., 7 November 1915.
39 E. H. Shackleton, op. cit., 19 November 1915.
40 R. W. James, op. cit., 24 January 1916.
41 A. H. Macklin, op. cit., 24 November 1915.
42 Frank Hurley, op. cit., 18 November 1915.
43 E. H. Shackleton, op. cit., 17 November 1915.
44 William Kinglake, *Eothen*, p. 15.
45 Frank Hurley, op. cit., 21 November 1915.
46 E. H. Shackleton, op. cit., 21 November 1915.

Chapter XXXVIII: From Ocean Camp to Patience Camp (pages 465–479)

1 F. A. Worsley, diary, 23 November 1915 (SPRI).
2 Ibid., 1 December 1915.
3 T. H. Orde-Lees, *Beset by Berg and Floe* (SPRI).
4 A. H. Macklin, letter to R. E. Priestley, 26 October 1926 (SPRI).
5 A. H. Macklin, letter to John Kendall, 19 February 1951 (SPRI).
6 Ibid.
7 Ibid.
8 Ibid.
9 L. Greenstreet, interview with James Fisher (SPRI).
10 H. McNeish, diary, 5 December 1915 (TBL).
11 E. H. Shackleton, *South*, p. 115.
12 Frank Hurley, diary, 27 November 1915 (ML).
13 Ibid., 30 November 1915.
14 Ibid., 23–25 November 1915.
15 Ibid., 16 December 1915.
16 Ibid.
17 A. H. Macklin, diary, 8 December 1915 (MFP).
18 Ibid., 10 December 1915.
19 F. A. Worsley, op. cit., 17 December 1915.
20 L. D. A. Hussey, *South with Shackleton*, p. 65.
21 A. H. Macklin, op. cit., 16 December 1915.
22 E. H. Shackleton, diary, 16 December 1915 (SPRI).
23 Ibid., 18 December 1915.
24 Frank Hurley, op. cit., 19 December 1915.
25 L. Greenstreet, op. cit.
26 F. R. Wild, unpublished memoirs, p. 227 (ML).
27 E. H. Shackleton, op. cit., 21 December 1915.
28 A. H. Macklin, op. cit., 21 December 1915.
29 E. H. Shackleton, op. cit., 25 December 1915.
30 F. A. Worsley, op. cit., 26 December 1915.
31 T. H. Orde-Lees, diary, 26 December 1915 (SPRI).
32 A. H. Macklin, op. cit., 13 November 1915.
33 BOT Crew List.
34 E. H. Shackleton, op. cit., 28 December 1915.
35 Gerald Bowman, *Men of Antarctica*, p. 73.
36 E. H. Shackleton, op. cit., 28 December 1915.
37 A. H. Macklin, op. cit., 29 December 1915.
38 E. H. Shackleton, op. cit., 29 December 1915.
39 H. McNeish, op. cit., 30 December 1915.
40 E. H. Shackleton, op. cit., 31 December 1915.
41 Frank Hurley, op. cit., 31 December 1915.
42 F. R. Wild, diary, 4 January 1909.
43 E. H. Shackleton, op. cit., 9 January 1916.
44 Ibid., 26 January 1916.

Chapter XXXIX: Escape by a hair's breadth (pages 480–487)

1 R. W. Richards, *Marooned in the Antarctic*, manuscript, p. 26.
2 E. Wild, diary, 25 January 1916 (SPRI).
3 E. M. Joyce, diary, 26 January 1916 (ML).
4 E. Wild, op. cit., 22 January 1916.
5 E. M. Joyce, op. cit., 22 January 1916.
6 A. Spencer-Smith, diary, 23 January 1916 (SPRI).
7 Ibid., 21 January 1916.
8 Ibid., 29 January 1916.
9 *Scott's Last Expedition*, Vol. i, p. 588.
10 E. M. Joyce, op. cit., 29 January 1916.
11 R. W. Richards, letter to the author.
12 A. Spencer-Smith, op. cit., 11, 15 February 1916.
13 E. M. Joyce, op. cit., 31 January 1916.
14 A. Spencer-Smith, op. cit., 18 February 1916.
15 E. M. Joyce, op. cit., 25 February 1916.
16 R. W. Richards, diary, 24 February 1916 (manuscript in possession of Richards).
17 Ibid.
18 R. W. Richards, *Marooned in the Antarctic*, p. 29.
19 E. M. Joyce, op. cit., 25 February 1916.
20 R. W. Richards, letter to the author.
21 E. M. Joyce, op. cit., 25 February 1916.
22 R. W. Richards, diary, 26 February 1916.

23 Ibid., 29 February 1916.
24 A. Spencer-Smith, op. cit., 29 February 1916.
25 Ibid., 1 March 1916.
26 R. W. Richards, op. cit., 9 March 1916.
27 E. M. Joyce, op. cit., 9 March 1916.
28 Ibid., 18 March 1916.
29 Ibid., 11 March 1916.

Chapter XL: "We can only wait and see"
(pages 488–502)

1 Winston Churchill, letter to his wife, 28 March 1916, *quoted*, Martin Gilbert, *Winston S. Churchill*, Vol. iii, Companion, 1914–16, p. 1468.
2 *The Times*; the *Daily Chronicle*, 25 March 1916.
3 *The Times*, op. cit.
4 *Daily Chronicle*, 27 March 1916.
5 *The Times*, 28 March 1916.
6 Winston Churchill, op. cit.
7 A. H. Macklin, diary, 15–18 March 1916 (MFP).
8 C. J. Green, interview with James Fisher (SPRI).
9 F. A. Worsley, diary, 3 February 1916.
10 Ibid., 14 February 1916.
11 E. H. Shackleton, diary, 7 February 1916.
12 F. A. Worsley, op. cit., 14 January 1916.
13 Ibid., 1 February 1916.
14 R. W. James, diary, 2 February 1916 (SPRI).
15 A. H. Macklin, op. cit., 2 February 1916.
16 Ibid., 20 March 1916.
17 H. McNeish, diary, 11 February 1916.
18 R. W. James, op. cit., 6, 11 February 1916.
19 C. J. Green, op. cit.
20 H. McNeish, op. cit., 8 February 1916.
21 F. A. Worsley, op. cit., 2 March 1916.
22 Ibid., 4 March 1916.
23 Ibid., 12 March 1916.
24 F. A. Worsley, 29 January 1916.
25 Frank Hurley, diary, 6 March 1916 (ML).
26 F. A. Worsley, op. cit., 31 December 1915.
27 A. H. Macklin, interview with James Fisher (SPRI).
28 R. W. James, op. cit., 11 February 1916.
29 A. H. Macklin, diary, 26 March 1916.
30 Frank Hurley, letter to Margery Fisher, 29 March 1956 (SPRI).
31 F. A. Worsley, *Endurance*, p. 64.
32 Ibid.
33 A. H. Macklin, op. cit., 29 March 1916.
34 Ibid., 13 March 1916.
35 F. A. Worsley, diary, 10 March 1916.
36 W. How, interview with James Fisher (SPRI).
37 R. W. James, op. cit., 6 February 1916.
38 T. H. Orde-Lees, *Beset by Berg and Floe* (SPRI).
39 F. A. Worsley, *Endurance*, p. 62.
40 E. H. Shackleton, op. cit., 9 March 1916.
41 Ibid., 10 March 1916.
42 H. McNeish, diary, 16 March 1916 (ML).
43 Frank Hurley, diary, 23 March 1916.
44 E. H. Shackleton, op. cit., 23 March 1916.
45 Frank Hurley, op. cit., 24 March 1916.
46 F. A. Worsley, diary, 24 March 1916 (SPRI).
47 F. A. Worsley, *Endurance*, p. 61.
48 R. W. James, op. cit., 24 March 1916.
49 A. H. Macklin, op. cit., 28 March 1916.
50 R. W. James, op. cit., 29 March; 11 February 1916.
51 F. A. Worsley, diary, 31 March 1916.
52 A. H. Macklin, op. cit., 30 March 1916.
53 Frank Hurley, op. cit., 30 March 1916.
54 Ibid., 1 April 1916.
55 Otto Sverdrup, *Nyt Land*, Vol. i, p. 150.
56 F. A. Worsley, op. cit., 8 April 1916.
57 A. H. Macklin, op. cit., 9 April 1916.

Chapter XLI: Into the open sea
(pages 503–519)

1 A. H. Macklin, diary, 9 April 1916 (MFP).
2 R. W. James, diary, 7 April 1916 (SPRI).
3 E. H. Shackleton, letter to Emily Shackleton, 1 January 1908 (SPRI).
4 A. H. Macklin, op. cit., loc. cit.
5 Ibid.

6 R. W. James, op. cit., 9 April 1916.
7 E. H. Shackleton, *South*, p. 57.
8 Ibid.
9 Frank Hurley, diary, 10 April 1916 (ML).
10 F. A. Worsley, *Endurance*, p. 67.
11 Frank Hurley, op. cit., loc. cit.
12 A. H. Macklin, op. cit., 10 April 1916.
13 A. H. Macklin, narrative (MFP).
14 W. How, interview with James Fisher (SPRI).
15 A. H. Macklin, op. cit.
16 A. H. Macklin, diary, 10 April 1916.
17 Frank Hurley, op. cit., 10 April 1916.
18 R. W. James, op. cit., 11 April 1916.
19 A. H. Macklin, narrative.
20 L. Greenstreet, interview with James Fisher (SPRI).
21 R. W. James, op. cit., 11 April 1916.
22 A. H. Macklin, diary, 13 April 1916.
23 A. H. Macklin, *Notes on the Boat Journey* (MFP).
24 R. W. James, op. cit., 12 April 1916.
25 F. A. Worsley, diary, 12 April 1916.
26 A. H. Macklin, narrative.
27 R. W. James, op. cit., 12 April 1916.
28 F. A. Worsley, op. cit., 15 April 1916.
29 T. H. Orde-Lees, *Beset by Berg and Floe*.
30 F. A. Worsley, op. cit., 13 April 1916.
31 T. H. Orde-Lees, diary, 14 April 1916.
32 Ibid.
33 A. H. Macklin, op. cit.
34 R. W. James, op. cit., 13 April 1916.
35 A. H. Macklin, op. cit.
36 A. H. Macklin, diary, 14 April 1916.
37 Ibid.
38 T. H. Orde-Lees, *Beset by Berg and Floe*.
39 T. H. Orde-Lees, diary, 14 April 1916.
40 F. A. Worsley, op. cit., 14 April 1916.
41 A. H. Macklin, narrative.
42 Ibid.
43 Ibid.
44 T. H. Orde-Lees, *Beset by Berg and Floe*.
45 T. H. Orde-Lees, diary, 14 April 1916.
46 Ibid., 15 April 1916.
47 F. R. Wild, unpublished memoirs, p. 148 (ML).
48 Ibid.
49 Ibid.
50 R. W. James, op. cit., 15 April 1916.
51 T. H. Orde-Lees, op. cit., 15 April 1916.
52 Frank Hurley, op. cit., 15 April 1916.
53 H. McNeish, diary, 16 April 1916 (TBL).
54 T. H. Orde-Lees, *Beset by Berg and Floe*.
55 A. H. Macklin, op. cit.
56 R. W. James, op. cit., 15 April 1916.

Chapter XLII: Half-way house (pages 520–527)

1 Frank Hurley, diary, 19 April 1916 (ML).
2 F. A. Worsley, *Endurance*, p. 80.
3 T. H. Orde-Lees, *Beset by Berg and Floe* (SPRI).
4 F. R. Wild, unpublished memoirs, p. 152 (ML).
5 A. H. Macklin, narrative (MFP).
6 F. R. Wild, op. cit., p. 153.
7 Ibid., p. 155.
8 F. A. Worsley, op. cit., p. 86.
9 F. R. Wild, op. cit., p. 156.
10 E. H. Shackleton, *South*, p. 80.
11 T. H. Orde-Lees, op. cit.
12 H. McNeish, diary, [20] April 1916 (TBL).
13 Ibid., 21 April 1916.
14 Ibid., 23 April 1916.
15 Ibid., 22 April 1916.
16 A. H. Macklin, interview with James Fisher (SPRI).
17 H. McNeish, op. cit., 24 April 1916.
18 T. H. Orde-Lees, diary, 24 April 1916 (SPRI).
19 Ibid.
20 Frank Hurley, op. cit., 24 April 1916.

Chapter XLIII: Tension on Elephant Island (pages 528–541)

1 T. H. Orde-Lees, diary, 12 June 1916 (SPRI).
2 Ibid., 24 April 1916 (TBL).
3 Ibid.
4 Ibid.
5 Ibid.
6 Ibid., 9 May 1916.
7 Ibid., 24 April 1916.
8 Ibid., 28 April 1916.
9 Ibid., 25 May–11 June 1916.
10 Frank Hurley, diary, 8 June 1916 (ML).

11 R. W. James, diary, 3 June 1916.
12 T. H. Orde-Lees, op. cit., 1 May 1916 (SPRI).
13 A. H. Macklin, diary, 5 August 1916 (MFP).
14 Frank Hurley, op. cit., 27 April 1916.
15 T. H. Orde-Lees, op. cit., 28 April 1916 (TBL).
16 Frank Hurley, op. cit., 29 April 1916.
17 Ibid., 30 April 1916.
18 Ibid., 8 May 1916.
19 Ibid., 12 June 1916.
20 A. H. Macklin, op. cit., 6 June 1916.
21 Frank Hurley, op. cit., 15 June 1916.
22 T. H. Orde-Lees, op. cit., 8 May 1916.
23 L. Greenstreet, diary, 15 June 1916 (Mrs Audrey Greenstreet).
24 A. H. Macklin, op. cit., 16 August 1916.
25 R. W. James, op. cit., 18 May 1916.
26 Frank Hurley, op. cit., 8 May 1916.
27 Ibid., 12 June; 7 July 1916.
28 A. H. Macklin, op. cit., 16 August 1916.
29 Ibid, 22 August 1916.
30 F. R. Wild, letter to "Dear Gussie", 31 December 1916 (Mr James-Martin).
31 T. H. Orde-Lees, op. cit., 30 June 1916.
32 Ibid., 7 June, 3 July 1916.
33 Ibid., 9–10 July 1916.
34 C. J. Green, interview with James Fisher (SPRI).
35 A. H. Macklin, interview with James Fisher.
36 C. J. Green, op. cit.
37 Frank Hurley, op. cit., 15 June 1916.
38 T. H. Orde-Lees, op. cit., 23 June 1916.
39 *Quoted*, A. G. E. Jones, "Frankie Wild's Hut", *Journal of the Royal Naval Medical Service*, Vol. 64, Spring 1978, p. 54.
40 T. H. Orde-Lees, op. cit., 6, 22 June, 2 July 1916.
41 C. A. Larsen, "Från vistelsen på Paulet-ön", in Otto Nordenskjöld, *Antarctic*, Vol. ii, p. 498.
42 Frank Hurley, op. cit., 1 August 1916.
43 Otto Nordenskjöld, op. cit., Vol. ii, p. 373.
44 T. H. Orde-Lees, op. cit., 19 July 1916.
45 Ibid., 3 August 1916.
46 Ibid.

Chapter XLIV: Relief preparations
(pages 542–545)

1 Notes of conversation between J. Scott Keltie and Douglas Freshfield, of the RGS, and J. K. Davis, 10 April 1916 (RGS, *Endurance* file).
2 RGS, letter to Capt. Parry, 30 March 1916 (RGS).
3 RGS, letter to Admiralty, 18 April 1916 (PRO ADM 116/1712).
4 Douglas Freshfield, letter to A. R. Hinks, 25 March 1916 (RGS).
5 E. H. Shackleton, letter to Lord Curzon, 13 January 1914 (RGS).
6 Hutchison Cuff, letter to RGS, 24 January 1916 (RGS).
7 Douglas Freshfield, letter to A. R. Hinks, 30 April 1916 (RGS).
8 Robert Graves, *Goodbye to all That*, p. 120.
9 Kathleen Scott, diary, 12 March 1912.
10 Kathleen Scott, *Self-Portrait of an Artist*, p. 140.
11 Admiralty minute, 26 April 1916 (PRO ADM 116/1712).
12 Ibid., 27 April 1916.

Chapter XLV: The open-boat journey
(pages 546–562)

1 F. A. Worsley, *Shackleton's Great Boat Journey*, p. 29 (SPRI).
2 Ibid., p. 18.
3 Ibid., p. 16.
4 E. H. Shackleton, *South*, p. 86.
5 H. McNeish, diary, 14 April 1916 (TBL).
6 F. A. Worsley, op. cit., p. 3.
7 Ibid., p. 5.
8 Ibid., p. 7.
9 Ibid.
10 Ibid.
11 Ibid.
12 Ibid., p. 5.
13 Ibid., p. 7.
14 *Admiralty Manual of Navigation*, p. 102.
15 F. A. Worsley, *Endurance*, p. 104.
16 E. H. Shackleton, op. cit., p. 169.
17 F. A. Worsley, *Shackleton's Great Boat Journey*, p. 24.

18 Ibid., p. 11.
19 Ibid., p. 10.
20 Ibid., p. 21.
21 Ibid., p. 9.
22 Ibid., p. 14.
23 Ibid.
24 E. H. Shackleton, op. cit., p. 166.
25 F. A. Worsley, op. cit., p. 9.
26 F. A. Worsley, *Endurance*, p. 106.
27 F. A. Worsley, *Shackleton's Great Boat Journey*, p. 15 (SPRI).
28 F. A. Worsley, *Endurance*, p. 115.
29 F. A. Worsley, *Shackleton's Great Boat Journey*, p. 15.
30 E. H. Shackleton, op. cit., p. 166.
31 F. A. Worsley, *Endurance*, p. 116.
32 F. A. Worsley, *Shackleton's Great Boat Journey*, p. 17.
33 Ibid.
34 Ibid., p. 18.
35 Ibid.
36 F. A. Worsley, log of voyage of *James Caird* from Elephant Island to South Georgia, 3 May 1916 (SPRI).
37 E. H. Shackleton, op. cit., p. 172.
38 Ibid., p. 173.
39 F. A. Worsley, *Shackleton's Great Boat Journey*, p. 19.
40 Ibid.
41 E. H. Shackleton, op. cit., p. 174.
42 F. A. Worsley, op. cit.
43 F. A. Worsley, diary, 6 May 1916.
44 E. H. Shackleton, op. cit., p. 175.
45 Ibid., p. 174.
46 E. H. Shackleton, op. cit., p. 172.
47 F. A. Worsley, op. cit., 6 May 1916.

Chapter XLVI: A slight change of course
(pages 563–565)

1 F. A. Worsley, *Shackleton's Great Boat Journey*, manuscript (SPRI).
2 Ibid.
3 Ibid.
4 A. H. Macklin, interview with James Fisher.
5 F. A. Worsley, op. cit.
6 Ibid.

Chapter XLVII: The line that divides success from failure
(pages 566–572)

1 Beaglehole, (ed.) *The Voyage of the Resolution and Adventure*, p. 625.
2 Debenham (ed.) *The Voyage of Captain Bellingshausen*, Vol. ii, p. 92.
3 F. A. Worsley, *Endurance*, p. 127.
4 E. H. Shackleton, *South*, p. 99.
5 F. A. Worsley, *Shackleton's Great Boat Journey* (SPRI).
6 Ibid.
7 F. A. Worsley, *Endurance*, p. 129.
8 F. A. Worsley, *Shackleton's Great Boat Journey*.
9 Ibid.
10 E. H. Shackleton, *South*, p. 101.
11 Ibid.
12 Ibid.

Chapter XLVIII: King Haakon Bay
(pages 573–580)

1 H. McNeish, diary, 10 [11] May 1916 (TBL).
2 F. A. Worsley, "Crossing South Georgia", *The Blue Peter*, August 1924, p. 224.
3 Ibid.
4 Ibid.
5 Ibid., p. 225.
6 E. H. Shackleton, *South*, p. 189.
7 F. A. Worsley, op. cit., loc. cit.
8 Ibid., p. 226.
9 H. McNeish, op. cit., 14 May 1916.
10 E. H. Shackleton, op. cit., p. 187.
11 F. A. Worsley, op. cit., loc. cit.
12 E. H. Shackleton, *South*, p. 190.
13 F. A. Worsley, op. cit., loc. cit.
14 Ibid., p. 228.
15 F. A. Worsley, *Endurance*, p. 143.
16 Ibid.
17 Ibid., p. 144.
18 F. A. Worsley, "Crossing South Georgia", *The Blue Peter*, August 1924, p. 228.
19 E. H. Shackleton, letter to H. McNeish, 16 May 1916 (TBL).

Chapter XLIX: The crossing of South Georgia
(pages 581–596)

1 F. A. Worsley, "Crossing South Georgia", *The Blue Peter*, August 1924, p. 229.
2 Ibid.
3 Ibid.
4 E. H. Shackleton, *South*, p. 195.
5 F. A. Worsley, op. cit., September 1924, p. 243.
6 Ibid.
7 Ibid.
8 E. H. Shackleton, op. cit., p. 197.
9 Ibid.
10 F. A. Worsley, op. cit., p. 244.
11 Ibid.
12 Ibid.
13 F. A. Worsley, *Endurance*, p. 154.
14 F. A. Worsley, "Crossing South Georgia", *The Blue Peter*, September 1924, p. 245.
15 Ibid., p. 247.
16 F. A. Worsley, *Endurance*, p. 157.
17 E. H. Shackleton, op. cit., p. 199.
18 F. A. Worsley, "Crossing South Georgia", *The Blue Peter*, September 1924, p. 245.
19 Ibid., p. 246.
20 The *Daily Mail*, 21 April 1911.
21 E. H. Shackleton, op. cit., p. 201.
22 F. A. Worsley, op. cit., p. 247.
23 E. H. Shackleton, op. cit., p. 201.
24 Ibid.
25 Ibid.
26 F. A. Worsley, op. cit., October 1924, p. 319.
27 E. H. Shackleton, op. cit., p. 202.
28 Ibid., p. 204.
29 F. A. Worsley, op. cit., loc. cit.
30 Ibid., p. 321.
31 Ibid.
32 E. H. Shackleton, op. cit., p. 205.
33 F. A. Worsley, op. cit., p. 322.
34 Ibid.

Chapter L: A trio of scarecrows
(pages 597–603)

1 F. A. Worsley, "Crossing South Georgia", *The Blue Peter*, October 1924, p. 322.
2 F. A. Worsley, *Endurance*, p. 164.
3 E. H. Shackleton, *South*, p. 206.
4 F. A. Worsley, "Crossing South Georgia", *The Blue Peter*, October 1924, p. 322.
5 Ibid.
6 E. H. Shackleton, op. cit., p. 210.
7 F. A. Worsley, *Endurance*, p. 164.
8 E. H. Shackleton, op. cit., p. 208.
9 F. A. Worsley, "Crossing South Georgia", *The Blue Peter*, October 1924, p. 323.
10 Ibid.
11 F. A. Worsley, "Crossing South Georgia", *The Blue Peter*, October 1924, loc. cit; *Endurance*, p. 165.
12 F. A. Worsley, *Endurance*, p. 165.
13 F. A. Worsley, "Crossing South Georgia", *The Blue Peter*, October 1924, p. 324.
14 Ibid.
15 E. H. Shackleton, *South*, p. 212.
16 F. A. Worsley, op. cit., August 1924, p. 228.
17 F. A. Worsley, *Endurance*, p. 167.

Chapter LI: "Urgent need immediate rescue"
(pages 604–619)

1 Governor of Falkland Islands, despatch to Sec. St. Colonies, 31 May 1916 (PRO CO 78/138. Despatch No. 25849).
2 Mid. Arthur Wellesley Clarke, diary, 1 June 1916 (Churchill College, Cambridge).
3 Ibid., 31 May 1916.
4 C. D. Mackellar, memorandum for H. R. Mill (SPRI).
5 *Vossische Zeitung* (Berlin), 15 June 1916.
6 Kathleen Scott, *Self-Portrait of an Artist*, p. 143.
7 The *Daily Chronicle*, 2 June 1916.
8 Ibid., 3 June 1916.
9 E. H. Shackleton, cable to the *Daily Chronicle*, 31 May 1916 (SPRI).
10 *John Bull*, 22 July 1916, p. 10.
11 *Magellan Times*, 21 September 1916.
12 Admiralty minute, 3 June 1916 (PRO ADM 116/1712).
13 E. H. Shackleton, letter to Emily Shackleton, 3 June 1916 (SPRI).
14 Douglas Mawson, letter to Emily Shackleton, 14 June 1916 (SPRI).
15 Emily Shackleton, letter to H. R. Mill, 4 June 1916 (SPRI).
16 E. H. Shackleton, cable to Ernest Perris, 31 May 1916 (SPRI).

17 Admiralty, letter to Foreign Office, 1 June 1916 (PRO CO 178/138).
18 "La Expedicion del 'Endurance' . . .", *Instituto Antarctica Uruguayo, Publicacion No. 18 Año 1975.*
19 Admiralty, telegram to Mitchell Innes, British Minister in Montevideo, 6 June 1916 (PRO ADM 116/1712).
20 Bjarne Aagaard, *Fangst og Forskning i Sydishavet*, Vol. i, p. 309.
21 *The Times*, 16 June 1916.
22 F. A. Worsley, diary, 16 June 1916 (SPRI).
23 F. A. Worsley, *Endurance*, p. 170.
24 Ibid., p. 170.
25 Commodore S.E.C. America, cable to Admiralty, 29 June 1916 (PRO ADM 116/1712).
26 The *Magellan Times*, 6 June 1916.
27 F. A. Worsley, diary, 13 August 1916.
28 F. A. Worsley, *Endurance*, p. 172.
29 Ibid., pp. 173–174.
30 E. H. Shackleton, letter to Cecily Shackleton, 1 August 1916 (SPRI).
31 F. A. Worsley, *Endurance*, p. 175.
32 E. H. Shackleton, cable to Hutchison & Cuff, 4 August 1916 (SPRI).
33 E. H. Shackleton, cable to Admiralty, 4 August 1916 (SPRI).
34 E. H. Shackleton, *South*, p. 218.
35 *Buenos Aires Herald*, 21 July 1916.
36 *Strathspey Herald*, 29 June 1916.
37 Admiralty, telegram to E. H. Shackleton, Punta Arenas, 16 August 1916 (PRO ADM 116/1712).
38 E. H. Shackleton, telegram to Admiralty, 17 August 1916 (PRO ADM 116/1712).
39 Admiralty, intercepted telegram from E. A. Perris to E. H. Shackleton, 20 August 1916 (PRO ADM 116/1712).
40 Ibid.
41 Admiralty, note by Sir Douglas Brownrigg, Chief Censor, 22 August 1916 (PRO ADM 116/1712).
42 Admiralty, cable to E. H. Shackleton, 26 August 1916 (PRO ADM 116/1712).
43 Tom Jones, *Patagonian Panorama*, p. 80.
44 The *Magellan Times*, 6 July 1916.
45 E. H. Shackleton, letter to Emily Shackleton, 22 August 1916 (SPRI).
46 *Buenos Aires Herald*, 29 September 1916.
47 F. A. Worsley, *Endurance*, p. 176.
48 Ibid., p. 178.

Chapter LII: Cape Wild
(pages 620–625)

1 L. Greenstreet, diary, 28 August 1916 (Mrs Audrey Greenstreet).
2 T. H. Orde-Lees, diary, 26 August 1916 (SPRI).
3 Frank Hurley, diary, 30 August 1916 (ML).
4 L. D. A. Hussey, *South with Shackleton*, p. 153.
5 T. H. Orde-Lees, op. cit., 30 August 1916.
6 Ibid.
7 F. R. Wild, letter to "My Dear Gussie", 31 December 1916 (H. J. James-Martin).
8 T. H. Orde-Lees, op. cit., ibid.
9 Ibid.
10 Frank Hurley, op. cit., 31 August 1916.
11 R. W. James, diary, 30 August 1916 (SPRI).
12 T. H. Orde-Lees, op. cit., ibid.
13 Frank Hurley, op. cit., 1 September 1916.
14 T. H. Orde-Lees, op. cit., ibid.
15 Tom Jones, *Patagonian Panorama*, p. 79.
16 T. H. Orde-Lees, op. cit., 3 September 1916.
17 R. W. James, op. cit., 3 September 1916.
18 Admiralty, cable to E. H. Shackleton, 26 August 1916 (PRO ADM 116/1712).
19 E. H. Shackleton, letter to Emily Shackleton, 3 September 1916 (SPRI).

Chapter LIII: *Aurora* and the end of the expedition
(pages 626–648)

1 T. H. Orde-Lees, diary, 3 September 1916 (TBL).
2 The *Magellan Times*, 21 September 1916.
3 Viscount Grey, cable to E. H. Shackleton, 7 September 1916 (PRO ADM 116/1712).
4 *San Francisco Chronicle*, 7 September 1916.
5 E. H. Shackleton, letter to Emily Shackleton, 23 October 1916 (SPRI).
6 T. H. Orde-Lees, conclusion of diary (TBL).
7 *El Pueblo de Los Andes* . . . [leaflet] (SPRI).
8 Douglas Mawson, letter to T. Edgeworth David, 17 September 1916 (MI).
9 T. Edgeworth David, letter to Douglas Mawson, 22 September 1916 (MI).
10 A. H. Macklin, diary, 18 October 1916 (MFP).
11 Governor, New Zealand, to Secretary of State for the Colonies, 23 October 1916 (PRO ADM 116/1712).
12 E. H. Shackleton, cable to E. A. Perris, n.d. (SPRI).

13 F. A. Worsley, diary, 30 October 1916 (SPRI).
14 E. H. Shackleton, letter to Emily Shackleton, 10 November 1916 (SPRI).
15 E. H. Shackleton, cable to Leonard Tripp, 9 November 1916 (TBL).
16 E. H. Shackleton, letter to Janet Stancomb-Wills, 10 November 1916 (HRM).
17 E. H. Shackleton, letter to Emily Shackleton, 10 October 1916 (SPRI).
18 Leonard Tripp, letter to Sir Harry Wilson, Secretary of the Royal Colonial Institute, 20 December 1916 (TBL).
19 Leonard Tripp, memorandum for H. R. Mill, 1 March 1922 (TBL).
20 J. K. Davis, *High Latitude*, p. 141.
21 Ibid., p. 240.
22 Ibid., p. 257.
23 Ibid., p. 259.
24 Leonard Tripp, op. cit.
25 E. S. Marshall, letter to John Kendall, 20 July 1952 (SPRI).
26 J. K. Davis, op. cit., p. 266.
27 Leonard Tripp, letter to Robert McNab, 6 December 1916 (TBL).
28 E. H. Shackleton, letter to Emily Shackleton, 20 December 1916 (SPRI).
29 Ibid., 6 December 1916.
30 E. H. Shackleton, cable to E. A. Perris, n.d. (SPRI).
31 Leonard Tripp, memorandum for H. R. Mill, 1 March 1922.
32 Leonard Tripp, letter to Sir Harry Wilson, 20 December 1916 (TBL).
33 J. K. Davis, op. cit., p. 261.
34 E. H. Shackleton, diary, 23 December 1916 (SPRI).
35 J. K. Davis, op. cit., p. 263.
36 E. H. Shackleton, letter to Emily Shackleton, 26 January 1908 (SPRI).
37 R. W. Richards, interview with L. Bickel, 25 November 1976 (ML).
38 E. M. Joyce, diary, entry for 3–10 May 1916 (TBL).
39 R. W. Richards, letter to author.
40 E. M. Joyce, op. cit., loc. cit.
41 R. W. Richards, interview with L. Bickel, loc. cit.
42 E. M. Joyce, *The South Polar Trail*, p. 187.
43 R. W. Richards, letter to author.
44 E. H. Shackleton, letter to E. M. Joyce, 8 March 1917, *quoted*, E. M. Joyce, *The South Polar Trail*, p. 216.
45 R. W. Richards, letter to the author; *Marooned in the Antarctic*, p. 42; interview with L. Bickel.
46 J. K. Davis, op. cit., p. 278.
47 E. H. Shackleton, letter to Emily Shackleton, 27 February 1917 (SPRI).
48 G. Moore, letter to Leonard Tripp, 14 March 1917 (TBL).
49 Leonard Tripp, memorandum for H. R. Mill, 1 March 1922, loc. cit.
50 Leonard Tripp, letter to R. W. Richards, 10 October 1955 (R. W. Richards).
51 E. Saunders, letter to Leonard Tripp, 24 June 1922 (TBL).
52 E. H. Shackleton, cable to Leonard Tripp, 17 March 1917 (TBL).
53 The *Sydney Morning Herald*, 21 March 1917.
54 Ibid.
55 E. H. Shackleton, cable to Leonard Tripp, 14 March 1917 (TBL).
56 E. H. Shackleton, letter to Leonard Tripp, 21 April 1917 (TBL).
57 Sir Shane Leslie, interview with James Fisher (SPRI).
58 Ibid.
59 Ibid.
60 Ibid.
61 F. R. Wild, letter to "My Dear Gussie", 31 December 1916 (H. J. James-Martin).
62 E. H. Shackleton, letter to Leonard Tripp, 13 July 1917.
63 Frank Hurley, letter to Douglas Mawson, 24 September 1917 (MI).
64 Frank Hurley, diary, 1 and 10 April 1916 (ML).

Chapter LIV: South America and Northern Russia
(pages 649–672)

1 E. H. Shackleton, cable to Leonard Tripp, 5 June 1917 (TBL).
2 E. H. Shackleton, letter to Leonard Tripp, 21 April 1917 (TBL).
3 E. H. Shackleton, letter to Janet Stancomb-Wills, 4 September 1917 (HRM).
4 E. H. Shackleton, letter to Leonard Tripp, 20 July 1917 (TBL).
5 Ibid.
6 *The National News*, 21 October 1917.
7 F. A. Worsley, "Crossing South Georgia", *The Blue Peter*, August 1924, p. 229.
8 Emily Shackleton, letter to Leonard Tripp, 18 July 1917 (TBL).
9 E. H. Shackleton, letter to Janet Stancomb-Wills, 17 August 1916 (HRM).

10 Janet Stancomb-Wills, letter to H. R. Mill, 30 April 1923 (SPRI).
11 E. H. Shackleton, letter to Janet Stancomb-Wills, 17 July 1917 (SPRI).
12 E. Shackleton, letter to Emily Shackleton, 28 August 1917 (SPRI).
13 Ibid., October 1914.
14 *Quoted, Siegfried Sassoon Diaries*, 19 June 1917, p. 176.
15 J. M. Wordie, letter to H. R. Mill, 29 January 1923 (SPRI).
16 Bernal Diaz, *The True History of the Conquest of New Spain, quoted*, J. H. Parry, *The Age of Discovery*, p. 33.
17 Leonard Tripp, letter to E. H. Shackleton, 25 April 1917 (TBL).
18 *Quoted, Siegfried Sassoon Diaries*, 24 February 1917, p. 136.
19 E. H. Shackleton, letter to his wife, 28 August 1917 (SPRI); letter to Janet Stancomb-Wills, 4 September 1917 (HRM).
20 Foreign Office, minute to Col. Buchan, 6 September 1917 (PRO FO 395/84).
21 Sir Edward Carson, letter to E. H. Shackleton, 20 September 1917 (SPRI).
22 E. H. Shackleton, letter to Janet Stancomb-Wills, 25 September 1917 (HRM).
23 Admiralty minute, 15 May 1918 (PRO ADM 1 8495/178).
24 E. H. Shackleton, letter to Emily Shackleton, 17 October 1917 (SPRI).
25 E. H. Shackleton, letter to Janet Stancomb-Wills, 12 September 1917.
26 E. H. Shackleton, letter to Emily Shackleton, 17 October 1917 (SPRI).
27 Ibid.
28 Ibid., 9 November 1917.
29 Ibid., 31 October 1917.
30 The *Standard and River Plate News*, 2 December 1917.
31 Sir Edward Carson, letter to E. H. Shackleton, 22 September 1917 (PRO FO/395).
32 E. H. Shackleton, letter to Department of Information, 15 January 1918 (PRO FO 395/251).
33 Roderick Jones, memorandum for Col. John Buchan, 15 January 1918 (PRO FO 395/251).
34 E. H. Shackleton, memorandum to Lord Robert Cecil, 18 May 1918 (PRO FO 395/251, p. 84921).
35 E. H. Shackleton, letter to Janet Stancomb-Wills, 15 September 1917 (HRM).
36 E. H. Shackleton, memorandum to Lord Robert Cecil.
37 Allan Macdonald, intercepted telegram to E. H. Shackleton, 12 June 1918 (PRO FO 395/251).
38 E. H. Shackleton, letter to Emily Shackleton, 22 May 1918 (SPRI).
39 E. H. Shackleton, letter to Cecily Shackleton, 21 June 1918 (SPRI).
40 M. P. Fisher, letter to his wife, 15 August 1918 (SPRI).
41 Dr J. A. McIlroy, interview with James Fisher (SPRI).
42 Edmond Ironside, *Archangel 1918–1919*, p. 192.
43 E. H. Shackleton, letter to Leonard Tripp, 11 October 1918 (TBL).
44 E. H. Shackleton, letter to Janet Stancomb-Wills, 19 October 1918 (HRM).
45 E. H. Shackleton, letter to Edward Shackleton, 26 October 1918 (SPRI).
46 E. H. Shackleton, letter to A. H. Macklin, 21 June 1917 (MFP).
47 A. H. Macklin, interview with James Fisher (SPRI).
48 Ibid.
49 E. S. Marshall, letter to Dr John Kendall, 3 September 1950 (SPRI).
50 A. H. Macklin, op. cit.
51 Ibid.
52 Maynard, *The Murmansk Venture*, p. 163.
53 Maynard, *quoted*, Mill, *The Life of Sir Ernest Shackleton*, p. 261.
54 Major General Sir C. Maynard, op. cit., p. 155.
55 E. H. Shackleton, letter to Emily Shackleton, 26 October 1918 (SPRI).
56 Ibid., 9 January 1919 (SPRI).
57 E. H. Shackleton, letters to Cecily Shackleton, 26 October 1918, 14 January 1919 (SPRI).
58 A. F. Birch-Jones, letter to Margery Fisher, 14 November 1956 (SPRI).
59 R. Greenhough, letter to Margery Fisher, 9 October 1955 (SPRI).
60 E. H. Shackleton, letter to Emily Shackleton, 29 January 1919 (SPRI).
61 Ibid.
62 Ibid.
63 Lermontov, *A Hero of our own Times*, p. 39.
64 E. H. Shackleton, letter to Emily Shackleton, 4 March 1919 (SPRI).
65 E. H. Shackleton, letter to the Assistant Governor-General, Murmansk, April 1919. *Quoted*, Vuillamy, *The Red Archives*, pp. 313–17.
66 E. H. Shackleton, letter to Emily Shackleton, 1 November 1918 (SPRI).
67 *The Times*, 4 April 1919.

Chapter LV: Quest
(pages 673–694)

1 E. H. Shackleton, *South*, p. 75.
2 L. D. A. Hussey, letter to Henry Wellcome, 21 August 1918 (Wellcome Institute).
3 R. Amundsen, the *Daily Chronicle*, 12 February 1917.
4 T. Crean, letter to A. Cherry-Garrard, 21 September 1917 (SPRI).
5 A. Cherry-Garrard, "The Boss", *The Nation*, 13 December 1919.
6 Bridges Adams, letter to James Fisher, 31 July 1955 (SPRI).
7 E. H. Shackleton, letter to Capt. E. R. G. R. Evans, 9 August 1920 (ML).
8 Commander E. R. G. R. Evans, "The Ideal Leader", the *Daily Chronicle*, 31 December 1913.
9 E. H. Shackleton, op. cit.
10 Ibid.
11 R. Amundsen, *Nordostpassagen*, p. 433.
12 E. H. Shackleton, op. cit.
13 Vilhjalmur Stefansson, *Discovery*, p. 238.
14 J. B. Harkin, memorandum for W. W. Cory, 2 March 1921 (PAC MG30, E169).
15 E. H. Shackleton, cable to A. Meighen, 6 May 1921 (PAC Meighen papers, Vol. 13, p. 7476).
16 Ibid., p. 7472.
17 A. Meighen, cable to E. H. Shackleton, 9 May 1921 (PAC Meighen papers, Vol. 13, p. 7479).
18 E. H. Shackleton, cable to A. Meighen, 12 May 1921 (PAC Meighen papers, Vol. 13, p. 7480).
19 A. Meighen, cable to E. H. Shackleton, 16 May 1921 (PAC Meighen papers, Vol. 13, p. 7484).
20 Sir Arthur Vicars, will (Record Office, Dublin).
21 E. H. Shackleton, letter to Emily Shackleton, 17 October 1921 (SPRI).
22 Ibid., "Tuesday".
23 E. H. Shackleton, *Plans for an Oceanographical and Sub-Antarctic Expedition* (SPRI).
24 E. H. Shackleton, letter to Janet Stancomb-Wills, 17 December 1921 (SPRI).
25 Vibert Douglas, letter to Margery Fisher, 29 November 1955 (SPRI).
26 Sir Hubert Wilkins, letter to Margery Fisher, 27 June 1956 (SPRI).
27 A. F. Birch-Jones, letter to Margery Fisher, 14 November 1956 (SPRI).
28 Hubert Wilkins, letter to his mother, 21 October 1921 (Mr Paul Rodzianko).
29 A. H. Macklin, diary, 23 December 1921 (MFP).
30 A. H. Macklin, interview with James Fisher.
31 E. H. Shackleton, cables to A. H. Macklin, 25 and 30 May 1921 (MFP).
32 James Dell, interview with James Fisher.
33 A. H. Macklin, op. cit., 31 December 1921 (MFP).
34 E. H. Shackleton, diary, 1 January 1922 (SPRI).
35 Ibid., 2 January 1922.
36 Ibid., 3 January 1922.
37 F. A. Worsley, diary, 4 January 1922 (ML).
38 D. G. Jeffrey, diary, 4 January 1922 (SPRI).
39 A. H. Macklin, diary, 4 January 1922 (MFP).
40 E. H. Shackleton, op. cit., 4 January 1922.
41 A. H. Macklin, op. cit., 5 January 1922.
42 F. A. Worsley, op. cit., 5 January 1922.
43 J. A. McIlroy, interview with James Fisher (SPRI).
44 James Dell, interview with James Fisher (SPRI).
45 The *Daily Mail*, 31 January 1922.
46 E. H. Shackleton, letter to Mrs Rowett, 18 July 1921 (SPRI).
47 A. H. Macklin, "Appendix V Medical", in F. R. Wild, *Shackleton's Last Voyage*, p. 365.
48 Frank Hurley, *Argonauts of the South*, p. 290.
49 R. Amundsen, diary, 11 July 1911.
50 R. Amundsen, *Sydpolen*, Vol. ii, p. 114.
51 J. Q. Rowett, letter to H. R. Mill, 4 September 1922 (SPRI).
52 L. D. A. Hussey, letter to H. R. Mill, 22 October 1922 (SPRI).
53 A. H. Macklin, diary, 25 March 1922 (MFP).

Epilogue: The Fourth Presence
(pages 695–697)

1 R. B. Robertson, *Of Whales and Men*, p. 56.
2 E. H. Shackleton, *South*, p. 209.
3 Leonard Tripp, memorandum for H. R. Mill, 1 March 1922 (TBL).
4 E. H. Shackleton, op. cit., loc. cit.
5 T. S. Eliot, notes to *The Waste Land* in *Collected Poems*, p. 85.

Sources

PUBLISHED SOURCES

Books

Aagard, Bjarne, *Fangst og Forskning i Sydishavet*, Oslo, Gyldendal Norsk Forlag, 1930.

Adburgham, Alison, *A Punch History of Manners and Morals*, London, Hutchinson, 1961.

Agostini, Alberto M. de, *Zehn Jahre im Feuerland*, Leipzig, F. A. Brockhaus, 1924.

Aktieselskapet Tønsbergs Hvalfangeri 1907–1957, Tønsberg, Selskapets Styre, 1958.

Amundsen, Roald, *Mitt Liv som Polarforsker*, Oslo, Gyldendal Norsk Forlag, 1927.

Nordostpassagen, Kristiania, Gyldendalske Boghandelk, 1921.

Nordvestpassagen, Kristiania, H. Aschehoug & Co., 1907.

Sydpolen, Kristiania, Jacob Dybwads Forlag, 1912.

Antarctic Pilot, The, The Hydrographer of the Navy, 1974.

Armitage, Albert B., *Cadet to Commodore*, London, Cassell and Co. Ltd., 1925.

Two Years in the Antarctic, London, Edward Arnold, 1905.

Bagshawe, Thomas Wyatt, *Two Men in the Antarctic*, Cambridge, at the University Press, 1939.

Bailey, Leslie, *Scrapbook, 1900 to 1914*, London, Frederick Muller, 1957.

Bamford, Francis, and Bankes, Viola, *Vicious Circle*, London, Max Parrish, 1965.

Barclay, W. S., *The Land of Magellan*, London, Methuen, 1926.

Barnett, Correlli, *The Collapse of British Power*, London, Eyre Methuen, 1972.

The Swordbearers, London, Eyre & Spottiswoode, 1963.

Barzini, Luigi, *Peking to Paris. An Account of Prince Borghese's Journey over Two Continents in a Motor Car*, London, Grant Richards, 1907.

Beaglehole, J. C. (Ed.), *The Voyage of the "Resolution" and "Adventure" 1772–1775*, Cambridge, published for the Hakluyt Society at the University Press, 1961. (The journals of Captain James Cook.)

Beckett, J. C., *The Anglo-Irish Tradition*, London, Faber and Faber, 1976.

A Short History of Ireland, London, Hutchinson, 1975.

Begbie, Harold, *Shackleton a Memory*, London, Mills and Boon, 1922.

Bennett, Geoffrey, *Coronel and the Falklands*, London, Batsford, 1962.

Bennett, Laura, and Dorman, Emily, *The Corona of Royalty*, London, Jones Blackwood, 1902.

Benson, E. F., *As We Were*, London, Longmans, Green, 1930.

Bernacchi, L. C., *Saga of the "Discovery"*, London, Blackie and Son, 1938.

To the South Polar Regions, London, Hurst and Blackett, 1901.

Bissett, Robert, *The Life of Edmund Burke*, London, George Cawthorne, 1798.

Blunt, W. S., *My Diaries*, London, Martin Secker, 1919.

Borchgrevink, Carsten E., *Nærmest Sydpolen, Aaret 1900*, København og Kristiania, Gyldendalske Boghandel Nordisk Forlag, 1905.

Bowman, Gerald, *Men of Antarctica*, New York, Fleet Publishing Corporation, 1959.

Bradley, John, *Allied Intervention in Russia, 1917–1920*, London, Weidenfeld and Nicolson, 1968.

Brittain, Sir Harry, *Happy Pilgrimage*, London, Hutchinson, 1949.

Brook-Shepherd, Gordon, *Uncle of Europe*, London, Collins, 1975.

Brown, R. N. Rudmose, *A Naturalist at the Poles*, London, Seely Service, 1923.

Mossman, R. C., Pirie, J., *The Voyage of the "Scotia"*, Edinburgh, William Blackwood, 1906.

Browning, Robert, *Poetical Works 1833–1864*, London, Oxford University Press, 1970.

Bruce, Sir Michael, *Tramp Royal*, London, Elek, 1954.
Bull, H. J., *The Cruise of the "Antarctic"*, London, Edward Arnold, 1896.
Byrd, Richard Evelyn, *Alone*, London, Putnam, 1938.
Little America, New York, G. P. Putnam's Sons, 1930.
Cecil, Robert, *Life in Edwardian England*, London, Batsford, 1969.
Charcot, J.-B., *Le "Français" au Pôle Sud*, Paris, Ernest Flammarion, Éditeur, 1906.
Le Pourquoi-pas? dans l'Antarctique, Paris, Ernest Flammarion, Éditeur, 1910.
Chesterton, G. K., *Autobiography*, London, Arrow Books, 1959.
"A Chronicler", *Archangel*, Chicago, A. C. McClurg, 1924.
Churchill, Randolph S., *Winston S. Churchill*, London, Heinemann, 1969.
Churchill, The Right Hon. Winston S., *The Great War*, London, George Newnes Ltd., n.d.
The World Crisis, London, Thornton Butterworth, 1923.
Clarke, Tom., *My Northcliffe Diary*, London, Gollancz, 1931.
Commission on the Loss of the s.s. "Titanic", Minutes of Evidence, London, His Majesty's Stationery Office, 1912.
The Complete Workings of Craft Freemasonry, London, A. Lewis, 1891.
Cook, Dr Frederick A., *Through the First Antarctic Night*, London, William Heinemann, 1900.
Cooper, Lady Diana, *The Rainbow Comes and Goes*, London, Rupert Hart-Davis, 1958.
Cowles, Virginia, *Edward VII and his Circle*, London, Hamish Hamilton, 1956.
Dangerfield, George, *The Strange Death of Liberal England*, London, McGibbon & Kee, 1966.
Dannevig, Petter, *Fjellboka*, Bergen, Nordanger, 1968.
Darwin, Charles, *The Origin of Species*, London, Dent, 1971.
David, M. Edgeworth, *Professor David*, London, Edward Arnold, 1937.
Davis, J. K., *High Latitude*, Melbourne, Melbourne University Press, 1962.
With the "Aurora" in the Antarctic, London, Andrew Melrose, 1919.
Debenham, Frank (Ed.), *The Voyage of Captain Bellingshausen*, London, The Hakluyt Society, 1945.
Deuxième Expédition Antarctique Française, Paris, Masson et cie., Éditeurs, 1914.
Die Reisen des "Jason" und der "Hertha", Separatabdruck aus den Mittheilunger der Geographischer Gessellschaft in Hamburg, 1891–92.
Diubaldo, Richard J., *Stefansson and the Canadian Arctic*, Montreal, McGill-Queen's University Press, 1978.
Dixon, Surgeon T. B., *The Enemy Fought Splendidly*, Poole, Blandford Press, 1983.
Doorly, Gerald S., *The Voyages of the "Morning"*, London, Smith, Elder, 1916.
Dubois, Bertrand, *Les Montagnes de L'Ocean*, Paris, Éditions du Pen Duick, 1980.
Dunnett, H. McG., *Eminent Alleynians*, Cranbrook, Neville & Harding, 1984.
Dupuy, R. Ernest, *Perish by the Sword*, Harrisburg, The Military Service Publishing Co., 1939.
Duse, S. A., *Bland Pingviner och Sälar*, Stockholm, Beijers Bokfölagsaktiebolag, 1905.
Drygalski, Erich von, *Zum Kontinent des eisigen Südens*, Berlin, Georg Reimer, 1904.
Eliot, T. S., *Collected Poems, 1909–1922*, London, Faber and Faber, 1974.
Ellis, A. C. *An Historical Survey of Torquay*, Torquay, published by the author, 1930.
Filchner, Wilhelm, *Ein Forscherleben*, Wiesbaden, Eberhard Brockhaus, 1951.
Zum Sechsten Erdteil, Berlin, Ullstein, 1922.
Fisher, Margery and James, *Shackleton*, London, Barrie, 1957.
Fuchs, Sir Vivian, *The Crossing of Antarctica*, London, Cassell, 1958.
Furse, Chris, *Elephant Island*, Shrewsbury, Anthony Nelson, 1979.
Gerlache, Adrien de, *Quinze Mois dans L'Antarctique*, Bruxelles, Imprimerie Scientifique Ch. Bulens, Éditeur, 1902.
Gibbs, Philip, *Adventures in Journalism*, London, William Heinemann, 1923.
The Pageant of the Years, London, Heinemann, 1946.
Gilbert, Martin, *Winston S. Churchill*, London, Heinemann, 1971.
Girouard, Mark, *The Return to Camelot*, New Haven and London, Yale University Press, 1981.
Girtin, Thomas, *The Abominable Clubman*, London, Hutchinson, 1964.
Gjæver, John, *Maudheim*, Oslo, Gyldendal Norsk Forlag, 1952.
Glazebrook, G. P. de T. (Ed.), *The Hargrave Correspondence*, Toronto, The Champlain Society, 1938.
Gran, Tryggve, *Slik var det*, Oslo, Gyldendal Norsk Forlag, 1945.
Graves, Charles, *Leather Armchairs*, London, Cassell, 1963.
Greely, Adolphus W., *Three Years of Arctic Service*, London, Richard Bentley and Son, 1886.
Hall, Captain C. F., *Life with the Esquimaux*, London, Sampson Low, 1864.

Halliday, E. M., *The Ignorant Armies*, London, Weidenfeld and Nicolson, 1961.

Hammond, William E., *What Masonry Means*, London, George Allen & Unwin, 1940.

Hanbury, David, *Sport and Travel in the Northland of Canada*, London, Edward Arnold, 1904.

Harstad, Herlof, *Erobringen av Antarktis*, Oslo, H. Aschehaug & Co. (W. Nygaard), 1968.

Hart-Davis, Rupert (Ed.), *Siegfried Sassoon Diaries, 1915–1916*, London, Faber and Faber, 1983.

Hayes, J. Gordon, *Antarctica*, London, The Richards Press, 1928.

The Conquest of the South Pole, London, Thornton Butterworth, 1932.

Headland, R. K., *South Georgia*, Cambridge, Cambridge University Press, 1984.

Hill, C. W., *Edwardian Scotland*, Edinburgh, Scottish Academic Press, 1976.

Hillary, Sir Edmund, *No Latitude for Error*, London, Hodder & Stoughton, 1961.

Hoare, Michael M., *The "Resolution" Journal of Johann Reinhold Forster*, London, The Hakluyt Society, 1982.

Hodges, Sheila, *God's Gift*, London, Heinemann, 1981.

Hoel, Adolf, *Svalbard*, Oslo, Sverre Kildahls Boktrykkeri, 1966.

Hope, Ronald (Ed.), *Seamen and the Sea*, London, George G. Harrap, 1965.

Hullah, Albert S., *The Presence*, London, The Epworth Press, 1928.

Hume, John R., and Moss, Michael S., *Beardmore*, London, Heinemann, 1979.

Hurley, Captain Frank, *Argonauts of the South*, New York and London, G. P. Putnam's Sons, 1925.

Hussey, L. D. A., *South with Shackleton*, London, Sampson Low, 1949.

Hyde, H. Montgomery, *Carson*, London, Constable, 1974.

Hynes, S., *The Edwardian Turn of Mind*, London, Oxford University Press, 1968.

Inglis, Brian, *The Story of Ireland*, London, Faber and Faber, 1966.

Ironside, Field Marshal Lord, *Archangel, 1918–1919*, London, Constable, 1953.

Jackson, Frederick G., *A Thousand Days in the Arctic*, London, Harper and Brothers, 1899.

The Lure of Unknown Lands, London, G. Bell and Sons, 1935.

Jacob, Margaret, *The Radical Enlightenment*, London, George Allen & Unwin, 1981.

Johnsen, Arne Odd, and Tønnesen, Joh. N., *Den Moderne Hvalfangsts Historie*, Oslo, H. Aschehoug & Co. (W. ...ard), 1959, and Sandefjord, Norges Hv...tforbund, 1969.

Joint Services Expedition E... Island 1970–71, London, Royal ...ical Society, 1971.

Jones, Sir Lawrence, *An Edwar...* London, Macmillan, 1956.

Jones, Tom C., *Patagonian Panora...* Outspoken Press, 1961.

Joyce, E. M., *The South Polar Trail*, Lo... Duckworth, 1929.

Kennett, Lady [Kathleen Scott], *Self-Po... of an Artist*, London, John Murray, 194...

Kirkwood, David, *My Life of Revolt*, Londo... George G. Harrap, 1935.

Kirwan, L. P., *A History of Polar Exploration*, London, Penguin Books, 1962.

Knight, E. F., *The Cruise of the "Alerte"*, London, Thos. Nelson and Sons, 1890.

Kohl-Larsen, Dr Ludwig, *An den Toren der Antarktis*, Stuttgart, Strecker und Schröder, 1930.

Lansing, Alfred, *Endurance, Shackleton's Incredible Voyage*, New York, McGraw-Hill, 1959.

Laseron, Charles Francis, *South with Mawson*, London, George G. Harrap, 1947.

Lawrence, John, *Freemasonry – a way of salvation?*, Bramcote, Notts, Grove Books, 1982.

Lee, Sir Sidney, *King Edward VII*, London, Macmillan, 1925.

Legg, Frank, *Once More on my Adventure*, Sydney, Ure Smith, 1966.

Leroi-Gourhan, *Les Explorateurs célèbres*, Genève, Paris, Editions d'Art Lucien Mazenod, 1947.

Leslie, Anita, *Edwardians in Love*, London, Hutchinson, 1972.

The Gilt and the Gingerbread, London, Hutchinson, 1981.

Leslie, Sir Shane, *American Wonderland*, London, Michael Joseph, 1936.

Lewis, David, *Ice Bird*, London, Collins, 1975.

Lewis, Roy, and Maude, Angus, *The English Middle Classes*, London, Phoenix House, 1949.

Liddell Hart, B. H., *History of the First World War*, London, Pan Books, 1979.

Lucas, J., *The Big Umbrella*, London, Hamish Hamilton, 1973.

Lucy, Sir Henry, *Sixty Years in the Wilderness*, London, Smith, Elder, 1916.

Mackellar, C. D., *A Pleasure Pilgrim in South America*, London, John Murray, 1908.

Scented Isles and Coral Gardens, London, John Murray, 1912.

McKenna, S en, *While I Remember*, London, T on Butterworth, 1921.

McKinlay, m Laird, *Karluk*, London, Weide d Nicolson, 1976.

M'Corm arles, *Memoirs of the Right Hon dmund Burke*, London, Lee 1798.

and, and Shackleton, Ernest

Mc *H.M.S.*, London, Simpkin Hamilton Kent, 1900.

ir Philip, *King Edward VII*, John Murray, 1964.

, Admiral Sir Albert H., K.C.B., *e of Sir Clements Markham*, London, Murray, 1917.

am, Sir Clements, *The Lands of ce*, Cambridge, The University Press, 1.

, Scout [James W.], *Into the Frozen uth*, London, Cassell, 1923.

son, A. E. W., *The Turnstile*, London, Hodder and Stoughton, 1912.

Masterman, C. F. G., *The Condition of England*, London, Methuen, 1909.

Matthews, L. Harrison, *South Georgia*, London, Simpkin Marshall, 1931.

Maurice, General Sir Frederick, *The Life of General Lord Rawlinson of Trent*, London, Cassell, 1928.

Maurois, André, *King Edward and his Times*, London, Cassell, 1949.

Mawson, Sir Douglas, *The Home of the Blizzard*, London, William Heinemann, 1915.

Mawson, Paquita, *Mawson of the Antarctic*, London, Longmans, 1964.

Maynard, Major-General Sir C., *The Murmansk Venture*, London, Hodder and Stoughton, 1928.

Meath, The Earl of, *Memories of the Twentieth Century*, London, John Murray, 1924.

Mellor, Alec, *Our Separated Brethren the Freemasons*, London, George G. Harrap, 1961.

Middlemas, Keith, *The Pursuit of Pleasure*, London and New York, Gordon & Cremonesi, 1977.

Mill, Hugh Robert, *An Autobiography*, London, Longmans, Green, 1951.

The Life of Sir Ernest Shackleton, London, William Heinemann, 1923.

The Record of the Royal Geographical Society 1830–1930, London, the Royal Geographical Society, 1930.

The Siege of the South Pole, London, Alston Rivers, 1905.

Moore, E. M., *Adventures in the Royal Navy; the life and letters of Admiral Sir Arthur Moore*, Liverpool, published by the author, 1964.

Morgan, Diana, *After My Fashion*, London, Samuel French, 1953.

Morris, James, *Heaven's Command*, Harmondsworth, Penguin Books, 1979.

Farewell the Trumpets, Harmondsworth, Penguin Books, 1979.

Motley, J. L., *The Rise of the Dutch Republic*, London, Bickers & Son, 1878.

Mountevans, Admiral Lord, *Adventurous Life*, London, Hutchinson, 1948.

The Antarctic Challenged, London, Staples Press, 1955.

South with Scott, London and Glasgow, Collins, n.d.

Müller, Johannes, *Einiges aus der Geschichte der Südpolforschung*, Berlin, Hermann Blanke's Buchdruckerei, 1914.

Munro, H. H. (Saki), *The Square Egg*, London, John Lane the Bodley Head, 1924.

Murdoch, W. Burn, *From Edinburgh to the Antarctic*, London, Longman, Green, 1894.

Murray, George (Ed.), *The Antarctic Manual*, London, Royal Geographical Society, 1901.

Murray, James, and Marston, George, *Antarctic Days*, London, Andrew Melrose, 1913.

Nansen, Fridtjof, *Fram over Polhavet*, Kristiania, H. Aschehoug & Co. Forlag, 1897.

Paa Ski over Grønland, Kristiania, H. Aschehoug & Co. Forlag, 1890.

Nordenskjöld, Otto, *Antarctic*, Stockholm, Bonniers Förlag, 1904.

Nowell-Smith, S. (Ed.), *Edwardian England, 1901–1904*, London, Oxford University Press, 1964.

O'Brien, Conor Cruise, *States of Ireland*, St Albans, Panther Books, 1974.

Pares, Bernard, *A History of Russia*, London, Jonathan Cape, 1926.

Partner, Peter, *The Murdered Magicians*, Oxford, Oxford University Press, 1982.

Pearsall, Ronald, *Edwardian Life and Leisure*, Newton Abbott, David & Charles, 1973.

Pearson, John, *Edward the Rake*, London, Weidenfeld and Nicolson, 1975.

Perrin, Robert, *Jewels*, London, Routledge and Kegan Paul, 1977.

Petersen, Carl O., *Med Byrd og Balchen mot Sydpolen*, Oslo, Gyldendal Norsk Forlag, 1931.

Pinochet de la Barra, Oscar, *La Antartica Chilena*, Santiago da Chile, Editorial Andres Bello, 1976.

Pochhammer, Hans, *Graf Spees Letzte Fahrt*, Berlin, 1918.

Poulson, Major Neville P., *The White Ribbon*, London, B. A. Sealey, 1968.
Prescott, *History of the Conquest of Peru*, London, Bickers & Son, 1878.
Read, Donald, *Documents from Edwardian England, 1901–1915*, London, Harrap, 1973.
Edwardian England, London, Harrap, 1973.
Report of the Inter-Departmental Committee on Physical Deterioration, London, His Majesty's Stationery Office, 1904.
Report of the Viceregal Commission appointed to investigate the circumstances of the loss of the Regalia of the order of Saint Patrick, London, His Majesty's Stationery Office, 1908.
Rich, E. E. (Ed.), *Journal of Occurrences in the Athabasca Department by George Simpson, 1820 and 1821*, Toronto, The Champlain Society, 1938.
Richards, R. W., *The Ross Sea Shore Party*, Cambridge, Scott Polar Research Institute, 1962.
Riiser-Larsen, *Mot Ukjent Land*, Oslo, Gyldendal Norsk Forlag, 1930.
Risting, Sigurd, *Kaptein C. A. Larsen*, Oslo, J. W. Cappelens Forlag, 1922.
Robertson, R. B., *Of Whales and Men*, London, Macmillan, 1956.
Ross, Captain Sir James Clark, R.N., *A Voyage of Discovery and Research in the Southern and Antarctic Regions*, London, John Murray, 1847.
Ross, M. J., *Ross in the Antarctic*, Whitby, Caedmon of Whitby, 1982.
Russell, The Rt. Hon. George W. E., *Half Lengths*, London, Grant Richards, 1913.
Sandison, Alan, *The Wheel of Empire*, London, Macmillan, 1967.
Scott, Captain Robert F., *The Diaries of Captain Robert Scott*, Facsimile Edition, Tylers Green, Buckinghamshire, University Microfilms, 1968.
The Voyage of the "Discovery", London, Macmillan, 1905.
Scott's Last Expedition, London, Smith, Elder, 1913.
Seaver, George, *Edward Wilson of the Antarctic*, London, John Murray, 1933.
Shackleton, Sir Ernest, *South*, London, William Heinemann, 1919.
The Heart of the Antarctic, London, William Heinemann, 1909.
Shepperton, A., *Symbolism in Craft Masonry*, London, A. Lewis (Masonic Publishers), 1976.
Silverlight, John, *The Victors' Dilemma*, London, Barrie & Jenkins, 1970.
Smith, D. Murray, *Arctic Expeditions from British and Foreign Shores*, Southampton, Charles H. Calvert, 1877.
Smith, F. B., *The People's Health, 1830–1910*, London, Croom Helm, 1979.
Sobral, José M., *Dos años Entre Los Hielos*, Buenos Aires, Imprenta de J. Tragant y cia, 1904.
Somerville & Ross, *Experiences of an Irish R.M.*, London, Everyman's Library, 1980.
Stefansson, Vilhjalmur, *Discovery*, New York, McGraw-Hill Book Company, 1964.
My Life with the Eskimo, London, Macmillan, 1913.
The Adventure of Wrangel Island, London, Jonathan Cape, 1926.
The Northward Course of Empire, London, George G. Harrap, 1922.
Sverdrup, Otto, *Nyt Land*, Kristiania, H. Aschehoug, 1903.
Synge, J. M., *The Playboy of the Western World*, Dublin, Maunsel, 1907.
Tannahill, R., *Food in History*, London, Methuen, 1973.
Taylor, Griffith, *With Scott: the Silver Lining*, London, Smith, Elder and Co, 1916.
Terriss, Ellaline, *Just a Little Bit of String*, London, Hutchinson, 1955.
Thomas, Lowell, *Sir Hubert Wilkins*, London, Arthur Barker, 1961.
Tuchman, Barbara W., *The Proud Tower*, London, Macmillan Press, 1980.
Underhill, Harold A., *Sailing Ship Rigs and Rigging*, Glasgow, Brown, Son & Ferguson, 1969.
Vamplew, Wray, *Salvesen of Leith*, Edinburgh, Scottish Academic Press, 1975.
Verne, Jules, *Twenty Thousand Leagues under the Sea*, London, Everyman's Library, 1908.
Vulliamy, C. E., *The Red Archives*, London, Geoffrey Bles, 1929.
Watkins, Julian Lewis, *The 100 Greatest Advertisements*, New York, Moore Publishing, 1949.
Weddell, James, *A Voyage towards the South Pole*, London, Longman, Rees, 1827.
Wellcome's Medical Diary, London, 1908.
The Wellcome Trust First Report 1937–1956, London, 1957.
White, Terence de Vere, *The Anglo Irish*, London, Victor Gollancz, 1972.
Wild, Commander Frank, *Shackleton's Last Voyage*, London, Cassell, 1923.
Willans, T. W., *Parachuting and Skydiving*, London, Faber and Faber, 1968.

Wilson, Edward, *Diary of the "Discovery" Expedition*, New York, Humanities Press, 1967.
Diary of the "Terra Nova" Expedition, London, Blandford Press, 1972.
Worsley, Frank Arthur, *Endurance*, London, Philip Allan, 1931.
First Voyage in a Square-Rigged Ship, London, Geoffrey Bles, 1938.
Shackleton's Boat Journey, London, Philip Allan, n.d.
Yesterday's Shopping, The Army & Navy Stores Catalogue, 1907, Newton Abbott, David & Charles, 1969.

Articles and Monographs

"A Great Explorer", *The Review of Reviews*, May 1923, pp. 520–2.
"Abominations of Dublin Castle Exposed", *The Gaelic American*, 4 July 1908.
"About Lieutenant E. H. Shackleton", *Royal Magazine*, June 1909, p. 192.
Amundsen, Roald, "Sir E. Shackleton", *Daily Chronicle*, 12 February 1917.
An Irishman, "Did Mr. Birrell Tell the Truth?", *John Bull*, 4 April 1908, p. 138.
"An Irishman at the South Pole", *The Weekly Freeman* (Dublin), 27 March 1909.
"Antarctic Discovery at the British Association", *Geographical Journal*, Vol. xl, No. 5, November 1912, pp. 541–50.
"Arrival of Lieut. Shackleton", *The Register* (Adelaide), 2 December 1907.
"Bei Lady Shackleton", *Vossische Zeitung* (Berlin), 15 June 1916.
Bruce, William S., "A new Scottish Expedition to the South Polar Regions", *Scottish Geographical Magazine*, Vol. xxiv, 1908, pp. 200–2.
"First Antarctic Voyage of the 'Scotia'", *Scottish Geographical Magazine*, February 1904, pp. 57–133.
Burley, M. K., "Climbing in the Antarctic", *The Alpine Journal*, Vol. lxvii, No. 305, November 1962, pp. 226–9.
"Combined Services Expedition to South Georgia 1964–5", *Explorers Journal*, Vol. xliv, No. 2, June 1966, pp. 106–18.
"Joint Services Expedition to Elephant Island", *Geographical Journal*, Vol. cxxxviii, September 1972, pp. 298–308.
"By Car to the South Pole", *The Car*, No. 283, 23 October 1907, pp. 393, 397–8.
"Call for Men. Shackleton's Address", *Sydney Morning Herald*, 21 March 1917.
Carse, Duncan, "In Shackleton's Tracks", *The Times*, 16 March 1956.
"Tracing the limits of endurance", *Geographical Magazine*, Vol. xlvi, 1974, pp. 561–8.
Cherry-Garrard, A., "The Boss", *The Nation*, 13 December 1919, pp. 397–8.
Chick, Harriette, "Early Investigations of Scurvy and the Antiscorbutic Vitamin", *Proceedings of The Nutrition Society*, Vol. 12, No. 3, 1953, pp. 210–19.
"Compania Argentina de Pesca S.A.", *Norsk Hvalfangst Tidende*, October 1954, pp. 553–581.
Cooper, A. B., "How I Began", *The Captain*, April 1910, pp. 42–5.
Cresswell, M., "Sir Ernest Shackleton", *The Marine Observer*, Vol. xv, No. 129, January 1938, p. 17.
David, T. G. Edgeworth, "The Ascent of Mount Erebus", *Aurora Australis*.
"The British Antarctic Expedition, 1907", *Daily Telegraph* (Sydney), 23 March–4 April 1908.
"Deutsche Antarktische Expedition. Vorläufige Berichte", Berlin, *Der Zeitschrift der Gesellschaft für Erdkunde zu Berlin*, No. 2, 1912, pp. 82–107.
Douglas, James, "Shackleton's Epic", *Sheffield Independent*, 4 November 1909.
"The Dublin Castle Scandals", *John Bull*, 11 April 1908, p. 341.
Dungan, Myles, "The Theft of the Irish Crown Jewels", *A Supplement to the "Irish Times"*, 10 July 1982.
Dunsmore, James, "Shackleton of the s.s. 'Flintshire'", *The United Methodist*, 4 May 1922, p. 213.
Eeg-Larsen, N., "Ernæring og helse", *Om norsk ernærings- og matforsynings- politikk*, St. meld. nr. 32 (1975–6).
"R. G. England", *The Window Card*, Christmas 1935, pp. 20–3.
"England's Latest Hero", *Pearson's Weekly*, 8 April 1909, p. 818.
"Ever a Fighter", *Evening Post* (New York), 4 August 1923.
Filchner, Wilhelm, "Die Deutsche Antarktische Expedition", Berlin, *Der Zeitschrift der Gesellschaft für Erdkunde zu Berlin*, No. 7, 1910, pp. 425–30.
"Following in the Steps of Shackleton", *Illustrated London News*, 19 June 1965, pp. 16–21.

Från Klara till Kosmopolis (History of the Primus Stove), Stockholm, 1929.

Gibbs, Philip, "Explorers I have met", *Daily Express* (Dublin), 18 February 1911.

Harris, Dr Leslie J., "Scurvy in Retrospect", *Nature*, 11 July 1953, p. 50.

Headland, R. K., "Wrecks, hulks and other vessel remains at South Georgia", *British Antarctic Survey Bulletin*, No. 65, p. 109.

"Heart of the Antarctic", *Daily Telegraph*, 4 November 1909.

Holst, Axel, and Frölich, Theodor, "Experimental Studies Relating to Ship-Beri-Beri and Scurvy", *Journal of Hygiene*, Vol. vii, October 1907, pp. 634–71.

Høygaard, Arne, and Rasmussen, Harald, "Vitamin C Sources in Eskimo Food", *Nature*, Vol. 143, 3 June 1939, p. 943.

"Hvalfangstbestyrer Toralv Sørlle", *Norsk Hvalfangst Tidende*, October 1914, pp. 136–137.

"The Impenetrable Ice. Shackleton Relief Expedition Fails", *Buenos Aires Herald – Weekly Edition*, 30 June 1916.

"In the Days of my Youth. My First Success. No. 572. – Lieutenant Shackleton", *M.A.P.*, 3 July 1909, pp. 17–18.

Irizar, J., "Partes officiales del viaje de 'La Uruguay'", *Boletin del Instituto Geográfico Argentino*, Tom 22, Nos. 1–6 [1907], pp. 57–82.

Jones, A. G. E., "Captain William Smith and the Discovery of New South Shetland", *Geographical Journal*, Vol. cxli, November 1975, pp. 445–61.

"Frankie Wild's Hut", *Journal of the Royal Naval Medical Service*, Vol. 64, Spring 1978, pp. 51–60.

"Shackleton's Amazing Rescue 1916", *The Falkland Islands Journal*, 1962, pp. 21–31.

Kendall, Dr E. J. C., "Scurvy during some British Polar Expeditions, 1875–1917", *Polar Record*, Vol. 7, September 1955, pp. 467–85.

"Konsul Lars Christensen", *Thor Glimt*, Sandefjord, No. 18, June 1966, pp. 6–15.

"La Expedicion del 'Endurance' de Sir Ernest Shacketon y el intento de su rescate por marinos uruguayos en el Pesquero 'B-1' del Instituto de Pesca, luego del 9 Junio 1916", *Instituto Antartica Uruguayo Publicacíon*, No. 18, 1975, pp. 41–6.

Larkman, A. H., "An Engineer's Antarctic Log", *N.Z. Engineering*, 15 August 1963, pp. 286–91; 15 September 1963, pp. 327–328.

Laurie, Peter, "The Rise and Fall of the Mad Major", *Sunday Times Magazine*, 28 April 1968, pp. 52–7.

Lewis, Dr H. E., Pugh, Dr L., and Holt, Dr Lewis, "Medical Aspects of Polar Exploration", *Proceedings of the Royal Society of Medicine*, Vol. 65, January 1972.

"Lieutenant Shackleton's Achievement", *Evening Telegraph* (Dublin), 24 March 1909.

"Life on Elephant Island", *Buenos Aires Herald – Weekly Edition*, 29 September 1916.

"Lionel Greenstreet's Great Adventure", *Book of Life Manual of Survival*, Part 3.

Macleod, Margaret, and Glover, Richard, "Franklin's First Expedition as Seen by the Fur Traders", *The Polar Record*, Vol. 15, No. 98, pp. 669–82.

Markham, Sir Clements, "The Antarctic Expeditions", *Geographical Journal*, Vol. xiv, No. 5, November 1899, pp. 473–81.

Marshall, Dr E. S., "An Antarctic Episode", *Off the Beaten Track*, 4th Series, No. 45.

Marshall, Edward, "Sir E. Shackleton and the Hidden World", *The National News*, 21 October 1917.

Mill, Hugh Robert, "Ernest Henry Shackleton, M.V.O., *Travel & Exploration*, Vol. ii, No. 7, July 1909, pp. 1–10.

"Sir Ernest Shackleton, C.V.O.", *Scottish Geographical Magazine*, 1922, Vol. 38, No. 2, pp. 118–21.

"Sir Ernest Shackleton, M.V.O.", *Nature*, 2 February 1922, pp. 143–5.

"The Voyage Southward of the 'Discovery'", *Geographical Journal*, Vol. xix, No. 4, April 1902, pp. 417–23.

Mossman, R. G., "The Physical Condition of the Weddell Sea", *Geographical Journal*, Vol. xlviii, No. 6, December 1916, pp. 479–500.

Naisbitt, Christopher, "I went with Shackleton", *Hampstead News and Golders Green Gazette*, 22 November 1956.

"National Antarctic Expedition: Report of the Commander", *Geographical Journal*, Vol. xxii, July 1903, pp. 20–37.

Nicolaysen, Ragnar, "Arktisk ernæring", *Det Norske Videnskabs-Akademi i Oslo Fridtjof Nansen Minneforelesninger*, No. 7.

"Nordenskjöld, Nils Otto Gustav", *Svenska Män och Kvinnor*, Vol. 5, Stockholm, Albert Bonniers Förlag, 1949.

Petersen, Dr Johannes, "Die Reisen des 'Jason' und der 'Hertha' in das Antarktische Meer 1893/94", *Mittheilungen der Geographische Gesellschaft in Hamburg 1891–92*, pp. 1–61.

"Plan Einer Deutschen Antarktischen Expedition", Berlin, *Zeitschrift der Gesellschaft für Erdkunde zu Berlin*, Jahrgang 1910, No. 3, pp. 3–6.

"Plasmon", *The Lancet*, 11 August 1900, p. 404.

Priestley, R. E., "Polar Exploration and the Twentieth Century", *The Nation*, 23 June 1923.

"Prof. J. W. Gregory, F.R.S", *Nature*, 25 June 1932, p. 930.

Przybyllok, Dr Erich, "Deutsche Antarktische Expedition", *Zeitschrift der Gesellschaft für Erdkunde zu Berlin*, 1913, No. 1, pp. 1–17.

"The Retirement of Captain England", *The Window Card*, Christmas 1938, pp. 15–17.

Rodahl, K., "Vitamin Sources in Arctic Regions", *Norsk Polarinstitutt Skrifter*, No. 91.

Rodahl, K., and others, "Effects of dietary protein on physical work capacity during severe cold stress", *Journal of Applied Physiology*, Vol. 17, No. 5, September 1962.

Roxburgh, "Cold and the Chinstraps", *Daily Telegraph Magazine*, No. 357, 27 August 1971, pp. 10–15.

Sarolea, C., "Sir Ernest Shackleton, A Study in Personality", *The Contemporary Review*, Vol. 121, 1922, pp. 321–8.

Schiavetti de Gómez, Lina, "El Camino de la Aurora Austral", *Revista de Marina*, July–August 1970, pp. 469–82; September–October 1970, pp. 644–56.

"Shackleton. Foredraget i Geografisk Selskab", *Aftenposten*, 16 October 1909.

Shackleton, E. H., "A New British Antarctic Expedition", *Geographical Journal*, Vol. xxix, March 1907, pp. 329–32.

"Lieutenant Shackleton's Own Story", *Pearson's Magazine*, September 1909, pp. 235–52; October 1909, pp. 347–67; November 1909, pp. 519–35.

"Life in the Antarctic", *Pearson's Magazine*, March 1904.

Plans for an Antarctic Expedition (pamphlet, no publisher or date.)

"The Adventurous Voyage of the 'Discovery', and the Sledge Journey to the Furthest Point South Ever Reached By Man", supplement to the *Illustrated London News*, 27 June, 5 July 1903.

"The Imperial Trans-Antarctic Expedition, 1914, *Geographical Journal*, Vol. xliii, February 1914, pp. 173–8.

"The Imperial Trans-Antarctic Expedition", *Geographical Magazine*, Vol. xliii, March 1914, pp. 318–21.

The Imperial Transantarctic Expedition (pamphlet), London, 1914.

"The Making of an Explorer", *Pearson's Magazine*, August 1914.

"Shackleton for Sentimentalists", *The Saturday Review*, 19 May 1923, pp. 667–8.

"Shackleton tilbage fra Finse" *Aftenposten*, 27 May 1914, p. 2.

"Shackleton's Experiences", *Buenos Aires Herald – Weekly Edition*, 16 June 1916.

"Shackleton's Men Rescued", *Magellan Times*, 7 September 1916.

Sharman, I. M., "Vitamin C: Historical Aspects", *Vitamin C*, ed. Birch and Parker, London, Applied Science Publishers, 1974.

"Sir Ernest Shackleton", *Dublin Express*, 15 December 1909.

"Sir Ernest Shackleton", *New Statesman*, 7 July 1923, pp. 399–400.

"Sir Ernest Shackleton", *The Times Literary Supplement*, 26 April 1923.

"Sir Ernest Shackleton, A Personal Interview with the Great Explorer", *Magellan Times*, 6 July 1916.

"Sir Ernest Shackleton in Budapest", *Pester Lloyd*, 12 January 1910, p. 6.

"Sir James K. Caird, Bart.", *Dundee Yearbook 1916*, pp. 53–4.

"Some Results of the Scottish National Expedition", *The Scottish Geographical Magazine*, August 1905, pp. 402–40.

"The South Pole. A New Imperial Expedition", *The Times*, 29 December 1913, p. 6.

"Speeches at the unveiling of the Shackleton Memorial", *Geographical Journal*, Vol. lxxxix, No. 3, March 1932, pp. 161–7.

Stackhouse, J. Foster, "The British Antarctic Expedition 1914", *The British Antarctic Expedition Discovery*, London, n.d.

"Studenternes Fakkeltog", *Aftenposten*, 16 October 1909.

Wallace, W., "James Murray, F.R.S.E., 1865–1914 – A Belated Biography", *Year Book of the Royal Society of Edinburgh*, 1976, pp. 15–20.

"Why to Explore the South Pole", *New Statesman*, 3 January 1914.

Wilson, L. G., "The Clinical Definition of scurvy and the discovery of Vitamin C", *Journal of the History of Medicine and Allied Science*, 30 (1) 40–60, January 1975.

Wordie, J. M., "Sir Ernest Shackleton, C.V.O.", *Geographical Journal*, Vol. lix, No. 3, 1922, pp. 228–30.

Worsley, Commander F. A., "Crossing South Georgia", *The Blue Peter*, Vol. 4, August 1924, pp. 223–9; September 1924, pp. 242–47; October 1924, pp. 318–24.

"Shackleton's Boat Journey", *The Blue Peter*, Vol. 4, May 1924, pp. 46–54; June 1924, pp. 104–10; July 1924, pp. 141–8.

Zaslow, Morris, "Administering the Arctic Islands 1880–1940", *A Century of Canada's Arctic Islands*, The Royal Society of Canada.

Newspapers

Aftenposten, Oslo (Christiania).
Aftonbladet, Stockholm.
The Age, Melbourne.
The Argus, Melbourne.
Belfast Evening Telegraph, Belfast.
Belfast News Letter, Belfast.
Buenos Aires Herald, Buenos Aires.
Canterbury Times, Canterbury, N.Z.
Cape Argus, Cape Town.
Cape Times, Cape Town.
Chicago Tribune, Chicago.
Cork Examiner, Cork.
Dagbladet, Oslo (Christiania).
Daily Chronicle, London.
Daily Express, Dublin.
Daily Graphic, London.
Daily Mail, London.
Daily Mirror, London.
Daily News, London.
Daily Telegraph, London.
Daily Telegraph, Sydney.
El Diá, Montevideo.
Dublin Evening Telegraph, Dublin.
Dundee Advertiser, Dundee.
Dundee Courier, Dundee.
Eastbourne Chronicle, Eastbourne.
Evening News, London.
Evening Telegraph, Dublin.
Financial Times, London.
Freeman's Journal, Dublin.
Gaelic American, New York.
Globe, London.
Hither Green Journal, London.
Hobart Mercury, Hobart, Tasmania.
Irish Times, Dublin.
Le Journal de St Petersburg, St Petersburg [Leningrad].
El Liberal, Madrid.
Liverpool Daily Post and Mercury, Liverpool.
Lyttelton Times, Lyttelton, N.Z.
Magellan Times, Punta Arenas.
Manchester Guardian, Manchester.
Le Matin, Paris.
Melbourne Argus, Melbourne.
El Mercurio, Santiago de Chile.
Montreal Gazette, Montreal.
Montreal Star, Montreal.
Morning Post, London.
New York Herald, New York.
New York Sun, New York.
New York Times, New York.
New Zealand Times, Wellington, N.Z.
News of the World, London.
Otago Daily Times, Lyttelton, N.Z.
Ottawa Evening Journal, Ottawa.
Pall Mall Gazette, London.
Pester Lloyd, Budapest.
La Prensa, Buenos Aires.
Rand Daily Mail, Johannesburg.
Record, Philadelphia.
Register, Adelaide.
San Francisco Chronicle, San Francisco.
Scotsman, Edinburgh.
South Pacific Mail, Valparaiso.
Standard and River Plate News, Buenos Aires.
Strathspey Herald, Grantown.
Sussex County Herald, Eastbourne.
Sydney Mail, Sydney.
Sydney Morning Herald, Sydney.
Tasmanian Mail, Hobart, Tasmania.
The Times, London.
The Times-Picayune, New Orleans.
Transcript, Boston, Mass.
The Tribune, London.
Western Daily News, Plymouth.
Westminster Gazette, London.

Press Cuttings
Collections at Scott Polar Research Institute, Cambridge; National Archives and Records Service, Washington, D.C.

Periodicals

The Alleynian, Dulwich.
Antarctic, Wellington, N.Z.
Book Review Digest, New York.
Boys' Own Paper, London.
Bystander, London.
The Captain, London.
Explorers Journal, New York.
The Field, London.
Geografisk Tidskrift, Copenhagen.
Geographical Journal, London.
Geographical Magazine, London.
Harper's Weekly, New York.
Illustrated London News, London.
John Bull, London.
Lloyd's List, London.
London Mail, London.
M.A.P. (Mainly about People), London.
Mitteilung Wiener Geographische Gesellschaft, Vienna.
The Nation, London.
Nature, London.
New Statesman, London.
Norsk Geografisk Tidskrift, Oslo.
Polar Record, Cambridge.
Polarboken, Oslo.
Review of Reviews, London.

Royal Magazine, London.
Scottish Geographical Magazine, Edinburgh.
Spectator, London.
Sphere, London.
Tatler, London.
The Times Literary Supplement, London.
Winning Post, London.
Ymer, Stockholm.
Zeitschrift der Gesellschaft für Erdkunde zu Berlin, Berlin.

UNPUBLISHED SOURCES

Archives and private collections consulted, with abbreviations.

The Alexander Turnbull Library (TBL), Wellington, New Zealand.
Antarctic Division, Hobart, Tasmania.
Associated Biscuits, company archives, Reading.
Australian Archives (AA), Dickson, A. C. T., and Brighton, Vic.
Churchill College, Cambridge, archives.
Det Kongelige Bibliotek (Royal Library), Copenhagen.
Edinburgh Public Library, Edinburgh.
Baron de Gerlache de Gomery papers of Adrien de Gerlache.
Mrs Audrey Greenstreet; Cdr. L. Greenstreet's papers.
Dr Derek Harbord, A. E. Harbord's diaries and papers.
Mrs Ruth Hatch, Capt. R. England's papers.
Hvalfangstmuseet (HVM) (Whaling Museum), Sandefjord.
Home Office, departmental records, London.
Hudson's Bay Company, archives, Winnipeg and London.
Imperial War Museum (IWM), London.
The Earl of Iveagh, Guinness family papers.
Mr H. J. James-Martin, letters of F. R. Wild.
Kungliga Biblioteket (The Royal Library), Stockholm.
Kungliga Vetenskapsakademien (KV) (Royal Swedish Academy of Sciences) Stockholm.
Mr Bjørn Tore Larsen, C. A. Larsen diaries.
Liverpool Record Office, Liverpool.
Mrs Jean Macklin; Dr A. H. Macklin's papers.
Mawson Institute for Antarctic Research (MI), Adelaide.
Memorial University of Newfoundland, St Johns, Maritime History Group.
Mitchell Library (ML), Sydney.
John Murray (Publishers) Ltd., London, company archives.
National Archives and Records Service (NAS), Washington, D.C.
National Library of Australia, Canberra.
National Library of Scotland, Edinburgh.
National Maritime Museum (NMG), Greenwich.
Norsk Sjøfartsmuseum (Norwegian Maritime Museum), Oslo.
Public Archives Canada (PAC), Ottawa.
Public Record Office (PRO), London; Admiralty, Army, Board of Trade, Colonial Office, Foreign Office, and Hudson's Bay Company archives.
The Registrar General of Shipping and Seamen, Cardiff.
Riksarkivet (RAS) (Swedish state archives), Stockholm.
Royal Archives (RAW), Windsor.
The Royal Geographical Society (RGS), London.
Scott Polar Research Institute (SPRI), Cambridge.
The State Library of Victoria, Melbourne.
Universitetsbiblioteket i Oslo (UB) (University Library), Oslo.
University of Edinburgh Library.
University of Glasgow, archives.
The University of Sydney, archives.
Mr J. van Haeften, letters and papers of Sir Philip Brocklehurst.

Diaries and Journals

Amundsen, R., *Belgica* diaries, 1898–9, UB.
Bernacchi, L. C., *Discovery* journals, 1902–3, SPRI.
Southern Cross diaries, 1899–1900, SPRI.
Clarke, A. W., diary kept on HMS *Royal Oak*, at Battle of Jutland, 31 May–1 June 1916 (Churchill College, Cambridge).
David, T. W. E., *Nimrod* diaries, 1908–9. University of Sydney archives.
Sledging diaries, ascent of Mount Erebus, 1908, and Magnetic Pole journey, 1908–9, University of Sydney archives.
Douglas, G. V., *Quest* diary, 1921–2.
Evans, F. P., diary kept on *Koonya* and *Nimrod*, 1907–9, TBL.
Ferrar, H. T., *Discovery* diaries 1902–3, SPRI.
Greenstreet, L., diary kept on Elephant Island, Mrs Audrey Greenstreet.

Harbord, A. E., *Nimrod* diary, 1907–9, Dr Derek Harbord.
Hare, C. H., *Discovery* diary, 1901–3, SPRI.
Hodgson, T. V., *Discovery* diary, 1901–3, SPRI.
Hurley, *Endurance* diaries, ML.
Jack, A. K., *Aurora* diaries.
James, R. W., *Endurance* diaries, 1914–16, SPRI.
Jeffrey, D. G., *Quest* diary, 1921–2, SPRI.
Joyce, E. M., Ross Sea diaries, 1915–17, TBL.
Sledging diaries, Ross Sea diaries, 1915–16, TBL.
King George V, diaries 1907–21, RAW.
Kinsey, Sir J. J., correspondence and papers, TBL.
Larsen, C. A., *Antarctic* diaries, 1902–3, B. T. Larsen.
Mackay, A. Forbes, *Nimrod* diary 1909, SPRI.
Mackintosh, Æ. L. A., *Nimrod* diary, 1909, copy in the possession of Dr Derek Harbord.
Aurora diary, 1915, RGS.
Macklin, A. H., *Endurance* diaries, 1914–16, Mrs Jean Macklin.
Quest diaries, 1921–2, Mrs Jean Macklin.
McNeish, H., *Endurance* diaries 1914–16, TBL.
Markham, Sir C. R., diaries, 1901–13, RGS.
Marshall, E. S., *Nimrod* diaries 1907–8, RGS.
Sledging diaries, Southern Journey, RGS.
Mawson, Sir Douglas, *Nimrod* diaries, MI.
Sledging diary, Magnetic Pole journey, 1908–9, MI.
Nordenskjöld, N. G. O., *Antarctic* diaries, KV.
Orde-Lees, T. H., *Endurance* diaries, 1914–16, SPRI, TBL.
Plumley, F., *Discovery* diaries, 1901–3, SPRI.
Priestley, R. E., *Nimrod* diaries, 1907–9, SPRI.
Richards, R. W., Sledging diary on Ross Sea Party, 1916, R. W. Richards.
Royds, C. W., *Discovery* diaries, 1901–3, Mrs Eyre.
Scott, Gilbert, *Discovery* diary, 1901–3, SPRI.
Shackleton, Sir Ernest.
Discovery expedition, 1901–3:
Diary kept on board *Discovery* at sea, ML.
Diaries kept at McMurdo Sound, SPRI.
Sledging diary, Southern Journey, SPRI.
Nimrod expedition, 1907–9:
Diary kept at McMurdo Sound, SPRI.
Sledging diary, Southern Journey, SPRI.
Endurance expedition, 1914–17:
Diaries kept on board *Endurance*, and on pack ice, SPRI.
Diary kept on board *Aurora*, Ross Sea relief, SPRI
Quest expedition, 1921–2.
Diary kept on board *Quest*, SPRI.
Skelton, R. W., *Discovery* diaries, 1901–2, SPRI.
Skottsberg, C., *Antarctic*, diaries, KV.
Spencer-Smith, A., Sledging diaries, kept on Ross Sea Party, 1915–16, SPRI.
Steuart, R. R., diary kept on HMS *Invincible* at Battle of the Falklands, 8 December 1914, (IWM).
Thomson, L., *Aurora* diaries, 1914–15.
Wild, E., diary kept on Ross Sea Party, 1914–16, SPRI.
Wild, F. R., Sledging diary, Southern Journey, *Nimrod* expedition, ML.
Williamson, T., *Discovery* diary, SPRI.
Worsley, F. A.:
Endurance expedition, 1914–17:
Diaries kept in London, on board *Endurance*, in pack ice, on Open Boat journey, on South Georgia, in the United States, South America and New Zealand, and on the relief voyages, SPRI.
Navigation books, SPRI.
Quest expedition, 1921–3:
Diary kept on board *Quest*, SPRI.

Letters and other manuscript sources

Admiralty records, PRO (ADM 1/7463 B, ADM 1/8367–8, ADM 1/8387, ADM 1/8483, ADM 1/8495, ADM 12/1392, ADM 116/943–4, ADM 116/1712, ADM 137/51–2, ADM 240/16).
Antarctic Petrel, TBL.
Armitage, A. B. A., Correspondence with H. R. Mill, SPRI.
Aurora and Ross Sea Party, Otago Harbour Board, SPRI, TBL.
Birch-Jones, A. F., letters to Margery Fisher, 14 November 1956, 3 April, 1957, SPRI.
Board of Trade records, PRO (BT 100/305).
Brocklehurst, Sir Philip, correspondence and papers, Mr J. van Haeften.
Bruce, W. S., correspondence, SPRI.
Christensen, Lars, correspondence, Framnæs mekaniske Værksted, Sandefjord.
Colonial Office records, PRO (CO 78/131, CO 78/138–41).

Company records, Companies House, Maxims (95839), PRO (BT 31), Cargo and General Transport (BT 31/25586/164050), Celtic Investment Trust (BT 1/11780/91392), Elstree Chemical Works (BT 31/24655/155473), F.I.A.T. Motor Cab Co. (BT 31/18175/94433), General Sponge Fishing Co. (BT 31/32162/130779), International Financial & Development Corp. (BT 31/18142/94007), ITA Film Syndicate (BT 1/22194/135095), City of Montevideo Public Works Corp. (BT 1/18958/104425), Northern Exploration Co. (BT 1/32080/112730), North Mexico Land & Timber Co. (BT 1/33782/109004), Potentia Ltd. (BT 1/8101/58435), Potentia Organization (BT 1/18504/99030), Tabard Cigarette Co. (BT 1/22818/140209), Tabard Cigarette & Tobacco Co. (BT 1/21067/125610), Water Softeners Ltd. (BT 1/19884/114364), West of England Rose Farm (BT 31/11032/83852).

Connaught, The Duke of, letter to the Duchess, 5 August 1907, RAW.

Coronel, battle of, eyewitness account by Navigating Officer of HMS *Glasgow*, IWM.

David, T. W. E., letters and papers, ML, University of Sydney Archives.

Davis, J. K., correspondence, SPRI.

Discovery, expedition records, RGS, SPRI.

Endurance, expedition records, Hudson's Bay Co. archives (PRO: BH1/2211 A12 FT 340/4/14, BH1/2214 A12/FT MISC/222 and A12/F340/4(Misc.), RGS, SPRI.

Ship, Framnæs mekaniske Værksted, Sandefjord.

England, R. G., correspondence and papers, Mrs Ruth Hatch, RGS, SPRI.

Filchner, W., correspondence, RAS, SPRI.

Fisher, J. and M., correspondence and papers, SPRI.

Foreign Office records, PRO (FO 118, FO 132/150, FO 371/3009, FO 371/3353–5, FO 371/3989, FO 385/251, FO 395/84, FO 395/304).

Greenstreet, L., letter to his father, 17 November 1914, Mrs Audrey Greenstreet.

Gregory, J. W., correspondence and papers, SPRI.

Hedin, S., correspondence, RAS.

How, W., letters and papers, SPRI.

Hurley, F., correspondence with Sir Douglas Mawson, MI.

James, R. W., correspondence, SPRI.

Joyce, E. M., correspondence and papers, SPRI, TBL.

Keltie, Sir J., correspondence and papers, RGS, SPRI.

Log books, *Discovery* RGS, *Endurance* SPRI, HMS *Glasgow* PRO (ADM 53/42843), *Nimrod* ML.

Løken, K., letters from South Georgia, HVM.

Mackellar, C. D., correspondence and papers, John Murray (Publishers) Ltd., archives.

Macklin, A. H., correspondence and papers, Mrs Jean Macklin.

Markham, Sir C. M., correspondence and papers, PRO (ADM 1 7463 B), RGS, SPRI.

Marshall, E. S., correspondence with Dr John Kendall, 1950–3, SPRI.

Mawson, Sir Douglas, correspondence and papers, MI.

Mill, H. R., correspondence and papers, SPRI.

Nansen, F., correspondence with RGS, RGS.

Correspondence with E. H. Shackleton, UB.

Nimrod expedition records, AA (CA 12 CRS A2 9/2497), RGS, SPRI.

Orde-Lees, T. H., *Beset by Berg and Floe*, SPRI.

Peary archives, NAS.

Petrides, N., correspondence, SPRI.

Priestley, R. E., correspondence and papers, SPRI.

Proposed Anglo-Swedish Expedition, 1915–19, records, KV.

Proposed Austrian Antarctic expedition, 1914–?, records, RGS.

Proposed British Antarctic expedition, 1914–? (J. Foster Stackhouse), KV, PRO (ADM 1/8368 and 8387), RGS.

Richards, R. W., interview with Lennard Bickel, 2 December 1976. Australian archives, Canberra.

Rowett, J. Q., correspondence 1921–3, SPRI.

Saunders, W., correspondence, TBL.

Scott, R. F., letters and papers, PRO (ADM 116/944), RAS, RGS, SPRI, UB.

Shackleton, Lady Emily, correspondence and papers, MI, SPRI, TBL, UB.

Shackleton, Sir Ernest, correspondence and papers held by Australian Archives, Canberra, Baron de Gerlache de Gomery, Lord Iveagh, ML, NAS, NMG, PAC, PRO (ADM 1/8368), RAS, RAW, RGS, Royal Scottish Geographical Society, SPRI, TBL, UB, Mr. J. van Haeften.

Letters to Elspeth Beardmore, 1906–14, NMG.

Letters to Emily Shackleton, SPRI.

Proposed Arctic expedition, 1920–1, PAC (MG 30 E 169, MG 26 I Vol. 13, pp. 7382–7476).
Ships' Articles and Crew Lists, *Hoghton Tower* Memorial University, St John's, Newfoundland; *Scotia, Discovery, Morning, Nimrod, Terra Nova*, PRO (BT 100).
Smith, F. L., letters from E. H. Shackleton, biographical note, SPRI.
Stancomb-Wills, Dame Janet, letters to H. R. Mill, SPRI.
Stefansson, V., letters concerning Shackleton, 1920, PAC (MG 26 I Vol. 13, pp. 7391–94, 7399–7400, 7423–24, 7429–30).
Stevens, A., correspondence, SPRI.
Report on the Ross Sea Party, SPRI.
Talbot, Capt. A. D., letters to Miss Turner from Gallipoli, 1915, IWM.
Tripp, L., correspondence and papers, R. W. Richards, TBL.
Whaling records, South Georgia, 1914–16, HVM.
Wild, F. R., correspondence and papers, SPRI.
Memoirs, ML.
Wilson, E. A., correspondence with E. H. Shackleton, 1907, SPRI.
Worsley, F. A., letters and papers, SPRI.

Index